Paradoxes of Mahathirism

Paradoxes of Mahathirism

An Intellectual Biography of Mahathir Mohamad

KHOO BOO TEIK

KUALA LUMPUR
OXFORD UNIVERSITY PRESS
OXFORD SINGAPORE NEW YORK

Oxford University Press

Oxford New York
Athens Auckland Bangkok Bombay
Calcutta Cape Town Dar es Salaam Delhi
Florence Hong Kong Istanbul Karachi
Madras Madrid Melbourne Mexico City
Nairobi Paris Shah Alam Singapore
Taipei Tokyo Toronto

and associated companies in
Berlin Ibadan

Oxford is a trade mark of Oxford University Press

Published in the United States
by Oxford University Press, New York

First published 1995
Third impression 1995

British Library Cataloguing in Publication Data
Data available

Library of Congress Cataloging in Publication Data
Khoo, Boo Teik, 1955-
Paradoxes of Mahathirism: an intellectual biography of
Mahathir Mohamad/Khoo Boo Teik.
p. cm.
Includes bibliographical references and index.
ISBN 967 65 3094 8: ISBN 967 65 3092 1 (boards):
1. Mahathir bin Mohamad, 1925-. 2. Malaysia—Politics and government.
3. Prime ministers—Malaysia—Biography. I. Title.
DS597.215.M34K47 1995
959.505'4'092—dc20
[P]
95-1217
CIP

Typeset by Indah Photosetting Centre Sdn. Bhd., Malaysia
Printed by Kyodo Printing Co. (S) Pte. Ltd., Singapore
Published by the South-East Asian Publishing Unit,
a division of Penerbit Fajar Bakti Sdn. Bhd.,
under licence from Oxford University Press,
4 Jalan U1/15, Seksyen U1, 40000 Shah Alam,
Selangor Darul Ehsan, Malaysia

To the memory of my friends,
Lim Boon Teik and Pramod Manaloor

Preface

Fin de Siècle, or the end of the century, has been notorious for inducing hope and dread, sometimes of millenarian proportions, among people in the world. But the coming end of the twentieth century may well find many Malaysians exhilarating in an atypical complacency.

So much of the developing world wallows in misery, underdevelopment, and turmoil, but Malaysia is prosperous, growing, and stable. So many among the developed nations appear to lack resolve, direction, and aspiration, but Malaysia is moved by determination, vision, and ambition. Whereas the New Economic Policy period of 1970–90 was characterized by trepidation, anxiety, and altercation, the National Development Policy era beginning with 1991 is seemingly blessed with assurance, certainty, and tolerance. If, in the mid-1980s, Malaysia was considered to be highly vulnerable to economic retrogression, it is, by the 1990s, widely assumed to be Asia's fifth newly industrialized tiger. If Malaysians then were held to be captive to inter-ethnic acrimony, now they seem to be scarcely troubled by ethnic matters. In short, if once the nation seemed unable to do anything right, now it seems unlikely to do anything wrong. For all its sloganeer's vulgarity, the 'can do' chant of 'Malaysia Boleh', regularly broadcast over Radio and Television Malaysia, captures the spirit of the times in which Malaysians now live.

However one views or assesses the impact a political leader can have on a society, many Malaysians will unhesitatingly credit Prime Minister Datuk Seri Dr Mahathir bin Mohamad with these recent changes in Malaysia's fortunes. They will thereby be attributing, perhaps unknowingly, their own change of heart—from the relative pessimism of the 1980s to the overflowing optimism of the 1990s—to the immense influence of Mahathirism, the ruling ideas of the Mahathir era in Malaysian political history.

That era officially began in July 1981 when Mahathir became the fourth Prime Minister of Malaysia. In ideological terms, its real beginnings, as this book suggests, are half a century old, if we date them to the days when Mahathir, using the pseudonym of C. H. E. Det, first expressed ideas that he has largely maintained to this day. Somewhere in between lay the evolution of Mahathir's world-view which is at once personal and shared. That world-view is filled with individual nuances and yet it also corresponds to the transformation of Malay and Malaysian society to which Mahathir's politics and policies have made no small contribution.

But if Mahathir has been in public view for nearly fifty years it is by no means clear that the man and the politician are well understood. To some, his vision is boundless. To most, he remains very much of an enigma who thrives on unfashionable ideas, controversial policies, and a contentious diplomacy. For me, he seems to be most approachable when regarded as a series of personae, and most comprehensible when taken as a composite of personal and social paradoxes—which this book explores and tries to explain.

As a study of political ideology, this book investigates Mahathir's ideas on nationalism, capitalism, Islam, populism, and authoritarianism, which, it maintains, form the core of Mahathirism. Within the context of Malaysia's recent political history, it charts the evolution of Mahathir's complex world-view to reveal paradoxes, and alternating patterns of consistency and contradiction, to explain Mahathir's politics, policies, and personality. In biographical terms, it examines the legacy of Mahathir's youthful immersion in the Malay world, the class background to his religiosity, and the medical influence on his political style. At the theoretical level, it offers some insights into the connections between ethnicity and class in Malaysian society and politics.

It may interest some to know that the genesis of this book, which concerns itself largely with matters of ideology and biography, lay in the conjuncture of personal and social circumstances which I encountered in the period of 1987–90.

In April 1987, while visiting Adelaide, just prior to taking up a Lecturer's position at Universiti Brunei Darussalam, I chanced to enquire at the Flinders University of South Australia if I might enrol as a part-time Ph.D. student in the Discipline of Politics in the Faculty of Social Sciences. My enquiry was received with much courtesy and encouragement. I was enrolled the following year.

In October 1987, the political crises that Malaysia was going through culminated, or so it seemed at first, in 'Operation Lalang', a police operation of mass arrests, which Mahathir, as Prime Minister and Minister of Home Affairs, justified as a pre-emptive measure to prevent what seemed like an imminent inter-ethnic bloodbath in the country.

Living and working in Brunei under the circumstances, I both faced the graduate student's problem of developing a workable thesis topic and felt the anger of a Malaysian abroad at the political repression at home. For a while, I dealt with them by drafting a thesis proposal that envisaged a detailed analysis of 'The 27th October of Mahathir Mohamad'. That proposal, presented at my first 'Work-in-Progress' Seminar at Flinders University in December 1988, was meant to grapple with the *problématique* of 'race, class, and state' in Malaysia during the Mahathir era. It accounted for most of my research and writing over the next two years.

But Malaysian politics after October 1987 kept producing twists and turns which threatened to broaden the scope of my thesis uncontrollably, were I to deal adequately with the unsettled developments, and even what had not yet emerged. At about the same time, excellent contemporaneous essays on the crisis of 27 October 1987, the UMNO split of February 1988, and the sacking of the Lord President of the Supreme Court in August 1988 were beginning to appear which made me wonder seriously whether I would have anything original left to say.

Perhaps one might say Mahathir came to my rescue. The Barisan Nasional's third decisive electoral victory under his leadership in November 1990 left him virtually unchallengeable. What was more, it gave him an unencumbered opportunity to consolidate the programme of modernization, industrialization, and deregulation which were principally the goals he started with in July 1981. As we now know, Mahathir shortly thereafter unveiled his 'Vision 2020', a statement of direction for Malaysia which paved the way for the promulgation of the National Development Policy. But 'Vision 2020' simultaneously expressed the maturation of Mahathirism—which had not yet been the subject of any full-length study.

It seems too easy now to say I switched thesis topics but in hindsight I did just that. One pleasant result was that I submitted my

Ph.D. thesis to Flinders University in January 1994. Suffice it to say that the thesis was a practical solution to an academic dilemma as well as an intellectual attempt to understand a man and politician whose ideology, politics, and personality have contributed to reshaping the Malaysian polity, and, I hope, a modest contribution to the understanding of Malaysian society itself.

One year has passed since this study was completed in its original form. In broad chronological terms, it may be said to begin with the period of 1948–50 which was when Mahathir wrote most of his C. H. E. Det articles for the *Sunday Times* (then based in Singapore). Substantively, the book concludes with some reflections on Vision 2020 although there are short references to some major events and issues which took place up to the end of 1993. I have not sought to revise or to add to the original study in order to record the latest happenings in the political life of Mahathir Mohamad, who is now entering his fourteenth year of office as Prime Minister. Naturally, it would be gratifying if the reader agrees that this omission does not result in the book being already dated.

There are several reasons why I have not attempted to play 'catch up' with Mahathir. First, no biography of an active politician, and Mahathir is an extremely energetic politician, can ever hope to chronicle fully or quickly enough the most recent comings and goings of its subject. Second, since this is fundamentally an intellectual biography, I cannot do better than to leave the task of updating Mahathir to the mass media whose journalists trail Mahathir, often breathlessly, in order to report the latest details of his politics, policies, and personality. Third, and more pertinently, I suggest in the concluding chapter that Mahathirism, in its ideological essentials, reached its culmination in Vision 2020. As far as I can see, post-Vision 2020 events which may have more than an indirect bearing on Mahathirism have so far thrown up little to merit a major modification or further substantiation of that argument. This is, of course, an opinion that is best left to the reader to consider. Fourth, and most important of all, Mahathir's characteristic response to changes and developments is not to change his mind, but to innovate and offer fresh policies; in that, he shows the singular talent of being able to provide seemingly new ideas while perceiving a changing world with his largely unchanged lenses.

I would be very happy if the following people considered that they had a share in the conception and completion of both the thesis and this book although I would not insist on their sharing the views, let alone any errors, that appear.

At Flinders University, I profited from the able and patient supervision of Leng Hin Seak when I started my thesis, and Bill Brugger when I finished it. I am grateful for their individual and combined interest, encouragement, and criticism, to say nothing of their forbearance when occasionally and silently I took mental walkabouts lasting months on end. I should also like to thank Brian Marks for his kind assistance in administrative matters, which made it feasible for me to work 'from afar', and Manjit Singh Bhatia for his timely interventions with the computer, which fished me out of trouble more than once.

I was not alone when making my switch in thesis topics. Khoo Khay Jin and Yeap Jin Soo, rarely short of conversation, and ever willing to offer their ideas and materials, helped to set aside many of my hesitations about undertaking a study of Mahathir. In the preparation of the manuscript for this book, I benefited from the careful and critical comments made by Loh Kok Wah and Tan Liok Ee, as well as the interest and help of Chang Yii Tan, Jomo K. S., and Lim Pao Li.

If I found research and writing in Brunei to be less lonesome and more practicable than I had initially dared to expect, it was largely because I enjoyed the company and assistance of John Funston, Kam Tin Seong, Roger Kershaw, Niew Shong Tong, and Wong Shuang Yann. That I found it possible at all to continue after 1991 was mainly due to the medical expertise of Iyaz, Tan Kok Hin, and Atun Wee.

One cannot write an intellectual biography without reflecting on one's own intellectual past. I wish to record my debt to Brijen Gupta, the late Christopher Lasch, and Peter Linebaugh, who showed me different ways of thinking about the world of nations while I was an undergraduate at the University of Rochester. At the Massachusetts Institute of Technology, Tunney Lee was always firmly but gently reminding me not to leave things unwritten. And I remember fondly the personal and intellectual camaraderie provided by S. Aravind, N. Balakrishnan, Jeyakumar Devaraj, Fong Chin Wei, James

Jesudason, Kwong Tai Chee, Lim Boon Teik, Ow Soon Guan, and Yeap Jin Soo with whom I spent several formative years under Malaysian schoolteachers at the Penang Free School.

My parents, Khoo Kay Yeow and Lim Ah Paik; my sisters, Ai Choo, Ai Poh, Ai Wah, and Ai Boey; my brother, Boo Hin; and my brothers-in-law, Kang Kong Peng, Lee Choo Tiat, and Yeoh Chip Beng demonstrated how unfailingly helpful and hospitable an extended family can be even though it is spread over Adelaide, Penang, and Singapore.

Will Pek Leng, Teng Jian, and Teng Xiang see something of themselves in this book? I hope so. Pek Leng bore much of the cost of my paper and book chase. Teng Jian's impending arrival in 1986 prompted my return to academic work. One and a half years later, Teng Xiang confirmed that it was not such a foolish decision.

Penang
January 1995

KHOO BOO TEIK

Contents

Preface *vii*
Plates *xv*
Note on the Use of Bahasa Malaysia Sources *xvi*
The Significance of Biography: A Tribute in Lieu of Theory *xvii*

1 **Paradoxes of Mahathirism** *1*

In Search of Mahathir Mohamad *1*
Paradoxes of Mahathirism *6*
Sources and Method *10*

2 **Dilemmas of Malay Nationalism** *17*

The Credentials of the 'Ultra' *17*
The Malay Dilemma: Malay Nationalism and Social Darwinism *24*
The Challenge: Islam and the West *34*
The Nationalist as Prime Minister *47*

3 **Dilemmas of Malaysian Nationalism** *54*

'Buy British Last': The Prime Minister as Nationalist *54*
North–South, East–West *57*
Look Out and 'Look East' *65*
The Little Guy's Diplomacy *74*
The Legacy of C. H. E. Det *81*

4 **Capitalism: Visions of a Free Economy** *103*

1990: *Fin de Siècle?* *103*
Capitalism as Liberation *109*
Capitalism as Liberalization *124*
The NEP in Abeyance: Recession's Solution *136*

5 **The Call of Islam** *159*

'Your Islam, My Islam' *159*
'Mahathir's Islam' *163*
Islamization *174*
The Religiosity of the Self-made Man *181*

6 **The Prime Minister as Populist** *198*

Mahathir's Populism *198*
Who's Sovereign?: The Constitutional Crisis, 1983 *202*
The Populist under Siege I: Financial Scandals, 1984–1986 *209*
The Populist under Siege II: Political Crises, 1984–1986 *219*
The Hour of the Populist: The August 1986 General Election *231*

7 **The Populist as Authoritarian** *261*

24 April 1987: Personal Mandate, Party Democracy, or UMNO Split? *261*
27 October 1987: The End of 'Liberalism'? *271*
27 May 1988: Who Will Judge the Judges? *286*
The Doctor and the Common Crowd *294*

8 **Mahathirism after Mahathir** *322*

1990: The Critical Year *322*
Vision 2020: Capitalism and Nationalism *327*
Melayu Baru: Mahathirism after Mahathir *331*

Bibliography *343*
Index *366*

Plates

Between pages 200 and 201

1 A selection of titles of C. H. E. Det articles, *c.*1948–50.
2 Mahathir succeeds Hussein Onn as UMNO President, UMNO General Assembly, Kuala Lumpur, 29 June 1981.
3 Mahathir signing the letter of appointment as Prime Minister, Kuala Lumpur, 16 July 1981.
4 Mahathir visiting his constituency, Kubang Pasu, Kedah, 22 August 1981.
5 Rally at Port Klang during the constitutional crisis of 1983, 6 December 1983.
6 Mahathir during a SEMARAK campaign at Lubok Jong, Kelantan, 6 March 1988.
7 Mahathir celebrating the Barisan Nasional victory in the general election, 4 August 1986.
8 Mahathir celebrating the Barisan Nasional victory in the general election, 21 October 1990.
9 Mahathir with other Commonwealth leaders at the CHOGM in Kuala Lumpur, October 1989.
10 Mahathir tabling the Sixth Malaysia Plan in Parliament, Kuala Lumpur, 11 July 1991.
11 Mahathir launching the Proton Satria, Kuala Lumpur, 25 November 1994.
12 Mahathir and Musa Hitam in response to rumours of Musa's resignation, Kuala Lumpur, 6 July 1985.
13 Mahathir and Ghafar Baba at the UMNO General Assembly, Kuala Lumpur, 7 November 1992.

Note on the Use of Bahasa Malaysia Sources

ALL quotations or excerpts which are based on original Bahasa Malaysia sources were translated into English by the author except where a prior or an official translation from Bahasa Malaysia to the English language is available or has been used. As an example, quotes taken from Mahathir, 'Ucapan di Upacara Pembukaan Rasmi Musabaqah Membaca Al-Quran Peringkat Kebangsaan', Kuala Lumpur, 24 April 1986, were translated into English by the author. But excerpts taken from Mahathir, 'Speech at the 33rd UMNO General Assembly', Kuala Lumpur, 10 September 1982, were directly taken from the English translation reprinted as 'UMNO in a World of Change and Challenge', *New Straits Times*, 11 September 1982.

The Significance of Biography: A Tribute in Lieu of Theory

THE study of politics in Malaysia has long been dominated by an 'ethnic perspective'. Studies informed by this perspective basically argue that the ethnic divisions and tensions in Malaysia's plural society decide the substance, character, trends, and limits of its politics. To them, the most important division is that between an 'indigenous Malay community' which possesses political power, and an 'immigrant non-Malay community' which controls the economy. Much of Malaysian politics may, therefore, be viewed as a process of managing inter-ethnic divisions, tensions, and conflicts amidst the efforts of avowedly ethnic-based political parties to advance the interests of 'their' communities. To the extent that these parties co-operate, compromise, and bargain, the inter-ethnic differences may be contained at non-dangerous levels. Where they cannot, or where they clash, inter-ethnic polarization may escalate and undermine political stability.

Equipped with these basic parameters, the ethnic perspective has prompted studies of a host of issues conventionally covered by the study of politics. Several political scientists, such as K. J. Ratnam, R. S. Milne, R. K. Vasil, and Gordon P. Means, studied Malaysia's electoral process and the programmes of political parties in the 1960s to show the powerful but potentially destabilizing appeals of communalism for a newly independent country trying to constitute itself as a politically cohesive entity.[1] Political mobilization along ethnic lines which finds institutional expression in party organization and ideology has also been examined by John Funston's study of UMNO and PAS, and Heng Pek Koon's study of the MCA.[2] Karl von Vorys's study of the Alliance model of consociationalism and its breakdown in 1969, and Mohamed Noordin Sopiee's work on the problems of political unification stressed the demanding role of the ethnic élites in mobilizing communal support and yet restraining communal appeals.[3] But Chandra Muzaffar has been more critical of the Malay élite's insistence on being the 'protector' of their community.[4] James V. Jesudason is critical of the Malay state élite because their attempt to bolster the Malays' 'relative group worth' resulted in economically inefficient state interventionism.[5] Differing treatment of the Malay-dominated state's approach towards 'subordinate ethnic groups' has been provided by Cynthia Enloe's analysis of state security concerns and Judith Strauch's idea of the 'encapsulation' of Chinese village politics.[6] The examination of particular issues pregnant with ethnic sensitivity has been undertaken by Ronald Mead on the Malay language and Tan Liok Ee on Chinese education.[7] In short, the ethnic perspective has been able to sustain a large body of scholarship with shifting focuses on the problems of Malaysia's plural society.

Since the 1970s, the ethnic perspective has been challenged by a 'class perspective' which has tried to substitute class for ethnicity as the primary factor in Malaysian politics. Writings from the class perspective have typically tried to highlight class transformation, domination, and contention in state policies, political ideology, and the struggles for the control of the state in Malaysia. To depict the Malaysian political economy as essentially 'a question of class', Jomo K. S. stressed the close links between state and capital, and state policies and class interests within a historical framework of capital accumulation.[8] Lim Mah Hui plotted corporate networks and interlocking directorships to demonstrate a pronounced degree of wealth concentration within Malaysian society.[9] In their various studies of the Malay state, Martin Brennan, B. N. Cham, Fatimah Halim, Lim Mah Hui, and William Canak traced the problem of 'class and communal conflict' in Malaysia primarily to the ideological conversion of an ethnically split intra-capital contention into inter-ethnic animosity.[10] There are other well-known class-based studies but I reserve those to make a different point below.

Briefly, it may be said that these two major theoretical approaches to Malaysian society and politics, having little to communicate, have largely bypassed each other, only to land themselves in different but equally baffling dilemmas. Writings from the ethnic perspective have maintained a studious silence over the class character of Malaysian society while those from the class perspective have barely confronted its ethnic divisiveness. One cannot hope to reconcile in theory a paradigm based on plural so ciety with another based on class society. And yet it seems almost self-evident that the theoretical acceptance of a simultaneous and intertwined influence of ethnicity *and* class makes a more rewarding point of departure for the study of Malaysian politics. It is beyond the scope of this study to provide a theoretical exegesis on this point. One can see it indirectly from the necessity, now accepted by leading proponents of both the ethnic and class approaches, of 'hyphenating' ethnicity and class. Thus Jomo refers to 'Malay statist capitalists' and 'Chinese capital'.[11] Ozay Mehmet discusses Malay 'distributional coalitions',[12] Jesudason opposes an 'enlarged [Malay] state' to 'Chinese business'[13] while Yoshihara Kunio differentiates between 'major indigenous capitalists' and 'major Chinese capitalists'.[14]

One can better illustrate this point by referring to a more tested method of grappling with the formidable *problématique* of ethnicity and class in Malaysia. This method essentially consists of exploring class structure, relations, and conflict within a single ethnic community. One may characterize it as a 'class-within-community' approach which investigates class while holding ethnicity 'constant'. Representative studies of this variety include Sinnapah Arasaratnam, *Indians in Malaysia and Singapore*;[15] Syed Husin Ali, *Malay Peasant Society and Leadership*;[16] Clive Kessler, *Islam in a Malay State: Kelantan, 1838–1969*;[17] Francis Loh Kok Wah, *Beyond the Tin Mines: Coolies, Squatters, and New Villagers in the Kinta Valley, Malaysia, c.1880–1980*;[18] Shamsul A. B., *From British to Bumiputera Rule*;[19] and Michael Stenson, *Class, Race, and Colonialism in West Malaysia: The Indian Case.*[20] Thematically, the studies of the immigrant Chinese and Indian societies by Arasaratnam, Loh, and Stenson share an underlying appreciation of the ethnic-and-class origins of Malaysia's plural society and its colonial division of labour. The studies by Syed Husin Ali, Kessler, and Shamsul lay bare the changing class structure and emerging lines of class conflict within the indigenous Malay society which have been accentuated by the socioeconomic developments promoted by the New Economic Policy. Strauch was not wrong to caution that 'class analysis, if it neglects or underestimates the salience of communal power structures, can offer only a partial understanding of social and political reality'.[21] But, equally, 'ethnic analysis', if it ignores the reality of class, only gains in apparent completeness what it loses in historical perspective and balance. This has been confirmed by studies of recent critical conjunctures in Malaysian political history, such as Simon Tan's account of the 27 October 1987 crisis, Khoo Khay Jin's analysis of the UMNO split in 1988, and Francis Loh Kok Wah's investigation of 'Kadazan consciousness' in Sabah during the 1980s.[22] Strictly speaking, not even these studies can 'reconcile' ethnicity and class in Malaysia with any finality, but then who can, in theory or in practice? At least, they collectively capture the Janus-like quality of the Malaysian polity, with its ethnic aspect beaming with public light while its class counterpart is shrouded in secrecy. The best practitioners of 'open ethnic politics', like Mahathir and former Deputy Prime Minister Musa Hitam, have tacitly acknowledged this. They have intuitively grasped that class without ethnicity in Malaysia gets one nowhere politically, whereas ethnicity without class gets one nowhere economically.

This intellectual biography of Mahathir hopes to offer another view of the *problématique* of ethnicity and class in Malaysia, this time through the ideological lenses of someone who may be said to personify his class while personifying his race. It will suggest of Mahathir that he is someone in whom the tensions of race and class are ever present, for example, in his twin impulses to engineer a capitalist class out of the Malay race, and his tendency to attribute to race the qualities needed for success under capitalism. We shall meet him as someone who pushes an Islamic religiosity, which is synonymous with Malay identity in Malaysia, but which is also tied to the ethos of a class of self-made men. Mahathir has been predisposed to use state power to bring about Malaysia's class transformation according to the logic of securing inter-ethnic parity, but he has been equally prepared to reduce the state's economic intervention because the emerging Malay capitalist class can itself do with less state regulation. Mahathir's much proclaimed vision proffers a new 'Malaysian race' led by a united capital while it calls for a 'new Malay' personified by the Malay entrepreneur. In the transition from C. H. E. Det and his Malay consciousness to the 'Malay ultra' and his anxieties to the Prime Minister and his ambition, his '2020' vision, and his legacy lies a personal biography of a complex man. It captures at the same time the political history of the transmutation of Malay nationalism into Malay capitalism.

I must register a small but critical disclaimer here. This study does not suggest any simplistic reflection of Mahathir's personal biography in the political history of the Malays or of Malaysia. It does not suggest 'Mahathir as individual' to be a perfect microcosm of his society. It only notes a correspondence of social issues and personal impulses, historical concerns and individual anxieties. It hopes to capture Mahathir's unusually complex personality in some of its main dimensions without constantly strait-jacketing it into a 'race and class' *problématique.* As an individual politician who felt a call to service, who possesses a sense of mission, but who has developed a taste for power, Mahathir would be the first to accept that he is both 'representative' and also 'peremptory'. That is to say, he is ultimately (a manifestation of) race *and* class *and* individual, with, need we say it, the whole being more than merely the sum of its parts.

The intellectual biography and ideological portrait of Mahathir which is attempted here finds little theoretical guidance from the existing literature on Malaysian politics. A review of the available biographies of Mahathir is given in Chapter 1. Biographies of other Malaysian politicians are not very helpful either. The biographies of figures like Hussein Onn, Musa Hitam, Tengku Razaleigh Hamzah, and Anwar Ibrahim are often quick productions meant to coincide with the rise of these politicians.[23] Their typical format of partly chronicling the ascendance of their subjects from youth to prominence and partly supplying a selection of speeches has its point. But it is mainly one of public relations and is not very instructive for the purpose of this book.

My study, however, has profited from reading William Shaw's *Tun Razak: His Life and Times* and R. K. Vasil's *Tan Chee Khoon: An Elder Statesman,* considerably finer examples of the genre of Malaysian political biography.[24] One can contrast the cosmopolitan character of Razak's student life in London with Mahathir's much more close-knit Malay students' experience in King Edward VII College of Medicine in Singapore. Vasil's account of the close connection between Tan Chee Khoon's medicine and politics, while he was starting out in both in urban Kuala Lumpur, provides a very useful sense of the path the young Dr Mahathir would tread in moving between medicine and politics in semi-rural Alor Star. I have drawn inspiration and instruction from other sources devoted in one sense or another to the art of political biography. In constructing his biography of Lee Kuan Yew, James Minchin drew upon numerous personal but unnamed sources, incomparably more than I can claim for my study of Mahathir. But I did learn from *No Man Is an Island: A Study of Singapore's Lee Kuan Yew* that one can analyse countless official speeches of a Prime Minister with profit.[25] I read in Hugo Young's biography of Margaret Thatcher, *One of Us: A Biography of Margaret Thatcher*, the story of a kindred spirit of Mahathir's, not least because the 'alderman's daughter'—like the 'schoolmaster's son'—became a 'personality expressed in contradictions'.[26] The idea of capturing Mahathir in a series of different personae—'the nationalist as Prime Minister', 'the Prime Minister as nationalist', 'the populist as authoritarian'—comes from Richard Hofstadter's *The American Political Tradition*.[27] Christopher Lasch's treatment of the American intellectual as a social type, in *The New Radicalism in America: The Intellectual as a Social Type, 1889–1963*, inspired my depiction of the colonial Malayan schoolmaster as a social type in my analysis of Mahathir's religiosity.[28] My understanding of Mahathir's populism owes a great deal to Ghita Ionescu and Ernest Gellner's *Populism: Its Meanings and National Characteristics*.[29] And although one can only tread extremely lightly along the pioneering path of Erik H. Erikson's *Young Man Luther*, it caused me to go boldly into the reconstruction of the 'world of C. H. E. Det'.[30]

1. K. J. Ratnam, *Communalism and the Political Process in Malaya*, Singapore: University of Malaya Press, 1965; K. J. Ratnam and R. S. Milne, 'The 1969 Parliamentary Election in West Malaysia', *Pacific Affairs*, 43, 2 (Summer 1970): 203–27; Gordon P. Means, *Malaysian Politics*, London: University of London Press, 1970; R. K. Vasil, *Politics in a Plural Society: A Study of Non-communal Political Parties in West Malaysia*, Kuala Lumpur: Oxford University Press, 1971.

2. John Funston, *Malay Politics in Malaysia: A Study of the United Malays National Organisation and Parti Islam*, Kuala Lumpur: Heinemann Asia, 1980; Heng Pek Koon, *Chinese Politics in Malaysia: A History of the Malaysian Chinese Association*, Singapore: Oxford University Press, 1988.

3. Karl von Vorys, *Democracy without Consensus: Communalism and Political*

Stability in Malaysia, Princeton: Princeton University Press, 1975; Mohamed Noordin Sopiee, *From Malayan Union to Singapore Separation: Political Unification in the Malaysian Region, 1945–65*, Kuala Lumpur: University of Malaya Press, 1976.

4. Chandra Muzaffar, *Protector?: An Analysis of the Concept and Practice of Loyalty in Leader-led Relationships within Malay Society*, Penang: Aliran, 1979.

5. James V. Jesudason, *Ethnicity and the Economy: The State, Chinese Business, and Multinationals in Malaysia*, Singapore: Oxford University Press, 1989.

6. Cynthia Enloe, *Ethnic Soldiers: State Security in a Divided Society*, Harmondsworth: Penguin, 1980; Judith Strauch, *Chinese Village Politics in the Malaysian State*, Cambridge: Harvard University Press, 1981.

7. Ronald Mead, *Malaysia's National Language Policy and the Legal System*, Yale University Southeast Asia Studies Monograph Series No. 30, New Haven, 1988; Tan Liok Ee, 'Dongjiaozong and the Challenge to Cultural Hegemony, 1951–1987', in Joel S. Kahn and Francis Loh Kok Wah (eds.), *Fragmented Vision: Culture and Politics in Contemporary Malaysia*, Sydney: Asian Studies Association of Australia in association with Allen and Unwin, 1992, pp. 181–201.

8. Jomo K. S., *A Question of Class: Capital, the State, and Uneven Development in Malaysia*, 2nd edn., New York: Monthly Review Press and Journal of Contemporary Asia Publishers, 1988.

9. Lim Mah Hui, *Ownership and Control of the One Hundred Largest Corporations in Malaysia*, Kuala Lumpur: Oxford University Press, 1980.

10. Martin Brennan, 'Class, Politics and Race in Modern Malaysia', in Richard Higgot and Richard Robison (eds.), *Southeast Asia: Essays in the Political Economy of Structural Change*, London: Routledge and Kegan Paul, 1985, pp. 93–127; B. N. Cham, 'Class and Communal Conflict in Malaysia', *Journal of Contemporary Asia*, 5, 4 (1975): 446–61; Fatimah Halim, 'Capital, Labour and the State: The West Malaysian Case', *Journal of Contemporary Asia*, 12, 3 (1982): 259–80; Lim Mah Hui and William Canak, 'The Political Economy of State Policies in Malaysia', *Journal of Contemporary Asia*, 11, 2 (1981): 208–24.

11. Jomo, *A Question of Class*.

12. Ozay Mehmet, *Development in Malaysia: Poverty, Wealth and Trusteeship*, London: Croom Helm, 1986.

13. Jesudason, *Ethnicity and the Economy*.

14. Yoshihara Kunio, *The Rise of Ersatz Capitalism in South-East Asia*, Singapore: Oxford University Press, 1988.

15. Sinnapah Arasaratnam, *Indians in Malaysia and Singapore*, Kuala Lumpur: Oxford University Press, 1970.

16. Syed Husin Ali, *Malay Peasant Society and Leadership*, Kuala Lumpur: Oxford University Press, 1975.

17. Clive Kessler, *Islam in a Malay State: Kelantan, 1838–1969*, Ithaca: Cornell University Press, 1978.

18. Francis Loh Kok Wah, *Beyond the Tin Mines: Coolies, Squatters, and New Villagers in the Kinta Valley, Malaysia, c.1880–1980*, Singapore: Oxford University Press, 1988.

19. Shamsul A. B., *From British to Bumiputera Rule*, Singapore: Institute of Southeast Asian Studies, 1986.

20. Michael Stenson, *Class, Race and Colonialism in West Malaysia: The Indian Case*, St Lucia: University of Queensland Press, 1980.

21. Strauch, *Chinese Village Politics in the Malaysian State*, p. 18.

22. Simon Tan, 'The Rise of State Authoritarianism in Malaysia', *Bulletin of Concerned Asian Scholars*, 22, 3 (July–September 1990): 32–42; Khoo Khay Jin, 'The Grand Vision: Mahathir and Modernization', in Joel S. Kahn and Francis Loh Kok Wah (eds.), *Fragmented Vision: Culture and Politics in Contemporary Malaysia*, Sydney: Asian Studies Association of Australia in association with Allen and Unwin, 1992, pp. 44–76; Francis Loh Kok Wah, 'Modernization, Cultural Revival and Counter-Hegemony: The Kadazans of Sabah in the 1980s', in Joel S. Kahn and Francis Loh Kok Wah (eds.), *Fragmented Vision: Culture and Politics in Contemporary Malaysia*, Sydney: Asian Studies Association of Australia in association with Allen and Unwin, 1992, pp. 225–53.

23. Bruce Gale, *Musa Hitam: A Political Biography*, Petaling Jaya: Eastern Universities Press, 1982; Ranjit Gill, *Razaleigh: An Unending Quest*, Petaling Jaya: Pelanduk Publications, 1986; J. Victor Morais, *Anwar Ibrahim: Resolute in Leadership*, Kuala Lumpur: Arenabuku, 1983; J. Victor Morais, *Hussein Onn: A Tryst with Destiny*, Singapore: Times Books International, 1981.

24. William Shaw, *Tun Razak: His Life and Times*, Kuala Lumpur: Longman Malaysia, 1976; R. K. Vasil, *Tan Chee Khoon: An Elder Statesman*, Petaling Jaya: Pelanduk Publications, 1987.

25. James Minchin, *No Man Is an Island: A Study of Singapore's Lee Kuan Yew*, Sydney: Allen and Unwin, 1986.

26. Hugo Young, *One of Us: A Biography of Margaret Thatcher*, rev. edn., London: Pan Books in association with Macmillan, 1990.

27. Richard Hofstadter, *The American Political Tradition*, New York: Vintage, 1948.

28. Christopher Lasch, *The New Radicalism in America: The Intellectual as a Social Type, 1889–1963*, New York: Vintage, 1965.

29. Ghita Ionescu and Ernest Gellner (eds.), *Populism: Its Meanings and National Characteristics*, London: Weidenfeld and Nicolson, 1970.

30. Erik H. Erikson, *Young Man Luther*, New York: W. W. Norton, 1958.

1

Paradoxes of Mahathirism

> Political scientists, of course, like to fit me into their assumptions. They assume first and then they fit me into those assumptions, they look for evidence that I'm confrontational. When you approach it in that manner, of course you're going to find I'm confrontational. Along those lines then, everybody's confrontational.
>
> Mahathir, quoted in S. Jayasankaran, 'Premier in Power', *Malaysian Business*, 1 January 1988, p. 6.

In Search of Mahathir Mohamad

LET us begin at a point which history may well judge to be nearly the end. In October 1990, Prime Minister Datuk Seri Dr Mahathir bin Mohamad led his ruling coalition, the Barisan Nasional (National Front), to its third consecutive victory at the general election under his leadership. The victory was not unexpected but it had not been easy either. It was only in January 1989 that Mahathir had undergone a coronary bypass operation; it was just over a year since he had returned to work. Mahathir and the Barisan Nasional triumphed over an opposition that presented itself as an alternative coalition that could rule the nation if it won. The leader of the opposition was Tengku Razaleigh Hamzah, who had been narrowly defeated by Mahathir in the contest for the presidency of the United Malays National Organization (UMNO) in April 1987. The Mahathir–Razaleigh battle of 1987 had led to a split in UMNO which, unhealed, caused UMNO's deregistration as a political party in February 1988. Shortly afterwards, Mahathir formed UMNO Baru (New UMNO) which denied membership to Razaleigh and his staunchest supporters. Razaleigh founded a new party, Semangat 46 (Spirit of '46), which led a broad coalition into opposition at the October 1990 election. That coalition was really made up of two smaller coalitions: Angkatan Perpaduan Ummah (APU, or Muslim Unity Force), comprising Semangat 46 and Parti Islam SeMalaysia (PAS), and Gagasan Rakyat, made up of Semangat 46 and the Democratic Action Party (DAP). The failure of the coalition of APU and Gagasan to defeat the Barisan Nasional at the October 1990 election effectively ended Razaleigh's ambition to replace Mahathir as the leader of the nation. It also meant the consolidation of Mahathir's position after several years of widespread disaffection with his leadership. By October 1990, Malaysia's economy, too, had completely recovered from the recession of 1985–6. Malaysia's fine economic performance from late 1987 to 1990 certainly aided Mahathir's electoral cause. More than that, it appeared to vindicate his policies and his management of the economy which had been much criticized during the mid-1980s. Four months after his October 1990 victory, Mahathir unveiled *Wawasan 2020* (Vision 2020), a programme to make Malaysia a 'fully developed country' by the year 2020. In many ways, that marked the fulfilment of a vision that Mahathir had foisted upon the nation ever since he became Prime Minister on 16 July 1981.

It was about then that this study of Mahathir was commenced. It does not pretend to having the fine sense of timing which Mahathir has said every good politician must possess. But his consolidation of power and the continuation of his vision made it plausible to think seriously of a 'Mahathir era' which has been dominated by his presence, of Mahathir's politics with its twists, turns, and dramas, and of 'Mahathirism' as a distinctive ideology. So to speak, Mahathir's moment of triumph in 1990 called for a study of a political career which has spanned almost half a century. The results of that career may be gauged in many personal and political ways. Mahathir has come a long way from being a small-town medical doctor cum Member of Parliament in the early 1960s to being a Prime Minister and a spokesman of the Third World by the 1980s. Mahathir's political progress may also be considered in terms of his evolution from being an occasional writer on Malay affairs for the *Sunday Times*, *circa* 1948–50, to being the most articulate ideologist to have inhabited Malaysia's political stage. Alternatively, one could contrast his misfortune of being an expelled party rebel in 1969 with his fortune of narrowly defeating the revolt against his party presidency in 1987. Mahathir has shown a remarkable ability to retrieve what seemed to be a politically lost position on more than one occasion. This ability, among other things, has helped him win three consecutive general elections in 1982, 1986, and 1990. To top it, he expects that before too long, Malaysia will have elevated itself from a humiliating colonial status, as he first encountered it, to a respected membership in the club of developed countries, with much of that advancement being scripted according to his own vision.

A serious study of Mahathir also seemed to be in order because despite being 'arguably the most analysed Prime Minister ever, the most relentlessly examined',[1] there is no consensus on the 'real' Mahathir, to use a cliché. Two months before he became Prime Minister, Adibah Amin confidently pronounced him to be a 'firm moderate, a natural at human relations'.[2] Six and a half years later, S. Jayasankaran was astonished to find that Mahathir the politician 'simply does not bother' about 'public relations'.[3] Three months after Mahathir had become Prime Minister, K. Das considered that his 'style of talking off the cuff—or appearing to—is the key to Mahathir's character and personality'.[4] Ten years later, Suhaini Aznam portrayed Mahathir as a 'mellowed maverick' who has mastered the art of turning adversity into fortune.[5] Yet, in November 1993, Jon Swain reasoned that Mahathir 'has made an art form of snubbing the Anglophone world' because 'his nationalism almost certainly stems from his early education, when he failed to gain admission to read law in Britain'.[6] Philip Bowring classified Mahathir with the 'single-minded visionary nationalists' (including Mao Zedong and Charles de Gaulle) who have been 'most frustrated' by their own people.[7] But Jomo K. S. argued that Mahathir is 'an economic nationalist, albeit a bourgeois one' but only 'in [the] limited sense' of having a 'vision of transforming Malaysia into a Newly Industrialising Country (NIC) under genuine *Bumiputera* capitalist entrepreneurial leadership'.[8] Roger Kershaw, however, proposed that it would be 'most meaningful to see the Malaysian Prime Minister as a man who responds to the inchoate visions of a new Malay intelligentsia as much as he moulds them'.[9]

If anything, Mahathir seems to continue to baffle—both in the abstract sense of leaving his watchers stranded in incomprehension and in the concrete ways by which he has outwitted his opponents. In that, as one of his interviewers intimated, Mahathir does exude 'a mystique ... out of proportion to the man himself',[10] like the proverbial famous figure whose public life is an open book but whose private being is blanketed by secrecy. Sometimes this Mahathirist 'mystique' is insinuated in platitudes: 'You either love him or hate him, but no one is neutral about him.'[11] Sometimes there can be a real attempt to decipher that mystique by recourse to Mahathir's political style or personality:

> He is a politician whose blunt, no-nonsense style clashes oddly with a political culture that is essentially consensual. More than anything else, according to his friends, he is a shy, reticent individual and yet his combative public image barely hints at this. And in an occupation where public relations is, to say the least, important, this man, much to the despair of many of his aides, simply does not bother.[12]

We can even advance additional reasons why Mahathir continues to defy any easy characterization. First, he appears to act 'out of sync' with his milieu. We know that from the way he behaved like a 'Malay ultra' amidst the Alliance's 'consociationalism' of the 1960s, or when he keeps praising enterprise in Malaysia's age of money politics. Second, he is capable of sudden and major policy voltes-face. Consider when he acted to 'hold the New Economic Policy [NEP] in abeyance' in 1986, or when he chose to host the Commonwealth Heads of Government Meeting after having refused to attend it at the beginning of his premiership. Third, he can quite readily swap political friends and foes. He turned against the Malay student movement in the mid-1970s, co-opted Anwar Ibrahim into UMNO in 1982 only to lose Musa Hitam and Razaleigh Hamzah from 1986 onwards. Fourth, he is not above spurning diplomatic conventions. He directed the 'Buy British Last' campaign in 1981 and pushed the Antarctica issue at the United Nations in the 1980s. Then there are simply times when, like all politicians, he says one thing and does another, or, having done one thing, says it how he pleases. He has even advised politicians that 'after you get your job, I think it is best to forget some of your promises'.[13] But at this level of understanding, useful yet shallow, all we get is a glimpse of Mahathir as 'something of an enigma',[14] not an explanation of the enigma itself.

That there are few biographies of Mahathir is part of the difficulty of explaining Mahathir in a fuller way. The other part is that his biographers have collectively left their work half-done. J. Victor Morais's biography of Mahathir, *Mahathir: A Profile in Courage*, contains some fairly long journalistic encounters but these are heavily drawn from two interviews by other journalists whom Morais failed to cite.[15] Besides, the biography is too deferential; its author is too intent on presenting 'our Prime Minister' to give us a balanced assessment of either the man or the politician. It is content to collate some facts about the man's background in order to sketch the politician's 'profile in courage'. Much of the rest of the book is an unsystematic collection of selected speeches by Mahathir, mostly given without comment. Robin Adshead's *Mahathir of Malaysia*[16] gains from long interviews with Mahathir. It records some of Mahathir's comments on his youth, his political ambition, his career as a doctor, and his medical approach to politics. It has lots of fulsome pictures of Mahathir, in private and in public, at home and abroad, at work and at play. It ends with a gracious appraisal of Mahathir's 'sincerity' by a comrade turned opponent (Musa Hitam), accolades from Mahathir loyalists such as Anwar Ibrahim and Leo Moggie, and an eloquent tribute from Margaret Thatcher. Had Adshead's book had a different format, it would have made an attractive 'coffee-table' edition. But its tone is entirely justificatory, and feeds rumours that the biography was commissioned to improve Mahathir's image around 1988–9 when public anti-Mahathir feelings ran highest.[17] Adshead's Mahathir did no wrong: he was either unappreciated or the victim of circumstances. It is not so much a question of judgement as that one will hardly think that Adshead's Mahathir was ever caught in political storms, so reduced are the controversies of his career to mere ripples of misunderstanding. On a minor note of contrast, *Profile of Dato' Seri Dr Mahathir Mohamad*, published by Malaysia's Ministry of Information, had the boldness at least to identify 'a combative nature' as 'the hallmark of Dr Mahathir's political career'.[18] It supplies a few engaging details of Mahathir's early family life, his passion for self-improvement, and the running of MAHA Clinic. Even its limited mention of Mahathir's manual skills—carpentry, gardening, decoration, and cooking—combines with a recitation of his daily schedule to confirm his reverence for time.[19] Mustafa bin Ali Mohamed's *Mahathir Mohamad*[20] is a light Malay-language biography which repeats most of the well-known personal details of Mahathir's life but contrives to confer a patrician lineage on the plebeian Mahathir. Its value may be judged by its claim that 'the blood that courses through Mahathir's body is the blood of leaders'.[21]

Other, not strictly biographical, studies of Mahathir do not do him much justice either. Murugesu Pathmanathan and David Lazarus's study of Mahathir's foreign policy, *Winds of Change*,[22] has little to commend it. In separate and short essays, the authors introduce Mahathir's foreign policy initiatives poorly and superficially. The rest of the book reproduces selected Mahathir speeches, without comment, without citing the occasions on which they were made, but with titles arbitrarily supplied by the authors. Rahmanmat's *Benarkah Dr Mahathir Pembela Bangsa Melayu?* gives some interesting details of Mahathir's attitudes towards the Malay student movement before and after his political exile.[23] But Rahmanmat, consumed by his own Malay nationalist passion, is too anxious to secure a one-dimensional conviction of Mahathir as someone who fell from the exalted position of a 'Malay saviour' the higher he ascended the rungs of power. Hasan Hj. Hamzah's *Mahathir: Great Malaysian Hero*, a work of 508 pages, cannot be taken seriously.[24] It is one thing if a writer's overriding aim is to ingratiate himself with his hero. It is quite another if entire chapters and smaller sections of his book are taken from other sources. The most brazen instances are the uncredited reproductions of Philip Bowring's 'Mahathir and the New Malay Dilemma'[25] as 'Chapter 10', K. Das's 'Mahathir's "Restoration"'[26] as part of 'Chapter 11', and David Jenkins's 'Proud and Prickly Princes Finally Meet Their Match' as 'Chapter 14'.[27]

Paradoxes of Mahathirism

Dr Mahathir deserves better. But this should not be taken as the author's self-flattery. The literature on Mahathir has left too many questions unanswered. Some of those pertain to deeply personal details which are unlikely to be revealed to outsiders. But, among Malaysian politicians, Mahathir has left an unparalleled record of his ideas in his books, essays, speeches, and interviews. These sources of Mahathir's political ideas, consolidated over forty years, have been inadequately tapped to fill the gap in our understanding of Mahathir. This study is a modest attempt to use mostly those sources in order to apprehend Mahathir's world-view, reconstruct his intellectual biography, and paint his ideological portrait.

The starting-point of the analysis in this study is that Mahathir's ideas constitute a relatively coherent political ideology which may be termed 'Mahathirism'. We may distinguish five core components within Mahathirism: nationalism, capitalism, Islam, populism, and authoritarianism. These four 'isms' plus Islam cover Mahathir's major ideas on politics, economics, religion, power, and leadership as he has expounded on them in three books, numerous essays, many more interviews, and countless speeches. They include ideas which can be discerned from his political praxis—through the policies he had supported at earlier stages of his career or those he has enacted since he became Prime Minister. Here Mahathir's politics may be regarded as the practical realization of his ideas and ideology. What is essential is to explore the meanings, quality, and implications of Mahathir's nationalism, capitalism, Islam, populism, and authoritarianism. This study argues that there is a sufficiently high degree of consistency in Mahathir's main ideas, held over his long political career, to make such an exploration meaningful.

There is a contrary motif that is no less important. There are tensions, contradictions, and paradoxes within Mahathirism, and between this ideology and Mahathir's politics. The core components of Mahathirism reveal not an uninterrupted consistency but significant changes and modifications at different points in Mahathir's career. The tensions between Mahathirist ideology and politics may be seen primarily as the dialectical interplay between a politician's ideas and the milieu within which they find their expression. In rudimentary conceptual terms, we may say that Mahathirism and the specific circumstances in which Mahathir operates as a politician sometimes reinforce, and sometimes alter, each other. This study hopes to highlight how some of the core components of Mahathirism can show discernible paths of evolution during the 'politician's progress'.

This method of tracking the dominant motifs of Mahathirism, and analysing their reaffirmation or amendment, depending on his assessments of his milieu, is the best way of dealing with Mahathir. One of his definitive characteristics is his constant concern to keep ahead of a rapidly changing world. In the life of a nation, as in that of an individual, to be forewarned is to be forearmed; Mahathir considers it the duty of a leader to forearm his people and his nation continuously. The Mahathir presented here will be found diagnosing environmental shifts (whether local or global), identifying emerging obstacles, pin-pointing opportunities, and taking steps to deal with them. Not for nothing are 'dilemmas', 'obstacles', and 'challenges' some of the key words in the Mahathirist lexicon.

The Mahathir who emerges from this study will undeniably assume an essentially political and ideological persona. But Mahathirism, it is suggested, is not just ideas. It incorporates Mahathir's deepest impulses, shades of his personality, and the imprint of his style. These intangible, but personally and politically significant, aspects of Mahathir have been observed, as noted towards the beginning of this chapter, but have not been adequately examined. The most critical of them pertain to Mahathir's youth, his class background, and his medical profession. To be specific, this study intends to clothe an ideological and political persona with what we know of some key personal aspects of Mahathir—his youthful immersion in the Malay world, his class background, and his professional identity as a doctor. By this, the study hopes to develop a more rounded portrait of Mahathir as politician, ideologue, and man.

Nevertheless, we have to reconcile not merely the political and the personal in Mahathir. We must reconcile Mahathir with his society if Mahathirism has any significance. Mahathir's ideas are no doubt individual to the extent that he articulates them and has the political power and authority to implement them in his own way. At the same time, those ideas cannot be isolated from Mahathir's lifelong attempt to grapple with socio-political developments in Malaysia. To that extent, Mahathirism goes beyond Mahathir, and his world-view captures the ethos of particular social groups in Malaysia. Who these groups are and how Mahathirism finally represents them will be discussed in the conclusion of this study.

Let us summarize what has been said so far. It is not just superficial nuances of style and personality—a brusqueness of speech here or an aptitude for controversy there—which lie at the unexplored character of Mahathir. There is a whole political ideology to be unravelled. There is a world-view to chart. There is a religiosity that has been assumed rather than analysed. Mahathir has a class background into which no one has inquired. And there is a medical influence on his politics which he openly refers to but which has hitherto only found trite mention. The fault does not lie in Mahathir's shyness. It is not the reticence of the man that stops us from understanding him. He has loudly proclaimed his views and disdained to hide his thoughts. But these thoughts need a systematic interpretation to give them coherence and clarity. Too often people comprehend Mahathir by apprehending small talk about the big man while they assume that the 'Malay dilemma' is the be-all and end-all of Mahathirist thought. It is the hope of this intellectual biography or ideological portrait to show that the Mahathirist world-view is deeper and more expansive, but that the 'enigma' of Mahathir is not unfathomably murky, so long as we look upon it with method and a critical eye.

How then do we decipher the enigma of Mahathir? It would be awkward to adopt the academic custom of listing some hypotheses and proceeding to test and prove their validity. How does one make hypotheses, a priori, about a subject of an intellectual biography or ideological portrait who has eluded simple and direct characterization? Here we must adopt a slightly maverick departure from the methodological norm. At all times, the concern of this study is to remain exploratory and to investigate the core components of Mahathirism for their meanings, quality, and evolution. It is not hypotheses about the enigma of Mahathir that this study will set out to prove, but the paradoxes and contradictions of Mahathirism which it will explore and try to resolve. If it succeeds, the enigma of Mahathir may become much less baffling. For this purpose, it sets out to examine a series of 'paradoxes of Mahathirism' which, although not exhaustive, seem to represent the mystique of Mahathir. These paradoxes are listed below without any strict order and without further comment. They will be found at suitable points in the study where their reappearance will sum up the exploration of a facet of Mahathir or Mahathirism and a resolution of the paradox itself. It is hoped that we shall then capture the political and ideological essence of Mahathir and Mahathirism.

- Anxious to secure the survival of the Malays, Mahathir seemed prepared to see the end of 'Malayness'.
- The foremost Malay nationalist of his generation, he transformed himself into a new Malaysian nationalist.
- His Social Darwinism accentuated his Malay nationalism. His Malay nationalism checked his Social Darwinism.
- Temperamentally undiplomatic, he fashioned a diplomacy to suit his temperament.

- The ideologue of state-sponsored constructive protection, he became the advocate of capitalist competition.
- In the name of work, he extols Islam. In the name of Islam, he casts work as an imperative. His is the religiosity of the self-made man.
- He would 'Look East' to catch up with the West.
- He personifies his class by personifying his race.
- He praised enterprise in an age of money politics.
- He left medicine for politics only to practise politics as medicine.
- Because he did not simply turn to the bureaucracy to realize his plans, but practically turned upon it, he turned the sceptical public perception of the bureaucracy into a mood more receptive of his vision.
- A rebel in 1969, he beatified loyalty in 1988.
- His frankness is his people's catharsis: that is the quality of his populism.
- His aspirations may not be those of his people: that is the character of his leadership.
- It was never quite clear where his populism dissolved and his authoritarianism congealed.
- He believes in History but is 'terrified' by it.

Sources and Method

There are three primary sources of information which this study relies on to reconstruct Mahathirism as an ideology.

First, there are Mahathir's writings which are indubitably his own efforts to publicize his ideas and arguments. These are made up of three books and numerous essays completed at various points during his political career. The first and best known of these is *The Malay Dilemma*[28] which was published in 1970. It remains the single best source for understanding Mahathir's Malay nationalism. Most observers know *The Malay Dilemma* fairly well, at least for its Malay nationalist content: an exposé of the unacceptable bases of inter-ethnic relations in the pre-1969 period, an insistence on the Malays as the definitive people of Malaysia, an explanation of the hereditary and environmental influences on the Malays, an analysis of Malay traits which are related to their economic backwardness, an advocacy of state-provided 'constructive protection' for the Malays, and a proposal for the 'complete rehabilitation of the Malays'. Observers tend to raid *The Malay Dilemma* for selective quotes which they can use to illustrate isolated points about Mahathir's convictions. Among scholars, Syed Hussein Alatas has tried at some length to refute Mahathir's association of certain Malay traits with economic backwardness as part of the former's broader attempt to debunk 'the myth of the lazy native'.[29] Shaharuddin Maaruf, much less successfully, offered a critique of Mahathir's 'capitalism' against the historical evolution of 'Malay ideas on development'.[30] This study tries, however, to examine *The Malay Dilemma* in its own right by engaging in a rigorous textual analysis. The most important part of this analysis, dealing with Mahathir's Malay nationalism, is to be found in Chapter 2. But we return to *The Malay Dilemma* in Chapter 7 to support the argument about the 'medical' dimensions of Mahathir's populism. The second important book by Mahathir is *The Challenge*,[31] a compilation of essays on various subjects. It is less well known and has been undeservedly neglected. The primary concern of *The Challenge* is to search for a system of values and ethics for the Malays which they might usefully imbibe now that the New Economic Policy was expected to open up new socio-economic opportunities. Here Mahathir deals with the insidious influences of a 'West in decline' and of obscurantist, retreatist, and militant tendencies in the Islamic resurgence in Malaysia during the early 1970s. Chapter 2 of this study undertakes a textual analysis of *The Challenge* to show its ideological significance and to suggest that it represents a transitional point in the evolution of Mahathir's nationalism. Mahathir's third book, *Guide for Small Businessmen*,[32] actually published before *The Challenge*, is a primer on how to start and maintain small-scale trading. It is directed towards prospective Malay entrepreneurs, and may be characterized as an exercise in good economic housekeeping on a small scale. The nature of this primer makes it less susceptible to full-scale analysis but it does reveal Mahathir's deeply held attitudes towards enterprise and good business habits. We can see that it indirectly expresses Mahathir's basic outlook on economic management. The *Guide for Small Businessmen* has been practically ignored. This study makes what use it can of it at specific points.

Of Mahathir's essays, the ones which are most extensively used in this study are those published in the *Sunday Times* (Singapore) from

1948 to 1950. These essays appeared under Mahathir's pseudonym of 'C. H. E. Det'.[33] This is the 'young' and virtually 'unknown' Mahathir. To our knowledge, the C. H. E. Det essays have never been seriously studied but they wonderfully illustrate the young Mahathir's immersion in the Malay world of the late 1940s and early 1950s. An examination of these essays appears in Chapter 3 as a way of concluding the treatment of Mahathir's Malay and Malaysian nationalism in both Chapters 2 and 3. This study contends that we can reconstruct a major part of Mahathir's world-view from the unexplored 'world of C. H. E. Det'.

The second important category of information on Mahathirism comes in the form of speeches given by Mahathir on official occasions, including debates in Parliament. Mahathir's speeches in the Second Parliament, 1964–9, are valuable for their range of subjects and the intensity of Mahathir's polemics, and for forming a picture of the first-term parliamentarian who, rightly or wrongly, then acquired his 'Malay ultra' reputation.[34] Mahathir's speeches from the time he became Prime Minister are especially important since many of them had policy implications of one kind or another.[35] In particular, this study widely uses his speeches on foreign policy, Islam, and the economy. One may well ask if these official speeches, often prepared by expert advisers cum speech writers, reflect the 'real' Mahathir. We can distinguish between minor speeches, such as those given during local ceremonial functions of secondary importance, and major speeches which spell out official positions of the Mahathir administration. We concern ourselves chiefly with the latter. There are three main reasons why we must regard Mahathir as being an active partner in the writing of these speeches, certainly more than a passive reader of prepared texts. First, it is well known that Mahathir handles major speeches with considerable care and responsibility and makes it a point to amend drafts of speeches submitted to him until they meet his approval. Second, many speeches contain phraseology and arguments that closely recall Mahathir's own writing, especially when the speeches deal with some of his favourite subjects, such as values, ethics, the press, and foreign investment. Third, even if some speeches carry nuances and rhetorical flourishes not normally employed by Mahathir in his own writings, he none the less delivers them with respectability and authenticity. This is very often confirmed by the ease with which Mahathir answers questions from journalists or audiences on the subjects addressed by those speeches. This study gives examples of these where appropriate.

The third major source of information is the large number of interviews which Mahathir has given, mainly to the local and foreign media but occasionally to someone of political significance like Tan Chee Khoon.[36] The 'unrehearsed' Mahathir, equally at home in English and Malay, gives no impression of being either reticent or contrived. He willingly discusses his policies and ideas. Ever prepared to roam over a wide range of subjects, he is typically spontaneous in reply, quick to wit, and, when faced with questions of a personal note, uninhibited in talking about himself. There is even a sense of occasion about some of his interviews, for example, the very lengthy ones held on his '100th day in office', his 'first year', and his 'second year' in office. This study has been able to draw upon several Mahathir interviews for insights into his ideas, policies, politics, and personality.

The study has employed several methods to take advantage of this sizeable collection of primary material on Mahathir. Where the material lends itself to an examination in its own right, it has been subjected to an in-depth textual analysis. This is evident in the treatment of *The Malay Dilemma*, *The Challenge*, and the body of C. H. E. Det essays. Where a group of discrete materials deals with a particular subject, excerpts are taken to build up a coherent picture of Mahathir's ideas on that subject. For example, Chapter 5 quotes extensively from his major speeches on Islam and the Muslim world between the 1970s and the 1980s to present 'Mahathir's Islam'. In this instance, reference is also made to Mahathir's numerous comments on Islam, such as those found in *The Challenge*, his presidential addresses at the UMNO General Assembly, and some of his interviews. In order to demonstrate threads of consistency, instances of discrepancy, or a discernible evolution in Mahathir's ideas, the study engages in comparisons of materials which appeared at different times in Mahathir's career. As an example, it uses *The Malay Dilemma*, *The Challenge*, and Mahathir's speeches and policies after he became Prime Minister to track an uneasy transformation of Mahathir's nationalism from its stridently Malay strain of the 1960s to its more Malaysian variety in the 1980s. On the other hand, by comparing C. H. E. Det with the mature Mahathir, the study argues that the former's youthful identification with the Malay cause has bequeathed a striking legacy to the latter's Malay nationalism, anti-Westernism, and Third World diplomacy.

The attempt of this study to reconstruct Mahathir's world-view and to present Mahathirism as a coherent ideology, by relying principally on primary materials, necessitates culling and reorganizing a great number of excerpts from original but diverse texts. Some may argue that this method is judgemental, even fundamentally discriminatory. It is, to the extent that we select excerpts we think are representative, useful, or illuminating, and weave them into the text in ways we consider to be logical and elegant. The result may not much resemble Mahathir's originals. But the study typically allows Mahathir to 'speak for himself': the vast majority of the excerpts are directly attributable to Mahathir himself. The study also tries to maintain a fidelity between text and context. Where it helps to explain a short excerpt or to justify its use, the study provides the full passage in which the excerpt appears. The study consistently clarifies the context in which an original whole text appears. These measures seek to limit our errors to those of interpreting 'what Mahathir really means', and to avoid those belonging to the realm of wilfully distorting 'what Mahathir actually said'.

1. S. Jayasankaran, 'Mahathir: The Man and the PM', *Malaysian Business*, 1 January 1988, p. 12.

2. Adibah Amin, 'Mahathir—A Committed Moderate', *New Straits Times*, 16 May 1981.

3. Jayasankaran, 'Mahathir: The Man and the PM', p. 12.

4. K. Das, 'A Tough Guy Takes Over', *Far Eastern Economic Review*, 30 October 1981, p. 30.

5. Suhaini Aznam, 'Mellowed Maverick', *Far Eastern Economic Review*, 18 July 1991, p. 24.

6. Jon Swain, 'Disgusted of Malaysia Aggravates the Anglos', *The Sunday Times*, London, 28 November 1993. Swain's view is typical of many unattributed and undocumented comments on 'the origin of Mahathir's Anglophobia', for example: 'Some have claimed that he [Mahathir] became "anti-British" after he was rejected for a Commonwealth Scholarship while a student at the University of Malaya (then in Singapore)' (Gordon P. Means, *Malaysian Politics: The Second Generation*, Singapore: Oxford University Press, 1991, p. 106, n. 23). Also see Michael Vatikiotis, 'The Making of a Maverick', *Far Eastern Economic Review*, 20 August 1992, pp. 18–19.

7. Philip Bowring, 'Mahathir and the New Malay Dilemma', *Far Eastern Economic Review*, 9 April 1982, p. 20.

8. Jomo K. S., *Growth and Structural Change in the Malaysian Economy*, London: Macmillan, 1990, p. 201.

9. Roger Kershaw, 'Anglo-Malaysian Relations: Old Roles Versus New Rules', *International Affairs*, 59, 4 (Autumn 1983): 647.

10. Jayasankaran, 'Mahathir: The Man and the PM', p. 12.

11. So spoke a 'veteran politician', cited in Suhaini, 'Mellowed Maverick', p. 24. Suhaini concluded an earlier article by noting that 'not easily ignored, Mahathir is either admired or resented, but even in the villages, very few feel ambivalent about him'. (See Suhaini Aznam, 'Love Him Or Not, You Can Never Lose Sight of Him', *Far Eastern Economic Review*, 2 January 1986, p. 24.)

12. Jayasankaran, 'Mahathir: The Man and the PM', p. 12. To compound the problem, 'I think he privately feels he's much misunderstood but he doesn't seem to give a damn' (ibid.).

13. Mahathir Mohamad, *Regionalism, Globalism and Spheres of Influence: ASEAN and the Challenge of Change into the 21st Century*, Singapore: Institute of Southeast Asian Studies, 1989, p. 22.

14. Jayasankaran,'Mahathir: The Man and the PM', p. 12.

15. J. Victor Morais, *Mahathir: A Profile in Courage*, Singapore: Eastern Universities Press, 1982. The interviews were by Leung Thong Ping, 'Mahathir', *Sunday Mail*, 2 April 1972, and Munir Majid, 'Datuk Seri Dr Mahathir Mohamad: Power and Responsibility', *Malaysian Business*, October 1980, pp. 4–10.

16. Robin Adshead, *Mahathir of Malaysia*, London: Hibiscus Publishing Company, 1989.

17. It would be interesting to know what other books are published by the 'Hibiscus Publishing Company' located in 'the United Kingdom', the 'hibiscus' being Malaysia's 'national flower'.

18. Even if it had an immediate qualifier: 'when confronting issues of injustice or inequality' (Malaysia, Ministry of Information, *Profile of Dato' Seri Dr Mahathir Mohamad*, Kuala Lumpur: Federal Department of Information, 1982, p. 11).

19. Ibid., pp. 20–4.

20. Mustafa bin Ali Mohamed, *Mahathir Mohamad*, Petaling Jaya: Pelanduk Publications, 1986.

21. Note: 'Mahathir's father was named Mohamad bin Iskandar and his mother was named Wan Tempawan, of Malay descent. His mother was descended from Malay leaders of long ago, so that the blood that courses through Mahathir's body is the blood of leaders. His mother is the descendant of Wan Su, that is, Dato' Temenggong Kulut, Bukit Lada, Kedah' (ibid.; no pagination given but third page of text). No time is wasted on Mahathir's paternal lineage, presumably because his father, Mohamad Iskandar, was half-Indian. Mahathir's old house in Alor Star, now converted into a Mahathir museum, displays a genealogical chart of Mahathir's lineage through the mother, Wan Tempawan, but has nothing on the father's side. This eager but lopsided emphasis on Mahathir's 'Malay' lineage is unjust to all parties concerned. On the basis of Mahathir's positive comments on

interracial marriages, belief in the hereditary influence on race, and complete identification with the Malay cause, one cannot imagine him being anything but proud of his mixed parentage.

22. Murugesu Pathmanathan and David Lazarus (eds.), *Winds of Change: The Mahathir Impact on Malaysia's Foreign Policy*, Kuala Lumpur: Eastview Productions, 1984.

23. Rahmanmat, *Benarkah Dr Mahathir Pembela Bangsa Melayu?*, Kuala Lumpur: Golden Books, 1982.

24. Hasan Hj. Hamzah, *Mahathir: Great Malaysian Hero*, Kuala Lumpur: Mediaprint Publications, 1990.

25. *Far Eastern Economic Review*, 9 April 1982, pp. 20–2.

26. *Far Eastern Economic Review*, 11 June 1982, pp. 38–41.

27. *Far Eastern Economic Review*, 22 February 1984, pp. 12–15. Some concluding sections of this article were unused.

28. Mahathir Mohamad, *The Malay Dilemma*, Singapore: Donald Moore for Asia Pacific Press, 1970.

29. Syed Hussein Alatas, *The Myth of the Lazy Native*, London: Frank Cass, 1977. See the section entitled 'Out of Malay Backwardness' in Chapter 4 of this study for a discussion of Alatas's critique of Mahathir's arguments.

30. Shaharuddin Maaruf, *Malay Ideas on Development: From Feudal Lord to Capitalist*, Singapore: Times Books International, 1988. See the section entitled 'Out of Malay Backwardness' in Chapter 4 of this study, for further references to Shaharuddin's comments on Mahathir's capitalism.

31. Mahathir Mohamad, *The Challenge*, Petaling Jaya: Pelanduk Publications, 1986; translated from *Menghadapi Cabaran*, Kuala Lumpur: Pustaka Antara, 1976.

32. Mahathir Mohamad, *Guide for Small Businessmen*, Petaling Jaya: Eastern Universities Press, 1985; translated from *Panduan Peniaga Kecil*, 2nd edn., Kuala Lumpur: Dewan Bahasa dan Pustaka, 1982; first published in 1973.

33. For full references to the C. H. E. Det essays and our discussion of them, see the section entitled 'The Legacy of C. H. E. Det' in Chapter 3.

34. Malaysia, *Dewan Ra'ayat, Parliamentary Debates*, Second Parliament, 1964–9.

35. The single best source of Mahathir's official speeches is the quarterly *Foreign Affairs Malaysia*, published by the Malaysian government. A complete list of the speeches cited in this study appears in the Bibliography.

36. A list of the interviews consulted for this study appears in the Bibliography.

2

Dilemmas of Malay Nationalism

> But supposing you gain independence and you have nothing, nothing in that independent country, you are still having to serve other people, then independence would be quite meaningless to the indigenous people. You are still at the same level with the same status that you were in when you were under the British. It seems pointless to struggle for independence from the British only to be dependent upon others. That is why countries insist that when they are independent there must be an identity for that country which is related to the indigenous people.
>
> Mahathir Mohamad, *Regionalism, Globalism and Spheres of Influence: ASEAN and the Challenge of Change into the 21st Century*, Singapore: Institute of Southeast Asian Studies, 1989, pp. 34–5.

The Credentials of the 'Ultra'

SINCE 1969 no one in Malaysia has arguably been so totally identified with the Malay cause as has Mahathir. In the public imagination, within political circles, on both sides of the ethnic divide between Malays and non-Malays, and to most domestic and foreign observers of Malaysian politics, Mahathir has been the foremost Malay nationalist of his time.

It is, one might say, almost enigmatically so. Because of his age, Mahathir was not to be found among the most famous names of pre-Merdeka Malay nationalism, for example, Dato Onn Jaafar, Ibrahim Yaakob, Burhanuddin al-Helmy, and Ahmad Boestamam. Nor would Mahathir be located among the vanguard of the UMNO-led independence movement which included Tunku Abdul Rahman, Tun Abdul Razak, and Tun Dr Ismail. Because he was not linked to any particular item of the Malay nationalist agenda, Mahathir, too, did not stand out as a single-issue advocate—unlike, say, Syed Nasir bin Syed Ismail, who emerged as the leading Malay language champion in the 1960s,[1] or Abdul Aziz bin Ishak, who suffered for his failed attempts to alleviate rural Malay poverty,[2] or Tengku Razaleigh Hamzah, who personified the 1970s push towards *bumiputera* economic development.[3] How then did Mahathir become the most forceful spokesman of the Malay community more than a decade before he became its principal leader?

His beginnings were modest. Before becoming a full-time politician, he made his name as a medical doctor in Alor Star. In 1957, Mahathir opened MAHA Clinic, one out of only five private clinics in Alor Star, and the first to be established by a Malay doctor in the town. Respected as a doctor among his community, Mahathir did not neglect performing his share of community service.[4] A considerate attitude towards his patients, poorer Malays especially, and an active involvement in local Malay politics led to his being called 'Dr UMNO'. It was a useful sobriquet for the doctor-politician who was elected as the Member of Parliament for Kota Star Selatan in 1964.

Mahathir's career as a first-term parliamentarian coincided with a period that experienced some of the most bitter reverberations of communal politics. The 1964–5 conflict between the ruling Alliance and the People's Action Party (PAP) of Singapore, the National Language Act controversy of 1967, the Labour Party-led hartal of 1967, and the electoral campaigns of 1969 all contributed to increasing ethnic confrontation which culminated in the violence of May 13 1969. During that period, few politicians of any persuasion were able to escape being ensnared in ethnic challenges. Many thrived on them. In this climate, it was not long before Mahathir became identified with those UMNO politicians and Malay intellectuals who reacted to any real or imagined threat of Chinese encroachment on the 'special position' of the Malays with great acerbity. These Malay politicians, well-known ones being Syed Ja'afar Albar, Syed Nasir, Harun Idris, Musa Hitam, and Abdullah Ahmad, were seen by their Malay admirers to be uncompromising Malay nationalists. Their non-Malay detractors tended to consider them as unbending Malay 'ultras', to use a label popularized by one of their main opponents, Lee Kuan Yew.[5]

Mahathir's Malay firster image went 'official' in Parliament on 26 May 1965. Still a relatively new backbencher, he was picked to lead the Alliance's offensive against the Socialist Front and, even more so, the PAP. Mahathir rose to the occasion by denouncing all the Alliance's opponents from trade unions to the opposition parties. But it was the 'Chinese communalism' of the 'so-called non-communal parties', that is, the Socialist Front and the PAP, that remained his ultimate target. 'The so-called non-communal parties', he declared, 'are the most communal and racialist in their attitudes. Basically they are pure Chinese chauvinists, or they derive their inspiration from a common dislike for the Malays.'[6]

The Socialist Front was 'almost purely a Chinese organization, led and supported by people whose only reason for coming together is their desire to propagate a "Chinese *über Alles*" ideology'.[7] But 'if the Socialist Front is communal ... behind the [PAP's] veneer of non-communalism is the most rabid form of communalism yet practised in Malaysia'.[8] The PAP's 'type of Chinese' were 'insular, selfish and arrogant' and 'have in most instances never crossed the Causeway. They are in fact overseas Chinese first—more specifically Chinese of the southern region as in their mind China is the centre of the world—and Malaysians a very poor second—a status so utterly artificial to them that it finds difficulty in percolating through their cranium.'[9] He allowed only one difference between the Socialist Front and the PAP: 'the Socialist Front is merely pro-Chinese and communist-orientated, while the PAP is pro-Chinese, communist-orientated, and positively anti-Malay'.[10]

So inflamed an attack on Chinese communalism might have been occasioned by the mutual provocations that had been passing between UMNO and the PAP which had taken turns, as it were, to encroach on what should have been recognized as each other's sphere of influence. Still, it ill disguised its own emotive appeal to a Malay communalism that was no less intemperate for its being alarmed by the PAP's 'Malaysian Malaysia' campaign.

Mahathir's 26 May 1965 'Address of Thanks' for the Yang di-Pertuan Agong's speech to Parliament was delivered when the Alliance–PAP conflict was approaching its climax, less than three months before Singapore was expelled from Malaysia on 9 August. Mahathir's 'rather vigorous tirade' which sparked off 'the emotionalism of the debate',[11] as Lim Chong Eu described it, enhanced Mahathir's standing among Malay political circles in another way. He had dared to lock horns directly with Lee Kuan Yew, whose brilliance as a politician and debater was taken for granted, if grudgingly, by contemporaries and opponents alike. Lim Chong Eu once remarked that 'when the Tunku makes a mistake, people say it is natural. When Lee Kuan Yew makes a mistake, they say it is impossible.'[12] Even Tun Dr Ismail, not someone who was unnerved by Lee Kuan Yew, was reported to have advised Razak: 'Don't talk to that fellow [Lee Kuan Yew] too long—he'll persuade you of anything!'[13] Mahathir was unintimidated by 'that fellow' and contemptuously dismissed 'the mad ambition of one man to see himself as the first Chinese Prime Minister of Malaysia'.[14] Mahathir took special pride in deflating 'the sort of stance that this Party [PAP] is fond of adopting: assume a brave front and dare everyone in the hope that it will overawe what it presumes to be the less clever and more timid groups into refusing to rise to the challenge'.[15]

Mahathir was already no less practised than the next politician in the art of ethnic accusation and counter-accusation. In later years, he often protested:

> I have been misinterpreted and misunderstood, even at the time when I was labelled as Ultra. I felt that the labelling was a political gimmick, and that image is unacceptable to a large majority of Malaysians. When I was a Member of Parliament, all I was talking about was that the Malays should have a fair share in this country—no more than that.[16]

Was it just gimmicks and labels and 'no more than that'? If so, Mahathir's rhetoric was at odds with the benignity of his intentions. He relished the display of his native ability for polemics. Apart from anything else, it permitted him to serve notice that he would be quick and able to rise to any—Chinese—challenge. As he recalled to Tan Chee Khoon two decades later: 'When there was a demonstration in 1967 . . . I told Tun Ismail that if they wanted it, I was prepared to bring 20,000 people from Kedah for a demonstration in Kuala Lumpur just to show how strongly the people supported the Government.'[17] Very likely it was just that sort of fighting talk,[18] or some variation of it, carelessly uttered in an environment of deteriorating ethnic relations, that lent credence to a rumour, widely held during the 1969 election campaign, that 'in Kedah Dr Mahathir advised his Chinese constituents not to vote for him, as he would not represent their interests in Parliament'.[19]

Robin Adshead, ever too eager to paint Mahathir's portrait without blemish, presents a victim's picture of his difficulties with the

Chinese voters prior to the 1969 election:

He had caused some difficulties for himself by his outspoken views on the advancement of the Malays. For his opinions, he was labelled 'a Malay Ultra' by the Chinese, who voted heavily against him. Once given such a label, he says, it was hard to live down, even when he had already done much for the Chinese in his constituency, including donating some scholarships in local schools. The tag of 'Ultra' made even the most innocent statement he made seem extreme and hampered his attempts to explain his stand in a rational manner.[20]

Chamil Wariya, maybe unwittingly, unveils a combative dimension to the indiscretion: 'As a result of his stridence in voicing the complaints of the Malays in their own homeland, he was not liked by the Chinese. When he knew the feelings of the non-Malays towards him, Dr Mahathir openly countered that he would not hope for their support in the election.'[21]

In the 1969 election, Mahathir failed to defend his Kota Star Selatan seat against the challenge made by Haji Yusof Rawa of Partai Islam SeMalaysia (PAS). Mahathir's defeat was one out of eight parliamentary losses suffered by UMNO, or out of twenty-three suffered by the Alliance, when the opposition parties made gains unprecedented in the history of Malaysian general elections. In trying to account for his defeat, Mahathir and his supporters have made much of his statement about not needing the support of the Chinese voters and the assumed loss of support from the Chinese because of Mahathir's 'ultra' label. Nineteen years after the event, Chamil Wariya's assessment, for all its caution, made much the same point:

His statement made an impact on his effort to defend the Kota Star Selatan parliamentary seat in the 1969 election. Because the Chinese voters in that parliamentary constituency were thought not to have voted for him but to have given their votes to the PAS candidate, thus Mahathir failed to defend his position in parliament.[22]

And if Karl von Vorys's account is accurate, Mahathir seemed to have had no doubt as to the cause of his defeat: 'When Dr Mahathir was confronted by his own defeat at 11.00 p.m. the preceding night, he concluded that the Chinese had "betrayed" him. It was after all as simple as that.'[23]

It was not as simple as that. Many factors featured in the 1969 election in general and would have influenced Mahathir's specific contest as well. Even if an explanation for Mahathir's defeat was to be sought strictly in terms of ethnic voting patterns, the Malay voters' disenchantment with UMNO led by Prime Minister Tunku Abdul Rahman was no less important a reason than the Chinese voters' unhappiness with Mahathir's ultra image. This Mahathir openly acknowledged—but only after May 13.

Before May 13, the continued participation of the Malaysian Chinese Association (MCA) in the government had become a serious issue. Following the party's poor showing in the election, the MCA leadership planned to keep the party out of the new Cabinet.[24] The MCA's intention matched the thoughts of some UMNO figures, notably Mahathir, Syed Nasir, and Syed Ja'afar Albar, who publicly called for the MCA's exclusion from the Cabinet and the State Executive Councils. Later, Mahathir supplied the most direct argument for their demand: 'The whole idea of having the MCA in the Cabinet is that the MCA represents Chinese views. It can be seen from the last election that the MCA is not supported by the large majority of the Chinese, so having the MCA in the Cabinet does not serve the purpose of giving representation to the Chinese.'[25]

But whereas the MCA conceived of its non-participation as a way to 'punish' the Chinese voters for their 'defection', Mahathir and his allies wanted the MCA's exclusion to mark the end of the former Alliance power structure. To put it differently, the latter demanded an UMNO-dominated government with a clear 'pro-Malay' orientation, hoping thereby to retrieve UMNO's own eroded Malay base.[26]

After violence broke out on May 13, Mahathir went even further. He blamed the Malay-initiated violence on the Chinese for making excessive demands on the Alliance government and he blamed the Tunku for placating them. In a letter to the Tunku, dated 17 June 1969, Mahathir derided him for holding 'opinions ... [which] ... were based on stories you heard from people who surround you, and who tell you only what they think you like to hear or should hear'.[27] 'Permit me', the letter continued, 'to tell you what the position, the thoughts and the opinions of the people are really.'[28] Mahathir sneered that the 'happiest prime minister in the world', as the Tunku once described himself, was now the object of hatred of 'the Malays whether they are UMNO or PMIP [Pan-Malayan Islamic Party] supporters ... especially those who had lost homes, children and relatives'.[29] But the ultimate object of the letter—'deliberately offensive' but representing 'the mood of many Malays'—was to call for the Tunku's resignation from office. Widely circulated before it was banned by the police, Mahathir's letter became symbolic of a party rebellion against the Tunku. In a last gasp, the Tunku managed, with Razak's and Tun Dr Ismail's support, to have Mahathir expelled from UMNO.[31] Other details of this confrontation between Mahathir and the Tunku are already well documented and need not be repeated here.[32]

However, the conjuncture of his electoral defeat, the violence of May 13, his letter to the Tunku, and his expulsion from UMNO became a turning-point in Mahathir's political career. It transformed him from being a failed electoral candidate into a living symbol of Malay nationalism. Before the confrontation, Mahathir was only one of several 'ultras'. After his expulsion—seen as a personal sacrifice—he became something of a martyr for the Malay cause. Interestingly, Mahathir recalled that 'after I was expelled, people were scared to come and see me. They felt they might be incriminated. There was a policeman watching the house.'[33] Others saw it differently: he 'immediately became a cult figure in exile, with prominent Malays beating a path to his door'.[34]

What accounted for Mahathir's confrontation with the Tunku—'a risky stance, as he [Mahathir] acknowledges, all previous critics of the Tunku having disappeared from the political scene permanently'?[35] Was it an impassioned outburst or a coldly calculated gambit, or a hybrid of both? Perhaps it had to do with 'cost-benefit' evaluation: compared to those who were in Parliament, he had less to lose by being the 'front man for the task' of 'making changes to the leadership' of UMNO.[36] Perhaps it was opportunism, shrewd political calculation allied to keen timing: 'the Tunku had already lost credibility among the Malays and Mahathir crystalised their disenchantment with him'.[37] Perhaps it was fundamentally a sheer instinct for survival that came from a deeper ambition. K. Das reported a conversation he once had with Musa Hitam to the following effect:

> The fact that Musa and Mahathir were once seen as extreme elements in UMNO was something Musa found amusing. He did not deny that he was a Malay politician with the need to nurse the Malay constituency and keep alive the notion of the sacredness of the totem of a Malay polity, to keep him secure in his party. That was not his language at all, but there was an eggs-must-be-broken-to-make-omelettes mood in our talk.

During a *tête-à-tête* at the E & O Hotel in Penang, I think it was in 1976, he told me that a young Malaysian politician had to play the race thing to the hilt even if there was not a single chauvinistic bone in his body. It had nothing to do with being a chauvinist. He said securing that constituency was critical—and he was not talking about any narrow electoral constituency. But once that was done, the politician could then consider how to become a statesman. Again those were not his words but that was the drift of his thinking.[38]

For a young and ambitious UMNO politician—needing to 'nurse the Malay constituency'—it was one thing to acknowledge Malay disaffection and quite another to blame Malay voters for one's defeat. It was perhaps psychologically less traumatic, certainly tactically more politic, to blame both Malay disaffection and one's defeat on the Chinese, and in time, the Tunku, too. If Mahathir lost his 'narrow electoral constituency' because of his 'ultra' label, as he believed it, he gained a 'national' constituency by engaging in even more strikingly 'ultra' action. Adshead records Mahathir's later appreciation of this turning-point in his political career: 'His criticism of the first Prime Minister and his subsequent expulsion from the Party appeared to have worked in his favour. Even he admits that it is possible that had he not gained notoriety due to his criticism of Tunku Abdul Rahman, he would not be Prime Minister today.'[39]

The Malay Dilemma: *Malay Nationalism and Social Darwinism*

Ban and Validity

During his political exile, Mahathir wrote *The Malay Dilemma*.* It contained such strong views, expressed in strong language, on many sensitive subjects that it would probably have kept the author in the public, if controversial, light for some time. The book was published in Singapore in 1970 but it was banned in Malaysia, thereby adding (if only by speculation as to its contents)[40] to Mahathir's fame as a Malay nationalist, or, alternatively, his notoriety as a Malay extrem-

*In this section, references to this book are accompanied by the relevant page numbers.

ist. Despite Razak's rehabilitation of Mahathir in 1972, the ban on *The Malay Dilemma* continued 'in deference to Tunku Abdul Rahman'[41] until after Mahathir became Prime Minister in July 1981. On 30 July 1981, his deputy, Musa Hitam, who was also Minister of Home Affairs, removed the ban, presumably out of deference to the new Prime Minister.

Mahathir himself thought that the lifting of the ban would allow 'the people to know what their Prime Minister thinks', to 'understand me more'[42] especially since 'I have not revised any of my views'. When Tan Chee Khoon asked Mahathir if he had 'modified [his] views as contained in that book', Mahathir replied:

> Well, that book was written in the late sixties.... Of course the situation then was quite different and there were many things I said which were valid then.
>
> [Question: Which [are] no longer valid today?]
>
> That they are not valid now I cannot say. All the views are still held by me. But certainly some of them are still valid and where they need to be acted on, we do act.[43]

However, the eleven-year ban on the book might have contributed to its general neglect by scholars of Malaysian politics. With notable exceptions,[44] studies which have cited *The Malay Dilemma*'s contents have tended to do so in a cursory manner. They typically use selective excerpts to illustrate discrete facets of Mahathir's political ideas, such as his explanation of the 'backwardness' of the Malays, his insistence on the Malays as the 'definitive people' of Malaysia, his defence of Malay company directors, and his calls for an 'affirmative action' programme in aid of the Malays. Given the polemical character of *The Malay Dilemma*, it is not difficult to extract portions of Mahathir's personal, peculiar, and sometimes idiosyncratic pronouncements to demonstrate particular and isolated points. But doing so, without considering the book as a whole, overlooks what is most forceful and striking about *The Malay Dilemma*, that is, it is the definitive document of post-Merdeka, pre-NEP Malay nationalism.

Definitive People, Backward Community

The scope of *The Malay Dilemma*'s concerns and the tone of its delivery suggested as much. First, it presented Mahathir's analysis of 'what went wrong' on May 13:

> In the first place the Government started off on the wrong premise. It believed that there had been racial harmony in the past and that the Sino-Malay cooperation to achieve Independence was an example of racial harmony. It believed that the Chinese were only interested in business and acquisition of wealth, and that the Malays wished only to become Government servants. These ridiculous assumptions led to policies that undermined whatever superficial understanding there was between Malays and non-Malays. On top of this the Government, glorifying in its massive strength, became contemptuous of criticisms directed at it either by the opposition or its own supporters. The gulf between the Government and the people widened so that the Government was no longer able to feel the pulse of the people or interpret it correctly. It was therefore unable to appreciate the radical change in the thinking of the people from the time of Independence and as the 1969 elections approached. And finally when it won by such a reduced majority the Government went into a state of shock which marred its judgement. And so murder and arson and anarchy exploded on 13 May 1969 (p. 15).

Ideologically, such a post-mortem fulfilled two purposes. It served as the oration at the funeral of the Tunku's regime and its associated Alliance power structure. By rejecting the 'ridiculous assumption' that 'the Chinese were only interested in business' while 'the Malays only wished to become Government servants', *The Malay Dilemma* thereby dismissed one of the commonly assumed achievements of the Alliance—the stable management of Malaysia's plural society on the 'separatist' formula of 'Malays in politics' and 'Chinese in economics'. As such the book's post-mortem on May 13 was also an ideological justification for scuttling the 'Alliance contract' and dismantling the political economy which it underwrote. An argument along this direction was already discernible in the post-election demand by Mahathir and others to exclude the MCA from representation in the Cabinet and State Executive Councils.

Second, *The Malay Dilemma* elaborated a theory of 'the Malay economic dilemma' which—even if its 'hereditary–environmental'[45] portions were not generally accepted—elevated the very notion of 'Malay economic backwardness' (p. 57) itself to the very top of the political and economic agenda of the post-Tunku era. Before the Tunku retired, Razak and a coterie of younger UMNO politicians had fastened on Malay discontent, arising out of Malay poverty, as the underlying cause of the May 13 violence. Along that line of reasoning, Malay economic backwardness and the need to overcome it became the *raison d'être* of the New Economic Policy (NEP). This, rather than the more unifying and abstruse Rukunegara, formed the dominant ideological framework of the post-1969 polity. Ideologically, the book's analysis of the 'Malay economic dilemma' paved the way for replacing the expediency of 'helping the Malays' during the Tunku's administration with the political imperative of 'restructuring' beginning with Razak's administration. Part of the spirit which moved that replacement was already evident in Mahathir's insistence that 'harsh punitive measures should be meted out to those who impede the elevation of the Malays to an equality with the other races' (p. 60).

Third, and above all else, *The Malay Dilemma* gave an unrestrained expression to the stock anxieties which beset the Malay nationalism of that period. It articulated the Malay community's deep and persistent unease about the 'far too many non-Malay citizens who can swamp the Malays' (p. 31) in a land that was 'no more *Tanah Melayu*' (p. 121). Its longest chapter (Chapter 8, pp. 115–53) was unswerving in its defence of the Malays as the 'definitive people' (p. 152, and *passim*):

> I contend that the Malays are the original or indigenous people of Malaya and the only people who can claim Malaya as their one and only country. In accordance with practice all over the world, this confers on the Malays certain inalienable rights over the forms and obligations of citizenship which can be imposed on citizens of non-indigenous origin (p. 133).

It was unbending in rejecting non-Malay claims to political, linguistic, and cultural parity with the Malays:

> Settlers willing to conform to the characteristics of the definitive citizen will in fact become definitive citizens and will exercise the same rights and privileges. But these rights and privileges do not include changing the characteristics of the definitive race. This emphasis on definitive characteristics rather than ethnic origin is an important principle and its application is also seen in the limitation of the rights of newer citizens to change these characteristics (p. 135).

The Malay Dilemma laid bare the Malay sense of humiliation at their economic backwardness which contrasted with the 'complete Sinocization [*sic*] of the economy of the country' (p. 51). It recorded the Malay resentment of the 'little effort made to right the economic wrongs from which they suffer' (p. 60). It argued that 'while Independence has definitely boosted Malay involvement in the commercial life of the nation' (p. 47), the 'Malay economic dilemma' (p. 51) 'is still there because for every step forward that the Malays make in the economic field other races make ten. It is there because other policies of the Independent Government of Malaysia offset the policy towards helping the Malays' (p. 47). *The Malay Dilemma* also captured the perplexity of the Malays in dealing with their own economic dilemma which, again, 'is there because the concept of business has changed and changed again, even as the Malays begin to understand the orthodox methods which had originally defeated them' (p. 47). And, finally, it posed the now familiar 'Malay dilemma': 'The Malay dilemma is whether they should stop trying to help themselves in order that they should be proud to be the poor citizens of a prosperous country or whether they should try to get at some of the riches that this country boasts of, even if it blurs the economic picture of Malaysia a little' (p. 61). To that, the book's reply was unambivalent:

> The cup of Malay bitterness must be diluted. A solution must be found, an equitable solution which denies nothing to anyone and yet gives the Malay his place in the Malayan sun. The Malay problem must be enunciated, analyzed and evaluated so as to enable us to find a solution. The problem must be faced, and it must be faced now before it is too late (p. 121).

After 'enunciating, analyzing and evaluating' the Malay dilemma in its various forms, as outlined above, *The Malay Dilemma* called on the state to work out a programme of 'constructive protection' (p. 31) for the Malays. In business, for example, it defended the policy of encouraging 'the appointment of Malays as directors in large non-Malay companies' (p. 43) without which 'Malay talent in business would never be able to manifest itself' (p. 45). That 'the much maligned "Ali–Baba" business set-up' (p. 46) would 'continue to be a feature of Malay participation in business for a long time' (p. 47) was 'unfortunate' (p. 47). But since 'ninety per cent of the wealth is in the hands of the Chinese, it is ridiculous to set up exclusively Malay companies which cater only for the poor Malays' (pp. 46–7).

The Malay Dilemma's underlying argument was that the economic inequality between the Malays and the non-Malays had become so severe under colonialism that the 'favoured position' (p. 43), 'privileges' (p. 46), and 'preferential treatment' (p. 47) accorded to the Malays, post-independence, were necessary to prevent their position from deteriorating. In particular, the constitutional provisions for Malay Land Reserve (pp. 69–72), scholarships for Malay students (pp. 73–6), and quotas for Malay employment in the civil service (pp. 76–8)—often criticized by the opposition parties—were completely justifiable.

The Malay Dilemma explicitly linked the Malay Land Reserve to the Malay anxiety of becoming dispossessed of their own homeland:

> The Malay Land Reserve Laws were by intention a measure to counter what was becoming quite obvious during the colonial era: that the Malays were losing all their land to richer immigrants and foreigners. Clearly, unless legal measures were adopted, the ultimate result would be that the Malays would become tenants of foreign and immigrant landlords in their own country. In other words, although the Malays called Malaya *Tanah Melayu* or Malay Land, there would in fact be no real land belonging to them. The possibility was distinct and credible at one time (p. 70).

In its defence of preferential treatment for Malay students in the government's award of scholarships, the book concluded:

> It is ... not for reasons of Malay superiority that preferential treatment for Malays in scholarship awards was insisted upon. The scholarships are not a manifestation of racial inequality. They are a means of breaking down the superior position of the non-Malays in the field of education. The Malays are not proud of this treatment. They are not proud of the 'privilege' of being protected by law like cripples. They would like to get rid of these privileges if they can, but they have to let pride take second place to the facts of life (p. 76).

A broadly similar 'inter-ethnic levelling' rationale was advanced in the case of the maintenance of a 'four-to-one' Malay-to-non-Malay ratio in the civil service:

> By no stretch of the imagination could it be said that the quota of Malays in the Civil [Administrative] Service contributes to or constitutes racial inequality. It is obviously a device to correct existing and potential racial inequality. One look at the annual school certificate results of the students

in higher educational institutions should be enough to give a picture of the Malaysian Government Service without the Civil Service quota. It is possible, with racial prejudice as evident as it is now, that without the quota provisions there would be no Malays in Government Service at all (p. 78).

The Malay Dilemma yielded nothing in the way of the 'special rights' reserved for Mahathir's economically backward community, not even to the 'financially handicapped' among the economically superior communities.[46] It was implacable in wanting 'the elevation of the Malays to an equality with the other races' (p. 60). Nevertheless, it regarded these ameliorative measures as only forms of rearguard action. They were limited, like 'laws [which] do not make people equal' but 'can only make equality possible' (p. 79). *The Malay Dilemma* held that 'in the final analysis it is the people, and the people alone who make themselves equal' (p. 79). No doubt. But Mahathir wanted no less than to remake the Malays. True redress lay elsewhere because the real problem lay deeper.

Social Darwinism and the Retreat of the Malays

The real problem, for Mahathir, lay in the Malays' 'inherent traits and character acquired over the centuries' (p. 31) as a result of 'the influence of heredity and environment on the Malay race' (Chapter 3, pp. 16–31). *The Malay Dilemma* did not flinch from saying that the effects of heredity and environment on the Malays were 'so debilitating' (p. 25) that it might have been 'perhaps kinder to leave this subject alone as it might prove rather discouraging to the Malays' (p. 16).

Mahathir was not one to leave well alone. He contended that the favourable physical geography of the Malay peninsula—'lush tropical plains with their plentiful sources of food' (p. 21)—made it possible for the early Malays to avoid 'hunger and starvation' (p. 21) without 'great exertion or ingenuity' (p. 21). One effect of such a lenient environment was that the 'process of weeding out the weak in mind and body' (p. 20) did not take place, and 'everyone survived. Even the weakest and the least diligent were able to live in comparative comfort, to marry and procreate. The observation that only the fittest would survive did not apply' (p. 21). The same physical environment left another effect: 'The hot, humid climate of the land was not conducive to either vigorous work or even to mental activity. Thus, except for a few, people were content to spend their unlimited leisure in merely resting or in extensive conversation with neighbours and friends' (pp. 21–2).

Those were the contributions of the 'environment' to the 'propagation of poorer characteristics' (p. 29) among the Malays. Heredity left its own mark. The 'absence of inter-racial marriages in the rural areas', 'the habit of family in-breeding' as seen in the frequency of 'first cousin marriages', and the Malay 'abhor[rence] [of] the state of celibacy' produced a 'cumulative effect ... [which] can be left to the imagination' (p. 29). There were also social practices that had a 'long term effect on community and race [which were] disastrous', namely, 'early marriages', 'the incapacity of the parents to take care of the children', and 'the upbringing of children [which] is distorted by the well-known excessive indulgence of the grandparents' (p. 29). 'In this sort of society,' commented Mahathir, 'enterprise and independence are unknown' (p. 29).

Contrast 'this sort of society' with 'the history of China [which] ... littered with disasters, both natural and man-made' dramatized the 'limitation of survival to the fit only' (p. 24). Moreover, the result of the 'Chinese custom [of 'cross-breeding']'[47] was to reproduce the best strains and characteristics which facilitated survival and accentuated the influence of environment on the Chinese' (p. 24). Thus 'the Chinese who flooded Malaya' (p. 25)—'people who were not content with their lot and were moved by a desire for a better life, and obviously by the determination to work for this' (p. 25)—were 'adventurous and resourceful' (p. 25).[48]

The Malay Dilemma conceded that it '[did] not pretend to be a scientific study' (p. 16). It meant to provide 'at best ... an intelligent guess' (p. 16) at the importance of heredity and environment in 'the development of the Malay race in the Malay Peninsula' (p. 16). It did not mean 'to imply that Malays are by nature inferior, and that this inferiority is hereditary and consequently permanent' (p. 1). Its 'intention was to spotlight certain intrinsic factors which retard the development of the Malays, particularly those which can be corrected' (p. 1). But the book ended up with something quite different and rather more than its 'intention'.

On the basis of tentative borrowings from Darwin[49] and Mendel,[50] and his brief excursions into 'Malay history' and the 'history of China', Mahathir plunged into a Social Darwinism all of his own. 'When races compete in a given field', he declared, many characteristics by which 'races are differentiated' play 'an extremely important role' (p. 84). Indeed, 'the moment different races come into contact with each other, these characteristics immediately make themselves felt and emphasize ethnic differences' (p. 84).

Hence, the history of Sino-Malay relations in the Malay Peninsula, 'according to Mahathir', was clear:

> The Malays whose own hereditary and environmental influence had been so debilitating, could do nothing but retreat before the onslaught of the Chinese immigrants. Whatever the Malays could do, the Chinese could do better and more cheaply. Before long the industrious and determined immigrants had displaced the Malays in petty trading and all branches of skilled work (p. 25).

Thus:

> It explains why the Malays are rural and economically backward, and why the non-Malays are urban and economically advanced. It is not the choice of the Malays that they should be rural and poor. It is the result of the clash of racial traits. They are easy-going and tolerant. The Chinese especially are hard-working and astute in business. When the two came in contact the result was inevitable (p. 85).

So it happened during colonial times, so it continued after independence. The Malayanization of the economy opened up vast opportunities for the taking but 'in the mad scramble that followed, the Chinese won hands down' (p. 50). And 'indeed Malaysian anxiety to Malayanize and Malaysianize meant complete Sinocization of the economy of the country' (p. 51).

But by now, any attempt to provide 'the Malay view of his inferior economic position' (p. 32) 'with as much objectivity as a Malay could muster' (p. 32) was engulfed by *The Malay Dilemma*'s recourse to racial stereotypes.

The Malays, the book pointed out, were noted for their '*laissez faire* and tolerance' (p. 84), 'unprotesting tolerance' (p. 158), 'politeness and ... abhorrence of unpleasantness' (p. 117), 'painstaking politeness' (p. 171), 'traditional politeness' (p. 172), 'courtesy and ... self-effacing habits' (p. 117), 'courtesy and fear of anarchy' (p. 120), 'natural courtesy' (p. 142), 'constant restraint' (p. 117), 'self-restraint' (p. 171), 'deference' (p. 116), 'temperance' (p. 160), and 'moderation' (p. 160). Mahathir saw in these attributes the ingrained aspects of a 'Malay character' (p. 116). They were the cultivated marks of 'good manners' (p. 116) and 'good breeding' (p. 116) in Malay society. But in politics, these attitudes were exploited by others and led to the Malays giving up, 'apparently, politely, almost every vestige of power and authority in their own land' (p. 118). In business and commerce, the Malays were severely handicapped by their 'code of ethics and value concepts' (p. 161)—in other words, their 'fatalism' (p. 158), 'inability to accept the inevitable' (p. 114),[51] 'failure to value time' (p. 163), attraction to 'immediate benefits' (p. 109), 'inability to understand the potential capacity of money' (p. 167), and 'failure to appreciate the real value of money and property' (p. 169).

In contrast, Mahathir saw in the Chinese 'not just almond-eyed people but ... also inherently good businessmen' (p. 84), but he could see 'no reason to believe that understanding and sympathy was a strong Chinese trait' (p. 39). He allowed that whenever they 'are in a minority, they always avoid provoking the Malays' (p. 5). Otherwise, he charged, 'Chinese demands increased as government concessions whetted their appetite' (p. 13). It was a charge that fitted in with his references to the 'predatory Chinese' (pp. 27 and 85) and the 'predatory immigrants' (p. 71). When the Chinese conducted business, 'not even the crumbs are left to others' (p. 56)—so complete was the Chinese 'stranglehold' on the economy (p. 39). *The Malay Dilemma* missed few opportunities to rail at 'non-Malay economic hegemony' (p. 43), 'Chinese economic hegemony' (p. 56), 'Chinese monopoly' (p. 56), 'Chinese economic domination' (pp. 60–1), 'total Chinese domination of the economy' (p. 61), and 'the menace of Chinese economic hegemony' (p. 125).

By resorting to such a blatant use of ethnic stereotypes to sustain the imagery of racial strife and unequal competition between two ethnic blocs which culminated in 'a Malay retreat before a Chinese onslaught', Mahathir showed how strongly his Social Darwinism accentuated his Malay nationalism. He held to the premises of a Social Darwinist world-view that seemed to have been custom-made to fit post-colonial Malaysia's plural society. *The Malay Dilemma* made scattered references to the 'completely unscrupulous' Portuguese, Dutch, and British—who between them completed the colonial subjugation of the Malays—but essentially ignored them. Instead, it directed the Malays' 'undercurrent of resentment' (p. 119), 'innermost' (p. 115) feeling of insecurity, and 'suppressed' (p. 115) sense of being wronged at 'the Chinese'—as an undifferentiated, alien, unassimilable, and dominating ethnic bloc—against whom the Malays had simply failed to compete successfully.

Paradoxically, Mahathir's Malay nationalism checked the extent of his Social Darwinism. He had dwelt upon its premises of racial traits and interracial strife and used them to fuel his polemics. But ideologically he would not countenance—and politically he could not admit—its conclusions. He could ruefully declare that 'politics created for the Malays a soft environment which removed all challenge to their survival and progress' (p. 31) and made them 'softer and less able to overcome difficulties on their own' (p. 31). But it was sure that 'subject[ing] the Malays to the primitive laws that enable only the fittest to survive' was 'equally without promise' (p. 31), since 'we do not have four thousand years to play around with' (p. 31),[52] to 'breed a hardy and resourceful race capable of competing against all comers' (p. 31). There could be no question of perpetuating 'competition based on so-called merit' (p. 93) because 'the obstacles of unequal opportunities emphasize and multiply every inequality existing between Malays and non-Malays' (p. 94). Faced with the logic of his own scenario of a 'clash of racial traits', the Social Darwinist faltered, so to speak, and the Malay nationalist rejected natural selection by 'so-called merit selection' (p. 92).[53] Perhaps there—in the tension between his Malay nationalism and his Social Darwinism—lay the source of so much of the post-Merdeka Malay anxiety and alarm which *The Malay Dilemma* so intensely expressed.

The Challenge: *Islam and the West*

From *The Malay Dilemma* to *The Challenge*

In forming impressions of Mahathir's political career, it would be easy, and not incorrect, to think of the ten years after the publication of *The Malay Dilemma*, the '1970s', as momentous years for Mahathir—when truly times changed.

The changes must have been dizzying in personal terms. No other Malaysian politician had returned from political exile to ascend to the highest ranks of political leadership in the very short span of eight years.[54] From being an ex-parliamentarian in 1972, Mahathir was made a Cabinet Minister in 1974 and became Deputy Prime Minister in 1976. From being an UMNO outcast in 1970, he was elected as one of the party's Vice-Presidents in 1975 and rose to become its Deputy President in 1978.

During the 1970s, conditions in Malaysia also changed substantially and in ways that seemed to match some of the most important ideas contained in *The Malay Dilemma.* The 'special rights' of the 'definitive people', which found a spirited defence in the book, found institutional fulfilment in UMNO's political supremacy which became obvious after the rule of the National Operations Council (NOC) and the establishment of the Barisan Nasional. 'Malay dominance' was intact in the 1970s and, unlike in the 1960s, was practically unchallengeable by the non-Malays. The 'Malay dilemma' itself had been resolved in the spirit of *The Malay Dilemma.* 'Malay economic backwardness' had been salved to a discernible degree by an extensive programme of 'constructive protection' launched by an 'enlarged state'.[55] Throughout the Razak and Hussein Onn administrations, '*bumiputera* economic participation' expanded via state and private Malay actions into strategic economic areas, in the process challenging and reducing *The Malay Dilemma*'s much-detested 'Chinese economic hegemony'. The book's call to 'urbanize the Malays' (p. 105) and facilitate their 'acquisition of new skills' (p. 114) appeared to have been met by the social engineering thrust of the NEP: large numbers of Malays had been inducted into the cities (especially Kuala Lumpur), the factories (notably those in the Free Trade Zones), and the universities (both at home and abroad).

But if Mahathir took satisfaction at the way things had turned out—personally, politically, economically, and socially—he gave little hint of it in *The Challenge*,* his other major book which was written during the 1970s.[56] Quite the contrary. At precisely the time when many an UMNO politician could have been forgiven for any boast of accomplishment or display of complacency over the progress of the Malays, Mahathir was troubled by 'the many forms of confusion threatening the Malays today' (Introduction). So far from wanting to celebrate their achievements under the NEP,

*In this section, references to this book are accompanied by the relevant page numbers.

Mahathir urged the Malays to 'act to overcome the thousand and one problems confronting them' (p. 1). And just in case the Malays were still unaware that 'the challenge is tremendous—the stake survival itself' (Introduction), Mahathir bluntly spelt it out: 'The Malays have emerged from a long period of backwardness only to be pulled in different directions by conflicting forces, some of which seek to undo whatever progress has been made and plunge the entire community back into the Dark Ages' (Introduction).

It would not be difficult to be put off by the alarmist tone in Mahathir's pronouncement. The tone resounds in most of the fourteen essays which make up *The Challenge* and is almost bizarre even by his standards of dire prognostication. Yet this book contains some of the most important of Mahathir's ideas after *The Malay Dilemma.* A close reading of *The Challenge*—that is partially deaf to its tone but fully attentive to its exploration of the 'conflicting forces' which threatened the Malays—reveals Mahathir's continued engagement with the Malay dilemma at its very core.

If *The Malay Dilemma*'s idea of 'the complete rehabilitation of the Malays' is taken to mean the ability of the Malays to adapt their values and attitudes to new challenges in new environments—that is, ultimately their ability to tackle the modern world on equal terms with all other communities—then the importance of *The Challenge* in reformulating and elaborating the Malay dilemma at its very core is quite clear. *The Malay Dilemma* focused on the weaknesses and the unsuitability of what *The Challenge* described as 'the old values and ways of life which have held the Malays back' (p. 113). *The Challenge* highlighted new 'conflicting forces' which challenged the Malays' values, ethics, and attitudes as regards religiosity (Chapters 5 and 8), education (Chapter 3), models for imitation (Chapters 4, 7, and 11), and issues of political economy (Chapters 2, 9, and 10). *The Malay Dilemma* identified the kinds of attributes and values—for example, fatalism, passivity, lack of appreciation of time, money, and property—that the Malays had to discard. *The Challenge* tried to specify the critical elements of a new system of values which the Malays should adopt. Whereas *The Malay Dilemma* sought to lift the deadweight of the past, *The Challenge* strove to provide the bearings for the future. The former was occasioned by the neglect of the Malays, the latter was necessitated by the opportunities open to them.

Islam: The Muslim Dilemma

Truly times had changed, and in *The Challenge*, Mahathir noted that

> one of the saddest ironies of recent times is that Islam, the faith that once made its followers progressive and powerful, is being invoked to promote retrogression which will bring in its wake weakness and eventual collapse. A force for enlightenment, it is being turned into a rationale for narrow-mindedness; an inspiration towards unity, it is being twisted into an instrument of division and destruction (Introduction).

'Some sections of the Malay [Muslim] community' were 'susceptible to the notion that Islam exhorts its believers to turn their backs on the world' while 'other sections of the community are being confused by attempts to equate Islam with socialism, using the ambiguity inherent in words like justice, equality and brotherhood' (Introduction).

The Challenge made no direct accusations at those different 'sections of the Malay community' and refrained from labelling any of those tendencies in Malaysian Islam. Some of these Islamic tendencies and groupings were proscribed by the religious organs of the state and the police for being 'deviationist'. Without agreeing to either Mahathir's omission or the state's inclination to condemnation, it would be reasonable to characterize these Islamic tendencies as 'radical', 'obscurantist', and 'retreatist' tendencies—although the boundaries between them could not be strictly and consistently demarcated.[57] First, there was PAS which broke away from the Barisan Nasional in 1977 and was thereafter led by a younger and more radical leadership committed to the ideal of an 'Islamic state' and very hostile towards the 'secular' government of the Barisan Nasional. Second, there was the socio-politically oriented Angkatan Belia Islam Malaysia (ABIM, or Islamic Youth Force of Malaysia) which was openly critical of the shortcomings of the government, especially on such issues as Malay poverty and official corruption. The ideologically oriented Partai Sosialis Rakyat Malaysia (PSRM, or Malaysian People's Socialist Party), too, made an attempt to reconcile socialism with Islam during this period. Third, there were Islamic groupings, like the Darul Arqam (House of Arqam), which enjoined its followers to withdraw to their own communitarian settings modelled after the early Islamic society of the Prophet. Despite their differences, these Islamic 'tendencies' were prepared to redefine the role of Islam in politics, government, and administration, and to extend the scope of Islam into education, as well as into civic and private life. In practice, they demonstrated an increasing preparedness to criticize UMNO and the Barisan Nasional government on Islamic grounds.

A more detached observer might be prepared to discover in the emergence of these 'radical', 'retreatist', and 'obscurantist' tendencies in Islam in Malaysia signs of a 'reflowering of Islam'[58] in Malay social and cultural life. But Mahathir took a different view of the emergence of doctrinaire and obscurantist Islam among Malay students, intellectuals, government officers, and in the rural strongholds of PAS.

The Challenge saw in the 'radical' tendency the failure to realize—at best because of genuine confusion—that 'a balance cannot be attained between spirituality and materialism' (p. 74) by which it meant an incompatibility between 'Islamic spirituality' (p. 73) and 'socialist and communist ideologies ... [which] ... are based on materialism' (p. 113).[59] Against the demands of 'socialist and communist ideologies' for 'material equality' (p. 62), it contended that these had nothing in common with the 'equality and brotherhood ... not in material wealth but in religion' (p. 65) that existed 'in a staunchly Muslim society' (p. 65). On the basis of overlapping arguments and repetitious assertions mainly contained in 'Materialism and Spirituality' (pp. 56–82) and 'Spirituality and the Modern Challenge' (pp. 104–16), the book summed up Mahathir's Islamic case against socialism:

> The materialistic motivation as found in a socialist society is not part of Islamic philosophy. Equality in property is not the basis of justice and brotherhood in Islam. Possession of property is not equal in a Muslim society and there is no demand that all Muslims should own property of the same value. Islam accepts the reality that in any society there will be rich and poor, king and commoner, leader and follower (p. 64).

If *The Challenge* insisted on the incompatibility between spirituality and materialism, it maintained—and very strongly—that 'a balance can be achieved between an interest in things spiritual and things worldly' (p. 73). It is futile for some groups of Muslims 'to try to preserve spirituality by closing their eyes and ears to reality. They reject everything that they deem worldly and try to isolate themselves from outside influences. To revive the faith in spiritual values that flourished in the days of the Prophet, they try to practise the way of life of those days' (p. 2). But 'this is not possible. Conditions have changed so vastly that nobody can escape the invasion of the modern world. Times and ways gone by cannot be revived. Attempts to do so will fail and the failure will further endanger the spiritual values that one seeks to defend and strengthen' (p. 72).

In abstract terms, *The Challenge* detected in the 'retreatist' tendency a fatal inability to understand that 'what Islam demands is not the rejection of the world' (p. 110). In less abstruse terms, it meant that 'Islam has never urged the rejection of worldly wealth' (p. 107). Indeed,

> the choice before the upholders of spirituality is not between rejecting and accepting the world and its wealth. The world and its wealth and a myriad social activities will exist irrespective of what philosophies of life and death dominate human minds. The choice before the spiritual group is whether to let greedy materialists own all the wealth of the world and the power that goes with it, or to own that wealth themselves. If the materialistic group owns that wealth, the spiritual group cannot but face destruction. On the other hand, if the spiritual group owns the wealth, there is some hope that they can still avoid moral decadence (p. 113).

What *The Challenge* found most objectionable in the 'obscurantist' tendency was its suspicion of 'secular' learning or 'Western' education that led to the deprecation of many fields of 'worldly knowledge' (p. 114) for fear that 'faith in Islam will ... be weakened by the mastery of such knowledge' (p. 36). Such an attitude stemmed from ignorance as to 'the contribution of Islam to world education since the fourteenth century' (p. 24). The Malays had to appreciate that Western or secular education, so-called, was 'neither Western nor secular' (p. 25), 'all [Western] knowledge and skills [having] originated from the contributions of Muslim pioneers' (p. 25), so that

> the education and knowledge that the West and that the Western people have spread throughout the world are in reality Islamic. When the Muslims mastered these, Islam spread rapidly. It would not be too much to say that the knowledge helped the spread of Islam. Knowledge which was so effective in helping the spread of Islam cannot be said to be in conflict with Islam (p. 25).

The Challenge offered a concrete lesson to help the Malays 'in overcoming their suspicion of fields of knowledge that the West calls "secular"or "Western" education' (p. 37). Noting that 'in West Asia . . . even now, where the technology of warfare is concerned [the Muslims] are still forced to be beggars' (p. 79), 'still dependent for defence on the Americans (capitalists) and the Russians (communists)' (p. 114), it charged that 'Muslims who hinder the mastery of knowledge related to the production and use of such equipment [of war], dubbing the knowledge "secular", may be committing treachery against their religion rather than preserving its integrity' (p. 31).

The moral of Mahathir's discussion of Islam and education was that 'spiritual and religious values can be preserved without abstaining from the mastering and use of modern ways which can safeguard the position and security of Muslims' (p. 81). Thus 'in Islam there is no dichotomy between the "religious" and the "secular". And where knowledge is concerned, there can be no division into "religious" and "secular" education. All education that is useful to mankind becomes part of the knowledge that Islam urges its believers to pursue' (pp. 27–8).

In *The Malay Dilemma*, Mahathir had briefly noted the historically beneficent impact of the coming of Islam into the Malay world. He saw the spread of a religion that was far more progressive than the animistic and Hinduistic influences which Islam replaced, albeit less successfully in the rural areas compared to the towns.[60] At the same time, the Arab and Indian Muslim bearers of Islam into the Malay world brought intrareligious intermarriages with 'town Malays' whose adaptation to new ways and whose sophistication grew.[61] But in the 1970s, for Mahathir, the kinds of values which were associated with the radical, retreatist, and obscurantist Islamic tendencies did not represent a new wave of values and influences which could become reliable tools for Malay progress. More ominously, by urging the Malays into one or another form of retrogression, they seemed to contain the seeds of the downfall of the Malays. Unable to pre-empt the expansion of Islam into the social and political life of the Malays, Mahathir for the time being grappled with it in the way he knew best—polemically.

The polemical habit dies hard with Mahathir despite his call to the Malays in *The Challenge* to forgo their 'habit of entering into polemics' (p. 1) which 'are found not only to be unproductive but also to add to the difficulty of overcoming challenges faced by Malay society' (p. 1). His discussion of socialism, communism, materialism, secularism, and spirituality—informed by his understanding of Islam—did not amount to a treatise on Islam. It was really one lengthy polemic aimed at what Mahathir considered to be unacceptable attitudes which the Malays had to avoid in the interests of their own progress. The substance of Mahathir's thinking on those Islam-related issues could ultimately be captured by the largely negative injunctions that *The Challenge* issued and which have been discussed above. To those could be added, for emphasis and variety, the following: 'Islam does not prohibit but encourages the pursuit of all knowledge' (p. 30); 'there is no place in Islam for extremist theories and practices' (p. 109); 'in Islam there are no hermits and no religious orders which reject the world' (p. 109); 'Islam evidently does not hold poverty in high esteem or disapprove of wealth' (p. 16); and 'organization and discipline are vital to the essence of Islam as the true faith' (p. 136).

To Mahathir's mind—that is to say, to the ideologue of Malay economic participation and the rehabilitation of the Malays—what Islam most urgently required of the Malays was for them to attain 'a balance between this world (*dunia*) and the next (*akhirat*)' (p. 107),[62] or, what comes to the same thing, a balanced attitude towards the pursuit of 'worldly wealth' and 'worldly knowledge' without which 'Muslims will be oppressed and finally spiritual values too will be lost' (p. 82). To the Social Darwinist who posited the scenario of a Malay retreat before the onslaught of the Chinese, it seemed absolutely, if not ominously, clear that 'a religion lives while its followers live' (p. 111).[63]

The Islamic resurgence in Malaysia compelled Mahathir to turn inward to the Islamic core of the Malay community to counter the 'retrogressive', 'narrow-minded', 'divisive', and 'destructive' interpretations of Islam advanced by some sections of the Malay [Muslim] community.[64] In *The Challenge*, Mahathir had not yet fully worked out his own Islamic system of values for the Malays beyond the principles, injunctions, and exhortations that he offered. But he had begun to offer a reading of Islam which came not from an Islamic theologian but a Malay nationalist. The result was that the Malay dilemma was recast as a Muslim dilemma.

The Decline of the West

Invariably that had to mean an 'intra-Malay' dilemma.

Mahathir made this shift in *The Challenge* so quietly, almost by intellectual stealth, that it concealed the enormity of its implication for his Malay nationalism. By focusing so entirely on the Muslim dilemma, by targeting so inwardly on the different Islamic tendencies, Mahathir was rechannelling Malay nationalism away from its age-old preoccupation with the Chinese or non-Malay threat which *The Malay Dilemma* itself had helped to establish. *The Challenge* does not contain forceful and combative, *Malay Dilemma*-like, appeals to Malay nationalism. There was no room for *The Malay Dilemma*'s ethnic preoccupations and accusations because the 'conflicting forces' which threatened the Malays in the 1970s, whatever they might be, did not issue from the non-Malay or Chinese quarters in Malaysia. Evidently the Mahathir of *The Challenge* no longer regarded the non-Malays as the primary threat to the Malays. *The Challenge* was practically devoid of any reference to the non-Malays or the Chinese; its only direct mention of 'the Chinese' in Malaysia appeared in the last essay, '*Quo vadis* Malaysia?', on page 160, five pages before the end of the book![65]

The persona of the Malay 'ultra' was nowhere to be seen. But the same strident voice of the Malay spokesman was everywhere to be heard: admonishing, berating, criticizing ... the Malays.[66] 'The fault may lie with others', conceded *The Challenge*, 'but the Malays will have to shape their own destiny' (p. 3). Or, putting it differently with an appeal to an unassailable authority, 'God will not change the fate of a nation unless that nation itself strives for improvement' (p. 3).

As always, for Mahathir, Malay 'destiny' and 'improvement' were inextricably bound up with Malay 'values'.[67] The Malays could only overcome the 'thousand and one problems' (p. 1) and confront them if they held fast to 'good Malay values' (p. 96). *The Challenge* did not fully list what the 'good Malay values' were although they included a respect for the elderly (p. 96) and 'administrators' (p. 97). Indirectly, it suggested that there was a need for the Malays to continue to observe 'rules and customs like proper attire, decent behaviour, and reverence for religion, marriage, the family, work, mutual respect, honesty' (p. 101). Elsewhere, it enjoined that the Malays must not just hold in 'high esteem' but practise as well 'industry, efficiency, honesty, discipline and other good values' (p. 3) so that 'progressiveness is certain to be achieved' (p. 3).

Paradoxically, it was in defence of all of these 'and a myriad other values' (p. 101) which he thought the Malays needed that led Mahathir to detect a new threat facing the Malays—the threat from 'a West in decline'. What was this 'West' that now posed as a threat? It was a 'West' of 'many undesirable Western values' (p. 103) that was suffering from a 'perversion of values, "good" being considered "bad" and "bad" being accepted as "good"' (p. 91). It was a 'West' where 'all the old values were cast aside, with no definite values to take their place' (p. 46). The 'West' had declined as a result of the collapse of 'the values which brought them success' in the past. In place of the observance of good old values, such as 'orderliness, discipline and firm social organization' (p. 47), the 'priority, devotion and adulation ... given to "basic rights"' (p. 101) paved the way for all kinds of objectionable social behaviour.

For example, workers in the West have abused the 'right to go on strike to prevent oppression by employers' (p. 102) and turned it into 'a weapon used to oppress others' (p. 102). Indeed, in Britain, 'certain groups of ['self-seeking'] workers ... do not even listen to their own leaders' (p. 138) with the result that 'if any society in the world comes close to anarchy, it is the socialist state, as found in Britain today' (p. 138). Students, on the other hand, formed pressure groups whose demonstrations—'whether or not the demonstrations are allowed by the laws of the country' (p. 119)—only led to 'the destruction of the rule of law and the creation of anarchy' (p. 119). In contrast to the discipline of Western forces which colonized the rest of the world, 'in the United States, demonstrations were used by students and other young men to avoid becoming Vietnam war casualties' (p. 118). Then again 'those whose task is law enforcement are abused and treated with contempt' (p. 94) and 'dubbing all policemen as "pigs" and oppressors' (p. 98) showed that 'the attitude of Western youth to the police is clearly unhealthy' (p. 97).

At the same time, there was the decadence bred out of 'the rejection of "normal" social behaviour' (p. 94). 'Too great a concern for minority rights in a democracy' (p. 93) allowed the 'deviant behaviour of a minority ... gradually [to] grow in numbers' (p. 93) until all kinds of licentiousness were permitted in the West: acceptance of nudity in public (p. 91), 'smoking marijuana' (p. 92), cohabitation among undergraduates (p. 93), 'male prostitution' (p. 94), homosexual marriages (p. 94), 'unisex' attire (p. 94), 'homosexual liaisons' (p. 101), and the screening of 'obscene films' (p. 102).

This post-war 'transformation of values' (p. 103), more accurately, the 'perversion of values' (p. 91) in the West, along with decolonization and the American defeat in Vietnam, had so 'enfeebled' (p. 48) the Western nations that they could 'no longer stand tall as models for the world to emulate' (p. 47). In short, *The Challenge* had little doubt where the West presently stood in the 'cycle of feebleness–progressiveness–feebleness [which] has a definite relationship with the system of values of a particular nation' (p. 3)—and which the 'history of any group of people' (p. 3) must pass through.

Historically, an ascendant West had completely subjugated the Malay States. But 'a West in decline' still posed a serious threat to the Malays in two different but related ways.

First, it was a source of 'enfeebling' values which could not be simply warded off 'in this age of instant communication' (p. 103) when 'human value systems in various parts of the world can no longer be kept apart from one another' (p. 103). Indeed,

> the invasion of the Malay system of values by the Western system has been taking place since the first contact between the Malay States and the West. The results of the invasion have not all been bad. Some outdated Malay values have been replaced by rather positive Western ones. But many undesirable Western values have seeped into the Malay system (p. 103).

The Challenge warned that

> today Malay values are changing without systematic study and without guidance. Anybody can attack the current system and set up new values. This results in senseless conflict and confusion. It is time the Malays realized this and thought out the right steps to ensure that such a vital and potent tool as a system of values was properly used for the good of the Malay community (p. 103).

A major problem was that the Malays were 'no less slavish in bowing to the domination of the West' (p. 44) than other 'Eastern peoples' (p. 47) by which *The Challenge* referred to the habitual copying of the West by the 'East'. In an expression of self-flagellation, albeit suffered on behalf of the Malays, Mahathir lamented:

'What the West does today, the East will do tomorrow and the Malays the day after. If the West stops doing it, the East will follow suit tomorrow and the Malays are likely to do the same thereafter' (p. 44).

The Challenge allowed that the copying had not been always undesirable. During colonial times, when the superiority of the West over the East was indisputable, it was 'logical' that 'the East copied the West in all fields' (p. 45). Now, when the West in decline had itself rejected its former 'Western qualities' (p. 45)—notably, of 'orderliness, discipline and firm social organization'—in favour of objectionable values, still the 'copying was done even when what was copied had clearly brought feebleness rather than success to the West' (p. 45).

The Malays—for whom 'the wild ways of the West are quickly assimilated, but not the values and norms which have given strength to the West' (p. 55)—had not fully awakened to the seeping danger of indiscriminately copying the 'forms rather than the substance of Western' civilization' (p. 55). Now 'as the value changes in the West are more towards bad than good, and as it is easier to copy the bad, Malay society is showing definite signs of changing for the worse' (p. 96).

However, the West did not simply pose a threat of 'value contamination', as it were. So to speak, deeper and darker motives lurked. According to Mahathir:

> Throughout human history, East and West have had contact with each other. As both have been centres of human civilization, their relations have seldom been peaceful. Each tries to dominate the other. There is constant rivalry. Sometimes the West conquers and dominates the East. This happened in the golden age of Macedonia under Iskandar Shah (Alexander the Great), of Rome under the Caesars, and most recently the era of the British empire and others. Sometimes the East conquers and dominates the West, as in the reign of Genghiz Khan and the early centuries of the spread of Islam (p. 54).

The Challenge was sure that 'the rivalry between East and West is by no means ended' (p. 48). The Western nations, having 'let go of [their] colonies one after another' (p. 48), and in decline, sought to protect themselves by 'various effective ways and means' (p. 48).

One way was to establish the 'European Economic Community as a means of controlling the world market so that the East would not be able to reverse the economic oppression which the West had inflicted on it' (p. 48). Another was to 'raise the production costs of Eastern manufactured goods' (p. 49) by having 'Western trade union leaders urge Eastern workers not only to demand more pay and less work but also to take all kinds of action that can weaken Eastern industries' (p. 49) so that 'Eastern countries cannot compete successfully with Western ones in world commerce' (p. 50). A third method was to employ the 'world mass media' to show that 'there was nothing good in the East' by 'highlighting bad happenings in developing countries, especially in the East' and not 'report[ing] [on] successes achieved by the East' (pp. 50–1).

By far, 'the most effective pressure inflicted by the West on the East' (p. 52) came in the form of 'democratic governments' which the West foisted on their former colonies 'as a condition of independence' (p. 53). But for many a newly independent nation, 'not very skilled in or knowledgeable about democratic administration' (p. 53), the 'obstacles and problems' (p. 53) and 'complexity of a democratic Government' (p. 53) tended to lead to failure in the practice of democracy and to its replacement by 'autocracy' (p. 54)—at which point 'the entire Western machinery will be used to condemn the nation concerned' (p. 54).[68]

Consequently, 'Malaysia and the Malays [who] are directly involved in the East–West conflict' (p. 55) had to understand the nature of the Western threat. If in its glory the West defeated the East by 'organization and discipline' (p. 130), in its decline it sought 'to perpetuate Western economic imperialism' (p. 49) by perfidy.

Mahathir is no theorist and *The Challenge* did not provide a coherent or sophisticated critique of Western imperialism in the 1970s. His warning that Western imperialism did not end with decolonization was true enough but locating it within a historical pattern of oscillating East–West domination hardly illuminated anybody's understanding of imperialism, let alone world history. It also did not pay to search long for subtleties in Mahathir's pronouncements on Western society or values. They were mostly outlandish and appealed to trite examples ('attire as indicator of discipline'), crude images (of sexual liberties), and dubious stereotypes (lazy workers and powerful unions). Ironically, he probably gained such distorted images from the Western media itself. Mahathir's exaggeration of Western sexual permissiveness was worthless without an informed discussion of numerous related issues bound up with the student, civil rights, and women's liberation movements of the 1960s. It was laughable and irresponsible to say that the 'young men of America' opposed the war in Vietnam simply because they 'could not honestly admit their cowardice about going to war' (p. 118). Post-war Britain was 'welfarist' but far from being 'socialist'; it was struck by protracted labour struggles but was far from being reduced to anarchy by workers' laziness and rebelliousness. Unable or uninterested in comprehending the complexities of the 'West', Mahathir only saw a monolith. Viewing the 'West' from an 'Eastern' perspective, he could only offer a vaguely drawn anti-Westernism, or what might be called 'Occidentalism'.[69]

Mahathir was not and is not a xenophobe.[70] He could be quite profuse and hearty in his praise of nations and peoples he thought were deserving of admiration and worthy of emulation. But, beginning with *The Challenge*, he fashioned and pushed a basically anti-Western message to the Malay community. The message and its timing, not its quality, was significant. Superficial or erroneous though his ideas might be, shrill and outlandish that some of his arguments were, they constituted, however unsatisfactorily, the ideological substrate which sustained Mahathir's attempts to depart from his own, UMNO's, and what he would have taken as the Malay nationalist's traditional, self-consuming preoccupation with the Malay position *vis-à-vis* the non-Malay communities. In other words, he had begun to reorientate Malay nationalism—as he had known and lived it—outwards: away from the divided state of Malaysia to the divided states of the world. Such a reorientation made it incumbent on the Malay community to shed its lingering images of the West which were no more than an outmoded remembrance of British protection.

The Nationalist as Prime Minister

Between the publication of *The Malay Dilemma* and *The Challenge*, Mahathir's Malay nationalism underwent an important transmutation. Its 'ultra' Malay nationalist edges of the 1960s, carried over into the pages of *The Malay Dilemma*, were blunted in the 1970s. Its direction at the Chinese was rechannelled. Mahathir's redefinition of the problems facing the Malay community in *The Challenge* turned him *inward* on to the Islamic core of the Malay community, and, simultaneously, *outward* on to the West.

If *The Malay Dilemma* represented the ideologue's aggressive and accusatory polemic in defence of Malay interests, *The Challenge* was a relatively more contemplative document. Here, and fittingly in an essay form, was the tentative tone of the would-be Prime Minister thinking aloud on issues which would occupy him in the near future: the future of the Malays, of Islam, of government, and of Malaysia's place in the world. *The Challenge* ended on the following note:

> In various parts of the world, nations that gained independence together with Malaysia have broken up or changed in character. Some are split in two; others are no longer national entities; yet others have become stooges of foreign powers. Nearly all these new nations have rejected or ceased to practise the forms of democracy that they inherited and chose on gaining independence.
>
> Will Malaysia too follow this trend? Will a democratic government prove too weak to overcome the problems mentioned above, and will it be replaced by a dictatorship? Or will Malaysia gradually become paralyzed and finally disintegrate because it cannot solve its problems? Or will realization of all this cause Malaysians and their leaders to work side by side to preserve the integrity and sovereignty of Malaysia and the characteristics which have so far managed to make Malaysia a multiracial nation that is successful and progressive in the true sense (p. 165).[71]

The Challenge gave an intimate glimpse of Mahathir surveying the scene, waiting to be Premier of all he could see. In that can be found both continuity and change in Mahathir's Malay nationalism up to the end of the 1970s. The continuity lay in his formulation and reformulation of his most cherished goal—'the complete rehabilitation of the Malays'. The change is to be sought in the shifting of the target of his Malay nationalism from 'the Chinese' to 'the West'. Only in hindsight has it become apparent that the essays on Islam and Malay values portended Prime Minister Mahathir's focus on ethics, values, attitudes, habits, and discipline in the 1980s, and that the anti-Westernism presaged new diplomatic directions in the same decade. By then, the dilemmas of Malay nationalism had become those of Malaysian nationalism.

1. For Syed Nasir's role in the 1967 National Language Act controversy, see Karl von Vorys, *Democracy without Consensus: Communalism and Political Stability in Malaysia*, Princeton: Princeton University Press, 1975, pp. 200–10. Although we do not know the specific reason for it, Mahathir maintained an unusual silence all through the parliamentary debate on the National Language Act, 1967.

2. Ibid., pp. 171–83.

3. Some UMNO members honoured Razaleigh as the 'Father of the Bumiputera Economy' (Ghani Ismail, *Razaleigh Lawan Musa, Pusingan Kedua, 1984*, Taiping: IJS Communications, 1983, p. 35).

4. See Robin Adshead, *Mahathir of Malaysia*, London: Hibiscus Publishing Company, 1989, pp. 44–6 and J. Victor Morais, *Mahathir: A Profile in Courage*, Singapore: Eastern Universities Press, 1982, pp. 21–2 for accounts of Mahathir's dedication to his medical practice. The section, 'The Doctor and the Common Crowd', which concludes Chapter 7, below, carries a fuller discussion of Mahathir's professional identity as a doctor.

5. There is a lengthy argument in John Funston, *Malay Politics in Malaysia: A Study of the United Malays National Organisation and Parti Islam*, Kuala Lumpur: Heinemann Asia, 1980, pp. 178–84, that the 'ultra' label was inappropriate, considering who the 'ultras' were, what they believed in, and where they stood within UMNO. Funston usefully distinguishes between two 'ultra' labels. The one given by Lee Kuan Yew was flung at those he accused of advocating an 'extremist' Malay position *vis-à-vis* the non-Malays (p. 179). The other given by the Tunku was meant for UMNO's 'young Turks' whom he suspected of being critical of the party leadership (p. 181). In practice, they were mostly the same people.

6. Malaysia, *Dewan Ra'ayat, Parliamentary Debat*es, II, 3, 26 May 1965, col. 77.

7. Ibid., col. 78.

8. Ibid., col. 79.

9. Ibid., cols. 84–5.

10. Ibid.

11. Ibid., 27 May 1985, col. 633.

12. Mohamed Noordin Sopiee, *From Malayan Union to Singapore Separation: Political Unification in the Malaysian Region, 1945–65*, Kuala Lumpur: University of Malaya Press, 1976, p. 215.

13. Quoted in James Minchin, *No Man Is an Island: A Study of Singapore's Lee Kuan Yew*, Sydney: Allen and Unwin, 1986, p. 169.

14. Malaysia, *Dewan Ra'ayat, Parliamentary Debates*, II, 3, 26 May 1965, col. 84.

15. Ibid., col. 79. Ten months earlier, Mahathir urged the Singapore government to finish with 'half measures' taken to combat 'the influence of the communist indoctrinated students [of Nanyang University]'. Since Lee Kuan Yew 'implied that the Singapore government is ruthless', Mahathir dared him not 'to have his cake and eat it as well' but to 'seriously consider as a final measure the merging of the Nanyang University with the University of Singapore ... despite the resistance of Chinese chauvinists within its ranks and the communists outside' (Malaysia, *Dewan Ra'ayat, Parliamentary Debates*, I, 11, 14 July 1964, col. 1441).

16. Tan Chee Khoon, *Without Fear or Favour*, Singapore: Eastern Universities Press, 1984, p. 61.

17. Ibid., p. 65. The figure of 20,000 does not match those given by Mahathir in Parliament. On 5 March 1965, he said: 'I proposed that we should send some UMNO members, roughly about 200,000 to demonstrate our support for the Government' (Malaysia, *Dewan Ra'ayat, Parliamentary Debates*, I, 51, 5 March 1965, col. 6752). On 7 December 1965, he recalled: 'I intended to bring some 60,000 members of the UMNO Youth' (ibid., II, 34, 7 December 1965, col. 4982).

18. In those days, Mahathir was even prepared to fight the Ian Smith regime! On the latter's 'Unilateral Declaration of Independence ... if possible, a further step should be taken by Malaysia by declaring a state of war between Malaysia and the rebel State of Southern Rhodesia' (ibid., II, 31, 3 December 1965, col. 4664).

19. Von Vorys, *Democracy without Consensus*, p. 284.

20. Adshead, *Mahathir of Malaysia*, pp. 57–8.

21. Chamil Wariya, *UMNO Era Mahathir*, Petaling Jaya: Penerbit Fajar Bakti, 1988, p. 10.

22. Ibid.

23. Von Vorys, *Democracy without Consensus*, p. 309.

24. As a result of its electoral losses, the MCA's parliamentary and state assembly seats were reduced from 27 to 13 and from 67 to 26 respectively.

25. Bob Reece, 'Alliance Outcast', *Far Eastern Economic Review*, 18 September 1969, p. 698.

26. 'Having lunch together to evaluate election results was a group of young UMNO leaders, including Syed Nasir, Musa Hitam, and Tengku Razaleigh. There was a broad anti-constitutional consensus among them. The contract had failed. The government and the country must be "returned" to the Malays.... A call went out to Dr Mahathir asking him to come to Kuala Lumpur' (Von Vorys, *Democracy without Consensus*, p. 317).

27. Mahathir, 'Letter to Tunku Abdul Rahman', 17 June 1969, reproduced in ibid., p. 372.

28. Ibid., pp. 372–3.

29. Ibid., p. 373.

30. Ibid., p. 372.

31. Musa Hitam, a close Mahathir ally, was dismissed from office and chose to go abroad. See Bruce Gale, *Musa Hitam: A Political Biography*, Petaling Jaya: Eastern Universities Press, 1982, pp. 29–31.

32. Von Vorys, *Democracy without Consensus*, pp. 371–85, provides the most detailed account. It is consistently critical of Mahathir. Mahathir's criticism of the Tunku's allegedly pro-Chinese policies and leadership later appeared in Reece, 'Alliance Outcast', p. 698. His fullest attack on the Tunku's leadership was contained in Mahathir Mohamad, *The Malay Dilemma*, Singapore: Donald Moore for Asia Pacific Press, 1970, pp. 4–15.

33. Leung Thong Ping, 'Mahathir', *Sunday Mail*, 2 April 1972.

34. Minchin, *No Man Is an Island*, p. 172.

35. Adshead, *Mahathir of Malaysia*, p. 63.

36. Chamil, *UMNO Era Mahathir*, pp. 10–11.

37. Minchin, *No Man Is an Island*, p. 172.

38. K. Das, *The Musa Dilemma*, Kuala Lumpur: K. Das, 1986, p. 11.

39. Adshead, *Mahathir of Malaysia*, p. 63.

40. A Malaysian ban on a book published in Singapore could not have been very effective. The book was widely, if surreptitiously, circulated in Malaysia, in some quarters by the author himself: 'When Anwar [Ibrahim] was a student leader at the University of Malaya ... Dr Mahathir gave Anwar some chapters of *The Malay Dilemma* to read and to circulate among the student leaders in the country' (Adshead, *Mahathir of Malaysia*, p. 170).

41. Morais, *Mahathir: A Profile in Courage*, p. 145.

42. Ibid., pp. 144–5.

43. Tan Chee Khoon, *Without Fear or Favour*, p. 78.

44. Syed Hussein Alatas takes issue with Mahathir's explanation of the 'indolence of the Malays' and his contribution to the 'distortion of Malay character' in *The Myth of the Lazy Native*, London: Frank Cass, 1977, pp. 155–61 and 173–81. Shaharuddin Maaruf, in *Malay Ideas on Development*, Singapore: Times Books International, 1988, Chapter 7, pp. 137–48, criticizes Mahathir's 'pursuit of a capitalistic millenium'.

45. The main 'hereditary–environmental' argument is contained in Chapte 3, 'The Influence of Heredity and Environment on the Malay Race', pp. 16–31. A discussion of this subject appears later in this section of our study.

46. 'It goes without saying that if the small number of non-Malays who are financially handicapped are assisted towards achieving what their richer countrymen have achieved, then the disparity between the educational status of the Malays and the non-Malays would increase even more' (Mahathir, *The Malay Dilemma*, p. 75).

47. '... in direct contrast to the Malay partiality towards in-breeding'(ibid., p. 24).

48. *The Malay Dilemma* was silent on the 'history of India' which was surely just as 'littered with disasters'. Was it because the Indian immigrants—also surely no less adventurous and resourceful than the Chinese immigrants—did not control the economy? It was also silent on the 'inherent traits and character' of the Westerners—no doubt 'completely unscrupulous' (p. 35)—who after all subjugated the 'hardy [Chinese] race' (p. 24) in China and the Indian race in India.

49. Note, however, Mahathir's ambivalence towards Darwin: 'Darwin's theory, explained in *The Origin of Species*, may be unacceptable for many reasons, but some of his arguments are nevertheless valid. Applied to man at a later stage in his development the theory seems logical' (p. 19). Mahathir seemed to hint that Darwin's theory, applied to an *earlier* stage of man's development, might offend certain Islamic tenets in the way that 'the theory of natural selection' was embroiled in polemics with certain Christian ecclesiastical authorities: 'Generally speaking, modern ideas on the evolution of man are not acceptable to Muslims and therefore to Malays' (p. 1).

50. See Mahathir's brief discussion of Mendel's Law in *The Malay Dilemma*, pp. 17–19.

51. Which seems rather like being 'fatalistic' but the context illustrates Mahathir's point: 'Malays working in non-Malay firms or under non-Malay

superiors invariably complain that they are being discriminated against. What they do not seem to be able to understand is that this is completely *natural.* Non-Malays working under Malays feel the same way. But whereas non-Malays accept this as a matter of course, Malays fight tooth and nail against it' (p. 113; emphasis added). And thus 'this inability to accept the inevitable represents a failure to adjust and adapt to circumstances' (p. 114).

52. '... unlike China which had no considerable immigrant settlers' (p. 31).

53. In Parliament, Mahathir once spoke on the low intake of Malay students into the Faculty of Medicine, University of Malaya and distinguished between 'qualification' which he thought the Malay students had and 'merit' which they lacked if they competed with the best of the non-Malays: 'There are enough *bumiputeras* to constitute 45% of the students in the university. What reduces their percentage and number is the method of selection.... For example, in the Faculty of Medicine, if there are places for 50 students and 200 people are qualified, have the basic qualification to apply for those places, those who are selected are the students with absolutely the highest certificates.... I have to admit ... that the *bumiputeras* are seldom at the top of the 50-best list. By this method of selection, I myself would not have become a doctor. But I know that when I was in Medical College, many others who were said to be more competent, smarter, whose Cambridge Certificates had more distinctions than me, failed and were compelled to leave College' (Malaysia, *Dewan Ra'ayat, Parliamentary Debates*, IV, 33, 12 February 1968, col. 5074).

54. Except for Musa Hitam, whose career trajectory simulated Mahathir's—dispatch into political exile by the Tunku and rehabilitation by Razak—but fell just 'slightly short' in other comparable facets. Musa was less controversial, his 'punishment' was lighter, his rise less dramatic, and his deputy premiership came later.

55. For a discussion of the 'enlarged state', its economic interventions, and its sponsorship of Malay capitalists, which is chiefly concerned with ethnic dimensions and rivalry, see James V. Jesudason, *Ethnicity and the Economy: The State, Chinese Business, and Multinationals in Malaysia*, Singapore: Oxford University Press, 1989, pp. 76–100.

56. Mahathir Mohamad, *The Challenge*, Petaling Jaya: Pelanduk Publications, 1986; translated from *Menghadapi Cabaran*, Kuala Lumpur: Pustaka Antara, 1976.

57. And without implying any direct association with the tendencies and groupings which were officially categorized as 'deviationist' and, in some cases, proscribed.

58. Judith Nagata, *The Reflowering of Malaysian Islam: Modern Religious Radicals and Their Roots*, Vancouver: University of British Columbia Press, 1984.

59. In the essay 'The Poor Are Poorer, the Rich, Richer!' (pp. 4–16) will be found Mahathir's own, inadequate, and confused definitions of 'materialism', 'communism', and 'socialism'.

60. Mahathir, *The Malay Dilemma*, pp. 22 and 26. 'Hinduism and animism ... had shaped and controlled the Malay psyche before the coming of Islam.... If the Malays were to become Muslims, these old beliefs must be erased and replaced with a strong and clear Islamic faith' (Mahathir, *The Challenge*, p. 19).

61. Mahathir, *The Malay Dilemma*, p. 28.

62. And 'thus Muslims are asked to work as if they were going to live forever and to perform religious duties as if they were going to die the next day' (Mahathir, *The Challenge*, p. 107).

63. 'A religion exists when it has followers' (p. 36), 'a religion is meaningless without followers' (p. 78), and 'a religion exists because its followers exist' (p. 78). At the beginning of *The Challenge*, Mahathir recalled a saying attributed to Hang Tuah—'The Malays shall not vanish from the face of the earth'—and added that whether 'this hope of Hang Tuah's becomes a reality depends on the Malays themselves' (p. 2).

64. Mahathir, *The Challenge*, Introduction.

65. Even that could have been left out without affecting the essay itself.

66. For their fondness for polemics (p. 1), their imitation of the West (p. 44), their lack of discipline in business (p. 134), or, as in the case of Malay students, for being 'unwilling to choose education and training according to the interests of society and the nation' (p. 39), for not mastering a second language (pp. 42–3), and for staging demonstrations (pp. 119–20).

67. 'In Malay society, as in others, a system of values plays the main role of destiny' (Mahathir, *The Challenge*, p. 103).

68. And then 'other Eastern nations join in the attack' (Mahathir, *The Challenge*, p. 54).

69. That is to say, the converse of 'Orientalism', for which, see Edward Said, *Orientalism*, Harmondsworth: Peregrine, 1985.

70. One should be on guard against the self-serving tendency of the Western media and academia to dismiss non-Western criticisms of the West for being 'xenophobic'.

71. '*Quo vadis* Malaysia?' (Mahathir, *The Challenge*, pp. 15–65).

3

Dilemmas of Malaysian Nationalism*

> All of us now claim to be masters of our own fate and fortune. If eloquence is the yardstick, our voices ring out loud and clear that we are free. But let us not delude ourselves. While we are legally free, the process of economic and political emasculation has rendered that freedom less than real. We cannot act freely because we have been so progressively emasculated that we will collapse if deprived of the crutches of our former imperial masters.
>
> Mahathir, 'Speech at the 8th Conference of Heads of State/Government of the Non-Aligned Countries', Harare, Zimbabwe, 3 September 1986, *Foreign Affairs Malaysia*, 19, 3 (September 1986): 47–54.

'Buy British Last': The Prime Minister as Nationalist

UP to the period of *The Challenge*, Mahathir's nationalism had an essentially negative ring to it. In *The Malay Dilemma* and *The Challenge*, most of Mahathir's nationalist messages showed his fears, worries, and anxieties—Chinese economic dominance at one point and Western machinations at another. There was little that was positive in terms of providing nationalist directions to the nation. Perhaps Mahathir was too much of an ideologue, spokesman, and critic, too fond of polemics, to change his style. Perhaps it was simply that he did not have the prerogative to spell out major directions for the country until he became Prime Minister.

But when he did have that prerogative, he seemed prepared to demonstrate the intensity of his nationalism in a higly visible, very curious, and seemingly negative manner. Around September 1981,

*An earlier version of the conclusion to this chapter was published as 'The Legacy of C. H. E. Det: Portrait of a Nationalist as a Young Man', *Kajian Malaysia*, XI, 2 (December 1993): 28–43. Permission to reproduce this essay, with very minor modification, is gratefully acknowledged.

the Prime Minister's Department itself appeared to be directing what amounted to an official but limited boycott of British goods and services (but not direct investment) known as the 'Buy British Last' policy.[1] All proposed government awards of tenders to British firms were to be sent, together with a second tender from a non-British firm, to the Prime Minister's Department for review. Then 'the Prime Minister's Department will decide whether the purchase shall be made from Britain or the non-British alternative'.[2] Only if non-British substitutes were not available or only if the British tenders were exceptionally competitive would the government purchase British goods.

The immediate event which prompted the 'Buy British Last' policy appeared to be the British media's and the London Stock Exchange's hostile reception to the Malaysian government's take-over of Guthrie Corporation, one of the oldest British plantation companies in Malaysia. The take-over was mounted by one of the government's major investment agencies, Permodalan Nasional Berhad (PNB, or National Equity Corporation),[3] and conducted so swiftly on the morning of 7 September 1981 that it surprised both Guthrie's management and the London Stock Exchange. Leading British newspapers, echoing the sentiment of Guthrie's managing director, chose to describe the take-over as an act of nationalization, whether 'front-door' or 'back-door'.[4] The take-over actually triggered off amendments to the London Stock Exchange's take-over rules.

The accusation of nationalization which imputed more than corporate motives behind the take-over badly stung Mahathir, who was known as a strong critic of nationalization.[5] Besides, talk of nationalization would distress any government committed to attracting foreign investment. Less than two months later, Mahathir remarked at a conference that 'as a result of our legitimate attempts to gain control of our own resources, we have been subject to various reports calculated to frighten away foreign investors from our country'.[6] The London Stock Exchange's amendments to its take-over rules, subsequent to the Guthrie's purchase, left him feeling badly wronged. The take-over was dramatic as market coups went. It involved a 'dawn raid' as the British press labelled it, but, as Patrick Smith's detailed account[7] suggested, it deftly observed prevailing rules of take-over which, Tengku Razaleigh noted, 'the British taught us'.[8]

The subsequent amendments to the take-over rules implied impropriety—that 'it's absolutely disgraceful that [the majority of Guthrie's shareholders] wake up to find that their company is owned by the Malaysian government'.[9] Once Mahathir had charged that 'there is still a colonialist mentality prevailing—and the British should get rid of it. If a company is up for grabs, then anybody should be able to go for it, whether Malaysian or British. If we have the money, we buy. We don't nationalize because it is ethically wrong. But must a British company remain one forever?'[10]

The take-over of Guthrie Corporation, the controversy it generated, and the unhappiness it caused did not seem significant enough to warrant an official reaction that was bound to have foreign policy repercussions.[11] There were suggestions that the 'Buy British Last' policy was Mahathir's act of retaliation coming after a series of frustrations at British attitudes towards Malaysia. Before the Guthrie take-over, Guthrie's trading subsidiary and Dunlop's plantation subsidiary had been sold to Multi-Purpose Holdings Berhad, the MCA's investment arm, 'without the knowledge of a major shareholder and tilted the balance against the *bumiputras*'.[12] The Malaysian government had also suffered severe financial losses when the London Metal Exchange abruptly amended its rules to limit the premiums payable by short-sellers who were unable to deliver on tin futures—at a time when the Malaysian government quietly but actively supported tin prices.[13] There was an earlier occasion, too, when the British government's decision to increase tuition fees for overseas students badly affected Malaysian students in Britain among whom were a large number of government-sponsored students.[14]

It is tempting enough to interpret Mahathir's 'Buy British Last' directive as a delayed outburst by the old Malay nationalist against the old mother country which he had already deemed to be decrepit anyway.[15] But as Philip Bowring astutely observed, 'Mahathir's antipathy to the British seems to be far more a consequence of his general philosophy than any personal prejudice. His campaign has an Ataturk-style symbolism about it. British technology is becoming outdated; Britain's social system shows signs of decay; the British are associated with the past.'[16]

Melodramatic but relatively short-lived, the 'Buy British Last' affair was undoubtedly important to Mahathir in symbolic ways. It indicated that any special relationship Britain used to enjoy with Malaysia had come to an end. In the same context, but putting it differently, he told Tan Chee Khoon that he 'doubt[ed] whether Britain would come to our aid if we have a confrontation now'.[17] It permitted him to make a visible and firm stand against the kinds of Western manipulations he had always resented and it probably vindicated the anti-Westernism he indulged in.[18] All the homilies he had so didactically preached on the critical importance of economic power to the fortune of a community or nation he at once demonstrated in the sensationalist form of a boycott.[19]

North–South, East–West

Among his Malaysian political contemporaries, Mahathir displayed the most acute sensitivity to the potentially damaging challenges and obstacles issuing from the 'global environment'.[20] In the 1980s, Mahathir decided that the world economy was unpromising for small and poor developing countries. A recession started in the industrialized countries and then swept across the globe, badly affecting the developing countries in the process. For the poor, small, and developing countries, times were very hard: barriers to international trade had multiplied, opportunities for economic development had dwindled, and challenges to their sovereignty had intensified.

This unfortunate situation was not the result of 'acts of God' but of 'mere decisions made by men, principally the powerful men in powerful countries'.[21] Mahathir questioned those 'mere decisions'—'made in the powerful countries by short-sighted people'[22]—which threatened to overwhelm the economies of the developing countries. On behalf of the 'Third World', the 'South', 'small countries', and 'developing countries', Mahathir spoke out against the 'powerful commercial and financial centres of the world'.[23] As the world economy slid into a prolonged recession in the early 1980s, developing countries could find little relief from the 'high interest rates, protectionism, the deliberate manipulation of commodity prices through outdated marketing systems and the release of stockpiles, disregard for GATT [General Agreement on Tariffs and Trade], refusal to implement the shipping code ... [and] the unilateral changes in the rules' which were 'cooked up in the capitals of some powerful industrialized countries'.[24]

For a start, 'no foresight [was] necessary to see that

> when an extremely rich country decides to live beyond its means it has to borrow bigger sums from the market. The consequence is not only to dry up the sources of funds but to push up the interest as well. High interest rates in a nation which lives on credit means lowered consumption, lowered inventories and lower investments.... When that country is also the biggest market, the effect on world trade is not difficult to foresee.... Depression in world trade is known and felt by everyone.[25]

From the point of view of the poor, commodity-producing countries, the terms of their trade with the rich, industrialized nations had steadily worsened. One important reason was the market manipulations of commodity prices over which the producers had no control:

> While the manufactured goods that we buy are priced according to the cost of production and marketing and of course a hefty profit ... primary products ... are priced according to the whims and fancies of a host of people who have nothing to do with production. The various exchanges located in the developed countries literally manipulate prices in order to make a profit for the brokers, the dealers, the speculators and others.[26]

Speaking from Malaysia's experience with 'the tin and rubber markets' which have 'played havoc with my country's economy',[27] Mahathir commented bitterly on 'the fate of the producers of primary commodities ... [who] now have to sell three to five times more of their produce in order to buy the same amount of manufactured goods from the developed countries as they did 20 years ago'.[28]

It was not even clear that the producers of primary commodities could continue to sell their commodities. Technological advances in the rich consumer nations had 'rendered the traditional raw materials obsolete' as manufacturing inputs.[29] Meanwhile, poor countries could not match the levels of subsidies which the rich nations gave to the production and marketing of their goods. The overall result was that

> if in the past, the terms of trade placed us in such a position whereby we were compelled to sell more primary commodities for less of their goods, now we cannot even sell more of our primary commodities to buy manufactured goods that have become more expensive. And our governments are finding it increasingly difficult to obtain foreign exchange to pay off their debts.[30]

If commodity production had become so fraught with problems that 'indeed many poor countries have literally to sell their soul in order merely to survive',[31] some developing countries' plans to change 'the pattern of trade whereby the poor countries produce cheap raw materials and buy expensive manufactured goods'[32] encountered an equally severe obstacle. Developing countries embarking on industrialization programmes, 'having bought expensive plants and machinery' and 'showing signs of success in exporting manufactured goods',[33] depended on world trade, free trade, and open markets in the rich countries of the West. But

> protectionism is rife, and the cry for more protection by industrialists and politicians from the developed countries can be heard almost daily.... Leaders of the developed countries piously call for more free trade, but at the same time they devise new restrictions—including quotas, tariffs, high interest rates and exorbitant freight charges in order to stifle imports into their countries.[34]

Mahathir denounced the 'free traders of convenience' who 'fanatically proclaim themselves to be the standard bearers of free trade except when it affects themselves adversely'.[35]

The basic reason for the prevailing abandonment of free trade seemed quite clear:

> When the Bretton Woods agreement was made the participants were the few countries which dominated the world at that time. They advocated free trade because to them it meant that they could freely enter the markets of those countries not in a position to export products which can compete with their own. Today the picture has changed. The countries which in the immediate post-war period were mere markets are now the manufacturers and exporters of competitive goods. These countries, having been persuaded that free trade is the ideal system, want to sell their goods freely in the industrially developed countries. Suddenly free trade takes on a different complexion for the formulators of the Bretton Woods agreement. And so free trade becomes a dirty word to be replaced by a newly salvaged protectionism.[36]

It would appear that Third World countries—'victims of an unjust and inequitable economic system that seeks to deny us the legitimate rewards of our labour and natural resources'—were subject to no end of 'economic bullying and manipulations'.[37] On the one hand, it could be seen that 'sovereign countries have no control over their currencies. Speculators, including banks, can push currencies up and down as they wish. Indeed the trade in commodities has been turned into a trade in currencies.'[38] On the other hand, some sovereign countries, the 'G-7' nations, could of their own accord tamper with foreign exchange rates to the great detriment of developing countries:

> When seven rich nations had trade imbalances, their solution was to force a currency revaluation of the yen and the Deutschmark. Many South-East Asian countries have borrowed a lot of yen. The appreciation in the value of the yen alone increased Malaysia's debt to Japan by sixty per cent. Other countries are in an even worse situation.
>
> If the real problem is Japan's excessive imports into North America and Europe, it will cause no less damage to the poor countries if high import duties are imposed. But revaluing the yen which wreaked havoc in our economy has no impact on the import of Japanese goods into North America and Europe.[39]

Perhaps the world was bewildered to find that 'in an age of instant communication, unlimited wealth and inspired application of man and material, we seem incapable of solving even the most simple of economic problems'.[40] But the developing countries could only look 'with despair and hopelessness' upon the 'deep-seated reluctance on the part of the industrialized countries to ameliorate the unhealthy situation the world finds itself in'.[41] It was already evident that 'the North–South dialogue, UNCTAD [United Nations Conference on Trade and Development] and other conferences that have been held have been futile'.[42] The 'big powers' now 'formed their own economic clubs to which developing countries were allowed to appeal from time to time. In any case, these clubs—like all other exclusive clubs—only give priority to the interests of their members.'[43]

As they had blatantly shown by their decision to revalue the Deutschmark and the yen, the 'economic club' of the industrialized nations behaved as if 'seven rich nations possess the exclusive right to force their method of solution on the problems of the world economy'.[44] Under the circumstances, 'how can we look at future meetings of the seven rich industrialized nations with equanimity'?[45]

Mahathir rejected the developed countries' attitude because

> we most certainly do not want to continue to be the plantations and mines for Europe or the rest of the world. We most certainly do not cherish the

dubious honour that ASEAN holds as a world leader in the production of various raw commodities whose prices are often dictated by the tender mercies of market manipulators and closed shop trading systems in Europe and other parts of the world. We most certainly do not want to see our peoples breaking their backs to till the soil and mine the land for depleting commodities, only to find that those who work the hardest are those who obtain the least economic benefits for their endeavours. Finally we most certainly do not want to perpetuate our manufacturing sectors at the lower ranges of the scale of world technology.[46]

Thus spake Mahathir. It was a tedious way of making a point but it made no secret of his growing antipathy to the rich industrialized nations. Throughout the 1980s, he filled out the anti-Western world-view he had only sketched in *The Challenge*. His criticism of the 'West', the 'North', the 'powerful commercial and financial centres of the world' and their 'economic dominance' grew harsher while his posture as a spokesman of the Third World stiffened.

It is necessary to see beyond Mahathir's posturing and rhetoric to appreciate the quality and substance of his anti-Westernism. Acting on the diplomatic stage has always required suitably adjusted modulations in tone, colorations in rhetoric, and shifts in posture to match occasions and audiences—and Mahathir knew it.

At the Seventh Conference of Heads of State/Government of the Non-Aligned Countries in New Delhi in 1983, Mahathir expressed his exasperation at the 'desperate need to prevent a total collapse of the world economy'. 'It is better that we fall back on our own resources than to place our hopes on understanding and help from the unfeeling North' if 'we will one day be free from the economic and technological oppression of an insensitive North'.[47] Let no one be mistaken, 'let us stop deluding ourselves': 'The North is not about to abdicate their role as the aristocrats of the world economies. For as long as the poor economies are incapable of striking back, we are not going to have one bit of concession from them.'[48]

At the United Nations in 1982, the voice of an emerging spokesman of the Third World could already be heard: 'The age of empires and imperial powers is practically over. But the world has not yet become a better place for the previously colonized. There are many reasons for this and among them is the banding together of the rich nations in order to maintain economic dominance, which some say is actually a form of imperialism.'[49]

Mahathir later argued that while the Commonwealth symbolized the end of 'political imperialism', the former colonies were still haunted by 'economic imperialism'. However, at the Foreign Policy Association in Washington, he only urged the enlightenment of self-interest on the 'big powers, the industrialized countries'. Having 'long sensed that Third World countries are unable to accept the monopolization of political and economic power by a few nations', he hastened to reassure his listeners that

> the majority of Third World countries do not favour the politics of radicalism in resolving these problems. All those who cherish peace and progress must therefore encourage and maintain the momentum toward peaceful negotiations based on fair give and take. The big powers, the industrialized countries, should not look upon this process with trepidation. It is not meant to deprive them of their legitimate gains, but rather it would help to protect those gains from precisely the sort of radicalism that prolonged deprivations and exploitation, whether political or economic, ultimately generate.[50]

Mahathir could as readily be plaintive as accusatory. For example, all that 'we most certainly do not want' could be avoided or shed—provided that an 'unfeeling North ... an insensitive North'[51] 'help ... release the stranglehold of the cycle of low income, lack of capital and know-how and continuing low income that entrap most developing nations'.[52]

In Japan, Mahathir was not above pandering to the anti-American sentiments of some Japanese by sneering that 'the economy of the United States is still in recession struggling to give credence to the frequent forecast of "seeing the light at the end of the tunnel"—without realising that this particular tunnel could well turn out to be the longest and a winding one at that'.[53] He not only said nothing about Japan's own protectionist policies but attacked the protectionism of 'certain developed countries' whose 'resistance to Japanese penetration of the traditional markets of the old developed countries has never abated' and with whose attitude 'Japan must be very familiar'.[54] To an important Japanese and Malaysian business audience meeting in Kuala Lumpur, he disingenuously detached Japan from his category of 'developed' countries by saying that 'Japan may be classified as developed but it is still developing vigorously'![55]

There was a stable core to Mahathir's anti-Westernism—his resentment at the reluctance of the rich Western nations to 'share ... what you have in abundance, [that is], technological know-how, capital, management and marketing skills' and 'of course, your own huge market'.[56] There was his anger at the readiness of the West to change the old rules of free trade. There was his indignation that as far as the 'free traders of convenience' were concerned, Bretton Woods could come or go so long as their own interests were protected. Evidently, they feared that 'the developing countries may cease to be a market for the simple manufactured products that they like to dump' and that 'these countries might actually invade and compete with them in their own markets'.[57]

It was not all rhetoric. Mahathir had encountered two direct and painful instances of a 'change of rules'. The less painful experience was the London Stock Exchange's amendments to the rules of take-over in the wake of the Guthrie take-over.[58] It was much more painful when the London Metal Exchange reduced the penalties imposed on short-sellers who could not meet their speculative commitments. That ended the Mahathir government's misadventure in the tin market and saddled Malaysia with an enormous financial loss which was hidden from public knowledge until 1986. It was with bitterness and a touch of self-mockery that Mahathir advised a Malaysian audience not to believe that 'the so-called liberal Western countries' had unregulated economies: 'Ostensibly there was no regulation on foreign purchase of shares when such purchases were rare and limited to acceptable countries. But the moment the practice becomes common and some upstarts get into the act, regulations were drawn up to limit free enterprise.'[59]

That one's plans and progress might be subverted by a 'change of rules' was an old apprehension of Mahathir's. He had noted before that the Malays found it difficult to catch up with the non-Malays because the 'concept of business has changed and changed again even as the Malays begin to understand the orthodox methods which originally defeated them'.[60] There was more than an incidental resemblance between Mahathir's earlier perception of the 'Chinese economic hegemony' and his later perception of 'Western economic dominance'. He thought the former was maintained by racial barriers and racial ground rules, while the latter was effected by 'big power' restrictions and changes in rules. In either case, he chafed at the threat of economic exclusion.

Mahathir's occasional declamation against 'a new form of colonialism' never did ring true. Too often it seemed as though it was an afterthought delivered for rhetorical effect, for example, ' ... which some say is a form of imperialism'. But his diatribes against the 'banding together of the rich nations', 'the exclusive clubs', and the 'closed shop trading systems' of the 'big powers' were genuine.[61] His outcries against an 'unfeeling' or 'insensitive' North were laden with such emotive charges as hypocrisy, deceit, trickery, conspiracy, intimidation, and even sabotage. At heart, it was a condemnation of Western motives, machinations, and manipulations.

Such was Mahathir's language of opprobrium employed against the West. It was a language of disillusionment, disenchantment, and indignation. But intemperate as the language sometimes sounded by diplomatic standards, it was not the anti-imperialist language of radical Asian, African, or Latin American nationalists. Mahathir would be unrecognizable among Ho Chi Minh, Frantz Fanon,[62] or Fidel Castro. Mahathir's anti-Westernism did not derive from earlier radical critiques of the capitalist origins, impulses, and structures of Western imperialism and the global pattern of dominance and dependence. He was not an anti-capitalist but a capitalist. He was only against 'imperialism' as protectionism but would hardly have conceived of imperialism in the form of 'foreign investments'. He defended transnational corporations against 'vilification' by the 'old protagonists of the superior race [and] also ... the working class in the developed countries' who pictured the transnationals 'as an economic octopus with tentacles stretching out among various countries and squeezing the lifeblood of these nations'.[63] He accepted that the transnationals had to take advantage of cheap labour which he continued to prohibit from unionizing in the Free Trade Zones of Malaysia. But he scorned the attempts of international labour federations to 'be the saviours of our workers [and] to instigate them to demand high wages and better working conditions' as a new form of infringement on the sovereignty of small nations.[64]

Most of all, Mahathir was worried that the rich nations of the West would shut out small, developing countries, such as Malaysia, which were trying to break free of underdevelopment by following the capitalist road—exactly as 'was taught to us'. He urged the European 'men of influence' attending the 1983 ASEAN–EEC Industrial Sectoral Conference 'to force a halt to the protectionist inward-looking policies that are aggravating an already dangerous situation'. Instead, 'let us return to sanity and the ways that in the 60s and the 70s brought prosperity to the world'.[65] That the 1960s and 1970s—which some would say was an era of wars of national liberation—represented a period of 'sanity and prosperity' for Mahathir only went to show how far away from radical 'anti-imperialism' he really stood.

When he addressed the Thirty-ninth Session of the United Nations General Assembly, Mahathir recalled:

> For a long time, the spirit of free trade was defended and the colonies of big powers were diligently taught the good values of free trade. At that time, and for many years after our independence, we were not able to export anything at all except our primary commodities, and our markets—as was taught to us—were wide open to imports of finished manufactured goods from the industrialized countries.
>
> Now that we have ourselves learnt the intricacies of industrialization and export a large proportion of our products, what has happened to the spirit of free trade that used to be esteemed? It has now faded in the industrialized countries.[66]

This was the language of an erstwhile neo-colony within the society of nations, the protest of an insecure parvenu spurned by the 'aristocrats of the world economies'. It was the sentiment of a man who felt he had been wronged for doing the right things. It was the lament of a dutiful pupil discovering the bad faith of his teacher. It was time to look for another teacher.

Look Out and 'Look East'

In *The Challenge*, Mahathir conceptualized an 'East–West' division of the world. After he became Prime Minister, he demonstrated at several important forums both at home and abroad that this division could just as readily be transposed along a 'North–South' axis. In either case, 'Mahathir's world' was made up of two basic camps. One side comprised poor, developing countries, former colonies, and other nations of the East and the 'South'. The other side consisted of rich, developed countries, former colonizers, and other nations of the West and the 'North'.[67] By Mahathir's scheme of things, such a division of the world, while it did not portend of mortal combat between the two sides, contained a leitmotif of ceaseless competition which determined the fates of nations.

Mahathir's world-view placed considerable emphasis on a nation's ability to compete successfully against other rivals, the goal being to survive, to remain independent, and to 'stand as tall as others'. The 1970s and the 1980s brought enormous changes to the global environment and the world economy which was Mahathir's primary concern. The West seemed to be in decline, eclipsed by the rise of 'Eastern' nations. To the extent that Mahathir linked true independence to economic success, he was inspired by Japan which was transformed into a world power by the Meiji Restoration and resurrected into an economic superpower after World War II. He admired South Korea which overcame the devastations of war to emerge as a strong industrialized and trading nation. There were also the impressive economic performances of Taiwan, Hong Kong, and Singapore, Asia's 'newly industrializing countries' (NICs) or 'little dragons', which had industrialized themselves out of backwardness into 'developed country' status.[68]

Mahathir probably shared the views of many, both in the West and in the East, that the rise of Japan and South Korea in particular had altered the global economic balance.[69] These two non-Western capitalist countries possessed powerful economies which the West respected, envied, and even feared. Mahathir found it logical that this change in the global balance of economic power (but not military might) was due to the competitiveness of Japan and South Korea (and the other Asian NICs)—which only exposed the inability of the West to compete in world trade. From the point of view of Mahathir's evolving nationalism, with its lengthening distance from the West, these changes to the global economic environment seemed to fit in logically with his Social Darwinism that was now transposed on to the world of nation states. The original proponents of Social Darwinism used it to justify the superiority of the white race over all other races. Mahathir stood Social Darwinism on its head and drew the grave but, for him, predictable, inference: the West had declined because its social values, moral system, and work habits had decayed. The West could not stiffen its moral fibre to reverse its reversal of fortunes. Thus, 'when challenged, and because they are unable to compete, they resort to negative action',[70] that is, unfair practices and unethical machinations to hold back the interlopers from the East.

In his first presidential address to the UMNO General Assembly, in 1982, Mahathir recollected that 'for centuries we have been awed by Western strength and ability. We have not only been impressed but we have also accepted the view that it is impossible for us or any Eastern nation to compete with the Westerners.'[71] Now, 'while generally the Western nations cannot solve the oil crisis and other problems, several Eastern nations can overcome them',[72] especially 'countries like Japan and [South] Korea in the East [which] have caught up with the Western nations'.[73] Very simply, the West had 'failed' in the matter of economic competition and, therefore 'we must adjust our attitude and direction. The West can no longer be an adequate example. Those who fail cannot be made examples to follow.'[74]

Elsewhere, he elaborated on the reasons for the failure of the West. For example:

> The Western nations have been labouring under an illusion. They believe only in their own intellect and expertise and to them no one else can compete with them. And because of this, they no longer work hard and instead prefer to take things easy. Through their unions, the Western workers agitate for all sorts of benefits, until there are Western nations which pay more allowances to their unemployed than salaries to those working. Thus many choose not to work.[75]

In other words, the people of the West 'have lost their drive. They still want the good life but are not prepared to face the realities of a world market which they can no longer dominate. Consequently, if we emulate them we will land ourselves in the quagmire that they are in without ever passing through the golden period that they went through.'[76]

Emulating those who succeed and spurning those who fail became one of Mahathir's favourite themes. Five years after he became Prime Minister, he concluded of the 'races in the East' that 'their methods of developing their countries have brought greater success and we do not want to copy those people who have failed'.[77] Six months before he became Prime Minister, he told the Third Islamic Summit Conference in Taif, Saudi Arabia, that it was time for the Muslim *Ummah* [community of believers] 'to cast off the traditional Eurocentric perception and approach'. He had discovered in the 'East' itself the reason and method for Malaysians to do so.

'Looking East', he perceived history to be on his side:

History has seen the shifting of the centre of civilization. At one time China claimed to be the centre of the universe. Events gradually moved it to the Mediterranean. For several centuries now it has been in Europe and latterly it is supposed to be more in the North American Continent. After the Second World War, it can be seen that the Pacific Basin has become more and more important.[79]

Notwithstanding differences in geography, history, and whatever else, he quickly moved to share destiny with the best from the Pacific Basin:

We are not listed in the Pacific Community but the fact remains that Malaysia and Japan are countries of the Pacific Rim. This vast area is predicted to be the growth area of the world, replacing the Atlantic shores. Malaysia and Japan, therefore, share a common economic destiny. Although we differ in terms of ethnicity, language, history, tradition and culture, there is sufficient commonality in terms of political philosophy and economic thrust that cooperation would be easy to achieve.[80]

Mahathir decided that the truly indispensable elements of the Japanese and South Korean 'economic miracles' were their moral and cultural pillars: a strong work ethic, worthy Eastern values, a capacity for learning, courage to compete, self-reliance, and national pride. To Prime Minister Yasuhiro Nakasone of Japan, he declared that he 'could not help but admire the fact that you and your predecessors, through sheer hard work and determination, helped to guide the first Asian nation from an island-based agrarian society to become what is perhaps the most technologically-efficient economy in the world today.'[81] To President Chun Doo Hwan of South Korea, he said he had 'no doubt in my mind that it is the Korean attitude towards work, their loyalty and discipline that have contributed to the economic miracle of the Republic of Korea'.[82] It was not diplomatic politesse alone which drove Mahathir to offer such profuse praise. He could think of no higher objective for himself and his country than to transform Malaysia into a productive and competitive industrial nation along the lines of Japan, South Korea, and the Asian NICs: 'If I can I would like to make this country as a whole a very productive country, in the sense that the people are productive and the government is productive also. If I can do that I think I will have achieved something.'[83]

However, in contrast to the Japanese and the Koreans, as Mahathir saw it, and as he was not too proud to admit at an international symposium: 'We have all the basic ingredients that will make it possible for Malaysia to become an important industrialized country in Asia after Japan and South Korea'[84] but 'something more is needed ... [which] is not found at home'[85]—'the work ethic' which is 'the most important thing that seems to have contributed to' the 'rags to riches story of Japan ... and the story of South Korea'.[86]

So it was 'in searching for a foreign model'[87] which could offer that 'something more' that Mahathir took to exhorting Malaysians to commit themselves to 'learning and practising Japanese and Korean work ethics'.[88] To his mind, 'if we desire success', Malaysia must 'look East where the people are hard-working, to rid ourselves of the Western values that we have absorbed', to emulate 'the diligence in work, efficiency in management and trade relations and other aspects found in the East'.[89] Such a national 'reorientation' from West to East was 'crucial at this juncture in the development of this country'[90] because only then would it become possible 'to rid ourselves of [a] past [when] we were looked down upon by the West because we were said to be lazy'.[91] Only then could a nation hope to claim equal status with other nations, assume a dignified standing in the global community of nations, and 'not be humiliated'.[92]

Mahathir's 'Look East' policy was first proclaimed in late 1981, soon after the 'Buy British Last' campaign. There was no mistaking Mahathir's enthusiasm for the 'Look East' policy, especially in the early days of its promotion of things Japanese among Malaysians. Then it seemed that Mahathir could not have his fill of mainly Japanese 'virtues of hard work', the 'democracy of the Japanese business organisation', 'the cradle-to-grave type of relationship' within Japanese companies, the attitude of 'making quality a point of honour', and the *sogoshosha*-led 'highly successful marketing strategies'.[93]

Some of Mahathir's praise for Japan bordered on idolization. He detested Western protectionism but considered that the 'concept of Japan Incorporated is interesting as a device for the development of the Malaysian economy', among other reasons, because of the 'large degree of protection ... afforded to Japanese companies at home which makes it difficult for foreign manufacturers to penetrate Japanese markets'.[94] He hated trade unions, whether Western or Malaysian, but he paid Japanese unions the supreme tribute of saying that 'even Japanese unions are conscious of the need to work hard'.[95] As some commentators have suggested, Mahathir was uncritically enthusiastic about what Malaysia could emulate from the examples of 'Japan Incorporated', *sogoshosha*, and 'in-house unions'.[96] On the matter of Japanese management–labour relations, one had to ignore the essence of hierarchy to share Mahathir's admiration of the 'democracy of the Japanese business organisation'.[97] One could conceivably approve of the 'paternalistic' 'cradle-to-grave type of relationship' in large Japanese companies which was 'reciprocated by workers being more loyal to the companies'[98] provided one suspended all questions about a concomitant lack of employee mobility.

It was dubious to praise the South Korean work ethic by abstracting it out of its basic social framework of the heavy repression of Korean labour by South Korea's military regimes.[99] Mahathir's analysis of the Japanese and South Korean 'economic miracles' allowed no room for the complex historical and geopolitical factors which had an important impact on Japan's post-war and South Korea's post-civil war economic performances. He glossed over critical points such as the role the United States of America played in Japan's post-war and South Korea's post-civil war reconstruction. His idealization of Japan and South Korea as models of national independence based on economic success was nowhere tempered by the reality of American military domination over these countries, including the maintenance of American military bases in both countries. His admiration of Japanese competition surely had to be weighed against Japan's domination of the South-East Asian economies, for example, 'which some would say is actually a form of imperialism'.[100]

One could further quarrel with Mahathir's views on the 'East' but that might only miss the unusual nationalistic impulses behind his 'Look East' policy.

First, Mahathir's admiration for Japan's economic success was a late twentieth-century variant of a historical and even more widespread Asian admiration for Meiji Japan's victory in the Russo-Japanese War of 1904–5. Where the early twentieth-century colonized Asians saw in Japan's military victory over Tsarist Russia the destruction of the myth of Western invincibility, Mahathir in the 1980s divined from Japan's surpluses in trade with the United States of America the end of an exclusively Western economic prosperity. Where earlier Asian nationalists could dream of independence and release from colonial shackles, Mahathir envisioned prosperity and deliverance from Western economic dominance. Japan's triumphs at the two ends of the twentieth century offered inspiration, example, and hope. They vicariously fed a much needed sense of 'Eastern' achievement but, deriving from that, an equally important sense of the 'attainability' of one's dreams and visions.[101] Once, after praising the Japanese, Mahathir remarked, almost incongruously, that the Japanese work ethic was a 'cultivated value system' and 'not traditional'. Maybe he did not express it very exactly but it scarcely suppressed his hope that 'if this work ethic could be acquired and developed artificially, it follows that Malaysians too can shape and develop their own work ethic'.[102] Mahathir differed from an earlier generation of Asians and Asian nationalists only in age, context, and vision. In the 1980s, Mahathir thought what many Asians thought in the early 1900s: Japan which succeeded by relentlessly copying the West lent itself to being copied by others. National salvation, be it from colonialism or underdevelopment, could be had but all roads led to Japan.

Second, it was an old obsession of Mahathir's to search for and imbibe 'values which I consider can make this country a great country, a developed country, a respected country'.[103] Like many nationalists in former colonized countries, he was prepared to copy a foreign model in order to 'stand on one's own feet'. Mahathir—who made it public knowledge that 'I always measure myself against people who are better than me, greater than me'[104]—had no compunction about calling on Malaysians to emulate the Japanese, the Koreans, and the Taiwanese. Sometimes he said that 'as we are from the East, looking East means looking at ourselves too—fostering existing good values, getting rid of the ones which we know are not beneficial'.[105] But if that was an attempt to de-emphasize the 'alien-ness' of those 'Eastern' values it was at best half-hearted, as was his effort to 'universalize' them: '[the Eastern] values are "universal" and acknowledged by all—but while we are good at talking about our good values, we are not that [good] in practising them'.[106]

This was partly because Mahathir had long been persuaded that 'left to themselves, the peoples of developing countries are more likely to subvert their own future than promote their well-being'.[107] How else could it be that 'a lot of us want to be mediocre'[108] or that 'we know Japan has succeeded but we do not emulate them until we are instructed to do so'?[109] But partly it was because

Mahathir was habitually touched by diffidence, not to say the frustration of 'single-minded, visionary nationalists at the fact that their peoples do not live up to the goals set for them'.[110] In *The Malay Dilemma*, he was pessimistic about the 'inherent' inability of the Malays to compete against the non-Malays. In *The Challenge*, he was anxious lest the Malays slipped back into 'the dark ages'. As Prime Minister, he worried that the 'inability of Malaysia until now to become a developed nation'[111] was due to the absence of 'something more' from the people. Seven years after launching the 'Look East' policy, he was still calling on Malaysians to emulate 'the Japanese, the Koreans, the Taiwanese' who 'work with their heart and soul' and 'have surpluses in the midst of a recession'.[112] In that sense, 'Look East' envisaged a 'transfer of ethics', the value-attitudinal-spiritual corollary to the transfer of technology.

Third, the full implication of 'Look East' could only be appreciated in light of his criticism of the Malay attitude towards work. On the eve of becoming UMNO President, Mahathir delivered a stinging attack on the supposed Malay 'disinclination to work'.[113] In essence, he blamed the historical downfall of the Malays on a widespread Malay predilection for 'comfort the easy way'. The Malay rulers lived off 'political pensions' and rentierist arrangements. They did not have to work but 'their people too did not want to work'. Malays 'with the slightest connections' aspired to be government officers, receiving fixed salaries without having to be competent or even to work. Because 'our Malay ancestors' were not 'willing to mine tin and tap rubber and manage businesses, small and big, and defend their own country', the 'control [of] the politics and economy of the Malay States' passed into foreign hands.[114] In consequence:

> From being a self-reliant race who administered themselves, traded on their own and defended their own country, the Malays were turned into a dependent race, compelled to let their country be administered by colonizers. We were labelled as reluctant and lazy at work, as people who considered commerce and industry to be lowering and were forced to surrender entirely the defence of their own country to foreigners and their weaponry.[115]

Henceforth 'the Malays lost all dignity' and 'were enslaved and humiliated in our own land by all immigrant communities, colonizer or otherwise'.[116] That was 'no fairy tale but history' but few Malays had learnt from it: 'Because we control the politics of this country, as our ancestors controlled the Malay States before, we think the easy way to live and die in luxury is to rely on others to work while we are paid compensation.'[117] That was an outlandish interpretation of Malay history but it allowed Mahathir to instil Santayana's 'terror of history' into his audience:

> They who do not learn from their mistakes shall be condemned to repeating them over and over again. Have we learnt from our mistakes? Do we wish to repeat them over and over again? Are we prepared to be colonized and humiliated again? Do we want to remain a dependent people who rely on other people for our own easy life?[118]

'Look East' was Mahathir's way of adding that they who did not learn from the success of others would suffer a similar fate.

'Looking East', Mahathir had come a long way from the days of *The Malay Dilemma.* Then he had defended sinecures and Malay 'frontman' directorships.[119] But bringing the subject up to date, he declared that 'the New Economic Policy does not merely mean the division of property and wealth among *bumiputras.* It is not merely the granting of licences, tenders or contracts for government supplies and construction to *bumiputras.* It is not merely the posts of secretary-general and clerk guaranteed until the age of 55 and a lifelong pension.'[120] Instead 'the New Economic Policy also means work for *bumiputras*—work in all fields, light and heavy, lucrative or otherwise. There must be meaningful Malay and *bumiputra* participation in all areas. Meaningful participation means *bumiputra* workers will ultimately not depend on non-Malay workers for competence, diligence and productivity.'[121] In other words, under Prime Minister Mahathir, Malay nationalism meant workaholism. For the theorist of the 'complete rehabilitation of the Malays', 'Look East' held the antidote for the 'disinclination to work' and immunization against the 'terror of history'. However one looked at it—'work ethics', 'good values', 'emulating the Japanese, the Koreans and the Taiwanese'—'Look East' meant work, hard work, and yet more work! Whereas the Mahathir of *The Malay Dilemma* demanded 'constructive protection', Prime Minister Mahathir demanded that '*bumiputras* will work together with non-*bumiputras* with equal responsibility'.[122] Such was Mahathir's diagnosis, outlook, and objective for the 1980s. Such became the familiar intonation of a

Prime Minister whose Malay nationalism had been stretched to breaking-point.

'Look East' contained Mahathir's hopes of Malay advancement. But if it could ensure that '*bumiputras* will work together with non-*bumiputras* with equal responsibility'—and thereby guarantee that the achievements of the 'twin aims' of the NEP will become 'less reversible'[123]—then, paradoxically, it also held out prospects of genuine, Malaysian, inter-ethnic co-operation. One might not be able to trace exactly the ideologically tortuous, if not personally tortured, path of Mahathir's reasoning, or plot the complete trajectory of qualitative leaps his mind had to perform to 'Look East'. Yet a mixture of old fears and new expectations seemed to have led him away from an older Malay nationalism to a newer Malaysian nationalism. 'Look East' was the policy expression of that maturation of Mahathir's nationalism. It had come full circle in the 1980s to redirect the gaze of the Malays and Malaysians away from the West to the East but, perhaps most important of all, not inwards at its old non-Malay target. K. Das was surely right about Mahathir's 'thinking in terms of decades into the future, and in terms of a Malaysian society in which the races stopped looking inwards with prejudice but rather outwards with pride'.[124]

The Little Guy's Diplomacy

From the early days of his premiership, Mahathir showed that he intended to keep foreign policy under his close control.[125] He appointed the experienced Ghazali Shafie as Minister of Foreign Affairs in his first Cabinet but he planned to direct Malaysia's outward gaze coherently and comprehensively. Mahathir himself set new terms and tones for the conduct of Malaysian foreign policy.

He established an official order of priority for the country's diplomatic relations with the rest of the world wherein ASEAN ranked first in importance, it being a regional grouping of neighbouring states that had been established for national and regional security. Second came the Islamic countries to reflect the growing significance of Islam to the conduct of public affairs in Malaysia.[126] The Non-Aligned Movement, 'a mini United Nations for the Third World',[127] was granted third place while the Commonwealth,[128] once important to Malaysia, only managed a fourth placing. After that came all other countries which did not belong to any of the first four groupings. 'This series of concentric circles', Munir Majid commented, 'is too neat to be adhered to strictly' but it 'provides Malaysian foreign policy executives with an ordered sense of priorities.'[129] The new sense of priority met the day-to-day demands of diplomacy. Still Mahathir supplied the diplomatic initiatives of real significance which could be quite startling as the 'Buy British Last' and 'Look East' campaigns demonstrated. On the whole, he preferred to 'talk economics and business, not the hallowed balance of power and spheres of influence'[130] but he equally knew how he wanted to handle issues related to the latter.

Malaysia, of course, could not ignore the superpowers but it could maintain a 'non-aligned' position *vis-à-vis* the United States of America, the Soviet Union, and China.[131] Mahathir upheld that 'equidistant' stance, albeit mostly by the negative method of continually criticizing the hypocrisy and self-serving policies and actions of the superpowers, notably the United States' support for Israel and South Africa, and the USSR's occupation of Afghanistan and support for Vietnam's occupation of Kampuchea.[132] That did not preclude a more positive option: as Chamil Wariya put it, 'to prove the [non-aligned] stance, Dr Mahathir visited America, Russia, and China'.[133] On a broader note, Mahathir derided 'the cavalier fashion with which even the United Nations has been dismissed by the rich and the powerful'[134] now that the United Nations was apparently no more the 'docile club whose members recognise the authority of the more equal among them'.[135] He even declared at the Commonwealth Heads of Government Meeting (CHOGM) in Nassau in 1985 that 'gunboat diplomacy is not dead'.[136]

Mahathir's abhorrence at any banding together of rich or 'more equal' nations led him to spurn the 'senior members' of the Commonwealth who did not seem to realize that it was 'no longer a club for nations founded by migrants from Europe'.[137] He accused them of dominating the Commonwealth, of not heeding the views of the non-White ex-British colonies, and of doing little to assist them.[138] He declined to attend the CHOGM in Melbourne in 1981 and in New Delhi in 1983. He attended the CHOGM in Nassau in 1985 only to regale his audience with 'my jaundiced view'[139] of it.

He refused to accept the potential carving up of Antarctica by the 'select' group of signatories to the 1959 Treaty of Antarctica such that its resources, 'the common heritage of all the nations of this planet', would be beyond the equitable reach of small and uninfluential countries.[140] For him, the Treaty of Antarctica was only 'an agreement between a select group of countries [which] does not reflect the true feelings of members of the United Nations'.[141] He worked to obtain the support of the Non-Aligned Movement and the United Nations to replace Antarctica's 'inadequate [and] deficient' system with 'an internationally accepted regime managed in the interest of all Mankind'.[142]

Mahathir denounced the 'insincerity' and the manipulations of the rich industrialized nations which have brought '[us] to a stage where we don't believe in [meaningful North–South relations] any more'.[143] On behalf of those nations, 'still overwhelmed by unbearable external debts, strait-jacketed by protectionism and beggared by volatile interest and exchange rates',[144] he pronounced the North–South dialogue dead,[145] and dismissed the New International Economic Order as a 'non-starter'.[146] His alternative was 'South–South co-operation' and he offered facilities for establishing the South Commission which might help to expand it.[147] His defence against the manipulation of the G-7 was the solidarity of the G-77.[148] He took the initiative of practising 'South–South cooperation' of a kind and embarked on a diplomatic campaign of befriending and assisting some of the very small countries of the Pacific and Africa whose levels of economic development were not as advanced as Malaysia's.[149] Nearer home, he half-emulated the European Community and half-prepared for 'Fortress Europe' by sponsoring the 'Group of 14 on ASEAN Economic Cooperation and Integration'.[150]

Mahathir liked to say that while he was 'no apologist for the Third World' and 'no admirer of the Second World', he could not be intimidated by 'the First World, some of whose leaders and many of whose commentators and analysts ... sermonize ... preach ... declaim on all that is wrong with the Third World ... [and] hurl abuse at the Third World'.[151] He wanted an end to the 'information imbalance between the developed and developing countries' which perpetuated 'the pattern of sensationalism and unmitigated embellishment of the truth that characterize the Western press' in its coverage of Third World countries.[152] He complained not just about the 'insufficient space given to us by the Western newspapers as against what our media give them' but of 'constant ill-treatment' by the

'Western controlled international media [which] have subverted the Governments of many developing countries until some are overthrown'.[153] He was cynical towards the trade unions in the developed countries which showed no concern over 'the fate of our workers—who were badly exploited' during colonial times but which have 'suddenly become the saviours of our workers, urging them to demand higher wages and better working conditions'.[154] He wondered if this 'extraordinary concern' of the Western trade unionists—who imagine they 'know better than our labour leaders how to protect the interests of our workers'—was not aimed at reducing 'the competitiveness of our products in the market'?[155] He saw no reason why the developed countries—which in colonial times 'paid no attention to the natural environment' when 'the bulk of our forests were felled for timber and to cultivate rubber, oil palm, tea, sugar cane, coffee and so on'—should now be so exercised when 'we strive to open our land for modern agriculture, energy generation and industrialization'.[156] He suspected that Western 'environmentalist groups'—'who have come to instigate our people's thinking on the preservation of the environmental beauty of our tropical forests'—meant to trap the developing countries in 'a condition where our rural people live and remain in poverty'.[157]

Before he became Prime Minister and actively embarked on his diplomacy, some observers might have thought that Mahathir had had rather 'limited foreign policy exposure'. Certainly, Munir Majid thought it necessary to show that the 'foreign policy aristocrats—at home and abroad, practitioners and their journalistic fellow-travellers' held a 'less than accurate' view of Mahathir as 'a foreign policy novice', essentially because 'he talked economics and business'.[158] But many probably thought he did not just talk 'different things' but he talked the 'wrong way'.

In the 1960s, Mahathir was part of Malaysia's delegation to the United Nations Committee on Decolonization. There he created something of a diplomatic huff by calling the 'Sultans and Sheikhs' of Arabia 'petty despots'.[159] Then, in the 1970s, and already Deputy Prime Minister, Mahathir created another and wider stir with his oft-quoted warning about 'shooting' Vietnamese refugees trying to land on Malaysian shores. As the leader of the Malaysian delegation to the Third Islamic Summit in Taif in 1979, he roundly criticized the faults of Muslims and the weaknesses of the Islamic world.[160] As Prime Minister, he practically commenced his diplomacy by snubbing Britain with his 'Buy British Last' policy and the Commonwealth by his loudly proclaimed absence from the CHOGM in Melbourne in 1981. It was true that Mahathir had led several trade missions abroad successfully when he was Minister of Trade and Industry in the 1970s. But, on balance, was it not becoming rather obvious, decade after decade, if it could be so expressed, that the man was temperamentally undiplomatic?

And, yet, one of the most astonishing things about the Mahathir era was its relative success, as the Mahathir administration and its admirers liked to express it, in 'putting Malaysia on the world map'. This could be seen in the growing recognition accorded to Malaysia by several international organizations by the latter half of the 1980s. In 1985, Mahathir was elected to be the President for the International Conference on Drug Abuse and Illicit Trafficking scheduled to meet in Vienna in 1987. In 1987, Malaysia was chosen to host the 1989 Commonwealth Heads of Government Meeting.[161] Malaysia was also elected to the Chairmanship of the G-77 for 1989. And in 1988, Malaysia was elected as Asia's representative for a two-year term in the Security Council of the United Nations. The diplomatic success could also be seen in terms of Mahathir's own enhanced reputation as a leading statesman of the developing world.

Mahathir was not naïve. He understood better than most that his or anybody else's call for a fairer world would always be something of a 'non-starter'. His diplomacy was also not morally unblemished. He was eloquent in opposing the continued occupation of Afghanistan, Kampuchea, Lebanon, and Palestine but his 'foreign policy executives' abjectly endorsed Indonesia's invasion of East Timor.[162] At the CHOGM in Nassau in 1985, he mocked that 'the only episode that we appreciate about the Commonwealth is when it expelled and made a pariah of South Africa'. At the CHOGM in Montreal in 1987, he became an apologist for Sitiveni Rabuka's racist regime,[163] pleading in vain for an end to Fiji's expulsion from the Commonwealth. Mahathir habitually bemoaned the plight of Muslims in the Middle East but at home a journal lost its publishing licence, among other reasons, for publicizing the plight of the Muslims of Southern Thailand.[164]

But Mahathir succeeded in fashioning an odd yet refreshing diplomacy that suited his temperament. Compared with the cautious foreign policies and the discreet ways of previous Malaysian administrations, Mahathir conducted his diplomacy with a heady mixture of high profile and plain speaking, of lofty principle and crude provocation. His performances at international forums were articulate and courageous, intelligent and polished. He had a quick wit and a sharp tongue. He had a ready opinion on anything and held a strong position on everything. He was seldom slow to castigate the powerful or to shame the hypocritical. He probed everywhere for 'double standards' and nailed them with a 'holier than thou' zest.[165] Mahathir's diplomacy seemed destined to lose friends if not designed to gain enemies. He was beholden to none and he relished wearing a 'truly independent look'[166]—so independent or so maverick that he claimed with some truth that 'we are aligned with no one ... not even ... the Non-Aligned'![167] However, he more often 'identified Malaysia with other developing countries'.[168] In their midst, he must have fancied himself to be befriending the lowly, supporting the oppressed, and rallying the underdog. He articulated their sense of grievance, their fear of exclusion, and their aspiration to development. On their behalf, he bristled at every real wrong or imagined slight, at every historical injustice or future threat.[169] In rhetoric, Mahathir could be alternately accusatory, polemical, or plaintive. In substance, he constantly claimed redress and demanded restructuring on a global scale.

Was it not appropriate that Mahathir should have emerged as an outspoken voice of the small nations, the developing countries, the powerless states—the little guys of the globe who are too frequently the objects and not the movers of international diplomacy? To many Third World countries, he was deserving. Few could equal the old Malay nationalist turned Third World spokesman when it came to expressing outrage at historical oppression and contemporary marginalization. To the statesmen of the powerful nations—for whom reasons of state come first and *realpolitik* is second nature—he was probably acceptable as a critic. They, who could rarely have time for a leader of an uninfluential nation, let alone one who purported to chastise them with an uninhibited mind and the force of moral suasion, would have noted that he offended only in verbal terms. He was against nationalization, he looked after foreign investors, and his political alignment was never truly threatening. He had also become available to the Non-Aligned Movement just when its old guard was passing away.

And Malaysia could also afford his brand of diplomacy because the country was a comparatively successful member of the wretched gathering of the little guys, too many of whom were too indebted, under-developed, and poor to thumb their noses at the developed world, or, at any rate, to be able to do so with any credibility. How many among the statesmen of the ex-colonies could condescend to tell Britain, in the shape of the Confederation of British Industry, that

> you have had your ups and downs, of course. But lately we noticed that you are on your way up again. We are happy regarding that turnaround because not only can we learn much from you but we may probably be benefiting from your success. Britain was once the biggest investor in Malaysia. There is no reason why you cannot regain at least some of your past glory.[170]

How many, besides the self-righteous initiator of the 'Buy British Last' campaign, would have rubbed it in by saying:

> We regret very much that the advantageous position that you had when we gained independence was not exploited by you. But partly this was your fault. We Malaysians looked up to you so much that you must have felt taller than you really were. It took the shock of dealing with a reputedly abrasive personality to correct an outdated patron–client relation[ship].[171]

Perhaps therein lies the answer to Philip Bowring's puzzlement that Mahathir's 'antipathy to the rich industrial world sometimes sounds more like Tanzania's President Julius Nyerere than the leader of a successful and fortunate developing nation'.[172] For Bowring, Mahathir 'gives the impression that he feels the NEP should be applied globally'.[173] With no small hint of pride, Mahathir had been known to 'reply':

> Certain quarters say that in the context of North–South relations and in the effort to have a New International Economic Order, Malaysia attempts to push the concept of its New Economic Policy—that is, balance and eradication of poverty. If aspects of the NEP are seen in Malaysia's suggestion in overcoming the problem of an unbalanced world economy, we will make no disclaimer.

Indeed, the foundations of the NEP are a good manifestation of social responsibility, and we are prepared to present it in international relations.[174]

Despite Mahathir's diplomacy, the world, not being Malaysia, was not open to 'restructuring' by its 'definitive people'. But Mahathir's small diplomatic triumphs encouraged some Malaysians to feel and act as if 'we've come a long way, baby'!

The Legacy of C. H. E. Det

The baby's pet name was 'Che Det'. It was formed by adding the common Malay honorific to 'det', 'a familiar shortening of the last syllable of his name'.[175] The adult converted the 'Che' into 'C. H. E.', a set of European-like initials. The resultant 'C. H. E. Det' became Mahathir's European-sounding pseudonym in a series of articles which he wrote for the *Sunday Times* in Singapore. As a pseudonym, 'C. H. E. Det' was an artful improvisation, probably born of the self-consciousness of young adulthood for Mahathir employed it to 'conceal the fact that the views expressed [in his articles] were being written by a Malay'.[176] We shall never really know, nor is it essential to be able to tell, whether this small guile was successful. But the little-explored 'world of C. H. E. Det' harboured the many dilemmas of the adult politician who became famous for disdaining to conceal any of his views.

The main collection of the C. H. E. Det articles[177] came out towards the end of 1948, appeared fairly regularly in 1949, and began to taper off in 1950, as the following chronology indicates.[178]

Date	*Title*
26 September 1948	Malays and the [*sic*] Higher Education
17 October 1948	Malays and Higher Education: Summing-up
9 January 1949	*Ronggeng* Is Popular[179]
23 January 1949	Picnic Time in the *Dusun*
6 February 1949	Rains Bring Fish to '*Sawahs*'
24 April 1949	Malay—'Modern' and Standard
24 July 1949	Malay Housewives Are Busy
7 August 1949	The Rulers Are Losing Loyalty
9 October 1949	Rulers and *Ra'ayats*—Climax Is Near
30 October 1949	Malay *Padi* Planters Need Help

20 November 1949	Changing Malay Marriage Customs
27 November 1949	Malay Progress and the University
8 January 1950	Malays in South Siam Struggle On
9 April 1950	New Thoughts on Nationality
23 April 1950	Plight of Malay Fisherfolk

The articles themselves may be categorized according to their contents as follows:

1. observations of Malay customs and social life—as in the articles on *ronggeng*, fish, durians, marriage customs, and the housewives;
2. analyses of the problems of the Malays—as in the articles on the Malay language, education, fisherfolk, and *padi* planters; and
3. political writings—as in the articles on nationality, royalty, and the Malays in South Siam.

The first category of articles found C. H. E. Det writing to inform an English-reading audience, presumably non-Malay and presumably with little acquaintance of Malay customs. C. H. E. Det wrote earnestly and with an underlying endearment for the customs and social life he knew intimately. He had an eye for detail. He knew his *ronggeng*, could ponder its origins and comment on the innovations in the music, the dance, and the *ronggeng* party hire arrangements.[180] He knew his *padi* field fishes, the methods of catching them, and the rewards which were 'never big enough to yield a profit'.[181] He was familiar with the eager preparations for the seasonal durian picnics in 'up-country' *dusun* where 'bathing may even be a serious problem'.[182] He could evoke the air of Hari Raya in the kampongs, of the housewives' hard work and the children's gaiety, the 'open house' custom and the homemade cakes, and 'the yards and yards of cheap Japanese textiles' bought from 'Indian and Chinese textile shops'.[183] C. H. E. Det was never facetious even if he sometimes meant to entertain. Here and there he inserted playful notes and light-hearted comments—on the *faux pas* of 'uninitiated *orang putehs* try[ing] to hold the *ronggeng* girls in their arms',[184] on 'how the picnickers can take *durians* for breakfast, tiffin, tea and dinner and in between meals', and on how likely the *padi* field fisherman's hand 'may close around a water snake' instead of a fish.

At his best, C. H. E. Det showed a feel for the changing texture of Malay social life without betraying a maudlin nostalgia at the passage of certain customs. He wondered how 'the seemingly crude

Malay dance, the *Joget* or *Ronggeng*, still holds its own among Malays' in spite of 'the popularity of Western dances and the large number of cabarets' but noted that '[e]ven the dancing has been modernized and shows influence of the rumba and samba'. He suggested that 'the employment of *ronggeng* parties by amusement parks' was a 'recent affair' which 'ensure[d] a comparatively steady income for them' so that 'relieved of their pecuniary worries they have more time to consider modernizing their profession'. He approved of 'do[ing] away with ... elaborate marriages' so as to 'curtail expenses' but conceded that 'many years may lapse before simple Registry marriages become fashionable'.[185] He appeared to be amazed that 'Malays are particularly sentimental about marriages' because 'the number of divorces among them seems to indicate otherwise'. He suspected it was because they 'attach[ed] greater importance to the various ceremonies than to the future happiness of the wedded couple'. He was relieved at the lifting of the ban on marriages between 'Royal ladies and commoners'—a ban 'no doubt motivated by a desire to preserve the mythical purity of the royal blood'. He could sense innovation at picnic time in the *dusun* where 'it was getting popular among the younger people' to spread the durian flesh on 'slices of bread just as one does with butter or jam', a practice which 'older people and true *dusun* dwellers are rather sceptical' of. Rearing *ikan darat* commercially seemed to him to be a 'simple affair' but he did not think it could become widespread because 'the demand for this type of fish is confined to kampong folk only' and they, 'like everyone else, enjoy going a-fishing'.

The second set of articles revealed C. H. E. Det in quite a different light. He was sensitive to the plight of the Malays and alert to their interests. To publicize the former and defend the latter, he could be sharply critical regardless of the target of his criticism. When its first Chancellor promised that the University of Malaya would be a 'truly Malayan institution ... where no race shall enjoy priority or privilege over others', he was told that 'a too stringent enforcement of this policy might end in bitter communal feelings'.[186] C. H. E. Det recalled that 'a considerable section of Malay opinion was against' the 'university project' for 'quite sound reasoning'—the low number of Malays in English secondary schools and, '[h]ard as it is for the Malays to admit ... [their] lo[w] average intelligence quotient'. C. H. E. Det was impatient with the kampong folk who, 'with their apathy towards English education and lack of faith in their own children's abilities ... never would send their children to English schools even if they could afford to as quite a high percentage of them undoubtedly could'. He, on the other hand, was concerned that 'the number of girls [attending schools] compares unfavourably with boys'.[187] He was all for the 'post-war innovation' of opening *Sekolah Menyesal* ('Schools for those who regret') to 'uneducated housewives' which 'ha[d] succeeded in widening the outlook of Malay women'.

'Malay *Padi* Planters Need Help' and 'Plight of Malay Fisherfolk', in particular, displayed a tremendous polemical ability that delighted in standing matters on their head. Malay leaders liked to call the *padi* planters 'the backbone of their race'. For C. H. E. Det, 'what they imagine is their backbone is made up of their most illiterate and tradition-bound members'—hence, 'the much talked of backwardness of the Malays'.[188] The Fisheries Department thought that banning the (Chinese-financed) '*kelong*' was 'retrogressive' since 'with the same number of fishermen, Malaya [may be] catching only a tiny fraction of the usual haul in the United States'. C. H. E. Det much preferred to 'keep [Malay] fishermen employed than to deprive them of their means of livelihood in the interest of "progress"'.[189] He was not a Malay Luddite, only not a naïve lover of 'mechanical farming' or 'modernization in fishing methods' unless prior social changes ensured that his 'inarticulate communit[ies]' would be 'the first to gain by whatever advancement is made'.

The third and final category of the C. H. E. Det articles made up a limited attempt at political commentary. 'Malays in South Siam Struggle On' expressed the tacit sympathy of a Kedah Malay for the insurrection in the 'Malay states of Setul, Yala, Patani and Nakon Sritamrat'.[190] But C. H. E. Det was guarded. He reported that the Malays of South Siam 'will be content with nothing less than union with the Federation of Malaya'. He concluded (cryptically?) that 'the possibility of such a union has never been explored with any seriousness in Malaya'. C. H. E. Det took an unequivocal stand on the 1949 conflict between 'diehard royalists' and 'supporters and members of UMNO'. His tone was polite, his language was mild, his position was clear: the royalty could compromise or 'lose, perhaps forever, the confidence and loyalty of their subjects'.[191] And when the conflict between 'Rulers and *ra'ayats*' was nearing its climax, he was bold enough to predict that it 'will be surprising if feudalism can hold its own' against the 'new force' of a 'new Malayan democracy'.[192]

By far C. H. E. Det's most remarkable piece of political writing was 'New Thoughts on Nationality'. Barring minor differences in terminology, it could qualify as a lengthy 'abstract' for *The Malay Dilemma*. It anticipated all the central issues of *The Malay Dilemma*: the assertion of the 'hereditary rights of the indigenous people', opposition to 'Equal Citizenship', Malay backwardness and the retention of Malay privileges, Chinese dominance and 'commercial discrimination', the inadmissibility of 'open competition' between the races, Malay Land Reservation Laws, 'sympathetic state governments', et cetera. Then there could not have been Mahathir's unrestrained attack on Tunku Abdul Rahman but, uncannily, there was C. H. E. Det's muted criticism of Dato Onn Jaafar's leadership. In 1950, C. H. E. Det thought of Singapore as the 'lost world' of the Malays. In 1970, Mahathir accepted the separated Singapore as a wholly different world.[193] To go to the heart of it all, C. H. E. Det had already grasped the essence of what Mahathir ideologized, two decades later, as the 'Malay dilemma'—'the necessity of retarding progress'.[194]

C. H. E. Det was attuned to Malay life everywhere and acquainted with the events which affected it: 'the experiments in mechanical farming carried out in Perak and Province Wellesley', 'the mood of discontent' in South Siam, the displacement of Malay fishermen in Penang, the Pahang government's ban on the *kelong*', 'the rashness of the Sultan of Johore's order to the Regent to accept Dato Onn's resignation',[195] the failure of the Peninsular Malays Union,[196] and the urgent need for 'Malay political parties and the Malay public [to] awaken to the danger that they are very far behind the Chinese and Indians in education'.[197] He knew Kedah best, of course, but he knew the Malay world better than most. He knew it well enough to know when plans for the formation of a Supreme Educational Council for the Malays went no further than 'a dinner ... attended by many responsible Malay leaders'.[198] He could see that 'Malay leaders have so far shown a singular lack of interest' in the 'encouraging results' of 'the experiments in mechanical farming'.[199] From Singapore, and as 'one who has had the opportunity of studying the Malays in the Federation', he could 'visualize', as even Dato Onn could not, 'the fate in store for the Federation

Malays if they decide to forego their privileges too soon'.[200]

The world, the Malay world, of C. H. E. Det was in transition. There was colonialism, there had been war, there was now political awakening. It seems anticlimactic to say merely that for C. H. E. Det the Malays' customs were passing, their social life was changing, and their political future was uncertain. But that was what C. H. E. Det was grappling with when he wrote from Singapore, physically distanced from the Malay world but emotionally immersed in it. Perhaps now we discover the identity of C. H. E. Det, that is to say, we see the qualities which prefigured the Malay nationalist persona of Mahathir Mohamad: an unwavering identification with the Malays, an intimate knowledge of their problems, and an uncompromising defence of their rights. Thus did C. H. E. Det come upon his vocation and an 'inarticulate community' find its ideologue in Mahathir Mohamad.

During the time when C. H. E. Det wrote his essays, he was a student at the King Edward VII College of Medicine in what was then the University of Malaya, Singapore. He was aged between twenty-three and twenty-five, an older age for his generation than is usually remembered in these times. By then he had already lived through the Second World War in the shape of the Japanese invasion and occupation of Malaya. His schooling was interrupted. He ran a small stall in Alor Star's Pekan Rabu. When the British returned to Malaya, he resumed and completed his secondary school education. Then he witnessed the rise of Malay politics in the form of the anti-Malayan Union campaign. He took part in Kedah's nascent Malay politics and joined the equally nascent UMNO. Only after all that did he 'go to college'.

Mahathir's recollection of that part of his life is relatively sparse. It is unadorned by youthful declarations and largely devoid of sentimental tones. But it is enough to confirm that those were formative years and definitive events for him. The Japanese occupation ended what placidity there was in the life of a sixteen-year-old student who had hitherto thought only of finishing secondary school and becoming a 'clerk', like some of his brothers and cousins.[201] But they, like others in the British colonial service, had lost their jobs during the Japanese occupation of Malaya.[202] When they turned to roadside hawking to survive, 'their lack of knowledge was pitiful, and they had a hard time making a living'.[203] For Mahathir, 'my education had not prepared me for poverty'[204] but he more or less took care of himself throughout this period. He had a share in the small stall at Pekan Rabu in Alor Star. He sold coffee and cakes, 'bananas fresh and fried', and even the stall itself when it proved to be profitable.[205] In short, he experienced personal poverty, discovered Malay poverty, and stumbled upon the means to overcome it.

Nor did the British return to Malaya restore much stability to the already uncertain times. Mahathir managed to resume and complete his secondary school education. Then came the colonial government's Malayan Union proposal which sparked off the rise of Malay politics. Mahathir took part in Kedah's Malay politics, joined the anti-Malayan Union campaign, and became a member of the emerging UMNO. Politics having become an inseparable feature of Malay life, it seemed set on becoming an integral part of his. Just then the young man was calculating enough to realize 'my need for a higher qualification in order to gain credibility in political circles, particularly among people older than me'.[206] He qualified for a scholarship. He would have preferred to read law but was 'offered' medicine.[207] So, in 1947, Mahathir, aged twenty-two, left Kedah for Singapore.

From Kedah one traversed the whole length of the Malay Peninsula to reach Singapore. It was a shorter journey for Mahathir than for those students who left Malaya for the United Kingdom. And yet we sense, from the C. H. E Det articles as well as the views of the older Mahathir, that 'Kedah-to-Singapore' entailed something of a momentous crossing for him.[208] It entailed a journey, as it were, between two worlds: from an almost purely Malay milieu to a predominantly Chinese society, from mostly rural Alor Star to the most highly urbanized region of Malaya, from the 'rice-bowl' to the commercial capital of Malaya. Scenes of grinding Malay poverty yielded to those of glittering Chinese prosperity, or, even worse, scenes of the one 'resided' in the other.[209] Images of humble Malay shacks made way for sights of 'palatial [Chinese] homes'.[210] *Kedai Cina*, the 'ubiquitous Chinese village shop' of rural Kedah, found its culmination in the 'Chinese economic hegemony'[211] of Singapore. One also moved from where there was a 'powerful Malay middle class' to a place 'filled with Malay syces, *kebuns*, cooks and *tambies*'.[212] Finally, one left a seat of traditional Malay rule for a place where 'they have never known Malay rule'.[213]

C. H. E. Det was no country hick. He was a 'sophisticated town

Malay' by his own reckoning,[214] 'cosmopolitan' in the way he grasped the Malay world. In contrast, 'the world of the Chinese' in Malaya appeared to him as if only in the imagery of Furnivall's 'market-place'. Despite, or perhaps because of, the six years C. H. E. Det spent in Singapore, it almost seemed as if his ventures out of the Malay world only took him past rows and 'rows of Chinese shops' and that his encounters with the Chinese were little more than contacts with shopkeepers, traders, petty traders, businessmen, merchants, small-time adventurers, and tycoons.[215] At another level he encountered the Chinese in Social Darwinist imagery—a race endowed with superior genes and traits which he admired but also a horde of predatory immigrants whom he resented. The closest he came to grips with Chinese society was when the Mahathir of *The Malay Dilemma* tried to understand and explain Chinese business methods, practices, and organizations[216]—that which made 'Chinese economic hegemony' tick. In the heat of a parliamentary debate in 1965, Mahathir accused Singapore's 'PAP Chinese' of never having crossed the Causeway.[217] Perhaps neither did C. H. E. Det.

Naturally the mature Mahathir broadened his horizon, so to speak, and Prime Minister Mahathir left Malaysia for the world at large. But the Malay world of C. H. E. Det never left him. It was superimposed on the 'world of Islam' and on the 'world of developing countries' so that his Malay dilemmas continued to resonate but as Muslim dilemmas and as the dilemmas of the Third World.[218] Mahathir reacted to the West, as he depicted it in *The Challenge*,[219] and the North, as he confronted it in the 1980s, not unlike the way he reacted towards the Chinese of *The Malay Dilemma*. Where the Chinese of *The Malay Dilemma* had appeared to Mahathir to have been only shopkeepers, traders, and businessmen, the West of *The Challenge* and the North of the 1980s practically stood for an undifferentiated lump of colonial oppressors, G-7 conspirators, human rights meddlers, and journalistic detractors.[220] The immigrant 'predator' was superseded by the Western 'protectionist', the hegemony of the one being simply replaced by the hegemony of the other. That was enough reason for Mahathir to react to each in turn with ill-disguised hostility, resentment, and suspicion.

Therein lay C. H. E. Det's legacy—of knowing one's own world while confronting alien and dominating worlds one tended to comprehend in caricature.

1. Mahathir denied there was a boycott: 'We have not severed trade relations with Britain and we also have not launched a boycott of British goods. What we have simply said is that the government will not buy something from Britain if we have an alternative choice, but we will buy if we do not have a choice ('100 Hari di bawah Mahathir', *Berita Harian*, 27 October 1981).

2. This was part of Mahathir's statement on the 'Buy British Last' directive, cited in Patrick Smith, 'The British Disconnection', *Far Eastern Economic Review*, 9 October 1981, p. 95.

3. For an interesting discussion of the relationship between the PNB and the Guthrie management prior to the take-over, see Patrick Smith, 'A Colonial Chapter Closes', *Far Eastern Economic Review*, 18 September 1981, pp. 144–5 and 147.

4. Ian Coates, Guthrie's managing director, described the take-over as 'front-door nationalization' (Patrick Smith, 'Dawn Raiders' Quiet Coup', *Far Eastern Economic Review*, 18 September 1981, p. 147) and as 'back-door nationalization' ('Guthrie Comes Home', *Asiaweek*, 25 September 1981, p. 32).

5. See his long and angry denial that any nationalization was involved in '100 Hari di bawah Mahathir', *Berita Harian*, 27 October 1981. His arguments against nationalization, and especially against the Malays resorting to nationalization, were set out most clearly in 'Nationalization of Foreign Industries', in Mahathir Mohamad, *The Challenge*, Petaling Jaya: Pelanduk Publications, 1986, pp. 121–9.

6. 'Speech at the 5th General Assembly of the Organization of Asian New Agencies (OANA)', Kuala Lumpur, 3 November 1981, reprinted as 'A New World Information and Communication Order', in Murugesu Pathmanathan and David Lazarus (eds.), *Winds of Change*, Kuala Lumpur: Eastview Productions, 1984, pp. 97–102.

7. Smith, 'Dawn Raiders' Quiet Coup', p. 147.

8. Cited in 'Guthrie Comes Home', p. 32.

9. Ian Coates, quoted in Smith, 'Dawn Raiders' Quiet Coup', p. 147. Coates was also quoted thus: 'That people should be allowed to achieve control of a business in the space of four hours without the majority of the shareholders being advised is grotesque' ('Guthrie Comes Home', p. 32).

10. Munir Majid, 'Datuk Seri Dr Mahathir Mohamad: Power and Responsibility', *Malaysian Business*, October 1980, p. 7. 'To me it seems more like British economic nationalism rather than Malaysian economic nationalism' (Mahathir, cited in K. Das, 'Problems and Power', *Far Eastern Economic Review*, 30 October 1981, pp. 33–4).

11. For an account of Lord Carrington's call on Mahathir to put 'Anglo-Malaysian relations back on an even keel', see Patrick Smith and Rodney Tasker, 'Look East, *Bumiputras*', *Far Eastern Economic Review*, 12 February 1982, pp. 15–16.

12. 'We are not saying that they cannot buy, but Guthries should know better. The same with Dunlop, they should know better, In fact, (PNB) was negotiating with them to buy' (Das, 'Problems and Power', p. 33). Mahathir charged that 'the British purposely offered [equity] to the non-*bumiputras* as a means of preventing *bumiputras* from acquiring their companies' (ibid.).

13. Around this time, the extent of the Malaysian government's financial loss on the tin market was as yet unknown to the public; see the section 'Maminco Sdn. Bhd.' in Chapter 6.

14. Mahathir complained: 'On the one hand, EEC students can study in Britain at the fees paid by British students. But people from the South, where the colonies used to be, must pay an inflated fee. Take it out of the EEC. Surely they can afford it much more than we can' (Das, 'Problems and Power', p. 34). In the midst of the 'Buy British Last' affair, the British–Malaysian Industry and Trade Association pledged to contribute up to RM1.5 million over three years to help Malaysian students abroad. This presumably placatory gesture floundered. Most British firms turned out to be reluctant to contribute. Malaysian officials regarded the RM1.5 million sum as 'paltry' (K. Das, 'Studiously Ignored', *Far Eastern Economic Review*, 18 December 1981, p. 52).

15. 'Britain is now known as a country which has lost the discipline it had in the days of its glory' (Mahathir, *The Challenge*, p. 135). 'British industry and economy have deteriorated to the state it is in today.... From a nation known for the quality and extensive circulation of its goods Britain has become a nation whose manufactures and supplies cannot be depended upon' (Mahathir, 'Speech to the Pemuda and Wanita UMNO General Assembly', Kuala Lumpur, 25 June 1981, reprinted as 'Cabaran di hadapan Pemuda dan Wanita UMNO', in Harun Derauh and Shafie Nor (eds.), *Mahathir: Cita-cita dan Pencapaian*, Kuala Lumpur: Berita Publishing, 1982, pp. 51–9). In Parliament, Mahathir once noted that 'Britain, Sir, is near bankrupt. The pound is tottering, the strike of seamen is crippling, the Empire, the blissful source of booty, is now disappearing.... And so for lack of anything else, the old lion must try and play metropolitan power with us. She wants to exert pressure and to assert herself' (Malaysia, *Dewan Ra'ayat, Parliamentary Debates*, III, 2, 16 June 1966, col. 598).

16. Philip Bowring, 'Mahathir and the New Malay Dilemma', *Far Eastern Economic Review*, 9 April 1982, p. 20.

17. Tan Chee Khoon, *Without Fear or Favour*, Singapore: Eastern Universities Press, 1984, p. 86.

18. Presumably without having to pay a high price for it, in Mahathir's view: 'The British say they are the third largest investor in Malaysia, but in fact this is old investment, not new investment. If we make a comparison over past years, British investment was very small compared with American, Japanese or even Singaporean investment' ('100 Hari di bawah Mahathir').

19. Mahathir might have learnt the power of the boycott from the Chinese. See his attack on a Chinese boycott he claimed was targeted at a 'well-known London firm' manufacturing cigarettes for allegedly discriminating against Chinese when it employed some Malays' (Mahathir Mohamad, *The Malay Dilemma*, Singapore: Donald Moore for Asia Pacific Press, 1970, pp. 94–5). For a short report on the effects of the 'Buy British Last' campaign on British firms which traditionally supplied the Ministry of Health and the Ministry of Education, see Das, 'Studiously Ignored', p. 52.

20. See, for example, Mahathir's analysis of the 'world situation'—which 'does not warrant complacency'—in his speech in Parliament on 14 February 1967 (Malaysia, *Dewan Ra'ayat, Parliamentary Debates*, III, 31, 14 February 1967, cols. 4459–67). Lim Chong Eu, a very successful promoter of export-led industrialization based in state-designated Free Trade Zones in Malaysia, was just as conscious

of the 'global environment' but he was limited to Penang politics and development.

21. Mahathir, 'Speech at the 7th Conference of Heads of State/Government of the Non-Aligned Countries', New Delhi, 8 March 1983, *Foreign Affairs Malaysia*, 16, 1 (March 1983): 1–9.

22. Mahathir, 'Speech at the 37th Session of the United Nations General Assembly', New York, 29 September 1982.

23. Ibid.

24. Mahathir, 'Speech at the 7th Conference of Heads of State/Government of the Non-Aligned Countries'.

25. Mahathir, 'Speech at the 7th Malaysian Economic Convention', Kuala Lumpur, 18 January 1983, reprinted as 'The Malaysian Economy: Policy Adjustment or Structural Transformation', in Murugesu Pathmanathan and David Lazarus (eds.), *Winds of Change*, Kuala Lumpur: Eastview Productions, 1984, pp. 171–9.

26. Ibid.

27. 'As if these are not enough', the United States employed its stockpile, maintained 'ostensibly for strategic reasons', as 'merely a rich nation's monopolistic weapon used to depress prices of commodities for the benefit of the consumers' (ibid.).

28. Ibid.

29. Mahathir, 'Speech at the 41st Session of the United Nations General Assembly', New York, 29 September 1986, *Foreign Affairs Malaysia*, 19, 3 (September 1986): 55–65.

30. Ibid.

31. Ibid.

32. Mahathir, 'Speech at the 7th Malaysian Economic Convention'.

33. Ibid.

34. Mahathir, 'Speech at the Banquet Hosted by His Excellency President Chun Doo Hwan of the Republic of Korea', Seoul, 9 August 1983, *Foreign Affairs Malaysia*, 16, 3 (September 1983): 297–302.

35. Mahathir, 'Speech at the Official Dinner Hosted by His Excellency the Prime Minister of Japan, Mr Yasuhiro Nakasone', Tokyo, 24 January 1983, *Foreign Affairs Malaysia*, 16, 1 (March 1983): 17–20.

36. Mahathir, 'Keynote Address at the ASEAN–EEC Industrial Sectoral Conference', Kuala Lumpur, 28 February 1983, reprinted as 'ASEAN–EEC Industrial Cooperation' in Murugesu Pathmanathan and David Lazarus (eds.), *Winds of Change*, Kuala Lumpur: Eastview Productions, 1984, pp. 189–97.

37. Mahathir, 'Speech at the Foreign Policy Association', Washington, 19 January 1984, *Foreign Affairs Malaysia*, 17, 1 (March 1984): 57–63.

38. Ibid.

39. Mahathir, 'Speech at the 41st Session of the United Nations General Assembly'.

40. Mahathir, 'Speech at the 7th Conference of Heads of State/Government of the Non-Aligned Countries'.

41. Mahathir, 'Speech at the Banquet Hosted by His Excellency President Chun Doo Hwan of the Republic of Korea'.

42. Ibid.

43. Mahathir, 'Speech at the 39th Session of the United Nations General Assembly', New York, 10 October 1984, reprinted as 'Mahathir kepada PBB: Nilai Revolusi Islam Secara Adil', *Utusan Malaysia*, 11 October 1984.

44. Mahathir, 'Speech at the 41st Session of the United Nations General Assembly'.

45. Ibid.

46. Mahathir, 'Keynote Address at the ASEAN–EEC Industrial Sectoral Conference'.

47. Mahathir, 'Speech at the 7th Conference of Heads of State/Government of the Non-Aligned Countries'.

48. Ibid.

49. Mahathir, 'Address at the 37th Session of the United Nations General Assembly'.

50. Mahathir, 'Speech at the Foreign Policy Association'.

51. Mahathir, 'Speech at the 7th Conference of Heads of State/Government of the Non-Aligned Countries'.

52. Mahathir, 'Keynote Address at the ASEAN–EEC Industrial Sectoral Conference'.

53. Mahathir, 'Speech at the Official Dinner Hosted by His Excellency the Prime Minister of Japan, Mr Yasuhiro Nakasone'.

54. Mahathir, 'Whither Malaysia?', Paper presented at the Keio International Symposium on 'Asia and Japan', Tokyo, 7–11 November 1983, reprinted in Andrew J. L. Armour (ed.), *Asia and Japan*, London: Athlone Press, 1985, pp. 150–9. This quote is from p. 152.

55. Mahathir, 'Speech at the 5th Joint Conference of MAJECA/JAMECA', Kuala Lumpur, 8 February 1982, *Foreign Affairs Malaysia*, 15, 1 (March 1982): 38–45.

56. Mahathir, 'Keynote Address at the ASEAN–EEC Industrial Sectoral Conference'.

57. Mahathir, 'Whither Malaysia?'.

58. The changes to the rules did not prevent the subsequent take-over of Harrisons and Crossfield, the last of the old 'Malayan plantation companies' to be based in London (Jeffrey Segal, 'Sunset on British Estates', *Far Eastern Economic Review*, 11 June 1982, pp. 120–2). It has been suggested that Mahathir would have understood the need for the City to change its take-over rules (Roger Kershaw, 'Anglo-Malaysian Relations: Old Roles versus New Rules', *International Affairs*, 59, 4 (Autumn 1983): 629–48).

59. Mahathir, 'Speech at the 7th Malaysian Economic Convention'.

60. Mahathir, *The Malay Dilemma*, p. 47.

61. Writing about how the British disregarded the Malays after making a half-hearted attempt to assist them economically, Mahathir noted: 'Now they were free once again to swill their whiskies in their clubs and give more contracts to British firms' (ibid., p. 41).

62. On 19 April 1985, Mahathir delivered an address at Trinity College, Oxford University, which began with a lengthy excerpt from Frantz Fanon's *The Wretched of the Earth*, only it turned out to be an excerpt from Sartre's Preface to

the book. Fanon himself found no mention in the address. See Mahathir, 'Holier than Thou—A Mild Critique', Speech at Trinity College, Oxford, 19 April 1985, *Foreign Affairs Malaysia*, 18, 2 (June 1985): 137–49.

63. Mahathir, 'Speech at the Seminar on Transnational Corporations and National Development', Petaling Jaya, 2 October 1979, *Foreign Affairs Malaysia*, 12 (1979): 392–5.

64. Mahathir, 'Speech at the 39th Session of the United Nations General Assembly'. In 1984, too, Mahathir reproached CUEPACS (Congress of Unions of Employees in Public, Administrative and Civil Services) for believing that 'the way to get more income is through threatening industrial peace and not through upgrading productivity', that is, for clinging to the 'old work ethic' of the West which 'was planted throughout the world through its international workers' organisations' (Mahathir, 'Speech at the 35th UMNO General Assembly', Kuala Lumpur, 25 May 1984, English translation reprinted as 'Making Sure the Spirit of UMNO Prevails', *New Straits Times*, 26 May 1984).

65. Mahathir, 'Keynote Address at the ASEAN–EEC Industrial Sectoral Conference'.

66. Mahathir, 'Speech at the 39th Session of the United Nations General Assembly'.

67. What does one do with Japan which is both 'East' and 'North'? Mahathir, as can be seen later, had other ideas for Japan.

68. There was considerable, unresolved, speculation whether Mahathir would have urged the Taiwan, Hong Kong, and Singapore 'models' on Malaysia (rather than the examples of Japan and South Korea) were these three not 'Chinese' states. He did say that 'Singapore's success story in the economic and social fields cannot but be a model for Malaysians rather than an object of envy' (Mahathir, 'Speech at a Dinner on the Occasion of an Official Visit to Singapore', Singapore, 18 December 1981, *Foreign Affairs Malaysia*, 14, 4 (December 1981): 311–16). At the 1987 UMNO General Assembly, he praised 'manufacturing countries like South Korea, Taiwan and Hong Kong [which] secure a higher trade surplus' amidst the world recession and falling commodity prices (Mahathir, 'Speech at the 38th UMNO General Assembly', Kuala Lumpur, 24 April 1987, English translation reprinted as 'Let Not Future Generations Condemn Us', *New Straits Times*, 25 April 1987).

69. Chamil Wariya, *Dasar Luar Era Mahathir*, Petaling Jaya: Penerbit Fajar Bakti, 1989, p. 65, suggests that Mahathir may have been influenced by Ezra Vogel's *Japan, Number One*, published 'two years before Dr Mahathir became Prime Minister' to think that 'if Malaysia wished to succeed it would be reasonable for it to learn from Japan's success'.

70. Mahathir, '25th National Day Message', reprinted as 'Kemerdekaan Negara di Bahu Generasi Muda', *Watan*, 3 September 1982.

71. Mahathir, 'Speech at the 33rd UMNO General Assembly', Kuala Lumpur, 10 September 1982, English translation reprinted as 'UMNO in a World of Change and Challenge', *New Straits Times*, 11 September 1982.

72. Ibid.

73. Mahathir, 'Speech at the 35th UMNO General Assembly'.

74. Mahathir, 'Speech at the 33rd UMNO General Assembly'.

75. Mahathir, 'Speech at the 35th UMNO General Assembly'.

76. Ibid.

77. Mahathir, 'Speech at the 37th UMNO General Assembly', Kuala Lumpur, 18 September 1986, reprinted as 'Sistem Tumpuan Luar Bandar Akan Dikekalkan', *Utusan Malaysia*, 19 September 1986.

78. 'Given the fact that the *Ummah* is blessed with more than 50% of the mineral resources, primary produce, food, human and intellectual resources, what is needed is for us to realign our interests and cast off the traditional Eurocentric perception and approach. This is a vital prerequisite for the prosperity and progress of the *Ummah*' (Mahathir, 'Speech at the 3rd Islamic Summit Conference', Taif, Saudi Arabia, 27 January 1981, reprinted as 'Towards Islamic Solidarity', in Murugesu Pathmanathan and David Lazarus (eds.), *Winds of Change*, Kuala Lumpur: Eastview Productions, 1984, pp. 57–68). Mahathir was then Deputy Prime Minister and leader of the Malaysian delegation.

79. Mahathir, 'Speech at the ASEAN Law Association General Assembly', Kuala Lumpur, 26 October 1982, reprinted as 'The Varieties of Justice', in Murugesu Pathmanathan and David Lazarus (eds.), *Winds of Change*, Kuala Lumpur: Eastview Productions, 1984, pp. 159–65.

80. Mahathir, 'Speech at the 5th Joint Conference of MAJECA/JAMECA'.

81. Mahathir, 'Speech at the Official Dinner Hosted by His Excellency the Prime Minister of Japan, Mr Yasuhiro Nakasone'.

82. Mahathir, 'Speech at the Banquet Hosted by His Excellency President Chun Doo Hwan of the Republic of Korea'.

83. Das, 'Problems and Power', p. 31.

84. Mahathir, 'Whither Malaysia?', p. 152.

85. Ibid., pp. 151–2.

86. Ibid., p. 153.

87. Ibid., p. 152.

88. Ibid., p. 154.

89. Mahathir, 'Speech at the 33rd UMNO General Assembly'.

90. Mahathir, 'Speech at the 5th Joint Annual Conference of MAJECA/JAMECA'.

91. Ibid.

92. '100 Hari di bawah Mahathir'.

93. Mahathir, 'Whither Malaysia?', pp. 154–5.

94. Ibid., pp. 155–6. But he was not unaware that 'protectionism is very strong especially in Japan' (Mahathir, 'Speech at the Symposium on ASEAN, Australia and Japan—Breaking Down the Barriers', Kuala Lumpur, 7 May 1984, *Foreign Affairs Malaysia*, 17, 2 (June 1984): 153–7).

95. Ibid., p. 155.

96. Chandra Muzaffar, 'Hard Work—The Cure All?' and 'Overkill?: In-House Unions for Malaysia'; Johan Saravanamuttu, 'Look East Policy: The Real Lessons'; Chang Yii Tan, 'Tilting East—The Construction Problem'; and Lee Poh Ping, '"Japan Incorporated" and Its Relevance to Malaysia', all in Jomo K. S. (ed.), *Mahathir's Economic Policies*, 2nd edn., Petaling Jaya: Institute of Social Analysis, 1989.

97. 'The democracy of the Japanese business organisation is quite unique.

Differences in status between the executives and the workers are not emphasized. They wear the same uniforms and the executives tend to spend more time on the shop floor than in their offices. When decisions are to be made everyone is consulted. Even the junior executives seem to have a say' (Mahathir, 'Whither Malaysia?', p. 154).

98. Ibid., p. 155.

99. Observe the militancy of South Korean labour after the fall of the military regime.

100. Bob Steven, *Japan's New Imperialism*, London: Macmillan, 1990. Chamil's admiring account of the 'Look East' policy none the less raised some doubts about Mahathir's expectations of Japan. 'It can be said that almost all the external loans after the policy was introduced were made in yen' but 'the creation of the "Look East" policy did not save [us] from the adverse effects of Japan's action' in revaluing the yen (Chamil, *Dasar Luar Era Mahathir*, pp. 74–6). Mahathir never castigated Japan's complicity in the G-7-initiated yen revaluation; Chamil offered the consolation that 'Japan did not intend to oppress [us]' (ibid., p. 76).

101. 'It is comforting to note that the reported cases of new and successful enterprises do not come from any given region, country or nationality. "Managing for excellence" is within the reach of any organisation, country or people' (Mahathir, 'Speech at the 20th World Management Congress', Kuala Lumpur, 3 November 1985, *Foreign Affairs Malaysia*, 18, 4 (December 1986): pp. 342–6).

102. Mahathir, 'Whither Malaysia?', p. 155.

103. Rehman Rashid, 'Standing Tall in the Face of Opposition', *New Straits Times*, 4 July 1986.

104. Rehman Rashid, 'Why I Took to Politics', *New Straits Times,* 5 July 1986.

105. Mahathir, 'Speech at the 33rd UMNO General Assembly'.

106. Mahathir, 'Speech at the 1981 Malaysia Press Award Presentation Ceremony', Kuala Lumpur, 28 November 1982, reprinted as 'Wartawan dan Tanggungjawab', *Berita Harian*, 29 November 1982.

107. Mahathir, 'Whither Malaysia?'.

108. Rehman Rashid, 'Why I Took to Politics'.

109. Mahathir, 'Speech at the 1981 Malaysia Press Award Presentation Ceremony'.

110. Bowring, 'Mahathir and the New Malay Dilemma', p. 20.

111. Mahathir, 'Whither Malaysia?', p. 151.

112. S. Jayasankaran, 'Premier in Power', *Malaysian Business*, 1 January 1988, p. 10.

113. This phrase is borrowed from Frank Swettenham who suggested that 'the leading characteristic of the Malay of every class is a disinclination to work' (Syed Hussein Alatas, *The Myth of the Lazy Native*, London: Frank Cass, 1977, p. 45). Mahathir did not actually use the phrase in his 'Speech at the Pemuda and Wanita UMNO General Assembly', 25 June 1981, but he meant the same thing and he argued that the Malays—rulers and 'their people', civil servants as well as workers, and even 'our ancestors'—avoided work.

114. Mahathir, 'Speech at the Pemuda and Wanita UMNO General Assembly', 25 June 1981.

115. Ibid.

116. Ibid.

117. Not realizing that 'others prefer us to be lazy and incompetent so that we will forever be dependent on them' (ibid.).

118. Ibid.

119. Mahathir, *The Malay Dilemma*, pp. 44–5.

120. Mahathir, 'Speech at the Pemuda and Wanita UMNO General Assembly', 25 June 1981.

121. Ibid.

122. Ibid.

123. Mahathir, 'Whither Malaysia?', p. 151.

124 K. Das, 'Mahathir's "Restoration"', *Far Eastern Economic Review*, 11 June 1982, p. 38.

125. Chamil, *Dasar Luar Era Mahathir*, pp. 123–4.

126. The reasoning for upgrading the status of diplomatic relations with Islamic countries is often terse: 'Since it is an Islamic country, it is logical for Malaysia to accord a special place in its relations with countries of similar character' and, hence, 'not surprising for Dr Mahathir to determine that in foreign policy relations with Islamic countries would be the second of his priorities' (ibid., p. 41). One might consider this as the diplomatic dimension to Mahathir's 'Islamization' policy. The argument is not presented here but Chapter 5 discusses Islamization in detail.

127. Ibid., p. 46.

128. Troops from Australia, New Zealand, and Fiji, for instance, brought in and maintained under Commonwealth auspices, had assisted the Malay[si]an government during the Emergency and the Confrontation with Indonesia.

129. Munir Majid, 'Knocking Foreign Policy into Shape', *New Straits Times*, 25 May 1983. Munir added: 'It is true that Malaysian foreign policy previously had already placed some kind of premium on relations with States in the categories Dr Mahathir defines, but it was in something of a jumble which did not give a proper backbone to policy—with some pulling the traditional Anglo-Saxon way, others the resurgent Islamic, still others in the non-aligned direction.'

130. Ibid.

131. 'Malaysia does not wish to be a member of any camp or bloc. We are aligned with no one. We are not even aligned with the Non-Aligned. We will criticize and condemn the Non-Aligned Movement or any of its members or groups as much as we would criticize the countries of the Eastern or Western blocs' (Mahathir, 'Speech in Conjunction with the Celebration of the 41st Anniversary of the United Nations', Kuala Lumpur, 25 October 1986, *Foreign Affairs Malaysia*, 19, 4 (December 1986): 16–19).

132. See Mahathir's speeches to the United Nations General Assembly in 1982, 1984, and 1986. He would not 'differentiate really between the role of China and the role of the Soviet Union. Both are equally disruptive. We want to keep them at arm's length' (Das, 'Problems and Power, p. 34).

133. Chamil, *Dasar Luar Era Mahathir*, p. 48.

134. Mahathir, 'Speech at the Commonwealth Heads of Government Meeting',

Nassau, Bahamas, 16 October 1985, *Foreign Affairs Malaysia*, 18, 4 (December 1985): 387–90.

135. Mahathir, 'Speech in Conjunction with the Celebration of the 41st Anniversary of the United Nations'. At the 41st Session of the United Nations General Assembly, New York, 29 September 1986, itself, Mahathir commented: '... for the majority of us, the small, developing nations, a world without the United Nations is unthinkable' because 'many nations here owe their independence to the work of the Decolonisation Committee of the United Nations'. But if the United Nations 'falls short of expectations', it was because the 'powerful nations ... expect the United Nations to be perhaps a creature in their own image, serving only perceived ends, for certain perceived interests'.

136. Mahathir, 'Speech at the Commonwealth Heads of Government Meeting', 16 October 1985.

137. Ibid. The reference to the 'senior members' came from his 'Speech to the Commonwealth Speakers and Presiding Officers Standing Committee Meeting', Kuala Lumpur, 6 January 1987, *Foreign Affairs Malaysia*, 20, 1 (March 1987): 7–9.

138. Especially over Britain's refusal to maintain economic sanctions against the Pretoria regime, in opposition to virtually all the non-White member countries of the Commonwealth. He instructed the newly established Institute of Strategic and International Studies (ISIS) Malaysia to carry out a review of Malaysia's membership in the Commonwealth. The ISIS study was never made public but Malaysia remained in the Commonwealth.

139. Mahathir, 'Speech at the Commonwealth Heads of Government Meeting', 16 October 1985.

140. Mahathir signalled the beginning of his 'Antarctica' campaign during his 'Speech at the 37th Session of the United Nations General Assembly', New York, 29 September 1982, reprinted as 'Towards Credibility in the United Nations', in Murugesu Pathmanathan and David Lazarus (eds.), *Winds of Change*, Kuala Lumpur: Eastview Productions, 1984, pp. 140–52. He called for a review of the 1959 Treaty of Antarctica in the spirit of the just concluded Conference on the Law of the Sea. 'Henceforth,' he declared, 'all the unclaimed wealth of this earth must be regarded as the common heritage of all the nations of this planet.'

141. Ibid.

142. Mahathir, 'Speech at the 8th Conference of Heads of State/Government of the Non-Aligned Countries', Harare, Zimbabwe, 3 September 1986, *Foreign Affairs Malaysia*, 19, 3 (September 1986): 47–54. He made an identical call at the 41st Session of the United Nations General Assembly, New York, 29 September 1986.

143. 'We don't believe there is any sincerity on the part of the North to do anything' (Das, 'Problems and Power', p. 34).

144. Mahathir, 'Speech at the 8th Conference of Heads of State/Government of the Non-Aligned Countries'.

145. 'We now know that we cannot squeeze blood from stone' (Mahathir, 'Speech at the 7th Conference of Heads of State/Government of the Non-Aligned Countries').

146. Mahathir, 'Speech at the South–South II Summit of Third World Scholars

and Statesmen', Kuala Lumpur, 5 May 1986, *Foreign Affairs Malaysia*, 19, 2 (June 1986): 23–31. The NIEO 'was an equitable proposal' but 'the developed countries turned it down flat'.

147. Mahathir urged South–South co-operation but was not uncritical of the lack of progress made in that direction. He saw the 1983 Delhi Declaration on Collective Self-reliance as 'no more than a paper pledge' and he thought 'no tangible benefit was derived by member states' from the 1981 Caracas Programme of Action (Mahathir, 'Speech at the South–South II Summit').

148. 'All we really need is the recognition that unless we help to strengthen each other we are not going to be in a position singly, or as a group to get fair treatment from the North. The North believes in strength. They deal differently with the strong and differently again with the weak' (Mahathir, 'Speech at the South–South II Summit'). Mahathir was elected to the Chairmanship of the G-77 in 1989.

149. Malaysia's ties with some of these countries (such as Fiji, Mali, the Maldives, and Mauritius), it has been explained, 'will not only bring benefit to them but also to Malaysia in terms of opportunities for trade and enhancing the name of Malaysia' (Intan, *Dasar Utama Kerajaan Malaysia*, 1988, cited in Chamil, *Dasar Luar Era Mahathir*, p. 49).

150. See Mohamed Noordin Sopiee, Chew Lay See, and Lim Siang Jin (eds.), *ASEAN at the Crossroads: Obstacles, Options and Opportunities in Economic Co-operation*, Kuala Lumpur: Institute of Strategic and International Studies (ISIS), n.d.

151. Mahathir, 'Holier than Thou—A Mild Critique'.

152. Mahathir, 'Speech at the 5th General Assembly of the Organization of Asian News Agencies'.

153. Ibid. He added that 'the sad thing is that the Governments which took over are often less democratic than the maligned predecessor. Whatever governments take over, they soon become subjects of international vilification by the western media.' Malaysia's suffering never reached such proportions but, after May 13 1969, Mahathir said, 'dire predictions were made which implied that the world could write off Malaysia'.

154. Mahathir, 'Speech at the 39th Session of the United Nations General Assembly'.

155. Ibid.

156. Ibid.

157. Ibid

158. Munir, 'Knocking Foreign Policy into Shape'.

159. In Parliament, Lim Chong Eu asked if Tunku Abdul Rahman 'was aware that considerable sections of our citizens are greatly concerned' by Mahathir's statement because 'to have the term—"petty despots"—which can be misinterpreted locally interposed so closely with the term "Sultan" which is also used locally could create misunderstanding'. In a partial rebuke of Mahathir, the Tunku replied that 'when one makes speeches at the United Nations, one feels that one gets plenty of support and hand clapping, and one can really overstate the fact and, I think, this is one of (those) cases' (Malaysia, *Dewan Ra'ayat, Parliamentary Debates*, II, 13, 12 November 1965, cols. 2332–5). However, 'Dr Mahathir, reflecting on what he said, says quite resolutely that he made his points in an atmosphere of complete

calm, within the Committee [on Decolonization], and that he meant every word' (Robin Adshead, *Mahathir of Malaysia*, London: Hibiscus Publishing Company, 1989, p. 55).

160. His injunctions to Muslims to seek knowledge, work hard, and become independent of non-Muslim countries have been cited in the section 'Islam: The Muslim Dilemma', in Chapter 2. His Taif speech is treated in greater detail in Chapter 5.

161. Mahathir explained thus: 'Why should we host the summit [CHOGM]? That's one way of getting your country known to others. We couldn't host a United Nations or a World Bank conference because the Israelis would want to come. But the Commonwealth has nobody that we've no relations with. So it gives us an opportunity. It's going to cost us money but it'll also put us on the map' (Jayasankaran, 'Premier in Power', p. 10).

162. See the statement delivered by Mustaffa Mohamad 'on the question of East Timor' at the United Nations General Assembly, 11 November 1982, *Foreign Affairs Malaysia*, 15, 4 (December 1982): 337–40. Mahathir's selective moralization over imperialist domination in the world was not new. In 1967, for example, Mahathir urged that 'Malaysia must never cease to help in the liberation of the Portuguese occupied territories and to condemn Portuguese recalcitrance over South Africa and South Rhodesia' (Malaysia, *Dewan Ra'ayat, Parliamentary Debates*, III, 31, 14 February 1967, col. 4466). But when Tan Chee Khoon asked if 'he [Mahathir] thinks that in Vietnam it is not a war of liberation', Mahathir replied, 'I have purposely avoided mentioning Vietnam in my little speech because I think this is far too big for us to put our fingers in ...' (ibid., col. 4469).

163. 'Dr M: Fiji Should Not Be Expelled', *New Straits Times*, 14 October 1987.

164. *Nadi Insan* lost its publishing licence, ironically during Mahathir's avowedly 'liberal' phase. Did those responsible for withdrawing the licence know that the young Mahathir wrote about the plight of the Malays of 'South Siam' in the *Sunday Times* (for which, see the concluding section of this chapter).

165. Mahathir, 'Holier than Thou—A Mild Critique'. This speech reveals, one hazards to guess, Mohamed Noordin Sopiee's literary style and rhetorical flourish but Mahathir was the only Malaysian Prime Minister who could have delivered it with conviction and effect.

166. Munir, 'Knocking Foreign Policy into Shape'.

167. Mahathir, 'Speech in Conjunction with the Celebration of the 41st Anniversary of the United Nations'.

168. Munir, 'Knocking Foreign Policy into Shape'.

169. A good example of Mahathir expounding the 'dilemmas of the developing world' may be seen from his 'Speech at the Luncheon Jointly Hosted by the Asia Society, the Far East American Business Council and the ASEAN–American Trade Council', New York, 16 January 1984, *Foreign Affairs Malaysia*, 17, 1 (March 1984): 50–4.

170. Mahathir, 'Speech at the Luncheon Hosted by the Confederation of British Industry', London, 23 July 1987, *Foreign Affairs Malaysia*, 20, 3 (September 1987): 59–62.

171. Ibid.

172. Bowring, 'Mahathir and the New Malay Dilemma', p. 21.

173. Ibid.

174. Mahathir, 'Speech at the 33rd UMNO General Assembly'.

175. Adshead, *Mahathir of Malaysia*, p. 26.

176. Datuk Zakiah Hanum of the National Archives, Kuala Lumpur, quoted in ibid., p. 34.

177. Two articles, unavailable for this study, were exhibited in Mahathir's old house but unfortunately without proper citations, that is 'Weekly Fair at Alor Star' and 'Malay Women Make Their Own Freedom'.

178. Subsequent references to the following articles will only give their titles. Note that the Malay words in the C. H. E. Det articles were not italicized in the original.

179. The byline for this piece appeared as C. H. E. Dett, an even more Anglicized spelling of 'Det' were it not an error.

180. '*Ronggeng* Is Popular'.

181. 'Rains Bring Fish to "Sawahs"'.

182. 'Picnic Time in the *Dusun*'.

183. 'Malay Housewives Are Busy'.

184. 'Ignorance is the usual plea though a few *stengahs* might also have something to do with it' ('*Ronggeng* Is Popular').

185. 'Changing Malay Marriage Customs'.

186. 'Malay Progress and the University'.

187. 'Malays and the Higher Education'.

188. 'Malay *Padi* Planters Need Help'.

189. 'Plight of Malay Fisherfolk'.

190. 'Malays in South Siam Struggle On'. A Kedah Malay of Mahathir's age and period lived under three colonial regimes: British before the war, Japanese during part of the war, and Siamese when Kedah was ceded to Siam by the Japanese—and then British again after the defeat of the Japanese.

191. 'The Rulers Are Losing Loyalty'.

192. 'Rulers and *Ra'ayats*—Climax Is Near'.

193. Mahathir, *The Malay Dilemma,* Chapter 11, 'Malaysia and Singapore', pp. 179–88.

194. 'New Thoughts on Nationality'. 'The Malay dilemma is whether they should stop trying to help themselves in order that they should be proud to be the poor citizens of a prosperous country or whether they should try to get at some of the riches that this country boasts of, even if it blurs the economic picture of Malaysia a little. For the Malays it would appear there is not just an economic dilemma, but a Malay dilemma' (Mahathir, *The Malay Dilemma*, p. 61).

195. 'Rulers and *Ra'ayats*—Climax Is Near'.

196. C. H. E. Det strongly sympathized with Hashim Ghani, 'the original proposer of the anti-Malayan Nationality Peninsular Malays Union' who was under no illusion as [to] the chances of his countrymen in competition with the superior organisation, financial position and education of the non-Malays' ('New Thoughts on Nationality').

197. 'Malays and the Higher Education'.

198. 'Malays and Higher Education: Summing-up'.

199. 'Malay *Padi* Planters Need Help'.

200. 'New Thoughts on Nationality'.

201. Adshead, *Mahathir of Malaysia*, p. 31.

202. 'The Japanese occupation period had exposed their [Malays'] backwardness and incompetence as nothing else could. The systematic retrenchment of white-collar workers carried out by the Japs [*sic*] resulted in untold misery to the Malays who form the majority of the Government employees. Unable to go into any lucrative trade, many were forced to turn to trisha pedalling, hawking and menial labour' ('New Thoughts on Nationality').

203. Adshead, *Mahathir of Malaysia*, p. 31.

204. Ibid.

205. Leung Thong Ping, 'Mahathir', *Sunday Mail*, 2 April 1972; Adshead, *Mahathir of Malaysia*, p. 31. Mahathir's business partner provided a brief recollection of the stall in Morais, *Mahathir: A Profile in Courage*, pp. 5 and 7. This evidently formative experience became part of the basis of Mahathir's primer on small-scale trading. See Mahathir Mohamad, *Guide for Small Businessmen*, Petaling Jaya: Eastern Universities Press, 1985; translated from *Panduan Peniaga Kecil*, 2nd edn., Kuala Lumpur: Dewan Bahasa dan Pustaka, 1982.

206. Adshead, *Mahathir of Malaysia*, p. 34.

207. Morais *(Mahathir: A Profile in Courage*, p. 7) was wrong about Mahathir being awarded 'a State Government Scholarship'. In fact, during his housemanship in Penang, Mahathir wrote to the State Surgeon of Kedah to request a medical officer's post in Kedah. He specifically mentioned that he was not a Kedah 'State scholar' but indicated his interest in working in his home state and being near to his ageing and ailing parents. This letter is on exhibit in Mahathir's old house, No. 18, Lorong Kilang Ais, Kampong Seberang Perak, Alor Star. Details of Mahathir's Federal Government scholarship are provided in Adshead, *Mahathir of Malaysia*, p. 34.

208. As it was to be for a later generation of Malay students sent to the United Kingdom and the United States of America. Mahathir's views on the experiences of those students, some of whom he thought were unable to deal with 'culture shock' in their encounter with the West, were cited in Mohd. Nor Shamsudin, 'Universiti Islam Antarabangsa Kembalikan Kegemilangan Dunia Islam', *Utusan Malaysia*, 16 March 1982.

209. 'The few Malays in the city live in the servants' quarters of Chinese and European houses' ('New Thoughts on Nationality').

210. In 'New Thoughts on Nationality', C. H. E. Det wrote of Singapore: 'And so in the island today the Malays, once the owners and rulers, are to be found only in the poorer quarters, living in dilapidated attap and plank huts sometimes only a stone's throw from the palatial residences of Chinese millionaires.' Fifteen years later, during an attack on Lee Kuan Yew's People's Action Party (PAP) in Parliament prior to Singapore's separation from Malaysia, Mahathir said: 'We Malays are very sensitive, but this is a total war declared by the P.A.P. and even if it hurts our feelings, it is still wiser to demonstrate that in this land the privileged Malays, Ibans, Dayaks and Kadazans live in huts whilst the underprivileged Chinese live in palaces,

go around in big cars and have the best things in life' (Malaysia, *Dewan Ra'ayat, Parliamentary Debates*, II, 1, 26 May 1965, col. 84).

211. See C. H. E. Det's reference to 'the ubiquitous Chinese village shopkeeper' in 'Malay *Padi* Planters Need Help' and his numerous remarks on 'Chinese economic hegemony' in *The Malay Dilemma*. In the interview which he gave to the local newspaper editors on the occasion of his '100th day in office', Mahathir said at one point: 'If we go to a shop, in our language, we say "go to a Chinese shop". As if the shop must be Chinese' ('100 Hari di bawah Mahathir', *Berita Harian*, 27 October 1981).

212. 'New Thoughts on Nationality'.

213. Malaysia, *Dewan Ra'ayat, Parliamentary Debates*, II, 1, 26 May 1965, col. 84. The passage containing this line is given under n. 217, below.

214. Mahathir, *The Malay Dilemma*, pp. 22–3 and 26. But in 'Malays and Higher Education: Summing-up', C. H. E. Det had distinguished between the attitudes of 'town Malays' and 'kampong folk'.

215. For the persistence of the Chinese shop in Mahathir's world-view, see 'rows of Chinese shops' in *The Malay Dilemma*, p. 25, '*kedai Cina*' in '100 Hari di bawah Mahathir', and 'the ubiquitous Chinese village shopkeeper' in 'Malay *Padi* Planters Need Help'. *The Malay Dilemma*, pp. 25, 35–6, 42–3, *passim*, contained frequent references to Chinese shopkeepers, traders, petty traders, businessmen, merchants, small-time adventurers, and tycoons.

216. Mahathir, *The Malay Dilemma*, pp. 53–6.

217. 'They have never known Malay rule and could not bear the idea that the people that they have for so long kept under their heels should now be in a position to rule them. They have in most instances never crossed the Causeway. They are in fact overseas Chinese first ... and Malaysians a very poor second' (Malaysia, *Dewan Ra'ayat, Parliamentary Debates*, II, 1, 26 May 1965, col. 84).

218. To that extent: 'He was apt to identify completely with a small human circle and with a vital set of local problems. When he later burst into universality, it was not on the basis of extensive knowledge of the state of universal questions, but rather because he was able to experience what was immediately about him in new ways' (Erik H. Erikson, *Young Man Luther*, New York: W. W. Norton, 1958, p. 87).

219. Mahathir, *The Challenge*. See especially the essays 'West and East' (pp. 44–55) and 'A System of Values and the Malays' (pp. 91–103).

220. Western 'investors' being the only and always welcome exception!

4

Capitalism: Visions of a Free Economy

> It is only recently that the Malays have been introduced to a monetised society. I have talked about the Malays' idea of money as a mere convenience; something lighter that you can put in your pocket instead of carrying a sack of rice to the town. Money in order to make money is a new concept.
>
> Mahathir, quoted in Rehman Rashid, 'Prime Minister Reveals His Hopes and Fears', Interview with Mahathir, Part 3, *New Sunday Times*, 6 July 1986.

1990: Fin de Siècle?

In 1970, the Razak government promulgated the New Economic Policy (NEP).[1] The NEP, very briefly, had two official objectives: 'poverty eradication irrespective of race' and 'restructuring to abolish the identification of race with economic function'. The NEP was designed as a policy response to the social discontent which underlay the violence of May 13 1969, and to assuage what the Razak-led National Operations Council regarded as the ultimate source of May 13: Malay frustration at their economic backwardness compared with the non-Malays'. The Razak administration declared that the NEP's ultimate goal was 'national unity' and argued that the successful attainment of the NEP's twin objectives over two decades, 1970–90, was indispensable to political stability in Malaysia.[2] All subsequent administrations have upheld that position.

Officially, the first objective of 'poverty eradication' expressed the government's basic intention to improve the socio-economic conditions of the Malaysian poor. That had the political advantage of reducing the incidence of poverty among mainly poor rural Malays who made up UMNO's base. The government's priority, however, was to entrench the second objective of restructuring the economy (to redress 'ethnic imbalances' in the ownership of wealth and the occupational structure) as the 'the overriding target' of the NEP.[3] In day-to-day terms, that meant making 'restructuring' an undisputed fact of Malaysian life. In the words of the Department of National Unity which had a prominent role in shaping the NEP, 'the economic objective of national unity may be expressed *as the improvement of economic balances between the races, or the reduction of racial economic disparities*'.[4] The strongest argument in favour of the NEP was probably that the NEP, or some version of it, in pursuit of roughly the same twin objectives, would have had to be invented no matter what one's premises and ideas about 'social justice' in Malaysia might be.[5] To the extent that the years of NEP implementation passed without a repeat of the 1969 racial violence, the Barisan Nasional government could claim that the NEP had helped to bring about political stability in the country.[6]

But 'national unity', if that implied closer inter-ethnic understanding and rapport, was more elusive. On balance, the NEP's implementation during its first ten years generated inter-ethnic tensions even as it was designed to dissipate them. Broadly, the Malay community favoured the NEP's creation of new opportunities for the *bumiputera* in education, employment, and business in the name of both 'poverty eradication' and 'restructuring'. The Malay community saw state sponsorship and assistance as essential forms of protection given their historical experience of exclusion from the modern sectors of the Malaysian economy. In that respect, nothing gave the NEP a sharper focus than its 'Outline Perspective Plan' target of raising the Malay share of corporate share capital from its 2.5 per cent level in 1970 to 30 per cent in 1990. This '30 per cent solution' became the minimum '*bumiputera* quota' for many things, including government contracts, new public share listings, and new (private sector) housing schemes. But what the Malay politicians and intelligentsia tended to laud as the NEP's affirmative action was apt to be resented as ethnic discrimination by many among the non-Malay communities.[7] Within the framework of ethnic politics, debates over such matters as civil service recruitment, university admissions and scholarships, and government contracts and licences often adopted a 'merit against discrimination' tone. The politicians and businessmen linked to the Barisan Nasional's Chinese-based component parties generally endorsed the NEP's objectives but frequently protested against the NEP's overzealous implementation by Malay bureaucrats, prompting many

Malays to suspect the firmness and sincerity of Chinese support for the NEP to begin with. The architects and formulators of the NEP had made it a point to say that the NEP would not be implemented at the expense of any community and would be carried out without creating any sense of loss or deprivation.[8] In reality, the NEP produced ethnically determined targets of corporate capital ownership, quotas in employment, and allocations of social services and development expenditure which accentuated a *bumiputera*–non-*bumiputera* divide. At their worst, the ethnically based targets spawned a certain quota fixation in the political and public imagination and fostered a close to 'zero-sum' attitude chiefly between the Malays and the Chinese.[9] By extension, the Barisan Nasional's self-styled power-sharing and 'consensus politics' were sometimes little better than political horse-trading behind the scenes, as happened when Pemuda UMNO opposed the MCA's attempt to gain control of the United Malayan Banking Corporation in 1981.[10] That also happened, for instance, when the university admissions quota for Chinese students was raised by 2 per cent after the government refused to approve the Chinese community-sponsored Merdeka University.

As the NEP years proceeded, inter-ethnic disagreements, instead of the avowed goal of multi-ethnic unity, were only the most glaring in a range of contradictions and controversies related to the NEP. First, there was a tension between the objective of 'poverty eradication irrespective of race' and that of 'restructuring'. In ethnic terms, few state-supported programmes of poverty eradication were ever targeted at the non-Malay poor, the official assumption being that poverty was largely a rural Malay condition.[11] Within the Malay community, however, the tension between poverty eradication and restructuring priorities had a different manifestation. Jomo K. S. and Ishak Shari have argued that the pattern of development plan allocations had showed a steady shift in emphasis from poverty eradication to restructuring since the NEP's inception.[12] In class terms, restructuring became a political cipher for the state's sponsorship of a Malay capitalist class which would assume 'the Malay share of wealth'. It has been strongly argued that the restructuring programmes disproportionately benefited those Malays of this new class who were politically and bureaucratically well-connected—members of 'distributional coalitions',[13] 'bureaucratic capitalists',[14] 'statist capitalists',[15] or 'bureaucrats and technocrat-politicians'.[16]

Second, the NEP generated tensions between the state and (largely) domestic capital which remained in the public imagination as the tensions between a Malay government and a (largely) Chinese private sector. The NEP had brought an end to the Alliance-dominated political economy where the state left 'economics' to private capital. The NEP state expanded in size to recruit and accommodate increasing numbers of Malays trained under restructuring auspices. The state strengthened its battery of regulatory powers by using the Industrial Co-ordination Act 1975 and the Foreign Investment Committee to ensure compliance with the restructuring requirements, namely share equity and employment quotas.[17] The state actively intervened in the economy, injecting massive amounts of public funds to acquire assets for and on behalf of the Malays. Its political appointees and bureaucrats operated Malay trusts, public enterprises, state economic development corporations, and regional development authorities for the purpose of promoting *bumiputera* participation in development and business.[18] The NEP state was simultaneously an expansive provider, a determined regulator, and an aggressive entrepreneur. Its relationship with private capital—popularly seen as a relationship between a Malay government and a Chinese private sector—was seldom easy.

Third, even among those sections of the Malay community most dedicated to restructuring (UMNO and Malay business), serious differences of opinion on extending the restructuring process beyond 1990 emerged in the 1980s. The NEP's restructuring exercise was originally premised on 'distribution' taking place within a 'growth' economy. When Malaysia's economic growth began to falter in the early to mid-1980s, mainstream Malay political and business opinion on the NEP's impact on the economy and its impending end in 1990 started to split between pro-'growth' and pro-'distribution' positions, as Malek Marican so clearly demonstrated in 1987.[19] Interestingly, Malay pro-'growth' ranks shared a wider concern, traditionally held by non-Malay and foreign capital, that excessive state regulation had led or would lead to a contraction in investment in the Malaysian economy. Pro-'distribution' advocates were committed to the retention of the NEP's restructuring objective.

Not everything good or bad that happened in Malaysia during the NEP years could be attributed to the NEP or blamed on it, or be explained in terms of support for and opposition to the NEP. But in reality so much had been carried out in the name of the NEP that inevitably opposition, dissent, and discontent fell upon the NEP, too. Thus the NEP, espousing the post-1969 ideology of national development and designed to be the social engineering foundation for the edifice of national unity, had become politically rather bedevilled.

The Mahathir era began in 1981, a symbolically important year inasmuch as it marked the mid-point of the NEP's two-decade span. The first NEP decade having passed in 1980, there were now ten years remaining for the NEP's objectives of poverty eradication and restructuring to be achieved. Expectations and apprehensions about the second half of the NEP were beginning to be felt and would intensify in subsequent years. There was little doubt then that a rigorous and politically motivated stocktaking of the attainments and shortfalls of the NEP's implementation would be conducted when the final stretch of the NEP loomed. Critical questions full of political implications were bound to be raised in earnest. For example, would the state be able to command the resources and direct the economy to produce results that would sufficiently satisfy all parties, classes, and communities that the NEP objectives had been attained? What would happen if the performance lagged considerably behind the targets? In the latter scenario, would the state bear the brunt of the blame, or would the ethnic political parties trade ugly accusations and make unreasonable demands with dangerous consequences for the Malaysian polity? Would the NEP end in 1990 as originally envisaged, or would it continue beyond that date? If there was to be a successor policy, would it be 'better' or 'worse'—from different viewpoints—than the NEP itself? No one in 1981 could as yet answer these and related questions with any real confidence. But the NEP's overarching impact on Malaysian society was such that many Malaysians focused on 1990, 'the end of the NEP', with sentiments akin to *fin de siècle* hope and dread—hope for some, dread for others, and uncertainty for all.

Mahathir had no hand in the official framing of the NEP. He was in political exile when the Department of National Unity issued its 'New Economic Policy' directive to all government departments and when the economic proposals contained in the *Second Malaysia Plan, 1971–75* were being drawn up. He had barely rejoined UMNO when the *Mid-Term Review of the Second Malaysia Plan* (and its accompanying 'Outline Perspective Plan, 1970–90' which fixed the corporate ownership division and poverty reduction targets) were formulated. Mahathir, however, shared the NEP's objective of reducing the inter-ethnic disparities in income, employment, and ownership so as, ultimately, to redistribute wealth more equitably in ethnic terms. He had spoken regularly enough in Parliament on this and related subjects. In spirit, restructuring as state policy matched the constructive protection advocated by *The Malay Dilemma*. Indeed, although 'the economic proposals in Mahathir's book (*The Malay Dilemma*) and in the Second Malaysia Plan had been voiced earlier in economic congresses organised by Government bureaucrats and billed as *Bumiputera* Economic Congresses',[20] many Malaysians found in *The Malay Dilemma* the strongest rationale and justification for the *bumiputera* economic participation programmes. Mahathir's Malay nationalist reputation led many Malaysians (and foreigners) to discern in Mahathir the ideological soul of the NEP. Given the popular identification of Mahathir with the NEP, and given Mahathir's own strong opinions of the NEP, it was a historical coincidence that he should have become Prime Minister in 1981 to preside over the NEP at its mid-point, and to stand somewhere between the hope and dread that *fin de NEP* inspired.

Mahathir approached the subject of the NEP with considerable care and balance. He gave early notice that the NEP in its basic objectives would continue under his leadership. Yet, beyond assuring the Malays that the NEP's restructuring target would be met, and reassuring the non-Malays (including foreign investors) that those targets would not be inflated, Mahathir stayed above the *bumiputera*–non-*bumiputera* recriminations that dogged most debates on the NEP. He told K. Das: 'As politicians, we know we are always under pressure from both sides. There is one pressure trying to force the percentage down and another trying to force the percentage up. As far as we are concerned, there is a target we set up for ourselves. We promise that we will achieve this target.'[21] And when he was asked if 'in short, you will not alter the targets?', Mahathir replied: 'No, we have no intention of altering the targets.'[22]

Mahathir did not mean to *replace* the NEP as a fundamental policy but it became apparent that he meant to *displace* it as the overriding target of the Malaysian economy. For him, the NEP was already a fact of Malaysian life and would retain a taken-for-granted presence. But the thrust of Mahathirist economics was reserved for a new agenda—to transform Malaysia into a modern and competitive newly industrializing country that could 'stand as tall' as other economically successful nations. Behind that agenda, or what came to be known as 'Mahathir's vision', lay certain impulses. Before it loomed various tasks.

Capitalism as Liberation

Out of Malay Backwardness

In *The Malay Dilemma*,* Mahathir's 'economic history of the Malays' was relatively simple, short, and sober. He observed that there had been 'a period of Malay economic independence' (p. 33) when 'the Malay sultanates of Kedah, Kelantan and Malacca' (p. 32) 'were already quite well-developed in commerce and industry, and had the facilities and the personnel for the import and export business that followed' (p. 33). In that halcyon period, 'there were skilled Malay craftsmen, artisans and skilled labourers' (p. 33) and 'the Malays were exclusively involved in marketing, petty trading, importing and exporting and even manufacturing' (p. 33). 'Money mean[ing] sophistication in business ... sophisticated commerce involving money instead of barter was already in progress' (p. 34) before the Europeans and Chinese arrived and 'destroyed the self-reliance of the Malays in craftsmanship, skilled work and business' (p. 27). 'Before the Chinese came to Malaya, the Malays had been shopkeepers and petty traders' but after that, 'because of the superiority of Chinese business tactics ... Malay shops have disappeared' (p. 110). Mahathir made it sound rather prosaic but *The Malay Dilemma* evinces a sense of native commerce being arrested and indigenous economic development marginalized by colonial subjugation and immigrant encroachment. It is a sentiment that bears a kindred spirit with many other post-independent retrievals or revisionist interpretations of the history of the Third World, Walter Rodney's *How Europe Underdeveloped Africa* being a leading scholarly case in point.[23]

*In this section, references to this book are accompanied by the relevant page numbers.

Few things about Malay history have occasioned a greater sense of loss for Mahathir than the Malays' historical economic decline. Yet nowhere in *The Malay Dilemma* will one find Mahathir searching for an ancient 'golden age' of Malay commerce as a response to that fallen past. He did not even seek it in the famed epoch of the Malacca Sultanate.[24] One speculates that that was so partly because Mahathir as a Social Darwinist would not have found much to glorify in the native ways which succumbed to the superiority of colonial capital and immigrant enterprise. Years after he wrote *The Malay Dilemma*, Mahathir used to say of foreign countries and peoples that 'those who fail cannot be made examples to follow'.[25] Hence, far from wanting to seek emotional refuge in a defeated past, Mahathir felt driven to criticize the elements of 'the Malay value system and code of ethics [which] are impediments to their progress' (p. 173).

Among the most serious 'impediments' to Malay progress were what Mahathir regarded as inadequate Malay attitudes to money, property, and time. The Malays, he argued, had only a very limited idea of 'property'. For the Malays who were mostly peasants, 'land and property are almost synonymous' (p. 166) so that the Malay 'attachment to the land as truly real property is deeply ingrained, and proprietorship of land becomes a status symbol' (p. 166). 'In the old Malay sultanates', a Malay could acquire land 'if he could show evidence that he had settled on the land, cleared it and cultivated it' (p. 166). The 'simplicity' of this process of land acquisition 'did not make for much initiative and ingenuity' (p. 166) but 'even more telling' was 'a feeling [among the Malays] of a right to property' which only 'promoted complacency and minimised any effort at self-enrichment' (p. 166). Other than land, 'jewellery and cash may sometimes constitute property, but the ease with which money and jewellery can be disposed of or just hidden and the lack of documentary evidence of title prevents these items from being accumulated as permanent inheritable possessions' (p. 167). Likewise, the Malays ill-understood the importance of money: 'Money is a convenience to the Malays. Money facilitates the exchange of goods and services. Money is not generally regarded as capital for investment. Whatever money is acquired, is acquired by selling property or services. The whole proceeds of the sale are then available for changing for services or for outright spending' (p. 167).

Mahathir observed that the rural Malays managed with a 'minimal use of money' (p. 168) in their basic livelihood of *padi* cultivation and depended on self-labour, '*gotong-royong*, good neighbours and haphazard cash advances' (p. 168) to see them through. Thus unable to make a proper 'computation of costs', or 'to put a money value on self-labour' and with 'the income from the next crop [having] usually been spent through unbudgeted credits in kind', they were incapable of transforming *padi* planting into 'a business proposition' (p. 168). They could only maintain it as 'a way of life' (p. 168).

In matters of money, Mahathir thought that 'the urban Malay is only slightly better' because 'again with him money is a convenience for spending. It is earned in the form of salary, and in the main it is almost completely spent. Savings are minimal and often the hire-purchase system means that money is spent well ahead of its being earned' (p. 168).

For the Malays, in short, 'the monetary system is still primitive, being merely a slight extension of the barter system' and money only signified the 'ability to facilitate the acquisition of goods and services' (p. 169). It was 'this inability to understand the potential capacity of money' that 'makes the Malays poor businessmen', so that 'beyond selling what they produce in work or in kind, the Malays appear unable to devise ways of acquiring money' (p. 167).

Consequently, 'budgeting, savings, banking, investments, credits, growth, transfers, and all the other refinements in the use of money are generally not appreciated' (p. 169). And 'it is only the few Malays involved in business who can understand the sophistication of a monetary system and how it could be made to work to earn a larger income' (p. 168).

Mahathir believed that 'the attitude to property and money is the key to the economic and social progress of a human community' (p. 166) and that 'a prosperous society depends very much on the ability of its members to manipulate money and to equate property not with land holdings alone, but with less and less tangible assets which may include prestige and goodwill in business' (p. 169). He could only conclude that 'Malay values with regard to property and money may therefore be said to be undeveloped' (p. 169).

Nor was the Malay sense of time any better developed, it seemed:

> Time does not seem to be appreciated by the Malays. Life is valuable but time is not. Time is therefore wasted or completely disregarded ... [as] seen

> in the careless way in which it is spent. Doing nothing, or sipping coffee, or talking is almost a Malay national habit. An invitation to a *khenduri* in a kampong is invariably for an indefinite time. One may arrive at any time, eat at any time and go off at any time. No one arrives on time for a meeting but once started there is no limit to the time it can last (pp. 162–3).

Mahathir himself had no doubt that 'the Malay failure to value time is one of the most important handicaps to their progress' because

> when there is no awareness of time, there can be no planning and work is never reliable. A time-table is an essential part of the life of modern man.... A community which is not conscious of time must be regarded as a very backward society. What is more, it will remain a backward society. It can never achieve anything on its own and it can never be expected to advance and catch up with superior time-conscious civilizations (pp. 162–3).

Mahathir's commentary on the Malay lack of awareness of time as well as other 'Malay traits', such as fatalism, lack of rationality, and a lackadaisical attitude towards work, was criticized by Syed Hussein Alatas as part of the latter's debunking of 'the myth of the lazy native'.[26] One does well to agree with Alatas's argument that Mahathir essentially shared colonial capital's prejudices against 'the natives' for their 'refusal to supply plantation labour' and their 'non-involvement in the colonially-controlled urban capitalist economic activity'.[27] But in suggesting that Mahathir's error was that 'he did not question the capitalist system',[28] implying he should have, Alatas misjudged what capitalism signified for Mahathir.

The historical consequence of the Malays' 'refusal to supply plantation labour' (which toiled under terrible conditions, as Alatas documented) was their marginalization in a capitalist economy increasingly dominated by colonists and immigrants. One distinguishing feature of the ensuing economic development of colonial Malaya was its stark ethnic division of labour which encapsulated the overwhelming part of the Malay community, the Malay peasantry, in a close-to-subsistence agricultural sector. Mahathir did not elaborate on this point. But he frequently noted its 'barter' character, highlighted by its unsophisticated, even 'primitive', attitude towards money: 'Now there are people in the villages who still [practise] or are close to a barter system. Money is something which they use because they can't carry their goods. They start by exchanging these goods for money which is afterwards exchanged for other goods.'[29]

Was Mahathir wrong when he concluded that the Malays had 'undeveloped values with regard to property', an 'inability to understand the potential capacity of money', and 'no awareness of time'? He was not, if by that it is understood that he not only 'did not question the capitalist system', he wanted the Malays to participate and succeed in that very system. For Mahathir there was no virtue, or what comes to the same thing, no wealth, to be gained from 'non-involvement' in capitalism. That could only mean the Malays would remain backward, unable to compare, compete, or catch up with the Europeans and the Chinese. One can surely dispute the 'Malayness' of those traits which Mahathir disapproved of. Those traits were not uniquely 'Malay' but quite common among peoples in pre-capitalist economic formations. Mahathir never shed his 'Malay' focus but he knew what was required if the Malays who 'only recently ... have been introduced to a monetised society'[30] were to make a 'transition from a barter system'[31] to capitalism in Malaysia: 'What we want is for these people [that is, rural Malays close to a barter system] to understand that money can also be used to make even more money. It can be invested, become an instrument of growth and maybe even more sophisticated matters.'[32]

This was Mahathir grasping at the very heart of capitalism and he was still at it as late as 1986, as can be seen from the quote given at the beginning of this chapter. Matters would have been clearer had he added that 'money in order to make more money'—the fructification of capital—was a 'capitalist' concept, as was his hope to see the Malays expand their notion of 'property' to embrace more and more things, including 'less and less tangible assets'. And no more but no less capitalistic than these 'new' concepts of money and property would be those of 'time-thrift', 'time value', 'time-budgets', and the idea that time should be 'husbanded' and not 'spent' or 'wasted' in 'doing nothing, or sipping coffee or talking'.[33]

Mahathir was hostile to colonial subjugation and immigrant encroachment in Malaya, but that was no reason to expect him to be hateful of the methods which gave them victory over the Malays. From the vantage point of a Malay who saw no prospects in subsistence agriculture and saw the defects of its 'barter' system, he read into the colonists' and immigrants' capitalism 'the superior tactics' of

European and Chinese business which held the 'key to the economic and social progress of a human community'. 'Their' capitalism—at any rate, its misnomer of 'free enterprise'—and its attendant imagery of 'competition', 'strife', and victory to the fittest could only have held a fascination for his Social Darwinism. Of course, Mahathir was opposed to the kind of 'competition which should be between individuals and business groups [but] has developed into a competition between racial groups in which one group has an absolute advantage over the other'.[34] Otherwise, he said, with even a small hint of pride, that 'the Malays are as much as everyone else for a free enterprise system' (p. 52) because 'free enterprise implies competition in commerce and industry. Free competition in such an economic system determines the price levels of goods, the wages, the distribution of wealth and the opportunities for employment and investment. By and large a free enterprise system is self-sustaining and self-correcting' (p. 51). If capitalism was indeed the way out of Malay backwardness, then no less than its hearty embrace, let alone a repugnance of it, would suit the Malay community.

The Imperative of Industrialization

When gazing upon the world and contemplating its economic history in 1979, then Deputy Prime Minister Mahathir Mohamad taught that 'once upon a time, the world was divided into a segment that produces raw materials and another segment where these raw materials are converted into manufactured goods to be resold to the first segment'.[35]

No doubt 'traditional development theories and traditional development policies' saw nothing anomalous about this global segmentation since they were 'based on the assumption, historically a perfectly valid one, that developing countries pay for imports of capital goods by exporting primary materials—farm and forest products, minerals, metals'.[36] But, as everyone knew, the business of producing and selling, buying, processing, and reselling raw materials allowed the manufacturing countries to become rich not 'by merely buying cheap raw materials' but 'by processing and selling the products'.[37] More to the point, the producers of raw materials remained poor developing countries which could do nothing about this global inequity 'because they did not have the technology and the skills to manufacture'.[38]

Mahathir spoke from experience. The resource-rich Malaysian economy had long been highly dependent on commodity exports to the industrialized countries.[39] Agricultural and mineral commodities which together contributed 88.3 per cent of Malaysia's exports in 1960 still accounted for 77.4 per cent of its exports in 1980.[40] During colonial times, the modern Malaysian economy had been founded on rubber and tin exports. A strong post-independent programme of commodity diversification added such products as palm oil, timber, pepper, and cocoa to Malaysia's range of primary commodity exports. The Malaysian economy and commodity exports in particular also received a huge boost in the 1970s with the production and sale of petroleum and natural gas. Mahathir noted that 'diversification paid fairly handsome dividends' over the 1960s and 1970s because 'it cushioned the effect of diminishing revenues from tin and rubber' and 'stood in good stead against the fluctuations in the commodity markets and the vagaries of the world economy'.[41]

By the 1980s, however, even 'this careful hedging by Malaysia has failed as a constellation of forces has driven down the prices of virtually all primary commodities produced and exported not only by Malaysia and other ASEAN countries but the whole world'.[42]

Part of the problem lay with the producers. Speaking for Malaysia, Mahathir judged that 'we were [so] lulled into a sense of security by the success of the diversification strategy' that 'despite the obvious trend with all commodities we felt that the fluctuations in the prices of different commodities would balance each other'.[43] To that extent, it was bewildering to encounter a 'new phenomenon'—the 'recent total collapse of all commodities'—and bitter to learn that 'all commodities can plunge at the same time no matter how rare or how much is the present demand for them'.[44] But the problem was partly created and aggravated by 'some powerful developed countries'. In principle, these countries refused to join commodity agreements 'because they negate free trade', were against the operations of stockpiles 'which disturb market forces', and took a dim view of subsidies which 'were regarded an unfair practice that artificially influence[d] prices'.[45] In practice, the governments of these countries took care to 'fix their prices, release their stockpiles and provide massive subsidies', and even to dump their excess produce 'as an aid item for needy countries, which effectively deprive[d] competing products of developing countries of their markets'.[46] Meanwhile, their 'agents, brokers, traders, and operators' of commodity exchanges speculated in commodities and manipulated their prices with the result that 'the producers suffer[ed]' from 'this sordid game'.[47]

However, the greatest problem was that 'a structural change has taken place in the commodity trade so that not only have the prices plunged severely and together but they are not ever going to recover to the old levels'.[48] 'Rapidly advancing technology' was 'the single most important factor which has caused the downfall of the commodities'.[49] First, 'new technology ... has enabled more of [any] particular commodity to be produced' which 'simply means the market is more easily and more frequently flooded' and 'the glut reduces [its] price'.[50] Second, 'new technology has also reduced the usage of various commodities'.[51] Third, 'new technology also results in a multitude of synthetic or natural substitute materials', thus reducing the overall demand for various commodities.[52]

In happier times, it was 'thought that diversification would solve the problem of fluctuating commodity prices and the lack of control over prices exercised by producer countries'.[53] Now the outlook was bleak. At last, 'we believe we understand commodities, particularly in the context of Third World producers. There was a time when the nations of ASEAN exchanged their spices for trinkets and glass beads brought by the merchants of the countries of the West. That situation has not changed. We are still getting trinkets.'[54]

But leaving aside developed countries' manipulations, technology's freakish triplets of over-production, reduced usage, and displacement by substitutes had made nonsense of diversification: 'that panacea is no panacea'.[55] One could protest that 'it is unthinkable that the world, particularly the manufacturing world, can do without commodities altogether' but it would be nearer the truth to see that 'for some commodities the end is near'.[56] Never one to flinch from painful truths, Mahathir forecast that 'what this means in commercial terms for the producers is that there is no future in commodities'.[57] Almost with an air of finality, Mahathir remarked that 'new technology has changed permanently the linkages between commodities and manufactured products'.[58] Extrapolate from that and one can virtually claim, in Social Darwinist fashion, that manufactured products had well and truly 'defeated' primary commodities. It was as if Mahathir, despite his anti-Marxism, had paraphrased Marx's 'fetishism of commodities': in Mahathir's reification, the relations between nations had taken on the fantastic form of a competition between 'primary commodities' and 'manufactured products'.[59]

During the mid-1980s, when Mahathir developed this coherent and gloomy assessment of the trade in commodities, Malaysia suffered great losses of export revenues as a result of collapsed commodity prices.[60] After a threefold increase in export earnings between 1975 and 1980, Malaysia's economic planners had forecast the country's total export earnings to rise to RM63.1 billion in 1985. Actual export earnings for 1985 were only RM37.6 billion. With the exception of saw logs, all the major Malaysian commodities recorded serious declines in earnings. Crude petroleum prices having fallen from US$36.5 per barrel in 1980 to US$14.7 per barrel in 1986, even a much higher volume of crude petroleum exports in 1986 earned less than in 1980. Palm oil earnings declined from RM4.5 billion in 1984 to RM3.0 billion in 1986. The value of tin exports in 1986 barely exceeded 25 per cent of the 1980 figure.

To that extent, Mahathir's analysis of the state of the trade in commodities bore the verisimilitude of painful experience. But his version of the commodities' collapse steadily took on more overtly ideological functions. He stressed the resulting loss of export earnings and state revenues to justify a regime of austerity measures and cut-backs in state expenditure.[61] He blamed an externally generated commodities' collapse to acquit the NEP of blame for the economic recession in the nation.[62] He underscored the helplessness of commodity producers in the face of external forces (developed countries, speculators, and 'new technology') to deflect domestic criticisms of his 'economic mismanagement'.[63]

Most consistently of all, Mahathir offered his commodities' argument as a vindication of his 'heavy industrialization' drive which had been widely criticized as a failure and a major debt burden during the recession of 1985–6. Arguing against a continuing dependence on commodities, Mahathir taught that Malaysia could not avoid or delay the imperative of industrialization: 'With the collapse of the commodities as the mainstay of the economies of the developing countries, we have no choice but to move into newer areas. We will have to depend more on manufacturing, for example.'[64] At the start of the 1980s, Malaysia already had a sizeable and fast-growing manufacturing sector.[65] The manufacturing sector's share of the country's Gross Domestic Product (GDP), for example, rose from 8.2 per cent in 1960 to 20 per cent in 1980.[66] Employment in the manufacturing sector grew from 6.4 per cent of total employment in 1957 to 15.7 per cent in 1980.[67] Similarly, manufacturing only accounted for 8.5 per cent of total exports in 1960 but that proportion had grown to 21.6 per cent by 1980.[68] The growing importance of the manufacturing sector in the economy could be traced back to the government's support for import-substitution industries shortly after independence, and its promotion of export-oriented industrialization in the 1970s.[69] The government promoted its export-oriented industrialization programme on the basis of an attractive regime of 'pioneer status' incentives and tax exemptions, low wages and stringent labour control, inexpensive land and adequate infrastructural support. The result was a fairly impressive record of persuading multinational corporations to relocate some of their labour-intensive operations to the Free Trade Zones of Malaysia. The well publicized attraction of several leading American and Japanese manufacturers of semiconductors or 'microchips' to the 'silicon island' of Penang was only the best known outcome of the Malaysian government's determined drive for foreign investment in manufacturing.

As Minister of Trade and Industry from 1978 to 1981, Mahathir had earnestly marketed Malaysia as a centre for direct investment by American, European, and Japanese manufacturing concerns. 'What are we after when we welcome the multinationals?' he asked. 'The first benefit ... is an inflow of capital. Next is the creating of job opportunities—the single most important raiser of living standards. Then there must be some form of technology and skill transfer ... [and] exports will earn foreign exchange. Local marketing, on the other hand, reduces the outflow of foreign exchange.'[70] Mahathir never lost sight of these specific, if limited, benefits of the multinational-based industries. But Prime Minister Mahathir had a bolder and more ambitious vision which neither the older import-substitution industries nor the multinational-based export-oriented industrialization could realize. 'Import substitution industries are good,' he explained, 'but their scope must necessarily be limited. If we want to grow we have to export our industrial products on the same scale as we export our agricultural products.'[71]

He was all for export-oriented industrialization but some types of export-oriented industrial products, though important, struck him as being not quite 'manufacturing' products. In the 1970s, Malaysia's export-oriented Free Trade Zones had turned the country into one of the world's largest producers of semiconductors or microchips for the electronics industry, but Mahathir introduced a caveat into that success story: 'We produce integrated circuits or microchips, an undifferentiated manufactured product which markets in almost the same way as primary commodities. For the purpose of trade, microchips may be considered a commodity.'[72]

Mahathir did not intend to be confined to the multinational-based type operations: 'We do not want to be grounded in the mediocrity of mere assembly operations' because 'our future lies in the greater value-added secondary and tertiary processing of our raw materials and the higher technology industries'.[73] He meant Malaysia to achieve the classical 'take-off' on to a higher stage of industrialization by way of a 'heavy industrialization' drive. In 1980, while he was still Minister of Trade and Industry, Mahathir had established the state-owned Heavy Industries Corporation of Malaysia (HICOM) and confidently anticipated the benefits of heavy industrialization: 'Large manufacturing enterprises need supporting industries and services. These must be provided by the locals mainly. The spillover is literally tremendous. Whole new towns spring up where industries are located. Urbanization means greater division of labour. And so new services and trades spring up.'[74]

Now the Prime Minister converted advocacy into policy. He brought HICOM directly under the Prime Minister's Department and used it to launch his 'heavy industrialization' drive. HICOM rapidly negotiated several large manufacturing joint ventures with Japanese and South Korean multinational corporations.[75] These were a 'national car project', Perusahaan Otomobil Nasional or National Automobile Industry (PROTON); a steel complex, Perwaja Trengganu Sdn. Bhd. (PERWAJA); two cement plants in Perak and Pulau Langkawi; and three motor-cycle engine factories. He shared his expectations of heavy industrialization with Malaysia's 'Top Business Leaders':

> The push towards the development of heavy industries represents another new dimension to national development. I believe heavy industries will bring substantial benefits to the economy in terms of technology, skills and the numerous spin-offs, and will lay the foundation for Malaysia to become an industrialized society. We will not give up being producers of various agricultural commodities but we should overcome the mental block which

condemns us to being the producers of primary commodities to fuel the growth of the industrialized countries. We must raise our sights and have the conviction that we have the 'dynamic comparative advantage' to sustain the development of heavy industries.[76]

Mahathir's heavy industrialization drive and the HICOM projects have been controversial ever since they were launched. Their suddenness and scale generated many reservations about their viability within the Cabinet, among state planners, and in academic circles. A serious economic and financial evaluation of their performance and impact on the Malaysian economy properly belongs elsewhere.[77] Suffice it here to summarize several sets of related problems which many critics predicted would beset Mahathir's programme of heavy industrialization.[78] First, the domestic market was too small and the products (especially automobiles and steel) had low export potential given the existing gluts for these products in the international markets.[79] Second, the absence of economies of scale made it likely that the projects would require considerable levels of subsidy and protectionism which in turn would burden the local consumers.[80] Third, the projects needed massive capital investments and foreign borrowings over long gestation periods which would divert funds from other projects and render profitability highly uncertain.[81] Fourth, the projects would remain overly dependent on foreign technology with a comparatively low degree of local participation in terms of content, expertise, and management.[82]

Mahathir, however, would not be distracted by Cabinet, civil service, or academic reservations over the scale, the cost, and the viability of the HICOM projects. His critics, he said, 'don't have the faintest notion of what they are talking about' because 'what they say is purely academic based on theories learnt in universities'.[83] He later deplored that 'the national car has been run down by nearly everybody' which 'makes things very difficult'.[84] As far as he was concerned, 'these industries are simply necessary for the process of industrialization to take place':

We are always being told that it is cheaper to buy than produce yourself. This is, of course, the propaganda of the developed countries: continue to be a market for them. Look at South Korea. When it wanted to start its first steel mill it was advised to produce 600,000 tons of steel, but they instead went for 1.5 million tons. Everybody said it was stupid, that South Korea could buy cheaper steel from Japan. But today South Korea is producing in one plant alone 11.5 million tons of steel, some of which is being sold to Japan. I am not saying that Malaysia is going to be another South Korea but the principle is the same.[85]

He had evidently thought through the most serious issues confronting his heavy industrialization projects. When asked if it was 'economically viable to build our own car', he gave a long and confident response:

No, it is not economically viable if we are looking for a cheaper domestic car or one which is comparable in price to imports. But let us look at the history of car making. As time goes on, the economies of scale demands greater and greater volume. Now we buy between 80,000 and 90,000 cars a year. If we imported that many cars in 1980, it would have been economical to build a plant of our own, because at that point of time, economies of scale required that kind of volume. By 1982, 80,000 units are adequate enough. Now we may need to produce say at least 200,000 to 250,000 to achieve the economies of scale. By 1995 or 2000 we may be buying 200,000 to 250,000 cars a year but the economies of scale then would require a much larger volume.

So you can see that we are chasing this volume and we will never catch up. We will never get to the stage where the volume is sufficiently big to justify the setting up of a motor car industry, which means of course that if we are going to follow that argument, we will never have a motor car industry in the country ever.[86]

If 'we are chasing this volume' but 'will never catch up', was he then not chasing a chimera? He was not, if one accepted that

the next question to ask is whether a motor car industry is necessary for this country? Well, we consider the capacity to produce the vehicles a necessary component of our industrialization programme. If it is a necessary component, then we must have it. It does not matter when. If we wait until 1995, we still would not have the advantage of economies of scale.[87]

As he told Tan Chee Khoon, 'If you want to produce a car that is for a small market, the economies of scale will mean that you will have to pay a higher price. It is cheaper to buy a foreign car but it may be necessary for us to pay the price of having cars made more costly.'[88]

Others may not have been for it, but Mahathir wanted to produce a car, 'not so much because of the car but because of the technology', and because 'the industry gives rise to a lot of spin-off effects, experience and knowledge for our people'.[89] Mahathir readily conceded that 'there is a cost here that we have to bear' but

> we have to be prepared to bear the cost and according to our calculation, the cost at this moment, considering the volume that we will produce, is something that the country can bear. It is not too great a cost and that is why we have decided that we will go in now. The sooner we go in, the sooner we will get acquainted with technology and the sooner the spin-off effects will benefit us.[90]

He was similarly confident of the profitability of the car project: 'It will bring in profit to the particular industry but the nation has a cost to pay in the sense that cars already have to bear a 15 per cent import duty on CKDs. That is the beginning of the cost.'[91]

That was an admission of the protectionism which the 'infant' national car would enjoy at a cost to be paid by the public. But Mahathir did not consider it to be a great cost compared to what post-war industrialization and reconstruction imposed on the people of Japan and Germany: 'For a long time they were not allowed to go abroad or to spend foreign exchange on personal needs. Only the industries were allowed to buy from abroad. Slowly at first but very quickly picking up momentum, they recovered. Today that sacrifice, that iron discipline, that strong will have paid handsomely.'[92] Mahathir did not deny the problem of Malaysia's 'small domestic market', only he had reasoned his way out of it quite differently from his critics. He envisaged that Malaysia's industrialization should go together with a 70-million population by the year 2100:

> We must have a sufficiently large domestic base if we are going to industrialize. Unlike the agriculturally-based economy where the smaller the population the better it is, an industrially strong nation is very difficult to build without a sufficiently large domestic market. Even for Japan, most of the cars that it produces are sold domestically. A big population is not harmful if the people are productive.
>
> The key word here is really 'productivity'. Seventy million people working very hard and producing a lot of goods could easily live in Malaysia. We think we can even produce sufficient food. I think a big population for Malaysia is important, particularly in a world that is becoming more and more protectionist.[93]

One begins to understand how it was that Deputy Prime Minister

Musa Hitam, who had his reservations about the PROTON project, cautioned Mahathir about 'the danger of the Japanese taking over if you did not know how to do it' only to receive the rebuke: '[I] kn[o]w how to do it!'[94]

It was reassuring to know how to do it. It was imperative to get it done. Maxime Rodinson, ideologically very different from Mahathir, once remarked that nations which had not done so 'must either industrialize, take off, develop, as the Euro-American nations have already done, or remain dependent on decisions taken by the world powers'—everything else, including 'protests against neo-colonialism' being 'just words'.[95] Mahathir would have agreed with Rodinson's stress on the power dimension of the imperative of industrialization. He conveyed a similar message to a largely American business audience in 1984 except his tone was softer, his argument disguised, and 'imperative' was replaced by the 'free-enterprise-friendly' term of 'choice':

> What choice have they [the developing countries]? A growing population, better communication and knowledge of the developments going on elsewhere in the world, better education and rising expectations demand that the developing countries move away from being mere producers of raw materials. On the other hand if they industrialize they are going to be faced with horrendous problems. This is their dilemma.[96]

In many ways, Mahathir's account of 'the fall of the primary commodities' paralleled his version of 'the economic decline of the Malays', albeit the 'fall' took place in the arena of world capitalism while the 'decline' occurred in Malaysia's multiracial marketplace. First, he judged the segmentation of the world between poor commodity producers and rich manufacturing countries to be Malaysia's ethnic division of labour writ large across the globe. Actually, he expressed it the other way around: 'the problem of [the] inequitable development of nations is reflected in the unequal development of the different races' in Malaysia.[97] Second, just as he saw the Malay economy to be backward in comparison with the non-Malays', so he held Malaysia's economy to be underdeveloped *vis-à-vis* the economies of the industrialized countries. Third, whereas the Malay economy was based on subsistence agriculture and, 'until recently', was not 'monetized', the Malaysian economy was bound to commodity production and was relatively 'non-industrialized'. And, in the final analysis, if the Malays had to learn the 'business tactics' of colonial and immigrant capitalism to emerge from backwardness, Malaysia had to adopt the 'manufacturing technology and skills' of the industrialized, capitalist nations to free itself from 'dependence on commodities'.[98]

Treading the path to heavy industrialization, Mahathir drew some lessons in comparative development from 'the Japanese miracle [and] the amazing performances of the Asian Newly Industrializing Countries'. They succeeded, above all, because of their 'adoption of a free enterprise system and the successful development of a dynamic and aggressive private sector'.[99] But they had also 'put their faith in export-led growth and adopted export-oriented policies' and 'achieved high savings rates, which have facilitated high rates of investment, especially in the industrial sector'.[100] They had been 'able to develop their agricultural capacity and productivity, even as they advanced on the industrial front', and 'to develop capabilities for rapid and dynamic adjustment policies'.[101] On the strength of these five 'common factors', the 'East' had stood up: Japan and the Asian NICs proved that 'competition with goods of the established industrialized countries was possible'.[102]

Capitalism as Liberalization

The New Economic Policy (NEP): The 30 Per Cent Solution

Mahathir took a very broad interpretation of the NEP. It was consonant with what he regarded as being necessary for the rehabilitation of the Malays: expanded opportunities for education, training, and employment; urbanization as deliverance from rural backwardness; and participation in business as a first step towards a fair share of the nation's wealth. Mahathir was fond of describing the NEP as 'social engineering' in a positive and optimistic sense. For him, there could be nothing amiss about its basic ethnic dimension. He had long accepted that ethnic problems needed 'openly' ethnic solutions[103] and believed Malaysia's ethnic politics to have aptly found its 'open' expression in the NEP. He reasoned that political stability dictated that 'the races must develop together; at par with each other'.[104] The NEP targeted a fair share of the nation's wealth for the Malays, and if the achievement of the fair share involves certain unpopular measures, it cannot be helped. Measures are apparently biased. This is interpreted by many people as being unfair to the non-Malays. But I don't think it's unfair because if you look around you the non-Malays have done even better since the New Economic Policy was implemented.[105]

Mahathir did not lose sight of the NEP's 1990 targets but he always kept a longer view of the NEP. He saw it moving the country gradually, if almost imperceptibly, away from its customary 'emphasis on race'. Since 'we can't remove the racial (vertical) divisions easily, so we must try to remove the social (horizontal) divisions': 'Then there will be poor Malays and rich Malays and poor Chinese and rich Chinese.'[106]

Perhaps in the future, when 'a Malay labourer [has] more in common with a Chinese labourer than he would have with a Malay millionaire', then 'the racial barriers [will] begin to be broken down'.[107] He regaled Tan Chee Khoon with an unusual anecdote for illustration:

You may have heard that in the last UMNO General Assembly there was one Malay who donated $9 million to the party. He has obviously gained very much by the implementation of the New Economic Policy. He has gained because this country is stable and economically doing well, that is why he is able to make this money. As the number of such people increases they will have a vested interest in this country's stability. When we have this vested interest, then the emphasis on race will diminish and they will have common ground with the Chinese who also have the need for a stable nation in order to maintain their position and wealth and their opportunities to make wealth.[108]

And just in case his old Labour Party adversary had missed the point, Mahathir tossed off the point that 'once you come to that, there may be class division rather than racial division'![109] Perhaps then would arise a non-ethnic division of wealth and labour which would become the basis of a new sort of multi-ethnic politics—but 'I do not know whether by 1990 we would be ready for this'.[110] Perhaps 'the day might come when the figures might balance'[111]—when 'in a Chinese firm there will be as many Malays as there are Chinese employees' and 'in the government there will be the same kind of distribution'—and 'then, and only then, will multi-ethnic politics become possible'.[112] But, coming down to earth, the NEP represented safeguards for the Malays, and one has to remember that the safeguards are not removed too early so that there is no recurrence of the old position. It is very difficult for me to judge when that will happen or whether that will be the attitude of coming Governments. Obviously it will not be this Government, because at this moment in the medical profession out of about 2300 doctors we have 250 who are bumiputras and that is not a very satisfactory situation yet.[113]

Mahathir was unperturbed by any accentuation of intra-Malay inequality. Apart from the NEP's kind of inter-ethnic levelling, or the 'spiritual' equality that might exist in a 'staunchly Muslim society',[114] Mahathir had never believed in social, 'materialistic' equality.[115] He had no sympathy for the kind of reasoning—'socialist and communist slogans'[116]—that led some Malays and non-Malays to protest that rich Malays were getting richer, poor Malays getting poorer.[117]

To the Malay intelligentsia attending the 1978 Bumiputera Economic Convention, held at Universiti Kebangsaan Malaysia, Mahathir attacked the idea that only a small group of Malays benefited from the NEP:

In fact almost every *Bumiputra* participant at this convention, whether on or below stage, has received a gift from the NEP. If they are already working, I believe their income is higher than their family income in the past. If they are still studying, this, too, means that their income has increased because their family may not afford a student's full expense at university.[118]

Hence, one could be satisfied that the NEP did its part to reduce the incidence of 'absolute poverty'. Beyond that, for Mahathir, poverty could only mean 'relative poverty' which 'would always be with us'. The NEP set out to improve the living conditions of the Malays and to open up opportunities to them, not to guarantee that each Malay, each poor *bumiputera*, would in turn become rich. He was satisfied that the NEP would diminish the disparities between rich and poor to the extent that 'someone may be the son of a taxi-driver, but there is nothing to prevent him from becoming the head of a corporation'.[119] There was no reason to despise, envy, or attack the new class of Malay capitalists for becoming rich owing to the NEP: theirs was also the success of the NEP itself. To those non-Malays who complained that the NEP was unfairly enriching a small group of Malays, he angrily declared that 'we are not socialists' and there was no reason why Malays could or should not become millionaires.[120] In fact, there had to be rich Malays to balance rich non-Malays.[121] Were there no rich Malays, there would still be rich Chinese—facing poor Malays.

Yet at heart Mahathir appeared to feel that all was not well in the NEP state. The core problem, as Mahathir saw it, was the unintended effect that the NEP had on the Malays themselves. Malays had a right to opportunities created by the NEP, he explained, but too many of them had begun to expect prosperity as a birthright.[122] Mahathir's previous warning about 'politics creat[ing] for the Malays a soft environment which removed all challenges to their survival and progress' seemed to have gone unheeded.[123] The many forms and levels of state sponsorship and financial assistance given to the Malays under the political ambit of the NEP had not led the Malays from backwardness to economic independence. Instead, the NEP state had become the 'soft environment' owing to wrong 'perceptions' and abuses of the NEP. Too many 'among the people for whom it was meant' tended to 'perceive the NEP as an open-ended opportunity machine, where what you want you just pick up'.[124] Or else 'they think that the NEP means a free gift'.[125] Yet others, *bumiputera* as well as the non-*bumiputera* who collaborate with them, 'regard the NEP not as an instrument of social and economic engineering' and 'not as a policy'—but 'as a convenience' and 'as a means to get rich quick'.[126]

Malay businessmen had been nurtured on easy credit, reserved corporate shares, business licences, government contracts, and other forms of preferential treatment, but they did not fulfil the NEP's vision of a class of competitive Malay entrepreneurs. Malay professionals were raised in MARA colleges and trained abroad on state scholarships to form a 'permanent Malay middle class'[127] but clung to the state for employment. The NEP's restructuring appeared to have removed the racial imbalances only in form because in reality the NEP had fostered a 'dole', 'subsidy', or 'get-rich-quick' mentality among the Malays. State protection had perpetuated Malay dependence on the state, and so, to Mahathir's disappointment:

> To say that the NEP has succeeded is to be optimistic. You say it has succeeded in creating this middle-class of Malay professionals. It has not. What has happened is simply the government makes it possible for them to

survive. The economy is still basically the same. All these people depend on the government—the Malay contractors, the Malay lawyers, the businessmen.[128]

To that extent, Mahathir was perhaps least impressed by the quota fixation which had been encouraged, most of all, by the NEP's 30 per cent corporate ownership target and the use of '*bumiputera* companies' to legitimize 'giving money to the Malays, for them to squander'—which 'is not helping them' to 'learn how to manage, how to be thrifty'.[129] The NEP made no sense unless one can manage and not squander one's new-found wealth. Nor did he think much of '100 per cent *bumiputera* companies' which 'invoked the NEP to get licences and contracts from the Government for themselves' but resold them to non-Malays, 'received a return on this sale ... had nothing more to do with the actual business' and 'instead ... would demand for more licences and more contracts'.[130] In the end, too few Malays understood that 'the weakness of the *bumiputra* in the economic field can be overcome, not by government aid, but by their own upgrading of their abilities to compete' simply because 'you can't be lifting a man up every time he falls'.[131]

The recession of the mid-1980s saw a lot of Malay businesses fall and made it difficult for the state to pick them up. An initial bout of counter-cyclical spending came to an end after 1984. Mahathir and his new Minister of Finance, Daim Zainuddin, chose to tackle the commodities collapse, trade and budget deficits, increase in external debt, and negative growth by imposing a regime of cut-backs in state expenditure, bureaucratic recruitment, and development projects. The medicine was bitter all round,[132] and fearfully so for the Malays, as Mahathir did not hesitate to say:

Now that the government is not having a lot of projects, all of them are suffering [a]nd they do not know what to do.... Now that the government is cutting back, these people have reverted to being, well, the bottom rung of the middle class.... Once the economy slides and there are no free gifts, they're in trouble. This so-called middle-class and rich Malays are all owing money to the banks. I think practically every one of them is bankrupt now.[133]

Were the NEP to continue unchanged, then its constructive protection, affirmative action, safeguards, and social engineering would not create a proud race of rugged and self-reliant Malay capitalists.

On the contrary, by 1990, twenty years of subsidies, scholarships, licences, contracts, share equity, quotas, and targets would not have culminated in Malay self-reliance and competitiveness but merely sculpted one gigantic 'crutch'[134]—while 'the economy is still basically the same'.

Well, it was not exactly the same. The NEP did have several bright spots. It had partially succeeded 'in the equity aspect, the nominal share aspect of wealth as characterized by PNB and so on'.[135] Permodalan Nasional Berhad (PNB or the National Equity Corporation) alone had assets of RM6.3 billion at the end of July 1986.[136] Official data showed that the total *bumiputera* equity ownership had increased from 2.4 per cent in 1970 to at least 19.1 per cent in 1985.[137] Between them, the *bumiputera* trust agencies controlled the 'commanding heights' of the economy—the largest banks, plantations, and mining companies. The NEP had also sponsored a number of *bumiputera* 'exceptions to the rule' (of failure),[138] in actual fact, some of the most powerful corporate figures in Malaysia.[139] To express it differently, there was already a pronounced degree of state capitalism and an appreciable presence of individual Malay capitalists. Perhaps it was not fully what Mahathir wanted, but it was enough of a basis for launching 'Privatization'.

Privatization: The 40 Per Cent Solution

Just over a month before he became Prime Minister, Mahathir disclosed the extent of his perceptiveness to the Malaysian International Chamber of Commerce:

> When you are inside something, roughly 50% will be behind you and will therefore be invisible. You may turn but then you would still see only 50%. But, of course, you will see that 50% at closer range and in greater relief. This is my experience in Government. I am blind to roughly 50% of what goes on in Government but what I see, I see very clearly.[140]

Among the things that made up the '50%' which Prime Minister Mahathir saw clearly were 'the size and extent of the government's involvement in the economy' which have 'surfaced in the Malaysian economy' as part of its 'structural problems'.[141] The size and extent of the state's intervention in the Malaysian economy had expanded vastly during the NEP years. Between 1970 and 1983, the bureaucracy grew fourfold, employing 521,818 persons in 1983 compared to 139,476 in 1970.[142] In roughly the same period, total public sector expenditure increased over tenfold, from RM3.3 billion in 1970 to RM35.4 billion in 1982.[143] Where there were an estimated 109 public sector enterprises in 1970, there were 656 in 1980. Under the Razak and Hussein Onn administrations, the NEP's social engineering functions and activities had become so diversified that the state's statutory bodies, state economic development corporations, and *bumiputera* 'trust agencies' were collectively involved in practically all sectors of the economy. This enormous expansion of the state was facilitated by strong economic growth in the 1970s and largely financed by petroleum-led state revenues.[144] Ideologically, this state expansion was justified as the necessary corrective to market-influenced and historically generated Malay economic weaknesses and inter-ethnic imbalances. As a result, the public enterprises were widely regarded by their officers as 'social enterprises' which 'are called upon to achieve legitimate social goals, not readily measured in terms of pecuniary values' and which 'may appear unprofitable when viewed by the criteria appropriately used to measure private sector efficiency'.[145] It also permitted the public enterprises' deficits, debts, and losses to be overlooked or absorbed by the state as the price of providing experience, employment, and skills to the Malays in order to achieve the NEP's objectives.[146]

Ideologically, Mahathir seemed to have held an ambivalent position *vis-à-vis* the expansionism of the state. To the extent that only the state itself could have implemented the NEP's grand scale of social and economic engineering, he was not opposed to having an enlarged and interventionist state, judging by his support for the Guthrie's take-over, and for the state-directed heavy industrialization drive. At the same time, Mahathir had long been sceptical about the efficiency of the public sector. He often made snide comments on the civil service, he was opposed to nationalization, and he believed in the dynamism of 'free enterprise'.[147] Mahathir demonstrated his scepticism about the civil service in practice by instituting several bureaucratic reforms immediately upon becoming Prime Minister.

At times, Mahathir, who observed that 'public[ly] owned enterprises never seem to be profitable or efficient', seemed to be genuinely perplexed: 'Even when they are monopolies they cannot seem to earn their way, much less pay tax or dividends to the owner—the Government.'[148] Whether it was because 'there was a lack of business acumen on the part of the management'[149] of state-owned companies, or whether 'because the government's management methods differ greatly from those of the private sector', the result was the same: 'with the exception of a few, most of the Government enterprises have lost money'.[150] This was not a startlingly new idea from Mahathir. It merely repeated his previous assessment of the failure of 'various commercial concerns (which) have been nationalized' in Malaysia:

The railway, MAS, the Electricity Board, PERNAS, PETRONAS, industries under several State Economic Development Corporations, MARA, FIMA, FAMA, FELDA and others are state enterprises. These state enterprises have sufficient capital and the types of industries are not only viable but sometimes constitute monopolies. Yet seldom do we hear of good profits and a large revenue through taxes. What we do know is that the Railway, the pineapple canning industry and several others are losing millions of dollars every year.[151]

He acknowledged that 'the Government had moved into business in the interests of the New Economic Policy' and 'because there were not enough capable *Bumiputras*, both in terms of skill as well as capital'.[152] But it worried Mahathir that 'the trend towards increasing government participation in business has led to competition with the private sector' whereby 'due to its power, the government can easily dominate private businesses and enterprises'.[153] In 1983, Mahathir announced a new 'Privatization' policy to resolve this contradiction between the state's involvement in business and its inability to achieve profitability. He perceived that 'private businesses and enterprises are usually profitable'[154] whereas 'the many constraints in the public sector have discouraged the full utilization of the wealth of the nation'.[155] He expected that 'Privatization', 'by releasing the full potential of the wealth of the nation', would 'overcome these constraints'.[156]

'Privatization', or simply 'the opposite of nationalization', as he explained, meant 'the transfer of government services and enterprises to the private sector'.[157] When 'Privatization' was first announced, the mechanics of that transfer were not disclosed; nor was it specified 'whether privatization should be complete, partial or selective'.[158] The implementation of 'Privatization' commenced in 1984, gained momentum during the recession years of 1985 and 1986, and by

1987 revealed what a full scope of privatization in Malaysia might mean. At its broadest, 'Privatization' encompassed the following: the sale or divestment of state concerns;[159] the sale of a portion of the shares of a state-owned public company;[160] the sale or lease of state-owned physical assets;[161] the private financing of public works projects on various kinds of 'build-and-operate' arrangements;[162] the contracting out of selected public services to private firms;[163] and the introduction of competition into areas of state monopoly.[164]

Mahathir's 'Privatization' policy found its logical supporters among the captains of Malaysian industry and commerce who sensed the opening of new business opportunities in the impending transfer of state enterprises and services to private capital.[165] It probably was welcomed by a more general public who thought it promised a measure of deliverance from years of bureaucratic ineptitude. 'Privatization', however, had its detractors among the employees of statutory bodies and public enterprises whose unions or staff consultative councils were unsure about its implications for their terms of employment.[166] Some critics of 'Privatization' who did not share Mahathir's belief in the inherent efficacy of private enterprise or the inherent inefficiency of the state wondered how the transfer of state assets to private capital would necessarily translate into public benefit.[167] Still others suspected that 'Privatization' within the existing Malaysian 'political/bureaucratic/business complex' was 'unlikely to be more than a rearrangement of economic and political power'.[168]

'Privatization' came with a twin—'Malaysia Incorporated' by which Mahathir intended to realize 'the concept of co-operation between the government and the private sector for the latter to succeed'.[169] 'Admittedly it [was] not very original', having been inspired by 'Japan Incorporated', but Mahathir introduced 'Malaysia Incorporated' to help 'the bureaucracy and the business community to change their attitudes towards each other'.[170] He instructed the bureaucracy to 'ensure that no undue hindrance is put in the way of the private sector'; in turn, 'the private sector must understand national policies, objectives and procedures in order to facilitate their dealings with the Government'.[171] 'A sovereign state cannot be a business company', Mahathir clarified, but 'it can ... be run like a corporation', with 'the private sector form[ing] the commercial and economic arm of the national enterprise' and 'the government lay[ing] down the major policy framework, direction and provid[ing] the necessary back-up services'.[172] He wanted 'no confusion between the involvement of the government in business and the Malaysia Incorporated concept' because 'the government becomes more the service arm of the [national] enterprise'.[173]

Whatever the wider arguments over 'Privatization' or 'Malaysia Incorporated' might have been, their most significant implications became evident in the mid-1980s. As policies went, 'Privatization' was rather more tangible than 'Malaysia Incorporated'. The former policy had to do with real companies, material assets, and actual services. The latter focused on a mutual reorientation of perceptions and attitudes within the ranks of the state and capital. But the timing of both policies was significant for several reasons. Beginning recession and the squeeze on state revenues later worsened into a condition of negative growth and the twin balance of payments and budget deficits. It would have been extremely difficult to sustain an expansionist state all the way to 1990. Mahathir, 'hav[ing] taken full cognizance of the continued uncertainties in the international economic environment and of the emerging resource constraints', chose to break with the past one and a half decades of state-led economic growth: 'The public sector will no longer play an expansionary role in spearheading economic growth.'[174] If anything, the reverse applied. Forced into austerity, the state instituted a job freeze on its bureaucracy, imposed financial discipline on its public enterprises, and postponed or cancelled many of the development projects budgeted under the Fourth Malaysia Plan.

That left capital to pick up the slack in investment. Or, to put it in Mahathir's terms: 'The alternative to Privatization may be to stop improving or providing [much] needed facilities. This will result in increasingly poor services and will stifle growth. Development will be retarded and the second [*sic*] prong of the NEP, poverty eradication, will not be accomplished.'[175]

He was more expansive on the 'major rationale' of 'Privatization', which was 'to relieve the financial burden of the government, promote competition in the economy, raise efficiency and productivity, accelerate growth of private investment and reduce the size and presence of the public sector'.[176]

This was the state turning to capital with touching faith. 'Privatization' and 'Malaysia Incorporated' provided the ideological turn away from an acceptance of unprofitable 'social enterprises', thus salvaging ideological virtue out of material necessity. Privatization's stress on the efficiency and competitiveness of private enterprise matched the rest of the Prime Minister's exhortations on work, productivity, thrift, and management as the antidotes to the 'subsidy' or 'dole' or 'dependent' or 'get-rich-quick' mentality. In short, it signified at least a partial end to the NEP's framework of statist protection, whether applied to individuals or enterprises. To show it in practice, Daim Zainuddin, the 'financial overseer' of this critical period in Malaysian economic history, ran the nation 'like a corporation' and 'worked the country's finances like the businessman he was'.[177]

'Privatization' and 'Malaysia Incorporated' had ideological value of another kind. Mahathir admitted that much as he had believed in capitalism and the private sector in the past, privatization could never have been permitted before the NEP had sponsored a respectable *bumiputera* presence in the Malaysian economy. Whereas the state had previously moved into business to stand in for the Malays, 'the position has now changed a great deal': 'In addition to a fairly large number of *Bumiputera* entrepreneurs, there are a number of funds owned by *Bumiputeras* which can be tapped as a source of capital.'[178] It was now plausible to talk of the 'private sector' without connoting 'non-Malay capital'.[179] Hence, 'Privatization', Mahathir emphasized, 'will not negate the objectives of the NEP' in that 'the *Bumiputeras* will get their share, both in terms of equity and employment'.[180] At the same time, the manner in which the *bumiputera* 'will get their share' also resolved a long-standing question of 'distribution'. In the NEP-dominated discourse, 'distribution' meant inter-ethnic 'redistribution' to redress 'racial imbalances'. But the NEP state was always under tacit pressure to 'distribute', *among the Malays*, the resources, assets, and corporate wealth it had garnered and held 'in trust' for them. In principle, the privatization of state enterprises, assets, services, and corporate equity provided a vehicle of distribution by which big Malay entrepreneurs as well as individuals of lesser wealth could 'get their share'.

Privatization was popular in the early 1980s when Reaganomics and Thatcherism ruled the ideological roost of the capitalist world and pledged to roll back the frontiers of the state. That would not have dismayed Mahathir for all his anti-Westernism and 'Buy British Last' directive. He would have seen privatization assuming its starkly 'denationalizing' and 'anti-socialist' form in the Thatcherite United Kingdom. Nearer home, where relations between the 'Malay state' and 'Chinese capital' were at least regulated if never quite warm—and the season of discontent, ushered in by financial scandals,[181] had not yet arrived—it was prudent to cast 'Privatization' in a celebratory rather than a confrontational mould. It was politically preferable to sing the praises of the private sector without a shrill refrain of 'rolling back the frontiers of the state'. To Mahathir's fortune, it was not even necessary to turn to privatization's ideological homelands of Reagan's United States and Thatcher's United Kingdom whose desolated economies could offer scant inspiration. Instead, Mahathir drew attention to the 're-flowering' of 'free enterprise' in the East—in Japan, in the Asian NICs, and, happily for all 'capitalist roaders', in Deng Xiaoping's China:

> We have seen the end of extreme socialist ideology, the severe loss of faith in the efficiency of rigid, over-centralized state planning with its concomitant state enterprises and monopolies; we have seen the flowering of the ideology of free enterprise even among newly independent developing countries, free enterprise which seeks to reward to each according to his effort, his contribution and to his ingenuity.[182]

In its time, the NEP represented a radical rupture in the pre-1969 state-and-capital alliance. Mahathir, who had framed the ideological parameters of that rupture more sharply than anyone else, must have looked back upon the NEP's constructive protection as only a rearguard action in the long battle for the complete rehabilitation of the Malays. In that sense, Mahathir's 1980s' rapture over 'Privatization' and 'Malaysia Incorporated' had a no less radical ideological significance: they offered a new basis for a new alliance between state and capital, or, should one say, capitals. NICdom's lure and the protectionist threat called for unity at home; constructive protection became less urgent than competitiveness. Here, at last, was the material basis for a new vanguard—a 'Malay state–Malay capital' alliance leading 'non-Malay capital'. 'Malaysia Incorporated', which many interpreted to mean an end to the divide between a 'Malay public sector' and a 'Chinese private sector', offered a resolution of the contradiction between 'incompetent state' and 'rapacious capital'.[183] In that it highlighted another important ideological point.

Mahathir repeatedly taught that the success of the private sector benefits the state. Where the state incurred losses, the private sector made profits—and thereby paid a 40 per cent tax to the state. Mahathir was fond of saying that the state 'owns a 40 per cent share' in all private enterprises.[184]

Had this '40 per cent solution' now superseded the '30 per cent target'? Had the NEP come into its own? And did that mean the NEP state had come to an end?

The NEP in Abeyance: Recession's Solution

The growth of the Malaysian economy has always been regarded as being essential to the NEP's success. The NEP's restructuring objective was premised on an expanding economy which would permit the Malays to attain their 30 per cent share of corporate wealth without provoking a sense of deprivation among the non-Malays. Economic growth, too, would generate employment opportunities to help abolish the 'identification of race with economic function'. The Malaysian economy did grow quite rapidly during the NEP's first decade. There was an average annual growth rate of 7.3 per cent for the Second Malaysia Plan period of 1971–5 and 8.6 per cent for the Third Malaysia Plan period of 1976–80. Employment expanded steadily, with total employment rising from 4.0 million in 1970 to 4.8 million in 1980. The unemployment rate fell from 7.8 per cent in 1970 to 5.7 per cent in 1980.

For ideological reasons, it was also necessary to have growth to demonstrate that the NEP's constraints on 'free enterprise' did not hamper economic performance or discourage investment. It was always moot whether Malaysia could have shown an even stronger economic performance had the economy remained 'free' of NEP-type regulations and impositions on local Chinese and foreign capital. To those who assumed so, Mahathir proudly pointed out that Malaysia's economic growth 'under NEP' was much higher than during the 'unregulated' pre-1969 period. For instance:

> If you look at Kuala Lumpur the growth took place after 1969. Before 1969 there was hardly any growth. Economic growth came after 1969 when the New Economic Policy was initiated in 1970. The reason why we want more growth is that we are committed to distributing growth, not distributing the original economic package. There will be no distribution if we

don't encourage growth and certainly all communities will want to see growth so that they will have a share. But of course, there must be sufficient to give to the *bumiputras*.[185]

Mahathir was not insensitive to Chinese and foreign capital's complaints about state over-regulation and intervention in the economy.[186] He was opposed to the rigid controls of the Industrial Co-ordination Act 1975, which was promoted by Hamzah Abu Samah, as well as the 'nationalistic' Petroleum Development Act 1974 sponsored by Tengku Razaleigh Hamzah.[187] Mahathir publicly frowned on those local businessmen 'who carp over the Industrial Co-ordination Act and the New Economic Policy'[188] but, as Deputy Prime Minister, he 'reiterate[d] the Government's determination to implement the Act with pragmatism and the maximum of flexibility' and gave the Federation of Malaysian Manufacturers his 'assurance that the Act will not be allowed to become a disincentive to private investment'.[189] As the Minister of Trade and Industry, he took pains to lead trade delegations to reassure potential investors in the West, Japan, and Hong Kong that the NEP's equity requirements and the Industrial Co-ordination Act did not preclude profitable investment in Malaysia. In fact, given the high growth of the 1970s and the fairly successful attraction of foreign investment into the economy, Mahathir could well contend that 'the NEP ... is one of the most liberal policies' and 'those who have decided to live with it have done extremely well'.[190]

But many among the Chinese business community who 'lived with it'—and did well—tended to develop short-term business perspectives and practices which were indicative of living with uncertainty. Yoshihara Kunio found that the old breed of Chinese entrepreneurs never quite adjusted to the NEP while a new generation of Chinese businessmen discovered rapid wealth in 'rent-seeking' alliances with Malay capitalists and politicians.[191] James V. Jesudason held that Chinese capital experienced the NEP as a 'restricted and uncertain economic environment'. Chinese capital thus stayed within 'easy and safe areas of expansion', avoided 'manufacturing which entailed larger risks and longer periods to recuperate investment outlays', and 'transferred assets abroad to diversify their economic and political risks'.[192] The Morgan Guaranty Trust Company estimated that 'capital flight' from Malaysia, originating mostly in the Chinese business community, totalled about US$12 billion between 1976 and 1985.[193]

One important part of the NEP state's strategy was to attract foreign capital to take up the slack in Chinese capital investment and to provide new employment opportunities.[194] The record of foreign investment in Malaysia under the NEP was mixed. Many multinational corporations took advantage of pioneer status benefits to relocate their more labour-intensive operations to Malaysia. But many potential foreign investors were reluctant to invest in Malaysia for fear of NEP-sanctioned 'nationalization'. Malek Marican suggested that foreign investors were often reluctant to form joint ventures with Malay partners since many of the latter were 'holding back payments or expected to be funded on easy terms'.[195] Other foreign investors were unwilling either to dilute their ownership and control within their own companies or to accept a minority position in a 'forced inter-racial corporate marriage'.[196] In any case, foreign corporate investment in Malaysia steadily declined in the 1980s, from its highest level of RM3,262 million in 1982 to RM2,926 million in 1983, RM2,138 million in 1984, RM1,725 million in 1985, and RM1,262 million in 1986.[197]

In 1985–6, the combination of the commodities collapse, diminished state revenues, reduced state expenditure, and decline in private capital investment sent the Malaysian economy into a recession. After almost a decade and a half of continuous growth, the economy contracted by 1 per cent in 1985 and only managed to register a 1.2 per cent growth in 1986. Negative growth, a freeze on state recruitment, and retrenchments in the private sector caused unemployment to rise from its record low of 4.6 per cent in 1982 to 7.6 per cent in 1985 to its record high of 8.5 per cent in 1986. For the first time since the NEP was launched, Malay graduate unemployment, estimated between 30,000 and 50,000, became a serious problem.[198] The shrinkage in state contracts and the Pan-Electric Industries-triggered stock market collapse of November 1985 severely exposed 'a continuing serious weakness among the *Bumiputeras* in business, particularly in project implementation and management'.[199] Many Malay businesses and businessmen, normally tied to state contracts, were highly geared on loans and too dependent on the '*bumiputera* share allotments' they preferentially acquired under the NEP. Mahathir later recalled that 'the recent recession made nearly all of them bankrupt and those that are not are heavily in debt'.[200] Then, he dismissed those Malay businessmen for 'hav[ing] neither credibility nor acceptance even among other *Bumiputeras*' because 'the wealth that some of them acquired and which many flaunt vanished under the slightest threat'.[201]

It seemed unlikely then that the NEP's 1990 target of 30 per cent *bumiputera* corporate ownership could be attained under such conditions of economic stagnation, high unemployment, and Malay business failures. And so in the climate of 1985–6, there lay in that act of vanishing wealth and receding target a political and ideological crisis which turned upon the NEP itself. UMNO and Malay business circles were soon polarized in an intense debate: What was to be done—about the NEP?

At one end of the polarity developed a basic position that demanded the extension of the NEP beyond 1990. The most 'extreme' argument advanced from this basic position, according to Malek Marican's candid analysis of that debate, wanted the state to be even 'more vigorous and aggressive in implementing the NEP'. Its proponents were 'aggrieved that we cannot even achieve a target like 30 per cent *bumiputra* participation and ownership when the *Bumis* comprise about half of the Malaysian population'.[202] The more 'moderate' variant of that position recognized the 'practical limitations to what may be achieved by 1990' and was 'quite willing to envisage a slower effort to push NEP restructuring given smaller financial resources available to the Government and the need to promote foreign as well as local investment'.[203]

At the opposing end of the debate stood a group which was primarily worried 'about the adverse impact on growth if the NEP as presently conceived continued to be implemented through the 1990s or even from now to 1990'.[204] Some within this group 'worry that we are now beginning to pay the price in trying to force interracial corporate marriages on unwilling foreign and non-*Bumi* entrepreneurs, in ways that ... favour the *Bumis* in our home country'.[205] Others 'believe that the NEP restructuring concepts can only be applied during a period of strong growth like the 1970s, and even then for only a limited period of time before the negative impacts inherent in a forced restructuring exercise would slow down national growth'.[206]

In policy terms, this second group, without giving up the NEP's vision, preferred to revert to the original premise of NEP restructuring—that is, 'distribution with growth', or, rather more pertinently under the prevailing conditions, 'no distribution without growth'. Or, as Mahathir said: 'NEP is based on growth.... Obviously if there is no growth there will be nothing to distribute.'[207]

Between 1985 and 1986, Mahathir's government initiated several measures to stimulate economic growth. In July 1985, it liberalized the guidelines for foreign equity ownership in manufacturing.[208] In December 1985, it amended the Industrial Co-ordination Act to make it easier for manufacturers to start new projects, expand their capacity, and diversify their products.[209] In May 1986, it passed the Promotion of Investments Act to provide further tax incentives to the manufacturing, agriculture, and tourism sectors. The government also launched a 'New Investment Fund' to channel funds at preferential rates of interest to finance new manufacturing, agricultural, and tourism projects.

But it was in August–September 1986 that Mahathir took a major decision on the question of 'restructuring vs growth'. During a trip to Australia to encourage foreign investment, he announced that the NEP would be 'held in abeyance', a politically circumspect phrase that became the code for suspending the NEP's *bumiputera* equity requirements. At the end of September 1986, while on an investment raising trip to the United States of America, Mahathir unveiled the policy implications of 'holding the NEP in abeyance'. He announced a set of new and more liberal conditions for foreign equity and expatriate staff which were to apply to investments made between 1 October 1986 and 31 December 1990. The new conditions favoured new foreign investments in industries whose products would not compete with products already being manufactured locally for the domestic market, and expansions of foreign-owned or partly foreign-owned industries which would not compete against existing local industries. Under the new conditions, a company that exported 50 per cent or more of its production, or sold 50 per cent or more of its production to companies in the Free Trade Zone or Licensed Manufacturing Warehouse, or employed 350 full-time Malaysian workers would be permitted whatever level of equity it applied for.[210] A company with foreign paid-up capital of US$2 million would be automatically allowed five expatriate posts at whatever level while changes of personnel would not require fresh work permits.[211] The conditions included a stipulation that the new foreign ventures should approximately reflect the ethnic composition of the country in their employment of Malaysians at all levels. Finally, Mahathir made clear that foreign investments committed between October 1986 and December 1990, under these conditions, 'will not be required to restructure their equity at any time'.[212] This was a critical concession which Mahathir justified on entirely pragmatic grounds:

> Growth which has long been taken for granted in Malaysia is not taking place. There is unemployment. Our emphasis now is on wealth creation rather than wealth distribution. We are sure we can manage our social engineering when the economy recovers. But it will not be at the expense of those who come when they are most needed.[213]

Some studies of the Malaysian political economy during this critical juncture regarded these new investment conditions as having had only minimal implications for the NEP, they being only the latest in a plethora of changes made to attract higher levels of foreign investment.[214] Undoubtedly 'holding the NEP in abeyance' was by no means a disavowal of the NEP itself. On record, Mahathir had repeatedly said that his government would not be the one to abandon the NEP. And if anything, during the Thirty-seventh UMNO General Assembly held barely a month after his Australian 'abeyance' statement, Mahathir issued one of his strongest defences of the NEP by attacking his non-Malay critics who blamed the economic malaise on the NEP. The NEP had become so embedded in the Malay imagination and so pervasive in its influence over the Malaysian political economy that neither Mahathir nor any other Malay politician could have risked declaring the NEP's end under 'ordinary' circumstances.

Under those constraints, Mahathir accomplished what was probably a 'second best' solution: if the 'extraordinary' economic and political turbulence of 1986 dictated placing 'wealth creation' ahead of 'wealth distribution', he would not balk at holding the NEP in abeyance. Mahathir was conscious that 'much political controversy was generated by [the] statement that the New Economic Policy will be held in abeyance'.[215] As he anticipated:

> Some will say, 'Ah, why do you hold the NEP in abeyance if it has nothing to do with recession?' The answer is that we are not expecting to become as prosperous as we were in the halcyon days of the commodities, merely because there will be more foreign investments. What we are really after is

jobs for the people laid off by the fall in commodity prices. The economic cake may not grow much but people must have jobs. They cannot wait for demand for tin to pick up.[216]

When the circumstances were politically less pressing than, say, at the UMNO General Assembly, Mahathir took pains to reason that the NEP had nothing to do with the economic crisis: 'We are in the throes of an economic recession. But is it due to the NEP? . . . When the prices of commodities collapsed by almost 60 per cent can the economy grow?'[217] But, significantly, that was only by way of proposing that 'holding the NEP in abeyance' had everything to do with stimulating economic growth: 'If certain conditions are found to inhibit growth at a given time, it follows that those conditions will have to be modified to remove the inhibitions', because the

NEP is not just equity distribution. It is equally important that job opportunities are also evenly distributed. In a situation where unemployment is rampant it is invidious to protect the interest of certain categories of investors at the expense of unemployment for workers. We will, therefore, modify the NEP conditions regarding equity in order to implement the stipulations regarding employment. The government is studying very specific conditions so that investors will not be left in doubt as to when and how we are prepared to forego equity participation in favour of jobs for Malaysians.[218]

Holding the NEP in abeyance by liberalizing the foreign equity ownership requirement was in a sense lopsided. It did not address the 'Chinese'—and, naturally, politically more risky—dimension of employment-generating investment. The Industrial Co-ordination Act which regulated firms with a paid-up capital of RM250,000 and employing more than twenty-five workers had been in force since 1975 despite a long-standing protest by the Chinese Chamber of Commerce. The Industrial Co-ordination Act was finally amended in 1985 to cover firms with more than fifty workers and with more than RM1 million in paid-up capital. After the foreign equity ownership liberalization in September 1986, the Industrial Co-ordination Act was further amended to cover only firms having more than seventy-five workers and RM2.5 million in paid-up capital. It was a 'concession in NEP implementation' made in the direction of Chinese capital.

Messing about with the NEP, so to speak, was a politically hazardous activity in which equivocation might have proven to be the better part of discretion. Mahathir took a plunge with his 'abeyance' decision, albeit by pleading the most compelling justification of 'economic crisis' requiring strong if bitter medicine. Yet, and if only in retrospect, might one not find behind the pragmatic justification of Mahathir's 'abeyance' something of a logical culmination of his personal convictions on economics and capitalism? It is, after all, during crises when politicians—indeed, all decent men and women—either defend their philosophy or compromise their principles. Moreover, a consummate politician like Mahathir, and one with strongly felt principles, might find a third way which was to advance his philosophy behind the very semblance of compromise! Ever since becoming Prime Minister, Mahathir had in practice committed himself to disciplining the NEP state, its bureaucracy, and its public enterprises. He had by 1984 abandoned the path of counter-cyclical spending in favour of an 'austerity drive' to combat the recession and rising foreign debt. He was already set on 'Privatization' as the alternative to the state's 'expansionary role'. Ideologically, he had inveighed against the 'soft environment' and the dependence on the '30 per cent solution' which NEP-sanctioned state protection had created for the Malays. He had himself taught the 'free enterprise' virtues of productivity, thrift, and managerial probity. He had detected a replicable workaholism behind the East Asian miracle of winning trade surpluses in times of global recession. Along the way, from 1981 to 1986, Mahathir often proclaimed an absence of any 'intention to be rigid or to regard policies and laws as sacred cows that may not be trifled with'.[219] He frequently claimed to have 'critically examined all the things that we have been doing or which we have taken for granted ... questioned old policies and approaches ... [and] assaulted many administrative and management methods that have been considered sacred'.[220] In 1984, he told the country's 'Top Business Leaders', premonition-like, that 'we are not about to abandon the New Economic Policy'—'but we can implement it without being too short-sighted'.[221] In that spirit, 'recession's solution' turned out to be the culmination of that premonition uttered two years before the advent of 'abeyance'.

1. The NEP is invariably mentioned in any social analysis of post-1969 Malaysia. The literature on the NEP is accordingly voluminous. For official documents on the NEP, see Department of National Unity, 'The New Economic Policy', a directive to government departments, dated 18 March 1970, reproduced as 'Document C' in Just Faaland, J. R. Parkinson, and Rais Saniman, *Growth and Ethnic Inequality: Malaysia's New Economic Policy*, Kuala Lumpur: Dewan Bahasa dan Pustaka, 1990, pp. 305–18; Malaysia, *Second Malaysia Plan, 1971–1975*, Kuala Lumpur: Government Printers, 1971, and *Mid-Term Review of the Second Malaysia Plan*, Kuala Lumpur: Government Printers, 1973. For a guide to analyses of the NEP from different viewpoints, see Business International, *Malaysia to 1980: Economic and Political Outlook for Business Planners*, Hong Kong, 1977; Faaland, Parkinson, and Rais, *Growth and Ethnic Inequality*; James V. Jesudason, *Ethnicity and the Economy: The State, Chinese Business, and Multinationals in Malaysia*, Singapore: Oxford University Press, 1989; Jomo K. S, *A Question of Class: Capital, the State, and Uneven Development in Malaya*, 2nd edn., New York: Monthly Review Press and Journal of Contemporary Asia Publishers, 1988; and Shamsul A. B., *RMK: Tujuan dan Pelaksanaannya. Satu Tinjauan Teoritis*, Kuala Lumpur: Dewan Bahasa dan Pustaka, 1977.

2. The NEP's two-decade span for achieving fixed targets of poverty eradication and restructuring were first set out in the 'Outline Perspective Plan', Malaysia, *Mid-Term Review of the Second Malaysia Plan*.

3. There were 'three basic objectives', namely 'reduction of racial economic disparities', 'creation of employment opportunities', and 'promotion of overall economic growth' but 'the Government is determined that the *reduction in racial economic disparities shall be the overriding target* even if unforeseen developments occur which pose a harsher conflict than now foreseen between the three objectives' (Department of National Unity, 'The New Economic Policy', in Faaland, Parkinson, and Rais, *Growth and Ethnic Inequality*, p. 309).

4. Ibid., original emphasis.

5. Non-ethnically bound but vocal critics of NEP 'malpractices' have often publicly said as much. For example, see Chandra Muzaffar, *The NEP: Alternative Development and Consciousness*, Penang: Aliran, 1989, pp. 88–9, and Jomo K. S., *Beyond 1990: Considerations for a New National Development Strategy*, Kuala Lumpur: Institute of Advanced Studies, University of Malaya, 1989, p. 15.

6. As did Mahathir, even after the 'instability' of 1987–8 (see Chapter 7): 'The fact is that it is the NEP which had made political stability possible after the race riots of 1969' ('Speech at the 10th Malaysian Economic Convention', Kuala Lumpur, 7 August 1989, reprinted as 'Charting Directions for Future Growth', *New Straits Times*, 8 August 1989).

7. Faaland, Parkinson, and Rais, *Growth and Ethnic Inequality*, Chapter 5, pp. 152–208, supplies a summary of 'the debate' over the NEP but it stays within a narrow, ethnic 'spectrum' of views. It omits the substantial but politically marginal non-ethnic, class-based critiques of the NEP, most comprehensively argued in Jomo, *A Question of Class*, or the 'anti-rentierist' critique in Ozay Mehmet, *Development in Malaysia: Poverty, Wealth and Trusteeship*, London: Croom Helm, 1986.

8. Razak explicitly stated that the Second Malaysia Plan 'will spare no efforts

to promote national unity and develop a just and progressive Malaysian society in a rapidly expanding economy so that no one will experience any loss or feel any sense of deprivation of his rights, privileges, income, job or opportunity' (Malaysia, *Second Malaysia Plan, 1971–1975*, 'Foreword', p. v).

9. Chandra Muzaffar's shorter but penetrating views of the heightened ethnic rivalry under the NEP are to be found in his essays, 'Has the Communal Situation Worsened over the Last Decade? Some Preliminary Thoughts', in Syed Husin Ali (ed.), *Ethnicity, Class and Development in Malaysia*, Kuala Lumpur: Malaysian Social Science Association, 1984, pp. 356–82, and 'The NEP and the Quest for National Unity', in Chandra Muzaffar, *The NEP: Development and Alternative Consciousness*, pp. 25–55.

10. Mehmet, *Development in Malaysia*. The take-over bid was made by the MCA-controlled Multi-Purpose Holdings Berhad. And 'in the end, the issue was settled quietly by the top political leadership in UMNO and MCA in a manner which maximized the common corporate interests of the parties involved' and 'MPHB and PERNAS were allowed to acquire 40% of the UMBC equity, on the theory that neither could then exercise a controlling interest' (ibid., p. 147).

11. This was starkly captured by the plight of the 'new villages' which had a very high incidence of poverty but were bypassed for rural development because of their predominantly Chinese population and despite their mostly rural and semi-rural locations. See Parti Gerakan Rakyat Malaysia, *Into the Mainstream of Development*, Kuala Lumpur, 1986.

12. Jomo K. S. and Ishak Shari, *Development Policies and Income Inequality in Peninsular Malaysia*, Kuala Lumpur: Institute of Advanced Studies, University of Malaya, 1986, p. 81. Table 29 (ibid., p. 82) showed the ratios of restructuring allocations to poverty eradication allocations to have been 0.22 in 1971–5, 0.37 in 1976–80, 0.47 in 1981–5, and 0.81 in 1981–3 (actual expenditure). The critical question is how much the poverty eradication goal had been achieved. The official position has been that the incidence of poverty among Malaysian households fell from 49.3 per cent in 1970 to 29.2 per cent in 1980. Jomo K. S., *Growth and Structural Change in the Malaysian Economy*, New York: Macmillan, 1990, pp. 145–54, disputes that claim with fairly complex statistical analysis. Mehmet, *Development in Malaysia*, p. 163, categorically concluded that 'the Malaysian trusteeship fits a *Zero-Sum Economic Game* in which the trustees have gained at the expense of the losers, the large number of poor families who have remained poor'.

13. See Mehmet, *Development in Malaysia*, pp. 151–3, on 'intra-Malay' inequality and pp. 132–47 for the view that the chief beneficiaries of the NEP's restructuring formed 'distributional coalitions' which profited from 'rent-seeking behaviour' while acting as 'trustees' of the Malay share of wealth.

14. Yoshihara Kunio, *The Rise of Ersatz Capitalism in South-East Asia*, Singapore: Oxford University Press, 1988, p. 74.

15. Jomo, *Growth and Structural Change in the Malaysian Economy*, pp. 263–8.

16. Business International, *Malaysia to 1980*, p. 61, and *passim*. '... it appears that the actual beneficiaries—and the coalition behind the NEP—are the political faction represented by the Razak group, the enlarged bureaucracy, and bureaucratic relatives and hangers-on' (ibid., p. 73).

17. A detailed analysis of the difficult state–Chinese business relationship can be found in Jesudason, *Ethnicity and the Economy*, Chapter 5, especially pp. 128–47.

18. Jesudason (ibid.) described such a state as an 'enlarged state'. Mehmet, *Development in Malaysia*, called the process 'bureaucratic expansion under the NEP trusteeship'. Jomo, *A Question of Class*, saw the entire process as the 'ascendancy of the statist capitalists'.

19. Malek Marican, 'The NEP from a Private Sector Perspective', Paper presented at the Seminar 'Dasar Ekonomi Baru Selepas 1990: Peranan Sektor Korporat Awam', Kuala Lumpur, 24–26 March 1987.

20. Khoo Khay Jin, 'The Grand Vision: Mahathir and Modernization', in Joel S. Kahn and Francis Loh Kok Wah (eds.), *Fragmented Vision: Culture and Politics in Contemporary Malaysia*, Sydney: Asian Studies Association of Australia in association with Allen and Unwin, 1992, p. 49, n. 16.

21. Mahathir, quoted in K. Das, 'Mahathir's "Restoration"', *Far Eastern Economic Review*, 11 June 1982, p. 40.

22. Ibid.

23. Walter Rodney, *How Europe Underdeveloped Africa*, London: Bogle-L'Ouverture Publications, 1972.

24. Mahathir Mohamad, *The Malay Dilemma*, Singapore: Donald Moore for Asia Pacific Press, 1970, p. 23, had a terse note on the Malacca Sultanate: 'The prosperity of the Malacca Sultanate came at a time when Islam was in the ascendancy in Malaya. Malacca attracted more foreign traders and eventually conquerors and settlers.'

25. Mahathir, 'Speech at the 33rd UMNO General Assembly', Kuala Lumpur, 10 September 1982, English translation reprinted as 'UMNO in a World of Change and Challenge', *New Straits Times*, 11 September 1982.

26. Syed Hussein Alatas, *The Myth of the Lazy Native*, London: Frank Cass, 1977, pp. 155–63, 172–81. Also see Shaharuddin Maaruf, *Malay Ideas on Development: From Feudal Lord to Capitalist*, Singapore: Times Books International, 1988, Chapter 7, pp. 137–48, which, however, rarely proceeds beyond dismissing *The Malay Dilemma* for its 'complete sympathy and identification with the history and cause of Malay capitalism in striking contrast to the condescending and contemptuous attitude towards non-capitalist, particularly rural Malays' (p. 142).

27. Alatas, *The Myth of the Lazy Native*, p. 80.

28. Ibid., p. 163.

29. 'Orang Kampung Masih Anggap Bank Itu Ceti', *Berita Harian*, 17 November 1982.

30. Rehman Rashid, 'Prime Minister Reveals His Hopes and Fears', *New Sunday Times*, 6 July 1986.

31. Exactly Mahathir's phrase, in 'Orang Kampung Masih Anggap Bank Itu Ceti'.

32. Ibid.

33. Mahathir's note on the Malay lack of awareness of time found a rebuttal in Alatas, *The Myth of the Lazy Native*, pp. 160–1, 171–3. On the historical relationship between a 'shift in time-sense' and the (not uncontested) imposition of a new work-discipline under industrial capitalism, see the classic essay by E. P. Thompson,

'Time, Work-discipline and Industrial Capitalism', *Past and Present*, 38 (1967): 56–97. Thompson poignantly observed that 'without time-discipline we could not have the insistent energies of industrial man; and whether this discipline comes in the form of Methodism, or of Stalinism, or of nationalism, it will come to the developing world' but 'the historical record is not a simple one of neutral and inevitable technological change, but is also one of exploitation and of resistance to exploitation; and that values stand to be lost as well as gained' (pp. 93–4).

34. 'This can hardly be termed fair competition' (Mahathir, *The Malay Dilemma*, p. 52).

35. Mahathir, 'Speech at the Seminar on Transnational Corporations and National Development', Petaling Jaya, 2 October 1979, *Foreign Affairs Malaysia*, 12 (1979): 392–5.

36. Peter Drucker, 'The Changed World Economy', *Foreign Affairs*, 64, 4 (Spring 1986): 768–91.

37. Mahathir, 'Speech at the 3rd General Conference of the United Nations Industrial Development Organization (UNIDO)', New Delhi, 22 January 1980, *Foreign Affairs Malaysia*, 13 (1980): 22–8.

38. Mahathir, 'Speech at the Seminar on Transnational Corporations and National Development'.

39. Mahathir, 'Speech at the Annual Dinner of Financial Institutions', Kuala Lumpur, 25 August 1986, *Foreign Affairs Malaysia*, 19, 3 (September 1986): 15–20.

40. Jomo, *Growth and Structural Change in the Malaysian Economy*, p. 56, Table 3.11. For a detailed discussion of the primary commodities' importance to the Malaysian economy, see ibid., pp. 53–66. An analysis of the role of exports from a limited 'dependency' perspective may be found in Khor Kok Peng, *The Malaysian Economy: Structures and Dependence*, Penang: Institut Masyarakat, 1983, pp. 86–103.

41. Mahathir, 'Speech at the International Seminar on Commodities', Kuala Lumpur, 21 July 1986, *Foreign Affairs Malaysia*, 19, 3 (September 1986): 6–11.

42. Ibid.

43. Ibid.

44. Ibid.

45. Ibid. Mahathir was disillusioned with commodity agreements: 'The test of the agreements comes when supply exceeds demand. The high prices maintained by the agreement encourages higher production by low-cost producers. The buffer stock manager must buy to prevent falling prices. What this really means is that the commodity producers are producing and selling basically to themselves. If they don't produce then illegal producers or non-members will take up the slack and profit. It's a case of tails I lose, heads you win' (Mahathir, 'Speech at the Seminar on Primary Commodities', Kuala Lumpur, 21 April 1986, *Foreign Affairs Malaysia*, 19, 2 (June 1986): 6–10).

46. 'Soya bean oil, butter and beef are among the aid items which create havoc with the exports of many developing countries' (Mahathir, 'Speech at the International Seminar on Commodities').

47. Ibid. See the section, 'North–South, East–West' in Chapter 3 for a longer discussion of Mahathir's attack on the developed countries' manipulation of commodity prices.

48. Mahathir, 'Speech at the Annual Dinner of Financial Institutions', 25 August 1986. 'What we are experiencing now is not the usual cyclical changes that have always afflicted the commodity trade. It is not the usual supply exceeding demand alternating with demand exceeding supply. The commodity trade is undergoing a much more fundamental change, a change that is structural in nature' (Mahathir, 'Speech at the Seminar on Primary Commodities').

49. Mahathir, 'Speech at the International Seminar on Commodities', pp. 6–11.

50. '... today's rubber tree produces ten times more rubber than the original rubber tree smuggled out of the Amazon forest' (ibid.).

51. 'Tin plating, for example, requires less tin now than in the past' (ibid.).

52. 'Now glass, paper, plastic and aluminium compete and displace tin. Copper is losing out to glass fibre. Aluminium and even titanium are gradually losing out to the new carbon fibres and synthetic composites in the manufacture of aircraft and soon in motor cars. Ceramics are creating a whole new world in terms of materials for manufacturing which will render out of date numerous metals in the manufacture of engines and components' (ibid.).

53. Mahathir, 'Speech at the Annual Dinner of Financial Institutions', 25 August 1986.

54. Mahathir, 'Speech at the 3rd ASEAN Council on Petroleum (ASCOPE) Conference and Exhibition', Kuala Lumpur, 2 December 1985, *Foreign Affairs Malaysia*, 18, 4 (December 1985): 348–52. Oil used to fetch trinkets, too: 'The story of oil is representative of the kind of practices found in commodity trade in particular. The payments made for the billions of barrels of oil to the oil-producing countries prior to 1973–74 were so niggardly low that for decades these countries remained poverty stricken. Not only was the posted price totally unrelated to the true value of oil as a source of energy and chemicals but the rate of royalty was so low that the oil-producing countries could hardly keep body and soul together' (Mahathir, 'Speech at the United Nations Conference on Trade and Development (UNCTAD) V Meeting', Manila, 15 May 1979, *Foreign Affairs Malaysia*, 12 (1979): pp. 154–67).

55. Ibid.

56. Mahathir, 'Speech at the International Seminar on Commodities'.

57. Ibid.

58. Mahathir, 'Speech at the Annual Dinner of Financial Institutions', 25 August 1986.

59. 'A commodity is therefore a mysterious thing, simply because in it the social character of men's labour appears to them as an objective character stamped upon the product of that labour; because the relation of the producers to the sum total of their own labour is presented to them as a social relation, existing not between themselves, but between the products of their labour. This is the reason why the products of labour become commodities, social things whose qualities are at the same time perceptible and imperceptible by the senses. ... There is a physical relation between physical things. But it is different with commodities. There, the existence of the things *qua* commodities, and the value-relation between the products of labour which stamps them as commodities, have absolutely no connexion

with their physical properties and with the material relations arising therefrom. There it is a definite social relation between men, that assumes, in their eyes, the fantastic form of a relation between things' (Karl Marx, *Capital*, Vol. 1, New York: International Publishers, 1967, p. 72).

60. This summary of the fall in Malaysian commodity prices in the mid-1980s is drawn from Jesudason, *Ethnicity and the Economy*, p. 121, Table 4.12.

61. For a summary account of Minister of Finance Daim Zainuddin's 'spurning of counter-cyclical spending' and 'contraction' of state expenditure from 1984 on, see Khoo Khay Jin, 'The Grand Vision', pp. 51–6.

62. 'We are in the throes of an economic recession now. But is it due to the NEP? Fifty percent of Malaysia's economy has been based on the production and export of tin, rubber, timber, palm oil, petroleum, cocoa, pepper, etc. When the prices of these commodities collapsed by almost 60 per cent, can the economy grow? Of course, it will have to reflect these reduced export earnings. When we earn less money from exports, demands for all sorts of domestic products and services must also be adversely affected. The nett result is economic recession' (Mahathir, 'Speech at the EMF Foundation Roundtable on Malaysia', Kuala Lumpur, 3 November 1986, *Foreign Affairs Malaysia*, 19, 4 (December 1986): 29–35).

63. See the section '24 April 1987: Personal Mandate, Party Democracy, or UMNO Split?', in Chapter 7, for a sample of Mahathir's plea of 'commodity collapse' as a response to his UMNO critics' attack on his and Daim's 'economic mismanagement'.

64. Mahathir, 'Speech at the International Productivity Conference', Kuala Lumpur, 3 November 1986, *Foreign Affairs Malaysia*, 19, 4 (December 1986): 20–4. Kit G. Machado argued that Mahathir's heavy industrialization drive was 'aimed at reducing Malaysia's economic dependence on advanced capitalist states in general and on world commodity markets in particular for both economic and nationalistic reasons' (Kit G. Machado, 'Japanese Transnational Corporations in Malaysia's State Sponsored Heavy Industrialization Drive: The HICOM Automobile and Steel Projects', *Pacific Affairs*, 62, 4 (Winter 1989–90): 507).

65. From 1971 to 1980, the manufacturing sector had an average annual growth rate of 11.4 per cent, compared with a GDP growth rate of 7.8 per cent (Mehmet, *Development in Malaysia*, p. 76, Table 4.1).

66. Jomo, *Growth and Structural Change in the Malaysian Economy*, p. 43, Table 3.4.

67. Ibid., p. 79, Table 4.1.

68. Ibid., p. 56, Table 3.11.

69. Mehmet, *Development in Malaysia*, pp. 76–8.

70. Mahathir, 'Speech at the Seminar on Transnational Corporations and National Development'.

71. Mahathir, 'Speech at the Top Business Leaders Conference on National Economic Development', Kuala Lumpur, 18 May 1984, *Foreign Affairs Malaysia*, 17, 2 (June 1984): 158–64. Mehmet, *Development in Malaysia*, p. 77, noted that Malaysia's import-substitution industrialization had reached its limit by the early 1970s 'with about 95 per cent of the consumer durables and 90 per cent of non-durables being produced locally, behind an effective, high rate of protection'.

72. Mahathir, 'Speech at the Seminar on Primary Commodities'.

73. Mahathir, 'Speech at the Malaysian Investment Seminar', New York, 30 September 1986, *Foreign Affairs Malaysia*, 19, 3 (September 1986): 66–9.

74. Mahathir, 'Speech at the Seminar on Transnational Corporations and National Development'.

75. Machado, 'Japanese Transnational Corporations', explores the coming together of 'Mahathir's and the Japanese transnationals' strategies' which made the joint ventures possible. That local Chinese capital was bypassed in all these has been frequently commented on, most clearly in Jomo, *Growth and Structural Change in the Malaysian Economy*, p. 129: 'Arguing—probably quite correctly—that the predominantly Chinese domestic investors had neither the interest nor technology to invest in projects offering uncertain, if not unattractive returns, the Malaysian authorities claim that foreign investors would be more inclined to get into joint-ventures, with the government providing capital subsidies and protection of the domestic market.'

76. Mahathir, 'Speech at the Top Business Leaders Conference on National Economic Development'.

77. See Machado, 'Japanese Transnational Corporations', a detailed and highly interesting account of the technological, financial, and managerial problems faced by PROTON and PERWAJA. Unfortunately, there are few other equally rigorous assessments of the HICOM projects.

78. The strongest criticism of the car project by an economist was made by Chee Peng Lim, 'The Proton Saga—No Reverse Gear: The Economic Burden of the Malaysian Car Project', in Jomo K. S. (ed.), *Mahathir's Economic Policies*, Kuala Lumpur: Insan, 1989, pp. 48–62. Machado, 'Japanese Transnational Corporations', confirmed much of the early doubt about PROTON's and PERWAJA's dependence on Japanese technology. Also see Jesudason, *Ethnicity and the Economy*, pp. 118–19, and Jomo, *Growth and Structural Change in the Malaysian Economy*, pp. 128–34.

79. Chee, 'The Proton Saga—No Reverse Gear', pp. 52–5.

80. Ibid., pp. 51–2.

81. For details of the capitalization of PROTON and PERWAJA, and the yen debts incurred, see the table in Machado, 'Japanese Transnational Corporations', p. 519.

82. From ibid., p. 530: 'On the question of prospects for reliance on Japanese transnational corporations to further Malaysian industrialization in ways that reduce dependence, the answer is probably no.' It was estimated that after 15 years of operation, the Malaysian car assembly industry showed the value of local content to be less than 18 per cent (Chee, 'The Proton Saga—No Reverse Gear', p. 49).

83. *Star*, 2 February 1982.

84. S. Jayasakaran, 'Premier in Power', *Malaysian Business*, 1 January 1988, p. 9.

85. 'A Vision for Malaysia', *Asiaweek*, 23 September 1983, p. 36.

86. Kadir Jasin, 'What Goes into the Making of the Malaysian Car', Interview with Mahathir, *New Straits Times*, 24 November 1982.

87. Ibid.

88. Tan Chee Khoon, *Without Fear or Favour*, Singapore: Eastern Universities Press, 1984, p. 83. To Tan Chee Khoon, Mahathir also said: 'Now in the case of

the automobile industry we made a big mistake right from the word go. We allowed all kinds of cars to come into the country. As a result there is no one single make or size that is used in sufficiently large numbers to justify the industry' (ibid.). That was surely a hint of an impending loss of market share for the existing assemblers of 'all kinds of cars' except the national one.

89. Kadir Jasin, 'What Goes into the Making of the Malaysian Car'.

90. Ibid.

91. Ibid.

92. Mahathir, 'Speech at the Seminar on Primary Commodities'.

93. Kadir Jasin, 'Need for a Bigger Population If We Are to Industrialize', *New Straits Times*, 24 November 1982. For a discussion of the '70 million' population policy, see Wan Abdul Manan Wan Muda, 'The Seventy Million Population Policy: Implications on Health, Nutrition and Aging', in Muhammad Ikmal Said and Johan Saravanamuttu (eds.), *Images of Malaysia*, Kuala Lumpur: Persatuan Sains Sosial Malaysia, 1991, pp. 224–59.

94. Musa Hitam, 'Malaysia: The Spirit of '46 Rises Again', *Correspondent*, November 1988, p. 18. Mahathir found it frustrating: 'In other countries people would have celebrated with joy if they had a car with a potential for export. Here it's different. We excoriate ourselves, we tell everybody that we're no good. How do we succeed with this kind of mentality?' (Jayasakaran, 'Premier in Power', p. 9).

95. Maxime Rodinson, *Marxism and the Muslim World*, London: Zed Press, 1981, p. 142.

96. Mahathir, 'Speech at the Luncheon Jointly Hosted by the Asia Society, the Far East American Business Council and the ASEAN–American Trade Council', New York, 16 January 1984, *Foreign Affairs Malaysia*, 17, 1 (March 1984): 50–4.

97. Mahathir, 'Speech at the 3rd General Conference of the United Nations Industrial Development Organization (UNIDO)'.

98. 'Malaysia's diversification in the primary industries field has not saved her in the present world-wide collapse of all commodities. We have therefore to come to terms with the reality of the situation: that is, dependence on commodities, no matter how diversified, is not enough. We have to think of other ways of achieving economic stability and growth' (Mahathir, 'Speech at the Seminar on Primary Commodities').

99. Mahathir, 'Speech at the International Monetary Fund Conference', Hong Kong, 3 June 1985, *Foreign Affairs Malaysia*, 18, 2 (June 1985): 159–68.

100. Ibid.

101. Ibid.

102. Mahathir, 'Speech at the Luncheon Jointly Hosted by the Asia Society, the Far East American Business Council and the ASEAN–American Trade Council'. 'South Korea, Taiwan, Hong Kong and Brazil took rather bold steps into industrialization. They disregarded the domestic market but concentrated on exports. Starting with garments which they frequently manufacture under buyers' labels, they were able to penetrate the huge markets in the industrialized countries. Encouraged by their success they moved into textiles, toys and other relatively simple consumer items. Soon they were moving into heavy machinery, ships and even manufacturing plants . . .' (ibid.).

103. Mahathir, *The Malay Dilemma*, Chapter 10, pp. 174–8.

104. Rehman Rashid, 'Why I Took to Politics'.

105. Tan Chee Khoon, *Without Fear or Favour*, p. 61.

106. Rehman Rashid, 'Why I Took to Politics'.

107. Ibid.

108. Tan Chee Khoon, *Without Fear or Favour*, p. 63.

109. Ibid.

110. Ibid.

111. Ibid., p. 79.

112. Jayasankaran, 'Premer in Power', p. 9.

113. Tan Chee Khoon, *Without Fear or Favour*, p. 79. Mahathir's reasoning perfectly illustrates one NEP tangle: was the 30 per cent target in corporate ownership or roughly proportional representation in the employment structure to be attained on a 'global' or 'firm-by-firm' basis? When K. Das asked him if the NEP target was 'for the economy as a whole' or to 'apply to every industry and every company', Mahathir categorically replied: 'Well, the target is global' (Das, 'Mahathir's "Restoration"', p. 40). But reasoning on a 'firm-by-firm' basis here, Mahathir highlights Malay 'under-representation' among the doctors. Yet by 1983, Malay professional establishments, from a 'global' perspective, had already accounted for 24.5 per cent of the total revenue earned by professional establishments in the country (Marican, 'The NEP from a Private Sector Perspective', p. 4, and Table IIA).

114. Mahathir Mohamad, *The Challenge*, Petaling Jaya: Pelanduk Publications, 1986; translated from *Menghadapi Cabaran*, Kuala Lumpur: Pustaka Antara, 1976, p. 65.

115. Mahathir, 'Materialism and Spirituality', in ibid., pp. 56–82.

116. Ibid., p. 16.

117. Mahathir, 'Speech at the Bumiputera Economic Convention', Universiti Kebangsaan Malaysia, Bangi, 19 March 1978, reprinted as 'Bumiputera Economy: A National Problem', *New Straits Times*, 1 April 1978. 'The Poor Are Poorer, the Rich, Richer', in Mahathir, *The Challenge*, pp. 4–17, contains Mahathir's general defence of the rich—who contribute to society by paying many forms of taxes (including 'the highest taxes ... on luxuries which the rich are so fond of'), employing 'those who may well be jobless otherwise' and, if they 'ha[ve] some money left', by investing it.

118. Mahathir, 'Speech at the Bumiputera Economic Convention'.

119. Rehman Rashid, 'Why I Took to Politics'.

120. Mahathir, 'Speech at the 37th UMNO General Assembly', Kuala Lumpur, 18 September 1986, reprinted as 'Sistem Tumpuan Luar Bandar Akan Dikekalkan', *Utusan Malaysia,* 19 September 1986.

121. Jesudason, *Ethnicity and the Economy*, argues that UMNO's sensitivity to the Malays' 'relative group worth' which was increased by the success of Malay *nouveaux riches* allowed it to retain the loyalty of its Malay base via the implementation of the NEP. For the theory behind 'relative group worth', see Donald Horowitz, *Ethnic Groups in Conflict*, Berkeley: University of California Press, 1985.

122. To an observation that 'there seems to be a sense among the rural poor that prosperity is their right', Mahathir replied: 'No, you have no right to prosperity

merely because you are a *Bumiputera*, but if there are opportunities going around, then you have a right to opportunities. You have to learn, to improve yourself' (Rehman Rashid, 'Why I Took to Politics').

123. Mahathir, *The Malay Dilemma*, p. 31.

124. Ibid.

125. Jayasankaran, 'Premier in Power', p. 9.

126. Mahathir, 'Speech at the 10th Malaysian Economic Convention'.

127. Jayasankaran, 'Premier in Power', p. 9.

128. Ibid.

129. Ibid.

130. Mahathir, 'Speech at the 10th Malaysian Economic Convention'.

131. K. Das, 'Problems and Power', *Far Eastern Economic Review*, 30 October 1981, p. 33.

132. Khoo Khay Jin, 'The Grand Vision', pp. 51–6, provides a concise analysis of Mahathir and Daim's abandonment of counter-cyclical spending, contraction in state expenditure, wage and job freeze, financial disciplining of public enterprises, and other austerity measures.

133. Jayasankaran, 'Premier in Power'.

134. Since 'these people have reverted to being, well, the bottom rung of the middle class', (the NEP as) 'the[ir] crutch therefore will have to remain until there is equitable distribution of wealth. I would not like to see the crutch taken off when Malay contractors can only get contracts from the government. Where are they to go?' (ibid.).

135. Ibid.

136. In 1983, the PNB, 'although barely five years old, was the largest single stockowner of the 145 top companies listed on the Kuala Lumpur Stock Exchange, owning 8.3 per cent of 5.2 billion shares in these companies' (Mehmet, *Development in Malaysia*, p. 142).

137. One should say *at least* because official data failed to clarify how much *more* was owned by *bumiputera* interests subsumed under 'nominee companies' and 'locally controlled companies' of unspecified ethnic identity which accounted for 20 per cent of corporate equity. For a considered analysis of this point, see Jomo, *Growth and Structural Change in the Malaysian Economy*, pp. 157–60.

138. 'It is true that there were *Bumiputeras* who actively participated', that is, in their own businesses, unlike those who merely used their *bumiputera* status to obtain and resell contracts and licences, 'but these were the exception rather than the rule' (Mahathir, 'Speech at the 10th Malaysian Economic Convention').

139. For biographical briefs on the leading Malay capitalists, see Yoshihara, *The Rise of Ersatz Capitalism in South-East Asia*, pp. 166–73 and Jesudason, *Ethnicity and the Economy*, pp. 105–8.

140. Mahathir, 'Speech at the Annual Luncheon of the Malaysian International Chamber of Commerce and Industry', Kuala Lumpur, 1 June 1981, reprinted as 'The Evils of Protectionism', in Murugesu Pathmanathan and David Lazarus (eds.), *Winds of Change*, Kuala Lumpur: Eastview Productions, 1984, pp. 77–82.

141. The other 'structural problems' mentioned in this statement were 'the increasing strains on the balance of payment' and the fact that 'private investment

has not shown much dynamism' (Mahathir, 'Speech at the Top Business Leaders Conference on National Economic Development').

142. Mehmet, *Development in Malaysia*, p. 9, Table 1.3. These figures exclude military and police personnel.

143. Ibid., p. 133, Table 6.1. Total public sector expenditure, as a proportion of gross national product (GNP), increased from 28.7 per cent in 1970 to 61.2 per cent in 1982.

144. Jesudason, *Ethnicity and the Economy*, p. 82, noted that 'Malaysia's petroleum policy gradually evolved into one of intensifying petroleum extraction and revenues for its NEP objectives'.

145. Mahathir, 'Speech at the ASEAN–West Asian Investment Conference', Kuala Lumpur, 9 March 1978, *Foreign Affairs Malaysia*, II, 1 (1978): 80–4.

146. According to estimates by Mehmet, *Development in Malaysia*, pp. 133–4, the total public sector deficit rose from RM0.4 billion in 1970 to RM15.2 billion in 1982 while state governments and major statutory bodies and public enterprises owed the federal government a total of RM8.743 billion in 1982.

147. See, for example, Mahathir's sarcasm about civil servants being 'on call twenty-four hours but never call for twenty years' (Malaysia, *Dewan Ra'ayat, Parkmentary Debates* I, 38, 17 December 1964, col. 4915), his opposition to salary increases for civil servants (ibid., I, 47, 1 March 1965, col. 6262), and his insistence that civil servants understood that 'tak(ing) their orders from different people' (in the event of changes of government) 'is the only independence that they are truly entitled to' (ibid., II, 41, 16 December 1965, col. 5914).

148. Mahathir Mohamad, 'Malaysia Incorporated and Privatization: Its Rationale and Purpose', in Mohd. Nor Abdul Ghani et al. (eds.), *Malaysia Incorporated and Privatization: Towards National Unity*, Petaling Jaya: Pelanduk Publications, 1984, p. 4.

149. Mahathir, 'Nationalization of Foreign Industries', in Mahathir, *The Challenge*, p. 126.

150. Mahathir, 'Malaysia Incorporated and Privatization: Its Rationale and Purpose', p. 4.

151. Mahathir, 'Nationalization of Foreign Industries', pp. 126–7.

152. Mahathir, 'Malaysia Incorporated and Privatization: Its Rationale and Purpose', p. 4.

153. 'Mahathir on Mahathir's Policies', *Malaysian Business*, September 1983, p. 42.

154. Ibid., p. 41.

155. Mahathir, 'Speech at the Top Business Leaders Conference on National Economic Development'.

156. Ibid.

157. 'Mahathir on Mahathir's Policies', p. 41.

158. He said it 'will depend on the circumstances' but added that 'guidelines on privatization have been worked out and will be made public soon' (Mahathir, 'Speech at the Top Business Leaders Conference on National Economic Development').

159. Syarikat Telekom Malaysia Berhad and Tenaga Nasional Berhad, public

companies specially incorporated for the purpose of privatization, took over the Telecoms Department and the National Electricity Board respectively.

160. As in the public flotation of Malaysia Airlines System's shares in 1985, together with a separate placement of 5 per cent of the stock with the Brunei government. This was followed in 1987 by the public issue of Malaysian International Shipping Corporation shares.

161. The Lady Templer Hospital was leased to Rampai Muda in 1984.

162. These were mostly the major highway projects—the North Port Klang bypass, the Jalan Kuching flyover, and the North–South Highway—which were financed by the contractor who retained the right to collect tolls on vehicles using the roads.

163. At the high end of these services was the operation of the container terminal at Port Klang; at the low end were local council garbage collection and disposal as well as car parking operations.

164. The nation's third television station, Sistem Televisyen Malaysia Berhad, popularly called 'TV3', was launched in 1984 to add to and compete with the two existing state-owned stations.

165. See the essays in Mohd. Nor Abdul Ghani et. al., *Malaysia Incorporated and Privatization*, especially Mohd. Ramli Kushairi, 'The View of the National Chamber of Commerce and Industry' (pp. 61–4), Ibrahim Mohamad, 'Implementing the Privatization Policy' (pp. 65–72), and Tan Koon Swan, 'New Opportunities' (pp. 73–82).

166. For example, see Mustafa Johan Abdullah, 'Ucapan Penutup' and 'Dasar Penswastaan Kerajaan Perlu Diulangkaji', in Mustafa Johan Abdullah and Shamsulbahriah Ku Ahmad (eds.), *Penswastaan: Tanggungjawab Sosial atau Untung Kapitalis*, Petaling Jaya: Ikraq, 1987, pp. 71–2 and pp. 73–7 respectively.

167. Jomo, *Growth and Structural Change in the Malaysian Economy*, pp. 215–18.

168. James Craig, 'Privatization in Malaysia: Present Trends and Future Prospects', in Paul Cook and Colin Kirkpatrick (eds.), *Privatization in Less Developed Countries*, Brighton: Harvester Press, 1988, p. 257.

169. 'Mahathir on Mahathir's Policies', p. 41.

170. Mahathir, 'Speech at the American International Group Investment Seminar', Kuala Lumpur, 6 October 1986, *Foreign Affairs Malaysia*, 19, 4 (December 1986): 6–11.

171. Mahathir, 'Malaysia Incorporated and Privatization: Its Rationale and Purpose', p. 3.

172. Ibid., p. 1.

173. Ibid., pp. 1–2.

174. Mahathir, 'Speech at the 9th MAJECA/JAMECA Joint Annual Conference', Kuala Lumpur, 24 April 1986, *Foreign Affairs Malaysia*, 19 2, (June 1986): 11–17. That statement had to be qualified: the state-owned HICOM still spearheaded the industrialization programme.

175. Mahathir, 'Malaysia Incorporated and Privatization: Its Rationale and Purpose', p. 5. Alas, we shall never know if calling 'poverty eradication' the *second*, instead of the usual *first*, prong of the NEP was a typographical error, or a Freudian slip betraying an identification of the NEP with restructuring.

176. Ibid.

177. Khoo Khay Jin, 'The Grand Vision', p. 54.

178. Mahathir, 'Malaysia Incorporated and Privatization: Its Rationale and Purpose', p. 4.

179. Especially since 'the non-*Bumiputeras* too have changed their attitude': 'Whereas before they would invest only in family-owned, now they are prepared to put money in large publicly owned and professionally run corporations' (ibid.).

180. Ibid., p. 5.

181. See the section 'The Populist under Siege I: Financial Scandals, 1984–1986' in Chapter 6.

182. Mahathir, 'Speech at the International Monetary Fund Conference'.

183. 'There is often a tendency to contrast the roles of the public and private sector in the development process; with the private sector cast as rapacious and unconcerned with social goals while public sector enterprises are often held up as inefficient and incompetent. Neither image is correct or deserved' (Mahathir, 'Speech at the ASEAN–West Asian Investment Conference'). Mahathir himself helped to promote the idea of a rapacious Chinese capital in Malaysia with his reference to the 'predatory immigrants' in *The Malay Dilemma* (see Chapter 2).

184. During an interview with the local press on the occasion of his second year in office, Mahathir said: 'As I have said many times, if they make profit, we will tax them 40 per cent. So why should we be envious of the private sector? It is they who bear the risk, their risk, the capital is also their capital, but the government owns a 40 per cent share in it without even placing a cent.' This interview was reproduced as 'Proses Islamisasi Bukan Bererti Memaksa Undang-undang Islam', in Rosnah Majid, *Koleksi Temuramah Khas Tokoh-tokoh*, Kuala Lumpur: Utusan Publications and Distributors, 1985, pp. 248–84.

185. Tan Chee Khoon, *Without Fear or Favour*, pp. 61–2.

186. Business International, *Malaysia to 1980*, p. 8, noted that 'it is known that the Deputy Prime Minister [Mahathir] himself does not agree with some of the [NEP sanctioned] policies, but he has had to go along with them'.

187. Ibid., p. 98, noted: 'The Petroleum Development Act and the Industrial Co-ordination Act have both been amended, though in the case of ICA, by no means to the satisfaction of investors. There has been great bureaucratic resistance to the ICA amendments, despite heavy pressure from Deputy Prime Minister Mahathir, who has privately stated his dissatisfaction with the bureaucratic obstructionism and has even publicly stated that the government is on the verge of revoking the act entirely.'

188. Mahathir, 'Speech at the Annual Luncheon of the Malaysian International Chamber of Commerce and Industry', Kuala Lumpur, 1 June 1981, reprinted as 'The Evils of Protectionism', in Murugesu Pathmanathan and David Lazarus (eds.), *Winds of Change*, Kuala Lumpur: Eastview Productions, 1984, pp. 77–82.

189. Cited in Jesudason, *Ethnicity and the Economy*, p. 141.

190. Mahathir, 'Speech at the 7th Malaysian Economic Convention', Kuala Lumpur, 18 January 1983, reprinted as 'The Malaysian Economy: Policy Adjustment or Structural Transformation', in Murugesu Pathmanathan and David Lazarus (eds.), *Winds of Change*, Kuala Lumpur: Eastview Productions, 1984, pp. 171–9.

191. Yoshihara, *The Rise of Ersatz Capitalism in South-East Asia*, p. 91.

192. Jesudason, *Ethnicity and the Economy*, p. 163.

193. Morgan Guaranty Trust, *World Financial Markets*, March 1986, p. 15, Table 12, cited in Jomo, *Growth and Structural Change in the Malaysian Economy*, p. 29, Table 2.4, and pp. 190–1.

194. The strongest argument along this line was advanced by Jesudason, *Ethnicity and the Economy*, Chapter 6, pp. 166–92.

195. Marican, 'The NEP from a Private Sector Perspective', p. 8.

196. Ibid., pp. 8–9. 'At its most restrictive phase, NEP restructuring policies were interpreted to require foreigners to sell shares of their companies especially those related to natural resources like mineral and land so that their shareholdings would be reduced to 30 per cent, thereby relinquishing majority ownership and control at the same time' (ibid., p. 9).

197. Jomo, *Growth and Structural Change in the Malaysian Economy*, p. 76.

198. 'Malaysia's Lost Generation', *Economist*, 8 August 1987, pp. 17–18.

199. Mahathir, 'Speech at the 10th Malaysian Economic Convention'.

200. Ibid.

201. Ibid.

202. Marican, 'The NEP from a Private Sector Perspective', p. 5.

203. Ibid., p. 6.

204. Ibid.

205. Ibid., p. 9.

206. Ibid., p. 7.

207. Mahathir, 'Speech at the Annual Dinner of Financial Institutions', 25 August 1986.

208. Essentially, the new guidelines tied the permissible levels of foreign equity ownership to a company's level of export of its products (Malaysia, Ministry of Finance, *Economic Report, 1985/1986*, Kuala Lumpur: Government Printers, 1985, p. 154).

209. For a summary of the December 1985 amendments to the ICA, see Jesudason, *Ethnicity and the Economy*, p. 188.

210. 'Where foreign equity is less than 100 per cent, the balance to be taken up by Malaysians should conform to the New Economic Policy rulings. Such rules will be applied without undue rigidity' (Mahathir, 'Speech at the Malaysian Investment Seminar', New York, 30 September 1986, *Foreign Affairs Malaysia*, 19, 3 (September 1986): 66–9).

211. 'Visas will be given automatically during the first ten years of the investment period. Additional expatriate posts will be given when necessary upon request' (ibid.).

212. Ibid.

213. Mahathir, 'Speech at the American International Group Investment Seminar', Kuala Lumpur, 6 October 1986, *Foreign Affairs Malaysia*, 19, 4 (December 1986): 6–11.

214. 'The Prime Minister's declaration on abeyance needs to be put in the proper context. The only feature that has been clearly identified for implementation has been the liberalization of foreign investment. In any case, there had already been

numerous successive relaxations of the terms for foreign investors' (R. S. Milne, 'Malaysia—Beyond the New Economic Policy', *Asian Survey*, XXVI, 12 (December 1986): 1381). Also see Gordon P. Means, *Malaysian Politics: The Second Generation*, Singapore: Oxford University Press, 1991, p. 173.

215. Mahathir, 'Speech at the Annual Dinner of Financial Institutions', 25 August 1986.

216. Mahathir, 'Speech at the EMF Foundation Roundtable on Malaysia'.

217. Ibid.

218. Mahathir, 'Speech at the Annual Dinner of Financial Institutions', 25 August 1986.

219. 'Indeed . . . the whole Government machinery ha(s) been clearly directed to re-examine everything, every policy and every practice, to see whether in fact they have served their purpose for which they were formulated or whether they are still relevant to the changing times' (Mahathir, 'Speech at the 7th Malaysian Economic Convention').

220. Mahathir, 'Speech at the 20th World Management Congress', Kuala Lumpur, 3 November 1985, *Foreign Affairs Malaysia*, 18, 4 (December 1985): 342–6.

221. Mahathir, 'Speech at the Top Business Leaders Conference on National Economic Development'.

5

The Call of Islam

The Quran promised the eternal survival of Islam; this promise does not extend to Muslims.

Mahathir, 'Speech at the 3rd International Seminar on Islamic Thoughts', Kuala Lumpur, 26 July 1984, *Foreign Affairs Malaysia*, 17, 3 (September 1984): 226–31.

'Your Islam, My Islam'

THE contemporary importance of Islam in Malaysian society and politics owes much to what has generally come to be regarded as the 'Islamic resurgence' of the 1970s. This Islamic resurgence was a complex and multifaceted phenomenon.

For one thing, the resurgence, taken in its totality, seemed to have been moved and sustained by a composite of personal, ethnic, and class impulses. The NEP-induced modernization and urbanization subjected the Malay community, and especially its youth, to many tensions and pressures, spatial and psychological dislocations, which a renewed religiosity and dedication to Islam helped to assuage.[1] Islam as 'the religion of the Malays'[2] also surpassed all other cultural distinctions as the *sine qua non* of Malay ethnic identity at a time when public consciousness of the Malays' *bumiputera* status, as distinguished from the non-Malays' 'immigrant' origin, was continually accentuated by the NEP's built-in discrimination in favour of the *bumiputera*.[3] The accelerated stratification of Malay society and the unequal access to economic opportunities during the NEP period were accompanied by a degree of class-based disaffection that appealed to Islamic concepts of social justice.[4]

The Islamic resurgence was also made up of a wide range of ideas and ideological tendencies most visibly linked to *dakwah* or Islamic missionary movements. These could be quite different in their orientation. Two well-known, generally apolitical, missionary movements were the Pertubuhan Kebajikan Islam Malaysia (Perkim, or Malaysian Muslim Welfare Organization) and the Jamaat Tabligh (Tabligh). Perkim was less involved in proselytizing activities and was better known for its welfare work among converts.[5] The Tabligh was an established and active missionary movement that had long been active among the Indian Muslim communities of the large towns but it had begun to extend into the Malay rural areas. The Tabligh stressed a combination of personal piety, religious rituals, and individual members' contributions towards missionary efforts.[6]

By comparison, the Darul Arqam (House of Arqam) was an anti-establishment missionary movement headquartered in its settlement in Sungei Pencala, Selangor. Life in the Sungei Pencala settlement—down to the donning of Arab costumes, using horses for transport, and eschewing 'Western' products—was meant to recapture what the Arqam regarded as the ideal setting of early Islam. This, together with their educational activities and practice of Islamic economics, was the movement's way of giving substance to its fundamental idea that the creation of an Islamic society had to be part of the struggle to create an Islamic state.[7]

The Angkatan Belia Islam Malaysia (ABIM) urged a different route to the Islamic ideal. It was the largest, best known, and most influential of the non-party-based Islamic groupings. ABIM promoted an activist, reformist Islam which argued the 'completeness' of Islam as 'a way of life' and the solution to Malaysia's social problems. ABIM was strongly critical of corruption and social injustice and openly critical of UMNO and the government it led.[8] ABIM's influence spread rapidly between 1977 when it began a tacit alliance with PAS against UMNO and 1981 when it led a broad public campaign against proposed amendments to the Societies Act.[9] ABIM's effectiveness as a dissident Islamic organization was abruptly lost when its president, Anwar Ibrahim, joined UMNO in 1982.[10]

PAS, too, made its own contribution to the Islamic resurgence of the 1970s. PAS had always portrayed itself—and had often been regarded—as the 'Islamic party-in-opposition'. In 1973, under post-May 13 circumstances, PAS relinquished its oppositionist position by joining the Barisan Nasional coalition forged by Tun Razak. But by 1978, PAS had fallen out with UMNO, departed from the Barisan Nasional, and lost control of the Kelantan state government. The influence of a PAS returned to political opposition was steadily revived by a set of younger PAS leaders, among them ex-ABIM leaders, who urged a more radical Islam and were prepared to adopt a more confrontational stance towards UMNO.[11]

The Islamic resurgence of the 1970s quickly gained a reputation for dissidence. The reasons were simple and clear enough. There was ABIM's readiness to criticize and confront UMNO and the government in broad-based public campaigns as well as on university campuses both at home and abroad. There was Arqam's 'counter-culture'. PAS revived an Islamic opposition. And intellectuals coming from divergent backgrounds, such as Kassim Ahmad of Partai Sosialis Rakyat Malaysia (PSRM) and Chandra Muzaffar of Aliran Kesedaran Negara (National Consciousness Movement), increasingly drew from Islam as the fount of social criticism and reformism.

At one end, albeit an extremist end, of the Islamic resurgence, lay a very small number of clandestine Islamic groups. They were shrouded in obscurity and usually gained notoriety through acts of violence. Members of one unnamed group were responsible for several incidents of desecration of Hindu temples.[12] Another group, likewise unnamed, attacked a police station in 1980, spurred by motives that were not altogether clear.[13] One named group had its entire leadership detained under the Internal Security Act in 1980 on suspicion of planning an armed campaign to set up an Islamic state in Malaysia.[14]

During the 1970s, UMNO attempted to meet the challenge of the Islamic resurgence by implementing government-sponsored programmes relating to Islamic instruction, the publication of Islamic literature, the establishment of an Islamic Research Centre and an Islamic Missionary Foundation, and the proclamation of a '*dakwah* month'.[15] UMNO offered these kinds of programmes and activities as evidence of its commitment to Islam. But UMNO's Islamic opponents tended to deride the government-sponsored programmes as largely symbolic and token concessions meant to control and manipulate the Islamic resurgence. No matter how they were perceived, those government-sponsored programmes added scope and variety to the Islamic resurgence.

The Islamic resurgence of the 1970s raised many more issues and spawned many more controversies. Suffice it here to summarize that at a basic level the resurgence seemed to express a gathering sense among Muslims in Malaysia that Islam ought to be accorded a larger role in the personal lives of Muslims and in the conduct of public affairs. Where the former was concerned, there was a feeling that Islam had to be more than a matter of personal conviction or individual observance and that, unlike other religions, it had to be fully practised as *ad-din* or a 'way of life'. As to how Islam was to influence the conduct of public affairs, there was a range of feelings: from mild expectations of a more public face for Islam, to calls for a government that would heed Islamic concepts of justice, to a strong insistence that an Islamic state based on *syariah* (Islamic law) must replace the secular state derived from the Malaysian Constitution. The Islamic resurgence thus meant many things to many Muslims. For that reason it demanded personal, ideological, and political responses from Malays in general and Malay politicians in particular. Those included Mahathir.

In approaching Islam between the 1970s and the 1980s, Mahathir was not concerned with offering startling premises on Islam or making profound interpretations of it. In so far as Islamic doctrines were concerned, he did not seem to seek a systematic engagement with the principal debates sweeping the Islamic world. He preferred not to 'waste … time on semantics and polemics, seeking differences rather than similarities'.[16] He never pretended to be an Islamic theologian, or an expert on Islamic jurisprudence, or an authority on the history of Islam.

He could, however, claim to be a Muslim politician who, in surveying the world of Islam, thought he had important insights into the contemporary Muslim condition, its failings, and what is more, its much-needed correctives. Mahathir rose to meet the challenge of the Islamic resurgence of the 1970s. He had made only scattered and undeveloped references to Islam in *The Malay Dilemma*. In *The Challenge*, he had set out his ideas on Islam at greater length. From then on, he appeared to have worked out a personalized but coherent view of Islam which informed the 'Islamization' policy of his administration during the 1980s. It is therefore plausible to speak of 'Mahathir's Islam'.

'Mahathir's Islam'

The World of Islam

The world of Islam had a glorious past which Mahathir, with other Muslims, could take genuine pride in. What Mahathir found to be especially glorious about Islam's past were Islam's 'success in the material, intellectual, cultural and scientific fields' and the civilizing mission of the early Muslims. The golden age of Islam was, for him, a 'great epoch of creative ability' and 'unprecedented flowering of human genius' which 'manifested itself in remarkable advances in the arts and sciences' and 'laid the foundation of modern knowledge and learning'.[17] Partly on account of the achievements of 'the Muslim scholars [who] were instrumental in generating the intellectual developments which prepared the ground for the European Renaissance', Islam 'gave birth to a civilization which continues to be a source of inspiration to mankind to this day, albeit unconsciously with most people'.[18]

At the 1978 Pemuda and Wanita UMNO General Assembly, Mahathir told his audience, possibly wistfully, that 'other than the glorious age of Islam during the beginning centuries of its blossoming, this is the era when Islam has the opportunity and the power to increase its followers and spread the holy teachings which were sent down by Allah s.w.t.'.[19] This was because 'with God's endowment Muslim countries have become the richest in the world' and they 'control a resource which can force the entire world to bow to them without having to wage war or do anything else': 'By right today Muslims and Muslim countries should make up the most powerful bloc in the world and can be depended upon to defend their religion and their countries, to spread *syiar* and to add to the number of followers of Islam.'[20]

Alas, as Mahathir reminded his audience then and kindred audiences in later years, it was not to be. Looking over the world of Islam in the 1980s, Mahathir discovered little that commended it to a man of his thinking and temperament. He judged it by its level of command of human knowledge, one of his favourite measures of achievement, and found it wanting: 'Where once Muslims led in the field of human knowledge now Muslims are the most backward people in all the arts and sciences.'[21] He judged it by another of his favourite measures, the relative strengths of cultures and peoples, and found it disconcerting: Muslims were 'being battered and bruised'[22] and 'quite unable to do anything by or for ourselves'.[23]

Lest anyone thought that the reassertion of Islam in the politics of Islamic, especially Middle Eastern, countries meant that he had the wrong picture of the Islamic world, Mahathir consistently voiced his concern over the three major 'Islamic'[24] issues of the period. These were the plight of the Palestinians, the Soviet occupation of Afghanistan, and the Iraq–Iran war.[25] The first two showed 'how frequently Muslim countries fall into the hands of non-Muslim enemies because of the weakness or incompetence of Muslims'.[26] The third proved that Muslims were so 'given to plotting and fighting among ourselves'[27] that 'in the Middle East more Muslims are killed by Muslims themselves than are Muslims killed by their non-Muslim enemies'.[28] For Mahathir who had always held that 'a religion lives while its followers live',[29] the consequence of these and other tragedies which had befallen the Islamic world was indeed grave: 'Already millions of Muslims have been lost. Some die of starvation even as other Muslims waste food. Some are killed in fratricidal wars. Some forsake Islam because Muslims forsake them in their hour of need. Some have lost their land to the enemies of Islam.'[30]

Under these far from satisfactory circumstances, Mahathir thought, Muslims could not have much use for 'talk of the past glories of Islam' because it 'really is an admission that Islam is not glorious now'.[31] If historically 'it was Islam which rescued the world from the Dark Ages and then launched it on the course which resulted in the so called modern civilization',[32] presently it was Islam and the Muslims who needed rescuing. Nor would Mahathir be comforted by any claim of an Islamic resurgence in the world. Were there 'a true Islamic resurgence presently', he reflected, 'Muslims would be dominant in the world'.[33] On the contrary, he warned that 'current trends show that Muslim society is heading towards an aimless future'[34] and that 'time may be running out on us as it has run out on a lot of Muslims'.[35]

The Fault, Dear Muslims

This difficult condition of the contemporary world of Islam had arisen, so Mahathir declared, 'not because Islam is in the way'[36] of the progress of Muslims and Muslim countries, for 'Islam wants its followers to be self-sufficient, independent and progressive'.[37] Wherever one looked, it was no doubt possible to espy the hand of the non-Muslim enemies of Islam who were 'intent upon disrupting the development of a genuine, progressive and united Muslim Brotherhood'.[38] But everywhere Mahathir looked, he detected that the fault lay with the Muslims themselves.

Muslims were agreed that they should follow the injunctions of Islam but too many 'were unable to understand ... [and] operationalise the injunctions of Islam with reference to contemporary reality'.[39] They tended to 'remain in a constant state of tension ... living in the past and only superficially coming to terms with the contemporary world'.[40] They seemed unable to find a practicable and satisfactory balance between holding on to a timeless faith and adapting to 'the changes which have occurred in recent decades [which] are fundamentally the biggest changes human society has ever experienced'.[41]

The confusion and tension hinted at a deeper malaise in the contemporary Islamic condition. Muslims were unable to 'ensure that Islam is responsive to the immediate requirements and concerns of modern man' or to 'look for the leading issues of our time'.[42] Certain wrong attitudes were the symptoms of that malaise. For example, 'we are so fond of making interpretations and devising methods which only obstruct and weaken us':[43]

> We say that we Muslims are entitled to our share of the bounties of Allah on this earth, but we interpret the teachings and devise procedures so that the bounties of Allah fall beyond our reach. The beliefs of the Jahiliah period, when sufferings on earth were supposed to confer merit, influence our thinking so that we seem to want to punish ourselves on earth in order to enjoy *akhirat* or the Hereafter.[44]

Alternatively, 'we concentrate on insignificant matters, on forms and appearances while the total welfare and well-being of the Muslims which are enjoined upon us to protect and promote are ignored'.[45] Why else would it be that 'more time and studies and debates are devoted to the subject of covering the head of a woman than the development of a capacity to defend Islam and the Muslims from their enemies'?[46] How else could it be that instead of interpreting the age-old injunction against *riba* as a limited prohibition of usury, Muslims mistake it for a blanket condemnation of all forms of interest, with self-damaging consequences?

> We define *riba* as any interest no matter how small. Even a service charge is considered as *riba* and cannot be taken. While profit sharing may be a method of financing, the fact is that Muslims have more money than there are businesses to finance. And so what happens? Billions of dollars of Muslim money are deposited in non-Muslim countries. Whether we accept the interest or not is irrelevant. The fact is that the money will be lent out by those banks with interest, sometimes to the enemies of Islam. These non-Muslim banks enjoy the interest earned by our money when the interest could very well finance the welfare of Muslims. We are deprived of this help because it is *riba* as a form that we abhor, not *riba* as a cause of misery—the reason why *riba* is forbidden by Islam.[47]

Could anyone then be confident that the world of Islam could successfully prepare itself for 'the two great challenges facing Muslims … to re-create a living civilization of Islam that was once dynamic and thriving, and to make a positive contribution to the predicament facing mankind'?[48]

Perhaps that was a tall order for a world of Islam that Mahathir diagnosed to be languishing 'in acute social, economic and political agony'.[49] And surely he was issuing a daunting challenge since 'in practical and intellectual terms, we Muslims have not been able to conceive of how to reorganize our political, social and economic life to take in the changes that have taken place'.[50] But at an abstract and didactic level, he offered some pointers to guide the way out of the 'agony'. First, 'we cannot re-create the world of the early years of Islam'.[51] Second, 'to retreat and withdraw from modern society is to deny that Islam is for all times'.[52] And, third, 'remember always that Islam, when it came, was a modernizing force that brought greatness to the early followers of the faith and greatness in the field[s] of economy, industry, the sciences, the arts and military prowess'.[53] In other words, be inspired by the past (if you must), keep your eyes on the present (which you must), and see your way through to the future (as we all must).

The elegant phrases and the lofty tone do not long disguise the true orbit of Mahathir's Islam. It circumscribed a religious concern that was oriented towards the mundane, the worldly, and the commonsensical. It was, at heart, a concern with 'the immediate requirements of modern man', 'our share of the bounties of Allah', the 'welfare and well-being of Muslims', 'the development of a capacity to defend Islam and the Muslims', 'greatness in [many] field[s]', et cetera. It would distort but little to paraphrase all that as: keep faith, safeguard the Muslims' worldly fate, and Islam will regain its exalted state. It held a sentiment which may be likened to that of a religiously inspired leader who said before the commencement of a critical battle: 'Trust in God and keep your powder dry.'[54] But, one asks, where in Mahathir's Islam was the 'powder' to come from?

The Power of Learning

That the improvement of the contemporary Islamic condition would not come automatically from 'above' was evident to Mahathir: 'Allah Subhanahu Wataala does not change the fate of a society unless they make an effort to change it for themselves. History offers no support for the idea that simply by the passage of time Muslims will suddenly undergo a miraculous revival.'[55] Possibly Mahathir was referring to those Muslims who searched for a 'miraculous revival' by travelling certain, say 'spiritualist', routes which he would not follow: 'Many Muslims have adopted a strangely false sense of security: reading the Quran will bring them *thawab* or blessings even if they do not understand or practisc it, going out on *tabligh* or propagation will secure a piece of paradise, writing pamphlets and propaganda sheets will win support for Islam.'[56]

But too many Muslims seemed to be unaware of this and seemed not to realize that Islam enjoined its followers to 'seek knowledge as far as China'. Mahathir found it scarcely comprehensible that 'many Muslims have accepted and to some extent have taken pride in their ignorance with unbelievable satisfaction'.[57] He made it sound quite contemptible that 'money for the pursuit of knowledge is a mere pittance compared to the vast sums spent on magnificent edifices'.[58] On the one hand, 'some Muslims profess to look upon scientific and technological advancement and regard them as Western and, therefore, un-Islamic'.[59] On the other hand, there were Muslims who 'believe that belief in God and piety alone will ensure a revival of Islam' and consider that 'what matters most ... is correct *aquidah* or faith' apparently because 'God will ensure the rest',[60] 'forget[ting] that in many regions of the world, Islam and the Muslims have been wiped out because they were not able to resist the onslaught of the intellectual and physical superiority of their adversaries'.[61]

Given 'a world of scientific advances and an accelerated process of change', Mahathir found it 'questionable' whether 'we from the Muslim world have taken our rightful place'.[62] There could be no refuge in devotion to 'religious' knowledge if that meant sacrificing a mastery of 'secular' knowledge, or if, being 'merely rich in religious knowledge and the performance of our *ibadat*, we ... find ourselves quite incapable of defending the faith effectively'.[63] There was no refuge in piety if it entailed 'the kind of negativism which for a long time rejected all kinds of images, still as well as moving, as against Islam'.[64] In this technological age, he argued, Muslims seriously had to choose, or, what comes to the same thing, had no real choice: voluntarily 'accept and apply modern technology to further spread the word of Islam' or 'be forced in the end to modify our views in the face of the realities around us'.[65] He supplied an example that went to the very heart of the Muslim countries:

> If we try to plunge ourselves into a field where we do not have sufficient knowledge, we will be cheated just as Muslim countries were cheated for nearly 100 years into selling oil at very low prices. We can blame those who cheat us but we are not free of the responsibility, demanded by Islam, of pursuing knowledge. Because we have no knowledge we are unable to extract the oil that lies in our earth and we do not know how to refine and market it. Because we have no knowledge, we are unable to have trade and industry which fulfil our needs. The fault lies with us, especially those who obstruct the command of knowledge.[66]

The world of Islam was inseparable from, and behind, the rest of the world: 'only by mastering knowledge and capabilities that are required can we save ourselves'.[67]

To Mahathir's mind, it was pointless for Muslims to be 'still arguing about acquiring knowledge of science and technology'.[68] It was enough that Muslims, once bearers of scientific knowledge, were enjoined by the Quran 'to study the stars and the environment and the animals created by Allah ... a study [which] cannot but be scientific in character even if it is also related to faith'.[69] It was 'fruitless' to be 'still talking about what is secular and what is not'.[70] There was no excuse not to 'get on with education, with the quest for knowledge and with research' because even 'if we don't like the results, as, for example, of Darwin's Theory of the origin of species, discard or disregard them and go on to others which are not against our belief. Do not condemn all knowledge simply because some areas of knowledge are bad or irreligious.'[71]

Again and again, Mahathir demanded learning, knowledge, technology, skills, and capabilities. Equipped with these, Muslims can 'sincerely try to regain the essence of Islam that so inspired the early Muslims so that not only did they manage to spread the teachings far and wide but they brought greatness to Islam in the fields of human endeavour'.[72] But if one is without them? Well, 'the Quran has said that poverty is close to a lack of faith. In other words, our faith weakens when we are poor. If we take poverty to mean not just monetary poverty but to include poverty of skills, of ideas, of education, of intellectual capacity, then we must realize how close we are to losing our faith.'[73] The ideal in Mahathir's opinion was a practical balance between 'religious' and 'secular' learning, a new synthesis of 'Muslim scholarship' and 'modern methods of study and research' which would once more inspire Muslims and non-Muslims alike. He delivered a lengthy exhortation to this end at the Third International Seminar on Islamic Thoughts in 1984:

> Muslim academicians should master all the modern disciplines, understand them completely and achieve an absolute command of all that they have to offer. This is, however, only the first prerequisite. Then they should integrate the new knowledge into the corpus of the Islamic legacy by eliminating, amending, reinterpreting and adapting its components according to the world view of Islam and its values. The exact relevance of Islam to the philosophy of the disciplines should be determined. A new way in which the reformed disciplines can serve the ideals of Islam should be adopted. Finally by their example as pioneers, they should teach the new generation of Muslims and non-Muslims how to follow in their footsteps, push the frontiers of human knowledge even further forward, discover new layers of the patterns created by Allah and establish new paths for making His will and commandments realized in history.[74]

The Quality of Thrift

As every Muslim knows, the oil-rich Muslim countries acquired untold wealth as a result of the OPEC-directed price increases of the 1970s. 'With this wealth,' Mahathir said, 'we could [have] strengthen[ed] the position of the Muslims generally ... free[d] them from oppression ... spread the faith and intensif[ied] the teachings of Islam among the faithful.'[75] But 'the truth is we did none of these'; instead, 'every Islamic country squandered its wealth'—on 'lavish developments', 'the purchase of arms', and 'the support of one Muslim nation ... against another Muslim nation'.[76]

There appeared to have been no attempt to save and properly re-invest the untold billions of petrodollars. 'When we were well-off we did not make preparations for leaner days' so that by the time of the 1980s 'lean days', when the oil prices had fallen sharply and 'our financial resources' were 'no longer unlimited', Muslim countries were faced with the prospect of 'revert[ing] to the stage prior to the oil boom'.[77] So it was with Muslim countries, so it could be with individual Muslims: fortunes can be had and lost by acts of waste and extravagance.

But Islam fundamentally enjoined thrift upon Muslims: 'while Islam enjoins its followers to be thrifty, Islam also forbids acts of waste'.[78] 'A livelihood can be had anywhere' provided 'we do not waste and we use God's endowed capital in a direct and proper manner'.[79] At the level of the individual, Mahathir's idea of thrift could become quite austere. All individuals should consider their personal talents and capabilities as 'God's gift to us', a gift that is sufficiently conferred upon all, even the handicapped and the crippled, because 'in truth, someone who is deficient in the five senses will show an exceptional ability with his non-handicapped limbs. A blind person possesses a sharp hearing and his fingers are extremely sensitive. On the other hand, a dumb person can see clearly. God confers this ability as a balance to the natural deficiency.'[80]

Thrift meant a coming to terms with and a proper employment of 'God's gift'. In the mid-1980s, when truly lean days were upon the Malaysian economy, Mahathir elevated thrift from being a matter of necessity to the status of an all-embracing quality which he honoured in Islamic terms: 'We should be thrifty for all time with all that is with us. We should be thrifty with time. We should be thrifty with our worldly possessions, with our health, with our Islamic comradeship, with our society's peace—with all prosperity that in truth is God's gift to us.'[81] When the prices of the country's primary commodities, including oil, fell sharply, when many debt-ridden

Malay (Muslim) businesses were fast becoming insolvent, and when there was speculation about Malaysia's ability to repay its international loans, Mahathir extolled thrift as the way out of economic and financial difficulties:

> By saving we can save ourselves from various pressures such as debts which cannot be repaid, the loss of property because of excess expenditure over income and others ... by being thrifty we as Muslims who cannot go back on our word will be able to pay back all our debts and maybe gather money to be invested or as capital for business. With wise investment we not only obtain profit but create job opportunities for the unemployed and enhance trading and commercial activities within our society, all of which will lighten the effects of economic recession on members of the society, including ourselves as Muslims.[82]

If the squandering of wealth by 'every Muslim country' was one problem, there was the accompanying problem of their inability to manage their wealth by methods which were acceptable and beneficial to Muslims. When oil prices and oil revenues escalated, 'the banking business became the largest business in the world of Islam' with 'non-Muslim banks [growing] like mushrooms in Muslim countries',[83] tapping the petrodollar deposits and earning untold amounts of interest. Or else, 'much of the wealth [was] invested in countries which have no friendly intention towards the Muslims or to Islam'.[84]

The 'Western financial system' could take advantage of the situation largely because the world of Islam had no 'Islamic' answer to the flood of money that it experienced. The 'international financial system no longer uses gold and silver, but the currency notes and cheques are not from the Islamic system'.[85] The Western system 'of banks, money exchanges, promissory notes, commercial letters of credit, investment, export-import, insurance and others' so controlled the whole world that 'we are unable not to use it'.[86]

Mahathir had no illusion that the world of Islam could quickly replace the Western financial system with its own[87] but he had no doubt that the wealth of Muslim nations, like 'God's gift' to individuals, had to be husbanded by thrift and safeguarded by proper management.

The Dignity of Work

Mahathir's faith in the power of learning and the quality of thrift was matched by an unbounded belief in the dignity of work. To his mind, lax attitudes towards work were closely allied to wrong attitudes towards learning. 'Muslims all over have been taught that indolence is a virtue' and 'because of this attitude our workers cannot even be relied upon by Muslims and few of our businesses are able to compete with others. Our workers are not prepared to work in the sun while non-Muslims coming from cold places endure the heat in doing their work.'[88]

'And as we stay away from work our skills get less and less'; consequently, Muslim countries suffered from an 'unnecessary weakness, the weakness to construct and develop our own countries' and were now so dependent on the exertions and the skills of non-Muslims that 'between our dependence on arms from other countries and [dependence] on non-Muslim workers and enterprises, our independence, despite the oil wealth, is almost completely eroded'.[89] 'It is incumbent upon us to extricate ourselves from this stranglehold,' he told his audience at the Third Islamic Summit Conference in Taif, Saudi Arabia, 1981, where he made one of his most impassioned speeches on the virtue of work. He added:

> This is not really difficult. All that is needed is for us to realize and admit our mistakes, and to motivate our workers and entrepreneurs. Work is an honourable thing. Nowhere in Islam is there an injunction against work, against working hard. Indeed we are enjoined to go and seek Allah's bounty when we have finished the *Sallat* [compulsory prayers]. There is a share of the wealth of this world for us. All that is needed is to work. Skills will come later—for Allah has caused skills to increase with practice.[90]

On another occasion, Mahathir was insistent that Muslim youth, hitherto 'unwilling and unproductive', 'should train and discipline themselves so that they can take the place of the civil mercenaries upon whom the Muslim countries have to depend now'.[91] He was especially clear that there was no call for Muslim youth to 'be carried away by visions of fame and power through youth-created upheavals' when 'what the Muslim world really needs is just skill and dedication to work'.[92]

As such, 'the need to work and work hard', since 'it is basic to everything we do', should be a 'relatively uncontroversial subject', only:

Let us apply ourselves to the task of Islamic motivation, so that our people can be depended on by us not merely to work but to work as hard or harder than others. Let us do away with false interpretations which depict work as unworthy of Muslims or that business is materialistic. It is much more materialistic to want wealth as we obviously do now without working for it.[93]

In the name of work, Mahathir extolled Islam: 'It was the diligence of the early Muslims and their willingness to face the hardship of migration that saved and spread Islam. Hard work is not the result of the ethical value[s] of the materialist world but is in fact the character of Islam and the Muslims.'[94] In the name of Islam, Mahathir cast work as an imperative: 'Our people must be encouraged to work *under every condition, as a duty* to Islam and the *Ummah, as a battle* to liberate Islam from dependence on the skills and the manipulation of others.'[95]

In Praise of Piety

It is legitimate to ask if Mahathir had not, consciously or otherwise, 'secularized' Islam in the very process of urging the correct—which some would read as 'selected'—injunctions upon the Muslims. Was it not beginning to seem as if one learnt in order to progress, one saved for prosperity, and one worked for one's share of Allah's bounty and ... well, to defend, liberate, and spread Islam? Despite the religious rhetoric, had Mahathir not abstracted learning and thrift and work—all 'honourable things'—out of the Islamic tradition, leaving little room for piety itself? No, but piety could be redefined.

Work was not only honourable. It was a many-splendoured thing. At his most rhetorical, Mahathir lauded work for its 'character of Islam' just as he had eulogized work as part of his 'Look East' policy. At his most determined, he conceived of work as an imperative from which no one was exempt, not even the crippled and the handicapped. He issued a stirring—even if he made it sound almost pitiless[96]—call to the handicapped and the crippled not to resign themselves abjectly to their disadvantages: 'Let us not use eyes that are blind as capital to beg for alms while our hands, our ears and our brain are still good and can be used to seek a livelihood in a legitimate way.'[97] *The Malay Dilemma* has a passage which links 'Malay fatalism' to work in a rather curious way. 'The effect of [the] resignation to fate', wrote Mahathir, 'is to relegate the struggle for worldly goods to a low priority. Pride in working to one's utmost ability and capacity is not common. Nor is there any great admiration for the man who refuses to give up working because of a handicap or because of old age.'[98]

Instead, he thought, the Malays held that 'the correct and acceptable attitude is one of sad recognition of the limitations of one's capacity and a willingness to submit to those limits'.[99] Mahathir's linking of a 'resignation to fate' and work is instructive because it demonstrates that he had thought of work as a counter-force against 'Malay fatalism' more than a decade before he offered work as the safeguard against a repetition of the Malays' historical decline.[100]

What then could one possibly want to say to 'people who are not handicapped', that is, those who are 'wealthy with the capability of every limb'?[101] All one can prescribe is work, hard work, making full use of what one has been endowed with, taking 'pride in working to one's utmost ability and capacity', thrift and discipline—and by these all things are possible: 'The son of a farmer today, a minister tomorrow, an office boy two or three decades ago, a millionaire now, the child of a cripple today, an *imam ulung* [chief imam] tomorrow, and a person of dignity who continuously fortifies his discipline may eventually become a leader.'[102]

Yes, work makes the man! But what if we remain poor? Mahathir's advice, and quite a telling piece of advice, was to search within us and ask 'if we have fully employed the gifts which have been confered by God as capital for us' or whether we have squandered that 'capital' which, as we have seen, was amply provided even to the blind, the dumb, and the crippled.[103] Mahathir maintained that finally 'it is ourselves who should be questioned whether we are poor or rich'.[104] He already knew his answer: if poverty befalls us, 'we cannot be leery because God has already conferred adequate capital on each of us'.[105] Success becomes piety itself.

Islamization

In Pursuance of Policy

Politically, Mahathir's 'Islamization' policy was a bold initiative, probably as bold as any that seeks to 'ride a tiger' under certain constraints. The first constraint was that the Muslim community owed varying degrees of allegiance to the wide range of organizations and movements that made up the Islamic resurgence in Malaysia. PAS was traditionally the 'party of Islam' while UMNO was not usually considered first among equals in matters of Islam. To the extent that an Islamization policy met a growing demand for 'more Islam' in the conduct of public affairs, it would find its share of supporters among the Muslims in Malaysia. But to the extent that it fell short of the radical demands of some Muslim dissidents, it would also have its share of detractors. Second, Islam was, constitutionally, the official religion of Malaysia, but half of the country's population was made up of non-Muslims. They (and many Muslims, besides) would be naturally wary lest an overt Islamization programme heralded the end of the secular state in Malaysia. Third, the government accorded an important economic role to foreign investors who were practically all from non-Muslim countries. Foreign investors who were already operating in Malaysia as well as those who were being courted by the country would wonder if Mahathir's Islamization meant the kind of Islamic 'fundamentalism' the Western world associated with the 1978 revolution in Iran.[106]

It is almost unnecessary to say that Mahathir took these and other considerations seriously. He addressed them variously when he launched his major Islamization projects. Perhaps his most complete reply to such questions and anxieties came from the content, quality, and tenor of the Islamization policy itself. A politician and his religion are not easily parted. When Tunku Abdul Rahman gave up his premiership, he carried what many considered to be his endearing ability to work with non-Malays into Perkim, an Islamic organization devoted to the welfare of new, and by definition non-Malay, converts to Islam in Malaysia. When Prime Minister Mahathir Mohamad enacted his Islamization policy, he gave institutional expression to his enduring belief in the power of learning, the quality of thrift, and, above all, the dignity of work.

The International Islamic University

On 7 March 1982, Mahathir announced his government's intention to establish an 'Islamic university' in Malaysia the following year. It would have been strange if Mahathir did not expect to derive political benefit from the timing of this important announcement—just one month before the April general election.[107] The university proposal was announced with a hint of endorsement by the world of Islam: Mahathir announced it upon arriving home after a ten-day visit to the Gulf States and Jeddah. It was a major and tangible step to boost UMNO's Islamic credentials *vis-à-vis* PAS.[108] It might also have been considered to be a way of strengthening Mahathir's personal credentials as an emerging statesman of the Islamic world.[109]

Mahathir supplied another political angle to the Islamic university. He thought that Muslim students studying in the West could be divided into three groups. One group comprised those 'culture shocked' into completely accepting things Western. A second group was made up of those 'culture shocked' into completely rejecting the West. Only a third group consisted of those who were able to 'retain a balance of values, accepting what was good from the West but continuing to hold firmly to Islamic values'—and they were 'only a small number'.[110] The two 'culture shocked' groups were of limited value since they 'could no longer comprehend the situation and the progress' in their countries and, 'moreover, there were those who felt that everything that took place or was implemented ... was totally wrong'.[111] In an Islamic context, it was politic to stress an adverse Western influence. In the Malaysian context, the influence of radical Islamic currents on Malay students studying in the West as well as the Middle East was a greater worry.[112] Hence, Mahathir concluded, it was necessary to have 'an international Islamic university in a Muslim country to provide facilities for learning and the pursuit of knowledge to students from Muslim countries'.[113]

The Islamic university, later bearing 'international' in its name, was described as being 'universal' in concept and character.[114] There seemed to be several dimensions to its 'universality'. The university would be located in and sponsored by Malaysia but 'not owned by the country but by the Islamic world'. The Organization of the Islamic Conference (OIC) later agreed to co-sponsor the university.[115] The academic staff and the student body would recruit and admit not only Muslims but also non-Muslims if the latter 'accept this [universal] concept and use Islamic philosophy as a basis [for learning]'.[116] The university would be free from 'political influence or factionalist sentiment', 'sectarian tendencies in Islam', and 'international political chess'.[117] It differed from the other universities in Malaysia in that it 'would not be subject to the local University Act or the National Education Policy'.[118] For example, English and Arabic would be the languages of instruction and not Bahasa Malaysia which would be used for administrative purposes.[119] And it was to be universal as regards to 'time and place' for its concept was 'based on the universities in the Islamic world during its age of glory, particularly those which were found in Spain and in the country now called Iraq'.[120] As Mahathir clarified: 'Before, these universities were called Islamic universities. In reality they were all centres of higher learning located in Muslim countries. The education was definitely based on religion, but other subjects were taught side by side. So the International Islamic University which we sponsor is a new concept from an old idea.'[121]

Fourteen months after Mahathir's announcement, on 11 May 1983, the university, named the International Islamic University (IIU) or Universiti Islam Antarabangsa (UIA), was officially registered. On 18 July 1983, the IIU opened at a temporary campus in Petaling Jaya, Selangor. It offered courses leading to degrees in law, economics, and business studies.[122] In due course, the IIU intended to set up faculties of engineering, basic sciences, and medicine. It has been suggested that the IIU's establishment had brought into place an institution of learning 'that accepts Revelation and reason as sources of knowledge'.[123] A keystone in the edifice of Mahathir's Islam was in place.

Bank Islam Malaysia Berhad

On 6 July 1982, Mahathir announced that the government would set up an 'Islamic bank'.[124] The nature of the Islamic bank, the first to be established in Malaysia, and its operations were progressively clarified in the ensuing months.[125] The Islamic bank expected to operate by two fundamental principles which would distinguish it from existing banks in the country. First, the Islamic bank would not offer any interest on deposits that it received. Instead, it would share the profits earned from investing the deposits with the bank's customers. For investment accounts, that is, accounts maintained by depositors who wish to have their deposits reinvested by the bank, the bank-to-customer profit-sharing ratio was set at 7 : 3.[126] Nor would the bank charge interest on credit that it extended. Depending on the type of credit facility it extended, it would either share in the profits made by the borrower or levy a 'cost of funds' on the borrower. This was demonstrated by the provisions of the four main types of credit facilities offered by the bank: equity financing, leasing, sale and purchase, and trade financing. In equity financing the bank would extend financing by taking up an appropriate share in a client's project. In leasing, the bank would incorporate a profit margin into the hire-purchase agreement it contracted with its client. For sale and purchase, the bank would acquire a required product and resell it to its client at a price that included a cost of funds. Under trade financing would come the provision of facilities such as letters of credit for importers.[127] Other than that, since 'Islam makes it sinful to receive interest' but 'does not prohibit profit' or 'disallow fees and commissions', the bank would be 'as profit-orientated as any other commercial bank in the country'.[128]

Second, the bank would 'only sanction *halal* [non-prohibited] projects' and 'businesses [which did] not clash with Islamic beliefs',[129] but it was not otherwise barred from conducting business with non-Muslims. Or, as Mahathir later emphasized, 'the Islam-ness of Bank Islam is based on the method of its management and not because Muslims are its owners, customers or managers'.[130]

At the launching ceremony of Bank Islam Malaysia Berhad on 1 July 1983, Mahathir spelt out the significance of this first Islamic bank in Malaysia. 'The establishment of Bank Islam in Malaysia [was] not a manifestation of the arrogance of the Muslims'[131] and did not portend any restriction on the existing 'non-Islamic' banks, much less their end. Bank Islam's establishment was not 'a symbolic effort to display the Islam-ness of this country' but 'an effort to convince that the assimilation of Islamic teachings by the economy of this country would not bring about any disaster'.[132]

Mahathir returned to the issue of the investment of Muslim funds in non-Muslim countries or non-Muslim banks without benefit to Muslims themselves. If this situation persisted, it was because 'we ourselves choose to restrict the development of the economies of Muslim countries', and 'we choose this damaging path because, first, the religious interpreters make narrow interpretations and, second, they do not give an alternative which can replace the Western system which they charge does not meet the requirements of Islam'.[133] On the other hand, 'if we have no answer to the questions and problems of the modern world, if we only say that this is prohibited and that is prohibited, then sooner or later the faith in Islam will be lost, especially the belief that Islam is for all ages and not for the age of the Prophet alone'.[134] Unlike the 'religious interpreters' who made 'narrow interpretations' but could 'offer no alternative to the Western system'—and to refute 'the idea that Islam is not compatible with progress'—Mahathir declared:

> Bank Islam which we establish today is our alternative: a way of complying with the laws of Islam in the management of money and a modern economy. There was no bank such as this in the time of the Prophet or the time of the caliphs which followed. But not having an Islamic bank during those times does not mean there cannot be one in this time.[135]

Bank Islam Malaysia Berhad was incorporated with an authorized capital of RM500 million and a paid-up capital of RM100 million. Its principal shareholders were the federal government, the State Islamic Religious Councils, Lembaga Urusan dan Tabung Haji (Muslim Pilgrim Saving and Management Authority), Islamic foundations and bodies, and Perkim.[136] Bank Islam formally opened for banking business on 1 July 1983. For Mahathir, there was now established an institution which obeyed age-old Islamic laws and answered the banking requirements of the modern era—a practical instrument for mobilizing Muslim funds and a symbol of thrift, savings, and wealth. Thus was a second keystone of Mahathir's Islam laid in place.

The Assimilation of Islamic Values

Unlike the International Islamic University and Bank Islam, the third major component of Mahathir's Islamization policy, *penyerapan nilai-nilai Islam* (or the 'assimilation of Islamic values') was an altogether deeper, not to say more amorphous, type of Islamic 'project'. Mahathir had previously written that 'there is no reason why the Islamic faith, properly interpreted, cannot achieve spiritual well-being as well as material success for the Malays'.[137] There was 'no reason', that is, if they learnt, saved, and worked—and assimilated the proper kinds of Islamic values. What values were these and how were they to be assimilated?

Between 1982 and 1987, Mahathir always found space in his

speeches to the UMNO General Assembly to refer to the need for UMNO, the Malays, and Muslims to assimilate worthy Islamic values. Mahathir never quite drew up an exhaustive list of Islamic values that merited assimilation but he came closest to doing so at the 1984 UMNO General Assembly when he called for 'putting in practice Islamic values like trust, discipline, loyalty, industriousness, and persistence, close bonds between Muslims, boldness arising from honesty, tolerance and consideration, justice, repentance and gratefulness and other honoured values'.[138] Mahathir frequently said that for the Muslims these values were necessary to assist them in 'seeking wealth in a moral and legal way'[139] or, ultimately, to 'obtain prosperity in this world and in the hereafter'.[140]

Mahathir conceded that these values were not 'easy to practise or portray'.[141] He decided that assimilation would begin at home—in his own administration, in the civil service. In that sense, although his early reformist drive was not explicitly couched in an Islamic idiom—not named 'Islamization'—it gave a number of indications of the kinds of 'Islamic values' Mahathir wanted assimilated primarily by the civil servants. Among those were '*bersih, cekap, dan amanah*' ('clean, efficient, and trustworthy'), the first important slogan of the Mahathir administration. It connoted an administration that would dedicate itself to being free of corruption, high in efficiency, and worthy of the public trust. The executive and the civil service were required, for example, to declare their assets and business involvement. There were companion campaigns and slogans such as '*kepimpinan melalui teladan*' ('leadership by example') which exhorted the civil service to take the initiative, not wait to be directed, or, interpreted more broadly, to become more self-reliant. The campaign to shut down state-owned companies which had become losing business concerns indicated not just a concern with profit and loss, but more with thrift and financial prudence.

Likewise several impositions were made on the civil service which sought to render it more accountable and more productive. All civil servants had to wear name tags to discourage anonymity, especially among those who had to service the public regularly. The punch-card system was introduced to reduce tardiness and absenteeism among civil servants. Drawing up a job manual for every civil service post was made mandatory to improve the civil servant's awareness of his or her duties and performance.

Mahathir was guarded when he spoke of the assimilation of Islamic values. He took care not to seem too hasty or pushy, nor to offend the non-Muslim half of the population, usually suggesting that the assimilation should begin with the administration and become gradually 'accepted by every stratum of the plural society of this country'.[142] Mahathir often pointed out the 'universalism' of those Islamic values he held up for assimilation: 'The Islamic values which we assimilate also represent universal values which are easily understood by all the people.'[143] The *Mid-Term Review of the Fourth Malaysia Plan, 1981–1985* explicitly suggested that 'the universality of Islamic values and the message of moderation it contains' did not conflict with 'the value system of the other faiths' and the 'sharing of these common values will further strengthen the bonds among Malaysians'.[144] One does best to think of it as half-hope and half-assurance.

The values listed in the *Mid-Term Review of the Fourth Malaysia Plan* were exactly the kinds of values Mahathir thought were needed to raise productivity at home, increase competitiveness abroad, and ensure political stability always. Among them were 'better discipline, more self-reliance and striving for excellence'[145] which, together with 'thriftiness'[146] and 'a more rational and scientific approach in overcoming problems'[147] were 'values which are progressive and consistent with the needs of a modernizing and industrializing plural society'.[148] That it was a 'plural society' that was being administered made it necessary to assimilate 'greater tolerance, moderation and greater understanding of the sensitivities of various ethnic groups' and specifically to reject 'extremism in any form', 'chauvinism', and 'excessive demand'[149]—'values consistent with the need to maintain stability'.[150] In the end, there was a surfeit of values!

The Religiosity of the Self-made Man

Among Mahathir's many cherished values, one stood above all others: 'Hard work should be a pervasive value among all Malaysians, irrespective of their status, social background and place in the economic life of the nation.'[151]

When Mahathir came to power, he tirelessly exhorted the Malaysian people to work hard, to 'Look East' at the Japanese, the Koreans, and the Taiwanese and emulate their dedication to hard work. No one has said it but it was surely a dreadful exhortation because it implied that Mahathir thought that most Malaysians were lazy.

On the eve of becoming UMNO President, as we have seen, he taught a version of history that attributed the downfall of the Malays to their ancestors' 'disinclination to work'. Upon becoming Prime Minister, he imposed the punch card on civil servants, many of whom he believed were seldom at their posts. He introduced the job manual because he suspected that just as many did not know their work. One hundred days into office, he told the domestic newspaper editors that his mission was to make Malaysia more productive so that foreigners would no longer look down upon Malaysians as a lazy people. At an international symposium in Japan in 1983, he said that Malaysia had all the basic ingredients to become an industrialized country except for a 'work ethic' which was not found at home.

The truth was Mahathir thought a lot more people than just Malaysians were lazy. To him, the decline of the Western, capitalist economies was a sure sign of the laziness of the Westerners, the workers especially. Nor did he think that the world of Islam was any better shielded from the debilitating affliction of indolence. One can go back to *The Malay Dilemma*, or to *The Challenge*, to Mahathir's numerous speeches, or, better still, to his very candid interviews as Prime Minister, and find that Mahathir's comments on hard work, or the lack of it, were good for all seasons.

For example, in the very flush of electoral victory in 1982, he lamented to an *Asiaweek* interviewer: 'We are not workaholics. We think we should be ... we should get away from the old value system for the new value system where you have to work very hard.'[152]

At the other extreme, in the very midst of a fierce battle for political survival in 1988, when S. Jayasankaran of *Malaysian Business* commented on the 'toning down' of his 'Look East' policy, Mahathir replied, somewhat wearily one suspects, that it was all about 'work ethics'—the work ethics of the Japanese, the Koreans, and the Taiwanese who worked 'with all their heart and soul'.[153]

One can, therefore, view the world with Mahathir's eyes and see that it can be divided—between the workaholic and the idle, between races or ethnic groups which progress on the basis of hard work and those which stagnate out of an aversion to hard work, and between nations which prosper because of a strong work ethic and those which flounder by its absence. Such a view of the world would have been considerably conditioned by Mahathir's own multifaceted identity—he being a Malay in the plural society of Malaysia, a Muslim in a Western-dominated world, and an Asian in a rising region of the globe. What these facets have in common are a historical leitmotif of humiliation, which has always affected Mahathir badly, and, correspondingly, an impulse towards achieving parity with the non-Malays, with the Westerners, and with the world, which has ever been Mahathir's goal in life. To achieve that goal, only a work ethic was wanting, only Islamic values needed assimilating. To meet the time, the mood, and the Islamic resurgence, workaholism, the credo of the Prime Minister, gave way to a broader ethic which, increasingly couched in an Islamic idiom, seemed only to reveal the religiosity of the man. But exactly what kind of a man was he?

It is said that behind every great man stands a woman. More likely, behind every pious man stands a pious mother. The short official profile of Mahathir as well as Adshead's longer biography tell us that it was at his mother's knee that Mahathir imbibed the religiosity and the Islamic precepts which 'remain a staunch foundation of his character'.[154] There is no reason to disbelieve or belittle it.

Yet it does seem that the real hero in our hero's story is his father. From available accounts, Mahathir's father, Mohamad Iskandar, was a caring but strict father who imposed his authority and order over home and hearth. Mahathir's brief recollections of his father turn out to be enduring memories of a firm hand which exercised a strong paternal influence over his children and other children who came under his charge.[155] The influence was aptly enough most strongly felt when it came to schooling and schoolwork—which in practice meant drilling into his charges the personal and work habits meant to last a lifetime.[156]

In professional terms, *Master* Mohamad Iskander, as he was called with the respect due to the teacher of an English-medium school, would have presented a familiar sight to the many generations of Malayan students who passed out of the élite English-medium schools of colonial Malaya. They would have no trouble recognizing in someone like Master Mohamad Iskandar a quasi-legendary figure of colonial yore—the capable, indefatigable, and stern schoolmaster who imparted knowledge, spread a mock disciplinary terror, and earned a grudging affection. In schooling terms, the Malayan schoolmaster was usually remembered for imposing a demanding but balanced regime of work and play and for enforcing 'English' authority and discipline.[157]

What is seldom remembered is that these schoolmasters, well known, sometimes even well loved by those whose minds they ruled over for several years, arguably the most genuinely colonial of the colonial social products,[158] were instrumental in implanting a world-view in the classrooms and on the playing fields of the English-medium schools of colonial Malaya. That that world-view was not inimical to the interests of the British Empire was obvious but in one sense beside the point. More to the point, these schoolmasters nurtured a world-view—and, at their best, performed this nurture as a labour of love—because, as much as anything else, that world-view corresponded to the circumstances and demands of their own social position as the prototypes of a new class of colonial Malaya.

By the time of the Japanese invasion of Malaya, these non-English schoolmasters, of Malay, Chinese, Indian, and Eurasian background,[159] trained in Malaya but modelled after their English counterparts, were already found in burgeoning numbers in the Penang Free School, Victoria Institution, St. Xavier's Institution, Anderson High School, the Malay College Kuala Kangsar, and wherever else in urban colonial Malaya the leading government and missionary schools were located. More precisely, they formed a distinct social type—the self-made man of a newly emerging urban *petite bourgeoisie.*

Theirs was the urban *petit bourgeois* version of the colonial success story, far more attainable if rather less spectacular than the rags-to-riches story of the proverbial 'coolie turned tycoon'. Today, when the economic demands, the occupational structure, and the patterns of social mobility of a post-colonial society have combined to reduce the earnings, status, and prestige of teachers below those of many other newer professionals—and just about obliterated an earlier sense of teaching as a calling[160]—it is easy to forget that the colonial schoolmaster found in being a schoolmaster a respectable niche in the urban colonial society.[161] The self-made schoolmaster—not being an English colonial, a Malay aristocrat, or a Chinese comprador—

discovered in an English education the necessary, and accessible, means of social advancement.

In return, these schoolmasters taught and many of them taught well. Generations of Malayan and Malaysian professionals and administrators, including many of the most prominent names in Malayan society, came under their charge, *in loco parentis*, and owed them no small debt. Equally, they superintended the birth of a new class of clerks, teachers, professionals, and administrators—their own class—and spread its ethos. In addition to their teaching duties, they would have conceived of their role, *vis-à-vis* their students, as proffering worthy values, inculcating good personal habits, imposing an essential work discipline, and instilling a sense of moral responsibility. For these reasons (possibly for others, too), that never charitable taunt—'those who can, do; those who can't, teach'[162]—would have been inappropriate by the high standards of collective achievement and individual commitment shown by these Malayan schoolmasters. It would have been cruelly unappreciative of their historical role.

Master Mohamad Iskandar belonged socially to this emerging class of the urban *petite bourgeoisie*. He was an accomplished man, already a senior schoolmaster in the Penang Free School when he was specially 'invited over by the Government of Kedah to commence the task of establishing the Government English School',[163] the first English-medium school in Kedah. He was committed to learning, having himself had to overcome obstacles to his own English education, and he went from house to house in Alor Star trying to recruit Malay children for his English school.[164] The Government English School, which he set up in 1908, went on to become Kedah's leading secondary school but under its new name of Sultan Abdul Hamid College. At a time when the headmasters of the English schools in Malaya were almost invariably English or European, Master Mohamad Iskandar became the first headmaster of the Government English School.[165] His individual ability, abetted by a successful English schooling in the Penang Free School and a Normal Class teaching qualification, had elevated him out of the confines of the social station to which men of his ethnicity and class would typically have been restricted.

In short, Master Mohamad Iskandar was self-made. One can visualize him to be exactly the type of man who made no distinction in school between rich and poor, royal and commoner students.[166] One can picture him to be just the type of father who ran his 'very disciplined home ... like a classroom'.[167] It is from such a disciplined and disciplining father that Mahathir acquired the dominant personal values which overshadowed most other considerations in his mature life: diligence, thrift, striving, perseverance, self-improvement, self-reliance, and attainment—collectively, the moral equipment of a regulated life, the ethos of self-made men.[168]

1. Chandra Muzaffar, *Islamic Resurgence in Malaysia*, Petaling Jaya: Penerbit Fajar Bakti, 1987, pp. 14–16. Also see Zainah Anwar, *Islamic Revivalism in Malaysia: Dakwah among the Students*, Petaling Jaya: Pelanduk Publications, 1987.

2. This phrase is used in awareness of the 'universalism' of Islam which is opposed to Islam being turned into the province of a particular ethnic group or nationality. However, and despite the presence of non-Malay Muslims, 'it is perhaps unavoidable that in a situation where all Malays are Muslims, Islam will be perceived as a Malay religion by both Malays and non-Malays' (Aliran, *The Universalism of Islam*, Penang, 1979, p. 1).

3. Islam as the badge of Malayness was far less likely to be rendered 'Malaysian' than the *Malay* language which state policy had turned into Bahasa *Malaysia*. See Chandra, *Islamic Resurgence in Malaysia*, pp. 24–6.

4. 'Given the atmosphere of Islamic revivalism, there are thus many reasons for the Malay "have nots", whether they are unemployed or underemployed graduates, or new entrepreneurs squeezed out of the economic pie because of low growth, or poor working class Malays, to turn to Islam in their quest for justice and to react against an economic policy that had benefited the secular Malay elites more' (Zainah, *Islamic Revivalism in Malaysia*, p. 94).

5. John Funston, 'The Politics of Islamic Reassertion: Malaysia', in Mohammed Ayoob (ed.), *The Politics of Islamic Reassertion*, New York: St. Martin's Press, 1981, pp. 165–89.

6. For a brief note on the Jamaat Tabligh, see Jomo K. S. and Ahmad Shabery Cheek, 'The Politics of Malaysia's Islamic Resurgence', *Third World Quarterly*, 10, 2 (April 1988): 846. The Tabligh Movement has been called 'Utopian' because of 'its obsession with personal piety as the decisive factor' ('in achieving social change') (Chandra, *Islamic Resurgence in Malaysia*, p. 46).

7. Jomo and Ahmad, 'The Politics of Malaysia's Islamic Resurgence', pp. 847–8. From Chandra, *Islamic Resurgence in Malaysia*, pp. 46–7, we note: 'Arqam is undoubtedly more traditional [than the Tabligh] in a sense, for it regards the restoration of the Meccan and Medinian social atmosphere associated with the Prophet Muhammad as a crucial pre-condition for the establishment of an Islamic society in today's world. Thus, its members eat Arab-style, Arqam males wear Arab-style green robes and turbans, and Arqam females are in purdah most of the time.

Indeed young male members are even encouraged to ride horses as the earliest followers of the Prophet used to in seventh-century Arabia.'

8. Chandra, *Islamic Resurgence in Malaysia*, pp. 48–51; Jomo and Ahmad, 'The Politics of Malaysia's Islamic Resurgence', pp. 845–6. See Funston, 'The Politics of Islamic Reassertion: Malaysia', pp. 174–8, for a discussion of ABIM's 'ideology'.

9. Jomo and Ahmad, 'The Politics of Malaysia's Islamic Resurgence', pp. 849–51, 853–5, 856–60.

10. 'His [Anwar's] resignation [as ABIM's President] created some confusion and a great deal of depression within ABIM. The movement lost its momentum; lethargy set in; there was no sense of direction' (Chandra, *Islamic Resurgence in Malaysia*, p. 51).

11. Ibid. It has been said of the ABIM–PAS relationship that 'many viewed ABIM as a transitional non-political Islamic organization for individuals not yet ready for further political involvement with PAS, while PAS provided the Islamic dissidents with a more explicitly political and electoral platform' (Jomo and Ahmad, 'The Politics of Malaysia's Islamic Resurgence', p. 850).

12. K. Das, 'Extremism Rears Its Head', *Far Eastern Economic Review*, 1 September 1978, pp. 12–13, and K. Das, 'The Chosen Ones Who Went Amok', *Far Eastern Economic Review*, 24 October 1980, pp. 10–11.

13. Das, 'The Chosen Ones Who Went Amok', pp. 10–11.

14. The police revealed that this group was called Pertubuhan Angkatan Sabilullah. It was thought that 'some government party officials have tried to exploit the similarity' in acronym between this group and the Parti Islam SeMalaysia (K. Das, 'From Killers to Crackpots', *Far Eastern Economic Review*, 3 March 1983, p. 22). The legitimate PAS denied any link to the clandestine 'PAS'.

15. For a summary of the government's Islamic activities, see Funston, 'The Politics of Islamic Reassertion: Malaysia', p. 180.

16. Mahathir, 'Speech at the International Islamic Symposium', Kuala Lumpur, 5 March 1986, *Foreign Affairs Malaysia*, 19, 1 (March 1986): 15–20. This speech was delivered just days after Musa Hitam's resignation as Mahathir's Deputy Prime Minister. We jump ahead of our story, but was it a coincidence that this speech, though directed to an international audience, contained a thematic call to 'stop the drive towards fragmenting the *Ummah*'?

17. Ibid.

18. Ibid. Mahathir's view of Islam's civilizing impact goes back to his observation in *The Malay Dilemma* (Singapore: Donald Moore for Asia Pacific Press, 1970) that Islam had a beneficent impact on the Malays: Islam enriched Malay culture (pp. 22–3), and 'intra-religious intermarriages' (p. 28) between Arabs and Indian Muslims with Malays in the town areas 'enriched Malay stock' (p. 28), thus giving the 'town Malays' a degree of sophistication which the rural 'purebred Malays' (p. 29) did not possess. Given the geneticist premises of *The Malay Dilemma*, perhaps Mahathir did not make the latter point without reservation, for he noted that Islam prevented *inter*-religious intermarriages: 'Hitherto, Malays had felt free to marry outside their religion. Now Islam forbade such marriage except when certain conditions were met' which helped to explain why 'intermarriage between Malays and Chinese was extremely rare' (p. 23).

19. Mahathir, 'Speech at the Pemuda and Wanita UMNO General Assembly', Kuala Lumpur, 14 September 1978, reprinted as 'Tradisi dan Pembangunan Kepimpinan', in Harun Derauh and Shafie Nor (eds.), *Mahathir: Cita-cita dan Pencapaian*, Kuala Lumpur: Berita Publishing, 1982, pp. 38–50.

20. Ibid.

21. Mahathir, 'Speech at the International Islamic Symposium'.

22. Mahathir, 'Speech at the 4th Regional Islamic Da'awah Council of Southeast Asia and the Pacific (RISEAP) General Assembly', Kuala Lumpur, 8 November 1986, *Foreign Affairs Malaysia*, 19, 4 (December 1986): 36–40.

23. Mahathir, 'Speech at the Seminar on Developing Islamic Financial Instruments', Kuala Lumpur, 28 April 1986, *Foreign Affairs Malaysia*, 19, 3 (June 1986): 18–22.

24. The quotation marks are not incidental. That Muslims were involved in each of the three conflicts mentioned here is obvious but how 'Islamic' that renders the conflicts is not.

25. Mahathir, Speeches at the United Nations General Assembly in 1982, 1984, and 1986.

26. Mahathir, 'Speech at the 4th RISEAP General Assembly'.

27. Mahathir, 'Speech at the Seminar on Developing Islamic Financial Instruments'.

28. Mahathir, 'Speech at the Pemuda and Wanita UMNO General Assembly', Kuala Lumpur, 25 June 1981, reprinted as 'Cabaran di hadapan Pemuda dan Wanita UMNO', in Harun Derauh and Shafie Nor (eds.), *Mahathir: Cita-cita dan Pencapaian*, Kuala Lumpur: Berita Publishing, 1982, pp. 51–9.

29. Mahathir Mohamed, *The Challenge*, Petaling Jaya: Pelanduk Publications, 1986; translated from *Menghadapi Cabaran*, Kuala Lumpur: Pustaka Antara, 1976, p. 111.

30. Mahathir, 'Speech at the International Islamic Symposium'.

31. Mahathir, 'Speech at the 4th RISEAP General Assembly'.

32. Mahathir, 'Speech at the 3rd Islamic Summit Conference', Taif, Saudi Arabia, 27 January 1981, reprinted as 'Towards Islamic Solidarity', in Murugesu Pathmanathan and David Lazarus (eds.), *Winds of Change*, Kuala Lumpur: Eastview Productions, 1984, pp. 57–68.

33. Mahathir, 'Speech at the 4th RISEAP General Assembly'.

34. Mahathir, 'Speech at the 3rd International Seminar on Islamic Thoughts', Kuala Lumpur, 26 July 1984, *Foreign Affairs Malaysia*, 17, 3 (September 1984): 226–31.

35. Mahathir, 'Speech at the International Islamic Symposium'.

36. Mahathir, 'Speech at the Seminar on Developing Islamic Financial Instruments'.

37. Mahathir, 'Speech at the International Islamic Youth Camp', Kuala Lumpur, 10 August 1981, reprinted as 'The Brotherhood of Islam' in Murugesu Pathmanathan and David Lazarus (eds.), *Winds of Change*, Kuala Lumpur: Eastview Productions, 1984, pp. 87–92.

38. Ibid.

39. Mahathir, 'Speech at the 3rd International Seminar on Islamic Thoughts'.

40. Ibid.

41. Ibid.

42. Ibid.

43. Mahathir, 'Speech at the Seminar on Developing Islamic Financial Instruments'.

44. Ibid.

45. Ibid.

46. Mahathir, 'Speech at the International Islamic Symposium'. For Mahathir's defence of women's rights against those who would 'use the religion of Islam' to 'deny the rights of women', see Mahathir's speech at the 'Nadwah Pertama Wanita Islam SeMalaysia', Kelana Jaya, Selangor, 28 November 1986, excerpts of which were carried by the *Berita Harian* of the following day. For example: 'The teachings which were presented to women focused more on the practice of all kinds of prohibitions and were added to religious practice but what women had to do to strengthen Muslim society was not given any attention.'

47. Mahathir, 'Speech at the Seminar on Developing Islamic Financial Instruments'. Mahathir continued that when 'profits of over 1000% were made at one time from the sale of petroleum', a 'very excessive profit' which 'caused misery' to 'many poor people, including the Muslim *ummah*', 'we interpret Islamic teachings as saying that excessive profit is not a crime as compared to the taking of even the smallest amount of interest'! To him this demonstrated 'our obsession with form rather than substance in our interpretation of Islam ... in commerce'.

48. Mahathir, 'Speech at the 3rd International Seminar on Islamic Thoughts'.

49. Ibid.

50. Ibid.

51. Ibid. This quote only seems to contradict an earlier quote (n. 49 above), but the 'fossilized' 'early years' of Islam (which 'we cannot re-create') should be distinguished from the 'living civilization' of Islam (which it is a challenge to re-create).

52. Mahathir, 'Speech at the 3rd International Seminar on Islamic Thoughts'.

53. Ibid.

54. Oliver Cromwell.

55. Mahathir, 'Speech at the 3rd International Seminar on Islamic Thought'. Mahathir's juxtaposition of 'Allah Subhanahu Wataala' and 'History' here is instructive. The first is an authority no Muslim can fault. The second is an 'authority' that Mahathir constantly cites.

56. Ibid.

57. Ibid.

58. Mahathir, 'Speech at the International Islamic Symposium'. There could have been an immediate reason behind the scorn in the statement, that is, several Islamic countries of the Middle East which had pledged financial support for the International Islamic University did not fulfil their pledges. The *Star* of 30 October 1985 wondered: 'What has happened to the pledges of funds and support from the Islamic countries that Prime Minister Datuk Seri Dr Mahathir Mohamad counted on when he initiated the concept of the International Islamic University?'

59. 'This is a wrong perception. Indeed it is the Muslims who rediscovered science and technology and enhanced their application for the betterment of mankind' (Mahathir, 'Speech at the International Islamic Youth Camp').

60. Mahathir, 'Speech at the 4th RISEAP General Assembly'.

61. Ibid.

62. Mahathir, 'Statement at the 5th Islamic Summit', Kuwait, 18 January 1987, *Foreign Affairs Malaysia*, 20, 1 (March 1987): 49–53.

63. Mahathir, 'Speech at the 4th RISEAP General Assembly'.

64. Ibid.

65. Ibid.

66. Mahathir, 'Ucapan di Majlis Perasmian Kursus Agama Anjuran Biro Agama UMNO Malaysia', Kuala Lumpur, 27 November 1981, reprinted as 'Faktor Persekitaran dalam Perjuangan UMNO', in Harun Derauh and Shafie Nor (eds.), *Mahathir: Cita-cita dan Pencapaian*, Kuala Lumpur: Berita Publishing, 1982, pp. 32–7.

67. Ibid. A fuller quote would include three preceding sentences which read: 'We also cannot isolate ourselves. To discard things manufactured by non-Muslims will neither make us more Islamic nor can it save us. Likewise merely wearing clothing that we produce and that we call Islamic clothing also will not save us.'

68. Mahathir, 'Speech at the 8th Meeting of the Islamic Foundation for Science, Technology and Development's Scientific Council', Kuching, 23 February 1987, *Foreign Affairs Malaysia*, 20, 1 (March 1987): 10–13.

69. Ibid.

70. Ibid.

71. Ibid. Recall that in *The Malay Dilemma* Mahathir proposed 'Darwinian' theses about Malay 'traits' while being conscious of Malay or Muslim unease with Darwin's ideas.

72. Mahathir, 'Speech at the International Islamic Symposium'.

73. Mahathir, 'Speech at the 4th RISEAP General Assembly'.

74. Mahathir, 'Speech at the 3rd International Seminar on Islamic Thoughts'.

75. Mahathir, 'Speech at the International Islamic Symposium'.

76. Ibid.

77. Mahathir, 'Speech at the Seminar on Developing Islamic Financial Instruments'.

78. Mahathir, 'Ucapan di Upacara Pembukaan Rasmi Musabaqah Membaca Al-Quran Peringkat Kebangsaan', Kuala Lumpur, 24 April 1986, reprinted as 'Berjimat Sepanjang Masa dalam Serba Serbi Kehidupan', *Utusan Malaysia*, 25 April 1986.

79. Ibid.

80. Ibid. Mahathir was not unaware of the 'vast differences in our respective resource endowments, our capital availabilities, our labour supplies and our technologies' (Mahathir, 'Speech at the 2nd Meeting of the Expert Group of Islamic Countries on Planning and Development', Kuala Lumpur, 3 December 1979, *Foreign Affairs Malaysia*, 12 (1979): 434–8). He accepted that 'some member nations are characterized by labour surpluses, others by scarcity; some are richly endowed with minerals, others poorly; some are land rich, others land poor; and some have excess capital while others are borrowers' (ibid.).

81. Mahathir, 'Ucapan di Upacara Pembukaan Rasmi Musabaqah Membaca Al-Quran Peringkat Kebangsaan'. The flavour of this praise of thrift is captured by the theme of the Quran reading competition: 'Berjimat Berkat, Membazir Mudarat' ('Thrift brings blessing, to waste brings disaster').

82. Ibid.

83. Mahathir, 'Ucapan di Majlis Perasmian Kursus Agama Anjuran Biro Agama UMNO'.

84. Mahathir, 'Speech at the International Islamic Symposium'. He had been more explicit before: 'In reality many Zionist banks make profit from keeping the money belonging to Muslims and a portion of this profit was surely used for the interest of Israel' (Mahathir, 'Ucapan di Majlis Perasmian Kursus Agama Anjuran Biro Agama UMNO').

85. Ibid.

86. Ibid.

87. 'The Islamic banks and financial institutions that exist today are but an embryonic form of the Islamic banking and financial systems that we need. They do business in a very restricted environment' (Mahathir, 'Speech at the Seminar on Developing Islamic Financial Instruments').

88. Mahathir, 'Speech at the 3rd Islamic Summit Conference'. It is not known who taught indolence as a virtue to Muslims all over the world. And, here, one wonders if the reference to 'our workers' has excluded the numerous Muslim migrant workers—Arabs, Bangladeshis, Pakistanis, and Palestinians—who occupied an important, if lowly paid, position in the Middle Eastern economies.

89. Ibid.

90. Ibid.

91. Mahathir, 'Speech at the International Islamic Youth Camp'.

92. Ibid. This address to 'Muslim youth' and Mahathir's 1981 address to the 'UMNO youth' (and women) are remarkably similar in their homily to youth: do not stir up trouble, work instead! The latter address was far more substantive and powerful, however.

93. Mahathir, 'Speech at the 3rd Islamic Summit Conference'. Was it possible that the 'need to work' could become controversial? It occurred to Mahathir that others might link his emphasis on work with the 'Protestant ethic'. Hence, 'let us not condemn this fundamental issue as something resulting from Western ethics'. He might have thought it safer to speak of an 'Islamic motivation' (ibid.) even though the term is by no means unambiguous.

94. Followed by the, by now, familiar qualifier: 'If Muslims are not working hard today it is because we have forsaken the teachings of Islam' (ibid.). The speech contained another thematic reference to 'migration': 'Muslims all over the world have been taught that indolence is a virtue, and are therefore unwilling to face the hardships of migration and the problems and risks that are present in all endeavours.' Mahathir was definitely evoking the *hijrah* here but might there not be a trace of influence from his reading of Malay history where the Malay 'disinclination to work' resulted in Chinese and Indian migration to Malaya? (See the discussion of Mahathir's 'Speech at the Pemuda and Wanita UMNO General

Assembly', 25 June 1981, in 'Look Out and "Look East"', Chapter 3.)

95. 'And they will be paid for it' (ibid.; emphases added).

96. The term is not used to connote ruthlessness but literally to mean a lack of pity. Mahathir's outlook, which denies self-pity and refuses the pity of others, may be compared with the 'bourgeois indifference' which left 'no trace of individual responsibility for the lot of others', or the 'lack of compassion in the bourgeois character (which) represented a necessary adaptation to the economic structure of capitalism' (Erich Fromm, 'Psychoanalytic Characterology and Its Relevance for Social Psychology', in Erich Fromm, *The Crisis of Psychoanalysis*, Greenwich, Conn.: Fawcett Publications, 1970, p. 183). Contrast this 'lack of compassion' with the 'admired and common trait among Malays' of displaying 'visible sympathy ... for the less fortunate' (Mahathir, *The Malay Dilemma*, p. 159).

97. Mahathir, 'Ucapan di Upacara Pembukaan Rasmi Musabaqah Membaca Al-Quran Peringkat Kebangsaan'.

98. Mahathir, *The Malay Dilemma*, pp. 158–9.

99. Ibid., p. 159.

100. See the section 'Look Out and "Look East"' in Chapter 3.

101. Mahathir, 'Ucapan di Upacara Pembukaan Rasmi Musabaqah Membaca Al-Quran Peringkat Kebangsaan'.

102. Mahathir, 'Hari Raya Aidilfitri Message', broadcast over Radio and Television Malaysia, 19 June 1985, reprinted as 'Marilah Kita Wujudkan Masyarakat Bersyukur', *Utusan Malaysia*, 20 June 1985.

103. Mahathir, 'Ucapan di Upacara Pembukaan Rasmi Musabaqah Membaca Al-Quran Peringkat Kebangsaan'. 'A person's poverty comes about because he is not thrifty but instead wasteful. Every human being is born with wealth if he realizes what he has with him. Because of that we can see that even handicapped people can use their intelligence to study an area of knowledge and their hands to write, carve and so on. What is only needed is that we do not squander this natural wealth of ours. We should not moan so long as we have this wealth. In truth if we say we are poor, we should ask whether we have fully used the wealth that was conferred by God upon us as our capital. If we have not then we are being ungrateful because we have been wasteful and not thrifty' (ibid.).

104. Ibid.

105. Ibid.

106. To foreign audiences, Malaysian politicians and diplomats took care to distinguish between the Sunni Islam of the Malays and the Shi'a Islam of the Iranian Revolution. See, for example, Musa Hitam, 'Malaysia's Strategic Vision: Into the 21st Century', Paper presented at 'A Conference on Malaysia', Tufts University, Massachusetts, 18–20 November 1984, reprinted in Institute of Strategic and International Studies, *Malaysia: Past, Present and Future*, Kuala Lumpur: ISIS Malaysia, 1987, pp. 1–8.

107. That Mahathir dismissed 'the talk among some circles' that his announcement of the IIU project 'during a general election period' was 'an election gimmick' (Mohd. Nor Samsudin, 'Universiti Islam Antarabangsa Kembalikan Kegemilangan Dunia Islam', *Utusan Malaysia*, 16 March 1982) is no reason to dismiss the very 'talk' itself. Musa Hitam denied that the IIU project was 'political capital'

by saying that it would become reality (*Berita Harian*, 14 April 1982).

108. This seemed to have been a really sensitive point with the supporters of the IIU. For example, Razak Rashid Ghows, 'Perbezaan Universiti Islam Antarabangsa dengan Lain-lain Universiti', *Utusan Malaysia*, 3 December 1982, recounted the assurances of support and expressions of praise that were made by many Middle Eastern Muslim leaders and scholars.

109. Md. Radzi Ismail ('Universiti Islam Antarabangsa: Apakah Implikasi Terhadap Malaysia?', *Utusan Malaysia*, 23 December 1982) claimed: 'Malaysia's initiative in establishing the IIU has opened the eyes of the world to this region and shown the stature of our leaders in realizing the true principle of recovering the glorious age of Islam. This has enhanced Malaysia's image in the world, especially among Muslim countries.'

110. Mohd. Nor Samsudin, 'Universiti Islam Antarabangsa Kembalikan Kegemilangan Dunia Islam'.

111. Ibid.

112. During the late 1970s, for example, Brighton became the centre of an 'anti-government', Islamic movement among the Malay students in Britain, virtually all of whom were sent by the Malaysian government. After the Iranian Revolution, radical Islam from the Middle East, where some Malay students studied, was especially feared.

113. Mohd. Nor Samsudin, 'Universiti Islam Antarabangsa Kembalikan Kegemilangan Dunia Islam'.

114. 'Sources said it was the Prime Minister's idea to create an Islamic university that was universal in concept, as preached by Prophet Muhammad' (Zainah Anwar, 'International University in '83', *New Straits Times*, 8 March 1982).

115. *Star*, 7 May 1983.

116. Mahathir, cited in *New Straits Times*, 8 March 1982.

117. The editorial, 'Konsep Sebenar Universiti Islam', *Utusan Malaysia*, 12 March 1982.

118. Ibid.

119. This point was emphasized in the *Utusan Malaysia* editorial ('Universiti Islam Antarabangsa Milik Semua') of 9 March 1982.

120. Amir Hamzah Shamsuddin, 'Universiti Islam: Konsep dan Hakikat', *Berita Harian*, 16 March 1982.

121. Ibid.

122. *New Straits Times*, 19 July 1983.

123. The IIU Rector recalled ten years later: 'In 1983, Dr Mahathir asked a group of Muslim educators and academics in Malaysia to plan a university based on the ideals of the Mecca conference: an institution that accepts both Revelation and reason as sources of knowledge, one that would create a Muslim intellectual with mastery of the modern professions, a keen awareness of the contemporary world and its problems, but at the same time appreciative of the Islamic heritage' (*New Straits Times*, 10 January 1992). Mahathir was Minister of Education when he attended the First World Conference on Muslim Education in Mecca in 1976.

124. *New Straits Times*, 6 July 1982.

125. For an explanation of the operations of Bank Islam and the Islamic

concepts which underlie them, see Halim Ismail, 'Bagaimana Bank Islam Beroperasi', *Utusan Malaysia*, 2 March 1983 and 4 March 1983.

126. At the time, the ratio for savings accounts was not yet decided. Current accounts bore no profit share. See *New Straits Times*, 17 May 1983.

127. There was to be a fifth facility called benevolent loans which were meant for applicants who had viable projects but not the capital to operate them. The borrower would have to repay the capital after he had earned his money but he was not obliged to share his profit or pay a cost for the funds.

128. *New Straits Times*, 30 May 1983. Mahathir himself seemed ambivalent about some aspects of the 'profit-sharing' concept. He cautioned that 'the system of forward reapportionment of profits results in repayments that are more onerous than interests' (Mahathir, 'Speech at the Seminar on Developing Islamic Financial Instruments'). He hoped that the Seminar 'succeeds in developing a system of Islamic banking that stresses not just the letter but the spirit of the injunctions of the Quran, that is, that loans should not be a burden to the borrower, rather it should help the borrower in his moment of need' (ibid.).

129. *New Straits Times*, 30 May 1983.

130. Mahathir, 'Ucapan di Majlis Pelancaran Operasi Bank Islam Malaysia Berhad', 1 July 1983, reprinted in *Utusan Malaysia*, 2 July 1983.

131. Ibid.

132. Ibid.

133. Ibid.

134. Ibid.

135. Ibid.

136. The federal government bought RM30 million worth of Bank Islam shares; the Islamic Religious Councils in various states, RM25 million; the Tabung Haji, Islamic foundations, and bodies, RM10 million; and Perkim, RM0.5 million (*New Straits Times*, 26 May 1983).

137. Mahathir, *The Malay Dilemma*, p. 173.

138. Mahathir, 'Speech at the 35th UMNO General Assembly', Kuala Lumpur, 25 May 1984, English translation reprinted as 'Making Sure the Spirit of UMNO Prevails', *New Straits Times*, 26 May 1984.

139. Mahathir, 'Speech at the 38th UMNO General Assembly', Kuala Lumpur, 24 April 1987, English translation reprinted as 'Let Not Future Generations Condemn Us: Mahathir', *New Straits Times*, 25 April 1987.

140. Mahathir, 'Speech at the 36th UMNO General Assembly', Kuala Lumpur, 27 September 1985, reprinted as 'Semangat Kebangsaan Beri Kekuatan pada Perjuangan dan Persaudaraan Islam', in *Utusan Malaysia*, 28 September 1985.

141. Mahathir, 'Speech at the 35th UMNO General Assembly'.

142. Mahathir, 'Ucapan Sempena Awal Muharram Hijrah 1406', reprinted as 'PM Ajak Rakyat Baharui Azam dengan Semangat Maju', in *Utusan Malaysia*, 16 September 1985.

143. Ibid.

144. Malaysia, *Mid-Term Review of the Fourth Malaysia Plan, 1981–1985*, Kuala Lumpur: Government Printers, 1984, pp. 28–9, para. 82.

145. Ibid., p. 28, para. 79.

146. Ibid., paras. 79 and 80.

147. Ibid., para. 79.

148. Ibid., p. 27, para. 77.

149. Ibid., p. 28, para. 81.

150. Ibid.

151. Ibid., para. 78. The preceding part of the paragraph declared that all attempts at attaining higher productivity and growth by increasing investment, better management, and raising skills 'would be nullified if they are not accompanied by a work force which is committed to hard work'.

152. 'An Opposition Is Not Absolutely Necessary', *Asiaweek*, 7 May 1982, pp. 42–3.

153. S. Jayasankaran, 'Premier in Power', Malaysian *Business*, 1 January 1988, p. 10.

154. Malaysia, Ministry of Information, *Profile of Dato' Seri Dr Mahathir Mohamad*, Kuala Lumpur: Federal Department of Information, 1982, p. 7; Robin Adshead, *Mahathir of Malaysia*, London: Hibiscus Publishing Company, 1989, pp. 27–8.

155. Mahathir recalled that 'I grew up in a very disciplined home. My father ran it like a classroom. The sound of his cough as he approached our house was enough to send us boys flying back to our books' (Leung Thong Ping, 'Mahathir', *Sunday Mail*, 2 April 1972).

156. Mahathir's cousin, Haji Mukti, said of Mahathir's father that he 'was a very strict man. When we were doing our homework, he would sit on the sofa, smoking his pipe and reading the papers. We could ask him anything, and he would help us, but he insisted on our working for regular periods, with breaks for tea and dinner, and back to work' (Adshead, *Mahathir of Malaysia*, p. 29).

157. In turn fostering an image of the ideal student (more schoolboy than schoolgirl, then) as one talented in studies and accomplished in sports. That this ideal may have been an import, an imitation of Etonian legend, say, did not make it any less 'real' for generations of Malayan and early Malaysian students.

158. One should add, together with the 'chief clerks' and other functionaries of the early colonial civil service.

159. Of course, the full complement of Malayan schoolmasters, headmasters, and educationists would have to include many of British origin, for example, Cheeseman and the early headmasters of the Penang Free School after whom the majority of the 'houses' are still named: Cheeseman, Hamilton, Hargreaves, and Pinhorn.

160. I say this not to ridicule the present teachers but to sympathize—without being patronizing, I trust. I recall a teacher from Westlands Primary School, Penang, telling my class how he became a teacher. A Penang Free School student, he had just finished sitting for his School Certificate examination when he and his classmates were asked by the headmaster what they wanted to be. Those who 'elected' to become teachers, like him, were recruited on the spot, sent to a teacher's college, and thus embarked on a 'teaching career'. Many like this teacher could say that they 'had always wanted to be teachers'—and proved it by their performance.

161. In contrast, 'the teachers in Chinese schools have always been insecure as

wage earners in this country, with the inevitable shifts and straits and lack of professional dignity and social status which have made them poor itinerants, packing bag and baggage for the annual mass migration to other jobs in other schools …' (*Annual Report on Education, 1952*, p. 9, cited in Tan Liok Ee, 'Dongjiaozong and the Challenge to Cultural Hegemony, 1951–1987', in Joel S. Kahn and Francis Loh Kok Wah (eds.), *Fragmented Vision: Culture and Politics in Contemporary Malaysia*, Sydney: Asian Studies Association of Australia in association with Allen and Unwin, 1992, p. 183). Measured by earnings, dignity, and status, teachers in the early Malay and Tamil schools were worse off.

162. Mahathir was fond of making that taunt. In 'Polemics' (Mahathir Mohamad, *The Challenge*, Petaling Jaya: Pelanduk Publications, 1986; translated from *Menghadapi Cabaran*, Kuala Lumpur: Pustaka Antara, 1976, p. 3), he rejected 'any attempt to challenge the writer so that the critic can display his prowess' thus: 'The saying goes: "Those who can, do; those who can't, teach (or criticize)"'. While defending his measures to 'revive the economy', Mahathir said: 'It is hoped that the kind of carping criticism which only hampers recovery will cease. We, the government, can and we do. Those who cannot should confine themselves to teaching' (Mahathir, 'Speech at the Annual Dinner of Financial Institutions', Kuala Lumpur, 25 August 1986, *Foreign Affairs Malaysia*, 19, 3 (September 1986): 15–20). Or: 'I don't like this stress on academics. It only turns out a lot of critics … who know how to run things (down?) but who've never actually run anything.… I'm looking for people who can do things' (cited in Jayasankaran, 'Premier in Power', p. 10).

163. The details of Mohamad Iskandar's association with the Government English School which are provided here are drawn from Mansur bin Ismail, 'Sejarah Perkembangan Government English School, Alur Setar, 1908–1935', in Khoo Kay Kim (ed.), *Beberapa Aspek Sejarah Kedah*, Kuala Lumpur: Persatuan Sejarah Malaysia, 1983, pp. 83–93.

164. The *Straits Echo*, 13 September 1961, paid a touching tribute to Mohamad Iskandar and his contribution to the education of the Malays in Kedah. He died in Alor Star on 11 September 1961.

165. The first five headmasters of the Government English School, inclusive of Mohamad Iskandar, were all Malays. That Kedah did not come under direct British rule until 1910 partly explains the selection of a non-English first headmaster. To account for the four others, Mansur ('Sejarah Perkembangan Government English School, Alur Setar, 1908–1935', p. 93) suggests that 'in the beginning, this institution was headed by Malays themselves, very likely so as to attract the attention of the local community that was initially prejudiced against English education'. The first five headmasters only held a total tenure of five years! Mansur (ibid.) continues that 'when it [the Government English School] had developed rapidly and new facilities were beginning to evolve, there came instead a new style of administration'—the arrival of the first British headmaster in 1914—and 'only after the early years of independence were important posts at SAHC [Sultan Abdul Hamid College] held once again by locals'.

166. Tunku Abdul Rahman, *Something to Remember*, Singapore: Eastern Universities Press, 1983, p. 51, recalled that Mohamad Iskandar, his headmaster at the Government English School, 'much preferred that I did not wear the regalia of

royalty in school' and, presumably with the right tact, 'objected to my wearing the gold studded cap on the grounds that if it was lost or stolen, he would have to bear responsibility for it'. And 'when my teacher, Master Hassan complained that I was making too much noise and disturbing the other pupils ... the headmaster placed my chair at Master Hassan's table where I had to behave myself'.

167. Leung, 'Mahathir'.

168. With Islamization, Mahathir might have wanted to, as Philip Bowring noted, 'create a new Malay man'. If so, if Mahathir meant to formulate an ethic for the 'future', he culled its ingredients from the 'past'—proving once again that 'the tradition of the dead generations weighs like a nightmare on the brain of the living' (Karl Marx, *The Eighteenth Brumaire of Louis Bonaparte*, New York: International Publishers, 1963, p. 15).

6

The Prime Minister as Populist

> I used to be very shy. I did not like crowds. I would not go to the stadium to watch a game. I would not go to an exhibition. In the old days, I would not go.... But this is different. This is a crowd I can be with. When they wave, shout a greeting, it is very touching. And coming from total strangers—that is what is so heartwarming about the experience.... Initially, when I used to go with Tun Razak, I would not walk on the red carpet. I would walk off it. He would tell me, 'This is laid for you.' I learnt then to gingerly walk on it.... I don't deserve that much respect. I'm nobody. I'm just one of them.
>
> Mahathir, quoted in Supriya Singh, 'The Man behind the Politician', *New Straits Times*, 14 April 1982.

Mahathir's Populism

POPULISM, populist movements, and populists have exhibited so many shades and variations in their meanings and characteristics that the difficulty of distilling their 'essence' is axiomatic.[1] To call Mahathir a populist, therefore, is not to fix him firmly in a well-screened gallery of 'ideal' populists, but mainly to suggest that several of Mahathir's ideological and personal characteristics as a politician are best captured by a 'populist' designation.

In common with most populists, Mahathir based his political appeal on a loose definition of 'the people' which for a long time meant the Malay *rakyat* because of his nationalism. Mahathir's deep-seated anxieties about Malay backwardness prevented him from praising 'Malay-ness' in the way that some African populists, in Peter Worsley's view, celebrated *négritude*.[2] But when Mahathir proclaimed the 'definitiveness' of the Malays he differed only in shades from the populists who discerned 'virtue' in the common people.[3] The obverse to this acceptance of a 'people-centred' world-view was a rejection of 'class' as an explanation of social issues and political conflict.[4] For example, C. H. E. Det noted that Singapore was 'filled with Malay syces, *kebuns*, cooks and *tambies*'. But he was not so much thinking about the making of a Malay working class as complaining about the low social status to which the Malays had fallen. Mahathir's disregard for 'class' was best, if peculiarly, revealed by his attitude towards 'the rich and the poor'. To his mind, the rich and the poor were not locked in an antagonistic polarity. They formed a poverty–wealth spectrum with the different positions along it being determined by aspiration, opportunity, and application.[5] So far from believing that the wealth of the one was the poverty of the other, Mahathir would have everyone believe that the rich best helped the poor by being rich.[6]

Mahathir was populist in another sense. His Malay-centred appeal was unavoidably 'rural' because, for a very long time, to be Malay was to be 'rural'. But the rural dimensions to Mahathir's populism need careful demarcation. Mahathir was not 'anti-urban' in the way that some agrarian populists disparaged the city for being alien and evil. In fact, he has always had an affinity for 'urbanity' and for the town as the locus of civilization and progress.[7] But C. H. E. Det's anger at the 'middlemen', the *padi kunca* system, and the loss of Malay land resulting from peasant insolvency—rural grievance, in a word—carried echoes of the American agrarian populist's fight against bank debt and farm foreclosure, both of which were seen as being imposed from outside—from the 'city'. In due course, Mahathir as a Third World spokesman frequently laced his anti-Western criticisms with overtones of traditional 'agrarian populism' and, in the process, expressed the agrarian (commodity) producer's hatred of 'metropolitan' 'brokers … dealers … speculators and others'.[8]

But there ends one similarity and there begins a difference between the rural aspects of Mahathir's populism and classical American agrarian populism. Whereas 'the character of American populism derive[d] in great part from the … entrepreneurial radicalism' of 'cash-conscious commercial farmers',[9] the character of Mahathir's rural populism sprang from the historical lack of entrepreneurship of the Malay middle class. In colonial Malaya, the Malay peasantry was poor but it was spared the worst ravages of early colonial capitalism. At the same time, there were well-to-do Malays but the incipient Malay middle class was denied a 'fair' share of colonial capital accumulation. Someone like Mahathir who was socially rooted between the Malay peasantry and middle class—but who had no ties to the Chinese and Indian working class which bore the worst conditions of colonial capitalism—tended to overlook the 'fortune' of being spared the ravages and to stress the 'injustice' of being denied the opportunities. There was, correspondingly, no revulsion against capitalism, only a resentment of the 'colonial administrators' and 'predatory immigrants' who deprived the Malay of his 'place in the Malayan (read: capitalist) sun'.

Populism, it has been suggested, 'tends to throw up great leaders in mystical contact with the masses'.[10] At first glance, Mahathir does not seem to fit this image of a populist leader. Privately shy, he tends to cut an austere rather than charismatic public figure. Yet Mahathir has consistently set great store by leadership qualities and claims to 'know how the people feel'. When he launched his *kepimpinan melalui teladan* ('leadership by example') campaign, he not only placed his leadership in public view, but sought to put in practice his conviction that the leaders of developing countries must 'influence the selection of systems and values of the people'.[11] Anyone could perform the ceremonial functions of a Prime Minister, he said, but true 'leadership' was 'the ability to provide guidance ... something *superior* to what your people can do by themselves'.[12] Would that make a leader 'different' from the led? When he was asked 'whether true leadership consists of being the embodiment of the hopes, dreams and aspirations of your people', Mahathir replied, 'Well, lots of people think they are such an embodiment; I don't really know whether my aspirations are the same.'[13] In fact, a leader 'must have initiatives and ideas that are not common'.[14] Mahathir held an almost unbounded belief in what 'leaders' could achieve. For example, he thought that responsible statesmanship, a form of global leadership, could virtually of its own accord overturn a world recession and protectionist trends.[15]

As for the masses, Mahathir believed he knew them thoroughly, their problems and weaknesses, as well as 'what is good for them'. Already during his C. H. E. Det days, Mahathir felt qualified to publicize the Malay condition. Later, he was confident that he had the Malay dilemma correctly diagnosed. He did not think that his diagnosis would be popularly received but he likened his role to that

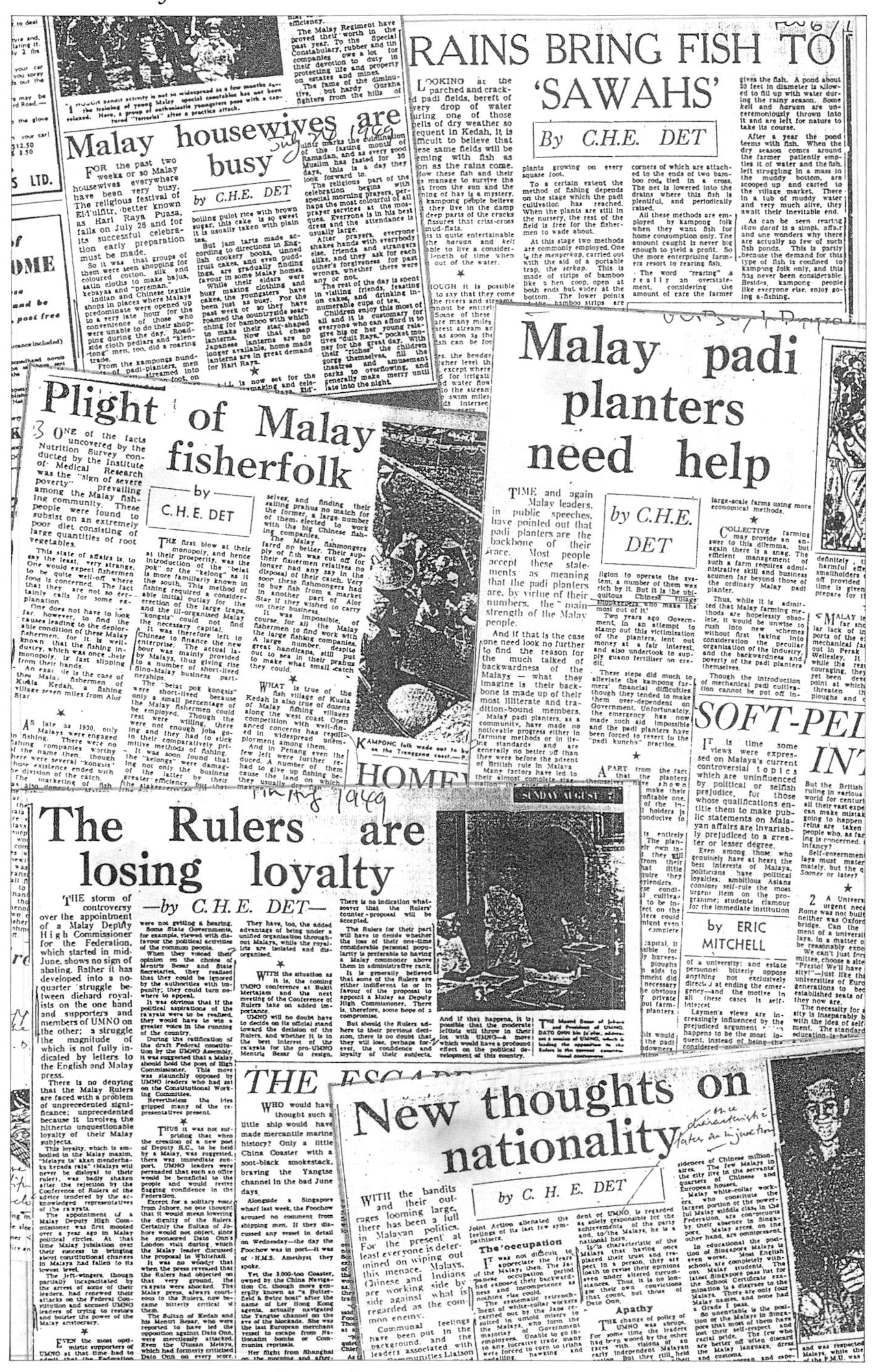

RAINS BRING FISH TO 'SAWAHS'

By C.H.E. DET

Malay housewives are busy

by C.H.E. DET

Plight of Malay fisherfolk

by C. H. E DET

Malay padi planters need help

by C.H.E. DET

SOFT-PE[illegible] IN[illegible]

by ERIC MITCHELL

The Rulers are losing loyalty

—by C.H.E. DET—

THE ESCAP[illegible]

New thoughts on nationality

by C. H. E. DET

1 A selection of titles of C. H. E. Det articles, *c.*1948–50.

2 Mahathir succeeds Hussein Onn as UMNO President, UMNO General Assembly, Kuala Lumpur, 29 June 1981.

3 Mahathir signing the letter of appointment as Prime Minister, Kuala Lumpur, 16 July 1981. (Jabatan Penerangan Malaysia)

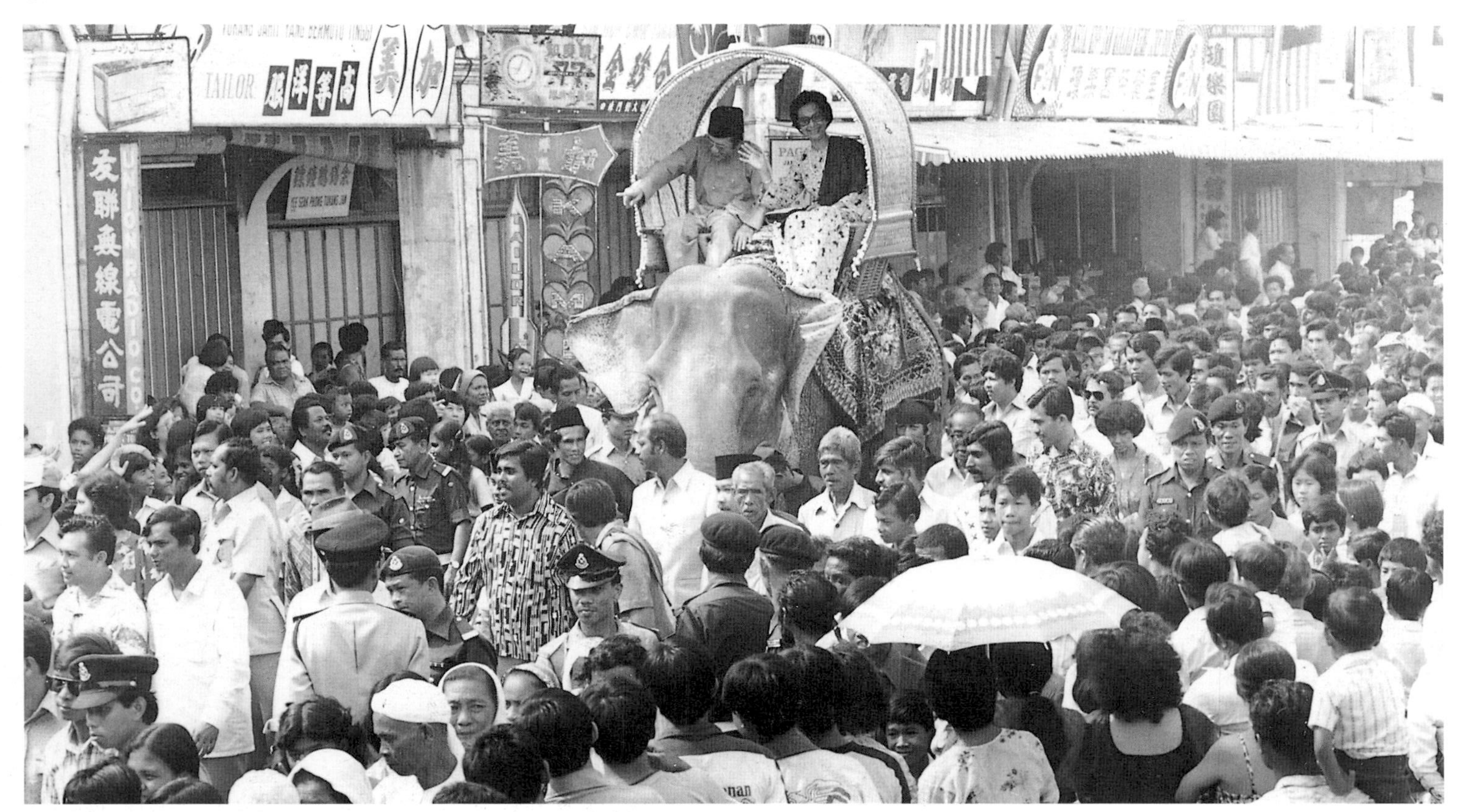

4 Mahathir visiting his constituency, Kubang Pasu, Kedah, 22 August 1981.

5 Rally at Port Klang during the constitutional crisis of 1983, 6 December 1983.

6 Mahathir during a SEMARAK campaign at Lubok Jong, Kelantan, 6 March 1988. (Jabatan Penerangan Malaysia)

The hour of the populist

7 Mahathir celebrating the Barisan Nasional victory in the general election, 4 August 1986. (Jabatan Penerangan Malaysia)

8 Mahathir celebrating the Barisan Nasional victory in the general election, 21 October 1990. (Jabatan Penerangan Malaysia)

9 Mahathir with other Commonwealth leaders at the CHOGM in Kuala Lumpur, October 1989. (Jabatan Penerangan Malaysia)

10 Mahathir tabling the Sixth Malaysia Plan in Parliament, Kuala Lumpur, 11 July 1991.

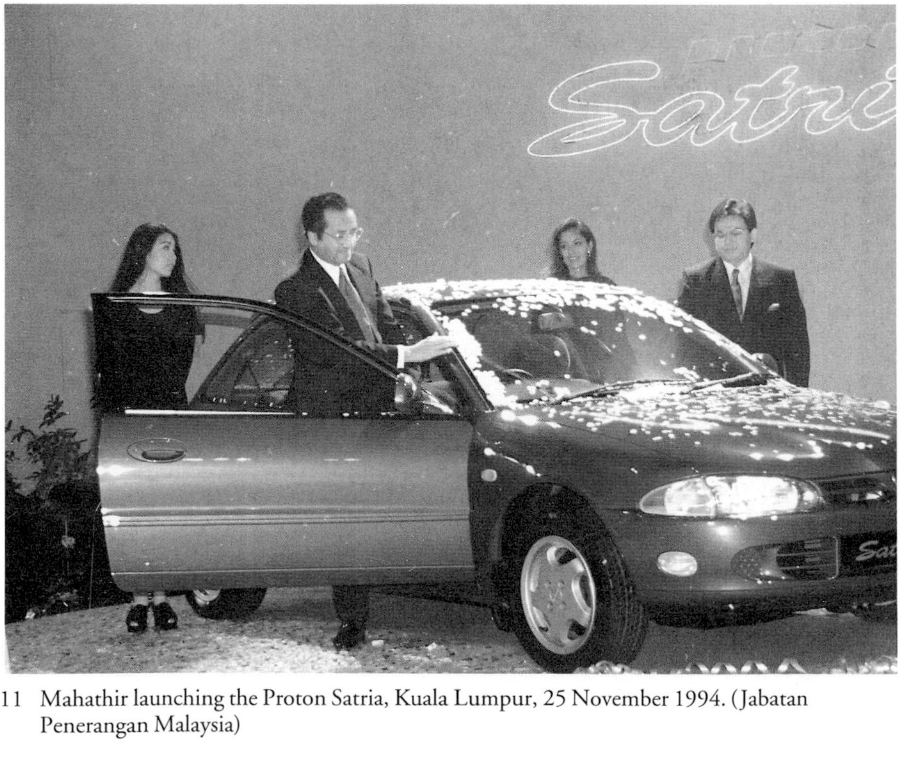

11 Mahathir launching the Proton Satria, Kuala Lumpur, 25 November 1994. (Jabatan Penerangan Malaysia)

Succeeding Mahathir is no laughing matter

12 Mahathir and Musa Hitam in response to rumours of Musa's resignation, Kuala Lumpur, 6 July 1985.

13 Mahathir and Ghafar Baba at the UMNO General Assembly, Kuala Lumpur, 7 November 1992.

of the 'few Negroes [who] achieved a breakthrough' and articulated the grievances of their people.[16] Later still, Mahathir professed not to have been greatly surprised when May 13 occurred: 'Living in a rural constituency, I heard the rumblings long ago.'[17] When he called upon the Tunku to resign, it was because, among other reasons, he faulted the Tunku for having lost contact with the Malays; thus, 'permit me to tell you what the position, the thoughts and opinions of the people are really ... ' .[18] After he was expelled from UMNO—for going above the heads of the leaders to reach the masses, so to speak—Mahathir 'always felt ... that he was popular among the party rank and file and that his views had wide support with them'.[19]

And when *The Malay Dilemma* argued the need to 'complete the rehabilitation of the Malays', Mahathir believed he had the right prescription: 'a carefully planned revolution [which] must be enlightened'[20] and 'executed with speed and thoroughness to produce a complete and radical change in the Malays'.[21] Only 'then would the nation be able to progress without the burden of a Malay problem'.[22] Mahathir admitted that 'revolution is a word that is unduly feared in Malaysia' but reassured the reader that 'revolutions can be creative and orderly if the mechanics are understood by those best able to carry them through'.[23] Only a man who thought he belonged among those 'best able to carry them through' would predict that the people, 'left to themselves', were 'more likely to subvert their own future than promote their well-being'.[24] It was not that Mahathir left no place in history for the masses. His own prime ministerial vision of reform and progress was 'mass-oriented' to the extent that his 'biggest challenge is to move all the people, not only government officers, but the whole population of this country so that they are aware of their respective responsibilities, their respective roles in national development'.[25] But as his policies, campaigns, and slogans showed, he far preferred the masses to play their part according to his script and under his tutelage.

The 'people-centred', 'non-class', and 'rural' aspects of Mahathir's populism overlapped with aspects of his nationalism which have been discussed in detail in Chapters 2 and 3. But this final aspect of Mahathir's populism helps to explain why Mahathir's most compelling persona has been that of a 'spokesman'—of the Malays, Malaysians, and Muslims, and the masses of the Third World. He was in contact with them, he knew them. He had a mandate from them, he would speak for them. In short, *vox* Mahathir *vox populi.*

If this does not automatically conjure an image of Mahathir as a 'great leader in mystical contact with the masses', Mahathir himself has hinted that it was not entirely without mystique:

> I feel good about making contact [with crowds]. My training as a doctor helps me to communicate. The touch of the hand, that is important. It is like the healing concept of the 'the laying of hands'. That is why I try and shake the hands of as many people as I can. It is not possible to shake everybody's hand in a large crowd, but as many as possible.... When people wave to me, shout greetings, I feel good.... Everything seems worthwhile. It's the way people greet you, the way they seem to accept you. You feel you are not a stranger. Your service is appreciated.[26]

It is this final dimension of Mahathir's populism—and its being subjected to the growing tensions between 'the leader' and 'the masses'—which sheds light on much of Mahathirist politics in the 1980s. Coincidentally, its most powerful political manifestation took the form of a show of strength between Mahathir, an elected Malay Prime Minister, and the royalty, the traditional emblem of Malay sovereignty.

Who's Sovereign?: The Constitutional Crisis, 1983

The crux of the 1983 constitutional crisis was Mahathir's attempt to amend Article 66 of the Constitution so as to explicitly require the Yang di-Pertuan Agong, the constitutional monarch, to give his assent to all acts passed by Parliament.[27] According to the proposed Constitution (Amendment) Bill, Article 66(5) would read: 'A Bill shall become law on being assented to by the Yang di-Pertuan Agong. If for any reason whatsoever the Bill is not assented to within fifteen days of the Bill being presented to the Yang di-Pertuan Agong, he shall be deemed to have assented to the Bill and the Bill shall accordingly become law.'

The Amendment Bill included a parallel and similar provision for the rulers' assent to legislation passed by the State Assemblies. The Amendment Bill was passed by Parliament in August 1983 and only awaited the Agong's assent and gazetting to become law. On the face of it, the amendment appeared only to contain a formality: to prevent in law what had never been attempted in practice. No Agong had actually failed to give his assent to bills passed by Parliament. But politically the amendment could permit Parliament to dispense with royal assent altogether. Before tabling the bill in Parliament, Mahathir had consulted with the Agong on the proposed amendments and had apparently obtained the Agong's verbal agreement to them. In any case, Mahathir was sensitive enough to the political ramifications of the amendments that he arranged to have the Constitution (Amendment) Bill 1983 passed 'with a secretiveness that [was] uncharacteristic of Mahathir's style' and 'surprising in view of the much-touted liberalism of the Mahathir administration'.[28]

The Prime Minister's Department instructed the domestic press to maintain a virtual silence on the parliamentary debates over the amendments. The editors of the local newspapers, 'with one exception ... were more than ready to comply with the request' from the Prime Minister's Department to 'report only Mahathir's speech introducing the bill, not the debate which would follow'.[29] The editor of a major daily recalled that 'we agreed among ourselves that we should treat this as a non-event'.[30] The report in the *New Straits Times* (2 August 1983) on the tabling of the Constitution (Amendment) Bill 1983 certainly rendered it a 'non-event'. No opinion besides Mahathir's was reported. The *New Straits Times* report discussed relatively uncontroversial amendments contained in the bill. Then it mentioned that the bill would 'clarify Article 150' but it did not clarify that the proposed alteration of Article 150 would remove the royal power to declare an emergency. The report maintained an absolute silence on the proposed amendment to Article 66, the most contentious part of the bill. Mahathir's instruction to the domestic press to keep silent on the constitutional amendments was obeyed for two months and the amendment was passed without much public notice.

But the silence was breached by Senu Abdul Rahman, an UMNO veteran and a former minister in the Tunku's Cabinet. In an open letter (dated 3 October 1983) which was widely circulated, Senu accused Mahathir of undermining the position of the Malay rulers.[31] Senu's exposé was followed by Tunku Abdul Rahman's criticisms of the amendments which were expressed in the latter's weekly column in the *Star*.[32] By then, the Agong had quietly retracted the verbal agreement to the amendments which he had given to Mahathir during their consultation. Upon legal advice, apparently apprised of the full extent of the amendments and their legal implications, and under pressure from the other Malay rulers, the Agong refused to give his assent to the Constitution (Amendment) Bill 1983. The Agong's refusal prevented the bill from becoming law and precipitated a political impasse between the executive and the Malay royalty.[33] Initial attempts to reach a compromise over the amendments failed. From October to December 1983, the legal impasse developed into a full-scale political crisis in which the federal government, the UMNO membership, and the Malay community became sharply divided into supporting one or the other side of the conflict.

The immediate impetus for Mahathir's proposed amendments was a calculated move to pre-empt the possibility that either of the two most senior contenders and likely successors to the Malaysian throne, Sultan Idris Shah of Perak and Sultan Mahmood Iskandar of Johore, might, upon enthronement, interfere with the process of parliamentary legislation.[34] It was widely assumed that disagreement between these Sultans and their Menteris Besar had played an important part in the latter's departure from office.[35] In 1982, the Sultan of Perak had declared that Hari Raya Puasa, the end of the Muslim fasting month of Ramadan, would be celebrated one day earlier in Perak than the date decided, according to custom, by the National Islamic Religious Affairs Council for the whole country.[36] In mid-June 1983, the Sultans of Perak and Johore decided that Ramadan and the fast would begin on 12 June 1983. When the National Islamic Religious Affairs Council later fixed the date for 11 June 1983, the Sultan of Johore withdrew Johore from the Council, and the Sultan of Perak indicated he would do likewise.[37] If tradition prevailed in the election of the next Agong—and there was no reason why it would not—then either the Sultan of Perak or the Sultan of Johore would become the next Agong in 1984. Mahathir probably wanted to minimize the possibility of a clash between the new Agong and the federal government should they find themselves in disagreement.[38]

There could have been a deeper inspiration for the proposed constitutional amendments. Mahathir was not necessarily an out and out 'anti-royalist'. He found heroes in strong modernizing sovereigns such as Peter the Great and the Meiji Emperor[39] but his attitude towards the Malay royalty was less admiring. Mahathir had not attempted a systematic critique of the Malay royalty before. Nor would he after 1970 when amendments to the Sedition Act made it seditious for anyone to question the constitutional position of the rulers.[40] Mahathir's disdain for the Malay rulers had, however, been expressed in oblique criticism before. C. H. E. Det had cast the 1949 conflict between the Malay royalty and the nascent UMNO leadership as a conflict between 'rulers and *ra'ayats*'.[41] Then C. H. E. Det stood with those who thought that the rulers had either to yield to the wishes of UMNO and its supporters or to forfeit the loyalty of the Malays. He also foresaw that the 'new force' of a 'new Malayan democracy' would eventually defeat Malay feudalism. In *The Malay Dilemma*, Mahathir's observations of the Malay rulers in history formed an implied criticism of their 'appropriation of a certain portion of goods belonging to their subjects' by which method 'vast amounts of clothing and jewellery were amassed by the rajas and the members of the courts'.[42] Mahathir also noted that the Chinese merchants' 'habit of giving expensive gifts to the ruling class ingratiated them with all levels of authority' and facilitated the 'greater influx of Chinese small-time merchant-adventurers' and allowed the 'system of [Chinese] retail shops [in] every nook and corner' to become 'an established feature of life in the old Malay sultanates'.[43] By far Mahathir's strongest criticism of the Malay rulers was made in his speech at the Pemuda and Wanita UMNO General Assembly in 1981, when he contended that the rulers' rentierist ways, disinclination to work, dependence on British pensions, and addiction to opium led to the retreat of the Malays before the colonists and immigrants.[44]

Mahathir probably conceived of trimming the royal prerogatives as a logical and legitimate part of his vision of transforming the Malaysian nation and society. His 1982 electoral triumph and the popular response to his reformist policies might have persuaded him that the political circumstances in August 1983 were favourable for translating administrative contingencies and personal sentiments into law. Leaving aside the Malay rulers, there was hardly anyone who was capable of challenging his move. It was unlikely that PAS would or could do it. In fact, the PAS leadership's general lack of sympathy for royalty was used as a red herring by Mahathir to fire the first shots in his constitutional amendment campaign.[45] On the sole issue of curbing the power of the royalty, Mahathir might even have fancied that the non-Malay opposition would adopt a neutral stance in what would be conducted as an exclusively Malay affair. He might have counted upon Malay and non-Malay liberal opinion, which was quietly critical of the excesses of certain rulers,[46] to regard the amendments sympathetically, that is, to see them as a rationalizing and 'anti-feudalist' rectification, albeit one that was being instituted late in the day.

Between October and November 1983, both sides to the conflict hinted at compromise but did not reach it. The Agong's unexpected absence from the Conference of Rulers' meeting on 9 October 1983 in Kota Kinabalu, Sabah, signalled the rulers' objection to the amendments. After a meeting in Selangor on 20 November 1983, the rulers publicly rejected the amendments. They questioned the legality of the Constitution (Amendment) Bill 1983 since Article 38(4) of the Constitution provided that no law affecting the privileges and position of the Malay rulers could be passed without the consent of the Conference of Rulers. Were the Constitution (Amendment) Bill 1983 to become law, the rulers and their supporters contended, Parliament could 'theoretically' transform Malaysia into a republic within fifteen days of the passage of an appropriate bill—without the assent of the rulers.[47] Aside from the legal debate, the Malay rulers were able to draw emotional support from a large number of Malays, traditional 'royalists' (including many within UMNO) who regarded the rulers as, among other things, one of the most important symbols of the special position of the Malays in Malaysia.

Mahathir and his supporters denied that the amendments were motivated by republican sentiment.[48] If anything, they claimed that the amendments only formalized what was tacitly expected of constitutional monarchy and would help to 'strengthen' it.[49] They insisted that the elected government must be able to function without obstruction from the rulers. As the crisis deepened, Mahathir, who had wanted to keep the amendments away from public purview, now swung the way of mass mobilization. He and his staunchest supporters in UMNO and the Cabinet—'younger, newer leaders who had risen meteorically in the last 2 or 3 years [and] owe[d] their positions to him'[50]—mobilized party and state resources to bring Mahathir's case 'before the people'.

And, now, in substance, rhetoric, style, and tactics, Mahathir's populism reached its height. The UMNO-owned newspapers, mainly the *New Straits Times* and *Berita Harian*, carried reports, features, analyses, and letters which were slanted against the Malay royalty.[51] The state-owned television stations ran a series of Malay films which depicted despotism and tyranny under the Malay equivalents of the *ancien régime*. Mahathir organized a series of rallies meant to re-enact the drama of the anti-Malayan Union campaign and to reinvoke 'the sovereignty of the Malays'. At rally after rally, the royalty were reminded of their initial acceptance of the Malayan Union—by implication, their surrender of Malay sovereignty—which would have turned the rulers into mere *kadi*.[52] It was repeatedly pointed out that it was the *rakyat*, under UMNO's leadership, who scuttled the Malayan Union, retrieved Malay sovereignty, and preserved the position of the Malay rulers.

The historical moment of unfolding Malay nationalism was relived as a continuing battle of Malay popular sovereignty against royal hegemony.[53] At a rally in Alor Star on 26 November 1983, Mahathir declared: 'It was the *rakyat* who had protested against the Malayan Union after the Second World War; it was the *rakyat* who wanted a democratic system that would enable them to choose their own leaders. It was always the people who had fought for their destiny.'[54]

To Anwar Ibrahim, it was 'the people, not the nobility, who obtained the independence of the nation' and they 'obtained [it] from the British colonialists, not the Malay rulers'.[55] At another rally, in Bagan Datok, Perak, on 27 November 1983, Mahathir was adamant that only the '*rakyat*'s representatives' who were 'responsible to the *rakyat*' could have the authority to run the country so that 'we should be aware that the destiny of the country is not in the hands of people who are not responsible to the *rakyat*'.[56] In Malacca, on 19 December 1983, Mahathir 'wanted the voice of the people to decide the destiny of the people'.[57] The destinies of the Malay people and the Malay rulers were no longer intertwined: so be it if constitutional formality required royalty to bow to popular sovereignty. Or else, as Anwar Ibrahim and his Pemuda UMNO executive council urged, the Constitution (Amendment) Bill 1983 should be gazetted without royal assent. And 'if that is challenged in court', Anwar Ibrahim said, 'let us go to court'.[58]

At his rallies, Mahathir's populist touch knew no end of deftness. In Malacca, the seat of Malay feudal glory, Mahathir pronounced that the 'age of the feudal system' had ended.[59] He returned to his home town, Alor Star, to be 'interviewed by the people' who, he knew, would know 'Che Det' even if he did not wear the government issue 'name tag' that Mahathir had directed all civil servants to wear.[60] And addressing himself to 'the more than 50,000 voters in my constituency who will interview me' (at the next election), he declared that, contrary to rumours, he would not resign. The 'voting slips have no feelings', he said, but 'a public rally like this proves the support of the people'.[61] In Batu Pahat ('where it all began' in 1946), Johore (whose ruler was a leading candidate to become the next Agong), Mahathir told his biggest rally: 'We weren't born ministers.... We're up here because we were chosen by all of you.'[62] The voice of the people has rarely sounded more plebeian.

The constitutional crisis turned out to be one of those political battles which neither of the major antagonists could win outright. The royalty were desperate in their resistance but managed to exert a strong hold on Malay loyalty and affection. Rallies held in support of the royalist cause were thought to have matched, if not exceeded, the UMNO rallies in spontaneity, attendance, and emotion.[63] Mahathir had state power and party resources but he could not push aside the royalty which UMNO had so long bolstered as the symbolic defender of the Malays *vis-à-vis* the non-Malays. The crisis had 'destabilized' Malay society and divided UMNO's leadership and membership. Mahathir had also miscalculated the tacit support or neutrality of the non-Malay opposition and liberal opinion. He forfeited much of their potential sympathy because his proposed amendment to Article 150 would transfer the power to declare a state of emergency from the Agong to the Prime Minister. That was regarded as an attempt at 'centralizing all power with the Prime Minister during an emergency' that was fraught with the danger of authoritarianism: 'Parliament can't check [the Prime Minister]; the judiciary can't counsel him; even his own Cabinet can't control him.'[64] The royalist opposition was worried about the erosion of royal prerogative and the prospect of republicanism. The 'non-royalist' critics were alarmed at the concentration of power in the executive and the danger of dictatorship.[65]

UMNO and the rulers reached a compromise towards the end of December 1983. The Agong agreed to give his assent to the Constitution (Amendment) Bill 1983. In return, Mahathir and

UMNO undertook to make further amendments to remove the provisions which were offensive to the rulers. A new bill was passed in 1984. It gave the Agong thirty days to study and assent to a bill passed by Parliament. If the Agong disagreed with the bill, he would return it with comments or objections. Parliament retained the right to pass the bill again, with or without incorporating those comments or objections, in which event the bill would become law within another thirty days, with or without royal assent. Mahathir had achieved his most important goal: the future Agong could not obstruct the legislative process by withholding assent from parliamentary bills.[66] But there was no follow-on provision of this nature at the state level. And Article 150 was left unaltered so that the Agong retained the prerogative of declaring an emergency.

The Populist under Siege I: Financial Scandals, 1984–1986

The compromise that was reached between UMNO and the Malay rulers brought Mahathir's political tussle with the very apex of Malaysian society to a close. (Only events in 1992 would show up the conclusion of the constitutional crisis of 1983 to have been only a cessation rather than a permanent solution.) But, ironically, that was followed by the commencement of a long siege of Mahathir's leadership by the 'grass roots', or at least certain sections of it. This siege was triggered off by a spate of financial scandals which affected Mahathir's administration and his political allies.

Bumiputra Malaysia Finance Limited (BMF)[67]

Between 1979 and 1982, Bumiputra Malaysia Finance Limited (BMF), a Hong Kong-based, wholly owned subsidiary company of Malaysia's state-owned Bank Bumiputra Malaysia Berhad (Bank Bumiputra), extended very large amounts of loans principally to three property-based companies in Hong Kong. The largest borrower among them, George Tan with his Carrian Group and private companies, borrowed more than US$700 million from BMF between June 1979 and October 1982. From November 1979 to September 1982, the Kevin Hsu Group of Companies borrowed approximately US$123 million, while Chung Ching Man and his

Eda Investments Limited had taken loans amounting to approximately US$40 million between September and December 1981.

Between late 1982 and late 1983, all three borrowers became insolvent and defaulted on their loans.[68] BMF was not the only lending bank to be affected by the collapse of these companies but it was heavily exposed. Just the Carrian and the Kevin Hsu groups together accounted for 79.4 per cent of BMF's total loan portfolio of HK$5.042 billion (up to 30 June 1982). BMF was Carrian's and Kevin Hsu's single largest creditor, having supplied, respectively, up to 45 per cent of Carrian's and about 40 per cent of Kevin Hsu's total debts.[69] By late 1983, when Carrian and Eda were liquidated, BMF—and through it, its parent company, Bank Bumiputra—had suffered an estimated total loss of RM2.5 billion, or more than twice the value of Bank Bumiputra's shareholders' capital of RM1.22 billion.[70]

Towards the end of 1982, the domestic press gave only an occasional intimation of BMF's impending crisis. Until November and December 1982, Bank Bumiputra continued to deny that there was any 'crisis' in its Hong Kong subsidiary.[71] BMF's problem was presented as one of over-exposure in terms of lending to property companies adversely affected by a sudden downturn in the Hong Kong property market,[72] or, at most, 'a situation of what you call an over-exposure of loans which I regard as exceeding usual banking prudence'.[73] The local press was unable to obtain a clearer account of BMF's position. Bank Bumiputra's chairman and board members were even absent from the press briefing held immediately after the bank's annual general meeting of 27 June 1983. 'Contrary to the practice of previous years, Dr Nawawi was not on hand for the Press briefing which followed the AGM',[74] leaving 'Bank Bumiputra's officers [to] parr[y] most of the questions posed by newsmen on the group's involvement with Carrian Holdings and Eda Investments'[75] with unsatisfactory results. On 16 July 1983, on the occasion of his second year as Prime Minister, Mahathir had a long interview with local news editors. He was sanguine about BMF. He considered BMF to be not very different from 'almost all banks in Hong Kong', which faced problems arising from the property slump in Hong Kong. 'Give us a chance,' Mahathir told his interviewers, '[because] we have faith that we can recover what has been committed by BMF.'[76]

Two days later, the chance evaporated. On 18 July 1983, Jalil

Ibrahim, a member of Bank Bumiputra's internal audit team who was recently seconded to BMF as an assistant general manager, was murdered in Hong Kong. His body was discovered on 19 July 1983. The Malaysian public, among others, quickly suspected a direct link between Jalil's murder and BMF's troubles.[77] The arrest, trial, and subsequent conviction of Mak Foon Than, a 'Malaysian businessman', for Jalil's murder in Hong Kong yielded a rich vein of information to sustain that suspicion.[78] In October 1983, George Tan and Bentley Ho (Carrian's executive director) were arrested by the Hong Kong police on charges of falsifying statements to defraud Carrian's shareholders. Their trial, which took place the following year, added another flow of information about BMF and its principal officers in Hong Kong—Lorraine Osman, Hashim Shamsuddin, Rais Saniman, and Ibrahim Jaafar. Continuing investigations of BMF revealed not merely imprudent banking let down by a property slump but highly irregular lending practices which reeked of criminality and corruption in Hong Kong. To the Malaysian public, mindful of Harun Idris and the Bank Rakyat affair, and cynical about the close relationship of politics to money in the country, what had happened in Hong Kong insinuated the complicity of unnamed politicians in Malaysia.[79]

BMF's débâcle contained several elements which sparked off a huge public clamour in Malaysia for a full investigation into the 'BMF scandal'. Through BMF, massive amounts of public funds had been lost by Bank Bumiputra, an agency which was established with explicit socio-political intent, that is, to help the Malay community to make inroads into commerce and banking.[80] Bank Bumiputra owned BMF and ultimately approved the disastrous loans. But, perhaps because the serious political ramifications had not been fully understood yet, it was not even clear who controlled Bank Bumiputra: both the Prime Minister and the Minister of Finance, Tengku Razaleigh Hamzah, seemed to disclaim final authority over the bank.[81] Several twists and turns in the initial unfolding of the BMF affair in 1983 lent it an air of mystery and disbelief so that each new disclosure of events and complicity stoked a gathering sense that 'the full story remains to be told'. The Prime Minister at times appeared to be only slightly more knowledgeable than the public about the whole affair: 'The moment the Hong Kong property market collapsed, I was informed. But the seriousness of the matter was realised a little late.'[82] At a press conference on 11 October 1983, Mahathir would not even mention the total amount of loans involved because of 'banking secrecy, which becomes a problem because we cannot, with freedom, disclose without taking into consideration the laws'.[83] For the first time, he conceded that acts had been committed within BMF and Bank Bumiputra which were 'morally wrong', and constituted a 'betrayal of trust', even a 'heinous crime'; but 'as of now, we have no evidence that any law has been broken'.[84]

But by then, 'Malaysians [could] not accept ... that in a "heinous crime" and "betrayal of trust" involving $2,000 million of public money ... 20 times more serious than the Bank Rakyat scandal, there [were] no criminals'.[85] Public disaffection over the BMF scandal was growing rapidly even though public sentiment was dominated by the constitutional crisis for the rest of 1983.[86] The year 1984 was different. The initial public calls for more 'information' intensified into a clamour for a 'full scale investigation' and crystalized into a demand for a 'Royal Commission of Inquiry'.[87] Cautious references to banking imprudence gave way to harsh attacks on fraud and corruption. The initial impatience with Bank Bumiputra's tardy and inadequate responses to the press congealed into an open suspicion of a government attempt at a 'cover up'.[88] From 1984 to 1986, 'BMF', the unsurpassed scandal of Malaysian banking, lay at the centre of a massive and protracted struggle, between Mahathir's administration and the 'people', over the highly politicized issue of executive accountability.

Maminco Sdn. Bhd.

The Maminco case developed differently. On 8 July 1981, eight days before Mahathir became Prime Minister, Hussein Onn chaired a Cabinet meeting which approved a price support scheme for tin and the creation of Maminco Sdn. Bhd., a company that would serve as the government's price-support vehicle.[89] Under Mahathir the 'price-support' intention was transformed into a secret plan to corner the international tin market.

Initially, Maminco's plan involved purchasing tin futures on the London Metal Exchange (LME) to counter the refusal of the major consumer members of the International Tin Council (ITC) to agree to the producers' proposal to raise the price of tin.[90] The plan was also meant to defeat a suspected spate of short-selling by LME traders to depress the tin prices. Maminco, a 'mystery buyer' at the time, made enormous tin purchases which raised the three-month tin futures prices from 6,880 pounds per tonne in July 1981 to 8,350 pounds per tonne in October 1981 and to its peak price of 8,970 pounds per tonne in February 1982.[91] For a brief period, Maminco's plan appeared to be working. The high prices were sustained and the short-sellers might soon be compelled to buy back tin at higher prices to meet their delivery requirements. The Malaysian government even earned an additional US$100 million from increased exports and duties.[92]

Two major developments drastically changed that scenario.[93] First, the higher tin prices stimulated a greater supply of tin, not least as a result of the United States General Services Administration's decision to unload part of its strategic stockpile of tin on to the international market. The increased supplies, still sold at high prices, were a market anomaly since tin consumption was beginning to fall because of the onset of recession in the major consumer countries. Second, many LME traders, who did not expect the 'mystery buyer' to be able to sustain its purchases, were further spurred to sell tin short three months forward. Around that time, Maminco altered its plan. It switched to cornering the tin market. It made large spot purchases of physical tin for cash, accumulating an estimated total stock of 40,000–50,000 tonnes. Its hope was to sustain this heavy buying operation for three months and then resell about half of its stock at premium prices to the short-sellers who would be desperate to buy tin back to meet their delivery requirements. By February 1982, tin prices reached their peak as many of the LME traders in fact scrambled for tin to be able to fulfil their forward contracts.

But on 13 February 1982, the LME intervened and changed its rules. The LME's new rules allowed traders to pay a fine in lieu of meeting a contractual delivery and sharply reduced the penalty on late deliveries of tin. The LME's rule changes, 'ostensibly to ensure market liquidity and probably to avoid the wholesale bankruptcies of many of its members',[94]—'cheating' in Mahathir's words[95]—effectively doomed Maminco's operations. Tin prices collapsed and Maminco was saddled with a huge stock of unsold tin.

For five years, Mahathir's government denied being the 'mystery buyer' on the tin market. Finally, Mahathir admitted Maminco's involvement and losses on 18 September 1986, at the Thirty-seventh UMNO General Assembly. Maminco's misadventure on the international tin market resulted in a loss of about RM660 million—public funds sourced from Bank Bumiputra and Malayan Banking Berhad.

Employees Provident Fund (EPF) and Makuwasa Sdn. Bhd.

Echoes of Maminco's 'market intervention' were heard in the Malaysian stock market between 1985 and 1986. In 1985, the Kuala Lumpur Stock Exchange (KLSE) was under 'heavy bearish pressure',[96] partly because of the deepening recession and partly because of the emerging political uncertainties. In mid-1985, it was reported that Minister of Finance Daim Zainuddin 'advised' the fund managers of several public institutions to 'go into the market'.[97] This move was taken, Daim explained, after 'a Cabinet committee decided that he should call all fund managers and advise them to support the market'.[98] It was not revealed exactly how many public institutions became involved but 'at least the Employees Provident Fund, Socso, and Bank Simpanan Nasional invested about RM150 million' in a 'common fund' set up by the Ministry of Finance and specially administered by an 'Investment Coordinating Committee' headed by Thong Yaw Hong, former Secretary-General of the Treasury and including Basir Ismail, the new Chairman of Bank Bumiputra and Chan Chin Cheung, the Acting General Manager of Bank Simpanan.[99]

But this 'common fund' and the public institutions subscribing to it lost heavily when the KLSE share prices plunged in November 1985 at the time of the financial collapse of Pan-Electric Industries Berhad.[100] The combined losses suffered by those public institutions were never fully revealed. Daim Zainuddin declined to comment on the EPF's 'investments' and maintained that the Ministry of Finance had 'no right to involve itself' in the EPF's investments since the EPF was 'completely autonomous'.[101] Zain Asraai, Secretary-General of the Ministry of Finance who was also the Chairman of the EPF, explained that the 'investments in the exercise (to support the stock market) were initially in blue chip companies' but 'subsequently went into other securities'. These 'other securities' were 'selective share counters which were volume leaders, that is, counters which have high turnovers and high price elasticity'.[102] Zain Asraai acknowledged that the EPF suffered overall 'paper losses' of RM141 million; its contribution of RM30 million to the 'common fund' of the Investment Coordinating Committee alone led to a 'paper loss' of RM11.5 million.[103]

This EPF episode was joined to a parallel controversy which surrounded Makuwasa Securities Sdn. Bhd. Ostensibly a 'private' company, Makuwasa became the 'secret beneficiary of 70 per cent of the EPF's allotments of public share issues by 13 companies during June 1984–March 1985'.[104] The EPF had first secured those share allotments but later resold them to Makuwasa at par value which was considerably below prevailing market prices. The EPF thereby deprived itself of approximately RM10 million which would have been its profit had the shares been sold at prevailing prices on the open market.

The 'private' Makuwasa turned out to be wholly owned by the government, and was 'far from being a RM2 company', as Zain Asraai clarified when Daim Zainuddin instructed that the EPF board 'should come out with a statement and explain the facts' about the EPF's share sale to Makuwasa.[105] Zain Asraai explained that the foregone RM10 million profit was never the EPF's to keep. In the share allotment exercise, the EPF's 'obligations would be that it subscribes to the allotted shares and subsequently transfers 70 per cent of the shares to Makuwasa at subscribed prices'; 'it was not open to the EPF' to transfer the shares at a higher price.[106] But 'it was open' to Makuwasa to do so.[107]

Zain Asraai would not discuss 'the question of Makuwasa itself [which] is for the Government to answer'.[108] In fact, it was Mahathir who answered on 18 September 1986. He revealed that Makuwasa was set up in June 1984 to recoup the losses the government had suffered as a result of Maminco's misadventure on the tin market. The shares which the EPF had channelled to Makuwasa were part of a scheme to obtain funds to repay some of the loans which Bank Bumiputra had extended to Maminco.[109]

Pan-Electric Industries (Pan-El)

On 19 November 1985, Pan-Electric Industries (Pan-El), a public company quoted on the Stock Exchange of Singapore (SES), was suspended by the SES. Pan-El had defaulted on its repayment of loans estimated to total S$400 million. Two other companies with major holdings in Pan-El—Growth Industrial Holdings and Sigma International—were also suspended. At the end of November, Pan-El collapsed after its creditors' attempt to implement a 'rescue plan' failed.[110] On 2 December 1985, the Monetary Authority of Singapore closed the SES for three days to forestall 'what would probably otherwise have been a disastrous share-price crash'.[111] The KLSE, closely linked to the SES, was likewise closed.[112] But both stock markets had registered severe losses by the time they were closed from 2 to 4 December. The KLSE alone was estimated to have shed RM18 billion in its capitalization. Pan-El's collapse has been described as 'the culmination of years of syndicate-led market manipulation in many quoted companies', involving, among other things, complex forward share contracts, 'webs of inter-broker credit' and the 'speculative ramping of share prices'.[113]

The man who stood at the centre of the Pan-El affair was Tan Koon Swan, who had just become the MCA's new President on 24 November 1985 after winning the party's longest and most bitterly contested presidential election. In the late 1970s, Tan Koon Swan and the MCA had prophesied a new economic strategy for the Chinese community. Malaysian business, it seemed to them, had become irreversibly politicized under the framework of the NEP.[114] The Chinese community could not expect its future to rest on its past: it had to 'think big', transcend the traditional, limited, family business unit and construct, as it were, a Chinese counterpart to the NEP's linking of ethnic politics to business. Moved by this kind of reasoning, the MCA not only claimed to be the political representative of the Chinese community; it sought to show the way for Chinese business as well.

In practice, this led to the party's deepening involvement in business. The MCA, with Tan Koon Swan playing a key role, built up the Multi-Purpose Holdings Berhad (MPHB),[115] a party-controlled conglomerate which was intimately linked to other Tan Koon Swan-controlled companies, such as the Supreme Group, Sigma, and Grand United Holdings, and, finally, Pan-El. Pan-El's collapse was a disaster for the Tan Koon Swan–MCA corporate empire of the 1980s. Its numerous associated and subsidiary companies saw their share prices plunge—to the detriment of Chinese shareholders and investors who had bought into those companies, not least because they were persuaded by the Tan Koon Swan–MCA vision of 'business-and-politics'.

On 21 January 1986, Singapore's Commercial Activities Investigation Department (CAID) arrested Tan Koon Swan in Singapore and charged him with 'conspiring with Tan Kok Liang, Pan-El's former financial director, to use S$3.78 million held by Trans Eastern to enable Orchard Hotel to acquire securities in Grand United Holdings'.[116] The CAID later added fourteen charges of alleged fraud and criminal breach of trust. Tan Koon Swan eventually pleaded guilty to the charge of abetting Tan Kok Liang; the remaining fourteen charges were dropped.[117] On 26 August 1986, Tan Koon Swan was sentenced to two years' imprisonment and fined S$500,000.

The Deposit Taking Co-operatives (DTCs)

In May 1986, a newspaper report on alleged financial irregularities in the Koperasi Belia Bersatu Berhad (Kosatu), a 'deposit taking co-operative' (DTC), led to a run on Kosatu when its depositors tried to withdraw their funds. A month later, growing fears that many other DTCs were also facing financial problems triggered a wider run by other depositors on other DTCs as well. Kosatu was a very large DTC which had 14,541 members, operated sixty-seven branches, and held nineteen subsidiary companies. As at 23 July 1986, Kosatu had collected about RM156.1 million in deposits from 53,000 depositors.[118] In early July, after Kosatu failed to stem the run by its depositors despite court injunctions and media advertisements, it suspended payments to its depositors. Malaysia's central bank, Bank Negara, raided Kosatu and its subsidiaries on 23 July and froze their assets.

This investigation of a DTC by Bank Negara occurred eleven days before the general election of 3 August 1986. On 8 August 1986, Bank Negara ordered twenty-three more DTCs to suspend their operations pending an official investigation of their activities, transactions, and financial positions for possible fraud and suspected criminal breach of trust.[119] These twenty-three DTCs had an estimated combined membership of 535,000 and held about RM1.4 billion in deposits at the time of their suspension.[120] Bank Negara froze the assets of the twenty-three DTCs as well as those of 136 of their principal directors and office-bearers.[121]

According to the government's White Paper on the DTCs, which summarized Bank Negara's investigation, only three of the twenty-four DTCs (including Kosatu) were financially solvent as of 8 August 1986: '21 of the 24 co-operatives had negative capital totalling RM629.5 million'[122] so that less than 60 per cent of the approximately RM1.5 billion in deposits held by the twenty-four DTCs was recoverable.[123] For the twenty-four DTCs as a whole, this meant a net return per ringgit deposited ranging from RM0.30 to RM1.00. Not all the DTCs were gravely insolvent, but there were major problems with nine DTCs which together accounted for RM609.6 million of the total 'negative capital'.[124] Of these, the largest DTC, the Koperasi Serbaguna Malaysia Berhad (KSM), alone showed a 'net capital deficiency of RM330 million' which meant an estimated return to depositors of 'not more than RM0.41 for each ringgit of deposit'.[125] Kosatu, whose troubles had triggered the Bank Negara move, was not expected to return more than RM0.30 per ringgit deposited.[126]

Bank Negara's investigation highlighted cases of 'gross mismanagement of funds',[127] 'imprudent ... lending of funds, including some to directors and interested parties',[128] directors' 'sale of land at inflated prices to the co-operatives' and their 'using co-operative assets to charge against loans for their own purposes',[129] and contravention or circumvention of the rules governing co-operatives.[130] Bank Negara cited six cases of apparent fraudulent conduct and thirteen cases of conflict of interest.[131]

Once more, Tan Koon Swan and the MCA played a prominent part in this matter of the DTCs. They had promoted the 'co-operative' as the vehicle to mobilize the Chinese community's savings and resources. The MCA, with Tan Koon Swan having a key role, had shown the way by building the KSM into a gigantic co-operative as if it embodied the 'Chinese alternative' to the NEP practice of channelling state resources into 'Malay trusts'.[132] Ironically, the DTC scandal vindicated Tan Koon Swan's idea with a vengeance. The DTCs had indeed become an effective 'savings vehicle'. Practically all the depositors of the twenty-four DTCs were Chinese; practically all the DTCs were completely 'Chinese-led'. If anything, some of the most seriously mismanaged DTCs were led by MCA leaders or businessmen closely linked to the MCA—for example, Tan Koon Swan in the KSM, and Kee Yong Wee and Wang Choon Wing in Komuda.[133]

The Populist under Siege II: Political Crises, 1984–1986

In the period from 1984 to 1986, there emerged in parallel with the financial scandals, which remained unsettled, a series of political crises which were unsatisfactorily 'resolved'. If the cumulative effect of the financial scandals was to undermine the credibility of the Mahathir administration, the gathering consequence of the political crises appeared to be the erosion of the extent of Mahathir's popular base. Under the combined stresses of the scandals and the crises, Mahathir finally uncovered the character of his populism.

Sabah: East Wind from Tambunan

Between December 1984 and May 1986, Sabah went through a severe political crisis.[134] In December 1984, Joseph Pairin Kitingan, State Assemblyman for Tambunan, once a Vice-President of Berjaya, and Huguan Siow ('Paramount Leader') of the Kadazans since 1983, resigned from Sabah's ruling Berjaya party. Pairin's resignation came following his disagreement with Harris Salleh, Berjaya's President and Sabah's Chief Minister.[135] Harris Salleh promptly 'enforced' Pairin's resignation from the Sabah State Assembly,[136] had Pairin's State Assembly seat of Tambunan declared vacant, and announced a by-election on 29 December 1984. Pairin regained his Tambunan seat, defeating Berjaya's Roger Ongkili by 3,685 votes to 637.

Berjaya responded to this defeat by abrogating Tambunan's district status, in effect depriving its residents of a range of administrative services. This move, designed to 'teach the Tambunan people a lesson',[137] only hardened the anti-Berjaya sentiments of a growing, Pairin-led, Kadazan-based movement which registered a new political party, Parti Bersatu Sabah (PBS), during the first week of March 1985. Harris Salleh called state elections for 20–21 April 1985, gambling on crushing Pairin's movement quickly.

The 20–21 April election was disastrous for Berjaya.[138] Entering the election with forty-two out of a total of forty-eight seats, Berjaya retained only six seats. Harris Salleh's entire State Cabinet, save for the Assistant Minister of Agriculture and Fisheries, was defeated. One major opposition party, the United Sabah National Organization (USNO), won sixteen seats. The PBS won twenty-five seats and gained another when the sole assemblyman from Pertubuhan Kebangsaan Pasok Ragang Bersatu (PASOK) immediately joined the PBS.[139] And so with twenty-six seats in Sabah's forty-eight-seat State Assembly, the PBS prepared to form Sabah's new government with Pairin as Chief Minister. Moreover, the PBS could count on gaining a further six seats which it could fill by appointment under the Sabah State Constitution.

But in the early hours of 22 April 1985, Mustapha Harun, USNO's leader, and Harris Salleh attempted a *coup d'état*. They met the Yang di-Pertua Negeri Sabah (Governor of Sabah) and had him swear in Mustapha as the new Chief Minister at about 6 a.m.[140] But this attempt to prevent the PBS from forming the state government failed later in the day. Acting Prime Minister Musa Hitam privately advised the Governor of Sabah to revoke Mustapha's 'appointment'. As Acting Chairman of the Barisan Nasional, Musa publicly acknowledged the PBS's electoral victory and disavowed any pact between Berjaya and USNO to rule Sabah.[141] At about 8.15 p.m. on 22 April 1985, Pairin was sworn in as Sabah's Chief Minister and the PBS formed its new government.

However, the PBS's political problems did not end there. For a whole year after the PBS came to power, the 'Sabah crisis' continued in one form or another. Different measures were adopted by different parties to undermine Pairin's government. On the legal front, Mustapha challenged Pairin's appointment as Chief Minister in court. A year passed before the High Court in Kota Kinabalu finally dismissed Mustapha's suit on 15 April 1985.[142] There were violent demonstrations and bombings in Kota Kinabalu and other parts of Sabah from late May to early June 1985 and again in March 1986 aimed at destabilizing Sabah and provoking an imposition of federal rule via a proclamation of emergency.[143] The federal government, which controlled internal security, responded by relative inaction. Despite many public calls for him to visit Sabah as a way of acknowledging the legitimacy of the PBS government, Mahathir declined. He wondered aloud who the rightful Chief Minister was since the issue was being heard in court.[144] The PBS applied to join the

Barisan Nasional but its application was put on hold while the party was accused of being 'anti-Muslim'.[145] In July 1985, the Barisan Nasional placed the PBS on a 'six-month probation' to allow the latter to prove it would look after the interests not only of its Kadazan and Chinese, that is, Christian and non-Muslim, supporters,[146] but of the Muslims in Sabah as well.

Many of the PBS's problems, and thus the tumult in Sabah, stemmed from Mahathir's seeming refusal to accept the PBS's electoral triumph because of several reasons. First, the PBS's victory was wholly unexpected, the PBS having been allowed to register as a political party only on 5 March 1985.[147] Second, Berjaya's defeat entailed the first ever loss of a Barisan Nasional state government despite the coalition's putting its media, machinery, and ministers at Berjaya's disposal. Mahathir might have felt personally slighted since he had pledged to 'sink or swim' with Berjaya during his 4 April 1985 campaign visit to Sabah. Third, the drastic anti-Berjaya electoral swing owed no small part to many Sabahans' 'anti-federal sentiment', most recently felt in 1984 when Pulau Labuan was ceded as a 'federal territory' to the federal government 'without legislative debate in Kota Kinabalu or in Kuala Lumpur' and without any compensation to Sabah, 'unlike Selangor's surrender of Kuala Lumpur to this status for RM3 billion'.[148] Fourth, Berjaya's defeat had severe ramifications for Peninsular Malaysian politics. The oppositionist sentiment in Peninsular Malaysia, which rallied behind Pairin after Tambunan and was outraged after the failed coup, took heart from the PBS victory. Having lost the state government so ignominiously, Berjaya could not expect to hold on to Sabah's parliamentary seats—a grim calculation for Mahathir given the rising disaffection with his administration.[149] And, fifth, if only it was suggested by later public knowledge of the growing rift between the two, Mahathir might not have been very pleased with Musa Hitam's being applauded by many quarters for his firm stand against the Mustapha–Harris coup attempt while Mahathir was abroad.[150]

By mid-1985, the PBS's position in the State Assembly had been strengthened by three defections from Berjaya to the PBS and the appointment of six nominated members, giving the PBS thirty-five seats against USNO's sixteen and Berjaya's three. The PBS's electoral support increased ironically as a result of attempts by USNO and Berjaya to force a series of by-elections. In October 1985, the PBS won the Ulu Padas by-election which was called when Harris Salleh vacated his parliamentary seat.[151] After that, four state by-elections were held on 24–25 January 1986—for the Balung, Buang Sayang, Karamunting, and Sukau constituencies. The PBS won in Balung and Karamunting while USNO won in Buang Sayang and Sukau.[152] But the PBS suffered a block of five defections in February 1986 and chose to dissolve the State Assembly and call for fresh elections 'rather than hang on to a weakened government under siege'.[153] Shortly after, Mahathir assured Pairin that there would be no emergency rule in Sabah and that the federal government would ensure a peaceful election.[154]

On 24 March 1986, Mahathir announced that he and Pairin had agreed in principle to a 'Sabah formula' which 'will bring political and economic stability back to Sabah'.[155] The formula envisaged a Barisan Nasional-style 'power sharing' between the PBS, USNO, and Berjaya whereby 'each party will have equitable rights', Mustapha would withdraw his suits against Pairin, and both the PBS and USNO would be admitted into the Barisan Nasional after the election.[156]

By the 'Sabah formula', the PBS would contest twenty-eight seats in the impending election, USNO sixteen seats, and Berjaya four. That way, Mahathir later emphasized, 'no one group' could gain a two-thirds majority in the State Assembly and 'change the State Constitution without the consent of other parties'.[157] Behind the insistence that the PBS should enter a pact with Berjaya and USNO was 'the federal view that the PBS—with ethnic Kadazan and Christian support—is not taking care of Malay-Muslim interests'.[158] As it happened, the PBS rejected the formula and its allocation of seats which 'will alienate us, perhaps permanently from the Muslims and turn the PBS into a communal party'.[159] The PBS presented a counter-proposal which was likewise rejected by the UMNO Supreme Council. Mahathir disapproved of the PBS's 'lop-sided' and 'unhealthy' proposal which showed that 'the PBS only want[ed] a two-thirds majority'.[160]

A month later, at the 5–6 May election, the PBS obtained more than a two-thirds majority. The PBS won thirty-four seats, including several 'Malay-Muslim' constituencies, thereby reducing USNO's tally to twelve seats and Berjaya's to a single seat.[161] But its new triumph marked the end of the PBS's heroic phase in Sabah's politics.

The PBS reapplied to join the Barisan Nasional and was finally accepted although it continued to govern Sabah on its own. USNO was also readmitted into the Barisan Nasional. When the PBS rejected the 'Sabah formula', Ghazali Shafie wrote that Mahathir's proposed PBS–USNO–Berjaya pact was really an offer of 'membership of the Barisan Nasional and not a coalition government'.[162] Ghazali was actually writing an apology for Mahathir on the Sabah crisis but he turned out to be correct: with the PBS's admission, the Barisan Nasional regained by 'coalition' what it lost by election.[163]

Papan: Local Resistance

Beginning in November 1983, Papan, the name of a small town of 2,000 people in Perak, located about 12 kilometres south of Ipoh, became synonymous with spontaneous activism and local resistance to the government's plan to site a radioactive waste dump-site in the town's vicinity. The source of the radioactive waste, thorium hydroxide, was Asian Rare Earth Sdn. Bhd. (ARE), a factory in Bukit Merah Industrial Estate, Perak, which processed monazite to obtain various rare earth chlorides.[164] Without consultation with the Papan community or the residents of the neighbouring towns, but with the agreement of Puspati (the Nuclear Energy Unit) and the Perak state government, ARE proceeded to construct the trenches to contain the radioactive waste. Papan was the second location of the dump-site, the latter having been shifted from Parit, Perak, after encountering opposition from the Parit residents.[165] The Papan residents discovered the existence of the trenches in November 1983 and began to oppose the siting of the ARE dump-site in their midst. Papan's residents, together with those in the surrounding towns of Pusing, Lahat, Siputeh, Batu Gajah, Bukit Merah, and Bemban New Village, set up the Perak Anti-Radioactivity Committee (PARC) and other community bodies to carry out protests and demonstrations against ARE and its dump-site.[166] Papan's cause found no favour with the Mahathir administration. The Minister of Science, Technology, and Environment, Amar Stephen Yong, and Mahathir himself merely reiterated the adequacy of safety standards to be adopted for the dump-site.[167] But the 'anti-radioactive' cause was very well supported by a broad spectrum of non-governmental organizations (NGOs).[168] Starting from mid-1984, the Papan community, including residents from neighbouring towns, mounted a concerted opposition to the radioactive waste dump-site. At the peak of their campaign, the Papan residents were able to maintain well-manned, publicized, and widely supported daily pickets as well as mass demonstrations in the vicinity of Papan and the ARE factory.[169]

In January 1985, the Papan cause seemed to have won. While Mahathir was overseas, Acting Prime Minister Musa Hitam visited Papan, 'knew that something was wrong ... and changed the site'.[170] But the dump-site was relocated to the nearby town of Bukit Merah and triggered off new protests from the Bukit Merah residents and their supporters.[171] The Bukit Merah campaign against the dump-site was just as relentless and was successful when PARC obtained a court injunction which ordered ARE to stop production pending an investigation into whether its processes were hazardous.[172] But when ARE resumed production in February 1987, on the strength of a one-year licence from the Atomic Energy Licensing Board, the Bukit Merah residents conducted fresh mass demonstrations and applied for new court injunctions.[173]

PAS's Opposition

PAS's political fortunes were not good during the first years of the Mahathir administration. PAS, which had lost control of the Kelantan state government after 1977, performed poorly at the 1982 general election. It was able to win some State Assembly seats in Trengganu but failed to recover the lost ground in its traditional base of Kelantan. In October 1982, PAS suffered a split. Its president, Mohammad Asri Muda, resigned his position at the party's Twenty-eighth General Assembly.[174] In fact, Asri had been ousted by a set of younger and more radical leaders (notably Abdul Hadi Awang, Fadzil Noor, and Nakhaie Ahmad) allied to older PAS figures (such as Yusof Rawa and Nik Abdul Aziz).[175] The post-Asri PAS was again defeated by UMNO in a series of by-elections held in the 'Muslim heartland' of Malaysia: Binjai, Trengganu (9 December 1982), Hulu Muda, Kedah (16 March 1983), Kemumin and Selising, both in Kelantan (8 September 1983).[176]

But by the mid-1980s, the new PAS leadership seemed to have steered the party towards a resurgence. One sign of PAS's resurgence was the expanding appeal and influence of several of the PAS leaders among the Malay-Muslim community. The best-known of them was Haji Abdul Hadi Awang, 'PAS's answer to Anwar [Ibrahim]' after the latter's defection to UMNO.[177] The highly charismatic Haji Hadi, a graduate of Medina University and Al-Azhar University, an ex-ABIM leader, and a religious teacher based in Rusila, Trengganu, was largely responsible for PAS's post-1978 revival in Trengganu. Haji Hadi had a strong, nation-wide following which was partly attained by the extensive dissemination of his sermons and talks in cassette form.[178] Another sign of the PAS resurgence was its widening spatial and social base. Before 1969, PAS was rooted in the Malay peasant societies of Kelantan and Trengganu; by 1969, PAS's influence had spread to the also predominantly rural states of Kedah and Perlis.[179] In the late 1970s and the 1980s, partly because of its close ties with ABIM, PAS's appeal reached the urban centres and the university campuses where the rising Islamic consciousness was most keenly felt among Malay-Muslim youth.

In conducting PAS's renewed challenge to UMNO, PAS's leaders seemed to shed part of the party's Malay nationalist character of the 1950s and 1960s.[180] They chose to adopt more distinctly Islamic criticisms and a more combative religious idiom to attack UMNO. By the mid-1980s, for instance, PAS projected itself as representing the *mustadhafin* ('the meek') against the *mustakbirin* ('the arrogant'), and fighting for the *adil* ('the just') against the *sasaad* ('the wicked').[181] The combative nuances in some of the PAS rhetoric opened them to charges of undermining the unity of the Muslim *ummah* and seeking a violent overthrow of the government.[182] At the local level, the intensified UMNO–PAS rivalry was quite divisive in ideological terms and mundane ways.[183] UMNO accused PAS of splitting the *ummah*—by holding prayers in separate mosques led by rival imams, issuing its own fatwa, boycotting local events, including feasts and funerals, that were sponsored by or involved UMNO members, and, ultimately, denouncing UMNO and the government as *kafir*.[184] The frequency of such 'divisive' acts might have been exaggerated by the UMNO and state-controlled mass media.[185] But they did dramatize the intensity of the UMNO–PAS conflict which was not softened by the government's open discrimination against PAS members and supporters in matters of development funds and state subsidies.[186]

The UMNO–PAS conflict of the 1980s took an unusual turn

when PAS not only attacked UMNO for the latter's espousal of *assabiya* or 'ethnic chauvinism',[187] but made overtures to the non-Muslim Chinese community. At a symposium on 'Islam and National Unity' held in Kuala Lumpur on 11 February 1985, Haji Hadi commented that under Islam a Chinese could become the Prime Minister of Malaysia—provided he was 'a Muslim who was pious and had the qualities of being a Muslim leader'.[188] Generally, PAS leaders had begun to suggest that 'the rights of both Muslims and non-Muslims would be better protected in a state governed by Islamic law'.[189] In a 'dialogue session' with the Chinese of Kuala Trengganu, on 14 September 1985, Haji Hadi reportedly declared that 'Islam does not set out special rights for Malays'.[190]

UMNO immediately protested that PAS had thereby pledged to 'eliminate Malay special rights' should it come to power. Musa Hitam directed his Ministry of Home Affairs to 'study' Haji Hadi's speech and determine what action should be taken against the party.[191] Mahathir instructed the Attorney-General to 'determine' if Haji Hadi's statement was 'seditious' under the Sedition Act.[192] Anwar Ibrahim called it 'the biggest mistake ever committed by [PAS] leaders'.[193] No action was ever taken against Haji Hadi or any other PAS leader over this issue, an indication that Hadi's statement 'pledged' less than what UMNO made it out to be.

It was unlikely PAS said more than that 'the concept of abolishing the special rights of the Malays doesn't arise if we govern because the Islamic laws we will introduce will guarantee a wider and better justice for Muslims and non-Muslims compared with the existing constitution'.[194] That basic position argued too fine an ideological concession for a Chinese community that was traditionally hostile to PAS. But these PAS overtures constituted its first ever attempt to reach and 'explain Islam' and PAS to the Chinese community 'directly, not as interpreted by UMNO or others'.[195] In 1985 and 1986, PAS held 'dialogues' with several Chinese associations, guilds, and educationists via the 'Chinese Consultative Committee' (CCC), all at least curious to know how Chinese 'language and culture will have a better future in an Islamic state under PAS'.[196]

PAS's overture to the Chinese community bespoke the party's historic, if belated, discovery of Chinese grievances over issues related to language, education, and the NEP. Even if no more than that, the PAS initiative threatened to encroach on UMNO's position as the

Chinese community's historical, though 'partial', ally. UMNO's reactions to the PAS–Chinese dialogues, hysterical in some instances,[197] revealed UMNO's sense of having been doubly 'betrayed'—by the only other major Malay political party seemingly jettisoning the ideological underpinning of Malay hegemony, and by the Chinese community rethinking its traditional distance from an Islamic party. It was lost on very few that PAS's rejection of UMNO's *assabiya*—'rousing the Malay spirit in an unhealthy manner'[198]—had an electoral angle to it. A general election was widely expected for 1986, and as Suhaini Aznam noted:

> With UMNO's major Chinese partner in the National Front, the Malaysian Chinese Association, in disarray, the Chinese vote is less certain to go to the front. In constituencies where UMNO and PAS hold almost equal sway, the Chinese vote can be decisive. Even if the Chinese merely boycott the election, PAS could probably increase its edge sufficiently to gain a few more seats.[199]

Ordinarily, neither PAS nor the Chinese electorate would have expected anything of each other. But the 1985–6 oppositionist mood was strong enough for PAS to hope that its Islamic dissidence might yet establish a meeting point with Chinese disaffection.

Incident at Memali

The severity of the UMNO–PAS rivalry and the challenge of Islamic dissidence to the state were tragically revealed by the 'Memali incident' of 19 September 1985. In this, a police attempt to arrest Ibrahim bin Mahmood, a local Islamic teacher and an ex-PAS electoral candidate, ended in a battle between the police and Ibrahim's followers and supporters in Kampung Memali, Kedah.[200] Ibrahim Mahmood and 17 other persons, including 4 policemen, were killed, 29 were injured, and 160, including children, were arrested. Musa Hitam, who was Acting Prime Minister when the 'Memali incident' happened, the police, and other UMNO leaders blamed the bloodshed on Ibrahim Mahmood and his followers, who allegedly ambushed the police.[201] According to the 'White Paper on the Memali Incident', Ibrahim Mahmood, also known as 'Ibrahim Libya', was a religious extremist who had threatened Muslim unity, preached violence, and repeatedly refused to surrender to police arrest since mid-1984.[202] PAS, other Islamic groups, and the Kampung Memali villagers saw the incident as an unwarranted attack conducted with excessive force on Ibrahim Mahmood and his followers.[203] The 'White Paper on the Memali Incident' strove to discredit PAS by emphasizing its links to Ibrahim Mahmood and his followers. PAS, on the other hand, condemned the police operation and proclaimed Ibrahim Mahmood and the slain Memali villagers as martyrs who died for Islam.[204]

In fact, there was considerable criticism of the government's versions of the Memali incident. The highly partisan 'White Paper on the Memali Incident' stressed the 'extremism' and 'criminality' of Ibrahim Mahmood and his followers.[205] Radio and Television Malaysia's 3 January 1986 screening of an edited police videotape of the Memali operation sought to exculpate the police role in the bloodshed and to discredit PAS. But with only seventeen minutes out of the forty-minute screening being directly related to Memali, the videotape 'showed very little of actual police action and gave exaggerated emphasis to the villagers' hysterical response', 'told us very little of how Ibrahim Libya developed a highly committed following', and 'failed to admit that government discrimination against PAS members and followers ... [and] repression against PAS activists ... and dire poverty in the area had contributed to the Memali incident'.[206]

'2 Ms' Minus Musa

On the night of 26 February 1986, Musa Hitam left Malaysia for Mecca to perform the *umrah*, the minor Muslim pilgrimage. Musa left behind for Mahathir a letter tendering his resignation from the positions of Deputy Prime Minister and UMNO Deputy President.

Musa's resignation was unexpected. There had been rumours of differences between Mahathir and Musa before, even a rumour of Musa's resignation in early July 1985, but these were repeatedly denied by one or the other of them.[207] The *Utusan Malaysi*a of 27 February 1986 had a front-page headline: 'Not True that Musa Has Resigned—Mahathir'.[208] Publicly, Mahathir's government had been labelled, probably by the press, the '2 M', that is, 'Mahathir–Musa', administration, giving the impression that it was headed by two like-minded and energetic leaders capable of working in tandem. There was much in their personal and political backgrounds to suggest that Mahathir and Musa were close. In 1981, when Musa battled against Tengku Razaleigh Hamzah for the UMNO Deputy President's post, Mahathir privately supported Musa.[209] Mahathir openly endorsed Musa at the 1983 UMNO General Assembly, one year before Razaleigh challenged Musa for the same post. Mahathir sought to bolster Musa's image as a Deputy President (and Deputy Prime Minister) 'I can work with'.[210] To all public appearances, Musa was Mahathir's heir apparent. The parting of the '2 Ms' left Mahathir with new political problems under already difficult circumstances.

Musa was widely regarded as a diplomatic, popular, and shrewd politician who enjoyed broad grass-roots support. From a very strong base in the powerful Johore UMNO, Musa showed the breadth and depth of his following in UMNO when he defeated Razaleigh in 1981 and 1984. Musa typically came across as being more suave, more flexible, and less confrontational than Mahathir. In Malaysia, the public, press, and politicians often regarded Musa rather than Mahathir as the man behind the 'liberalism' of the '2 Ms'. By the time of his resignation, Musa also enjoyed more 'credibility' than Mahathir with the non-Malay community and many NGOs for his opposition to the Mustapha–Harris attempt to seize power in Sabah.

In addition to a formal letter of resignation from his deputy premiership, Musa left a seven-page letter to Mahathir, copied and already circulated to all the UMNO Supreme Council members. The letter set out the reasons for his resignation as UMNO's Deputy President. Most of all, Musa explained, he could no longer remain as Deputy Prime Minister because Mahathir had accused him of privately discrediting Mahathir so as to 'bring him down'.[211] Musa admitted that he had 'questioned' several of Mahathir's 'policies and methods of policy implementation' but maintained that he had deferred to Mahathir's seniority and adhered to 'the principle of collective responsibility'. Musa had decided to resign since his loyalty to Mahathir had been repaid with a lack of confidence and a lot of suspicion about the activities of 'Musa's boys'.

One serious problem which Musa's resignation created for Mahathir was that it seemed to confirm what a lot of people thought of the Prime Minister—that he was abrasive, blunt, combative, irascible, tactless, and uncompromising. These perceptions of Mahathir might not have mattered during the balmiest days of his administration. When his popularity was high, his admirers could nuance those perceptions of Mahathir positively: the man was firm, he called a spade a spade, he got things done the way he wanted. But with Mahathir's credibility undermined by the financial scandals, his popularity whittled down by the political crises, and his leadership now weakened by Musa's desertion, the nuance went mostly the other way: his detractors criticized his 'non-consultative', even 'dictatorial', ways.[212]

At the hurriedly convened UMNO Supreme Council meeting of 28 February to discuss Musa's resignation, Mahathir countered by producing another, earlier, letter from Musa Hitam to Mahathir, dated 5 July 1984. By making available this 'Top secret—Personal' letter—in which Musa wanted to 'register *my strongest views against* TR's [Tengku Razaleigh's] appointment at MTI [Ministry of Trade and Industry]'—Mahathir meant to show that Musa resigned because Mahathir would not comply with Musa's demand that Razaleigh be removed from the Cabinet after Razaleigh lost his second contest against Musa.[213] This emergency UMNO Supreme Council meeting turned out to be the first terrain upon which Musa's and Mahathir's supporters commenced their tactical manoeuvres to outflank one another.[214] The Supreme Council more or less reached a compromise, at least for the time being and seemingly for the sake of the party's image: it stated its allegiance to Mahathir's leadership but sent a party delegation to meet with Musa and to persuade him to withdraw his resignations.[215]

Eventually, Musa agreed to withdraw his resignation as UMNO's Deputy President—but *not* his resignation from the Deputy Prime Minister's position. He reasoned that he was elected by the party to be its Deputy President, but was appointed by Mahathir to be his Deputy Prime Minister. But that only exerted additional pressure on Mahathir and exposed another of his vulnerable points. Never having been a real 'party boss' with a personal grass-roots base in UMNO, Mahathir owed his appeal to the party membership primarily to his Malay nationalist credentials and his ideological influence. That did not quite matter so long as an unchallenged Mahathir remained above the intra-party fray by virtue of being UMNO President and Prime Minister. But Musa's manner of desertion effectively dragged Mahathir into the intra-party fray and 'reduced' Mahathir to being only one of three contenders (Mahathir, Musa, and Razaleigh) at UMNO's very summit—exactly where Mahathir's damaged prestige as Prime Minister and his largely untested party President's claim to rank-and-file loyalty had to contend with the broad bases and deep support which Musa and Razaleigh had built up throughout UMNO.[216]

The Hour of the Populist: The August 1986 General Election

Mahathir responded to the public outcry over the financial scandals as might be expected of a Prime Minister who had an overwhelming majority in Parliament and who was an heir to a political tradition that was not known for 'executive accountability'. Where he could, he ignored or dismissed most of the public criticisms. Hence, for five years, there was simply no admission of the Maminco affair. Mahathir left Daim Zainuddin to 'clarify' the EPF–Makuwasa transaction, and Daim in turn instructed Zain Asraai to 'explain' it. Mahathir's administration had earlier known of the DTCs' troubles but left it until five days after the 3 August 1986 election to act against the DTCs. Mahathir did become partially unstuck over the BMF affair. He refused public demands for a Royal Commission of Inquiry into the BMF affair but was compelled to set up a Bank Bumiputra 'in-house panel of inquiry', later known as the 'Committee of Inquiry', headed by Ahmad Noordin, the former Auditor-General. After the Committee submitted its 'Final Report', Mahathir initially refused to make it public on grounds that the government might become subject to libel suits arising from the contents,[217] and the 'possibility that public release of the report will affect the performance of Bank Bumiputra'.[218] But there were strong public demands for the release of the report and Ahmad Noordin and Chooi Mun Sou, two out of the three Committee members, expressed their willingness to accept responsibility for its publication.[219] Mahathir questioned the Committee's authority and impartiality[220] but finally agreed to release it. But, 'to be fair to everybody', the government supplied its own 'White Paper on the BMF' in parallel with the Committee's 'Final Report'.[221]

To all appearances, Mahathir's other political difficulties had also become more pressing. The Prime Minister had been critical of 'pressure groups in a democracy'; now, public outrage over BMF, Papan, and Sabah in particular seemed to have galvanized the major NGOs into a movement of mass dissent.[222] In the 1982 general election, the early '2 M' administration's dynamism, reformism, and gestures of liberalism had helped to erode the DAP's strength in Parliament. But beginning from the by-election of September 1983, when it won back the Seremban parliamentary seat from the MCA, the DAP had regained its ground among the urban non-Malay electorate.[223] PAS had similarly performed poorly in the 1982 election. But the massive attendances at PAS *ceramah* (political talks) in the mid-1980s seemed to herald the party's resurgence among the Malay electorate, more so if its overtures to the non-Muslim electorate could result in a swing against UMNO in keenly contested Malay-majority constituencies. In 1981 and 1984, Mahathir had been elected UMNO's President without contest but Musa's resignation had begun to cast doubts over Mahathir's ability to contain the party's factionalism for long. Tensions grew within the Barisan Nasional. UMNO was worried that the MCA was too badly divided after the Neo Yee Pan–Tan Koon Swan presidential contest to be able to retain Chinese support for the Barisan Nasional.[224] On its part, the MCA was upset that the government had 'allowed' Tan Koon Swan to be arrested by the Singapore authorities over the Pan-El collapse. The Gerakan Rakyat Malaysia, the self-proclaimed 'conscience of the Barisan Nasional', professed to differ with Mahathir and UMNO over the handling of the BMF affair, Papan, Sabah, and other issues, and even pondered aloud the wisdom of remaining within the coalition.

Mahathir's responses to the political crises were likewise varied. He publicly accepted the decisions which Musa as Acting Prime Minister had taken in his absence, namely over Papan, Sabah, and Memali. But the proposal to build a radioactive waste dump-site was not abandoned; the relocation of the ARE dump-site from Papan to Bukit Merah started off another round of local resistance. After the Memali incident, several more PAS leaders were arrested under the Internal Security Act, one of them for publishing his version of the incident. The Kedah Islamic Religious Council issued a fatwa that denied PAS's claim of martyrdom for Ibrahim Mahmood and his slain Memali followers which technically proscribed any further PAS agitation over the issue.[225] In Sabah, where it served Mahathir's purpose and salved his pride to leave the PBS government in a prolonged state of instability, he 'did nothing'. Even so, Herman Luping, Sabah's Attorney-General and a PBS leader, was arrested in October 1985, coincidentally the month in which the Ulu Padas by-election was held, and charged with corruptly receiving RM464,000 on behalf of the PBS.[226] And to shore up his position in UMNO after Musa's resignation, Mahathir appointed Ghafar Baba, UMNO's 'perennial' Vice-President and much less of a potential rival than Razaleigh Hamzah, as the new Deputy Prime Minister.[227]

Mahathir's public image was already marked by irony. The Prime Minister who had started office on an anti-corruption crusade found himself bestriding the most sordid period in Malaysia's financial history. The politician who had decried 'money politics' as a threat to his party's soul hesitated to investigate the conspiracies linking money and politics which gnawed at the bowels of his administration.[228] The populist who had placed popular sovereignty above royal prerogative resisted public demands for 'executive accountability'.

Against this adverse view of him and his administration, Mahathir pleaded the innocence of his administration. Whatever the scandal, whatever the crisis, he claimed to have been moved by honourable motives and to have acted in good faith. At most, he conceded that his administration was an unfortunate victim of circumstances. On the BMF affair, he spoke at one point of a 'betrayal of trust' and 'heinous crimes' being committed by BMF's principal officers, but fundamentally he attributed the BMF affair to the collapse of the Hong Kong property market. He reasoned that the colony's property market had been every banker's choicest lending target, and 'had there been no collapse in the [Hong Kong] property market ... certainly there would not have been a problem' and then 'maybe everyone would praise what has happened'.[229]

This basic plea of having being foiled by unforeseen and unfavourable market fluctuations presaged Daim Zainuddin's explanation of the EPF affair. Daim recalled that the Cabinet decided to support the weakened market 'on [*sic*] the behest of captains of industry' who 'approached Prime Minister Datuk Seri Dr Mahathir Mohamad and me. We were initially against the idea but in view of the large number of people in serious trouble because of market conditions, we agreed'.[230]

Like Mahathir, Daim admitted no culpability for instructing managers of public funds to enter the stock market. He was in fact close to being indignant: 'Fund managers were making money until the crash of Pan-El and the stock market which we did not expect.'[231]

And when Mahathir finally revealed the Maminco losses, he defended the government's intervention: 'it is true that governments could not enter the tin market' but 'whatever was done by the government was intended to save the tin industry' because 'the large scale cheating that was going on at the LME at that time was ruining us'.[232] 'For some time,' he noted, 'the government managed to collect higher revenue' and 'were it not for the cheating carried out in London where the rules were altered to protect the LME members, the government would not have lost and the question of the government's involvement in defending the price of tin would not have been raised at all'.[233]

But increasingly Mahathir did not simply plead good intentions and honourable motives. Over the BMF affair, he criticized Britain's 'hamfisted handling of the relationship with Hong Kong' which caused the collapse of the colony's property market.[234] Recalling that 'relations between Hong Kong and Malaysia were not good at one time' and that 'there were differences between me and the governor there in 1975', Mahathir questioned the Hong Kong police's seizure of BMF documents in connection with their investigation of the Jalil Ibrahim murder.[235] He repeatedly wondered— 'the ways things are reported'—why, of the 'not less than 50 banks, maybe as many as 100 banks, involved in loans' to the Carrian Group, 'it looks as if only BMF has lent money to this customer'.[236]

Those were relatively mild, 'veiled hints of Hong Kong or British antipathy toward Malaysia' in the context of the BMF affair.[237] By 1986, they had yielded to explicit accusations of a more invidious design. Mahathir claimed to detect a pattern whereby 'tendentious', 'unfair', and 'unsubstantiated' articles damaging to Malaysia 'were timed to appear just before certain occasions, particularly when there was a meeting that may affect the economy of the country'.[238] He charged that 'foreign powers' and the 'foreign press', abetted by local critics and oppositionists, were attempting to misrepresent the country's condition, malign its leaders, and sabotage its economy. He denounced 'some of the local journalists' for being the 'tools' of 'Jewish-owned' 'foreign magazines' which sought to 'create chaos' within the country.[239] He 'gave warning' that the government 'knew several organizations were managed by groups which received foreign assistance from certain quarters in order [to ensure] that Malaysia would not progress in the field of industrialization'.[240] Some of the NGOs received funding from overseas, which was no secret, but he accused them of harbouring 'crypto socialists' whose identities forever remained a secret—because, 'no', he would not name them.[241] He characterized the local environmentalists who opposed the proposed Bakun Dam project as the 'slaves' and 'hirelings' of 'developed countries which do not want to see this country's industries compete with their industries'.[242]

In a manner reminiscent of some populists, Mahathir redefined the criticisms of his administration as threats from alien ideas, hidden hands, and insidious means. The 'crypto socialists' 'realized they had no place in the country' but in 'the guise of intellectuals', they '[were] invited to seminars and conventions where they deliver[ed] working papers aimed at spreading the socialist philosophy'.[243] His critics from the NGOs were not just critics: 'These people have political motives but they cannot form political parties and so they hide behind their organizations to prevent development.'[244] There were 'foreign newspapers and magazines' which 'gave strong support to PAS and DAP' so that 'both would have renewed spirit to oppose the Barisan Nasional government'.[245] There were 'groups' which, 'by using the BMF issue ... [were] trying to oust the Malay leaders',[246] or were insinuating that the Mahathir administration had its 'Watergate' and its 'Lockheed': 'They talk of a scandal such as the one in which Tanaka [of Japan] was involved. They know they cannot win through the ballot box so they are trying to topple us through a whisper campaign.'[247] Were not Mahathir's protestations of innocence too transparent and his allegations of intrigue too wild to be persuasive?

They probably were to the urban non-Malay constituency—that section of Malaysian society most outraged by the scandals. From mid-1981 to the 1982 general election, the Barisan Nasional under Mahathir had managed to win significant support from this urban electorate. During the constitutional crisis of 1983, Mahathir had a measure of the urban constituency's quiet sympathy. But from 1984 onwards, the urban constituency—whose political sentiments were most strongly expressed by the DAP but whose sense of moral outrage was best captured by Aliran—had come to regard Mahathir's promise of a 'clean, efficient, and trustworthy' administration as merely base coin. And, by 1986, when the general election approached, the urban non-Malay constituency had largely been lost to the Barisan Nasional. In the urban electoral contests, the DAP could look forward to a field day against the MCA and Gerakan. That which was sown by the financial scandals and political crises was expected to be reaped by Mahathir's partners in the Barisan Nasional.

From Mahathir's perspective, what mattered was to retain the loyalty of UMNO's traditional rural Malay base. In that sense, one has to discover—exactly in Mahathir's seemingly unconvincing protestations of innocence and wild 'anti-foreign', 'anti-pressure group', 'anti-opposition', and 'anti-press' allegations—a distinctly populist appeal made to a select audience: UMNO's rural Malay constituency. For this rural Malay constituency—as opposed to the urban, middle class, fiscally conscious, market-literate electorate—BMF and Carrian, LME and Maminco, EPF and Makuwasa, DTCs and Pan-El were alien entities which did not inhabit their quintessentially localized political world of UMNO–PAS rivalry. It was not rustic idiocy but social milieu which compelled the rural Malay constituency to find greater political immediacy in issues affecting 'Malay-Muslim unity'—*kafir-mengkafir, dua imam*, separate burial grounds for UMNO and PAS supporters, boycott of local functions, and the break-up of families[248]— than in the financial scandals. As the political campaigning during the 1986 election showed, not just UMNO but PAS (in sharp contrast to the DAP) took leave of the financial scandals to conduct their electoral battles on other terrain.

But at another ideological level, just as the urban constituency held Mahathir to his early promise of 'clean government', so the rural Malay constituency could readily hold fast to the idea of 'rightful government' which Mahathir insisted was *his* and *theirs* by virtue of an electoral majority and mandate. Add an 'anti-urban' flavour ('it's the poor who will suffer—not these do-gooders in the cities')[249] and a dash of ethnic appeal (the DAP meant to perpetuate Malay economic backwardness, the PAS was ready to sell the Malay birthright)—and to that rural Malay constituency, a 'strong government'[250] palpably made more sense than an 'effective opposition'. By conjuring up an image of his elected government and his personal leadership coming under siege by alien quarters and non-elected groups, Mahathir made his populist appeal to the rural Malay constituency perhaps not only comprehensible but compelling, perhaps not only natural but just: one either commanded a majority or followed it, one either possessed a mandate or heeded it. Mahathir, having a prior claim to both majority and mandate, by virtue of the 1982 election, appealed to have them extended.

During the first half of 1986, Mahathir traversed the country in a series of official visits and public rallies. During these occasions, he gauged the political sentiments of the masses, attacked his critics, and evaluated the state of preparation of the Barisan Nasional's election machinery. In July, Mahathir called for a general election to be held in early August, having judged that this was the 'best time for the Barisan Nasional to win'. He was aware that the populace was politically restive. He meant the election to end the anticipation of election: 'Until this election is over, the people cannot settle down to do anything. They have been thinking about the election all the while. It is a syndrome that we must get rid of. We do not want the people to go on talking and speculating about the election, and depressing the stock market with their talk.'[251]

Many local and foreign observers expected or forecast that the financial scandals and political crises of the Mahathir era, taking place during a continuing economic recession, would inflict serious losses upon the Barisan Nasional. The opposition parties, mainly the DAP and PAS, seemed poised to make significant electoral gains. They were optimistic enough to call on the electorate to deny the Barisan Nasional its traditional and symbolically important 'two-thirds majority' in Parliament. The major NGOs supported this 'no two-thirds' call. However, the August 1986 election returned the Barisan Nasional to power with 148 out of a total of 177 parliamentary seats, thirty seats more than what was required to safeguard the Barisan Nasional's two-thirds majority. UMNO's performance was close to perfect. It won eighty-three out of eighty-four parliamentary contests. PAS, on which much oppositionist hope had rested, managed a solitary parliamentary victory in Pengkalan Cepa, Kelantan. It 'disappointed' Mahathir that the DAP won twenty-four parliamentary seats and inflicted heavy defeats on the MCA and Gerakan.[252]

August 1986 held a deep personal triumph for Mahathir. There could be no mistaking that. Under siege over the scandals, facing widespread disaffection, and suffering from Musa's abandonment, he had defeated his opponents in a show of electoral force. His mandate had been renewed and his leadership extended.

But one might also detect in that triumph a peculiar culmination of Mahathir's populism. As a consequence of the August election results, there now loomed a curious 'rural–urban divide' in the electoral topography (of Peninsular Malaysia) which reflected different but overlapping hues.[253] With UMNO having devastated PAS in the Malay 'country', and the DAP having humiliated the MCA and Gerakan in the non-Malay 'town', the Malaysian Parliament now featured a 'strong government' facing a reinforced, if still far from 'effective', opposition. Of course, that could be interpreted in strictly ethnic terms as a Malay-dominated government facing a Chinese-based opposition. It was instructive that Mahathir partly interpreted this as the triumph of 'rural loyalty' over 'urban defection'. In his presidential address to the Thirty-seventh UMNO General Assembly, on 18 September 1986, which might be regarded as his 'victory speech' proper, Mahathir brushed aside criticisms that excessive rural weightage (in the distribution of electoral constituencies) had allowed the Barisan Nasional to win four-fifths of the seats with only 57 per cent of the popular vote.[254] From his point of view, the loyal rural constituency served as the government's bulwark against 'the current of chauvinism among many Chinese in the urban areas in this recent election'.[255] That the 'urban voters were not very bound to any party'[256] gave him no pause to ponder the disaffection of the DAP supporters but instead reason to charge that 'the Chinese in the urban areas have shown proof of their chauvinism and spurned our hand of friendship in this recent general election'.[257] Who was it, Mahathir asked, who had attacked the government over BMF, Maminco, and Makuwasa, who was responsible for Pan-El and the DTCs, and who was indirectly to blame for the country's economic decline and the reduction in foreign investment: 'Who caused all this to happen? The people in the villages? ... Or the people in the towns who so readily condemned the government, people who always faulted the government, people who were so angry that they wanted to see the Barisan Nasional lose?'[258]

Immediately after the election, Mahathir had commented that 'in the past [1982] they [the urban voters] supported us ... maybe they will support us at another time'; but basically he thought that the 'urban voters did not have the same loyalty as rural voters and they easily changed parties'.[259] Thus Mahathir pledged 'to perpetuate the system which gives weightage to rural areas because this is the best system for political stability and balanced development'.[260]

Before the 1986 elections, there were UMNO members and leaders who had some misgivings about the people's continued support. Mahathir had called the election to slay all talk that the government, in other words his leadership, no longer enjoyed the support of the people. Now, as he commented on the night of his triumph, he had 'proof that the government practised the right policies and all accusations of corruption and mismanagement which were flung at its leaders were made purely out of political interest'.[261] Now, as he told the UMNO delegates to the Thirty-seventh General Assembly, 'we know the position of the people'. Evidently, 'the people' were not those who had 'spread various rumours to erode the faith of the people and UMNO members in the party's leadership' and who had charged that certain leaders were involved in corruption, including embezzling BMF money.[262] They were not 'the enemies of UMNO and their supporters from abroad, including several Zionist-controlled magazines and newspapers'; not the PAS which engaged in 'self-deception' and 'deified their leaders'; not the DAP which had no Malay representative 'as if there were no Malays in Malaysia'; not 'a number of highly educated *bumiputeras* in the city who do not support UMNO' but did not dare 'to try their luck in the democratic process'; not 'our own journalists and newspapers who have been brain-washed'; and, perhaps, not even those Malaysians who 'sometimes denigrate the image of our country'.[263] Feeling vindicated by the election, Mahathir was yet unforgiving in his hour of victory—as if the leader who knew the people should not have had to vindicate himself in the first place.

1. Ghita Ionescu and Ernest Gellner (eds.), *Populism: Its Meanings and National Characteristics*, London: Weidenfeld and Nicolson, 1970. Also see the treatment of populism as a distinctive mode of political mobilization in newly independent countries in Peter Worsley, *The Third World*, London: Weidenfeld and Nicolson, 1974, Chapter 4, pp. 118–74.

2. Worsley, *The Third World*, pp. 119–26.

3. A basic notion of diverse populist movements, as suggested by Peter Wiles,

'A Syndrome, Not a Doctrine: Some Elementary Theses on Populism', in Ghita Ionescu and Ernest Gellner (eds.), *Populism: Its Meanings and National Characteristics*, London: Weidenfeld and Nicolson, 1970, p. 166. Bill Brugger and Dean Jaensch, *Australian Politics: Theory and Practice*, Sydney: George Allen and Unwin, 1985, p. 8, takes an early note of this point in discussing Australian populism.

4. One of the 'principal features' of the Third World 'variant of populism' is that 'the class struggle is ... an irrelevant conception' (Peter Worsley, 'The Concept of Populism', in Ghita Ionescu and Ernest Gellner (eds.), *Populism: Its Meanings and National Characteristics*, London: Weidenfeld and Nicolson, 1970, p. 229). 'In particular populism avoids class war in the Marxist sense' (Wiles, 'A Syndrome, Not a Doctrine', p. 167). It was not entirely clear what Mahathir thought the 'war against communism' was about, but he was clear that it was 'not a class war' (Mahathir, 'Speech at the Pemuda and Wanita UMNO General Assembly', Kuala Lumpur, 1 July 1976, reprinted as 'Asas dan Matlamat Perjuangan UMNO', in Harun Derauh and Shafie Nor (eds.), *Mahathir: Cita-cita dan Pencapaian*, Kuala Lumpur: Berita Publishing, 1982, pp. 17–27).

5. See the discussion of Mahathir's conception of piety in Chapter 5. It may be instructive to note Musa Hitam's view on this subject: 'There will be a growing class distinction between the wealthy and not wealthy Malays ... because this is the society we are striving for within the context of the NEP—to create a class that could occupy the top of a pyramid as against a class which occupies the very bottom of the pyramid. This is inevitable, but this does not necessarily create a situation of conflict. I personally do not subscribe to the Marxist perception of inevitability of conflict within the context of our society—especially within the Malay community. I think this is something which we feel we will be able to diffuse by an injection of the spiritual value of development; by ethics, by religion, by making them realise that one has to strive in order to reach the top. It is our bounden duty to respect the success of whoever reaches the top as a result of hard work and striving for it' (Tan Chee Khoon, *Without Fear or Favour*, Singapore: Eastern Universities Press, 1984, p. 100).

6. See the essay, 'The Poor Are Poorer, the Rich, Richer', in Mahathir Mohamad, *The Challenge*, Petaling Jaya: Pelanduk Publications, 1986; translated from *Menghadapi Cabaran*, Kuala Lumpur: Pustaka Antara, 1976, pp. 4–16.

7. 'In the context of our economy, we find that the town represents facilities for economic activities including trade, finance, communications, services and others.... In this broader context, we see that the town has a positive role and is not a "parasite" upon its surrounding.... [A] town should become the manifestation of the material wealth and spirituality of society' (Mahathir, 'Ucapan di Upacara Perletakan Batu Asas Projek Dayabumi', Kuala Lumpur, 14 November 1981, reprinted in Arkib Negara Malaysia, *Ucapan-ucapan Dato' Seri Dr Mahathir Mohamad, 1981*, Kuala Lumpur, 1986, pp. 91–7).

8. See the section 'North–South, East–West' in Chapter 3.

9. Richard Hofstadter, 'North America', in Ghita Ionescu and Ernest Gellner (eds.), *Populism: Its Meanings and National Characteristics*, London: Weidenfeld and Nicolson, 1970, p. 9.

10. Wiles, 'A Syndrome, Not a Doctrine', p. 167.

11. Mahathir, 'Whither Malaysia', Paper presented at the Keio International Symposium on Asia and Japan, Tokyo, 7–11 November 1983, reprinted in Andrew J. L. Armour (ed.), *Asia and Japan*, London: Athlone Press, 1985, p. 152.

12. Rehman Rashid, 'Why I Took to Politics', *New Straits Times*, 5 July 1986; original emphasis.

13. Ibid.

14. Ibid.

15. In that sense he spoke of the global recession, protectionism, and related problems as being 'man-made' and could therefore be 'un-made' by responsible leadership (see Chapter 3). That the G-7 leaders could do harm was, however, more obvious, as in Mahathir's oft-cited example of the yen and Deutschmark revaluation of the Plaza Accord.

16. 'Inevitably a few Negroes achieved a breakthrough, and it is they who most see and feel the resentment of their community and desire to right the wrongs which have been wrought on Negroes through the generations' (Mahathir Mohamad, *The Malay Dilemma*, Singapore: Donald Moore for Asia Pacific Press, 1970, pp. 65–6). By now, Mahathir would have substituted 'blacks' for 'Negroes'.

17. Leung Thong Ping, 'Mahathir', *Sunday Mail*, 2 April 1972.

18. Mahathir's letter to Tunku Abdul Rahman, dated 17 June 1969, reproduced in Karl von Vorys, *Democracy without Consensus: Communalism and Political Stability in Malaysia*, Princeton: Princeton University Press, 1976, pp. 372–3.

19. Robin Adshead, *Mahathir of Malaysia*, London: Hibiscus Publishing Company, 1989, pp. 61–2. After his 'Buy British Last' campaign, he said: 'Over large areas I have no complaints against the British. Indeed I can get on with the ordinary Englishmen quite easily' (Munir Majid, 'Datuk Seri Dr Mahathir Mohamad: Power and Responsibility', *Malaysian Business*, October 1976, p. 7). His 'ordinary Englishmen' were probably businessmen; otherwise it is difficult to see how he could 'get on' with the 'ordinary', working-class blokes whose 'laziness', 'socialism', and 'tendency towards anarchy' he detested.

20. Mahathir, *The Malay Dilemma*, p. 103.

21. Ibid., p. 114.

22. Ibid.

23. Ibid., p. 103. Mahathir's 'revolution' was really 'social engineering': 'Urbanization, acquisition of new skills and the acceptance by the Malays of new values which are still compatible with their religion and their basically feudal outlook would constitute a revolution' (ibid., p. 114).

24. Mahathir, 'Whither Malaysia', p. 152.

25. '100 Hari di bawah Mahathir', *Berita Harian*, 27 October 1981.

26. Supriya Singh, 'The Man behind the Politician', *New Straits Times*, 14 April 1982. But 'I don't like adoration, adulation. That is why when people try to kiss my hand, I pull away' (ibid.).

27. H. F. Rawlings, 'The Malaysian Constitutional Crisis of 1983', *International and Comparative Law Quarterly*, 35, 2 (April 1986): 237–54, provides the most detailed analysis of the 1983 constitutional crisis. Also see Roger Kershaw, 'Malay Monarchy since Yahya Petra: Riding for a Fall?', *Contemporary Review*, 245, 1424 (September 1984): 113–20, and Vincent Lowe, 'Redefining the

"Constitutionality" of the Monarchy: The 1983 Constitutional Amendment Crisis in Malaysia', *Kajian Malaysia*, 11, 2 (December 1984): 1–15.

28. K. Das, 'Less Ado about Anything', *Far Eastern Economic Review*, 25 August 1983, pp. 20–2.

29. David Jenkins, 'Proud and Prickly Princes Finally Meet Their Match', *Far Eastern Economic Review*, 23 February 1984, pp. 12–15.

30. Ibid.

31. ' . . . the chief editors were again summoned to Mahathir's office' and 'once again Mahathir found most of them more than understanding and hardly had to ask them to ignore Senu's letter; they had decided to do as much themselves' (ibid.).

32. Tunku Abdul Rahman, 'As I See It . . . ', *Star*, 17 October 1983. In contrast to the *New Straits Times* report, the Tunku had no doubt that 'only three provisions' in the Constitution (Amendment) Bill 1983 had 'controversial significance'—'the power of the Yang di-Pertuan Agong to assent to bills', 'the power of the Yang di-Pertuan Agong to declare an emergency', and 'the curtailment of the powers of the State Rulers under the State Constitutions following the new amendment'.

33. Jenkins, 'Proud and Prickly Princes Finally Meet Their Match', suggested that one of the reasons for the Agong's refusal to assent was because he discovered that it included a provision which made the Sultans, in their own states, subject to the same '15 day assent period'—which the Sultans objected to and which the Agong was not briefed about in his meeting with Mahathir in July.

34. Kershaw, 'Malay Monarchy since Yahya Petra', pp. 113–15, gives an interesting background to the impending succession to the throne.

35. The Menteris Besar in question were Othman Saat of Johore and Ghazali Jawi of Perak and his successor, Wan Mohamed (David Jenkins, 'Sultans as Symbols', *Far Eastern Economic Review*, 30 June 1983, pp. 26–32). In Pahang, home of the then reigning Agong, Sultan Ahmad Shah, Menteri Besar Rahim Bakar left office after a crisis during which the then Regent of Pahang refused to sign money bills (Kershaw, 'Malay Monarchy since Yahya Petra', p. 114).

36. David Jenkins, 'Princes and Palaces, and a Possible Battle Royal', *Far Eastern Economic Review*, 30 June 1983, pp. 30–1.

37. K. Das, 'Locking Horns over the Timing of the Ramadan Fast', *Far Eastern Economic Review*, 30 June 1983, p. 34.

38. See Kershaw, 'Malay Monarchy since Yahya Petra', and Rawlings, 'The Malaysian Constitutional Crisis of 1983', for detailed explanations on why the Sultan of Perak and the Sultan of Johore were respectively first and second in line to become the next Agong in 1984.

39. Adshead, *Mahathir of Malaysia*, p. 51.

40. On the implications of the Sedition Act within the context of the 1983 Constitutional Crisis, see Rawlings, 'The Malaysian Constitutional Crisis of 1983', pp. 248–9.

41. See the section 'The Legacy of C. H. E. Det' in Chapter 3.

42. Mahathir, *The Malay Dilemma*, p. 33.

43. Ibid., p. 35.

44. Mahathir, 'Speech at the Pemuda and Wanita UMNO General Assembly',

Kuala Lumpur, 25 June 1981, reprinted as 'Cabaran di hadapan Pemuda dan Wanita UMNO', in Harun Derauh and Shafie Nor (eds.), *Mahathir: Cita-cita dan Pencapaian*, Kuala Lumpur: Berita Publishing, 1982, pp. 51–9. 'In the old days the rulers and the aristocrats had no need to work' and 'Malay rulers had only to collect regular payments' from 'trade in opium' or the 'collect[ion] [of] state revenue'. Hence 'Malay administrators smoked opium and received payments from the holders of trade and tax monopolies'. It was 'only seventy years ago' that 'the British gave political pensions to the royal families so that they did not have to work'.

45. The *Utusan Malaysia* editorial of 13 June 1983 began by saying that Mahathir criticized 'groups' which wanted to start a 'revolution' to 'replace the system of monarchy in this country' because they believed that the monarchy was 'not good' and 'not necessary'. Was this a veiled attack on radical Islamic elements in and out of PAS who might have tried to take advantage of the disagreement between Perak and Johore, and the National Islamic Council? In mid-June, there were several calls for a 'review of the Constitution' following that disagreement with the National Islamic Council but none sounded 'republican'. Examples are Tunku Abdul Rahman's comment and ABIM's statement, both in *New Straits Times*, 18 June 1983; and PAS's statement in *New Straits Times*, 21 June 1983. Also see K. Das, '1028 and All That', *Far Eastern Economic Review*, 14 July 1983, p. 16. Or were Mahathir and the *Utusan Malaysia* subtly laying the ground for a later claim that the constitutional amendments were necessary to 'uphold constitutional monarchy' as Musa Hitam 'pledged' in the midst of the crisis? (*Star*, 7 June 1983). Musa felt 'sad that there were Malaysians, especially from the opposition parties, who were attracted to ... the idea of creating an Islamic republic through the politics of force' (*Star*, 7 November 1983). For an analysis of an earlier Musa statement as a message 'to indicate to the sultans where their salvation lay', see K. Das, 'A Battle Royal', *Far Eastern Economic Review*, 13 October 1983, pp. 17–18.

46. For example, Chandra Muzaffar argued that 'some aspects' of the institution of royalty in Malaysia 'can and should be discussed in public'—'the alleged utilization of public funds for private purposes, the apparent extravagance in lifestyles, involvement in businesses, interference in strictly political matters, the inability to uphold high ethical standards and most of all the absence of an image of excellence which can inspire emulation' (cited in K. Das, 'Sultans as Symbols', *Far Eastern Economic Review*, 30 June 1983, p. 27).

47. This was the royalists' strongest objection and the Tunku raised it in his column in the *Star* (17 October 1983).

48. At a rally in Bagan Datok, Perak, on 27 November 1983, Mahathir said that 'our enemies have tried to deceive the people by saying that we wish to set up a republic' (*Star*, 28 November 1983). Musa Hitam pledged UMNO's commitment to 'defending the sovereignty of the Malay Rulers and constitutional monarchy in Malaysia' (*Star*, 12 November 1983).

49. Abdullah Badawi, for example, argued that the amendments would 'strengthen their [the rulers'] position as constitutional monarchs' (*Berita Harian*, 2 November 1983). Ghafar Baba claimed that 'the Bill will forever secure the sovereignty of our Rulers' (*New Straits Times*, 5 November 1983). Against these 'reassurances', the Sultan of Perak replied: 'No one has told us how it [the amendment]

would strengthen us' (K. Das, 'The Sultans Dig In', *Far Eastern Economic Review*, 24 November 1983, p. 18).

50. Chandra Muzaffar, 'Constitutional Crisis: The Aftermath', in Chandra Muzaffar, *Freedom in Fetters: An Analysis of the State of Democracy in Malaysia*, Penang: Aliran, 1986, p. 230. Later, Musa Hitam identified seven Cabinet Ministers as Mahathir's 'magnificent seven': Abdullah Badawi (Prime Minister's Department), Adib Adam (Information), Anwar Ibrahim (Culture, Youth and Sports), Rafidah Aziz (Public Enterprises), Rais Yatim (Land and Regional Development), Sanusi Junid (National and Rural Development), and Shahrir Samad (Federal Territory).

51. See, for example, two features written by unnamed 'Special Writers' attached to *Bernama*—'The Malaysian Constitution—What Is It?', *New Straits Times*, 7 November 1983, and 'The Basis of Malay Nationhood', *New Straits Times*, 16 November 1983, as well as a letter to the editor, 'Where Does Raja Tun Azlan Shah Stand?', *New Straits Times*, 30 November 1983.

52. 'Initially, the British tried to turn our rulers merely into kadis', but 'our unity defeated the British Empire so that it was forced to abort the Malayan Union and forced to restore our rights and the power of the rulers' (Mahathir, quoted in *Berita Harian*, 28 November 1983).

53. See Cheah Boon Kheng, 'The Erosion of Ideological Hegemony and Royal Power and the Rise of Malay Nationalism, 1945–46', *Journal of Southeast Asian Studies*, XIX, 1 (March 1988): 1–28, for an insightful treatment of the ideological tensions in the 1946 tussle between the emerging 'Malay nation' and the Malay royalty which, in Cheah's view, resulted in the former's victory.

54. *Star*, 27 November 1983.

55. Quoted in Zulkefli Abu, 'Pindaan: Anwar Kecam Pemimpin yang Diam Diri', *Berita Harian*, 28 November 1983.

56. *Star*, 28 November 1983.

57. Quoted in Sharom Suboh, 'Hanya Sistem Parlimen Jamin Keadilan bagi Negara: PM', *Berita Harian*, 20 December 1983.

58. Quoted in K. Das, 'Mahathir Plays It Tough', *Far Eastern Economic Review*, 15 December 1983, p. 15. Thus, it might be said, Anwar remained true to his political benefactor, Mahathir, his Islamic credentials, and the intemperance that was the Pemuda UMNO tradition.

59. Quoted in Sharom Suboh, 'Hanya Sistem Parlimen Jamin Keadilan bagi Negara'.

60. Quoted in Ahmad Puad Onah, 'PM Tidak Akan Letak Jawatan', *Berita Harian*, 27 November 1983.

61. Ibid.

62. Quoted in Raphael Pura, 'Mahathir Whips Up Support at Rallies', *Asian Wall Street Journal*, 12 December 1983.

63. See 'The Hidden Facts', a letter signed 'Lover of True Democracy', in *Far Eastern Economic Review*, 22 December 1983, which gave details of a massive and emotional 'public audience with the people' given by the Sultan of Trengganu on 1 December 1983. The letter was accompanied by two photographs of the huge crowd at the palace grounds in Kuala Trengganu.

64. Chandra Muzaffar, 'The Constitutional Crisis: Clearing the Confusion', in Chandra Muzaffar, *Freedom in Fetters: An Analysis of the State of Democracy in Malaysia*, Penang: Aliran, 1979, p. 207.

65. See Lim Kit Siang, 'Speech on the Constitutional (Amendment) Bill 1984', Parliament, Kuala Lumpur, 9 January 1984, reprinted in Lim Kit Siang, *Malaysia: Crisis of Identity*, Petaling Jaya: Democratic Action Party, 1986, pp. 118–34. For his opposition to the constitutional amendments, Lim Kit Siang was branded by Mahathir as a 'royalist'!

66. Cheah Boon Kheng, 'The Erosion of Ideological Hegemony and Royal Power', p. 28, concluded: 'It is said that the veto powers they retained under the Malaysian Constitution have led the rulers to believe that they, and not the *rakyat*, are the paramount authority in the country. Jurists are likely to debate over this indefinitely without reaching any agreement. But it is my contention that the resolution of the 1983 constitutional amendment crisis was very much to the favour of the Malaysian Parliament and the *rakyat*. However, it was never put to the test whether the "Will" of the people, or the sovereignty of the rulers is paramount. Both sides have preferred to call the settlement a "compromise".'

67. To date, the single most complete published source of information about BMF's operations and losses in Hong Kong comes from the *Final Report* (Kuala Lumpur: Bank Bumiputra Malaysia Berhad, 1986), prepared by the Bumiputra Malaysia Finance Limited Committee of Inquiry, headed by Ahmad Noordin. This discussion of the BMF affair relies on summaries of the *Final Report*, presented variously in 'BMF: 'The Final Report' (*Star*, 12 March 1986) and INSAN, *BMF: The People's Black Paper*, Kuala Lumpur, 1986. The Malaysian government's view of the BMF affair is contained in its 'White Paper' which was tabled in Parliament on Tuesday, 11 March 1986. For the 'politics' of the BMF affair, this discussion relies on the extensive local and regional press coverage as well as numerous statements and documents which emerged in the period from 1983 to 1986.

68. For useful background information on Carrian's dramatic rise and disastrous fall in the Hong Kong stock and property markets, see Philip Bowring and Robert Cottrell, *The Carrian File*, Hong Kong: Review Publishing Company, 1984.

69. Or about HK$4.6 billion out of Carrian's total debt of over HK$10 billion (ibid., p. 13) and US$123 million out of Kevin Hsu's debt of about US$300 million ('Rise and Fall of Kevin Hsu', in 'BMF: The Final Report', *Star*, 12 March 1986).

70. Of which RM600 million was suddenly injected into Bank Bumiputra by Permodalan Nasional Berhad (PNB) in early 1983 'to shore up Bank Bumiputra's finances because of problems in Hong Kong' (Cheah Cheng Hye, 'Colony Loans May Hurt Malaysian Agency', *Asian Wall Street Journal*, 11 October 1983).

71. Some time around November 1983, Bank Bumiputra wrote to 'monetary and banking authorities at home and abroad' and 'categorically denie[d] that there [was] any crisis', describing reports from 'regional and financial newspapers and periodicals' about BMF's problems as 'speculative, misleading and unfair' (Kadir Jasin, 'Bank Bumi: No Crisis in HK Unit', *Business Times*, 27 November 1983). In December 1983, Nawawi Mat Awin, Chairman of Bank Bumiputra, was reported to have said: 'I really don't know what the fuss is all about.... We don't have a

problem there. I assure you that the subsidiary is sound' ('Bank Bumi Chief Hits Out at Reports', *Sunday Star*, 19 December 1983).

72. See 'HK Unit Gets the Jitters', *Star*, 8 November 1982, a summary report on Carrian and the 'financial crisis in the HK property market'.

73. As the Governor of Bank Negara described it in March 1983; cited in Raphael Pura and Matt Miller, 'For Bank Bumiputra, Some Troubling Questions Remain', *Asian Wall Street Journal*, 1–2 July 1982.

74. 'Dr Nawawi, the Press was told, had to leave for Tokyo to sign a 10 billion yen (about RM100 million) loan, representing the second tranche of a loan totalling 20 billion yen ($200 million) to finance the construction of UMNO headquarters in Kuala Lumpur' (Kadir Jasin, 'No Answer from Bank Bumi AGM', *Business Times*, 28 June 1983).

75. 'Bank's Officers Stay Mum on Eda and Carrian', *New Straits Times*, 28 June 1983.

76. 'Proses Islamisasi Bukan Bererti Memaksa Undang-undang Islam', in Rosnah Majid, *Koleksi Temuramah Khas Tokoh-tokoh*, Kuala Lumpur: Utusan Publications and Distributors, 1985, pp. 248–84. The quotations are taken from pp. 280–1.

77. As in fact it was. N. V. Raman, P. K. Katharason, and Rusdi Mustapha, 'Probe into BMF Link' (*Star*, 22 July 1983) was an early local press report on the suspected link. Later 'police raids on offices of the troubled Carrian group in Hong Kong took a new turn ... with reports that their searches were linked to the murder of Bumiputra Malaysia Finance official Jalil Ibrahim' ('New Turn in Probe', *Star*, 14 September 1983). Reporting from Kuala Lumpur, Raphael Pura commented that 'Malaysian newspapers', 'Jalil's relatives', and 'public pressure' were united in trying to 'draw a connection between Mr Jalil's killing and the lending scandals' ('Malaysian Banker's Murder Escalates Scrutiny on Loans', *Asian Wall Street Journal*, 25 July 1983).

78. Bowring and Cottrell, *The Carrian File*, pp. 138–40, gives a useful synopsis of the Mak Foon Than trial which led to Mak's conviction on 17 May 1984 and his being sentenced to death.

79. To this day, no politician has officially been charged in connection with the BMF affair. But the 'average' Malaysian scarcely believes that no politics was involved.

80. State support had turned Bank Bumiputra into the nation's largest bank. For relatively early analyses of Bank Bumiputra's problems and some political ramifications arising out of BMF's losses, see Pura and Miller, 'For Bank Bumiputra, Some Troubling Questions Remain', and Wong Sulong, 'BMF Loans Cause Growing Concern', *Business Times* (Singapore), 30 March 1983.

81. In February 1983, Razaleigh Hamzah said that Bank Bumiputra was under the Prime Minister's charge. At his 11 October press conference, Mahathir said that Bank Bumiputra was controlled by the Ministry of Finance. Lim Kit Siang recalled in Parliament that 'when I asked the Finance Minister the next day on 12th October during question time who was in real charge of Bank Bumiputra, Tengku Razaleigh replied that if the Prime Minister said he was in charge, then he was in charge' ('Speech on the 1984 Budget', Parliament, 24 October 1983, reprinted

as 'BMF Scandal—Let the Chips Fall Where They Should', in Lim Kit Siang, *Malaysia: Crisis of Identity*, Petaling Jaya: Democratic Action Party, 1986, pp. 260–86).

82. 'Carrian: The Storm Breaks', *Asiaweek*, 21 October 1983, p. 54. For a considered speculation that Mahathir was not fully briefed about BMF's position, see 'A Furore over the Loans', *Asiaweek*, 28 October 1983, pp. 40–4.

83. Mahathir, Press Conference, Kuala Lumpur, 11 October 1983. Mahathir's statement, and the questions and answers which followed it were reproduced as 'Cards on the Table', *Malaysian Business*, November 1983, pp. 39–41.

84. He was referring to large 'consultancy fees' which Kamarul Ariffin, Chairman of Bank Bumiputra until April 1982, and BMF's principal officers took for approving the BMF loans. 'Cards on the Table' gives most of Mahathir's important press conference of 11 October 1983 but it left out Mahathir's comments on the 'betrayal of trust' and the 'heinous crime' for which see N. V. Raman, 'BMF Loan Scandal: Four to Go', *Star*, 12 October 1983.

85. Lim Kit Siang, Press Statement, 12 October 1983.

86. For a sample of expressions of dissatisfaction with the level of disclosures up to that point, see the editorials by the *New Straits Times* ('Not Personal Freedom', 17 October 1983), the *Star* ('BMF—Overdue Explanation', 6 October 1983), and *Watan* ('What Is This?', 18 October 1983). 'Questions That Need to be Answered: Aliran', *Star*, 15 October 1983, was fairly typical of the kinds of doubts that the NGOs had. That many sensed an unnamed 'puppeteer' behind the 'scapegoats' whom Mahathir had mentioned was captured in 'Bumiputra Tulen', 'Skandal Bank Bumiputra. Wayang Kulit: Dari Cerita Sedih kepada Cerita Lucu', *Mimbar Sosialis*, November–December 1983.

87. The most articulate call for a Royal Commission of Inquiry was made by Lim Kit Siang in Parliament on 18 October 1984. See 'Call for a Royal Commission of Inquiry into the BMF Scandal', in Lim Kit Siang, *Malaysia: Crisis of Identity*, Petaling Jaya: Democratic Action Party, 1986, pp. 303–31.

88. Lim Kit Siang, 'Speech When Moving a RM10 Cut on the Finance Minister's Salary', Parliament, 20 November 1984, reprinted as 'BMF Scandal—Malaysia's Watergate', in Lim Kit Siang, *Malaysia: Crisis of Identity*, Petaling Jaya: Democratic Action Party, 1986, pp. 346–51.

89. 'Briefs', *Far Eastern Economic Review*, 18 December 1986, p. 10.

90. The proposed increase was about 4.5 per cent (Nick Seaward, 'Blowing a Tin Trumpet', *Far Eastern Economic Review*, 2 October 1986, p. 103). Gill Burke, 'The Rise and Fall of the International Tin Agreements', in Jomo K. S. (ed.), *Undermining Tin: The Decline of Malaysian Pre-eminence*, Sydney: Transnational Corporations Research Project, University of Sydney, 1990, pp. 43–69, is excellent for a lay understanding of the background to the Maminco episode; see especially pp. 55–8.

91. Maminco kept its identity hidden by trading through David Zaidner and Marc Rich 'who used the LME metal-trading firm of MacLaine Watson ... and one or two others to place orders' (Raphael Pura, 'Malaysia Plan to Control Tin Led to Disaster', *Asian Wall Street Journal*, 22 September 1986).

92. Jomo K. S., 'Malaysia's Tin Market Corner', in Jomo K. S. (ed.),

Undermining Tin: The Decline of Malaysian Pre-eminence, Sydney: Transnational Corporations Research Project, University of Sydney, 1990, p. 71.

93. The following account is based on Pura, 'Malaysia Plan to Control Tin Led to Disaster'.

94. Jomo, 'Malaysia's Tin Market Corner', p. 74.

95. Cited in Seaward, 'Blowing a Tin Trumpet', p. 103.

96. To quote Zain Asraai, Chairman of the EPF, which was a 'key player' in the government's attempt to support the KLSE (*Star*, 25 June 1985).

97. *Star*, 25 June 1986. Daim Zainuddin was the country's first unelected Minister of Finance. A close friend of Mahathir's and a successful businessman with a reputation for corporate 'wizardry', Daim was an UMNO-nominated Senator when Mahathir appointed him to replace Razaleigh Hamzah after Razaleigh's defeat in the 1984 UMNO deputy presidential contest.

98. *Star*, 25 June 1986.

99. Ibid.

100. See the discussion of the Pan-Electric Industries collapse, below.

101. 'Daim Asks EPF Board to Clarify', *Star*, 25 June 1986.

102. '$30m Investment That Resulted in RM11.5m "Loss"', *Star*, 2 July 1986.

103. 'Zain: EPF Suffered "Paper Loss" of RM141m' and '$30m Investment That Resulted in RM11.5m "Loss"', *Star*, 2 July 1986.

104. Nick Seaward, 'Without Portfolio', *Far Eastern Economic Review*, 24 July 1986, pp. 82–3.

105. Daim's statement was made on 24 June 1986 ('Daim Asks EPF Board to Clarify') while Zain's clarification came out one week later ('EPF on Makuwasa', *Star*, 2 July 1986).

106. 'EPF on Makuwasa'.

107. But Makuwasa 'instead realized significant losses on its share transactions in the aftermath of the Pan-El stock market collapse in late 1985' (Jomo, 'Malaysia's Tin Market Corner', p. 75).

108. 'EPF on Makuwasa'.

109. Seaward, 'Blowing a Tin Trumpet'.

110. For an account of the closure of the SES in the wake of Pan-Electric's collapse, see Paul Sillitoe, 'Markets Blow a Fuse', *Far Eastern Economic Review*, 12 December 1985, pp. 87–9. The creditors' failed rescue plan is discussed on p. 89.

111. Ibid., p. 87.

112. For accounts of the impact of the Pan-El collapse on the KLSE, see Anthony Rowley, 'Pan-Electric Shock Jolts Kuala Lumpur', *Far Eastern Economic Review*, 12 December 1985, pp. 88–9; James Clad, 'Daim Buys More Time', and 'A Tangled Web of Deals', both in *Far Eastern Economic Review*, 19 December 1985, pp. 88–9.

113. Sillitoe, 'Markets Blow a Fuse', p. 87.

114. Bruce Gale, *Politics and Business: A Study of Multi-Purpose Holdings Berhad*, Singapore: Eastern Universities Press, 1985, p. 103.

115. Ibid.

116. Suhaini Aznam and Michael Malik, 'Trapped in a Storm', *Far Eastern*

Economic Review, 6 February 1986, pp. 12–15. An account of the arrest is available in 'The Singapore Sting', *Far Eastern Economic Review*, 30 January 1986, pp. 10–11.

117. Nigel Holloway, 'End of the Line', *Far Eastern Economic Review*, 4 September 1986, pp. 48–9; 'The Jailing of Tycoon Tan', *Asiaweek*, 7 September 1986, p. 31.

118. Malaysia, *Investigation Report on Twenty-four Deposit Taking Co-operatives*, Appendix to Command Paper 50, 1986, tabled in Parliament, 10 November 1986, hereafter cited as the 'White Paper on the DTCs'. See especially 'Reports on Individual Co-operatives' (no pagination). Report No. 24 deals with Kosatu.

119. 'Freeze on 23 Co-ops', *Star*, 9 August 1986, gave a full list of the DTCs which were affected by Bank Negara's order. For a fuller analysis of the DTC scandal, see Edmund Terence Gomez, *Money Politics in the Barisan Nasional*, Kuala Lumpur: Forum, 1991, pp. 47–104.

120. For reports on Bank Negara's move, see 'Freeze on 23 Co-ops', *Star*, 9 August 1986, and Nick Seaward, 'Cooperatives Purged', *Far Eastern Economic Review*, 21 August 1986, pp. 50–1.

121. Initially, 136 directors and officers were listed but the number was reduced to 72 as the other 64 were able to disclose their assets to the satisfaction of Bank Negara prior to a 15 August deadline (Seaward, 'Cooperatives Purged', p. 50).

122. 'White Paper on the DTCs', p. 17.

123. Nick Seaward, 'White Paper, Black Sheep', *Far Eastern Economic Review*, 20 November 1986, p. 103.

124. 'White Paper on the DTCs', p. 17.

125. Ibid., 'Report on Individual Co-operatives', Report No. 1.

126. Ibid., Report No. 24.

127. Ibid., p. 6.

128. Ibid., p. 9.

129. Ibid., p. 10.

130. Ibid., p. 16.

131. Ibid., p. 11.

132. On the KSM's history and growth, see Gale, *Politics and Business*, pp. 15–40. On the links between politics and the DTCs, see Gomez, *Money Politics in the Barisan Nasional*, pp. 49–55.

133. Gomez, *Money Politics in the Barisan Nasional*, pp. 52–55. Kosatu's chairman, Tee An Chuan, was President of the People's Progressive Party, a very minor component party of the Barisan Nasional. Tee was an ex-MCA member.

134. Just for clarification, since it is outside the scope of this discussion, it would be more accurate to say that the crisis continued in one form or another even after 1986 and intensified after the 1990 general election.

135. For a brief account of Pairin's immediate differences with Harris Salleh, see 'A Battle over Democracy', *Asiaweek*, 25 January 1985. Pairin's personal ascendancy to the position of Huguan Siow coincided with the rise of Kadazan 'cultural consciousness' which included a strong resentment of Berjaya and the Harris Salleh government's ethno-cultural policies (Francis Loh Kok Wah, 'Modernization, Cultural Revival and Counter-Hegemony: The Kadazans of Sabah in the 1980s', in Joel S. Kahn and Francis Loh Kok Wah (eds.), *Fragmented Vision: Culture and*

Politics in Contemporary Malaysia, Sydney: Asian Studies Association of Australia in association with Allen and Unwin, 1992, pp. 249–50).

136. By dating a letter of resignation, previously signed by Pairin, and delivering it to the Speaker of the State Assembly. All Berjaya candidates for elections left signed but undated letters of resignation with the Berjaya President. At first Pairin challenged the validity of his 'resignation' in court but then chose to stand in the by-election once it was called. A short but informative account of Pairin's differences with Harris Salleh and of the Tambunan by-election and its aftermath, is available in Mavis Puthucheary, 'What after Tambunan?', *Star*, 6 January 1985.

137. Among other effects of the abrogation of Tambunan's district status were the termination of the services of more than 100 native chiefs, district chiefs, and community development officers based in Tambunan and the transfer out of Tambunan of 73 Public Works Department personnel (Kalimullah Hassan, 'Over 100 in Tambunan Get Termination Letters', *Star*, 21 January 1985). Berjaya's Secretary-General, Muhammad Noor Mansor, provided the bluntest rationale for this vindictive move: 'Berjaya acted according to the wishes of the Tambunan people.... Ours is a political government. What will a political government do under these circumstances when the people clearly rejected us?' ('It's Our Right: Berjaya', *Star*, 11 January 1985).

138. Kalimullah Hassan and Zainal Epi, 'Berjaya Trounced', *Star*, 22 April 1985. A complete record of the election results was published in the *Star* of the same day.

139. For an analysis of some factors which contributed to the PBS's victory, see Suhaini Aznam, 'A Failed Coup in Sabah', *Far Eastern Economic Review*, 2 May 1985, pp. 10–11.

140. Mustapha and Harris argued that their 'coalition' of twenty-two elected representatives, once accepted as the new government (before Pairin could be sworn in as Chief Minister), would appoint six more assemblymen and thereby enjoy a two-seat majority over the PBS's twenty-six seats ('Chronology of Events after PBS's Win', *New Sunday Times*, 28 April 1985; 'The Morning After: Pairin's Full Account', *New Straits Times*, 29 April 1985; John Berthelsen, 'Electoral Tumult Hits Malaysian State', *Asian Wall Street Journal*, 24 April 1985).

141. See the statements by Musa Hitam as Acting Prime Minister and Acting Chairman of Barisan Nasional in 'Musa: Respect the Wishes of the People', *Star*, 23 April 1985.

142. An excellent account of the legal arguments and constitutional implications of the court case is given in A. J. Harding, 'Turbulence in the Land below the Wind: Sabah's Constitutional Crisis of 1985–86', *Journal of Commonwealth and Comparative Politics*, XXIX, 1 (March 1991): 86–101.

143. Presumably the organizers hoped to repeat the 1977 Kelantan crisis in Sabah. In 1977, politically motivated riots and demonstrations became an excuse for the imposition of emergency rule which ended PAS's control of the state government. For an idea of how the 'Sabah opposition trie[d] to force a state of emergency' in 1986, see Suhaini Aznam, 'Bombs and Ballots', *Far Eastern Economic Review*, 27 March 1986, pp. 14–15. For details and a brief but revealing 'photographic record' of the USNO-led demonstration of 14 March 1986 which turned riotous, see 'Sabah Storm', *Asiaweek*, 30 March 1986, pp. 34–40.

144. For a criticism of Mahathir's handling of the Sabah crisis—which reflected a large segment of pro-PBS public sentiment in Peninsular Malaysia—see K. Balasundaram, 'The Hidden Hand of Kuala Lumpur', *National Echo*, 22 March 1986.

145. A typical example of the Malay press' use of unsubstantiated allegations that the PBS government was anti-Malay and anti-Muslim was contained in the *Berita Harian* editorial, 6 May 1985 (reprinted as 'The Danger of Using Govt Servants as a Tool', *Star*, 9 May 1985). The source of *Berita Harian*'s 'news [of] action taken against Malay civil servants in the State by the two-week old Parti Bersatu Sabah government' (which, 'if true ... will tarnish the credibility and integrity of PBS') was ... Harris Salleh! The *Berita Harian* editorial 'hope[d] that the real situation is not as bad as reported', that is, by Harris Salleh to Anwar Ibrahim, President of Pemuda UMNO. Pairin himself called for a Royal Commission to investigate allegations that the PBS was anti-Islam which was never set up ('Pairin: Look into Anti-Islam Claims', *New Straits Times*, 24 March 1986).

146. 'Six months of fruitless waiting to be accepted into the National Front plus the federal government's obvious tolerance of Usno's war of attrition are ample indication that Kuala Lumpur is not happy with the present situation and will continue to keep PBS waiting' (Suhaini Aznam, 'The Sabah Stalemate', *Far Eastern Economic Review*, 21 November 1985, pp. 16–17).

147. While campaigning for Berjaya, during his visits to Sabah on 17 February 1985 and on 4 April 1985, Mahathir concentrated his attacks on Mustapha and USNO, apparently thinking they formed Berjaya's real threat ('Penentang-penentang Parti Berjaya Golongan Pelampau—Mahathir', *Utusan Malaysia*, 18 February 1985; Kalimullah Hassan, 'PM Denies Owning "a Lot of Land" in Sabah', *Star*, 5 April 1985). Ismail Kassim was right that 'it's between Berjaya and Parti Bersatu [*sic*]' (*Singapore Monitor*, 20 April 1985).

148. James Clad, 'Elected to Power But Left Out in the Cold', *Far Eastern Economic Review*, 6 February 1986, p. 65. The resentment over Labuan was not felt by Kadazans alone. USNO was expelled from the Barisan Nasional in 1984, among other things, for opposing Labuan's transfer to the federal government (N. V. Raman, 'What Happens Now to Harris and Berjaya?', *Star*, 24 April 1985). The resentment over Labuan was openly expressed during the PBS's first General Assembly, held on 22–23 August 1986, after the PBS had joined the Barisan Nasional (Suhaini Aznam, 'The Labuan Issue', *Far Eastern Economic Review*, 4 September 1986, pp. 14–15). Many Kadazans suspected that Harris Salleh's 'downgrading' of Kadazan status and his zeal in proselytizing Islam were sanctioned by Kuala Lumpur (Suhaini Aznam, 'Politics of Ethnicity', *Far Eastern Economic Review*, 21 March 1985, pp. 54–5; Loh, 'Modernization, Cultural Revival and Counter-Hegemony').

149. This last point is arguable. Pairin acknowledged the support he obtained from the opposition in Peninsular Malaysia by immediately cancelling Berjaya's ban on Lim Kit Siang entering Sabah ('Pairin Lifts Entry Ban on Kit Siang', *New Straits Times*, 24 April 1985). But Pairin at the same time expressed the PBS's intention to apply to join the BN—to which, interestingly, Musa Hitam seemed more receptive ('Barisan Will Consider If PBS Applies', *New Straits Times*, 24 April 1985) than Mahathir ('Sink-or-swim Pledge Still Holds', *Star*, 30 April 1985).

150. On his return, Mahathir said he supported Musa's handling of the crisis in Sabah ('Musa Did Right—Dr M', *New Straits Times*, 30 April 1985). But in contrast with Musa's categorical disapproval of the USNO–Berjaya 'pact' and attempted coup, Mahathir (one week later) cautioned that 'these matters could have happened in the heat of the moment and one has to give due consideration to the atmosphere prevailing' ('Sink-or-swim Pledge Still Holds', *Star*, 30 April 1985).

151. For which Musa Hitam was gracious enough to congratulate the PBS ('Accept Choice of the People: Musa', *New Straits Times*, 14 October 1985; Zainon Ahmad and Eddy Hiew, 'PBS Entrenches Itself in Sabah', *New Straits Times*, 14 October 1985).

152. 'Stronger Case for PBS in BN: Pairin', *New Straits Times*, 27 January 1985.

153. As Pairin himself put it ('Assembly Dissolved', *Star*, 27 February 1986).

154. 'PM Assures Pairin', *Star*, 18 March 1986.

155. K. Baradan, 'A Sabah Formula', *Star*, 25 March 1986. 'Shaping a Deal on Sabah', *Asiaweek*, 6 April 1986, asked 'Why did the PBS agree to a coalition now when it rejected the idea just five months ago?' (p. 27) and a 'political analyst' answered: 'With their backs to the walls, the federal government holding the gun of emergency and Mustapha reminding them of the April 15 court verdict, they had to accept a compromise' (p. 27).

156. Baradan, 'A Sabah Formula'. Mustapha had added one other suit to nullify the dissolution of the State Assembly.

157. Rusdi Mustapha and Winslow Wong, 'PM: PBS Plan Is Not Healthy', *Star*, 7 April 1986.

158. Suhaini, 'The Sabah Stalemate', p. 16. Also see Ismail Kassim, 'Kitingan Firm on Not Forming a Coalition', *Straits Times*, 17 May 1985.

159. Pairin added that 'the Prime Minister seems to stand firm on the one point that we find most difficult to compromise—our intention to contest all seats and under our own banner' (K. Baradan, 'PBS Offers a Way Out', *Star*, 8 April 1986).

160. Rusdi and Wong, 'PM: PBS Plan Is Not Healthy'.

161. And the sole elected representative from the Sabah Chinese Consolidated Party announced that he would join the PBS (K. T. Arasu and K. Baradan, 'PBS Gets Two-thirds', *Star*, 7 May 1986).

162. Ghazali Shafie, 'Sabah: Better to Have a Pact before Elections', *Star*, 9 April 1986.

163. Ghazali Shafie made a virtue out of the federal government's 'refusal' to declare a state of emergency when 'there was a public order situation' (whatever that meant) and there were 'cries of demand for emergency rule' (from USNO? Berjaya? UMNO?). He added that 'even Datuk Pairin will admit that he had received the highest consideration and collaboration from the Prime Minister and other Cabinet Ministers' (ibid.).

164. The government, through the Lembaga Urusan Tabung Haji, had a 20 per cent share in ARE. Mitsubishi Chemicals and BEH Minerals each owned 35 per cent while the remainder belonged to Malay individuals.

165. Sahabat Alam Malaysia, *Papan Radioactive Waste Dump Controversy*, Penang, 1984, pp. 11–12, has useful background information on ARE's search for a dump-site.

166. See ibid., pp. 37–44, for an account of the campaigns waged by the Papan Residents Action Committee up to 1984.

167. Lim Chin Chin and Tong Veng Wye, 'The Papan Protest', *Aliran Monthly*, IV, 9, pp. 1–5. Sahabat Alam Malaysia, *Papan Radioactive Waste Dump Controversy*, pp. 37–44, recounted the unsuccessful 'dialogue' attempts between the Papan residents and the government/ARE.

168. The Environmental Protection Society of Malaysia (EPSM) co-ordinated a 'Papan Support Group' made up of prominent NGOs and unaffiliated individuals. The Papan Support Group provided technical assistance and helped to create a nation-wide, even international, awareness of Papan's fight against ARE, and, by extension, an unsympathetic government.

169. Sahabat Alam Malaysia, *Papan Radioactive Waste Dump Controversy*, pp. 39–43, gives an account, supplemented by photographs, of Papan's pickets and demonstrations.

170. Musa Hitam, 'Malaysia: The Spirit of '46 Rises Again', *Correspondent*, November 1988, p. 18. 'When he [Mahathir] came back', Musa claimed, 'he told me that what I did was admitting a mistake.'

171. Suhaini Aznam, 'Waste Land Revisited', *Far Eastern Economic Review*, 21 May 1987.

172. Tan Sooi Beng, 'The Papan–Bukit Merah Protest', in Committee Against Repression in the Pacific and Asia, *Tangled Web: Dissent, Deterrence and the 27 October 1987 Crackdown in Malaysia*, Haymarket, NSW: CARPA, 1988, pp. 28–31.

173. Ibid., pp. 29–30.

174. 'Feuding among the Fundamentalists', *Asiaweek*, 5 November 1982, pp. 10–11.

175. Hadi, Fadzil, and Nakhaie were ex-ABIM leaders who openly endorsed PAS around the time of the Kelantan crisis of 1977–8 (Jomo K. S. and Ahmad Shabery Cheek, 'The Politics of Malaysia's Islamic Resurgence', *Third World Quarterly*, 10, 2 (April 1988): pp. 849–51). For some of the demands of these influential figures in the anti-Asri alliance, see ibid., pp. 851–3.

176. The by-elections were reported in K. Das, 'Putting Up a Good Front', *Far Eastern Economic Review*, 17 December 1982, p. 10, on Binjai; Harold Crouch, 'Green at the Grassroots', *Far Eastern Economic Review*, 31 March 1983, pp. 33–5, on Hulu Muda; and K. Das, 'Passing on Pas', *Far Eastern Economic Review*, 22 September 1983, pp. 32–3, on Kemumin and Selising.

177. Jomo and Ahmad, 'The Politics of Malaysia's Islamic Resurgence', p. 853.

178. See 'Resolute and Patient', *Inquiry*, February 1988, pp. 13–15, for an interview with Haji Hadi. Vignettes of Hadi are found in Jomo and Ahmad, 'The Politics of Malaysia's Islamic Resurgence', pp. 852–3, and K. Das, 'The East Is Green, and the Rest Are Worried', *Far Eastern Economic Review*, 3 March 1983, p. 24. For a hostile view of Hadi—'deeply obsessed with political power' and 'inclined to see himself as the new messiah of the Muslims in this country'—by Ghafar Baba's press secretary, see Alias Mohamed, *Malaysia's Islamic Opposition: Past, Present and Future*, Kuala Lumpur: Gateway Publishing House, 1991, pp. 82–3.

179. Clive Kessler, *Islam in a Malay State: Kelantan, 1838–1969*, Ithaca: Cornell

University Press, 1978, was instrumental in showing how PAS's 'Islamic idiom of political discourse' spoke to the 'social experience of the Kelantanese peasant'.

180. 'PAS ... inherited its policies from three ideological traditions: the nationalist and socialist approach of MNP, the Islamic modernism of *Hizbul Muslimin*, and the more strongly communal views of the anti-UMNO protest movement of the 1950s' (John Funston, *Malay Politics in Malaysia: A Study of the United Malays National Organisation and Parti Islam*, Kuala Lumpur: Heinemann Asia, 1980, p. 161).

181. Jomo and Ahmad, 'The Politics of Malaysia's Islamic Resurgence', p. 862. For an UMNO-type view of Haji Hadi's '*ceramahs* on the so-called *mustadhafin* (the oppressed)', see Alias, *Malaysia's Islamic Opposition*, p. 83.

182. For example, an excerpt from a 1981 Haji Hadi speech, which contained references to *mati syahid* ('martyr's death') was reproduced in the 'White Paper on the Memali Incident' (Appendix 2), purportedly as evidence of Haji Hadi's extremism. A less partisan view might conceivably consider Hadi's references to *mati syahid* as largely rhetorical.

183. Mahathir once claimed that 'there were no feelings of disunity among us, no misunderstanding at all among us' before PAS was founded (Mahathir, 'Ucapan Ketika Merasmikan Mesyuarat Perwakilan UMNO Bahagian Hulu Kelantan', Kuala Kerai, Kelantan, 16 April 1983, reprinted as 'Ulama yang Gila Kuasa Menggugat Perpaduan', *Berita Harian*, 21 April 1983).

184. *Kafir* means 'infidel'. By '*dua imam*', literally 'two imams', UMNO accused PAS of exhorting its members and supporters not to join in prayers led by a state-appointed imam, but only prayers led by a 'PAS' imam. Legally, fatwas (Islamic rulings) could only be issued by state religious authorities. Some marriages reportedly underwent two ceremonies, once before a state-appointed kadi and then again before a PAS kadi (Suhaini Aznam, 'Memali Revisited', *Far Eastern Economic Review*, 16 January 1986, p. 14).

185. PAS was usually assumed to be the instigator of such divisive acts. Rodney Tasker ('The Muslim Heartland', *Far Eastern Economic Review*, 6 December 1984, p. 46) reported an 'UMNO mother' throwing away a fish that her son had bought from a 'PAS fisherman'.

186. Mustafa Ali, a PAS Youth leader, said: 'We admit the fact that there is some sort of split in the Malay community because of this (Umno–Pas friction). The question is, what are the underlying reasons? To us, the many discriminatory policies of Umno are the main cause' (ibid.).

187. *Assabiya* referred to 'tribalism' in early Islam. PAS used it to criticize UMNO for basing its politics on 'Malay nationalism' rather than Islam which did not discriminate on the basis of ethnicity. See Suhaini Aznam, 'Islam's Open Arms', *Far Eastern Economic Review*, 25 April 1985, p. 18, for a report on PAS's criticism of *assabiya* and 'narrow, communal interests' during the party's General Assembly in April 1986.

188. Quoted in 'Orang Cina Boleh Jadi Pemimpin Negara Ini—Haji Hadi', *Utusan Malaysia*, 12 February 1986.

189. 'Islam's guarantees for preserving the rights of citizens are founded on justice. What we wish to state and have stressed is that more complete guarantees of

the rights of Muslims and non-Muslims can be justly realized if this country is governed according to the teachings and system of Islam.' So spoke Nakhaie Ahmad, PAS Vice-President, as quoted in 'Nakhaie: Hak Istimewa Melayu Hapus dengan Sendiri Jika PAS Kuasa', *Utusan Malaysia*, 19 September 1985.

190. Cited in Suhaini Aznam, 'No Special Rights', *Far Eastern Economic Review*, 3 October 1985, p. 22.

191. 'Musa Akan Kaji Ucapan Hadi', *Utusan Malaysia*, 18 September 1985.

192. 'Peguam Negara Akan Tentukan', *Utusan Malaysia*, 19 September 1985.

193. 'Musa Akan Kaji Ucapan Hadi'.

194. 'Nakhaie: Hak Istimewa Melayu Hapus dengan Sendiri Jika PAS Kuasa'.

195. Subky Latiff, cited in Suhaini Aznam, 'Everyman's Islam', *Far Eastern Economic Review*, 29 May 1986, p. 16.

196. As Ismail Kassim put it, in 'Political Scene May be Altered in Long Run', *Straits Times*, 9 October 1985. Also see Ismail Kassim, 'Pas Steps Up New "Moderate" Strategy', *Straits Times*, 24 September 1985, and Suhaini, 'Everyman's Islam', p. 16, for analyses of PAS's attempts to reach the Chinese. On the CCCs, see Ong Hock Chuan, 'PAS Reaches Out to the Chinese', *Sunday Star*, 20 April 1986.

197. Note *Utusan Malaysia*'s racist attacks on PAS's use of 'banners written in Mandarin' ('PAS Guna Pemidang Tulis Cina', *Utusan Malaysia*, 11 February 1985) during the symposium on 'Islam and National Unity' which was held in the Chinese Town Hall, Kuala Lumpur, 'a hall that is normally used to serve pork and liquor' ('Tempat Simposium PAS Dipersoal', *Utusan Malaysia*, 12 February 1985).

198. Yusof Rawa, quoted in Ismail Kassim, 'Political Scene May be Altered in Long Run', *Straits Times*, 9 October 1985.

199. Suhaini, 'No Special Rights', p. 22. Realistically, PAS could only work towards gaining a measure of Chinese electoral support in the long run. Suhaini cited Subky Latif, a PAS leader: 'If our aim [is] to win Chinese voters, then this is a long-term aim.'

200. 'Kedah's Day of Carnage', *Asiaweek*, 29 November 1986, pp. 14–15; Suhaini Aznam, 'The Battle of Memali', *Far Eastern Economic Review*, 5 December 1985, pp. 28–9. A. C. Milner, 'Rethinking Islamic Fundamentalism in Malaysia', *Review of Indonesian and Malaysian Affairs*, 20, 2 (Summer 1986): 48–69, locates the Memali incident in 'a history of Islamic fundamentalism', but only cursorily. Jomo and Ahmad, 'The Politics of Malaysia's Islamic Resurgence', pp. 862–6, places it in the spate of repressive police actions against PAS leaders and supporters.

201. The police were trying to arrest Ibrahim Mahmood and two other persons under the Internal Security Act, as well as thirty-two of Ibrahim's followers who 'were suspected of having being involved in several criminal activities who were taking refuge in Ibrahim bin Mahmood's house' (Malaysia, *Peristiwa Memali*, Command Paper 21, 1986, pp. 19–20; hereafter cited as the 'White Paper on the Memali Incident').

202. The 'White Paper on the Memali Incident' lists several charges against Ibrahim Mahmood, for example, 'socially divisive activities' (pp. 3–5), 'extremist activities' (pp. 5–8), and repeated refusal to surrender to a warrant for his arrest pp. 10–12).

203. A total of 576 police personnel took part in the operation although only 228 actually approached Ibrahim Mahmood's house ('White Paper on the Memali Incident', pp. 19–20). A 'Pas leader from a nearby village' was quoted as saying that '[i]f the police had not come down 200-strong with riot squads and armoured vehicles, bloodshed could have been avoided' (Suhaini, 'The Battle of Memali', pp. 28–9).

204. PAS's 'proclamation' was formally disavowed by a Rulers' Council fatwa which denied that Ibrahim and his slain supporters had died a martyr's death (*mati syahid*).

205. The charges against Ibrahim Mahmood were inadequately substantiated. The 'White Paper on the Memali Incident', for example, listed three of Ibrahim's utterances as evidence of his call for a violent confrontation with the state. In the third of these utterances, Ibrahim allegedly called on the people to 'rise to oppose the 2M administration with whatever means, and, if necessary, by the sacrifice of life and property'. But that utterance, preceded by another to his audience 'not to be afraid or scared of arrest by the Government' (p. 7, paras. 20 and 23), was allegedly made on 19 July 1986, that is, nine days after several PAS leaders had been detained under the ISA (p. 8). Might the context not suggest that Ibrahim's utterance sounded a note of 'defiance' but did not necessarily constitute a serious 'incitement'?

206. Chandra Muzaffar, 'The Memali TV Show', in Aliran, *Issues of the Mahathir Years*, Penang, 1988, pp. 84–5. Chandra added that 'the lack of emphasis upon the intellectual, rational dimension in PAS's approach to Islam is one of the causes'. Suhaini, 'Memali Revisited', p. 14, gives a general sense of how the 'official video ... fail[ed] to answer all the questions'.

207. On the July 1985 rumour, see 'Saya di Sisi PM—Musa', *Mingguan Malaysia*, 7 July 1985, which reported: 'When asked by the journalists whether it was true that [Musa] had resigned, Datuk Seri Dr Mahathir immediately turned to the right and asked Datuk Musa, "Is it true?", Datuk Musa spontaneously said: "I'm definitely still by the side of the Prime Minister".' Musa's handwritten letter to Mahathir, dated 31 July 1984, showed that Mahathir's and Musa's replies skirted the question which was 'on target'. Part of the letter read: 'I plan to retire from the post of Deputy Prime Minister beginning from 1 August 1985. This decision of mine is final.' Musa then requested three months' leave to be taken from 1 May 1985 'or any other suitable date'.

208. 'Tidak Benar Musa Letak Jawatan—Mahathir', *Utusan Malaysia*, 27 February 1986.

209. Ghani Ismail, *Razaleigh Lawan Musa, Pusingan Kedua, 1984*, Taiping: IJS Communications, 1983, p. 16.

210. 'A Vision for Malaysia', Interview with Mahathir, *Asiaweek*, 23 September 1983, p. 36. At the 1984 UMNO General Assembly, Mahathir 'thanked' the delegates who in 1981 had chosen Musa, 'a deputy president who could cooperate with me as a team' and with whose co-operation 'leadership has been easy' ('First Blows for Battle '84', *Asiaweek*, 2 September 1983, p. 34).

211. Musa, 'Letter to Mahathir' (in his capacity as UMNO President), 26 February 1986. Musa recalled of a conversation he had with Mahathir on

16 January 1986 that each time he denied complicity in 'anti-Mahathir' activities, Mahathir just said that 'too many Senior Government officials and journalists have reported it'.

212. Musa's later comments on the 'Mahathir style' well illustrated the point: 'The problem with Dr Mahathir is that he is crass, rough and hard. This man pushes things down your throat ... the trouble with what is going on is simply this: what Dr Mahathir wants, Dr Mahathir gets. What does that mean? It actually means one-man rule ... we have a so-called economic planning unit and, under Dr Mahathir it has become less and less useful. The job of the economic planning unit is merely to justify a *fait accompli*, something that has already been decided' (Musa, 'Malaysia: The Spirit of '46 Rises Again', p. 18).

213. Musa Hitam, 'Letter to Mahathir', 5 July 1986. Razaleigh was removed from the Ministry of Finance. Musa's letter was 'written with a very heavy heart and the greatest reluctance' and delivered 'before your [Mahathir's] final decision' to offer Razaleigh appointment as Minister of Trade and Industry—which Razaleigh accepted.

214. Interesting details and able analyses of this meeting may be found in John Berthelsen and Raphael Pura, 'Malaysia's UMNO Faces Leadership Rift', *Asian Wall Street Journal*, 3 March 1986; Suhaini Aznam, 'Mahathir's Dilemma', *Far Eastern Economic Review*, 13 March 1986, pp. 10–12; and 'Rift at the Top', *Asiaweek*, 16 March 1986, pp. 31–4 and 39–40.

215. 'MT Ikrar Setia Pada Mahathir', *Utusan Malaysia*, 1 March 1986.

216. Jockeying for the 1987 UMNO election had effectively begun, as Suhaini Aznam, 'Overplaying His Hand', *Far Eastern Economic Review*, 20 March 1986, pp. 17–18, and 'Survival of the Fittest', *Asiaweek*, 6 April 1986, p. 28, commented.

217. Attorney-General Abu Talib Othman was against releasing the report since, with respect to the extradition proceedings which Hong Kong authorities were conducting against two former BMF officers in London, 'it is very likely to frustrate their prosecution and prejudice a fair trial' ('Don't Do It: A-G', *Star*, 12 December 1985). 'But the public ... wants the report to be made public because it is concerned about the loss of so much money and rightly wants to know who is involved,' responded former Prime Minister, Hussein Onn ('Explain Stand on Report: Hussein Onn', *Star*, 13 December 1985).

218. 'Bank Bumiputra did not ask for the report to be made only to jeopardize its performance.... We have already lost RM2 billion and if BBMB faces financial problems because of the report, we will lose more, probably RM200 million, RM1 billion or possibly (God forbid) the bank may have to close down. This will pose a burden to the people and we, as the Government, cannot say, "Ah, if we let the people know they will not accuse us, so it is better for us to let them know"' ('Mahathir Answers the Critics', *Star*, 23 February 1986).

219. Ahmad Noordin and Chooi Mun Sou explained their position at length in their 11 January 1986 memorandum to Mahathir (reprinted in *New Straits Times*, 17 January 1986). It responded to Mahathir's statement that 'the report can be made public but someone has to take the responsibility.... The ball is now in the court of the Committee if it wants to take any action' (*New Sunday Times*, 5 January 1986). The third member of the Committee, Ramli Ibrahim, did not sign the memorandum.

220. Basically, Mahathir, wondering why Ramli Ibrahim, the third member of the Committee, had not signed the 11 January 1986 memorandum, noted that 'you [presumably only Ahmad Noordin and Chooi Mun Sou] have on so many occasions acted beyond your authority', stated that 'the terms of reference ... did not say that you should seek publicity for your work', and warned that 'if, as a result of your publishing the report damage is done to the credibility or credit-worthiness of BBMB, the bank will be fully justified in suing you for damages' (Mahathir, 'Letter to Ahmad Noordin' [n.d.], reprinted in *New Straits Times*, 18 January 1986).

221. 'We Want to Be Fair: PM', *Star*, 10 March 1986. Information Minister Rais Yatim justified the parallel release of a White Paper thus: 'Within the [final] report, there might be aspects, actions and statements which the government must explain just like in the Kampung Memali case' ('Govt to Publish BMF Report', *Star*, 23 January 1986).

222. The 'Informal Movement for Freedom and Justice'—which, for instance, strongly supported the publication of the BMF Committee's *Final Report* ('Group of 15 to Govt: Release BMF Report', *Star*, 21 December 1985).

223. DAP's 'Seremban Declaration', its by-election manifesto, called for a full investigation into the BMF affair. See I. Rajeswary, 'DAP Confident of a Better Showing', *Star*, 28 April 1986.

224. Mahathir had issued a thinly veiled warning to the MCA: 'Ordinarily the component parties in Barisan Nasional do not interfere in the domestic problems of respective parties' but 'if events in a component party not only destroy it but threaten the strength of Barisan Nasional, then Barisan Nasional will not remain quiet' ('Speech at the 36th UMNO General Assembly', Kuala Lumpur, 27 September 1985, reprinted as 'Semangat Kebangsaan Beri Kekuatan pada Perjuangan dan Persaudaraan Islam', *Utusan Malaysia*, 28 September 1985).

225. For the Council's full statement, see 'Ibrahim Libya Tak Mati Syahid', *Utusan Malaysia*, 3 February 1986.

226. Herman Luping was arrested on 7 October and charged in court the next day ('Charging Sabah's Top Lawman', *Asiaweek*, 18 October 1985, p. 20). The Ulu Padas by-election was held on 12 October.

227. 'Sizing Up Ghafar for No. 2', *Asiaweek*, 13 April 1986, pp. 29–30, gives an interesting analysis of how Ghafar fit into Mahathir's attempt to consolidate his position in UMNO.

228. Mahathir first attacked the growth of 'money politics' in UMNO in 1984 (Mahathir, 'Speech at the 35th UMNO General Assembly', Kuala Lumpur, 25 May 1984, English translation reprinted as 'Making Sure the Spirit of UMNO Prevails', *New Straits Times*, 26 May 1984).

229. 'Proses Islamisasi Bukan Bererti Memaksa Undang-undang Islam', in Rosnah, *Koleski Temuramah Khas Tokoh-tokoh*, pp. 280 and 283.

230. *Star*, 25 June 1986.

231. Ibid.

232. Mahathir, 'Speech at the 37th UMNO General Assembly', Kuala Lumpur, 18 September 1986, reprinted as 'Sistem Tumpuan Luar Bandar Akan Dikekalkan', *Utusan Malaysia*, 19 September 1986.

233. Ibid.

234. 'Cards on the Table', p. 39.

235. And the release in court of Mak Foon Than's statement that Razaleigh Hamzah and other Malaysian ministers were involved ('BMF: Why the Lies', *Star*, 28 May 1984). Later, Mak retracted his statement about Razaleigh.

236. 'Cards on the Table', p. 40. 'You must look at all the banks in Hong Kong. Almost all of them gave loans to the property sector. This matter is evident. But only Bank Bumiputra has been singled out' ('Proses Islamisasi Bukan Bererti Memaksa Undang-undang Islam', in Rosnah, *Koleski Temuramah Khas Tokoh-tokoh*, p. 283).

237. Raphael Pura and Matt Miller, 'Mahathir Tilts to Theories Faulting Motives of Colony', *Asian Wall Street Journal*, 30 May 1984.

238. 'Malaysia Will Bow to No One—Mahathir', *Malaysian Digest*, October 1986, p. 12. 'When the Asian Development Bank met in Manila, an article came out in the *AWSJ* which was very unfair to the minister of finance, accusing him of all kinds of crimes without substantiation. Just before the IMF meeting in Washington recently, another article appeared accusing the minister of finance of certain transactions, of his relationship with the prime minister and how he was chosen as the finance minister. This time, just before the UN General Assembly and the investment seminar organized by the Malaysia Industrial Development Authority, the *Wall Street Journal* carried a number of tendentious articles, including a story on Malaysia's intervention in the tin market.'

239. 'Ada Pemberita Jadi Alat Yahudi—PM', *Mingguan Malaysia*, 17 August 1986. Contrast this with Mahathir's previous ridicule of unnamed UMNO members who tried to start an 'anti-Freemason' and 'anti-Zionist' campaign: 'Today their target is the Freemasons. But there are already signs that after the Freemasons, the Rotary Club, Apex Club, Lions Club and other service and welfare organizations will be targets and their ban will be demanded' (Mahathir, 'Speech at the 33rd UMNO General Assembly', Kuala Lumpur, 10 September 1982, English translation reprinted as 'UMNO in a World of Change and Challenge', *New Straits Times*, 11 September 1982).

240. 'PM Tegur Pejuang Bakun Pura-pura Bela Rakyat', *Utusan Malaysia*, 8 February 1986.

241. 'PM: Ada Kumpulan Sosialis Guna Seminar Burukkan Kerajaan', *Utusan Malaysia*, 7 February 1986, and 'PM Tegur Pejuang Bakun Pura-pura Bela Rakyat'.

242. 'PM Tegur Pejuang Bakun Pura-pura Bela Rakyat'.

243. Kalimullah Hassan and Lee Min Keong, 'Socialists Trying to Make Comeback: PM', *Star*, 7 February 1986.

244. Kalimullah Hassan and Lee Min Keong, 'Mahathir Hits Out at Environmental Groups', *Star*, 8 February 1986.

245. 'Ada Pemberita Jadi Alat Yahudi—PM'.

246. 'Golongan Cuba Jahanamkan Bank Bumiputra Dibidas', *Utusan Malaysia*, 25 October 1986; 'Dr M Hits at Groups Out to Shame Leaders', *Star*, 25 October 1986.

247. Kalimullah and Lee, 'Socialists Trying to Make Comeback: PM'.

248. Maria Samad, 'The UMNO–PAS Fight in Terengganu', *Sunday Star*, 13 April 1986.

249. Kalimullah and Lee, 'Mahathir Hits Out at Environmental Groups'.

250. 'You would have heard it said that the government is now too strong, and it is not right that it be given a two-thirds majority. You would appreciate that we have governed with a two-thirds majority since Merdeka. From the ranks of the developing countries, is there any that can be said to have performed better than our country?' (Mahathir, 'Surat Terbuka kepada Rakyat Malaysia', reprinted in *Utusan Malaysia*, 26 July 1986).

251. *Malaysian Digest*, July 1986.

252. 'PM Kecewa Kekalahan MCA, Gerakan', *Utusan Malaysia*, 5 August 1986.

253. Sankaran Ramanathan and Mohd. Hamdan Adnan, *Malaysia's 1986 General Election: The Urban–Rural Dichotomy*, Occasional Paper No. 83, Singapore: Institute of Southeast Asian Studies, 1988, pp. 50–67.

254. Mahathir, 'Speech at the 37th UMNO General Assembly'.

255. Ibid.

256. 'Bukti Kerajaan Amal Dasar yang Betul—Dr M', *Utusan Malaysia*, 5 August 1986.

257. Mahathir, 'Speech at the 37th UMNO General Assembly'.

258. Ibid.

259. 'PM Kecewa Kekalahan MCA, Gerakan'.

260. Mahathir, 'Speech at the 37th UMNO General Assembly'.

261. 'Bukti Kerajaan Amal Dasar yang Betul—Dr M'.

262. Mahathir, 'Speech at the 37th UMNO General Assembly'.

263. Ibid.

7

The Populist as Authoritarian

> Why not call a spade a spade? Why not say bravely that the people of Malaysia are too immature for a workable democracy? Why not say that we need some form of authoritarian rule? We are doing that anyway and it looks as if we are going to do that for a very long time to come.... Authoritarian rule can at least produce a stable strong government.... We must accept that there is not going to be a democracy in Malaysia; there never was and there never will be.
>
> Mahathir, quoted in Bob Reece, 'Crimes for Democracy?', *Far Eastern Economic Review*, 18 September 1969, p. 688.

24 April 1987: Personal Mandate, Party Democracy, or UMNO Split?

PRIOR to 1987, there had only been a single instance of someone challenging UMNO's incumbent President in the party's triennial election. That was in 1978 when Sulaiman Palestin, an unknown with no chance of winning, stood as a 'protest candidate' against Hussein Onn, and obtained 250 votes to Hussein's 898.[1]

Prior to 1981, there had also been only one instance of an incumbent Deputy President being challenged. In 1956, Tun Dr Ismail unsuccessfully challenged the incumbent Tun Razak in an obscure contest. Traditionally, there had been little more to the selection of the Deputy President than a general endorsement of the President's choice. But in 1981, Hussein Onn's retirement and Mahathir's elevation to the presidency created a vacancy for the Deputy President's post which sparked off the first Musa Hitam–Razaleigh Hamzah battle.[2] Musa was junior to Razaleigh in the party hierarchy but he was privately supported by Hussein Onn and Mahathir, and won the 1981 election. In 1984, Razaleigh challenged Musa but again Razaleigh lost.[3]

When Hussein Onn announced his plan to retire in mid-1981, Mahathir was returned unopposed as the new President during the General Assembly in June 1981. Three years later, Mahathir's presidency was likewise unchallenged. Musa's parting of the ways with Mahathir in February 1986, however, left open the possibility that UMNO's highest posts would all be contested the following year. There were four likely contenders for the summit of UMNO's hierarchy in 1987—Mahathir, the incumbent President; Musa, the ex-Deputy Prime Minister but incumbent Deputy President; Ghafar Baba, the new Deputy Prime Minister and a party Vice-President; and Razaleigh, who has been a twice unsuccessful candidate for the Deputy President's post and a 'four-time' unsuccessful contender for the deputy premiership. From late 1986 to early 1987, as the UMNO divisions met to elect their delegates to the 1987 UMNO General Assembly and to nominate their candidates for the high party positions, there was much rumour and speculation as to what the top four party figures planned. One journalistic report summarized it well:

> Will Musa run against Mahathir or settle for a defence of the No. 2 post? Will Razaleigh run against Mahathir or against Ghafar Baba, an old friend and ally who supported him in two contests against Musa? Will there be a three-way fight between Mahathir, Musa and Razaleigh for the top post or a Ghafar–Musa–Razaleigh struggle for deputy? Might not old foes Razaleigh and Musa team up to take on Mahathir and Ghafar? Or perhaps Razaleigh, not fancying his chances against Ghafar or Mahathir, might team up with them to take on the common enemy: Musa. When it comes to the crunch, will Mahathir and Ghafar stick together?[4]

The final electoral configurations began to clarify around February 1987 when, first, Musa declared that he would defend his Deputy President's position,[5] and, second, Razaleigh indicated that he would challenge Mahathir.[6] On 27 February 1987, Razaleigh was specially invited to open the assembly of the Musa-led UMNO Segamat (Johore) division. On 20 March, Musa reciprocated by inaugurating the Razaleigh-led UMNO Gua Musang (Kelantan) divisional assembly. By this symbolic show of mutual support, the 'old foes' indicated they had become allies.[7] In Segamat, Musa publicly offered to support Razaleigh if the latter chose to challenge Mahathir. In Gua Musang, Razaleigh pledged to 'offer myself to lead your struggle'—the nearest thing to an official announcement of his challenge to Mahathir which he made on 11 April 1987, the nomination day for the election.[8] On 21 March 1987, Ghafar entered the fray by way of Mahathir's announcement that Ghafar would challenge Musa for the Deputy President's post.[9] Some saw the announcement of 'Ghafar's decision' as 'Mahathir's way of steering Ghafar into a firm commitment' since Ghafar had 'assiduously avoided declaring his intentions'.[10] On 4 April 1987, Ghafar publicly confirmed that he would contest the deputy presidency. As for Mahathir, he had always maintained that he would not be 'kicked out' but would 'definitely fight if challenged or forced to withdraw'.[11] There were some half-hearted calls for the rival factions to work out 'no-contest' compromises which would avoid the repercussions of debilitating battles for the party's highest posts. But there was no one left in the party who was sufficiently influential and disinterested to mediate. The nation's elder statesmen, Tunku Abdul Rahman and Hussein Onn, former premiers and ex-UMNO presidents, were, respectively, openly and discreetly sympathetic to the Razaleigh–Musa alliance. And the harsh truth was that there were 'four leaders and only two posts'.[12]

The party election of 24 April 1987 brought UMNO's factionalism to a head. Down the party hierarchy, UMNO's élite—Cabinet Ministers, Deputy Ministers, and Chief Ministers—quickly divided into being supporters of 'Team A' (the Mahathir–Ghafar faction) and 'Team B' (the Razaleigh–Musa faction), and prepared to engage in desperate contests for the three Vice-President's posts and the twenty-five Supreme Council seats. As early as 26 February 1987, all the UMNO Menteris Besar had issued a collective pledge of support for Mahathir and Ghafar 'in their steering of the government and their leadership of the party'.[13] Of the UMNO Cabinet Ministers, Abu Hassan, Anwar Ibrahim, Daim Zainuddin, Rafidah Aziz, and Sanusi Junid belonged to Team A. Team B's share of the Cabinet (aside from Razaleigh) was scarcely less impressive: Abdullah Badawi, Ajib Ahmad, Rais Yatim, and Shahrir Samad. The gathering divide of UMNO's élite was crowned with the cleavage of its membership. For example, Rafidah Aziz managed to obtain a Wanita UMNO endorsement of Mahathir–Ghafar, Anwar Ibrahim could only extract a less than unified Pemuda UMNO announcement of support for Mahathir's policies, while many among UMNO's old guard came out in support of Razaleigh–Musa.[14] It was thought, too, that the Team A–Team B split had spread beyond UMNO's party structure into the Malay community at large, the bureaucracy in particular, and even the royalty.[15]

In explaining why the 24 April 1987 election was 'special compared to others before it', Safar Hashim argued that UMNO's expansion into a party of 1.5 million members and the increased rewards of political office induced a higher degree of contestation, while the enhanced educational levels and the much altered occupational profile of the members made them more ready to challenge the party leadership.[16] Shamsul A. B. was more specific in tracing the emergence of Team B to 'competing interests and aspirations' within the NEP-created Malay upper and middle classes; as it were, their 'negative expressions' were being mediated through UMNO politics against a backdrop of economic recession and financial scandals.[17] Khoo Khay Jin's political economy of UMNO's split into Team A and Team B showed how Mahathir's modernizing vision and privatizing policies, bureaucratic reform and austerity programme diverged from previous NEP premises, state interventionist practices, and counter-cyclical measures.[18] The policy divergence had painful effects for many Malays and UMNO members, business people, and bureaucrats who found themselves 'squeezed', 'disciplined', or sidelined, and they tended to blame their difficulties on Mahathir and Daim's 'mismanagement' and 'cronyism'.[19] Malek Marican gave an insightful analysis of a widening split in Malay opinion between those who were committed to the NEP-based 'restructuring' ('Group B Malays') and those who were persuaded by private sector-led 'growth' ('Group A Malays').[20] A prominent Malay banker himself, Malek tactfully refrained from drawing the obvious correspondence between his 'Group A' and 'Group B' Malays, and UMNO's Team A and Team B.

In the critical period of 1986–7, the personal ambitions and private resentments of key UMNO figures had intersected with the social contradictions within the party and the Malay community to produce a brooding dissension against Mahathir's leadership. As Khoo Khay Jin noted, it only required the willingness of someone to 'take up the cudgels' for the dissension to erupt into an 'electoral war'. To give only the most prominent examples on Team B's side, there were Razaleigh's disappointment at being repeatedly denied the Deputy Prime Minister's post, Musa's 'loss of Mahathir's trust', Abdullah Badawi's resentment of Anwar Ibrahim's intrusion into Penang, Rais Yatim's antagonism towards the 'personality cult' purportedly built up around Mahathir, and the unhappiness of veterans like Harun Idris, Suhaimi Kamaruddin, and Marina Yusoff.[21]

From an ideological perspective, it required the readiness of Mahathir's key rivals to test the limits of UMNO's 'tradition' and 'doctrine' of not challenging incumbent leadership. The most sophisticated treatment of this point was made by Roger Kershaw whose examination of the 'doctrinal differentiation' between Team A and Team B exhaustively analysed the polemics of both teams as it ranged over UMNO's history, party politics, the national economy, and even Islam.[22] In doctrinal terms, Team A appealed to part tradition, the incumbent President's mandate, and continuity.[23] Team B called upon 'the party to control the government', and argued the legitimacy of Razaleigh's contest and change. But as Kershaw's study confirmed, the crux of the Team A–Team B quarrel was whether to retain or replace Mahathir's leadership.

In that, some of Mahathir's non-UMNO critics and opponents might have detected a certain poetic justice about this wrinkle in Mahathir's political career. With UMNO behind him, Mahathir had renewed his embattled executive's electoral mandate in 1986 but now many in UMNO were against him. His triumph over disaffection 'abroad' had won him no immunity against dissension 'at home'. He had wanted the people to settle down after the general election; instead his party was gearing up for an all-out election. And if his leadership of the nation was only 'questioned' in August 1986, his leadership of the party was 'challenged' in April 1987.

Mahathir reacted to this latest political crisis in ways which were reminiscent of his handling of the financial scandals and political crises of the 1984–6 period. He acknowledged no wrongdoing as party President or Prime Minister. 'If required', he was prepared to 'swear on the Quran in a mosque' that all the accusations of corruption and nepotism which had been flung against him 'had no basis'.[24] Mahathir strenuously defended Finance Minister Daim Zainuddin who, for Team B, personified 'corruption', 'incompetence', and 'cronyism' under Mahathir.[25] Mahathir denied that he had mismanaged the economy or that the economic climate was unfavourable because he had antagonized the Western countries with his brand of diplomacy, his 'Buy British Last' and 'Look East' policies.[26] He pleaded that the economy had earlier fallen victim to collapsed commodity prices which 'I don't think ... fell because of our quarrel with the Zionists [and which] I don't think will ... rise if we are on good terms with the Zionists'.[27] He also denied he had forced 'mammoth' or 'luxury' projects on the nation which had exacerbated the recession. To prove his point, Mahathir declassified and disseminated the minutes of Cabinet meetings where decisions were taken to implement three controversial projects—the Dayabumi complex, the Penang Bridge, and the national car (Proton Saga).[28] Mahathir rejected the criticisms that under him the 'government controlled the party'[29] and that he was himself 'dictatorial'. He insisted that the principle of Cabinet responsibility made Musa, Razaleigh, and the other Team B ministers accountable for the policies of his administration. He chided that it was 'impossible [that] I can speak for hours [and] no one else talks' at the UMNO Supreme Council meetings and that only an 'outright liar' would claim that members of the Supreme Council were prevented from voicing their opinions.[30]

Mahathir defended himself by attacking his opponents. He doubted their motives and questioned the legitimacy of their challenge. His only consideration as party President was 'to serve' for 'in the end we will die ... not able to take what we have in this world'[31] but 'they' only sought to use 'UMNO as a ladder for them to rise' to the 'positions of Deputy Prime Minister or Prime Minister'.[32] He, Mahathir, 'became Minister of Education after 28 years of being in UMNO, became Deputy Prime Minister after 30 years ... and became Prime Minister after 36 years' but 'they' wanted to topple him hastily, forgetting that by UMNO tradition one had 'to wait for very long before becoming Prime Minister' and even that was 'up to God'.[33] In his time, 'even though there were many matters' over which he disagreed with Hussein Onn,[34] he did not challenge his party President. Now some of his own appointees surreptitiously attacked him while remaining in the Cabinet. He much preferred the stance of Rais Yatim, who 'burnt his bridges' and openly declared his allegiance to Razaleigh–Musa: 'Datuk Rais alone has bravely done this.... Who else besides Datuk Rais will be brave enough?'[35] Initially he had wanted to 'stay quiet' on the issue of the election, but as the nomination day approached he condemned the 'traitors to the

Malays' who would 'split UMNO'.[36] Had UMNO suffered defeat in the 1986 election, he noted, it would have been reasonable for the leadership to be expelled. Instead, he warned, 'there were signs that certain countries are trying to influence [the election] so that leaders who are not strong will be elected to lead Malaysia, so that those leaders will easily bow to them'.[37]

This was vintage Mahathir. But he no longer had a choice. The crux of the Team A–Team B quarrel being the desirability of his leadership, his only alternative to an unrestrained battle was to resign from office. Resignation was an option that had precedents of sorts. In 1970, the Tunku resigned from office, aware that May 13 had undermined his authority and eroded his support. In July 1981, Hussein Onn retired from active politics for reasons of personal health. Curiously, Mahathir himself thought aloud on resignation from office on several occasions prior to April 1987. In June 1981, he paid UMNO's outgoing president, Hussein Onn, a glowing tribute that specially praised his voluntary departure from power. Speaking as Hussein's successor, with pride in party tradition, out of one politician's appreciation of another's graciousness, and from personal gratitude, Mahathir stated:

> There would be no point in my being a hypocrite and denying that I am proud to hold this post. But I am even more proud of Datuk Hussein Onn's utter selflessness in relinquishing the post of UMNO President, the nation's most vital post, one with myriad implications, one that many might covet.
>
> Few would easily give up such an important post. A person who holds such a post would normally strive to perpetuate his position....
>
> If at all such a post is relinquished, it would normally be through pressure and compulsion from certain quarters....
>
> I wish ... to thank Datuk Hussein for facilitating the process of change of leadership in the party. In a world where leaders are loath to withdraw without compulsion, Datuk Hussein's stand is admirable. We in UMNO, in fact in the whole nation, are proud of Datuk Hussein's statesmanlike stand.[38]

At the 1984 UMNO General Assembly, Mahathir could 'offer nothing to UMNO and the nation but the service which I can still provide. Only I pray to God that when my service is no longer required, I will become aware of it and recognize the signs and retire with all sincerity.'[39]

In 1985, Mahathir admonished that 'all UMNO leaders, including myself, should withdraw if [we] no longer have the support of party members'.[40] In January 1986, according to Musa Hitam's letter of resignation, Mahathir was momentarily 'determined to resign' so troubled was he by the allegations of corruption and dictatorial conduct that had been spread about him.[41] Even as late as March 1987, Mahathir repeated his pledge to leave office if his leadership was no longer required and in fact called on UMNO members or the people to tell him so.[42] When it was clear that Razaleigh would contest the UMNO presidency in April 1987, Mahathir yet appealed: 'If party members want me, I will continue to serve. If party members do not want me, tell me so, do not push me down.'[43]

'On and off', Mahathir seemed to have considered the idea of resigning 'abstractly', as any veteran politician was wont to do. But he rejected it during the constitutional crisis of 1983 and insisted he would remain in office as long as he had popular support and his leadership was required. If Musa was right, Mahathir rejected it in January 1986 after which it was Musa who resigned. If his rivals in UMNO hoped that a poor performance at the 1986 election would compel Mahathir to resign, they were mistaken. UMNO triumphed and three weeks later, Mahathir told an important gathering of bankers and financiers that 'I'm not so daft that I should lead my party to victory in order to resign'.[44] No other Malaysian Prime Minister or leading politician had so publicly contemplated resignation, so indulgently expressed this political equivalent of a 'death wish', so to speak, without consummating it—for Mahathir again rejected resignation in 1987. Perhaps at that critical juncture, Mahathir, who had habitually spoken his fears of a repetition of Malay history, pondered the tragicomic dimensions of his position and found the prospect of resignation unbearable.

Eighteen years before, Mahathir the commoner had led a revolt against the Tunku, a prince of Kedah, in the aftermath of UMNO's worst electoral set-back. Now, a prince from Kelantan led a rebellion against Mahathir in the wake of UMNO's biggest electoral triumph.

Seventeen years before, by being expelled from UMNO just before the NEP was formulated, the champion of 'Malay economic participation' had missed his chance of directly influencing its specific forms. Now, under challenge three years before the NEP expired, the Prime Minister with the most decided views on

Malaysia's economic transformation risked finding no place for his vision in a post-1990 programme.

After May 13 1969, the princely Tunku had lost power but Razak and Tun Dr Ismail safeguarded the Tunku's honour by putting down a party rebellion, expelling his most vocal detractor, and allowing the Tunku to retire as an elder statesman for whose past service the nation was yet grateful. On the eve of 24 April 1987, Mahathir's prospects were bleaker: surely a *mamak*[45] who possessed no noble birth and little personal grace could hardly expect to salvage an honourable retirement out of a retreat from an acrimonious battle?[46] In short, a defeat in April 1987 would have cast Mahathir not into the wilderness of 1969–71 but into political oblivion. One can be sure he would have been stung by the 'injustice' of it all.

If Team B harboured hopes that a respectable share of the vote would give them a 'moral victory'[47]—hopes that were ironically sustained by Mahathir's initial plea that a '55 per cent President' would be weak[48]—Mahathir disabused it of such notions: 'There are people saying that I will resign if I win the party President's post by a 55–45 per cent vote or even 51–49 per cent. But even if I obtain a majority of one vote, I will continue to hold my post.'[49]

Towards the end of the election campaign when a very close result was expected, Mahathir warned that he might not resign as Prime Minister if he lost the contest! 'Technically it is up to the Prime Minister to make his own decision'[50] and not up to UMNO to terminate his tenure. And 'if the Prime Minister does not want to resign and there are others who want him to be removed, they can move a motion of no-confidence against him in the Dewan Rakyat'.[51] Despite Team A's appeal to 'UMNO tradition', which at its core assumed a coterminacy between the UMNO presidency and the nation's premiership, Mahathir insisted that he had a 'national mandate'—'which he claimed not as President of the multiracial coalition but as the man who received a personal vote of confidence from the electorate in the General Election of August 1986'.[52] He implied that he would concede his 'appointment by the monarch' if and only after his 'national mandate' was nullified by a parliamentary vote of no confidence.[53]

On 24 April 1987, this 'national mandate' argument was not tested.[54] Mahathir defeated Razaleigh by 761 votes to 718, a majority of 43 votes or 1.5 per cent of the total vote. Ghafar triumphed over

Musa by 739 votes to 699, winning by 40 votes in an electoral count which included 41 spoilt votes.[55] In the contest for the three Vice-President's posts, Team B's Abdullah Badawi came in second, between Wan Mokhtar and Anwar Ibrahim. Team B contestants also won eight out of the twenty-five Supreme Council seats.

Team B had been defeated but only just. Razaleigh's 48.5 per cent of the delegates' votes alone exposed an extensive dissatisfaction with Mahathir's leadership. Yet there could be no 'moral victory' for the losers as Mahathir had warned before the contest—(and 'isn't [my] majority more than one vote?')[56]—and as he repeated in his closing speech to the General Assembly: 'We must realize that if we win we get something and if we don't win we don't get.... I realized myself and accepted that if I failed it would be impossible for me to live in Sri Perdana and be Prime Minister.... What is the use of our contesting if, on winning, we surrender the fruits of our victory to other people?'[57]

After the General Assembly, Mahathir showed that there was to be no reconciliation either, indeed no quarter at all. He clarified that he 'did not pick the Cabinet from the ranks of those loyal to me' but it was understood that all Cabinet appointees undertook to 'keep secrets', 'abide by collective responsibility', and 'work with one another'.[58] Those who did not or could not, he implied, or those who opposed the leader of the party, he specified, should resign their Cabinet positions 'as in other countries'; but 'this didn't happen, so what can one do?'[59] What Razaleigh and Rais Yatim did on 28 April was to tender their resignations from their ministerial positions which Mahathir formally accepted two days later. Ghafar believed that 'all problems can be overcome if two primary factors, that is a clean and healthy Cabinet line-up and Supreme Council, are inherited and nurtured'.[60] Mahathir accomplished the one even if he could not the other. He purged the Cabinet of its seven remaining Team B figures: Ministers Abdullah Badawi, Ajib Ahmad, and Shahrir Samad, and Deputy Ministers Abdul Kadir Sheikh Fadzir, Radzi Sheikh Ahmad, Rahmah Othman, and Zainal Abidin Zin—not bothering that Abdullah Badawi had been elected Vice-President with the second highest vote, and that the remaining six had been elected to the Supreme Council.

There was a parallel between Mahathir's post-24 April treatment of Team B's dissent against his leadership of the party and his post-

August 1986 disregard for the opposition to his leadership of the country. It was not simply that Mahathir once mocked that Team B leaders 'talked as if they were Lim Kit Siang'.[61] It was that Mahathir demonstrated that a dissenting minority—no matter that it may be as large as Razaleigh's 48.5 per cent of the UMNO General Assembly delegates or DAP's 23 per cent of the national electorate—meant nothing to him, that a majority and the mandate it conferred upon his leadership meant everything. Perhaps it was all the more so as his popular base kept dwindling and his constellation of opponents kept broadening. 'What kind of a leader would I be, what kind of credibility would I have,' Mahathir asked, 'if the people who support me are left out . . . and replaced by people who are against me?'[62] And he answered: 'I would lose the support of the people who supported me. Nor would I gain the support of those who have been accommodated.'[63]

Twenty-fourth April 1987 saw the stripping of the last pretence Mahathir might have had as a populist commanding mass popular support. His purge of Team B drew many rationalizations and recriminations. There were those who thought Team B figures waited to be sacked so that 'they can prove how dictatorial was the Prime Minister who dropped them even though they had support from the delegates'.[64] Others felt that 'when you win by one vote, you win' but 'how you exercise your power reflects your leadership capabilities'.[65] Some, like Anwar, defended Mahathir's 'wanting a cabinet that has confidence in him and in whom he has confidence'; others, like Shahrir, called it 'victimization'.[66] These were partisan voices. So, too, was that of Abdullah Badawi, who remarked, most perceptively of all, that Mahathir operated by 'the corporate concept, whereby the majority shareholder gets his way'.[67] Somehow it was apt that the leader who saw his nation as a corporation should choose to run his party like a boardroom.

27 October 1987: The End of 'Liberalism'?

In the aftermath of the political events of 1987–8, the most persuasive academic perspective of the Mahathir administration has cast it as an authoritarian regime.[68] Harold Crouch considered that the Mahathir era was a continuation and consolidation of the Malaysian ruling élite's post-1969 trend of replacing the country's 'modified democratic system' with a 'modified authoritarian system'.[69] Simon Tan traced 'the rise of state authoritarianism' under Mahathir to the crisis in Malaysia's 'state monopoly capitalism' during the 1980s.[70] For Johan Saravanamuttu, Mahathir's authoritarianism was wedded to his bureaucratically driven industrialization programme, thus making it the Malaysian variant of the 'bureaucratic authoritarian state' in newly industrializing countries.[71] Kershaw concluded that Mahathir's 'autocracy' stemmed from his 'historic interventions' in 'various delicate equilibriums' because of his readiness to 'enhance his own prerogatives by usurpation from other institutions'.[72] And, yet, Prime Minister Mahathir did not start out being authoritarian.

To a nation which remembered the Tunku's paternalistic ways, Razak's imperturbable manner, and Hussein Onn's self-effacing demeanour, Mahathir seemed to enter the Prime Minister's office with a rude slamming of doors. Immediately in office, he embarked on a well-publicized campaign of bureaucratic reform, diplomatic initiative, economic modernization, and Islamization as if to show that his new government would be driven by his personal dynamism. Many saw him as a man in a hurry. No doubt Mahathir saw himself acting out his conception of what a good leader should do: foresee challenges, identify problems, supply ideas, and present solutions. He was not the first Prime Minister to want to set an example of good leadership, cleanse the bureaucracy, and set it moving in the directions he planned. Razak had a reputation for a great capacity for work, capable administration, and placing stringent demands on his senior staff. Hussein Onn was noted for his personal integrity and his boldness in tackling political corruption. Was the apparent novelty of Mahathir's approach merely a matter of his 'style' as he claimed when he insisted that he was retaining the policies of his predecessors?

In part it was. It was said of Mahathir, just before he became Prime Minister, that 'unlike Hussein, he has courted unpopularity with civil servants, and might openly demand performance when Hussein simply expected it'.[73] The relentless manner in which Mahathir set out to tackle the bureaucracy at the beginning of his administration proved the truth of this observation. But, importantly, the campaign had 'content'—a more thorough diagnosis of the problems,[74] an urgent treatment[75] inspired by managerial methods[76] which were adapted from a successful model, and a clear goal.[77] Mahathir's reformism was just so much balm to a public weary of bureaucratic ills. Not merely a new 'style' in governing, the reformism was a promise of better government. And because Mahathir had not merely turned to the bureaucracy to realize his plans, but had practically turned upon it, he turned the long sceptical public perception of the bureaucracy into a mood more receptive of his modernizing vision.

In the early months of his administration, it did seem as if Mahathir's modernizing vision engendered his populism, the latter being a kind of tutelary populism which sought to join a purposeful mass mobilization to an enlightened leadership. As Mahathir soon clarified, it needed more than for him to lay down precepts and directions for mass guidance, and present ideas and values for mass learning; it needed 'the people themselves [to] undergo radical changes in outlook and attitude'.[78] Starting from July 1981, as if creating a pattern of ripples radiating from himself, Mahathir called on UMNO, the Barisan Nasional, the bureaucracy, the private sector, and 'the whole population' to change their ways, redefine their priorities, and strengthen their commitment to the nation. It was this 'mass-oriented' appeal which distinguished Mahathir's approach from the *laissez-faire* mood of the Tunku's era, and the state-directed character of NEP implementation under Razak and Hussein Onn. In that sense, Mahathir, unlike his predecessors, had a populist aura, appeared to be all things to all men, and to have something to say to different sections of Malaysian society—which was why diverse dissidents and opponents, such as ABIM's Anwar Ibrahim, PSRM's Kassim Ahmad, the Dongjiaozong's Kerk Choo Ting, and Syed Hussein Alatas of the original Gerakan, could rally to Mahathir's banner.[79]

Possessing the leader's mantle, donning the populist's aura, and reaching a 'national' and not merely a 'Malay' constituency, seemed finally to free Mahathir from the Malay adulation and non-Malay suspicion which had enmeshed the better part of his political career. The many 'isms' of his early administration gave a sense that he sought to 'rise above ethnicity' in order that the former 'ultra' could genuinely become the premier of a multi-ethnic nation. His nationalism, judged by the 'Buy British Last' directive, the 'Look East' policy, and his 'Third World' diplomacy, had evolved into a more Malaysian, and less Malay, variety. His reformism targeted the Malay community and the Malay-dominated bureaucracy for criticism without attaching attendant blame on the non-Malays. His 'Privatization' and 'Malaysia Incorporated' called for closer relations between the 'Malay' public sector and the 'Chinese' private sector. He was eager to promote his Islam but careful to point out that its universalism made it compatible with non-Muslim values.

In more directly political ways, Mahathir projected himself as the leader of a multi-ethnic coalition who would fairly adjudicate issues which had a bearing on ethnic sensitivities. He realized that the Barisan Nasional's component parties tended to bicker over policies and issues that had real or imputed ethnic implications. He conceded that some degree of intra-coalitional squabble was unavoidable;[80] perhaps it was even necessary so that each party could periodically reaffiirm its claim to represent its community. But there remained an inherent danger that when push came to shove, an intra-Barisan Nasional quarrel could inflame inter-ethnic antagonism and threaten the coalition's integrity.

UMNO and the MCA, the two senior and most avowedly 'communal' of the Barisan Nasional's component parties, were the most likely to indulge in the kind of 'ethnic championing' which Mahathir meant to curb. He had told the 1981 Pemuda and Wanita UMNO General Assembly that Pemuda UMNO should discard its former 'ginger group' mould, cease its 'ethnic championing', and adopt a new mission of propagating a 'work ethic' among the Malays. When he first addressed the MCA in his capacity as the Barisan Nasional leader, he cautioned that the MCA had to be able to 'distinguish possible from impossible demands'.[81] He was prepared to chide the Malays for not appreciating the efforts made by non-Malays to learn the Malay language and accept the education policy.[82] He was equally willing to admonish the MCA, and, by implication, the Chinese, that the sooner they helped to achieve the NEP objectives the more likely inter-ethnic competition would end.[83] Mahathir would not be drawn into the '3Rs' and 'second Deputy Prime Minister' disagreements which developed between UMNO and the MCA soon after he became Prime Minister.[84] He refused to apportion blame to any specific party or else blamed all the parties involved in the disputes.[85] And when Tan Chee Khoon interviewed him, Mahathir promised to protect freedom of worship for non-Muslims and dissociated government policy from the actions of bureaucrats who made it difficult for non-Muslim religious organizations to obtain land and buildings for religious uses.[86]

At the same time that he tried to 'mute' ethnicity, Mahathir professed to practise an 'open' and 'liberal' style of administration. His reservations about the practicability of democracy were well known but he and Musa offered no shortage of pledges that the '2 M' leadership would respect basic civil rights and liberties. In principle, Mahathir loathed the idea of the press being the 'fourth estate' and he opposed allowing the press too much freedom and power.[87] But the '2 Ms' promised a freer, at any rate a less restricted, press under them and routinely envisioned a 'role' in national development for a 'responsible' press.[88] Later, during a television interview in 1984, Mahathir claimed that 'KDNs' (licences for newspapers, journals, and magazines) had been widely granted under his administration except to those magazines and journals which tried to 'sensationalize sex and exploit communal feelings'.[89] He was wary of lawyers and affected to pick a doctor's quarrel with the legal profession but promised to respect the independence of the judiciary.[90] Mahathir was not about to dismantle the existing battery of repressive legislation or to repeal the Internal Security Act (ISA). Yet, within days of his assumption of power, he chose to release many political prisoners who had been detained for years without trial under the ISA.[91]

Mahathir's 'open' and 'liberal' style of governing was perhaps unexpected. On record he was not a model of tolerance of dissent. As Deputy Prime Minister, he did not hesitate to use the ISA to detain unionists of the Malaysia Airlines System–Airline Employees Union which took industrial action in 1979.[92] When he was the Minister of Education, he supported the police repression of the student movement of the mid-1970s and was instrumental in enacting the Universities and University Colleges Act 1975 which ended university autonomy in the country.[93] While he was an Alliance backbencher, he loudly supported Tunku Abdul Rahman's use of emergency powers to force out the Kalong Ningkan government in the state of Sarawak.[94] After May 13 1969, he, a newly defeated parliamentarian, wasted no tears over the suspension of Parliament.

Mahathir held a dim view of democracy. Sometimes it could be as harsh as the one he pronounced at the first 'National Conference on National Security' organized by the Institute of Strategic and International Studies (ISIS) Malaysia just three weeks before the August 1986 general election:

> The modern world is against autocracy. It believes in democracy on the assumption that the majority, even if it is illiterate and not well-versed in politics, must always be right. The problem is that opportunists, rogues and foreigners also have access to the minds of the electorate. In the end it is not so much the wishes of the majority that count. It is the perception of things presented to them by frequently unscrupulous and ambitious politicians who may or may not be in league with various ideologies or agencies.[95]

In fact, long before it was fashionable for the 'Western press' to hallow the dissent in the 'East' of the late 1980s with the term 'pro-democracy', Mahathir had concluded that the spectre which haunted newly independent countries was 'democracy' which the departing colonial powers foisted upon nations and peoples who had had no experience of it.[96] In a democracy, argued Mahathir, 'pressure groups' and 'systems of lobbies' made heavy demands on the government while local and foreign criticism undermined its authority. Democracy made for difficult government because an elected government was compelled to run as much on popularity as efficiency, and it often became unpopular because it became inefficient. Thus did the 'democratically elected politician' frequently turn 'authoritarian', or so Mahathir lectured an Oxford audience in 1985.[97] But if the authoritarian government was overthrown, there could be little cause for rejoicing because it was usually replaced by a regime that was neither less authoritarian nor more efficient. Mahathir meant his government to be more efficient. He probably preferred it to be less authoritarian, that is to say, he preferred to 'teach by precept and by example' and to 'believe that by constant reminders we can sow good values'.[98] But to be precise, Mahathir's 'liberalism', the last of the many 'isms' of the early, balmy days of his administration, proffered a semblance of mutuality between him and the masses which softened the reality of the imposition of his vision upon the masses. Hence his 'liberalism' stood as a buffer, dare one say, between populism and authoritarianism. In 1987–8, the buffer disintegrated.

From about 1984, under the siege of financial scandals and political crises, Mahathir had tried to curb the flow of information which he saw as being used to expose the scandals and exaggerate the crises which embarrassed his government. As early as March 1985, Mahathir had warned that the 'government would rethink its liberal policy towards the press'.[99] Later in the year, two journalists were arrested for violations of the Official Secrets Act (OSA).[100] In March

1986, the government proposed new and harsher amendments to the OSA. The proposed amendments would broaden the definition of 'an official secret', remove judicial review of what constituted an 'official secret', and impose mandatory imprisonment in the event of conviction.[101] These proposed amendments to the OSA sparked off a broad 'anti-OSA' campaign which was co-ordinated by the National Union of Journalists and supported by many NGOs, opposition parties, and labour unions. The campaign was defeated by the Barisan Nasional's heavy domination of Parliament.[102] But outside Parliament, Mahathir did not always have his way. At the end of September 1986, the government suspended the publishing permit of the *Asian Wall Street Journal* for three months and expelled its Kuala Lumpur-based correspondents, John Berthelsen and Raphael Pura, who had written extensively on the BMF, Maminco, and UMBC affairs.[103] On 3 November 1986, the Supreme Court overturned a High Court decision and granted Berthelsen's appeal against the Immigration Department's cancellation of his work permit.[104] In light of the Supreme Court decision, the government conceded Pura's application to the High Court in Kuala Lumpur to set aside his expulsion order and revoked the *Asian Wall Street Journal*'s suspension.[105]

The next court decision which went against the government again involved a dispute over a publication. In April 1987, Mahathir, who was also Minister of Home Affairs, rejected Aliran's application for a permit to publish a monthly magazine in the Malay language. On 2 September 1987, the High Court allowed Aliran's appeal against the Ministry of Home Affairs' rejection of its application for a permit. The Ministry of Home Affairs appealed against the ruling to the Supreme Court. In August 1987, several participants at an Aliran-sponsored conference suggested that the 'Merdeka Constitution' should be reviewed after thirty years of independence. Mahathir responded by attacking an 'élitist group which numbered between 200 and 300 people', 'only a small group who are frustrated because they are not able to rule the country' but who 'would wrest power from the people if given the chance'.[106] Such an attack on Aliran's 'Conference on the Constitution' was out of proportion to what its participants said or the contents of the memorandum which they chose to send to the government.[107] But Mahathir detested those '200 [to] 300 people'—mostly the organizers and activists of

NGOs—for 'consider[ing] themselves more powerful than the Government elected by the people and presum[ing] to make policies for the Government'.[108] He could barely conceal his contempt for them: 'during the elections, none of them dared to come out for fear that they would lose' and they were 'even reluctant to openly show their support for political parties'.[109] All the same, the NGOs had their moments of victory. The Perak Anti-Radioactivity Committee also won an Ipoh High Court injunction which ordered the suspension of Asian Rare Earth's operations. Asian Rare Earth, which had the support of the federal and Perak state governments, likewise appealed against the decision to the Supreme Court.

In a politically critical case, the DAP's Lim Kit Siang, the leader of the parliamentary opposition, tried to stop the government from awarding a RM3.4 billion 'North–South Highway' contract to United Engineers (M) Berhad (UEM).[110] He alleged a conflict of interest in the award because Mahathir, Ghafar, Daim, and Sanusi, who had taken part in the Cabinet decision to give the contract to UEM, were trustees of Hatibudi, an UMNO-owned holding company which controlled 50 per cent of UEM.[111] Lim Kit Siang's initial attempt to obtain an order from the Penang High Court restraining UEM from signing the contract with the government failed. But a week later, the Supreme Court overturned the High Court decision and granted Lim Kit Siang an interim injunction which stopped UEM from entering into a contract with the government.[112] UEM sought to remove the restraining order in the High Court but on 5 October 1987 the High Court also decided against UEM. UEM and the government then appealed the High Court ruling to the Supreme Court but pending the outcome of the appeal the North–South Highway contract could not be signed. His charge that 'an opposition party had alleged that the Government indulged in corrupt practice while the [élitist] group had said that the Government had no power' captured Mahathir's mood in his confrontation with the opposition and the NGOs.[113]

The most serious lawsuit facing Mahathir stemmed from the UMNO election of 24 April 1987. His open dismissal of Team B Ministers and Deputy Ministers and the covert purge of Razaleigh's and Musa's supporters at lower government and party levels led to a continuation of the 'electoral war' by other means and by proxy.[114] On 25 June, twelve UMNO members from seven separate party divisions (the 'UMNO–12', later 'UMNO–11' after one member dropped out) filed a suit in the Kuala Lumpur High Court seeking to nullify the 24 April election. The defendants were UMNO's Secretary-General, Sanusi Junid, the secretaries of the seven affected divisions, and the Registrar of Societies. The plaintiffs argued that there were irregularities in the election of a number of delegates to the General Assembly.[115] About fifty-three unregistered, therefore illegal, UMNO branches had sent 'unapproved' delegates to divisional conferences which in turn sent delegates to the General Assembly. The plaintiffs claimed that about 78 of the eventual total of 1,479 delegates who voted at the General Assembly were legally not entitled to attend. They maintained that given the narrow election margins for the highest positions, the presence of those 'illegal' delegates had 'substantially' affected the election results. In short, the election process was 'tainted' from its early to its final stages and contravened UMNO's constitution and the country's Societies Act. Consequently, the UMNO–11 wanted the court to declare the 24 April election 'null and void', and order all party posts to revert to the pre–24 April position pending the conduct of fresh UMNO elections. Mahathir and his allies failed to persuade the UMNO–11 to drop the suit while the UMNO Supreme Council was unable to effect more than a token attempt to negotiate between the opposing factions.[116] At the end of September, the High Court gave UMNO until 14 October to reach an out-of-court settlement.[117] For the time being, UMNO's leadership could not lead the party, its internecine factionalism having shifted to the courts and, to Mahathir's mind, 'robbed the party Supreme Council of the power to decide the fate of the party' so that 'now it is the courts which will decide who should lead the party while the UMNO members have been rendered redundant'.[118]

Finally, the 'ethnicity' which Mahathir tried to mute at the beginning of his administration surfaced with a vengeance. During the mid-1980s, UMNO, MCA, and DAP politicians had periodically conducted their share of inter-ethnic skirmishes over real grievances, imagined slights, and manipulated provocations. From the 'Chinese point of view', issues such as the proposed development of Bukit China in Malacca, the mandarin orange boycott, the conversion of non-Malay minors to Islam without parental consent, and the NEP's ethnic discrimination contained real grievances.[119] The BMF,

Maminco, Pan-El, and DTCs scandals were, however, cases where public demands for executive accountability and the prosecution of culpable individuals were twisted into imagined slights upon one or the other community's leaders. Other instances, like Lee Kim Sai's *pendatang* statement and Abdullah Ahmad's 'Malay supremacy' speech, were seized upon as provocations now by UMNO figures, now by MCA figures in the familiar mould of ethnic championing. For most of the 1980s, such inter-ethnic skirmishes remained at the level of irksome but non-explosive one-upmanship, and not without contributions from Mahathir, either by omission or commission. Over Sabah, for example, Mahathir tormented the PBS with his silence while many quarters in UMNO accused the PBS's 'Christian' government of being anti-Muslim at the same time that the 'Muslim' USNO was trying to destabilize Pairin's government. The public clamoured for 'accountability' and 'disclosure' in the BMF affair but Mahathir accused his critics of wanting to topple the 'Malay leadership'. Tan Koon Swan and several other MCA leaders were disgraced over Pan-El and the DTCs, not least 'in the eyes of the Chinese', but Mahathir detected a 'silence' over these scandals because they were not 'Malay' institutions.[120] After winning the 1986 election, he praised the 'rural voter's loyalty' and pledged to retain 'rural weightage' but he could only think of 'hard core chauvinism' to explain why the urban (non-Malay) electorate had deserted his cause. Mahathir defended Abdullah Ahmad's 'democratic right' to make his offensive 'Malay supremacy' speech[121] but then his speech to the 1986 UMNO General Assembly barely disguised its own intemperance. And, whereas Mahathir denounced the 'anti-Freemason' antics of an unnamed UMNO figure during the 1982 UMNO General Assembly, by 1986 he perceived the unseen hand and the unnamed tools of 'Zionists' everywhere.

But in a period of six months ending in October 1987, the ethnic championing intensified.[122] In April, the Malacca state government instituted the practice of having all schoolchildren take a pledge during regular school assembly. Chinese associations and political parties took exception to the pledge which they claimed contained Islamic overtones. In May, the MCA formulated its scheme for a government-backed 'dollar-for-dollar' refund to the DTCs' almost completely Chinese depositors and threatened to leave the Barisan Nasional if the government refused to support the scheme.[123]

Towards the end of June, the University of Malaya decided that its first-year elective courses in the English, Chinese, and Indian Studies departments would be taught in Malay. The head of the Chinese Studies Department and the acting head of the Indian Studies Department resigned over the decision while Chinese and Indian educational, social, and political groups protested against the change.[124] Some DAP leaders and supporters demonstrated against the ruling just outside the University of Malaya grounds, barely separated from some Malay students who counter-demonstrated within the campus. Between June and August, there were rumours that the Ministry of Education had established an 'all-Malay' committee to review the Education Act 1961 which might affect the character of Chinese (and Indian) schools despite the Barisan Nasional's 1986 election pledge to maintain the character of those schools. The Dongjiaozong launched an 'awareness campaign' and set up state committees to monitor how the government planned to fulfil its election pledge. Leaders from the MCA, Gerakan, and the DAP met separately with the Chinese educationists on this issue. The MCA was the first of the political parties to commit itself to 'sink or swim' on the issue of the Chinese schools. From July to August, the MCA protested the use of the *songkok* and the *tudung* as the headgear for all, including non-Malay and non-Muslim, graduands at the Universiti Teknologi Malaysia convocation. In August, Chinese hawkers who participated in a state-sponsored seafood carnival in Johore Bahru were directed to erase or remove the Chinese characters written on their signboards, contrary to the practice of previous years. September saw five incidents of arson against mosques in Pahang which were rumoured to be the work of either 'Christians' or 'Muslim apostates' among illegal Indonesian migrants.[125] There were also allegations that 2,000 FELDA settlers had become Christians, and 60,000 Muslims had renounced Islam as a result of proselytizing activities being carried out among Malays and the Orang Asli by Christian missionaries and 'Muslim apostates'.[126] And at the end of September, Pemuda UMNO petitioned Mahathir to terminate the government's financial aid to the MCA-operated Tunku Abdul Rahman College on grounds that the college did not use Bahasa Malaysia as its medium of instruction and had no 'fair quota' for both non-Chinese admissions and the recruitment of non-Chinese lecturers.[127] One critical result of these months of inter-ethnic quarrels was that the Barisan Nasional's ability to resolve its inter-component-party disagreements came under tremendous strain. Towards the end of August, Anwar Ibrahim, Lim Chong Eu, Ling Liong Sik, and Samy Vellu had called on their respective party members to 'stop bickering'.[128] Mahathir himself regretted that the 'component parties ha[d] done [no]thing to counter' the allegations of the opposition and the 'élitist group' while instead they had blown up the disagreements between them 'out of proportion'.[129]

Then came October 1987 and the 'promotion of non-Mandarin-educated teachers' issue. One-upmanship degenerated into brinkmanship and the Barisan Nasional's 'unity' vanished. In September, the Ministry of Education promoted several Chinese, but non-Mandarin-educated, teachers as headmasters and senior assistants and posted them to Chinese schools in Malacca, Penang, Selangor, and Kuala Lumpur.[130] These promotions and postings prompted protests from parents, Chinese educationists, Chinese associations and guilds, the MCA, Gerakan, and the DAP. Minister of Education Anwar Ibrahim insisted that the promotion exercise would stay, while his Cabinet colleague, MCA's Ling Liong Sik, maintained that the exercise went against the Barisan Nasional's pledge not to change the character of Chinese and Indian schools.[131] The Barisan Nasional's framework failed to resolve the rising inter-ethnic tensions. The Ministry of Education under Anwar, a Cabinet committee under Ghafar, and negotiations between the MCA, Gerakan, and UMNO were unable to break the deadlock. On 5 October, the Malacca MCA, Gerakan, DAP, Dongjiaozong, and Chinese Chamber of Commerce sent a joint memorandum to the Malacca Education Department, giving the department 'until 14 October' to resolve the issue. The MCA's Lee Kim Sai was adamant that the MCA would not yield on the issue 'just for the sake' of maintaining the Barisan Nasional 'spirit'.[132] The 'anti-promotions' campaign began to organize a students' boycott of classes in Chinese schools for three days beginning on 15 October. On 11 October, about 2,000 leaders and representatives from the MCA, Gerakan, DAP, Dongjiaozong, and Chinese associations and guilds held a meeting at the Thean Hou Temple in Kuala Lumpur to reaffirm the Chinese community's stand on the issue.

On the face of it, the Thean Hou Temple gathering was a solemn and rare attainment of 'Chinese unity' which cut across party lines.[133]

But the Thean Hou Temple gathering equally depicted the desperate coming together of the two horns of the 'Chinese dilemma' *vis-à-vis* Malay-UMNO dominance—the 'agony of coalition', represented by the MCA, and the 'futility of opposition', experienced by the DAP. In 1987, the MCA had only 17 parliamentary seats almost none of which was won in an obvious Chinese-majority constituency. The MCA could only claim to represent the Chinese community in the narrow sense of being virtually UMNO's 'Chinese adjunct', precisely vindicating Mahathir's curt reminder that UMNO could rule the country by itself but chose to 'share' its power.[134] The DAP commanded the support of the largest urban, Chinese-majority constituencies and took 20 per cent of the popular vote in 1986. But the DAP's 24 seats in Parliament fell far short of UMNO's 87 and meant almost nothing against the Barisan Nasional's 143 in a Parliament that had steadily diminished the scope and role of the opposition since the 1960s.

UMNO, however, regarded the MCA's (and, to a lesser extent, Gerakan's) 'collaboration' with the DAP as a breach of Barisan Nasional discipline if not a betrayal of its principles.[135] A badly divided UMNO chose to retaliate against the MCA–Gerakan–DAP's forlorn show of 'Chinese unity' with its own equally forlorn calls for 'Malay unity'. Pemuda UMNO staged a huge rally of Malays at the Kelab Sultan Suleiman grounds in Kuala Lumpur on 17 October to protest against the MCA and Gerakan's joint presence with the DAP at the Thean Hou Temple and to call for Lee Kim Sai's expulsion from the Cabinet.[136] A heavy police presence at the Pemuda UMNO rally and heavy rain were thought to have prevented any untoward incident during the rally which featured fiercely anti-Chinese speeches and banners.[137] UMNO itself organized a 'civics course' for 8,000 divisional delegates in Kuala Lumpur on 18 October and planned an even bigger rally at Stadium Merdeka in Kuala Lumpur on 1 November.[138] UMNO had originally planned to hold the rally in Malacca to commemorate UMNO's birth as a party. Now it chose to shift the venue of the rally to Kuala Lumpur to accommodate an estimated 300,000 UMNO members and an additional 200,000 'Malays who support[ed] the party'.[139] Sanusi Junid, who chaired the organizing committee for the rally, 'described its theme—"Malay unity gathering to commemorate UMNO's birth"—as significant, particularly at this time when too many people were challenging the integrity and status of the Malays'.[140]

Despite the fearful implications of holding a 500,000-strong rally which would be attended by feuding UMNO factions and other Malays already incited to defend 'Malay dignity', Deputy Minister of Home Affairs Megat Junid gave an assurance that 'the rally will be peaceful'.[141] Despite the Kuala Lumpur police chief's hesitation to issue a permit for the rally—'because the magnitude of the gathering is expected to be unlike the other rallies ever held in the city'—Ghafar Baba saw nothing 'to be afraid of' as 'we guarantee the safety of everyone'.[142] Despite growing public dread that the 1 November rally would ignite violent clashes—probably between Malays and Chinese but possibly between Team A and Team B supporters—Megat Junid claimed that 'in view of recent events, it [the rally] is indeed timely as Dr Mahathir can speak about the importance of solidarity and how to live in a multiracial country'.[143]

At that critical juncture, Mahathir returned from the Commonwealth Heads of Government Meeting in Montreal. In retrospect, one can imagine Mahathir's tortured view of 'democracy' and its 'failings' returning to haunt him. August 1986 and April 1987 renewed his mandates 'back to back' but gained him no respite from disquiet and discontent. The opposition parties and the NGOs continued to dissent and had gained successive landmark decisions against the government on the 'independent' terrain of the courts. The discord in UMNO persisted and had ominously shifted to the court as well. And now the bitter recriminations between a discredited MCA and a divided UMNO threatened to break up the Barisan Nasional. Mahathir had won election upon election and yet his leadership of the nation, of his party, and his coalition was spurned, and, perhaps like the Tunku's in 1969, was about to be consumed by an inter-ethnic conflagration.

But unlike the Tunku in May 1969, Mahathir was not about to 'demonstrate a failure to judge the mood that gripped the opposition as well as the supporters of the Government'.[144] On Tuesday, 27 October 1987, the police launched 'Operation Lalang'.[145] Within the first day, 'Operation Lalang' made fifty-five arrests, all under the ISA, of DAP MPs, a DAP state assemblyman, second-echelon MCA leaders,[146] Chinese educationists, prominent NGO figures, and university lecturers.[147] Three newspapers, the *Star*, *Watan*, and *Sin Chew Jit Poh*, were suspended indefinitely.[148] Over the next few days, more people were arrested, including politicians from Pemuda UMNO (three, and all from Team B), Gerakan, PAS and the PSRM, local Muslim teachers, members of some Christian groups, and other NGO activists. The arrests spread geographically from Peninsular Malaysia to Sarawak where local environmentalists and anti-timber-logging natives were also detained. The waves of arrests, though lessening after October, continued until the number of detainees reached a peak figure of 119 in December.[149]

On 28 October 1987, Mahathir explained in Parliament that the arrests were necessary to forestall a repeat of the ethnic violence of May 13 1969. 'Operation Lalang', he emphasized, was a police initiative. The police blamed the deteriorating ethnic tensions first and mostly on the DAP, then the MCA for having to keep apace of the DAP in fanning Chinese discontent, and the press 'for having fanned the hearts of the races involved'.[150] Mahathir omitted any direct mention of UMNO's role but he tersely noted that 'the reaction of the Malays has also increased ... and the response has exceeded its limits'.[151] Again he stressed that it was the police who 'were of the opinion, and I agree with that opinion, that the government should not wait for an outbreak of rioting to take action'.[152] In that sense, the first wave of arrests of mostly Chinese oppositionists, educationists, and even Barisan Nasional politicians was necessary to defuse the tense situation and for Mahathir, through the police, to re-exert his control over the nation.

But in another sense, the arrests were a trade-off for the only 'decision' which Mahathir took 'as Minister of Home Affairs'—which was 'to ban all rallies nation-wide' and which meant that 'the proposed giant UMNO rally on November 1 is cancelled'.[153] Even before 27 October 1987, as everyone was aware, it was the UMNO rally which posed the greatest threat of violence, so that its cancellation 'was applauded by all'.[154] In Parliament, Mahathir did not comment directly on the danger posed by the 1 November UMNO rally but there was no mistaking his anxiety about it which he communicated to an *Asahi Shimbun* interviewer one week later:

> What I wanted to do was to demonstrate that at the grass roots there is unity, although among some of the leaders there may be divisions. That is why we planned to have a rally. The rally was to show that the grass roots are one group. But unfortunately the character of the rally changed from being an UMNO rally to an anti-Chinese rally. Because of that, I had to stop it.[155]

From that point of view, the first wave of arrests in the name of beating back chauvinism, Chinese chauvinism, permitted Mahathir to stop the rally without appearing to back down in the eyes of Team B. It also permitted him to appease his own Team A which had held the Pemuda UMNO rally and threatened to hold the 1 November rally with or without a police permit. Only after Mahathir's decision to ban the rally were three UMNO members arrested (not coincidentally all three being Team B leaders in Pemuda UMNO),[156] a mild indication, by the scale of the October arrests, that Mahathir would now rein in his own party. As for the Barisan Nasional, it was simply brought to heel. The coalition was designed to pre-empt ethnic crises, not to act when they erupted. Ghafar was brusque when asked if the Barisan Nasional Supreme Council would be convened to discuss the arrests: 'The arrests have been made ... all is quiet. What is there to be said.'[157]

Mahathir said that that was the end of his liberalism. The NGOs, such as Aliran, the Environmental Protection Society of Malaysia, INSAN, and the Perak Anti-Radioactivity Committee, whose representatives were arrested although they had no role in the escalating racial tensions, would have had to concur. And although it was 'that kind of liberalism, yes ... which spawn[ed] a lot of misfits who want to project themselves as champions',[158] Mahathir sounded regretful about its end:

> I wanted to be liberal because I thought people would be responsible and would not misuse their rights. Unfortunately, after six years, I found out people are misusing their rights and again trying to aggravate the bad relations between different races. Because of that I think I need to be less liberal. I am disappointed because I have had to change my mind.[159]

But was it really a 'disappointment'? Or was it a long-standing prophecy become self-fulfilled when this 'democratically elected politician' turned 'authoritarian'?

27 May 1988: Who Will Judge the Judges?

The political crisis of 27 October 1987 brought the latent authoritarianism in Mahathirist ideology to the fore. But if the repression and mass arrests of Operation Lalang constituted the tragedy of Mahathirist populism under stress, its farce was enacted seven months later.

Mahathir's main achievement on 27 October 1987 was to crush the challenge of the opposition, the dissent of the NGOs, and the recalcitrance of the 'Chinese' components of the Barisan Nasional, leaving him with a freer hand to tackle Team B's continuing dissidence within UMNO itself. That Team B's dissidence was far from being spent was shown by the UMNO-11's persistence in seeking a court decision to nullify the results of the 24 April 1987 UMNO election. The UMNO-11's suit was scheduled to be heard in the Kuala Lumpur High Court in late January 1988. Perhaps the UMNO-11 felt they had no choice other than to seek redress from the court, given Mahathir's purge of Team B leaders and the failure of both factions, Team A and Team B, to reach a compromise. Perhaps the UMNO-11 placed their hopes in the independent arbitration of the court because of the series of landmark decisions that had been given against the executive in 1986–7. In the political climate of 1986–7, many Malaysian dissidents of different shades—the press, the NGOs, and the opposition parties—might have found reason to be exuberant about the independence of a Malaysian judiciary that had decided the *Asian Wall Street Journal*, Aliran, Papan, and Lim Kit Siang–United Engineering Malaysia cases against the powers that be.

Certainly, Mahathir would not share that exuberance because 'since anyone can sue the government, the government can no longer decide on anything with certainty. Every decision can be challenged and perhaps overruled. Thus the government is no longer the executive. Others have taken over that function.'[160]

Others might argue that the 'government' was only 'one-third' executive—co-existing and functioning with the legislature and the judiciary according to the doctrine of the separation of powers. Certainly, the Malaysian judiciary appeared to hold that it had 'no interest, nor desire, to embark upon trespassing into the domains of the legislature or the executive'.[161] Its Lord President, Tun Salleh Abas, in dismissing several applications for *habeas corpus* by detainees arrested under Operation Lalang, emphasized that 'our duties are not to substitute our decision for that of the executive' and that 'we are only concerned with the procedural aspects of the exercise of executive discretion'.[162] This was a relatively conservative view of the judiciary's role and bailiwick, *vis-à-vis* the exercise of executive power, as Salleh Abas himself later conceded.[163] Salleh Abas's view went beyond constitutional doctrine because he, together with two other Supreme Court judges, ruled in a 3 : 2 decision on 15 January 1988 that Lim Kit Siang had no *locus standi* to bring a suit against the executive for alleged corruption in its award of the North–South Highway project to UEM.[164] Salleh Abas's pronouncements would also have struck few people as being the views of a 'conspicuously liberal judge'[165] seeking confrontation with the executive.

But from Mahathir's point of view, under the gathering cloud of the impending UMNO-11 suit, the fatal flaw in Salleh Abas's reasoning might have been that 'it is now accepted that the judiciary whilst in the process of resolving disputes does also at the same time develop the law'.[166] Mahathir jealously guarded the prerogative of the legislature to 'develop the law', as it would seem to be suggested by his remarks to *Time* magazine, on 24 November 1986:

> The judiciary says: 'Although you passed a law with a certain thing in mind, we think that your mind is wrong, and we want to give our interpretation'. If we disagree, the Courts will say, 'We will interpret your disagreement'. If we go along, we are going to lose our power of legislation, we know exactly what we want to do, but once we do it, it is interpreted in a different way, and we have no means to reinterpret it our way. If we find out that a Court always throws us out on its interpretation, if it interprets contrary to why we made the law, then we will have to find a way of producing a law that will have to be interpreted according to our wish.[167]

These remarks, which were made in reference to the *John Berthelsen* v. *Minister of Home Affairs* case when the Supreme Court ruled in favour of the *Asian Wall Street Journal* correspondent,[168] have been taken to mark the commencement of Mahathir's assault on the judiciary in 1987–8. Uncannily, Mahathir had expressed a similar sentiment when he supported a proposed amendment to the Internal Security Act twenty years earlier:

> As to the matter of amending the Internal Security Act, the Member for Ipoh is concerned that this amendment seems to have cropped up because certain judges have made certain decisions in courts, and it seems to me he is suggesting that we should do nothing about amending it. To me, a law is promulgated in order to attain a certain end; and if, having made the law, we find that it is ineffective, I think the best thing is to amend the law to make it effective.[169]

Under the climate of dissent that he had faced until 27 October

1987, and under the gathering cloud of the UMNO-11 suit scheduled for late January 1988, Mahathir's sentiment was increasingly expressed as insinuations about the impartiality of 'certain courts' or a 'particular court' which heard cases involving the executive. When he was asked if the Malaysian judiciary was 'fiercely independent', he tried to sound fair-minded about it: 'That's a label blown up by the Press. I don't think the judiciary is fiercely independent. It's merely fair and just.'[170] But really what came through in his reply was a faltering tolerance of a judiciary which 'always throws us out on its interpretation':

> There are black sheep in any group who want to be, as you say, fiercely independent. What is it anyway? When you want to be fiercely independent, you're implying that you'd forget your duty to be just and fair. You're only interested in being independent and in order to do that, you have to stretch things a bit, you have to prove you can hammer the government, for example.
>
> But in doing so you lose your independence because now you're following public trends. You want to ingratiate yourself, you want to be well thought of by the public. You are no longer independent. You're subject to public opinion.[171]

After Karpal Singh was ordered to be released by the Ipoh High Court on 9 March 1988, when the Court found material errors in the 'charge sheet' used to detain him during Operation Lalang, Mahathir warned that 'judges must apply the laws made by Parliament and not make their own laws as is happening now'.[172] In fact, the *Asian Wall Street Journal*, Aliran, Papan, the initial Lim Kit Siang–UEM, and Karpal Singh cases—which went against the government between 1986 and 1988—had led Mahathir to discern 'signs that matters which were deemed to be the sole powers of the executive have been assumed to be open to judicial interference'.[173] After Sultan Azlan Shah and Tun Mohamed Suffian had supported calls for a review of the Malaysian Constitution, and Justice Harun Hashim had recommended that the Senate be transformed into an elected body (these suggestions being made at separate conferences on Law and the Constitution in late 1987), Mahathir cautioned the judiciary to be 'neutral' in politics. And when the UMNO-11 shifted Team B's dissidence from the party to the court in September 1987, Mahathir regretted that 'now it is the courts which will decide who should lead the party while the UMNO members have been rendered redundant'.[174]

It was with this sense that the courts had 'interfered' in politics, 'taken over' executive functions, and misinterpreted the wishes of the legislature, that Mahathir said of the impending UMNO-11 suit in January 1988: 'Don't get me wrong. If it [the UMNO-11 suit] goes to the courts ... I don't care what the result is.'[175]

On 4 February 1988, the result of the High Court hearing on the UMNO-11 suit was that UMNO ceased to be a political party. Justice Harun Hashim accepted the UMNO-11's argument that illegal UMNO branches had taken part in the process leading to the 24 April 1987 election. But he would not accept their plea to nullify only the election. He ruled that the presence of illegal UMNO branches made UMNO an illegal party under the Societies Act. Consequently, he ordered the deregistration of UMNO itself.

Others might have been shocked that suddenly the country was being ruled by a defunct party! Mahathir seemed to be unperturbed. He virtually repeated his 'national mandate' argument—which he had made on the eve of the 24 April 1987 UMNO election—when he insisted that 'the government is founded on elections where we stand as individuals even though we use party symbols'.[176] In contrast to the cases immediately preceding the UMNO-11 suit, when the executive had appealed against virtually all court decisions made against it, Mahathir would not appeal the High Court's deregistration of UMNO. For a moment, it was as if having 'lost' his party, Mahathir prepared to rule without a party. One did not have to be a Team B partisan or to be wholly cynical to note that 'without a party, and thus party elections, Mahathir's rivals cannot challenge him as party president'.[177]

But when the UMNO dissidents, gathered around the Tunku, tried to resurrect UMNO by registering an 'UMNO Malaysia', Mahathir thwarted and outmanoeuvred them. The Tunku's 'UMNO Malaysia' application was rejected by the Registrar of Societies as being premature for being lodged at a time when the Registrar herself had not technically deregistered UMNO! At the precise moment of UMNO's deregistration, best known only to the Registrar (who served directly under Mahathir as the Minister of Home Affairs), Mahathir's application to register UMNO Baru, or 'New UMNO', was accepted.[178] Thereafter, no other 'UMNO' could legally emerge. Other details surrounding UMNO's deregistration and re-registration have been ably recounted elsewhere and need not be repeated here.[179] Suffice it to say that 'the joy of total re-registration of the party for Mahathir and his Team A [was] that Team B supporters [were] excluded from the reconstituted party'.[180]

With hindsight, it is clear that the judiciary, itself under verbal assault by the executive from 1987 to 1988, had in fact 'chosen' to remain 'neutral' in the most critical political case of all. Whatever its legalities, the 4 February deregistration of UMNO had effectively tossed the Team B dissidents' case back into the political arena. There Mahathir proved once more he could reign supreme. Once again, however, the UMNO-11 tried to shift its battle from 'politics' to 'law', from the closed grounds of UMNO Baru to the contestable terrain of the judiciary. It was in that conjuncture of Team B's persisting dissidence and the judiciary's uneasy independence that Mahathir's authoritarianism of 27 October 1987 completed its course.

In January 1988, Attorney-General Abu Talib Othman echoed Mahathir's growing impatience with the independence of the judiciary. Abu Talib warned that it would be 'unfortunate if the trust and confidence the public has in the actual function of the judiciary is undermined as a result of the urge to champion freedom in secondary matters'.[181] He added that the 'independence of [the] court does not necessarily mean deciding a case against the state' because then 'although the verdict might be legally sound the judgement might contain side comments or reflect personal opinions of the judge which might offend certain groups'.[182] Abu Talib had candour if not subtlety. In a direct reply, although 'we need no reminders from the Attorney-General, nor from anyone else, as to our responsibilities and duties', Salleh Abas retorted: 'Not only must the subjects have confidence in the judiciary, the executive and the legislature too should not do anything to undermine that confidence.... Judicial independence must not be seen as a national liability but as a single most important asset.'[183]

In mid-May 1988, Salleh Abas 'noticed that the UMNO-11 case seemed to engage much public attention' and that 'the press carried reports of the Prime Minister's speeches attacking the so-called conflict between the oral and written judgements of Harun J. in [the 4 February UMNO-11] case'.[184] Since the UMN-11's appeal was 'of great national importance', and perhaps because Salleh considered that it would demonstrate the impartiality of the Supreme Court, he 'fixed the appeal to be heard by a full panel of 9 members of the Supreme Court on 13.6.88', realizing that 'never had any appeal been heard by a full panel before—either in the practice of the Federal Court or the Supreme Court'.[185] Perhaps Mahathir took a different view of having his political future decided by a 'full panel' of nine Supreme Court judges, or 'the King's judges', who were, constitutionally speaking, protected from executive interference.

Salleh Abas never did hear the UMNO-11's appeal. On 27 May 1988, he was invited to meet Mahathir in the latter's office. There he was informed that the Yang di-Pertuan Agong had instructed the Prime Minister to suspend the Lord President. The Agong had been displeased with Salleh's conduct, primarily for his writing a letter, dated 25 March 1988, to the Agong and the Malay rulers. The letter touched on the executive's criticisms of the judiciary and had been written after a meeting of High Court judges in Kuala Lumpur decided to 'reply' to the Prime Minister's assault on the judiciary by the 'non-public' method of writing to the Agong and the Malay Rulers.

Faced with suspension, Salleh Abas first opted to resign from the Lord President's position. Later, he retracted, choosing to face impeachment by a specially constituted tribunal. Nearly everything connected with the impeachment proceedings was controversial.[186] Certainly, Salleh Abas's lawyers considered them improper. The tribunal consisted of six members, an even-numbered panel which made it possible that the chairman might have a casting vote. Five out of the six tribunal members were either junior to Salleh Abas or even tainted by 'conflicts of interest'; for instance, Chief Justice Hamid Omar, Acting Lord President during Salleh's suspension and due to become Lord President should Salleh lose the case, was chairman of the tribunal. Salleh Abas wanted the tribunal proceedings to be public; the tribunal chose to keep its deliberations closed. The documentation of the charges seemed to have contained mistakes or errors—critical ones in Salleh's view, 'innocent' slips according to Mahathir.

Salleh Abas was concerned that these unresolved issues made it impossible for him to obtain a fair hearing. When the tribunal commenced its proceedings, his lawyers withdrew and instead filed in the High Court for a stay order against the tribunal. The Attorney-General failed to attend the High Court hearing on this suit but the High Court made no decision. With the tribunal proceedings still continuing, Salleh Abas appealed to the Supreme Court for a stay order against the tribunal. In a special sitting on 2 July, five members of the Supreme Court heard the case and granted a stay order against the tribunal. What the five judges thought was an act in pursuance of justice became the very grounds for their suspension the next day by the Acting Lord President, Hamid Omar. Upon the conclusion of its proceedings, the tribunal recommended Salleh Abas's dismissal from office. The dismissal, conveyed by letter to Salleh on 6 August, took effect from 8 August 1988. On 9 August, the UMNO-11's appeal, which had been postponed under unclear circumstances when Salleh was suspended, was heard in the Supreme Court and dismissed.

The DAP called Salleh Abas's impeachment a 'deliberate, calculated and orchestrated move … to intimidate the judiciary in view of the UMNO suit which is due for hearing very soon before the Supreme Court'.[187] The voters at the 25 August Johore Bahru by-election—which was called when Shahrir Samad resigned to force a by-election against UMNO Baru—seemed to agree: Shahrir won a huge victory against the UMNO Baru candidate. But that was practically the last dramatic gasp of the anti-Mahathir, ex-UMNO dissidents. Shahrir dedicated his victory to Salleh Abas, but UMNO Baru had come to stay. On 10 October 1988, Razaleigh and thirteen 'ex-UMNO' parliamentarians crossed over to the 'opposition' in Parliament.

At the first UMNO Baru General Assembly in late October 1988, Mahathir pointed out that 'until recently judges had never been sacked in Malaysia' but 'this is probably because until recently judges had not violated any law'.[188] He asked, rhetorically, one gathers: 'What is so special about judges in Malaysia that they are considered to be above the law?'[189] In any case, he took pains to explain that the 'Government, or *rakyat* or a ruler, has no power to sack the judges. Only the judges themselves have the authority to sack a brother judge through a tribunal made up of judges. The Ruler is bound by the advice of that tribunal. Politicians cannot interfere in these matters.'[190] Perhaps therein lay the final injustice of the Salleh Abas affair which brought the authoritarianism of 27 October 1987 to its completion in May 1988. In the judiciary's losing battle against the executive, the judiciary had ultimately turned upon itself.

The Doctor and the Common Crowd

It is sufficient to recall only the most prominent examples of Tun Dr Ismail, Dr Tan Chee Khoon, Dr Lim Chong Eu, Dr Chen Man Hin, and Dr Mahathir Mohamad to realize that the Malaysian political roll of honour has been replete with the names of 'doctor-politicians' who successfully made the transition from being a medical practitioner to being a politician.[191]

Are there peculiar reasons for the striking performance of these doctor-politicians? Many would admit the advantages of using a private medical practice as the launching pad for a political career: the doctor's rapport with his 'patient-constituents', his social standing in the 'community-constituency', and the personal–professional–financial independence which comes from thriving 'self-employment'.[192] None would disparage the individual qualities, talent, and dedication which went into the making of each renowned case of 'medicine-to-politics' transition, including, as Mahathir described it, 'a certain degree of restlessness ... which would make total commitment to medicine quite unsatisfying'.[193]

Mahathir, the only doctor to have become Prime Minister in Malaysia, appeared to have benefited from those advantages:

> Medicine had all along been his planned route to gaining credibility among people older than himself. He found it natural that having become recognized as a person of some standing within his community, a doctor in a small town, he should make his move into politics. After all, he had a fall-back position, represented by the clinic, and if he should fail in politics, he could simply resume his medical practice.[194]

But it would be churlish to imagine that Mahathir viewed medicine only through the careerist lenses of an aspiring politician. Like the best known of the 'doctor-politicians', 'Dr UMNO', as he was popularly called, was a good doctor before and on the way to becoming a good politician. From 1953 to 1957, he worked as a government doctor in Penang, Alor Star, Perlis, and Pulau Langkawi. In 1957, he started his MAHA Clinic, the first Malay private medical practice to be set up in Alor Star. He built up a reputation for competence, diligence, and dedication. He had compassion for his patients whether judged in terms of his 'bedside manners' or his willingness to forgo charging the poorer among them for consultation and medicine.[195] In 1958, the General Hospital in Alor Star faced difficulties in scheduling surgical operations because its surgeon was 'incapacitated'. This was just one year after Mahathir set up private practice. He wrote to the Kedah State Surgeon and offered to help conduct some of the General Hospital's emergency cases, 'to stand by' or 'to assist' at operations. Mahathir cited his own considerable experience in operations and offered his services 'gratis'.[196]

In Parliament, Mahathir the doctor-politician spoke lengthily and feelingly during debates involving medicine, doctors, and hospitals. One of his earliest speeches in Parliament called for a review of laws related to 'patent rights' in view of 'price fixing' abuses carried out by some pharmaceutical companies.[197] He favoured a more stringent regulation of the medical profession 'to see that the public is protected from people who might profess to be doctors but who are not really doctors'.[198] He boldly recommended using existing hospitals to conduct a 'crash programme' to 'step up the production of doctors',[199] 'without waiting until we have big universities and big hospitals'.[200] Sensing 'no desire on the part of the administrators to enquire ... why doctors resign and to try somehow or other to influence doctors to stay in Government service', Mahathir spoke for the doctors whose night and 'on-call' duties were genuinely arduous, unlike 'the Civil Service type of duty, that is, on call twenty-four hours, but never call for twenty years'.[201] He knew that 'there are doctors who resign in order to make more money in [private] practice' but then 'there are also doctors who are willing to work for the Government but their position in Government is made so untenable that they have to resign'.[202] He spoke for women doctors whom 'we are so short of' and yet who 'are treated not as equals ... not given any incentive to work at all ... not asked to specialize ... and if they are married ... are discriminated against'.[203] He argued that it would be 'grossly unfair to expect' non-Malay doctors to sit for a Malay language examination unless they were 'at least ... given one month's leave to prepare themselves'.[204] But he had no sympathy for lower-ranking hospital employees whose unions instituted 'work-to-rule' actions in the government hospitals.[205] The dispensers only 'want to work overtime and to get extra pay'.[206] For the ambulance drivers, 'their comfort comes first' while 'the sick, especially those in rural areas, do not count at all'.[207] The X-ray assistants, 'want(ing) high ranks but not conditions that go with it [*sic*]', refused overtime work by 'claim(ing) that exposure to X-ray causes sterility'.[208] Nor did Mahathir approve of the University of Malaya's role in the training of doctors. To his mind, its faculty of medicine had too few Malay students, too many disgruntled teaching staff, and a 'rarified atmosphere' while its University Hospital unnecessarily duplicated the specialized facilities of the Kuala Lumpur General Hospital.[209]

Mahathir stopped practising as a doctor in 1974. His appointment to Razak's Cabinet required it, but since he had had twenty years of the medical profession, and 'the study of medicine was at least partly in order to further my career as a politician', 'it was not too difficult to give up medicine for my other and more abiding love, politics'.[210] Still, he recollected that the 'practice of medicine came easily to me. I discovered I was naturally sympathetic to people and their problems. It was very satisfying to be able to cure a sick person.'[211]

And whether it sprang out of nostalgia, that very 'gratifying' remembrance of his patients' 'gratitude for helping them',[212] or from the yearning for instant 'job satisfaction'[213] which politics seldom supplied, Mahathir was given to mentioning his medical background in numerous different contexts. For example, he exulted in drawing the differences in the perceptions of law that he, a doctor, might have in contrast with the legally trained participants at the 1982 ASEAN Law Association General Assembly.[214] He took it as 'a signal honour for a doctor of medicine who has had no training whatsoever in economics' to address the Economic Society in Singapore but he thereby half-excused himself 'if what I pronounce is unconventional and at times verges on the absurd and errs in terms of theory and even understanding of economic principles'.[215] He advised Malaysian bankers and financiers to distinguish between borrowers 'who deserve to be made bankrupt' and those who 'are in a bad way through no fault of their own' although 'it is really superfluous for a medical doctor' to tell the bankers so.[216] At a seminar on Malaysian–British 'invisible trade links', he taught that 'a deficit in the current account' should be demystified to mean simply 'borrowing to finance consumption' because 'as a medical doctor, I know only too well the danger of self-deception, whether by the patient or the doctor'.[217] At the 1985 Commonwealth Heads of Government Meeting in Nassau, he derided Britain's excuse of 'black suffering' for not applying economic sanctions against South Africa: 'The fact is the blacks are already suffering. Cures are always painful. As a doctor I should know....'[218] When an Indonesian interviewer asked him to comment on his being a doctor and a writer, he confidently stated that 'it is easy for me to examine a patient and then prescribe an appropriate medicine' but humbly added that 'to be a writer is more difficult'.[219] When a local interviewer asked if he missed being a doctor, he replied: 'Yes, I miss that. Medicine is something like detective work. You know that Conan Doyle who wrote *The Adventures of Sherlock Holmes* was a doctor. I read Conan Doyle first, then read medicine. The way Conan Doyle solves his problems is the way the doctor solves his cases.'[220]

Mahathir might have 'read Conan Doyle first, then read medicine' and considered himself to have been 'a politician earlier than becoming a doctor'.[221] But medicine, once he had embarked upon it, suffused his whole life and career in Erik Erikson's sense that the first discipline a young man encounters is the one he identifies with. Mahathir the politician habitually looked back to Dr Mahathir for the lessons which his medical training held for political praxis:

> The first lesson is the methodical way that doctors approach medical problems. Observance, history taking, physical examinations, special examinations, narrowing the diagnosis and then deciding on the most likely diagnosis and the treatment required. These are most useful in any problem in life, and they serve me well in attending top political problems.[222]

He meant his doctor's skills to address directly the demands of politics: 'If the ailments of a society or nation are attended *in the same way as* the illness of a patient, some good results must follow. The essential thing is to develop diagnostic skills.'[223]

Deputy Prime Minister Mahathir even let out his 'trade secret' at the Conference on Business in Southeast Asia, held on 4 February 1977, in Kuala Lumpur:

> As a doctor, one is always tempted to look at problems as diseases, and the people affected by them as patients.
>
> Since taking up politics and the chores of running a Government, that temptation has seldom been resisted by me, and I must admit that the clinical approach to problems pays.[224]

There were others who saw Mahathir's medical skills applied to his politics in a different light. Mahathir, it was thought, operated with a 'medical' or 'surgical' style. For Musa Hitam, that generally meant that the 'good doctor wanted to push things down your throat'.[225] For an unnamed delegate to the 1987 UMNO General Assembly, that specifically meant that when faced with the Team B problem, Mahathir chose a 'medical solution ... to cut out the cancer'.[226] In an allusive way, Musa and the unnamed UMNO delegate were right. Mahathir never hesitated to say that 'as a doctor I know how to choose good medicine'.[227] Nor, as a good doctor, would he shrink from employing strong medicine: 'When the indications are irrefutable, amputations, however painful, must be undertaken.'[228] For that matter, a medical approach informed his observation that although a government might respond to a 'potentially dangerous internal security threat' too early as to 'elicit criticisms for heavy handedness ... [y]et it is at the early stages that positive results can be obtained'.[229] And quite a few people would have reason to rue Mahathir's peculiar idea that the 'sense of compassion and deep understanding that a doctor develops towards patients are also useful in politics. An ability to look at the other side of the picture, the patient's or the opponent's side enables understanding and appreciation. Countermeasures can then be developed.'[230]

But 'pushing things down your throat' or 'cutting out' one's opponents are time-honoured political practices and not exclusively Dr Mahathir's in Malaysian political history. In their own time, the Tunku dismissed Aziz Ishak, Razak dropped Khir Johari, and Hussein Onn prosecuted Harun Idris.[231] We must seek the real significance of Mahathir's application of medicine to politics elsewhere.

For a start, it now appears quite unmistakable that *The Malay Dilemma* was structured very much according to 'the methodical way that doctors approach medical problems'. It will be recalled that *The Malay Dilemma* begins with a pathologist's report on 'what went wrong' on May 13 1969 which emphasizes that things went wrong, among other reasons, because 'the Government was no longer able to feel the pulse of the people'.[232] The book continues with a 'history taking' of the 'influence of heredity and environment on the Malay race'. Thereafter it proceeds with a 'therapeutic analysis' of 'the Malay value system and code of ethics'.[233] Along the way, it likens the violence of May 13 1969 to a collective *amok* by the Malays, 'an overflowing of [their] inner bitterness' after, if one will, a long history of collective repression.[234] As to the choice of remedies for the 'Malay problem', it rejects the 'meaningless' palliative of 'legal equality'.[235] Instead, it prescribes an immediate treatment by 'constructive protection' but recommends a 'creative and orderly ... revolution' for a 'complete rehabilitation'.

Mahathir's later analyses of the Malay 'disinclination to work' and the Muslim dilemma as well as his insistence on the adoption of an Eastern work ethic likewise showed his 'diagnostic skills' and prescriptive ability operating on political subjects. But a 'special examination' turned upon the doctor himself would isolate the most curiously 'medico-political' of Mahathir's analyses in his suggestion that 'frankness ... is not a part of the Malay social code':[236]

> This analysis and criticism of Malay values, largely disparaging as it must seem, is uncharacteristic and atypical of a Malay. In modern psychology seeking out and identifying causes serves not only to facilitate treatment but is also part of the treatment. There is an almost immediate relief when a cause is identified. From then on it is a question of either removing the cause or nullifying or reversing its effect. The process of identifying the cause is often painful and depressing. Events are recalled which seem far better forgotten. Yet without this laborious and painful process, treatment cannot begin. And so it is with the ailments of a community. To cure, it is imperative that the painful process of identifying the causes of the ailment be examined.[237]

Mahathir held that 'by and large, the Malay value system and code of ethics are impediments to their progress', but he counselled that 'if they admit this, and if the need for change is realized, then there is hope; for as in psychiatry, success in isolating the root cause is in itself a part of treatment. From then on planning a cure would be relatively simple.'[238] For 'Dr UMNO', medicine and politics were unified: 'There is no other way but to face boldly the pain of self-examination, the admission that one is wrong, and the acceptance that the cure lies in the rejection of some ideas and concepts no matter how dear to the heart they may be.'[239]

If no one else would 'admit this', he would, no matter how 'disparaging' he sounded, how 'uncharacteristic and atypical of a Malay' he appeared to be, or how much of an 'ultra' he was labelled. He maintained that 'if you examine all that I have said, I will admit to *forthrightness* and *frankness* but I will not admit to being extreme'.[240] Here emerges the deepest medical dimension of Mahathir's politics. Here medicine becomes more than a metaphor for the diagnosis and treatment of the body politic: the doctor's 'frankness' is his people's 'catharsis', his voice their very own—which is the quintessential quality of any triumphant populist.

In that, *Doctor* Mahathir differed from the Tunku, Tun Razak, and Hussein Onn, three lawyers who headed Malaysia's first three post-1957 administrations which were fundamentally suspicious of any populist mobilization of the masses. The Tunku's Alliance government, widely regarded as a model of 'consociationalism', was by that characterization decidedly élitist and profoundly anti-popular.[241] It was not for nothing that Mahathir accused the Tunku of not knowing how the Malay masses felt. In the post-1969 period, Razak's 'NEP government' was predicated on recognizing and satisfying Malay mass grievances. But equally Razak left little room for any politics besides the élitist accommodations and administrative formulas based on the 'consensus' of the UMNO-dominated Barisan Nasional. Hussein Onn's administration inherited Razak's parameters and extended them to the point of banning political rallies and introducing the Societies Act. The Tunku, a prince of Kedah, and Razak and Hussein Onn, Malay aristocrats closely linked to the Pahang and Johore royal houses respectively, were likely to have found it politic to speak in terms of *leading* the Malays when in fact it might be more accurate to say that they found it habitual to *rule* over the (Malay) masses.

Not so Mahathir. Other Malay politicians had tried their hand at populist mobilization and succeeded to some extent, like Harun Idris in Selangor and Razaleigh Hamzah in Kelantan. But Harun's populism relied heavily on his powerful position as the Menteri Besar of Selangor while 'Ku Li' skilfully tapped a reservoir of Malay respect for the royalty. Only Mahathir, a plebeian of anti-patrician bent, staked his claim to Malay support on the basis of his total identification and empathy with the Malay masses. Whatever his political persona—C. H. E. Det, Dr UMNO, party rebel, or Prime Minister—Mahathir was never far from claiming to understand the common Malays, to diagnose their condition, to represent their interests, to articulate their grievances, to offer solutions to their dilemmas, and to uplift their status. Only Mahathir with his intellectual's inclination, ideologue's temperament, doctor's skills, and Prime Minister's vision managed to fashion a populist politics out of the assemblage of the realities and contradictions of Malay and Malaysian society.

And the populist politics was matched by Mahathir's exceptional fondness for the public rally as a vehicle to mobilize popular support. In the days before the Hussein Onn government banned public rallies,[242] Malaysian politicians spoke and debated at political rallies which were held during the election campaigns. When Mahathir became Prime Minister, he practically ignored the continuing ban on rallies. Instead, he made the political rally his definitive mode of campaigning, or, as he would no doubt have regarded it, reaching out to the people. As a vehicle of mass communication and as a spectacle of mass mobilization, the political rally suited Mahathir admirably. He liked to hold the rallies in series, swinging through the entire country in a 'state-by-state' progression which reinforced his image as the leader of the entire nation. He held these rallies at all critical junctures of his administration: during the 1983 constitutional crisis, prior to the 1986 election and just after Musa's resignation, in his battle against Razaleigh, following his narrow 24 April 1987 victory, and after UMNO's split in 1988.

The typical Mahathir rally wore at least a semi-official atmosphere no matter how overtly political the occasion for the rally might be. It was organized and staged by his UMNO lieutenants and amply supported by a mix of state and party personnel and resources. The rally would feature Mahathir with a coterie of loyalists—Cabinet Ministers, UMNO and Barisan Nasional politicians, and high government officials. Its programme would incorporate elaborate gestures of welcome, official ceremonies, emotional speech-making, and even oath-taking. Free transport, food and drinks, and, sometimes, it was rumoured, an 'attendance fee' were provided to some of those who were able, willing, or even directed to attend the rally. There would be ample press, radio, and television coverage of the rally to ensure its transmission to the rest of the nation.

Such an approach to mass mobilization scarcely distinguished between what was overtly political and what should have been strictly administrative. In its crudest form, it involved an abuse of governmental power and resources for partisan politics, as his critics, especially Aliran, never ceased to point out. Certainly, the rally participants, spectators, or anyone else could not properly and separately keep in perspective the different personae of the Prime Minister, the UMNO President, or simply the politician when Mahathir spoke. By default, the rally gained an official aura and Mahathir an automatic legitimacy.

The rest was a matter of intuition and technique. Mahathir was no mean public speaker although he is not stylistically as eloquent as Musa Hitam, Razaleigh Hamzah, Anwar Ibrahim, or Rais Yatim, among his UMNO contemporaries. He is certainly not as fiercely charismatic as PAS's Haji Hadi Awang. But always combative and provocative, Mahathir was uncannily sensitive to the mood of the 'common crowd' who could be teased into being his accomplice by the sharing of a sneer or the throwing of a taunt. Imperious of intellect, proud of his polemics, and secure in the knowledge that nothing he uttered 'could be used against him',[243] Mahathir was at his best when caricaturing *in absentia* opponents who did not or were not permitted to have a comparable means of replying.[244] Donning a populist aura and never discarding his ideologue's garb, Mahathir exploited the tangible and symbolic advantages of the political rally which he first used in a systematic and massive way during the 1983 constitutional crisis when there was no better way to demonstrate the power of popular sovereignty against the royalty than to 'return to the people'.[245] By way of the symbolic power of the political rally, Mahathir, as it were, kept faith with the crowds from whose midst he must have perceived himself re-emerging from time to time as 'a man of the people', each time blessed with a reaffirmed mandate, and reassured that his services as a leader were still required.

In time, the manipulative elements of the staged rally—with its bussed-in crowds, its use of executive power, and its deployment of state resources—may have been overlooked by Mahathir himself so that only the contrived images of loyal crowds and demonstrative rallies lingered to feed an imagery of spontaneous popular support. That is to say, Mahathir, like many another politician, came to believe in his own propaganda and to cling fervently to his notion of a popularly derived mandate which, he once went so far as to insist, was 'personal to holder'.[246] Not coincidentally, then, and not out of cynicism alone did Mahathir repeatedly ask to be 'interviewed by the people'—if he was to be 'interviewed' at all.

But note. On the one hand, Mahathir could admonish 'leaders

whose support had diminished' to withdraw from active office. On the other hand, he counselled on several occasions that if a leader is good and still has contributions to make to his cause, he should be left where he is, unchallenged, much less deposed, in order that he might continue his work. Many a time Mahathir pledged to retire graciously if the 'signs' showed that he was no longer required.[247] At critical times, he vowed to continue in office even if he won by one vote.

It was surely a measure of the man's boundless inventiveness that he could endlessly hold together ideological tensions and contradictions of this nature for which his opponents and critics quite readily, not unreasonably, but none the less simplistically, accuse him of distortion, repeated voltes-face, and hypocrisy. Perhaps it was just Mahathir's own way of passing 'the test of a first-rate intelligence [which] is the ability to hold two opposed ideas in the mind at the same time and still retain the ability to function'.[248] It was this same ideological inventiveness in the face of political adversity that led the 'Rebel of '69', to beatify loyalty in 1987–8: loyalty to himself as Prime Minister of a divided nation and as President of the rump of UMNO, loyalty to the spirit of a legally defunct party, and loyalty to a royalty he had tried to curb in 1983.[249]

Mahathir's use of the political rally as a vehicle of mass mobilization, as an instrument for enacting political spectacle, conjuring up populist imagery, and symbolically reaffirming the reciprocal bonds of faith between him and the people, reached its pinnacle in the SEMARAK campaign when his political career hung by a thread. The SEMARAK campaign consisted of a state-by-state sequence of highly publicized and closely choreographed public rallies by which Mahathir, his principal UMNO allies, and Cabinet members 'returned to the people'.[250] SEMARAK, a Malay word meaning 'glow', 'lustre', or 'shine', was the acronym for the campaign slogan, 'Setia Bersama Rakyat', itself a linguistic sleight of hand—for it proclaimed not Mahathir's loyalty to the people, not even the people's loyalty to Mahathir, but Mahathir's 'loyalty *with* the people'.[251] There was the rub. Believing he had kept faith with the people, Mahathir turned around to demand that they keep faith with *him*. It became less and less clear where a limited mandate ended and an indefinite tenure began, where populism dissolved and authoritarianism congealed.

1. The 'protest' was mounted by UMNO's old guard in retaliation for Hussein Onn's prosecution of Harun Idris. Sulaiman Palestin was later suspended from the party.

2. Not becoming President until after the General Assembly, 'Mahathir had no choice but to concede to the party delegates to decide their choice for Deputy President' (Chamil Wariya, *UMNO Era Mahathir*, Petaling Jaya: Penerbit Fajar Bakti, 1988, p. 82) although on the quiet, Mahathir set his 'gurkhas' to campaign for Musa (ibid., pp. 85–6). Ghani Ismail interpreted it as Mahathir's 'self-interested' manoeuvre against Razaleigh, who was senior to Musa but whom Mahathir considered to be a more dangerous rival (Ghani Ismail, *Razaleigh Lawan Musa, Pusingan Kedua, 1984*, Taiping: IJS Communications, 1983, p. 17). It has been argued that it was Hussein Onn who threw the Deputy President's contest open by resigning just before the General Assembly (Roger Kershaw, 'Within the Family: The Limits of Doctrinal Differentiation in the Malaysian Ruling Party Election of 1987', *Review of Indonesian and Malaysian Affairs*, 23 (1989): 129).

3. The two Musa–Razaleigh contests were highly fractious affairs. That Musa privately urged Mahathir to drop Razaleigh from the Cabinet after the 1984 contest was a good indication of the stakes and bitterness involved. Ghani, *Razaleigh Lawan Musa*, is a fascinating account of the run-up to the 1984 contest.

4. 'Gearing for Battle', *Asiaweek*, 7 December 1987, p. 27.

5. Musa gave a lengthy explanation for his decision to defend his incumbency—but not to challenge Mahathir for the presidency—in an interview ('An Offer to the Party', *Asiaweek*, 8 March 1987, pp. 13–14). Briefly, Musa explained that he had been elected by the party, that the party was 'more important than the government', and that his disagreement with Mahathir did not stem from a personal ambition to supplant him.

6. See 'Sounds of Battle', *Asiaweek*, 1 March 1987, pp. 21–4, for a thoughtful consideration of Razaleigh's 'options'.

7. Suhaini Aznam, 'In Everything But Name', *Far Eastern Economic Review*, 12 March 1987, p. 14.

8. 'Razaleigh's "Offer to Lead"', *Asiaweek*, 29 March 1987, p. 14; 'Razaleigh Tanding Presiden', *Utusan Malaysia*, 12 April 1987. In Gua Musang, Razaleigh said he 'understood' Musa's action in asking Mahathir to drop him (Razaleigh) from the Cabinet in 1984. The Gua Musang meeting, a rapturous affair, was largely ignored by the UMNO-controlled Malay press but captured on videotape by Razaleigh's supporters.

9. 'Mahathir Umum Ghafar Bertanding', *Utusan Malaysia*, 22 March 1987. For a contemporary assessment of Ghafar's position, see 'Battle for Survival', *Asiaweek*, 15 March 1987, pp. 18, 21–2.

10. Suhaini Aznam, 'Divided Shows of Unity', *Far Eastern Economic Review*, 2 April 1987, p. 12.

11. 'Mahathir: Saya Tetap Melawan', *Mingguan Malaysia*, 22 March 1987. A useful review of Mahathir's position was provided by 'Mahathir's Big Test', *Asiaweek*, 12 April 1987, pp. 12–15.

12. So, 'how can there be a compromise?', explained 'a high-ranking UMNO leader' ('Razaleigh's "Offer to Lead"', p. 14). Suhaini Aznam reported that Mahathir

scorned the possibility of a compromise after officiating at the meeting of the Kuala Kubu (Selangor) division on 14 March 1987 ('Daim for the Wolves?', *Far Eastern Economic Review*, 26 March 1987, p. 34).

13. 'Semua MB Sokong Mahathir, Ghafar', *Utusan Malaysia*, 27 February 1987.

14. Suhaini, 'Daim for the Wolves?', p. 36. The best known of the UMNO veterans who supported Team B were Harun Idris, Othman Saat, Rahim Bakar, Manan Osman, and Suhaimi Kamaruddin ('The Battle Is On', *Malaysian Business*, 16 April 1987, p. 7).

15. 'The Battle Is On', pp. 5–8. One can sense what the Team A–Team B cleavage meant at the grass-roots level from a description of the division caused by the two Musa–Razaleigh battles: 'This time [the division] went down to the grass roots—to the *warung* (stall) and Malay-dominated trade union meetings in the urban areas and to the *kedai kopi* (coffee shop) and *surau* (small prayer house) in the rural areas. *Orang Musa* [Musa's man] and *orang Razaleigh* [Razaleigh's man] were not only labels but often became the "key phrases" which opened or terminated a business or any other discussion, guaranteed or denied an individual getting a contract or a scholarship, and expedited or delayed an application for a job, a licence, or even the transfer of a school teacher from an *ulu* [remote] to an urban school and vice versa.' The passage is taken from Shamsul A. B., 'The "Battle Royal": The UMNO Elections of 1987', in Institute of Southeast Asian Studies, *Southeast Asian Affairs, 1988*, Singapore: ISEAS, p. 172.

16. Safar Hashim, 'Pemilihan UMNO: Antara Tradisi dengan Amalan Demokrasi', *Dewan Masyarakat*, May 1987. 'It seems that the urge to challenge the President did not arise from a few leaders only but was widespread among the members' (p. 7). Safar (p. 8) cited the following 'occupational profile' ('prepared by Sdr Anwar Ibrahim') of the 1,506 delegates to the 1987 General Assembly: teachers (19 per cent), traders and business people (25 per cent), government officers (23 per cent), MPs and state assembly representatives (19 per cent), Kemas members (5 per cent), professionals, *penghulu*, and others (9 per cent).

17. Shamsul, 'The "Battle Royal"', p. 174.

18. Khoo Khay Jin, 'The Grand Vision: Mahathir and Modernization', in Joel S. Kahn and Francis Loh Kok Wah (eds.), *Fragmented Vision: Culture and Politics in Contemporary Malaysia*, Sydney: Asian Studies Association of Australia in association with Allen and Unwin, 1992, pp. 44–76.

19. See 'A Fight for Principles', *Malaysian Business*, 16 April 1987, pp. 12–13, for Marina Yusoff's candid discussion of how a party leader and businesswoman like her found herself sidelined and with her debt burden unrelieved. But Marina denied that she was with Team B because of 'her personal financial problems' and because 'positions' were denied her. Marina's charges were later elaborated in Marina Yusoff, *Time for Change*, Kuala Lumpur: Champ Press, 1990.

20. See the section 'The NEP in Abeyance: Recession's Solution' in Chapter 4.

21. On Abdullah Badawi's differences with Anwar Ibrahim, see 'Friends and Foes into the Fray', *Malaysian Business*, 16 April 1987, p. 14. Rais Yatim explained his stand against the 'personality cult' in 'Rais "Membakar Jambatan" untuk Razaleigh–Musa', *Era*, 2 (1987): 34–5. Suhaimi Kamaruddin lost his Pemuda

UMNO presidency to Anwar, who first and narrowly defeated Suhaimi in 1982 with Mahathir's backing. Marina Yusoff's predicament was noted under n. 19 above.

22. Kershaw, 'Within the Family'. The doctrinal quarrel was dogged by scurrilous attacks, sometimes at 'closed-door' sessions, often by *surat layang* (flying letters), a sample of which, duly rendered suitable for academic hearing, was given in Shamsul, 'The "Battle Royal"', p. 177.

23. In a sense, Rafidah Aziz may be said to have personified Team A's position: she supported Razaleigh in 1981, Musa in 1984, and Mahathir in 1987—each time, in her view, backing 'tradition' and 'incumbency' ('Why I Back the PM', *Malaysian Business*, 16 April 1987, pp. 11–12).

24. 'Mahathir: Saya Tetap Melawan'. 'Menentang Kemungkaran Politik dan Ekonomi', Razaleigh's 'policy speech', delivered on 19 April 1987 during a meeting at Hotel Regent, Kuala Lumpur, could be taken as Team B's most comprehensive criticism of Mahathir's leadership. The speech was reproduced in Tengku Razaleigh Hamzah, *Mengapa Saya Tentang Mahathir*, Petaling Jaya: AZ Distributors, 1989.

25. For an academic analysis of the Daim–UMBC episode, see Edmund Terence Gomez, *Politics in Business: UMNO's Corporate Investments*, Kuala Lumpur: Forum, 1990, pp. 41–3. The *Asian Wall Street Journal* articles on possible conflict of interest in Daim's United Malayan Banking Corporation deal had so angered Mahathir that the work permits of two Kuala Lumpur-based *AWSJ* journalists were revoked in September 1986. 'Pemindahan Milik UMBC kepada Bumiputera Usaha Daim—PM', *Utusan Malaysia*, 23 March 1987, reported Mahathir saying that Daim, then 'only a businessman', had 'played an important role' in transferring UMBC from 'non-*bumiputera*' to '*bumiputera*' ownership. Daim may have been especially unpopular with Team B because he 'worked the country's finances like the businessman he was' (Khoo Khay Jin, 'The Grand Vision', p. 54) which, during the recession, did not relieve the debt burdens of many Malay business people.

26. 'Our anti-Western attitude resulted in Western investors and traders losing interest in investing and trading with us. Our pro-Eastern attitude, which ought to have attracted investment and trade from the developed countries of the East, also brought adverse consequences for us' (Musa Hitam, 'Speech at the UMNO Johor Convention', Johore Bahru, 2 April 1987).

27. 'PM Nafi Nak Letak Jawatan', *Utusan Malaysia*, 31 March 1987.

28. Incidentally revealing his personal contempt for the Official Secrets Act (OSA), which was passed in December 1986 at his insistence and against strong public opposition (see the next section '27 October 1987: "The End of Liberalism"?'). Mahathir explained that the OSA allowed for such declassification to safeguard 'truth' against 'people who spread lies' ('Documents De-classified', *New Straits Times*, 14 April 1987). An official statement from the Prime Minister's Department on the three 'mammoth projects' was reprinted as 'Kedudukan Sebenar Tiga Projek Raksasa', *Berita Harian*, 23 April 1987.

29. Whether the 'party' controls the 'government' became a highly contentious issue 'not because another party, let alone another race or a democratic electorate, was challenging UMNO for control, but simply because UMNO itself had fallen prey to extreme factionalism' so that 'the "government" that was conceptually

distinct from "the party" in the out-group's arguments was none other than the incumbent party faction, using state machinery, including the media, to sustain themselves, and running a closed government unresponsive (allegedly) to the councils of the party as a whole' (Kershaw, 'Within the Family', pp. 132–3).

30. 'PM: Tiada Larangan Bercakap dalam MT dan Kabinet', *Mingguan Malaysia*, 12 April 1987.

31. 'Mahathir: Saya Tetap Melawan'.

32. 'Saya Sokong Ghafar Kerana Khidmat Cemerlangnya—Dr M', *Utusan Malaysia*, 23 March 1987.

33. Ibid.

34. 'PM: Tiada Larangan Bercakap dalam MT dan Kabinet'.

35. 'Perdana Menteri Sanjung Sikap Rais Yatim', *Utusan Malaysia*, 25 March 1987.

36. 'Siapa Pecah-belahkan UMNO Pengkhianat—Dr M', *Utusan Malaysia*, 11 April 1987.

37. 'PM Nafi Nak Letak Jawatan'.

38. Mahathir, 'Speech at the Closing Session of the 32nd UMNO General Assembly', Kuala Lumpur, 28 June 1981, reprinted as 'Today My Burden Is My Burden', in J. Victor Morais, *Mahathir: A Profile in Courage*, Singapore: Eastern Universities Press, 1982, pp. 77–83.

39. Mahathir, 'Speech at the 35th UMNO General Assembly', Kuala Lumpur, 25 May 1984, English translation reprinted as 'Making Sure the Spirit of UMNO Prevails', *New Straits Times*, 26 May 1984.

40. 'Mahathir: Saya Sedia Undur', *Mingguan Malaysia*, 12 May 1987, and 'Dituju pada Semua Pemimpin UMNO', *Utusan Malaysia*, 13 May 1985.

41. Musa Hitam, 'Letter to Mahathir', 26 February 1986, p. 3.

42. *Watan*, 21–23 March 1987; *Mingguan Malaysia*, 15 March 1987. Kershaw, 'Within the Family', pp. 168–9, nn. 42–4, discusses this point at some length.

43. Cited in Suhaini, 'Daim for the Wolves?', p. 35.

44. Mahathir was responding to the 'latest,' 'fantastic myth' churned out by the 'rumour mills' that 'the Prime Minister is going to resign' (Mahathir, 'Speech at the Annual Dinner of Financial Institutions', Kuala Lumpur, 25 August 1986, *Foreign Affairs Malaysia*, 19, 3 (September 1986): 15–20).

45. A local Malay, and derogatory, term for 'Indian Muslim'. This crude and undeserving reference to Mahathir's lineage was often made in Team B's closed-door sessions, sometimes as a contrast with Razaleigh's princely status.

46. 'The Battle Is On', p. 6, quotes 'an aide' of Mahathir as saying: 'You know, he even told me once that he felt like chucking it all, that it was not worth it, but he knows that if he did that and these guys took over, Musa would make him out to be a Marcos.'

47. A Razaleigh loyalist confidently said that 'if Ku Li could get around 40 to 45 per cent of the votes, that would be enough'; in that sense, 'if he wins, he wins but if he loses, he still wins' (ibid., p. 5).

48. On 14 March, Mahathir declared in Kuala Kubu Baru that 'a leader would be weak and not respected if he only received 55 per cent support' (ibid.).

49. Ibid. In 'Di Mana Silapnya Mahathir', *Era*, 2 (1987): 14, Sanusi Junid

gave the 'one-vote win' argument a twist: 'Earlier we said that the Tengku Razaleigh–Dr Mahathir contest would be an act of democratic practice; that being so, we don't need a big win. A win by one vote is still called a win. That's the name of democracy.'

50. 'How to Remove PM Who Won't Resign: Dr M', *New Straits Times*, 1 April 1987.

51. Ibid.

52. Kershaw, 'Within the Family', p. 139.

53. Under the heading of 'Constitutional arguments' (ibid., pp. 139–42), Kershaw treated Mahathir's attempt at a 'notional shift of the *arena* of power from the party General Assembly to Parliament, but not a shift of power *from* party to Parliament as such' (p. 140) with considerable subtlety.

54. See 'The Price of Victory', *Asiaweek*, 3 May 1987, pp. 12–18; Suhaini Aznam, 'The Vital Forty-three', *Far Eastern Economic Review*, 7 May 1987, pp. 12–15; and Shamsul, 'The "Battle Royal"', for accounts of the election, related happenings, and various views on the outcome.

55. For a sample of the post-election speculation about the forty-one spoilt votes, see Suhaini, 'The Vital Forty-three', p. 13. It was widely believed that some Razaleigh supporters with a long memory of the 1981 and 1984 fights against Musa were persuaded after 'heavy [Team A] lobbying', just before vote casting, not to vote for their 'old foe' even if they would not vote for Ghafar.

56. 'Dr M Ajak Ahli-ahli Parti Bersatu Semula', *Utusan Malaysia*, 25 April 1987.

57. 'Siapa Yang Kalah Tanggung Risiko—Dr M', *Utusan Malaysia*, 27 April 1987.

58. Ibid.

59. 'Orang Lawan Ketua Parti Patut Letak Jawatan', *Utusan Malaysia*, 27 April 1987.

60. 'Ghafar Mahu Kabinet dan MT yang Bersih', *Utusan Malaysia*, 27 April 1987.

61. 'Siapa Pechah-belahkan UMNO Pengkhianat—Dr M'.

62. S. Jayasankaran, 'Premier in Power', *Malaysian Business*, 1 January 1988, p. 7.

63. Ibid.

64. Idzan Ismail, 'Siapa Kalah, Siapa Gugur dalam Kabinet Mahathir', *Utusan Malaysia*, 29 April 1987.

65. Ajib Ahmad, quoted in Suhaini Aznam, 'Dr Mahathir's Surgery', *Far Eastern Economic Review*, 14 May 1987, p. 14. Also see 'Mahathir Cracks the Whip', *Asiaweek*, 10 May 1987, pp. 27–8.

66. Suhaini, 'Dr Mahathir's Surgery', pp. 14–15.

67. Ibid.; also see Shamsul, 'The "Battle Royal"', p. 186.

68. For an instructive non-academic view of the authoritarian legacy and Mahathir's contribution to it, offered by someone who has been no stranger to political harassment in Malaysia, see Fan Yew Teng, *The UMNO Drama: Power Struggles in Malaysia*, Kuala Lumpur: Egret Publications, 1989, Chapter 11, pp. 144–89.

69. Harold Crouch, 'Authoritarian Trends, the UMNO Split and the Limits of State Power', in Joel S. Kahn and Francis Loh Kok Wah (eds.), *Fragmented Vision: Culture and Politics in Contemporary Malaysia*, Sydney: Asian Studies Association of Australia in association with Allen and Unwin, 1992, pp. 21–43.

70. Simon Tan, 'The Rise of State Authoritarianism in Malaysia', *Bulletin of Concerned Asian Scholars*, 22, 3 (July–September 1990): 32–42.

71. Johan Saravanamuttu, 'The State, Authoritarianism and Industrialisation: Reflections on the Malaysian Case', *Kajian Malaysia*, V, 2 (December 1987): 43–75.

72. Kershaw, 'Within the Family', p. 158.

73. K. Das, 'After Hussein, What?', *Far Eastern Economic Review*, 8 May 1981, p. 11.

74. Civil servants had to put an end to their 'disinclination to work' and stop treating a government post as a sinecure, 'getting a salary without working', as Mahathir put it in his 'Speech at the Pemuda and Wanita UMNO General Assembly', Kuala Lumpur, 25 June 1981, reprinted as 'Cabaran di hadapan Pemuda dan Wanita UMNO', in Harun Derauh and Shafie Nor (eds.), *Mahathir: Cita-cita dan Pencapaian*, Kuala Lumpur: Berita Publishing, 1982, pp. 51–9.

75. As implied in his '*bersih, cekap, amanah*' and '*kepimpinan melalui teladan*' campaigns as well as his promotion of a 'work ethic'.

76. The inspiration came from the 'East'. Some quick-fix methods included the punch card, the job manual, the desk file, the 'Quality Control Circles', and the 'Joint Consultative Councils'.

77. To build a more productive nation which could 'stand as tall, sit as low' as other nations.

78. Philip Bowring, 'Mahathir and the New Malay Dilemma', *Far Eastern Economic Review*, 9 April 1982, p. 20.

79. To sum it up, Anwar went for 'Islamization', Kassim of the old Malay left saw something in Mahathir's 'nationalism', Syed Hussein Alatas was impressed by the anti-corruption campaign, while Kerk Choo Ting, formerly legal adviser to the 'Merdeka University', thought Mahathir's 'liberalism' made it worthwhile to work for Chinese interests 'from within' the Barisan Nasional.

80. Which was why he repeatedly stressed the importance of resolving 'demands and counter-demands' within the Barisan Nasional framework amiably ('100 Hari di bawah Mahathir', *Berita Harian*, 27 October 1981).

81. Mahathir, 'Speech at the 29th MCA General Assembly', Kuala Lumpur, 19 September 1981, reprinted as 'Peranan MCA dalam Memperkukuhkan Perpaduan Negara', in Harun Derauh and Shafie Nor (eds.), *Mahathir: Cita-cita dan Pencapaian*, Kuala Lumpur: Berita Publishing, 1982, pp. 71–5. One example of an 'impossible demand' was the MCA's call to have a second, presumably Chinese, Deputy Prime Minister ('Timbalan Ke-2 Tidak Timbul', *Berita Harian*, 10 October 1981, and 'Dr M Tolak Timbalan Ke-2', *Berita Harian*, 22 October 1981).

82. 'We insist the Education Policy be accepted by all communities, and the National Language be used, yet when these two are well followed by other communities we don't give a proper appreciation of their efforts. On the contrary,

we do not differentiate those who follow the Education Policy and use the National Language from those who don't. As such they feel there is no benefit in following the Education Policy and using the National Language because we set them apart when we evaluate a venture or even a candidacy' (Harun Derauh and Shafie Nor, 'Temuramah Khas dengan Perdana Menteri Malaysia Datuk Seri Dr Mahathir bin Mohamad', in Harun Derauh and Shafie Nor (eds.), *Mahathir: Cita-cita dan Pencapaian*, Kuala Lumpur: Berita Publishing, 1982, pp. 8–9).

83. Mahathir, 'Speech at the 29th MCA General Assembly'.

84. See K. Das, 'The *Bahasa* Backlash', *Far Eastern Economic Review*, 22 January 1987, pp. 10–11, for a report on the '3Rs' controversy.

85. '100 Hari di bawah Mahathir'. Note the Malay editors' ethnic slant in their questions on those disputes which Mahathir tactfully set aside.

86. Tan Chee Khoon, *Without Fear or Favour*, Singapore: Eastern Universities Press, 1984, pp. 88–90.

87. Mahathir stated his views of the press most clearly and strongly in 'Fact and Fallacy', *New Straits Times*, 9 July 1981, and 'A Prescription for a Socially Responsible Press', *Far Eastern Economic Review*, 10 October 1985.

88. Mahathir, 'Speech at the 1981 Malaysian Press Awards Presentation Ceremony', Kuala Lumpur, 28 November 1982, reprinted as 'Wartawan dan Tanggungjawab', *Berita Harian*, 29 November 1982. Also see Musa Hitam, 'Speech at the Seminar on the UNESCO Report on Information and Communication', Kuala Lumpur, reprinted in *Watan*, 30 November 1982.

89. Mustafa K. Anuar, 'Liberal Attitude towards KDN?', in Aliran, *Issues of the Mahathir Years*, Penang: Aliran, 1988, pp. 41–2. Aliran was unable to obtain a KDN for publishing a Malay language monthly. PAS had no permit for a newsletter for years.

90. Mahathir, 'Speech at the 3rd ASEAN Law Association General Assembly', Kuala Lumpur, 26 October 1982, reprinted as 'The Varieties of Justice', in Murugesu Pathmanathan and David Lazarus (eds.), *Winds of Change*, Kuala Lumpur: Eastview Productions, 1984, pp. 159–65. *Berita Harian*, 27 October 1982, headlined its report on this event, 'Kebebasan Hakim: Ikrar PM'.

91. The release of political detainees was the single most 'liberal' act of the Mahathir administration. Twenty-one out of 540 political detainees were released in July 1981, followed by the release of another 146 detainees over the next year ('The First 250 Days of the Double-M Administration', *Far Eastern Economic Review*, 9 April 1982, pp. 16–17). In February 1982, Musa Hitam offered the remaining detainees—'those involved with communist or pro-communist activities, with subversive activities and with proscribed organizations which had the avowed aim of toppling the government by force'—for 'adoption' by other countries (ibid., p. 17).

92. For accounts of the MAS–AEU dispute, including references to Mahathir's 'tough image', see K. Das, 'Mana Ada Sistem?', *Far Eastern Economic Review*, 16 February 1979, pp. 31–2; 'Fight to Clip a Union's Wings', *Far Eastern Economic Review*, 23 February 1979, p. 15; and 'Flying Home to a Fanfare', *Far Eastern Economic Review*, 30 March 1979, p. 26.

93. Ministry of Information, *Akta Universiti dan Kolej Universiti (Pindaan)*

1975: Soal-jawab dengan Menteri Pelajaran, contained Mahathir's view of 'autonomy' for the universities, given in an interview with Radio and Television Malaysia held one day after the UUCA 1975 was passed. Mahathir clarified that the universities were 'given autonomy, meaning the autonomy to make their own plans, to administer themselves, to carry out their own activities even though they are supported by Government funds'. Moreover, 'if they wish to study "Communism", they are free to study, to have books and study and make analyses and so on'. But 'if they say that within the university campus, they want to be followers of Communism, and run the administration in a communist way, this cannot be permitted because it violates the laws of the country'.

94. Part of Mahathir's argument in support of the Emergency (Federal Constitution and Constitution of Sarawak) Bill passed during an Emergency Meeting of Parliament is worth noting: 'I think the Deputy Prime Minister in his address made it quite clear that *de jure* the Government of Kalong Ningkan is the Government of Sarawak. But is it in fact the Government of Sarawak? In a recent case the High Court in Rhodesia ruled that the Smith's [*sic*] regime was illegal but that does not remove the fact the Smith's [*sic*] regime is the *de facto* Government of Rhodesia.... And in the case of Sarawak quite obviously, if you follow democratic practices, the Government of Tawi Sli would be the real Government of Sarawak, while the Government of Kalong Ningkan, though it would be the legal Government, is not in fact the acceptable Government from the democratic sense' (Malaysia, *Dewan Ra'ayat, Parliamentary Debates*, III, 12, 19 September 1966, col. 2129).

95. Mahathir, 'Speech at the First ISIS National Conference on National Security', Kuala Lumpur, 15 July 1986, *Foreign Affairs Malaysia*, 19, 3 (September 1986): 1–5.

96. Mahathir's views on 'democracy' and its problems for developing countries are drawn from his essays, 'West and East' and 'Pressure Groups in a Democracy', in *The Challenge*, Petaling Jaya: Pelanduk Publications, 1986; translated from *Menghadapi Cabaran*, Kuala Lumpur: Pustaka Antara, 1976.

97. Mahathir, 'Holier than Thou—A Mild Critique', Speech at Trinity College, Oxford, 19 April 1985, *Foreign Affairs Malaysia*, 18, 2 (June 1985): 159–68.

98. Mahathir, 'Speech at the Annual Dinner of Financial Institutions of Malaysia', Kuala Lumpur, 18 August 1985, *Foreign Affairs Malaysia*, 18, 3 (September 1985): 246–50.

99. 'Now I find with this liberal attitude, the press does not value it because there are those who would say anything they like and would be safe from the consequences of what they say', which 'consequences' he suggested were leading the country towards 'chauvinism, racialism and extremism' ('Dasar Liberal Akhbar Akan Difikir Semula', *Utusan Malaysia*, 25 March 1985).

100. James Clad of the *Far Eastern Economic Review* pleaded guilty to two charges of 'receiving, possessing and divulging secret information and of knowing that this contravened the [Official Secrets] Act' ('Review Man Fined for Breaching Secrets Act', *Straits Times*, 15 October 1985). Shortly after Clad's arrest, Sabry Sharif of *New Straits Times* was arrested for another violation of the OSA.

101. Aliran, *Issues of the Mahathir Years*, Chapter 2, 'The Official Secrets Act (OSA) Controversy', pp. 102–43, provides an excellent 'anti-OSA' perspective on the issues involved. Also useful is 'Official Secrets Act: Tougher Penalties?', *Asiaweek*, 11 May 1986, p. 90, which gave the opposing views of Rais Yatim, Minister of Information, and Bob Teoh, Secretary-General of the National Union of Journalists. Bob Teoh thought that the 1986 amendments to the OSA had different targets: 'the opposition' and, since 'a lot of information has been given to the PAS', 'to frighten civil servants so that they don't give out information to the opposition'.

102. Gerakan (and the PBS after it joined the Barisan Nasional) expressed reservations about the OSA but all their MPs were directed to vote for the OSA in Parliament. Thus did Gerakan run with the hares and hunt with the hounds.

103. Deputy Home Affairs Minister Megat Junid said that the *Asian Wall Street Journal* spread 'feelings of uncertainty among the people' which 'in a way' was 'a sabotage of the economic development of this country' (Suhaini Aznam, 'Silenced Voices', *Far Eastern Economic Review*, 9 October 1986, p. 16). Mahathir was reported to have said in New York on 2 October 1986 that 'if foreigners have the right to come to our country and run us down, we also have the right to expel them' ('Kita Juga Berhak Singkir Orang Luar—Dr M', *Utusan Malaysia*, 3 October 1986).

104. Suhaini Aznam, 'Journalist Reprieved', *Far Eastern Economic Review*, 1 November 1986, p. 17. In retrospect, Mahathir's assault on the judiciary in 1989 had its origins in the Berthelsen case; see Lawyers Committee for Human Rights, *Malaysia: Assault on the Judiciary*, New York, 1990, pp. 17–19.

105. Suhaini Aznam, 'Publishing Ban Lifted', *Far Eastern Economic Review*, 27 November 1986, pp. 22–3.

106. 'PM Warns against Elitist Group', *New Straits Times*, 18 August 1987. For a report on the Conference, including Mahathir's response to it, see Suhaini Aznam, 'Princes, Power, People', *Far Eastern Economic Review*, 3 September 1987, pp. 8–9.

107. The memorandum issued after the conference was published together with the conference papers in Aliran, *Reflections on the Malaysian Constitution*, Penang, 1987. For replies to Mahathir's attack, see the statements by Chandra Muzaffar, 'Constitution Review: Response to Hostile Reactions', in ibid., pp. 310–14, and 'Editorial', *Insaf*, XX, 3 (September 1987): 4–8.

108. 'PM Warns against Elitist Group'.

109. Ibid.

110. See Lawyers Committee for Human Rights, *Malaysia: Assault on the Judiciary*, pp. 22–3, from which this summary is drawn.

111. On Hatibudi's formation, structure, trusteeship, and link with UEM, see Edward Terence Gomez, *Politics in Business: UMNO's Corporate Investments*, Kuala Lumpur: Forum, 1990, pp. 107–39. When, in relation to the UEM controversy, the Tunku said that UMNO should not go into business, Mahathir said he would 'subscribe' to the idea if 'there are people willing to give $360 million to pay for the UMNO headquarters building' ('Dr M: Do Not Use the Law to Stop Progress', *New Straits Times*, 29 August 1987).

112. On the High Court decision against Lim Kit Siang's suit, see 'UEM Deal:

Court Throws Out Lim's Writ', *New Straits Times*, 19 August 1987. On the Supreme Court decision to allow his appeal, see 'Don't Sign It, UEM Told', *New Straits Times*, 26 August 1987.

113. Attributed to Mahathir, 'PM to BN Parties: Rally Behind Government', *New Straits Times*, 18 August 1987. When he spoke at the opening of a community hall in Kampung Pok, 60 kilometres from Johore Bahru, on 27 August 1987, Mahathir told his audience that 'we must defend democracy as it is and beware of the campaign that has been begun to destroy it' ('PM: Defend Constitution', *New Straits Times*, 28 August 1987).

114. For an account of the continuing factionalism in UMNO, see 'The Battle Within', *Asiaweek*, 2 October 1987, pp. 12–13.

115. Suhaini Aznam, 'See You in Court ...', *Far Eastern Economic Review*, 9 July 1987, p. 14. Stephen Duthie, 'UMNO Dissidents' Lawsuit Is Flawed, Lawyers Argue', *Asian Wall Street Journal*, 27 January 1988, and 'Dissidents Should Have Appealed to UMNO Council, Lawyer Says', *Asian Wall Street Journal*, 28 January 1988, summarized the plaintiffs' case. The suit was heard six months later.

116. The UMNO Supreme Council set up a five-member committee to 'look into the matter'; a Council member recalled that 'Sanusi read out a few names and we all nodded' ('Searching for a Compromise', *Asiaweek*, 9 October 1987, p. 18). There was not even an agreement on who should chair the committee—Secretary-General Sanusi or Vice-President Abdullah Badawi. Sanusi was a defendant in the UMNO-11 suit while Mahathir said of Team B's Abdullah that 'he's an interested party' ('No Offers Made to UMNO 12 Who Filed Suit: PM', *New Straits Times*, 30 September 1987).

117. 'UMNO Given Two Weeks', *New Straits Times*, 1 October 1987.

118. 'These 12 Out to Destroy UMNO: Mahathir', *New Straits Times*, 14 August 1987.

119. On Bukit China, see James Clad, 'No Place to Rest', *Far Eastern Economic Review*, 23 August 1984, pp. 13–14.

120. 'It is obvious from Dr Mahathir's interpretation of the Pan-El and BMF scandals, that he is the one blinded by communal sentiments. He sees Pan-El as a Chinese issue and BMF as a *Bumiputra* issue. He is wrong on both scores' (Chandra Muzaffar, 'Integrity, Not Ethnicity', in Aliran, *Issues of the Mahathir Years*, pp. 246–7).

121. Abdullah Ahmad, *Issues in Malaysian Politics*, Singapore Institute of International Affairs Occasional Paper Series No. 7, Singapore: Heinemann Asia. Dollah Ahmad, as Abdullah is better known, was arrested for being a 'communist'—which he protested he never was—in the 1976 UMNO 'communist hunt' (Harold Crouch, 'The UMNO Crisis: 1975–1977', in Harold Crouch, Lee Kam Hing, and Michael Ong (eds.), *Malaysian Politics and the 1978 Election*, Kuala Lumpur: Oxford University Press, 1980, pp. 11–36).

122. The analysis in this section is concerned to plot briefly the rising inter-ethnic tensions of April–October 1987. It is beyond its scope to explain whether 'coincidence', administrative ineptitude, or 'manipulation' was behind the spate of inter-ethnic disagreements over seemingly insignificant issues. It is instructive to note the general applicability of Suhaini Aznam's perceptive comment, made in

relation to the University of Malaya issue (see below): 'The crux of the debate addressed anew the issue of conformity to a Malaysia based on things Malay—sometimes too vehemently insisted upon by Malaysia's 48 per cent Malays, and at times opposed to the point of exaggeration, by Malaysia's 32 per cent ethnic Chinese and 8.5 per cent Indians' (Suhaini Aznam, 'Of Races and Tongues', *Far Eastern Economic Review*, 30 July 1987, p. 9).

123. Suhaini Aznam, 'Staying on the Inside', *Far Eastern Economic Review*, 9 July 1987, pp. 13–14. By 'ethnic reasoning', the MCA argued that if Petronas could bail out Bank Bumiputra over the BMF collapse—a 'Malay' bail-out—then the Chinese DTC depositors deserved a bail-out, too. Of course, it was the MCA which most needed to be bailed out of the DTC scandal.

124. Suhaini, 'Of Races and Tongues', pp. 9–10, gave a balanced and critical report on the controversy.

125. 'Small Group behind Arson', *New Straits Times*, 5 September 1987. Megat Junid, Deputy Minister of Home Affairs, denied that there were 'racial, religious or political links' to the five cases of mosque-burning.

126. 'Don't Listen to Speculation: Dr M', *New Straits Times*, 8 September 1987.

127. As explained by Fahmi Ibrahim, head of Pemuda UMNO Education Bureau, and a Team B man ('MCA Youths [*sic*] Send Letter to PM', *New Straits Times*, 30 September 1987).

128. 'Stop Bickering, Say Leaders', *New Straits Times*, 22 August 1987.

129. 'PM to BN Parties: Rally behind Govt', *New Straits Times*, 18 August 1987.

130. Thirty-three such teachers were posted to twenty-six schools in Penang; corresponding figures were fourteen and seven for Malacca, seven and seven for Selangor and the Federal Territory.

131. 'Decision Stays, Says Anwar', *New Straits Times*, 5 October 1987.

132. 'Kim Sai Tells Woon: Settle Issue or Quit', *New Straits Times*, 12 October 1987. 'Woon' was Woon See Chin, MCA Vice-President and Deputy Minister of Education, who 'was caught between loyalty to his ministry and party' (Suhaini Aznam, 'The Language of Politics', *Far Eastern Economic Review*, 29 October 1987, p. 14).

133. The DAP's Lim Kit Siang spoke of the need for the '3 Lims' to work together: Lim Kit Siang, Lim Keng Yaik, and Ling Liong Sik (whose 'Ling' is written the same way as 'Lim' in Mandarin).

134. Mahathir, 'Speech at the 37th UMNO General Assembly', Kuala Lumpur, 18 September 1986, reprinted as 'Sistem Tumpuan Luar Bandar Akan Dikekalkan', *Utusan Malaysia*, 19 September 1986.

135. For a summary of UMNO's quarrel with the MCA, expressed in such terms, see Suhaini, 'The Language of Politics', pp. 14 and 21. Gerakan was generally less emotive and more circumspect during this controversy.

136. Ostensibly in retaliation for Lee Kim Sai's purported call for Anwar's resignation as Minister of Education. The animosity between Lee Kim Sai and Pemuda UMNO in fact went back a few disputes. The man behind the Pemuda UMNO rally was its Acting President, Najib Tun Razak. Initially regarded as neutral in the run-up to 24 April 1987, Najib swung his support to Team A at the last moment

when Anwar Ibrahim vacated his Pemuda UMNO presidency to enter the Vice-President's contest. In the normal course of events, Najib would have to seek election as Pemuda UMNO President in 1988.

137. Local papers censored their coverage of the Pemuda UMNO rally but it was widely known that 'many inflammatory speeches were made' by Pemuda UMNO and other UMNO politicians, 'with no attempt by the authorities to curb them' (M. G. G. Pillai, 'Political Brinkmanship Raises Malaysian Tension', *Bangkok Post*, 29 October 1987).

138. Suhaini, 'The Language of Politics', p 14.

139. This was Sanusi's estimate ('500,000 Expected for Rally', *New Straits Times*, 26 October 1987).

140. 'Rally to Mark Birth of UMNO', *New Straits Times*, 16 October 1987.

141. 'UMNO Rally on Sun Will be Peaceful, Says Junid', *New Straits Times*, 26 October 1987.

142. 'Rally: No Need to Be Alarmed, Says Ghafar', *Star*, 28 October 1987. Up to 27 October 1987, the police had still not decided whether to give a permit for the rally. Ghafar realized that but insisted that 'the rally will go on'.

143. 'UMNO Rally on Sun Will Be Peaceful, Says Junid'. But Megat Junid warned that 'banners' for the rally would be screened ('Rally: No Need to Be Alarmed, Says Ghafar')—a warning believed to be partly aimed at Team B supporters rumoured to be heading for the rally with 'anti-Mahathir' banners.

144. Mahathir Mohamad, *The Malay Dilemma*, Singapore: Donald Moore for Asia Pacific Press, 1970, p. 14.

145. For a sample of analyses of 27 October 1987, see Chandra Muzaffar, 'Whitewash! White Paper on ISA Arrests', in Chandra Muzaffar, *Challenges and Choices in Malaysian Politics and Society*, Penang: Aliran, pp. 163–79; Jomo K. S., 'Race, Religion and Repression: "National Security" and the Insecurity of the Regime', in Committee Against Repression in the Pacific and Asia, *Tangled Web: Dissent, Deterrence and the 27 October 1987 Crackdown in Malaysia*, Haymarket, NSW: CARPA, 1988, pp. 1–27; Fan Yew Teng, 'The Mahathir Concoction: An Alternative White Paper on the ISA Detentions', in Fan Yew Teng, *If We Love This Country . . .*, Kuala Lumpur: Egret Publications, 1988, pp. 50–68; and Simon Tan, 'The Rise of State Authoritarianism in Malaysia'.

146. Lee Kim Sai, the central MCA figure in the 'anti-promotions' campaign, was neither expelled from the Cabinet nor detained. He went on indefinite leave from 28 October 1987, on Ling Liong Sik's 'advice' ('Kim Sai Takes Leave', *Star*, 28 October 1987); he left for Melbourne, Australia.

147. 'Detained', *Star*, 28 October 1987.

148. See Suhaini Aznam, 'Taming the Guerillas', *Far Eastern Economic Review*, 12 November 1987, pp. 21–2.

149. For an almost complete list of the detainees, see Committee Against Repression in the Pacific and Asia, *Tangled Web: Dissent, Deterrence and the 27 October 1987 Crackdown in Malaysia*, pp. 72–7.

150. Mahathir, 'Speech in Parliament', 28 October 1987, English translation reprinted as 'Mahathir Explains Why the Crackdown Was Necessary', *Straits Times*, 30 October 1987.

151. Ibid.

152. Ibid.

153. Ibid. Mahathir only announced his decision to ban the 1 November UMNO rally at the very end of his speech.

154. Rendering 'the theory that the arrests were a trade-off for the cancellation of the mammoth UMNO "unity rally" ... increasingly credible' (Suhaini Aznam, 'The Great Crackdown', *Far Eastern Economic Review*, 12 November 1987, p. 13). See also the *Nanyang Siang Pau* editorial of 29 October 1987, 'Maintenance of Harmony and Stability Is the Most Urgent Task', translated into English and reprinted in *Straits Times*, 30 October 1987, which said that 'the extension of the ban [on rallies] to UMNO shows that the government is fair and puts security considerations above others'.

155. 'Interview with *Asahi Shimbun*', reprinted as 'Situation Is Very Stable, Says Mahathir', *Straits Times*, 5 November 1987.

156. Fahmi Ibrahim, Ibrahim Ali, and Tajuddin Ahmad.

157. Untitled 'boxed' item, *New Straits Times*, 30 October 1987.

158. Jayasankaran, 'Premier in Power', p. 7.

159. 'Interview with *Asahi Shimbun*'.

160. Cited in Suhaini Aznam, 'A Judicial Shake-up', *Far Eastern Economic Review*, 14 January 1988, p. 27.

161. Ibid.

162. Cited in Suhaini Aznam, 'Removing the Hardcore', *Far Eastern Economic Review*, 7 January 1988, p. 14. The hearing on the applications for *habeas corpus* was concluded on 23 December 1987.

163. Salleh Abas, *The Role of the Independent Judiciary*, Kuala Lumpur: Promarketing Publications, 1989, p. 49.

164. Nick Seaward, 'Clearing the Highway', *Far Eastern Economic Review*, 28 January 1988, p. 35. Salleh Abas argued that only the Attorney-General had the authority to initiate any such suit.

165. Hugo Young, 'Commentary', *Guardian*, 8 November 1988. The relevant passage read: 'It should be said that the Lord President [Tun Salleh Abas] had not hitherto shown himself to be a conspicuously liberal judge. No Denning he, nor even a Donaldson! By his own account, he had sided with the State in numerous cases. When Dr Mahathir's original attack in *Time* was cited for contempt, he rejected the complaint.'

166. Salleh Abas, *The Role of the Independent Judiciary*, p. 5.

167. *Time*, 24 November 1986, p. 18.

168. See the preceding section '27 October 1987: The End of "Liberalism"?'.

169. Malaysia, *Dewan Ra'ayat, Parliamentary Debates*, II, 48, 22 March 1966, col. 6881.

170. Jayasankaran, 'Premier in Power', p. 8.

171. Ibid.

172. Cited in Suhaini Aznam, 'The Tilt of Power', *Far Eastern Economic Review*, 31 March 1988, p. 15.

173. Remarks made during a speech in Parliament on 18 March 1988, cited in ibid.

174. See the preceding section '27 October 1987: The End of "Liberalism"?' where this remark was earlier quoted.

175. Jayasankaran, 'Premier in Power', p. 6.

176. Cited in Rodney Tasker and Suhaini Aznam, 'Challenge of Elders', *Far Eastern Economic Review*, 18 February 1988, p. 12.

177. Ibid.

178. For a contemporary account of this manoeuvre to register a new UMNO, see Rodney Tasker, 'A Grand Master Move', *Far Eastern Economic Review*, 3 March 1988, pp. 14–15.

179. Ibid.; also see Gordon P. Means, *Malaysian Politics: The Second Generation*, Singapore: Oxford University Press, 1991, pp. 223–8.

180. Rodney Tasker, 'The Balance of Power', *Far Eastern Economic Review*, 25 February 1988, pp. 12–13. As Mahathir put it, UMNO Baru excluded those who 'worked against UMNO's interests' (Tasker, 'A Grand Master Move', p. 14).

181. Abu Talib, statement of 11 January 1988, cited in Suhaini Aznam, 'Judging the Judges', *Far Eastern Economic Review*, 28 January 1988, pp. 34–5.

182. Ibid.

183. Cited in ibid., p. 35.

184. Salleh Abas, *The Role of the Independent Judiciary*, p. 16.

185. Ibid., pp. 13–14.

186. The following summary of the Salleh Abas impeachment was mostly drawn from Salleh Abas, *The Role of the Independent Judiciary*; Lawyers Committee for Human Rights, *Malaysia: Assault on the Judiciary*; Raja Aziz Addruse, *Conduct Unbecoming*, Kuala Lumpur: Walrus, 1990; Suhaini Aznam, 'Sending Off the Umpire', *Far Eastern Economic Review*, 9 June 1988, pp. 12–13; Suhaini Aznam, 'The King's Bench', *Far Eastern Economic Review*, 23 June 1988, p. 22; and Suhaini Aznam, 'The Judge in the Dock', *Far Eastern Economic Review*, 30 June 1988, pp. 12–13. Powerful incumbents will always attract apologists; in this context, see Peter Alderidge Williams, *Judicial Misconduct*, Petaling Jaya: Pelanduk Publications, 1990.

187. Cited in Suhaini Aznam, 'Sending Off the Umpire', p. 13.

188. Mahathir, 'Speech at the UMNO General Assembly, 1988', Kuala Lumpur, 28 October 1988, English translation reprinted as 'UMNO Is UMNO', *New Straits Times*, 29 October 1988.

189. Ibid.

190. Ibid.

191. Among those named, Tan Chee Khoon and Chen Man Hin retained their medical practices alongside their lifelong involvement in opposition politics.

192. Tan Chee Khoon's experience as a young doctor just started on his own practice gives a sense of how the confluence of medicine and personal dedication could help to transform a 'community of patients' into a political constituency: Tan Chee Khoon 'chose Batu Road for his dispensary as the area had a heavy concentration of his type of Hokkiens, that of the Hin Hua clan who were mostly engaged as trishaw riders, spare-part dealers, bicycle repairers, and small hotel-keepers. These were "my people" as Tan Chee Khoon puts it and they provided a ready made practice for him.... Very soon Tan Chee Khoon built up a large

thriving practice. It brought people from all along Batu Road, the Batu village and from the new villages of Kepong and Jinjang. There was always a large crowd of patients waiting to see their doctor. These were the Tan Chee Khoon people who later were to become his chief political supporters' (R. K. Vasil, *Tan Chee Khoon: An Elder Statesman*, Petaling Jaya: Pelanduk Publications, 1987, pp. 19–20).

193. Robin Adshead, *Mahathir of Malaysia*, London: Hibiscus Publishing Company, p. 65.

194. Ibid., p. 48.

195. Ibid., pp. 45–6.

196. Mahathir, 'Letter to the Kedah State Surgeon', dated 31 August 1958, on exhibit in Mahathir's old house, No. 18, Lorong Kilang Ais, Kampung Seberang Perak, Alor Star, Kedah.

197. Malaysia, *Dewan Ra'ayat, Parliamentary Debates*, I, 5, 6 July 1964, cols. 723–6.

198. Ibid., II, 49, 25 March 1966, col. 7216, and III, 33, 16 February 1967, col. 4716.

199. Ibid., II, 33, 6 December 1965, col. 4873.

200. Ibid., II, 35, 14 December 1964, cols. 452–6. Also see ibid., IV, 33, 12 February 1968, col. 5077.

201. Ibid., I, 38, 17 December 1964, col. 4915, and II, 33, 6 December 1965, col. 4867. See the previous discussion of this point about the civil service in the section 'Privatization: The 40 Per Cent Solution' in Chapter 4.

202. Ibid., II, 33, 6 December 1965, col. 4868. This brought a rare 'Hear! Hear!' from Dr Tan Chee Khoon.

203. Ibid., col. 4875.

204. Ibid., col. 4874.

205. Ibid., II, 1, 26 May 1965, cols. 73–4, and III, 33, 16 February 1967, col. 4714–15.

206. Ibid., II, 1, 26 May 1965, cols. 74–5.

207. Ibid., col. 74.

208. Ibid.

209. Ibid., IV, 23, 24 January 1968, col. 3990, and ibid., IV, 33, 12 February 1968, cols. 5076–8.

210. Adshead, *Mahathir of Malaysia*, p. 65.

211. Ibid., p. 65. To Supriya Singh ('The Man behind the Politician', *New Straits Times*, 14 April 1982), Mahathir said: 'A man has appendicitis. After an operation, he walks out after a week. To be able to make a sick man well is very satisfying.'

212. Adshead, *Mahathir of Malaysia*, p. 65.

213. 'There is challenge. There is a lot of job satisfaction' (Supriya Singh, 'The Man behind the Politician').

214. 'As this is the first conference of lawyers that I have ever addressed it is proper for me to say something about my attitude towards the law'; but before that he regaled his audience with a couple of anecdotes about doctors being short-changed by lawyers to illustrate 'how quick they [lawyers] are on the uptake' (Mahathir, 'Speech at the 3rd ASEAN Law Association General Assembly').

215. Mahathir, 'Speech at the Economic Society Dinner, Singapore', 31 October 1980, *Foreign Affairs Malaysia*, 13 (1980): pp. 395–409.

216. Mahathir, 'Speech at the Annual Dinner of Financial Institutions', 25 August 1986.

217. Mahathir, 'Speech at the Opening of the Seminar on Malaysian–British Invisible Trade Links', Kuala Lumpur, 17 July 1984, *Foreign Affairs Malaysia*, 17, 3 (September 1984): 219–24.

218. Mahathir, 'Speech at the Commonwealth Heads of Government Meeting', 16 October 1985, Nassau, Bahamas, *Foreign Affairs Malaysia*, 18, 4 (December 1985): 387–90.

219. Interview with *Sinar Harapan*, reprinted as 'Menjadi Seorang Sasterawan Lebih Sulit dari Doktor', *Mingguan Malaysia*, 2 February 1986.

220. Supriya Singh, 'The Man behind the Politician'.

221. Adshead, *Mahathir of Malaysia*, p. 65. He meant, of course, his involvement in the Kedah Malay Union, SABERKAS, and the anti-Malayan Union campaign before he studied medicine, but he was a doctor for most of the time before he became the politician that everyone knows.

222. Ibid., p. 53.

223. Ibid. (emphasis added).

224. Mahathir, 'Speech at the Conference on Business in Southeast Asia', Kuala Lumpur, 4 February 1977, *Foreign Affairs Malaysia*, 10, 1 (1977): 70–2.

225. 'I would provide a completely contrasting style to the current prime minister, who says, like the good doctor that he is, "this is good for you, take it".... The problem with Dr Mahathir is he is crass, rough and hard. This man pushes things down your throat' (Musa Hitam, 'Malaysia: The Spirit of '46 Rises Again', *Correspondent*, November 1987, p. 18).

226. Cited in Suhaini, 'Dr Mahathir's Surgery', p. 15.

227. 'Menjadi Seorang Sasterawan Lebih Sulit dari Doktor'.

228. Thus concluded Mahathir's speech in Parliament on 14 July 1964 which urged the 'merger' of Nanyang University with the University of Singapore to keep the former's 'communist indoctrinated students' under 'a more effective supervision by a staff more dedicated to academic progress and by the Government itself' (Malaysia, *Dewan Ra'ayat, Parliamentary Debates*, I, 11, 14 July 1964, col. 1442). The merger did take place with the effect that Mahathir envisaged but it is not known whether Mahathir's 'prescription' was incidental or instrumental to the Singapore government's action.

229. 'Often, of course, the government acts too late and a really serious security situation will develop' (Mahathir, 'Speech at the First ISIS National Conference on National Security'.

230. Adshead, *Mahathir of Malaysia*, p. 53.

231. As Mahathir recalled with some indignation (Jayasankaran, 'Premier in Power', p. 6). The MCA, Gerakan, the MIC, and the DAP were not immune to their leaders' habit of peremptorily dismissing recalcitrants and would-be challengers.

232. Mahathir, *The Malay Dilemma*, p. 15.

233. Ibid., p. 172.

234. Ibid., pp. 103 and 117–18.

235. Ibid., p. 67.

236. Ibid., p. 171.

237. Ibid., pp. 171–2.

238. Ibid., p. 173.

239. Ibid., p. 172.

240. Emphasis added. This line was preceded by 'I believe I have moderate views—I'm not an *ultra* or extremist. These are just labels politicians like to give their rivals in order to colour everything they say' (Munir Majid, 'Datuk Seri Dr Mahathir Mohamad: Power and Responsibility', *Malaysian Business*, October 1980, p. 5).

241. Karl von Vorys, *Democracy without Consensus: Communalism and Political Stability in Malaysia*, Princeton: Princeton University Press, 1975, remains the most rigorous and most approving analysis of the élitism which undergirded Malaysia's consociational 'democracy without consensus'. In practice, the Tunku's regime was anti-labour, anti-leftwing popular movements, and, as Aziz Ishak's detention showed, wary of Malay populism itself.

242. More accurately, police permits are required but seldom granted, at least to opposition parties or dissident groups.

243. He could not be held accountable in many senses. After all, he was Prime Minister, and, after Musa's resignation, also Minister of Home Affairs. Once he prided himself on being able to 'escape through as many loopholes as I can create': 'Between the vagueness of a politician and the peculiarities of the English language, I think I can escape any attempt to hold me to my words' (Mahathir, 'Speech at the Annual Luncheon of the Malaysian International Chamber of Commerce and Industry', Kuala Lumpur, 1 June 1981, reprinted as 'The Evils of Protectionism', in Murugesu Pathmanathan and David Lazarus (eds.), *Winds of Change*, Kuala Lumpur: Eastview Productions, 1984, pp. 77–82). He spoke in Malay at his rallies but the point remains. Finally, as we have noted before, he advised politicians that 'after you get your job, I think it is best to forget some of your promises'.

244. As Team B found out in 1987, their speeches were not reported or telecast—except by way of being attacked!

245. See the section 'Who's Sovereign?: The Constitutional Crisis, 1983' in Chapter 6.

246. 'Personal to holder' is a Malaysian civil service provision for permitting the *ad hoc* creation of a senior or special post for an individual officer. Recall our discussion of Mahathir's argument that he had a 'national mandate' as the man who led the Barisan Nasional to victory in August 1986 (see the section '24 April 1987: Personal Mandate, Party Democracy, or UMNO Split?' above).

247. At one point during Anwar Ibrahim's recent (and successful) campaign to challenge Ghafar Baba for the UMNO deputy presidency at the UMNO General Assembly in November 1993, Mahathir said: 'I pray to God to show me when I should say goodbye.... I fear that when the people don't want me, I'll still be sitting here. That is why I want to know when I am not wanted. *But it is very difficult to know this*' ('Dr M: It Won't Be a Disgrace If One Withdraws from Contest', *New Straits Times*, 11 September 1993; emphasis added).

248. F. Scott Fitzgerald, 'The Crack-up', in F. Scott Fitzgerald, *The Crack-up with Other Pieces and Stories*, Harmondsworth: Penguin, 1979, p. 39.

249. In 1988–9, a 'song of loyalty'—'Lagu Setia'—extolling loyalty and allegiance to king and country, leaders and people, religion and race was actively promoted over Malaysian radio and television and regularly sung at political, government, and civic functions. See Clive Kessler, 'Archaism and Modernity: Contemporary Malay Political Culture', in Joel S. Kahn and Francis Loh Kok Wah (eds.), *Fragmented Vision: Culture and Politics in Contemporary Malaysia*, Sydney: Asian Studies Association of Australia in association with Allen and Unwin, 1992, pp. 133–55, for a discussion of the 'Lagu Setia' as an instance of 'invention of tradition', here attempted by Mahathir in 1988 in order to consolidate his support base in UMNO and the Malay community.

250. The SEMARAK campaign 'took Mahathir to towns all over the country to address crowds of thousands bussed in from neighbouring villages' (Suhaini Aznam, 'Mellowed Maverick', *Far Eastern Economic Review*, 18 July 1991, p. 23). The SEMARAK campaign, repeatedly shown on Malaysian television, was carefully choreographed and pregnant with political symbolism: 'The media faithfully recorded him (Mahathir) planting a tree, helping to build a house for a destitute grandmother, helping to haul in a fishing boat in Trengganu state' (ibid.).

251. For a brief discussion of the SEMARAK campaign in conjunction with the promotion of 'Lagu Setia', see Kessler, 'Archaism and Modernity: Contemporary Malay Political Culture', p. 154.

8

Mahathirism after Mahathir

> I couldn't care less if people remember me or not. What does it matter if I (have made) history or not when I am dead. As minister of education I forbade schools being named after living people, including myself. It's totally irrelevant to perpetuate oneself in history. You can't determine what kind of judgement history is going to pass on you. Even alive I find that people are passing all kinds of judgements over which I have no control.
>
> Mahathir, quoted in 'A Vision for Malaysia: Interview with Prime Minister Mahathir', *Asiaweek*, 23 September 1983, p. 37.

1990: The Critical Year

ONE has to acknowledge the political skills, personal tenacity, and measure of good luck which enabled Mahathir to overcome the continuing challenges to his position following his slim victory in UMNO's 24 April 1987 election. From 1988 to 1989, there were arguably three critical moments when Mahathir's political career hung in the balance. The first came when UMNO's deregistration in February 1988 left Mahathir without a political party to legitimate his leadership of the nation. UMNO's deregistration had technically transformed the party's elected representatives into 'independents' who, had they wanted to, could have disengaged themselves from Mahathir's control. But the Barisan Nasional's component parties and a majority of the legally defunct UMNO's parliamentarians stood by Mahathir so that his premiership was not questioned. Second, UMNO's deregistration sparked off a race between Mahathir and his opponents to form UMNO's successor party which would recover both its membership and assets. While UMNO's membership and the Malay community, particularly, were shocked by the deregistration of the party, the Tunku, generally regarded as working in concert with Razaleigh, moved ahead to register an 'UMNO Malaysia'. But, as we have seen, Mahathir won the UMNO 're-registration' race and immediately used UMNO Baru to legitimate his position and reconstitute an UMNO without Razaleigh, the UMNO-11, and other Team B dissidents. And as we have also seen, the UMNO dissidents' appeal against the High Court's decision to deregister the 'old' UMNO was embroiled in the impeachment and dismissal of the Lord President. Subsequently, the Supreme Court rejected the appeal. Razaleigh and those Team B parliamentarians who were out of UMNO Baru also tried in vain to resurrect the old UMNO by legislation in the Mahathir-controlled Parliament. As a last resort, Razaleigh and the UMNO dissidents founded a new party, Semangat 46 (Spirit of '46), which claimed the old UMNO's 1946 Malayan Union legacy. By now, UMNO was irrevocably split. Semangat 46 had become, if reluctantly, an opposition party. Third, Mahathir almost lost everything when he suffered a heart attack in January 1989. On 24 January, he underwent an emergency coronary bypass operation in Kuala Lumpur. He recovered from the operation, went abroad to rest, and returned to resume his control of the political situation.

The ferment of Malaysian politics, seen in its leitmotif of challenge to Mahathir's leadership, continued unabated until 1990. In 1988–9, a series of state and parliamentary by-elections tested, first, the relative strengths of Semangat 46 and UMNO Baru, and, second, the potential of an emerging Semangat 46-led 'multi-ethnic coalition'. An examination of the details of these by-elections is available elsewhere.[1] Here it is sufficient briefly to recount their major features and outcomes. The first three by-elections took place in Johore in 1988—Tanjung Puteri, Johore Bahru, and Parit Raja. In Tanjung Puteri, UMNO Baru defeated the PSRM by a mere 31 votes out of a total of 20,331. In Johore Bahru, Shahrir Samad, standing as an 'independent' candidate, rode a strong wave of Malay and non-Malay anti-Mahathir sentiment to overwhelm UMNO Baru's Ma'sud Abdul Rahman. But UMNO Baru won in Parit Raja by a margin of 413 votes out of 14,111. The year 1989 saw a somewhat different set of by-elections. The first by-election took place in Ampang Jaya where Harun Idris stood for Semangat 46 and lost to an MCA candidate.[2] The Bentong (Pahang), Tambatan (Johore), and Telok Pasu (Trengganu) by-elections were held in mid-1989. The DAP lost to the MCA in Bentong, Semangat 46 lost to

UMNO Baru in Tambatan, but PAS defeated UMNO Baru in Telok Pasu.

One important point about the by-elections in Tanjung Puteri and Johore Bahru (when Mahathir's leadership was the dominant campaigning issue), and in Parit Raja, Tambatan, and Teluk Pasu (all heavily Malay-populated constituencies) was that the Malay divide remained as strong as during the April 1987 period. The other significant point about the by-elections of 1989 was the uneasy manner in which a 'multi-ethnic coalition' of sorts was emerging to challenge the Barisan Nasional. In May 1989, Semangat 46 and PAS formed the Angkatan Perpaduan Ummah (APU, or Muslim Unity Force). The DAP would not enter into a direct electoral pact with APU because PAS would not discard its 'Islamic state' programme. But, as expectations of a general election in 1990 heightened, Semangat 46 and the DAP (with other small non-Malay and non-Islamic parties) formed a separate alliance, Gagasan Rakyat Malaysia (Gagasan). It was a tortuous way for Semangat 46 to span the deep ideological chasm between the DAP (and, later, the PBS) and PAS. But APU and Gagasan enthusiastically saw in their electoral pact the introduction of a 'two-coalition system' in Malaysia.

Could the mid-1980s' broad-based dissent against Mahathir's leadership have evolved into a serious alternative to the Barisan Nasional itself?[3] Purely as a conjecture, it might have done so if the recession which was widely blamed on Mahathir and Daim's economic 'mismanagement' had continued into the late 1980s. In reality, the reverse was true. The three years after Mahathir's twin crises of 24 April 1987 and 27 October 1987 witnessed a very strong recovery from the recession of 1985–6.[4] From a negative growth of 1 per cent in 1985, the economy grew by just over 2 per cent in 1986 and by about 5.2 per cent in 1987. During the three-year, pre-election, period of 1988–90, the economy grew by an average annual rate of 9.1 per cent. Unemployment fell from its peak level of 8.3 per cent in 1986 to 6 per cent in 1990. Improved prices for some of Malaysia's major commodities combined with substantially higher production and export volumes to raise commodity earnings from RM23.93 billion in 1985 to RM28.97 billion in 1990.[5] Between the recession year of 1985 and the election year of 1990, the value of manufacturing exports rose nearly fourfold, from RM12.47 billion to RM48.05 billion, thus recording a remarkable average annual growth rate of 31 per cent. Manufacturing sector employment also grew at a high average annual rate of 12 per cent between 1986 and 1990.[6] The trend of declining private investment during the recession was reversed. In the manufacturing sector, the proposed capital investment of all approved industrial projects for 1990 was RM28.17 billion compared to RM5.69 billion for 1985, while the total for 1986–90 amounted to RM58.58 billion.[7] Foreign investment in approved industrial projects amounted to RM17.63 billion in 1990 compared to RM959 million in 1985 while the corresponding figure for 1986–90 was RM34.91 billion.[8] In all these, Mahathir could claim that the economic revival vindicated his economic policies and his and Daim's economic management. Their austerity measures, curbs on state expenditure, and reliance on the private sector had brought the budget deficit under control while the increased values of exports had helped to overturn the balance of payments deficit. Mahathir's decision to hold the NEP in abeyance, aided by the foreign exchange factor of a depreciating Malaysian ringgit, among others, encouraged a massive inflow of foreign investment from Taiwan, Japan, and Singapore in particular.[9]

Against this background of economic growth, Mahathir called for general elections to be held in October 1990. He, of course, judged the moment to offer the best chances for the Barisan Nasional's return to power. But it would have been politically awkward to delay calling the election until the government had reached its full term in 1991. That would have been a significant break with precedent and it would have postponed his chance of promulgating a post-1990 economic policy to succeed the NEP. Around 1987–8, Mahathir had consolidated his political power by authoritarian means that left him publicly judged to be dictatorial. But following his consolidation of UMNO Baru, he began to try to soften his dictatorial image, seeking to appear more 'consensual' than authoritarian. Starting with the Parit Raja by-election, Mahathir had offered to bring Razaleigh and the former Team B dissidents back into the UMNO (Baru) fold. In time, his supporters mounted 'Malay unity' forums which accomplished little in the way of ending Malay disunity but progressively split Musa Hitam's Johore base and isolated Razaleigh and Semangat 46. Mahathir also agreed to a call by the Barisan Nasional's non-Malay components to set up some form of multi-ethnic 'consultative' forum at the national level which would be akin to the post-1969 National Consultative Council which prepared the 'national ideology', the Rukunegara, and laid the 'consensual' framework for the NEP. Mahathir set up the National Economic Consultative Committee (NECC) in early 1989, ostensibly to prepare a multi-ethnic consensus that would lay down the parameters of a post-1990, post-NEP economic policy.[10] In reality, Mahathir remained aloof from the NECC which was largely a public relations exercise to mollify the Barisan Nasional's non-Malay component parties (whose loyalty had become more important given the UMNO–Semangat 46 split), and placate some of the NGO-based dissent (which was veering towards the APU–Gagasan's vision of a 'two-coalition system').[11]

Again, only the outcome rather than the elaborate details of the 1990 election need be repeated here.[12] Mahathir was confident of the Barisan Nasional's return to power. APU and Gagasan Rakyat, too, were confident that minimally they could deny the Barisan Nasional a two-thirds majority in Parliament. Midway through the election campaigning period, Sabah's PBS broke away from the Barisan Nasional and joined Gagasan Rakyat.[13] That probably inspired the opposition's most optimistic scenario of displacing the Barisan Nasional from power. But in October 1990, the Semangat 46-led coalition could not even secure one-third of the seats in Parliament, let alone dislodge the Barisan Nasional from power. This time, unlike PAS's dismal performance in 1986, it was Semangat 46 which could not deliver on the oppositionist promise. Semangat 46's parliamentary representation fell from thirteen to eight. PAS won seven parliamentary seats, the PBS got fourteen, and the DAP retained twenty.[14] The PBS remained in power in Sabah. UMNO met with calamity in Kelantan: it lost every single state and parliamentary contest. After a break of thirteen years, PAS again formed the state government in Kelantan, this time with Semangat 46 as its junior partner. In a reflection of UMNO's losses in Kelantan, the MCA suffered a total defeat in the Chinese-majority urban constituencies of Kuala Lumpur and Penang. The DAP was only three seats short of capturing the state government in Penang. UMNO's débâcle in Kelantan and the PBS's defection from the Barisan Nasional were new landmarks in the post-electoral topography. But in essence it was not greatly different from what it was in 1986: the Barisan

Nasional was back in power, UMNO was dominant, and Mahathir was in charge.

The critical year of 1990 having ended in twin economic and political triumphs for Mahathir, Mahathirism could now and truly look 'beyond 1990'.

Vision 2020: Capitalism and Nationalism

Beyond 1990 lay 2020, or so Mahathir informed the newly established Malaysian Business Council (MBC) at its inaugural meeting on 28 February 1991. Mahathir used the occasion to present a working paper, 'Malaysia: The Way Forward', to this 62-member body which brought together the élite of the state and the captains of Malaysian commerce and industry.[15] Before this MBC (rather than the NECC), together with these people who mattered (rather than those who bickered), Mahathir wanted to share the 'inaugural' exposition of his agenda for Malaysia under his third term of office and 'beyond'. Judging from his tone, he meant to offer his agenda as their common 'legacy' to the nation: 'Most of us in this present council will not be there on the morning of 1 January 2020' to see the agenda fulfilled, he said, or at any rate, 'not many, I think'.[16]

The agenda that was mapped out in 'Malaysia: The Way Forward' has since been officially promoted and popularized as *Wawasan 2020* or Vision 2020. In its skeletal form, it envisaged Malaysia transforming itself into a 'fully developed country' by the year 2020. Such a propitious advancement out of the world of developing countries could be targeted in 'growth' terms: the country's Gross Domestic Product (GDP) in 2020 would become eight times larger than its GDP in 1990.[17] It would mean doubling the GDP every ten years, or having it grow at an average annual rate of 7 per cent, from 1990 to 2020. But that was a 'realistic (as opposed to aspirational) target' because 'we grew at an annual average of 6.9 per cent' over the past twenty years, and 'what is needed is an additional 0.1 per cent growth'.[18] The accompanying level of prosperity could be generally determined: Malaysians in 2020 would be 'four times richer (in real terms) than they were in 1990'.[19] One could also sketch out the qualitative profile of a developed Malaysia's 'diversified and balanced economy' in 2020: it would have 'a mature and widely based industrial sector, a modern and mature agricultural sector and an efficient and productive and an equally mature [services] sector'.[20]

Several socio-political parameters framed Vision 2020. These were somewhat tendentiously set out in Mahathir's working paper as 'nine strategic challenges' which lay over the path to becoming a 'fully developed country'.[21] Some of these 'nine challenges' recapitulated NEP-type expressions of national unity and an 'economically just society' with a 'fair and equitable distribution of the wealth of the nation'. But there was Mahathir's characteristic reminder that since 'no nation can achieve full progress with only half of its human resources harnessed ... the *Bumiputeras* must play their part in the achievement of the national goal'. Indeed, the whole people—in the 'correct mix with regard to professionals, sub-professionals, craftsmen, and artisans'[22]—were to be mobilized 'to make the 1990s the most economically productive decade in our history'. Other parts of Vision 2020 carried shades of the major policies of the Mahathir era. There was the 'Look East' stress on attaining 'excellence', 'a high and escalating productivity', 'the knowledge of what to do and how to do it', an 'economy that is technologically proficient', and 'an exemplary work ethic'. There was Islamization's call to establish 'a fully moral and ethical society whose citizens are strong in religious and spiritual values and imbued with the highest of ethical standards'. Yet other portions of Vision 2020 reasserted the imperatives of 'an accelerated industrialization drive', 'economic liberalization', and 'deregulation'—these being praised as the active ingredients of a 'winning formula' that had rescued the nation from recession and would safeguard its 'economic defence capabilities'. Vision 2020 retained an important place for 'Privatization' and the reliance on the private sector as the 'primary engine of economic growth'. And it planned to make a 'flourishing reality' of 'Malaysia Incorporated'—that 'productive partnership [which] will take us a long way towards our aspirations'.

Vision 2020 has been officially promoted as the ideological pillar of the National Development Policy which was promulgated in mid-1991 to succeed the NEP.[23] In that light, Vision 2020 seemed new and fresh, not least because its catchy slogan with its numerical twists[24] sought to focus national attention on its agenda for the twenty-first century. Yet, on the strength of the kinds of pronouncements noted above, the substance of Vision 2020 was largely familiar rather than novel. The substance of Vision 2020 had been mostly drawn from the core components of Mahathirist ideology as we have explored it—an evolving nationalism, a freer capitalism, a universalizing Islam, and a scripted populism. Even its seemingly fresh hope of 'fostering and developing a mature democratic society' hardly promised to end Mahathir's authoritarianism. One had only to remember his post-27 October 1987 regrets about the people's immature abuse of his early liberalism.[25]

Perhaps that is apt. Perhaps one should really see Vision 2020 not so much as the launching of a new Mahathirist project which its association with the post-1990 National Development Policy implied but as the culmination of Mahathirism, as an ideological 'summing up', as it were. Mahathirism culminates in Vision 2020 because its deepest ambition of transforming Malaysia into a 'developed country' represents the maturation of Mahathir's nationalism. As our analysis of the evolution of Mahathir's nationalism shows, it has its roots in the intensely Malay nationalist impulse to catch up with the non-Malays. But it aspires to find its fulfilment in an equally committed Malaysian nationalist goal of competing equally with the advanced nations of the world. Mahathir himself has alluded to all this before. But Vision 2020 links the two—Malay and Malaysian nationalism—when it speaks of

> creating a psychologically liberated, secure and developed Malaysian society with faith and confidence in itself, justifiably proud of what it is, of what it has accomplished, robust enough to face all manner of adversity. This Malaysian society must be distinguished by the pursuit of excellence, fully aware of all its potentials, psychologically subservient to none, and respected by the peoples of other nations.[26]

But on the evidence of Mahathir's comments on the need to liberate the Malay from feelings of inferiority and insecurity *vis-à-vis* the non-Malay, one can be sure that the first part of the above passage refers to the 'rehabilitation of the Malays'. The second part summarizes what 'standing tall as others' must mean in the world of nations.

Philosophically, Mahathir has always been something of an idealist who believed that attitudes, value systems, and ethics were what made and shaped races and nations. In practice, he has been a determined economist, almost an economic determinist, for whom politics or psychology or ideology led nowhere without economics. From his view, whereas Malay nationalism had to redeem itself through Malay parity in the Malaysian economy, Malaysian nationalism must project itself on to the global economy where 'entry into the world market pits our companies against all-comers and subjects them to the full force of international competition'.[27] The nation's 'winning formula' to survive this pitiless competition calls for 'persist[ing] with export-led growth despite the rise of protectionism, trade blocs and managed trade' which 'we must oppose' because 'the trend towards the formation of trading blocs will damage our progress'. In the global scramble to trade, 'just as we must diversify the products we export, so we must diversify the markets we export to'. One, therefore, had to acquire 'new knowledge, new networks, new contacts and new approaches towards dealing with unfamiliar laws, rules and regulations' in order to penetrate the individually small markets but collectively big market of 'the developing Asian, African and Latin American countries'. So intense is this impulse to trade that diplomacy must speak with the merchant's tongue: 'Small though we may be, we must strive to influence the course of international trade.' Simultaneously, international trade reverberates with tones of 'national defence' because a 'country without adequate economic defence capabilities and the ability to marshal influence and create coalitions in the international economic arena is an economically defenceless nation and an economically powerless state'[28] which 'Malaysia cannot afford to be'. To build up the necessary 'economic defence capabilities', the '2020' state would assist 'small and medium industries ... to grow bigger', mobilize 'surplus savings and domestic capital' for productive investment, supply infrastructural support, and facilitate 'the birth of tomorrow's entrepreneurs'. But it would leave behind the NEP's state interventionism.[29] The '2020' state would prefer to oversee and guide, liberalize, and deregulate, except 'where absolutely necessary'.[30] For their part, the 'infants' of the national economy—especially those 'over-protected' industries—will 'simply have no choice but to be more lean ... and more competitive'. They will have to be weaned from 'artificial profits and ... protection'. They 'must grow up to be sturdy and strong'. They must measure up to 'the full discipline and rigour of market forces'. In a word, they must become 'more able to take on the world'.

This language of contest and preparation for combat is not

derived from any militaristic tradition in Malaysian politics; there is none. But it is fitting that Vision 2020, the ideological expression of Mahathir's 'mature' nationalism, should be so permeated with capitalism's idiom of combat and contest. Within this scenario of trade wars and struggles for market shares, Vision 2020 specifies that its 'first strategic challenge' lies in 'establishing a united Malaysian nation' possessed of 'a sense of common and shared destiny', shored up by a 'full and fair partnership', and 'made up of one *Bangsa Malaysia*' or 'Malaysian race'. *Bangsa Malaysia* is Vision 2020's truly novel proposal audaciously mooted before the Malaysian Business Council's august union of 'state and capital'. The erstwhile neo-colony remakes itself into a market colonizer. The plural society unifies as 'one Malaysian nation'. *Fin de siècle* capitalism offers itself as the 'market nationalism' of twenty-first-century Malaysia.

Melayu Baru: *Mahathirism after Mahathir*

In the preceding chapters, we explored Mahathir's ideas on nationalism, capitalism, Islam, populism, and authoritarianism. These ideas form the core components of 'Mahathirism', a relatively coherent ideology. To that we added a more personal investigation of Mahathir in his youthful C. H. E. Det pose, the class background to his religiosity, and the medical influence on his political style. The result is a two-tiered analysis of what Mahathirism encompasses and what the politician Mahathir is like—'up to this point', we should note, for there can be no end to this kind of analysis, not least because Mahathir remains Prime Minister. He continues to supply ideas and policies: for him, that is the *sine qua non* of leadership. He continues to engage in political moves: that is the politician's *raison d'être*. It is possible that some of these new ideas, policies, and political moves may call the themes of this study into question. We leave it to some future study to demonstrate that.

For now, one feels that further policies and moves by Mahathir will more likely reflect those basic Mahathirist themes resonating now in new variations, now according to old scores. Towards the end of 1992, for example, the 1983 constitutional crisis was replayed according to the old theme of trimming royal power and prerogatives. In 1992, the specific battle was fought over legal immunity for rulers who transgressed against the law. A more anti-royalist

UMNO,[31] a more partisan public mood, and even the DAP's support in Parliament made up some of the changed circumstances in 1992 which helped Mahathir to gain victory whereas he only had a stalemate in 1983.[32] Mahathir's 'Sabah problem' resurfaced in 1990 when the PBS defected from the Barisan Nasional to join Gagasan Rakyat. In 1985–6, when the Barisan Nasional was besieged by popular disaffection, Mahathir neutralized the 'east wind from Tambunan' by co-opting the PBS into the Barisan Nasional. Since 1990, he has been far more threatening towards the PBS. UMNO has 'spread its wings to Sabah',[33] several PBS figures have been detained on suspicion of planning Sabah's secession from Malaysia, and PBS President and Sabah Chief Minister, Pairin Kitingan, has been tried in court on charges of alleged corruption. The 1990 election saw the total eclipse of UMNO in Kelantan by PAS and Semangat 46. It remains to be seen how Mahathir's Islamization will respond to the PAS-led state government's plans to deepen Islam's role in Kelantan's public and political life, most dramatically by introducing *hudud* laws for the Muslims in the state.[34] At the international level, Mahathir's role as an opponent of protectionism and trade barriers, and as a Third World spokesman, has become generally acknowledged. His anti-Westernism is more urgently directed against Fortress Europe and the North America Free Trade Agreement. Looking East, he has initiated the East Asian Economic Caucus which seeks to bypass the Asia–Pacific Economic Council, started by Australia but now dominated by the United States of America. In 1981, he declined to attend the Commonwealth Heads of Government Meeting. He refused to attend the Asia–Pacific Economic Cooperation Summit in Seattle in November 1993. In 1981, he snubbed Britain with his 'Buy British Last' directive. In 1990, he snubbed Australia by downgrading official ties after his protest against an Australian television's distortion of Malaysia went unheeded.

To say that Mahathirist ideology is relatively coherent and that its core themes can be expressed in new variations is not to suggest that Mahathirism is free of contradictions. At many points, we have demonstrated that the reverse is true: Mahathir has been full of paradoxes and Mahathirism abounds in contradictions and tensions. We may briefly but usefully recapitulate this theme of Mahathirist 'contradictoriness' as a way to conclude the study.

Since his C. H. E. Det days, Mahathir's identification with the Malays has never wavered. He has ever been their ideologue. But his identification with the Malay cause has co-existed with a pronounced rejection of 'Malayness' which he thought had hindered their progress.[35] It is as if anxious to secure the survival of the Malays, Mahathir wished an end to 'Malayness'. Mahathir's nationalism has also experienced a tension between an older Malay nationalism and a nascent Malaysian nationalism to the extent that he oscillates between wanting to promote Malay economic participation and wanting to end their retardation of national economic progress. This tension finds an alternative expression in his capitalism when he comes under a simultaneous compulsion to preserve the Malays' 'NEP crutches' and a need to prevent the Malays from ossifying under layers of state protection. Once the most articulate ideologue of 'constructive protection', Mahathir has become the foremost promoter of 'productivity'; once the advocate of state interventionism on behalf of the Malays, he has become the initiator of privatization. The Social Darwinist rejector of 'merit selection' within the plural society has made merit the highest value of a freer Malaysian capitalism in the global community. And Mahathir never ceased to praise enterprise during his premiership which has palpably been an age of money politics. Mahathir has tried to encourage the assimilation of a 'universalizing' Islam in Malaysia but here we can locate his religiosity in the particularity of his class background. His spiritual qualities of an Islam of 'learning, work, and thrift', considered to be acceptable to the ethnic sensitivities in Malaysia, more pertinently blend with the specific demands of an ascending Malay capitalism: 'new' attitudes towards work, rugged individualism, self-reliance, and the piety of worldly success. His populism, too, has been uneasily allied to his authoritarianism. He has been the most successful populist in Malay politics without really commanding UMNO's grass roots. No Malaysian politician had set so much store by his popular mandate, and yet no other Malaysian leader had taken his electoral mandate so personally. Mahathir has always fancied himself to be the voice of the people—with justification—but he has always steeled himself to speak with the voice of the leader. In the end, his populism and authoritarianism were scarcely divisible. His only attempt to resolve that by recourse to 'liberalism' was tentative and short-lived. Among Malaysian politicians, Mahathir's record of raising hopes and creating fears, inspiring adulation and provoking hostility, has not been equalled. He has supplied the boldest of visions only to induce the most intense opposition. He has initiated many policies with flair but also altered courses with equanimity. From another angle, complexities and contradictions have dotted his long political career, often resulting in the swapping of friends and the making of foes.

Hence, when Mahathir expresses a dream of creating a *Bangsa Malaysia*, a single Malaysian nation, albeit in the year 2020, it seems like another Mahathirist contradiction. After all, the dream comes from a man whose politics has been predicated on the passions of the Malay cause and who has always argued for an openly ethnic approach to ethnic issues. But we must imagine Mahathir being serious and contemplate his dream of a *Bangsa Malaysia* which Vision 2020 lays down as 'a full partnership [of Malays and non-Malays] in economic progress'.[36]

If so, the beginning of Mahathir's dream has always been the ending of the 'Malay dilemma', the removal of this (Malay) 'millstone around the nation's neck', for otherwise 'our progress is going to be retarded'.[37] This is, of course, an echo of the 'Malay dilemma', descended all the way from C. H. E. Det, but now emitted with an altered lilt. Vision 2020 is explicit about having to 'reach a stage where no one can say that a particular ethnic group is *inherently* economically backward and another is economically advanced'.[38] It envisages a 'fair balance with regard to the participation and contribution of all our ethnic groups ... in the high-growth, modern sectors of the economy' and 'a fair distribution with regard to the control, management and ownership of the modern economy'. Beyond that, it plays down the NEP's idiom of 'restructuring' and 'distribution', 'targets' and 'quotas'. It even stands the NEP's 'distribution fixation' on its head by warning against 'growth fixation'.[39] Vision 2020 sets its sights on an eventual 'creation of an economically resilient and fully competitive *Bumiputera* community' and 'the healthy development of a viable and robust *Bumiputera* commercial and industrial community'. But it allows that 'we have already come a long way towards the fulfilment of these objectives'.[40]

In material terms, this is supported by *bumiputera* economic gains between 1985 and 1990. The corporate restructuring which took place between 1985 and 1990 resulted in the *bumiputera* ownership of share capital reaching at least 20.3 per cent of the total,[41] despite holding the NEP in abeyance. The abolition of 'the identification of race with economic function' proceeded apace. In 1990, while they still accounted for the largest proportion of the labour force engaged in agriculture, the *bumiputera* constituted 50.3 per cent of all manufacturing employment.[42] The *bumiputer*a share of 'certain higher-paying professional occupations' was 29 per cent.[43] *Bumiputera* also 'gained as much as 60 per cent of all new jobs generated during [1985–90]'.[44]

These represent important contributions to 'Malaysia's success'. And even if 'the world has not given sufficient credit to the Malays and *Bumiputeras*',[45] these achievements had surmounted a critical socio-psychological barrier: 'Getting the Malays and *Bumiputeras* to improve their achievements in areas where they are now lacking is not something impossible. If they can progress in many fields to various levels now, there is no reason why they can't go much higher.'[46] Evidently 'national human resource development' can now take care of most of the rest: 'What may be considered a burden now can, with the correct attitude and management, be the force that lightens our burden and hastens our progress.'[47] Given the generally sombre tone which underlay most of Mahathir's previous comments on the Malay condition, that is a relatively optimistic indication that the Malay dilemma is nearing its end: 'Some may think that this is a dilemma that cannot be reconciled. This is not true. It may, however, reflect the lack of self-confidence on one's part. If we are prepared to face our problems positively and are also prepared to overcome our own weaknesses, this so-called dilemma will no longer exist.'[48]

To put it more positively, the 'complete rehabilitation of the Malays'—the definitive end in Mahathirism—is in sight. What is needed to attain it is a 'culture [that] values mastery of knowledge and sophisticated and relevant technology highly and encourages learning and hard work'.[49] That 'new' culture can be 'ours' but

> we must raise our effort to make ourselves into people who are able to take their appropriate place in this modern world.
>
> For this we require a new Malay and *bumiputera* race which possesses a culture suitable to the modern period, capable of meeting all challenges, able to compete without assistance, learned and knowledgeable, sophisticated, honest, disciplined, trustworthy and competent.[50]

Thus did Mahathir reveal his vision of creating a *Melayu Baru*, or 'New Malay', who will assume his 'full and fair partnership' in *Bangsa Malaysia*.[51] In 'generic', that is, ethnic, terms, *Melayu Baru* denotes Malays who are prepared to undergo 'a mental revolution and a cultural transformation',[52] and leave behind the feudalistic and fatalistic vestiges of an older Malay culture, value system, and mental make-up. Linking *Melayu Baru* and Vision 2020, Mahathir holds out hopes for all Malays except those who, being so 'fanatical in their belief[s], shun *Wawasan 2020* in favour of *Wawasan Akhirat*, or "Vision Hereafter"'.[53] But Muslim 'fanatics' aside, there are new Malays and new Malays, and it is essential to determine which of them lie closest to Mahathir's *Melayu Baru* heart.

That place will not be occupied by the Malay peasants and agriculturalists whom C. H. E. Det described as the 'most backward and illiterate' of the Malays. Mahathir, too, has long believed that it is necessary to urbanize and retrain these rural Malays for life in the 'modern' and 'urban' sector. He has always regarded the diminution in rural population and the declining importance of the small Malay agricultural sector with a detached approval. He favours further reductions in rural population by mechanization of agriculture, by 'cooperatization' of small farms into large corporate agri-businesses, and by rural-to-urban migration of surplus agricultural labour.

Nor will pride of place among the *Melayu Baru* go to the Malay working class, arguably the unsung hero of the NEP. The Malay working class has undergone the enormous social and psychological transition of being plucked out of the patterns of rural life and incorporated into the multinational factories producing for the world market. With their induction into the modern capitalist sector, the Malay workers have had to imbibe exactly the complex of 'time-thrift', 'industrial discipline', and 'work ethic' which lay behind Mahathir's 'Look East' policy. The Malay working class has undergone a more thorough 'mental revolution' and 'cultural transformation' than virtually all other Malay social groups. Beyond the NEP's employment quotas, which may only have facilitated its induction into manufacturing employment, the Malay working class has not enjoyed the forms of subsidies and state sponsorship which other classes of Malays have had. If anything, the making of the Malay working class has proceeded in the face of state protection of the multinational companies against trade union formation and collective industrial action in the Free Trade Zones. Mahathir who prescribes 'work' and 'productivity' to Malays and Malaysians alike has said little that is favourable to the Malay working class. Indeed, Mahathir's typical comment on Malay workers is not only unfavourable, it blames them for the 'Malay' failure to succeed in business.[54] Dedicated to the dignity of work, Mahathir has shown himself to be opposed to the interests of the working class.

Mahathir has never been enamoured of the Malay aristocrats. His 'historical judgement' upon them is that they were rentiers who lived off the labour of others and led to the ruin of the Malay States.[55] Finally, Mahathir has rarely regarded the Malay civil servants with favour. He often thinks of (Malay and non-Malay) civil servants as people who treat their jobs as sinecures, who prefer comfort to risks, and, most damning of all, who are unable to make profits for the (state-owned) businesses which they run.[56]

We are left with the Malay entrepreneurs and the (non-government) Malay professionals who broadly make up the '*Bumiputera* commercial and industrial community'. Before the 1990s, Mahathir had often expressed disappointment with their progress, considering the financial assistance, education and training, and political sponsorship which the state lavished upon them. But he has more frequently acknowledged their collective achievement towards the 1990s. At the UMNO General Assembly in November 1993, Mahathir spoke with a rare pride of the 'achievements of the Malays and *Bumiputeras*' which indicate that they 'have the talent and ability to progress and be successful in whatever fields they undertake':

> Today we have Malays and *Bumiputeras* as heads of departments, scientists, actuaries, nuclear physicists, surgeons, experts in the fields of medicine and aviation, bankers and corporate leaders. In fact, some are already managers of major conglomerates with assets worth billions of ringgit and able to acquire bigger companies in the open market or participate in mergers and acquisitions which are complex and sophisticated.[57]

He considered that it is all the more remarkable that 'most of these Malays and *Bumiputeras* originate from the rural areas, from families of farmers, fishermen and settlers'.[58] The NEP and immediate post-NEP years have undoubtedly been an era of unparalleled social mobility for the Malays. Individuals of ability, as Mahathir himself noted, have arisen from the 'old' Malay backgrounds to join the highest ranks of the *bumiputera* commercial and industrial community'. They are, for him, the best examples of the Malays who will be 'capable of meeting all challenges, able to compete without assistance, learned and knowledgeable, sophisticated, honest, disciplined, trustworthy and competent'. They are, for him, the true *Melayu Baru*, a new breed of self-made men, 'individuals [who] through their own efforts and skills ... will achieve progress'.[59]

But they are not just individuals: they are historically the 'new' class of Malay capitalists and the 'new' Malay middle class which were largely 'engineered' by the state according to the logic of Malay parity with non-Malays in a capitalist economy. Mahathir knows no other class to whom the Malay future can be entrusted. The complete rehabilitation of the Malays can now be seen in their rise as a class able to claim parity with the non-Malays and the rest of the world. From the point of view of Mahathir and his *Melayu Baru*, the 'prehistory' of the Malays has ended. Their history, and, by extension, the history of *Bangsa Malaysia* may perhaps begin. In the beginning, so to speak, a race set out to remake itself in class terms: that was the promise of Mahathirism. It has largely succeeded. In the end, so it appears, a new class offers itself as the social basis of a new nation. Whether it will succeed remains to be seen. Perhaps therein repose the contradictions of Mahathirism after Mahathir.

1. For example, see Gordon P. Means, *Malaysian Politics: The Second Generation*, Singapore: Oxford University Press, 1991, pp. 243–8 and 263–4.

2. The Ampang Jaya by-election was the first since the Tanjung Puteri contest in which Mahathir's leadership was not the primary issue. Ampang Jaya's non-Malay voters were highly suspicious of Harun's role in the May 13 1969 violence. The DAP pointedly refused to endorse Harun. Ironically, Harun seemed to have preempted Semangat 46's choice of candidate for Ampang Jaya by announcing himself as their candidate! For a critical analysis of the Ampang Jaya by-election, see Chandra Muzaffar, 'Ampang Jaya: Why the Semangat '46 Group Lost', in Chandra Muzaffar, *Challenges and Choices in Malaysian Politics and Society*, Penang: Aliran, 1989, pp. 88–94.

3. The most articulate advocacy of this 'two coalition system' was made by Lim Kit Siang, after his release from prison, and recorded in the DAP-produced videotape, 'Tanjung'.

4. Malaysia, *Sixth Malaysia Plan, 1991–1995*, Kuala Lumpur: Government Printers, 1991, pp. 6–10.

5. Ibid., pp. 22–3, Tables 1.3 and 1.4.

6. Ibid., p. 131, Table 4.3.

7. Ibid., p. 133, Table 4.4.

8. Ibid., p. 135, Table 4.6.

9. In the Fifth Malaysia Plan period, Taiwan became the biggest single source of foreign investment in Malaysia. Taiwanese investments rose from RM32 million in 1985 to RM6.34 billion in 1990. Their total for 1986–90 was RM9.58 billion (ibid).

10. See Means, *Malaysian Politics*, pp. 265–70, for a useful discussion of the NECC.

11. It was unclear how committed Mahathir was to the NECC, to say nothing about 'consensus' being alien to his 'strong-leader' style. The NECC was chaired by Ghazali Shafie, not someone Mahathir would entrust the preparation of a post-NEP economic policy to, but someone who might be remembered for his role in formulating the Rukunegara. UMNO's team was led by Abdullah Badawi whom Mahathir had purged from the Cabinet after 24 April 1987. The NECC's *modus operandi* called for individual and institutional submissions and representations by its 'equally balanced' *bumiputera* and non-*bumiputera* members. Apparently all submitted with the exception of UMNO which gave, and presumably gave away, nothing! Subsequently, the opposition and several dissenting NGO or 'individual' participants openly broke with the NECC.

12. A useful summary of the 1990 election is given in Harold Crouch, 'Authoritarian Trends, the UMNO Split and the Limits to State Power', in Joel S. Kahn and Francis Loh Kok Wah (eds.), *Fragmented Vision: Culture and Politics in Contemporary Malaysia,* Sydney: Asian Studies Association of Australia in association with Allen and Unwin, 1992, pp. 35–9. A detailed analysis is available in Khong Kim Hoong, *Malaysia's General Election, 1990: Continuity, Change and Ethnic Politics*, Research Notes and Discussion Papers No. 74, Singapore: Institute of Southeast Asian Studies, 1991.

13. There were strong, but in the end untrue, rumours that the Parti Bansa Dayak Sarawak (PBDS)—a 'national-level' member of the Barisan Nasional but a 'state-level' opposition to Sarawak's ruling Barisan Nasional component, the Parti Bumiputera Bersatu (PBB)—would completely break with the Barisan Nasional and follow the PBS into the Gagasan.

14. 'Coalition' cost the DAP, which 'conceded' four parliamentary seats to the PBS in Sabah! Hence the DAP had 'only' twenty seats in 1990 compared with twenty-four in 1986.

15. Mahathir, 'Malaysia: The Way Forward', Working Paper presented at the Inaugural Meeting of the Malaysian Business Council, Kuala Lumpur, 28 February 1991, reprinted in *New Straits Times*, 2 March 1991. All subsequent citations under this section are taken from this text, unless specified otherwise.

16. 'The great bulk of the work that must be done to ensure a fully developed country called Malaysia a generation from now will obviously be done by the leaders who follow us, by our children and grandchildren. But we should make sure that we have done our duty in guiding them with regard to what we should work to become. And let us lay the secure foundations that they must build upon' (ibid.).

17. That is, the GDP would increase from RM115 billion in 1990 to 'about RM920 billion in real (1990) terms' (ibid.).

18. Ibid.

19. Ibid.

20. Ibid.

21. Such a format, tending towards long litanies, was indicative of Mohamed Noordin Sopiee's influence in the formulation of 'Vision 2020'. Noordin Sopiee's Institute of Strategic and International Studies (ISIS) served as the MBC's Secretariat.

22. '... and the correct balance with regard to those with competence in science and technology, the arts and the social sciences' (ibid.).

23. Malaysia, *Sixth Malaysia Plan*, pp. 4–5.

24. With '2020' connoting 'perfect vision', and Malaysia poised to become the '20th' member of an existing club of the 'present 19 countries' that are generally regarded as 'developed countries' (Mahathir, 'Malaysia: The Way Forward').

25. 'The third challenge we have always faced is that of fostering and developing a mature democratic society, practising a form of mature consensual, community-oriented Malaysian democracy that can be a model for many developing countries' (ibid.). Would it not have been less opaque to say that there would be no immature, dissenting, individual, 'rights'-based, 'Western' democracy unsuited to a 'not-yet-fully-developed' Malaysia?

26. Ibid.

27. Ibid.

28. Ibid. In the aftermath of the so-called 'Gulf War' against Iraq in 1991, Mahathir added a foreboding tone to this line of argument: 'If Malaysia is to defend its independence, this country must have its own power. What is meant is not military power although military power has a role. What is meant is economic power and the ability to develop one's own country. Only if we do become a developed country can we defend [ourselves] should trade sanctions and other non-military threats be launched at us' (Mahathir, 'Speech at the UMNO General Assembly, 1991', Kuala Lumpur, 8 November 1991, English translation reprinted as 'PM: Avoid Corruption in Any Form', *New Straits Times*, 9 November 1991).

29. During an interview on Malaysian television, held ten days before Vision 2020 was presented, Mahathir counselled: 'Well, the public sector should confine itself to creating an environment looking after law and order. Business is really not the business of government. When we do go into business, we do it very badly' ('We Are Masters of Ourselves: Mahathir', *Malaysian Business*, 1–15 March 1991, p. 20).

30. 'The Government will continue to downsize its role in the field of economic production and business' but 'where absolutely necessary the Government will not be so completely bound by its commitment to withdraw from the economic role, that it will not intervene' (Mahathir, 'Malaysia: The Way Forward').

31. Chamil Wariya, *Politik dan Raja*, Petaling Jaya: Penerbit Fajar Bakti, 1992.

32. Syed Husin Ali, *Isu Raja dan Pindaan Perlembagaan*, 2nd edn., Petaling Jaya: S. Husin Ali, 1993.

33. This phrase, 'mengembangkan sayap ke Sabah' in Malay, refers to the estab-

lishment of 'UMNO Sabah'. With this move, UMNO eventually replaced its ally, USNO, and got ready to challenge the PBS directly. See Chamil Wariya, *UMNO Sabah: Mencabar dan Dicabar*, Petaling Jaya: Penerbit Fajar Bakti, 1992. UMNO's 'incursion' into Sabah must be compared with the PAP's decision to contest the 1964 election in Peninsular Malaysia. UMNO's bitter opposition to the PAP's (abortive) move to 'spread its wings' beyond Singapore was one critical factor in Singapore's later separation from Malaysia.

34. So far, Mahathir and UMNO hesitate to confront PAS's introduction of *hudud* laws openly. They 'pass the buck' by claiming that any attempt to introduce *hudud* laws for the nation by amendments to its 'secular' Constitution will fail because of non-Muslim opposition. At the 1992 UMNO General Assembly, for example, Mahathir dwelt lengthily on the danger of Muslim 'fanaticism' in Malaysia, but generally, without once referring to PAS's concrete moves (Mahathir, 'Speech at the UMNO General Assembly, 1992', Kuala Lumpur, 6 November 1992, English translation reprinted as 'No Place for Religious Fanatics', *New Straits Times*, 7 November 1992).

35. Islam was an important exception.

36. Mahathir, 'Malaysia: The Way Forward'.

37. Ibid.

38. Or where there was neither the 'identification of race with economic function' nor the 'identification of economic backwardness with race'. The emphasis is added to draw attention to the persisting, if softened, Social Darwinist tone.

39. That is, 'the danger of pushing for growth figures oblivious to ... [among others], the achievement of our other social objectives' (ibid.)—a reminder that the NEP tilt towards 'distribution' has been overturned.

40. The original statement refers to these objectives as well as others in Vision 2020's full list of 'strategic challenges'.

41. In 1990, ethnically indeterminate 'nominee companies', presumably including *bumiputera* interests operating through these companies, held 8.4 per cent of total share capital (Malaysia, *Sixth Malaysia Plan*, pp. 13–14). In comparison, the Chinese-held proportion of total share capital declined from 48.2 per cent to 44.9 per cent between 1985 and 1990.

42. Ibid., p. 36, Table 1.11.

43. Ibid., p. 13.

44. Ibid., p. 12.

45. Mahathir, 'Speech at the UMNO General Assembly, 1992.'

46. Ibid.

47. Mahathir, 'Malaysia: The Way Forward'.

48. Mahathir, 'Speech at the UMNO General Assembly, 1992'.

49. Ibid.

50. Mahathir, 'Speech at the UMNO General Assembly, 1991'. Here Mahathir for the first time spoke openly of creating a 'New Malay'. His intention was evident much earlier. See Philip Bowring, 'Mahathir and the New Malay Dilemma', *Far Eastern Economic Review*, 9 April 1982, p. 20: 'Mahathir is keenly aware that the pace of change for Malays must be sustained. Shape up! Be disciplined! Work hard! Follow new leads! Create a New Malay Man!'

51. In 'Perkembangan Sebuah Konsep', *Mastika*, October 1992, pp. 7–8, Rustam A. Sani sees Mahathir's raising of *Melayu Baru* as a way to offset Malay unease over the idea of a *Bangsa Malaysia* in the process of realizing Vision 2020.

52. Mahathir, 'Malaysia: The Way Forward'.

53. The Malays 'should not allow themselves to be influenced by groups which charge that what is important is not Vision 2020 but a vision of the hereafter' (Mahathir, 'Speech at the UMNO General Assembly, 1991'). 'Those who purposely hinder Muslims from achieving success in this world, who try to confuse Muslims regarding Vision 2020, and who advocate *Wawasan Akhirat* are actually conspiring with the enemies of Islam' (Mahathir, 'Speech at the UMNO General Assembly, 1992').

54. For example: 'The failure of the Malay businessman is in no small way caused by Malay workers themselves who do not work hard and with honesty' (Mahathir, 'Speech at the Pemuda and Wanita UMNO General Assembly', Kuala Lumpur, 25 June 1981, reprinted as 'Cabaran di hadapan Pemuda dan Wanita UMNO', in Harun Derauh and Shafie Nor (eds.), *Mahathir: Cita-cita dan Pencapaian*, Kuala Lumpur: Berita Publishing, 1982, pp. 51–9). From his '100th Day Interview' comes an example which diverts class prejudice into ethnic differences: 'Sometimes Malays who have industries don't want to pick Malays; they say Malays are "a bit difficult". So we can't get angry at other people. It's true, go and ask the Malay contractor, say, who his workers are, and why he doesn't subcontract to other Malays? Frequently, if possible, he subcontracts to the Chinese. Because he knows if he gives to a Chinese, the work will be done' ('100 Hari di bawah Mahathir', *Berita Harian*, 27 October 1981).

55. See the section 'Look Out and "Look East"' in Chapter 3 for a discussion of Mahathir's reading of Malay history which blamed Malay rulers and aristocrats for the Malay 'disinclination to work'.

56. 'Any Malay who had a little connection with powerful men dreamt of becoming a salaried Government officer, that is, someone who doesn't need to be efficient or to work, but receives a fixed income' (Mahathir, 'Speech at the Pemuda and Wanita UMNO General Assembly', 25 June 1981). On the inability of civil servants to make profits, see the section 'Privatization: The 40 Per Cent Solution' in Chapter 4.

57. Mahathir, 'Speech at the UMNO General Assembly, 1991'.

58. Ibid.

59. Mahathir, 'Speech at the UMNO General Assembly, 1992'.

Bibliography

SOURCES for quotations from newspapers and magazines are given in the endnotes, together with bibliographic details. This Bibliography is selective and comprises the more important works consulted during the preparation of this study.

Mahathir Mohamad: His Books, Essays, Speeches, and Interviews

Books and Essays by Mahathir (arranged chronologically)

C. H. E. Det, 'Malays and the [*sic*] Higher Education', *Sunday Times*, 26 September 1948.

_____, 'Malays and Higher Education: Summing-up', *Sunday Times*, 17 October 1948.

_____, '*Ronggeng* Is Popular', *Sunday Times*, 9 January 1949.

_____, 'Picnic Time in the *Dusun*', *Sunday Times*, 23 January 1949.

_____, 'Rains Bring Fish to "Sawahs"', *Sunday Times*, 6 February 1949

_____, 'Malay—"Modern" and Standard', *Sunday Times*, 24 April 1949.

_____, 'Malay Housewives Are Busy', *Sunday Times*, 24 July 1949.

_____, 'The Rulers Are Losing Loyalty', *Sunday Times*, 7 August 1949.

_____, 'Rulers and *Ra'ayats*—Climax Is Near', *Sunday Times*, 9 October 1949.

_____, 'Malay *Padi* Planters Need Help', *Sunday Times*, 30 October 1949.

_____, 'Changing Malay Marriage Customs', *Sunday Times*, 20 November 1949.

_____, 'Malay Progress and the University', *Sunday Times*, 27 November 1949.

_____, 'Malays in South Siam Struggle On', *Sunday Times*, 8 January 1950.

_____, 'New Thoughts on Nationality', *Sunday Times*, 9 April 1950.

_____, 'Plight of Malay Fisherfolk', *Sunday Times*, 23 April 1950.

Mahathir Mohamad, *The Malay Dilemma*, Singapore: Donald Moore for Asia Pacific Press, 1970.

———, *Guide for Small Businessmen*, Petaling Jaya: Eastern Universities Press, 1985; translated from *Panduan Peniaga Kecil*, 2nd edn., Kuala Lumpur: Dewan Bahasa dan Pustaka, 1982; first published in 1973.

———, *The Challenge*, Petaling Jaya: Pelanduk Publications, 1986; translated from *Menghadapi Cabaran*, Kuala Lumpur: Pustaka Antara, 1976.

———, 'Fact and Fallacy', *New Straits Times*, 9 July 1981.

———, 'Malaysia Incorporated and Privatisation: Its Rationale and Purpose', in Mohd. Nor Abdul Ghani et al. (eds.), *Malaysia Incorporated and Privatisation: Towards National Unity*, Petaling Jaya: Pelanduk Publications, 1984, pp. 1–6.

———, 'Whither Malaysia?', Paper presented at the Keio International Symposium on 'Asia and Japan', Tokyo, 7–11 November 1983, reprinted in Andrew J. L. Armour (ed.), *Asia and Japan*, London: Athlone Press, 1985, pp. 150–9.

———, *Regionalism, Globalism and Spheres of Influence: ASEAN and the Challenge of Change into the 21st Century*, Singapore: Institute of Southeast Asian Studies, 1989.

———, 'Malaysia: The Way Forward', Working Paper presented at the Inaugural Meeting of the Malaysian Business Council, Kuala Lumpur, 28 February 1991, reprinted in *New Straits Times*, 2 March 1991.

Speeches by Mahathir (only those cited, arranged chronologically)

'Speech at the Pemuda and Wanita UMNO General Assembly', Kuala Lumpur, 1 July 1976, reprinted as 'Asas dan Matlamat Perjuangan UMNO', in Harun Derauh and Shafie Nor (eds.), *Mahathir: Cita-cita dan Pencapaian*, Kuala Lumpur: Berita Publishing, 1982, pp. 17–27.

'Speech at the Conference on Business in Southeast Asia', Kuala Lumpur, 4 February 1977, *Foreign Affairs Malaysia*, 10, 17 (1977): 70–2.

'Speech at the ASEAN–West Asian Investment Conference', Kuala Lumpur, 9 March 1978, *Foreign Affairs Malaysia*, 11, 1 (1978): 80–4.

'Speech at the Bumiputera Economic Convention', Universiti Kebangsaan Malaysia, Bangi, 19 March 1978, reprinted as 'Bumiputera Economy: A National Problem', *New Straits Times*, 1 April 1978.

'Speech at the Pemuda and Wanita UMNO General Assembly', Kuala Lumpur, 14 September 1978, reprinted as 'Tradisi dan Pembangunan Kepimpinan', in Harun Derauh and Shafie Nor (eds.), *Mahathir: Cita-cita dan Pencapaian*, Kuala Lumpur: Berita Publishing, 1982, pp. 38–50.

'Speech at the United Nations Conference on Trade and Development (UNCTAD) V Meeting', Manila, 15 May 1979, *Foreign Affairs Malaysia*, 12 (1979): 154–67.

'Speech at the Seminar on Transnational Corporations and National Development', Petaling Jaya, 2 October 1979, *Foreign Affairs Malaysia*, 12 (1979): 392–5.

'Speech at the 2nd Meeting of the Expert Group of Islamic Countries on Planning and Development', Kuala Lumpur, 3 December 1979, *Foreign Affairs Malaysia*, 12 (1979): 434–8.

'Speech at the 3rd General Conference of the United Nations Industrial Development Organization (UNIDO)', New Delhi, 22 January 1980, *Foreign Affairs Malaysia*, 13 (1980): 22–8.

'Speech at the Economic Society Dinner', Singapore, 31 October 1980, *Foreign Affairs Malaysia*, 13 (1980): 395–409.

'Speech at the 3rd Islamic Summit Conference', Taif, Saudi Arabia, 27 January 1981, reprinted as 'Towards Islamic Solidarity', in Murugesu Pathmanathan and David Lazarus (eds.), *Winds of Change*, Kuala Lumpur: Eastview Productions, 1984, pp. 57–68.

'Speech at the Closing Session of the 3rd Islamic Summit Conference', Taif, Saudi Arabia, 28 January 1981, reprinted as 'The Resurgence of Islam', in Murugesu Pathmanathan and David Lazarus (eds.), *Winds of Change*, Kuala Lumpur: Eastview Productions, 1984, pp. 69–72.

'Speech at the Annual Luncheon of the Malaysian International Chamber of Commerce and Industry', Kuala Lumpur, 1 June 1981, reprinted as 'The Evils of Protectionism', in Murugesu Pathmanathan and David Lazarus (eds.), *Winds of Change*, Kuala Lumpur: Eastview Productions, 1984, pp. 77–82.

'Speech at the Pemuda and Wanita UMNO General Assembly', Kuala Lumpur, 25 June 1981, reprinted as 'Cabaran di hadapan Pemuda dan Wanita UMNO', in Harun Derauh and Shafie Nor (eds.), *Mahathir: Cita-cita dan Pencapaian*, Kuala Lumpur: Berita Publishing, 1982, pp. 51–9.

'Speech at the Closing Session of the 32nd UMNO General Assembly', Kuala Lumpur, 28 June 1981, reprinted as 'Today My Burden Is My Burden', in J. Victor Morais, *Mahathir: A Profile in Courage*, Singapore: Eastern Universities Press, 1982, pp. 77–83.

'Speech at the International Islamic Youth Camp', Kuala Lumpur, 10 August 1981, reprinted as 'The Brotherhood of Islam', in Murugesu Pathmanathan and David Lazarus (eds.), *Winds of Change*, Kuala Lumpur: Eastview Productions, 1984, pp. 87–92.

'Speech at the 29th MCA General Assembly', Kuala Lumpur, 19 September 1981, reprinted as 'Peranan MCA dalam Memperkukuhkan Perpaduan Negara', in Harun Derauh and Shafie Nor (eds.), *Mahathir: Cita-cita dan Pencapaian*, Kuala Lumpur: Berita Publishing, 1982, pp. 71–5.

'Speech at the 5th General Assembly of the Organization of Asian News Agencies (OANA)', Kuala Lumpur, 3 November 1981, reprinted as 'A

New World Information and Communication Order', in Murugesu Pathmanathan and David Lazarus (eds.), *Winds of Change*, Kuala Lumpur: Eastview Productions, 1984, pp. 97–102.

'Ucapan di Upacara Perletakan Batu Asas Projek Dayabumi', Kuala Lumpur, 14 November 1981, reprinted in Arkib Negara Malaysia, *Ucapan-ucapan Dato' Seri Dr Mahathir Mohamad, 1981*, Kuala Lumpur, 1986, pp. 91–7.

'Ucapan di Majlis Perasmian Kursus Agama Anjuran Biro Agama UMNO', Kuala Lumpur, 27 November 1981, reprinted as 'Faktor Persekitaran dalam Perjuangan UMNO', in Harun Derauh and Shafie Nor (eds.), *Mahathir: Cita-cita dan Pencapaian*, Kuala Lumpur: Berita Publishing, 1982, pp. 32–7.

'Speech at a Dinner on the Occasion of an Official Visit to Singapore', Singapore, 18 December 1981, *Foreign Affairs Malaysia*, 14, 4 (December 1981): 311–16.

'Speech at the 5th Joint Conference of MAJECA/JAMECA', Kuala Lumpur, 8 February 1982, *Foreign Affairs Malaysia*, 15, 1 (March 1982): 38–45.

'25th National Day Message', reprinted as 'Kemerdekaan Negara di Bahu Generasi Muda', *Watan*, 3 September 1982.

'Speech at the 33rd UMNO General Assembly', Kuala Lumpur, 10 September 1982, English translation reprinted as 'UMNO in a World of Change and Challenge', *New Straits Times*, 11 September 1982.

'Speech at the 37th Session of the United Nations General Assembly', New York, 29 September 1982, reprinted as 'Towards Credibility in the United Nations', in Murugesu Pathmanathan and David Lazarus (eds.), *Winds of Change*, Kuala Lumpur: Eastview Productions, 1984, pp. 140–52.

'Speech at the 3rd ASEAN Law Association General Assembly', Kuala Lumpur, 26 October 1982, reprinted as 'The Varieties of Justice', in Murugesu Pathmanathan and David Lazarus (eds.), *Winds of Change*, Kuala Lumpur: Eastview Productions, 1984, pp. 159–65.

'Speech at the 1981 Malaysian Press Awards Presentation Ceremony', Kuala Lumpur, 28 November 1982, reprinted as 'Wartawan dan Tanggungjawab', *Berita Harian*, 29 November 1982.

'Speech at the 7th Malaysian Economic Convention', Kuala Lumpur, 18 January 1983, reprinted as 'The Malaysian Economy: Policy Adjustment or Structural Transformation', in Murugesu Pathmanathan and David Lazarus (eds.), *Winds of Change*, Kuala Lumpur: Eastview Productions, 1984, pp. 171–9.

'Speech at the Official Dinner Hosted by His Excellency the Prime Minister of Japan, Mr Yasuhiro Nakasone', Tokyo, 24 January 1983, *Foreign Affairs Malaysia*, 16, 1 (March 1983): 17–20.

'Keynote Address at the ASEAN–EEC Industrial Sectoral Conference', Kuala Lumpur, 28 February 1983, reprinted as 'ASEAN–EEC Industrial Cooperation', in Murugesu Pathmanathan and David Lazarus (eds.), *Winds of Change*, Kuala Lumpur: Eastview Productions, 1984, pp. 189–97.

'Speech at the 7th Conference of Heads of State/Government of the Non-Aligned Countries', New Delhi, 8 March 1983, reprinted as 'Non-alignment: Patterns of Conflict and Cooperation', in Murugesu Pathmanathan and David Lazarus (eds.), *Winds of Change*, Kuala Lumpur: Eastview Productions, 1984, pp. 198–210.

'Ucapan Ketika Merasmikan Mesyuarat Perwakilan UMNO Bahagian Hulu Kelantan', Kuala Kerai, Kelantan, 16 April 1983, reprinted as 'Ulama yang Gila Kuasa Menggugat Perpaduan', *Berita Harian*, 21 April 1983.

'Ucapan di Majlis Pelancaran Operasi Bank Islam Malaysia Berhad', 1 July 1983, reprinted in *Utusan Malaysia*, 2 July 1983.

'Speech at the Banquet Hosted by His Excellency President Chun Doo Hwan of the Republic of Korea', Seoul, 9 August 1983, *Foreign Affairs Malaysia*, 16, 3 (September 1983): 297–302.

'Speech at the 34th UMNO General Assembly', Kuala Lumpur, 19 August 1983, English translation reprinted as 'Running on Team Spirit—For Now and Future', *New Straits Times*, 20 August 1983.

'Speech at the Luncheon Jointly Hosted by the Asia Society, the Far East American Business Council and the ASEAN–American Trade Council', New York, 16 January 1984, *Foreign Affairs Malaysia*, 17, 1 (March 1984): 50–4.

'Speech at the Foreign Policy Association', Washington, 19 January 1984, *Foreign Affairs Malaysia*, 17, 1 (March 1984): 57–63.

'Speech at the Symposium on ASEAN, Australia and Japan—Breaking Down the Barriers', Kuala Lumpur, 7 May 1984, *Foreign Affairs Malaysia*, 17, 2 (June 1984): 153–7.

'Speech at the Top Business Leaders' Conference on National Economic Development', Kuala Lumpur, 18 May 1984, *Foreign Affairs Malaysia*, 17, 2 (June 1984): 158–65.

'Speech at the 35th UMNO General Assembly', Kuala Lumpur, 25 May 1984, English translation reprinted as 'Making Sure the Spirit of UMNO Prevails', *New Straits Times*, 26 May 1984.

'Speech at the Seminar on Malaysian–British Invisible Trade Links Jointly Organised by the British Invisible Exports Council and the Council on Malaysian Invisible Trade', Kuala Lumpur, 17 July 1984, *Foreign Affairs Malaysia*, 17, 3 (September 1984): 219–25.

'Speech at the 3rd International Seminar on Islamic Thoughts', Kuala

Lumpur, 26 July 1984, *Foreign Affairs Malaysia*, 17, 3 (September 1984): 226–31.

'27th National Day Message over Radio and Television Malaysia', 30 August 1984, reprinted as 'Mullah Sistem Jenis Diktator', *Utusan Malaysia*, 31 August 1984.

'Speech at the 39th Session of the United Nations General Assembly', New York, 10 October 1984, reprinted as 'Mahathir kepada PBB: Nilai Revolusi Islam Secara Adil', *Utusan Malaysia*, 11 October 1984.

'Speech at the Global Community Forum', Kuala Lumpur, 3 November 1984, *Foreign Affairs Malaysia*, 17, 4 (December 1984): 316–21.

'Holier than Thou—A Mild Critique', Speech at Trinity College, Oxford, 19 April 1985, *Foreign Affairs Malaysia*, 18, 2 (June 1985): 137–49.

'Speech at the International Monetary Conference', Hong Kong, 3 June 1985, *Foreign Affairs Malaysia*, 18, 2 (June 1985): 159–68.

'Hari Raya Aidilfitri Message Broadcast over Radio and Television Malaysia', 19 June 1985, reprinted as 'Marilah Kita Wujudkan Masyarakat Bersyukur', *Utusan Malaysia*, 20 June 1985.

'Speech at the Annual Dinner of Financial Institutions', Kuala Lumpur, 18 August 1985, *Foreign Affairs Malaysia*, 18, 3 (September 1985): 246–50.

'Ucapan Sempena Awal Muharam Hijrah 1406', Kuala Lumpur, reprinted as 'PM Ajak Rakyat Baharui Azam dengan Semangat Maju', *Utusan Malaysia*, 16 September 1985.

'Keynote Address at the World Press Convention', Kuala Lumpur, 18 September 1985, *Foreign Affairs Malaysia*, 18, 3 (September 1985): 251–60.

'Speech at the 36th UMNO General Assembly', Kuala Lumpur, 27 September 1985, reprinted as 'Semangat Kebangsaan Beri Kekuatan pada Perjuangan dan Persaudaraan Islam', *Utusan Malaysia*, 28 September 1985.

'Speech at the Commonwealth Heads of Government Meeting', Nassau, Bahamas, 16 October 1985, *Foreign Affairs Malaysia*, 18, 4 (December 1985): 387–90.

'Speech at the 20th World Management Congress', Kuala Lumpur, 3 November 1985, *Foreign Affairs Malaysia*, 18, 4 (December 1985): 342–6.

'Speech at the 3rd ASEAN Council on Petroleum (ASCOPE) Conference and Exhibition', Kuala Lumpur, 2 December 1985, *Foreign Affairs Malaysia*, 18, 4 (December 1985): 348–52.

'Speech at the International Islamic Symposium', Kuala Lumpur, 5 March 1986, *Foreign Affairs Malaysia*, 19, 1 (March 1986): 15–20.

'Speech at the Seminar on Primary Commodities', Kuala Lumpur, 21 April 1986, *Foreign Affairs Malaysia*, 19, 2 (June 1986): 6–9.

'Ucapan di Upacara Pembukaan Rasmi Musabaqah Membaca Al-Quran Peringkat Kebangsaan', Kuala Lumpur, 24 April 1986, reprinted as 'Berjimat Sepanjang Masa dalam Serba Serbi Kehidupan', *Utusan Malaysia*, 25 April 1986.

'Speech at the 9th MAJECA/JAMECA Joint Annual Conference', Kuala Lumpur, 24 April 1986, *Foreign Affairs Malaysia*, 19, 2 (June 1986): 11–17.

'Speech at the Seminar on Developing Islamic Financial Instruments', Kuala Lumpur, 28 April 1986, *Foreign Affairs Malaysia*, 19, 2 (June 1986): 18–22.

'Speech at the South–South II Summit of Third World Scholars and Statesmen', Kuala Lumpur, 5 May 1986, *Foreign Affairs Malaysia*, 19, 2 (June 1986): 23–31.

'Speech at the First ISIS National Conference on National Security', Kuala Lumpur, 15 July 1986, *Foreign Affairs Malaysia*, 19, 3 (September 1986): 1–5.

'Speech at the International Seminar on Commodities', Kuala Lumpur, 21 July 1986, *Foreign Affairs Malaysia*, 19, 3 (September 1986): 6–11.

'Speech at the Annual Dinner of Financial Institutions', Kuala Lumpur, 25 August 1986, *Foreign Affairs Malaysia*, 19, 3 (September 1986): 15–20.

'Speech at the 8th Conference of Heads of State/Government of the Non-Aligned Countries', Harare, Zimbabwe, 3 September 1986, *Foreign Affairs Malaysia*, 19, 3 (September 1986): 47–54.

'Speech at the 37th UMNO General Assembly', Kuala Lumpur, 18 September 1986, reprinted as 'Sistem Tumpuan Luar Bandar Akan Dikekalkan', *Utusan Malaysia*, 19 September 1986.

'Speech at the 41st Session of the United Nations General Assembly', New York, 29 September 1986, *Foreign Affairs Malaysia*, 19, 3 (September 1986): 55–65.

'Speech at the Malaysian Investment Seminar', New York, 30 September 1986, *Foreign Affairs Malaysia*, 19, 3 (September 1986): 66–9.

'Speech at the American International Group Investment Seminar', Kuala Lumpur, 6 October 1986, *Foreign Affairs Malaysia*, 19, 4 (December 1986): 6–11.

'Speech in Conjunction with the Celebration of the 41st Anniversary of the United Nations', Kuala Lumpur, 25 October 1986, *Foreign Affairs Malaysia*, 19, 4 (December 1986): 16–19.

'Speech at the EMF Foundation Roundtable on Malaysia', Kuala Lumpur, 3 November 1986, *Foreign Affairs Malaysia*, 19, 4 (December 1986): 29–35.

'Speech at the International Productivity Conference', Kuala Lumpur, 3 November 1986, *Foreign Affairs Malaysia*, 19, 4 (December 1986): 20–4.

'Speech at the 4th Regional Islamic Da'awah Council of Southeast Asia and the Pacific (RISEAP) General Assembly', Kuala Lumpur, 8 November 1986, *Foreign Affairs Malaysia*, 19, 4 (December 1986): 36–40.

'Speech to the Commonwealth Speakers and Presiding Officers Standing Committee Meeting', Kuala Lumpur, 6 January 1987, *Foreign Affairs Malaysia*, 20, 1 (March 1987): 7–9.

'Statement at the 5th Islamic Summit', Kuwait, 18 January 1987, *Foreign Affairs Malaysia*, 20, 1 (March 1987): 48–53.

'Speech at the 8th Meeting of the Islamic Foundation for Science, Technology and Development's Scientific Council', Kuching, Malaysia, 23 February 1987, *Foreign Affairs Malaysia*, 20, 1 (March 1987): 10–13.

'Keynote Address at the First ASEAN Economic Congress', Kuala Lumpur, 13 March 1987, in Noordin Sopiee, Chew Lay See, and Lim Siang Jin (eds.), *ASEAN at the Crossroads: Obstacles, Options and Opportunities in Economic Cooperation*, Kuala Lumpur: ISIS Malaysia, n.d., pp. 1–4.

'Speech at the 38th UMNO General Assembly', Kuala Lumpur, 24 April 1987, English translation reprinted as 'Let Not Future Generations Condemn Us', *New Straits Times*, 25 April 1987.

'Speech at the Luncheon Hosted by the Confederation of British Industry', London, 23 July 1987, *Foreign Affairs Malaysia*, 20, 3 (September 1987): 59–62.

'Speech at the UMNO General Assembly, 1988', Kuala Lumpur, 28 October 1988, English translation reprinted as 'UMNO Is UMNO', *New Straits Times*, 29 October 1988.

'Speech at the 10th Malaysian Economic Convention', Kuala Lumpur, 7 August 1989, reprinted as 'Charting Directions for Future Growth', *New Straits Times*, 8 August 1989.

'Speech at the UMNO General Assembly, 1991', Kuala Lumpur, 8 November 1991, English translation reprinted as 'PM: Avoid Corruption in Any Form', *New Straits Times*, 9 November 1991.

'Speech at the UMNO General Assembly, 1992', Kuala Lumpur, 6 November 1992, English translation reprinted as 'No Place for Religious Fanatics', *New Straits Times*, 7 November 1992.

'Speech at the UMNO General Assembly, 1993', Kuala Lumpur, 4 November 1993, English translation reprinted as 'Be Grateful for the Benefits of NEP', *New Straits Times*, 5 November 1993.

Interviews with Mahathir (only those cited, arranged chronologically)

Bob Reece, 'Alliance Outcast', *Far Eastern Economic Review*, 18 September 1969, pp. 698–700.

Leung Thong Ping, 'Mahathir', *Sunday Mail*, 2 April 1972.

Interview with Radio and Television Malaysia [1975], reprinted in Ministry of Information, *Akta Universiti dan Kolej Universiti (Pindaan) 1975: Soal-jawab dengan Menteri Pelajaran*, Kuala Lumpur, 1975.

Munir Majid, 'Datuk Seri Dr Mahathir Mohamad: Power and Responsibility', *Malaysian Business*, October 1980, pp. 4–10.

Interview by the Local Press on the Occasion of Mahathir's 100th Day in Office [24 October 1981], reprinted as '100 Hari di bawah Mahathir', *Berita Harian*, 27 October 1981.

K. Das, 'Problems and Power', *Far Eastern Economic Review*, 30 October 1981, pp. 31–5.

Supriya Singh, 'The Man behind the Politician', *New Straits Times*, 14 April 1982.

'An Opposition Is Not Absolutely Necessary', *Asiaweek*, 7 May 1982.

K. Das, 'Mahathir's "Restoration"', *Far Eastern Economic Review*, 11 June 1982, pp. 38–41.

Interview by the Local Press on the Occasion of Mahathir's First Year in Office [16 July 1982], reprinted as 'Setahun Bersama Mahathir', in Rosnah Majid, *Koleksi Temuramah Khas Tokoh-tokoh*, Kuala Lumpur: Utusan Publications and Distributors, 1985, pp. 145–73.

Tan Chee Khoon, 'Interview with Datuk Seri Dr Mahathir bin Mohamad' [*c.* August 1982], in Tan Chee Khoon, *Without Fear or Favour*, Singapore: Eastern Universities Press, 1984, pp. 60–91.

Harun Derauh and Shafie Nor, 'Temuramah Khas dengan Perdana Menteri Malaysia Datuk Seri Dr Mahathir Mohamad', in Harun Derauh and Shafie Nor (eds.), *Mahathir: Cita-cita dan Pencapaian*, Kuala Lumpur: Berita Publishing, 1982, pp. 3–11.

Kadir Jasin, 'What Goes into the Making of the Malaysian Car' and 'Need for a Bigger Population If We Are to Industrialize', *New Straits Times*, 24 November 1982.

Interview by the Local Press on the Occasion of Mahathir's Second Year in Office [16 July 1983], reprinted as 'Proses Islamisasi Bukan Bererti Memaksa Undang-undang Islam', in Rosnah Majid, *Koleksi Temuramah Khas Tokoh-tokoh*, Kuala Lumpur: Utusan Publications and Distributors, 1985, pp. 248–84.

'A Vision for Malaysia', *Asiaweek*, 23 September 1983, pp. 36–7.

Interview with *Sinar Harapan*, reprinted as 'Menjadi Seorang Sasterawan Lebih Sulit dari Doktor', *Mingguan Malaysia*, 2 February 1986.

Rehman Rashid, 'One-on-one with the Premier': Part 1, 'Standing Tall in the Face of Opposition', *New Straits Times*, 4 July 1986; Part 2, 'Why I Took to Politics', *New Straits Times*, 5 July 1986; Part 3, 'Prime Minister Reveals His Hopes and Fears', *New Straits Times*, 6 July 1986.

Interview with *Asahi Shimbun*, reprinted as 'Situation Is Very Stable, Says Mahathir', *Straits Times*, 5 November 1987.

S. Jayasankaran, 'Premier in Power', *Malaysian Business*, 1 January 1988, pp. 5–11.

Interview over Radio and Television Malaysia, 18 February 1991; excerpts reprinted as 'We Are Masters of Ourselves: Mahathir', *Malaysian Business*, 1–15 March 1991, pp. 18–27.

Books

Abdullah Ahmad, *Issues in Malaysian Politics*, Singapore Institute of International Affairs Occasional Paper Series No. 7, Singapore: Heinemann Asia, 1988.

Adshead, Robin, *Mahathir of Malaysia*, London: Hibiscus Publishing Company, 1989.

Ahmad Shabery Cheek (ed.), *Cabaran Malaysia Tahun Lapan Puluhan*, Kuala Lumpur: Persatuan Sains Sosial Malaysia, 1989.

Alatas, Syed Hussein, *The Myth of the Lazy Native*, London: Frank Cass, 1977.

Alias Mohamed, *Malaysia's Islamic Opposition: Past, Present and Future*, Kuala Lumpur: Gateway Publishing House, 1991.

Aliran, *The Universalism of Islam*, Penang, 1979.

_____, *Reflections on the Malaysian Constitution*, Penang, 1987.

_____, *Issues of the Mahathir Years*, Penang, 1988.

Anderson, Benedict, *Imagined Communities: Reflections on the Origins and Spread of Nationalism*, London: Verso, 1983.

Arasaratnam, Sinnapah, *Indians in Malaysia and Singapore*, Kuala Lumpur: Oxford University Press, 1970.

Ashgar Khan (ed.), *Islam, Politics and the State*, Kuala Lumpur: Ikraq, 1986.

Bedlington, Stanley, *Malaysia and Singapore: The Building of New States*, Ithaca: Cornell University Press, 1978.

Bowring, Philip and Cottrell, Robert, *The Carrian File*, Hong Kong: Review Publishing Company, 1984.

Brugger, Bill and Jaensch, Dean, *Australian Politics: Theory and Practice*, Sydney: Allen and Unwin, 1985.

Business International, *Malaysia to 1980: Economic and Political Outlook for Business Planners*, Hong Kong, 1977.

Chamil Wariya, *UMNO Era Mahathir*, Petaling Jaya: Penerbit Fajar Bakti, 1988.

_____, *Dasar Luar Era Mahathir*, Petaling Jaya: Penerbit Fajar Bakti, 1989.

_____, *Pandangan Politik Era Mahathir*, Petaling Jaya: Penerbit Fajar Bakti, 1990.

———, *Politik dan Raja*, Petaling Jaya: Penerbit Fajar Bakti, 1992.

———, *UMNO Sabah: Mencabar dan Dicabar*, Petaling Jaya: Penerbit Fajar Bakti, 1992.

Chandra Muzaffar, *Protector?: An Analysis of the Concept and Practice of Loyalty in Leader-led Relationships within Malay Society*, Penang: Aliran, 1979.

———, *Freedom in Fetters: An Analysis of the State of Democracy in Malaysia*, Penang: Aliran, 1986.

———, *Islamic Resurgence in Malaysia*, Petaling Jaya: Penerbit Fajar Bakti, 1987.

———, *Challenges and Choices in Malaysian Politics and Society*, Penang: Aliran, 1989.

———, *The NEP: Development and Alternative Consciousness*, Penang: Aliran, 1989.

Cheah Boon Kheng, *A. Samad Ismail: Journalism and Politics*, Kuala Lumpur: Singamal Publishing Bureau, 1987.

Chung Kek Yoong, *Mahathir Administration: Leadership and Change in a Multiracial Society*, Petaling Jaya: Pelanduk Publications, 1987.

Committee Against Repression in the Pacific and Asia, *Tangled Web: Dissent, Deterrence and the 27 October 1987 Crackdown in Malaysia*, Haymarket, NSW: CARPA, 1988.

Crouch, Harold, *Malaysia's 1982 Election*, Singapore: Institute of Southeast Asian Studies, 1982.

Crouch, Harold; Lee Kam Hing; and Ong, Michael (eds.), *Malaysian Politics and the 1978 Election*, Kuala Lumpur: Oxford University Press, 1980.

Das, K., *The Musa Dilemma*, Kuala Lumpur: K. Das, 1986.

Das, K. and SUARAM (eds.), *The White Paper on the October Affair and the Why? Papers*, Kuala Lumpur: SUARAM, 1989.

Enloe, Cynthia, *Ethnic Soldiers: State Security in a Divided Society*, Harmondsworth: Penguin, 1980.

Erikson, Erik H., *Young Man Luther*, New York: W. W. Norton, 1958.

Faaland, Just; Parkinson, J. R.; and Rais Saniman, *Growth and Ethnic Inequality: Malaysia's New Economic Policy*, Kuala Lumpur: Dewan Bahasa dan Pustaka in association with Chr. Michelson Institute, Norway, 1990.

Fan Yew Teng, *If We Love This Country ...*, Kuala Lumpur: Egret Publications, 1988.

———, *The UMNO Drama: Power Struggles in Malaysia*, Kuala Lumpur: Egret Publications, 1989.

Fisk, E. K. and Osman-Rani, H. (eds.), *The Political Economy of Malaysia*, Kuala Lumpur: Oxford University Press, 1982.

Funston, John, *Malay Politics in Malaysia: A Study of the United Malays National Organisation and Parti Islam*, Kuala Lumpur: Heinemann Asia, 1980.

Gale, Bruce, *Musa Hitam: A Political Biography*, Petaling Jaya: Eastern Universities Press, 1982.

_____, *Politics and Business: A Study of Multi-Purpose Holdings Berhad*, Singapore: Eastern Universities Press, 1985.

George, T. J. S., *Lee Kuan Yew's Singapore*, Singapore: Eastern Universities Press, 1984.

Ghani Ismail, *Razaleigh Lawan Musa, Pusingan Kedua, 1984*, Taiping: IJS Communications, 1983.

Gomez, Edmund Terence, *Politics in Business: UMNO's Corporate Investments*, Kuala Lumpur: Forum, 1990.

_____, *Money Politics in the Barisan Nasional*, Kuala Lumpur: Forum, 1991.

Gurmit Singh K. S., *Malaysian Societies: Friendly or Political*, Petaling Jaya: Environmental Protection Society Malaysia, 1984.

Hall, Stuart, *The Hard Road to Renewal: Thatcherism and the Crisis of the Left*, London: Verso, 1988.

Harun Derauh and Shafie Nor (eds.), *Mahathir: Cita-cita dan Pencapaian*, Kuala Lumpur: Berita Publishing, 1982.

Hasan Hj. Hamzah, *Mahathir: Great Malaysian Hero*, Kuala Lumpur: Mediaprint Publications, 1990.

Heng Pek Koon, *Chinese Politics in Malaysia: A History of the Malaysian Chinese Association*, Singapore: Oxford University Press, 1988.

Higgot, Richard and Robison, Richard (eds.), *Southeast Asia: Essays in the Political Economy of Structural Change*, London: Routledge and Kegan Paul, 1985.

Hiroshi Matsumoto and Sopiee, Noordin (eds.), *Into the Pacific Era: Southeast Asia and Its Place in the Pacific*, Kuala Lumpur: ISIS Malaysia and APIC, 1986.

Hofstadter, Richard, *The American Political Tradition*, New York: Vintage, 1948.

_____, *The Paranoid Style in American Politics and Other Essays*, New York: Vintage, 1967.

Horowitz, Donald, *Ethnic Groups in Conflict*, Berkeley: University of California Press, 1985.

Husin Ali, Syed, *Malay Peasant Society and Leadership*, Kuala Lumpur: Oxford University Press, 1975.

_____, *Kemiskinan dan Kelaparan Tanah di Kelantan: Satu Penyelidikan Sosio-ekonomi*, Petaling Jaya: Karangkraf, 1978.

_____, *The Malays: Their Problems and Their Future*, Kuala Lumpur: Heinemann Asia, 1983.

——, *Isu Raja dan Pindaan Perlembagaan*, 2nd edn., Petaling Jaya: S. Husin Ali, 1993.

—— (ed.), *Ethnicity, Class and Development in Malaysia*, Kuala Lumpur: Malaysian Social Science Association, 1984, pp. 356–82.

Ibrahim Mahmood, *Sejarah Perjuangan Bangsa Melayu*, Kuala Lumpur: Pustaka Antara, 1981.

INSAN, *BMF: The People's Black Paper*, Kuala Lumpur, 1986.

Institute of Strategic and International Studies, *The Bonding of a Nation: Federalism and Territorial Integration in Malaysia*, Kuala Lumpur: ISIS Malaysia, 1986.

——, *Malaysia: Past, Present and Future*, Kuala Lumpur: ISIS Malaysia, 1987.

Ionescu, Ghita and Gellner, Ernest (eds.), *Populism: Its Meanings and National Characteristics*, London: Weidenfeld and Nicolson, 1970.

Ismail Kassim, *Race, Politics and Moderation: A Study in the Malaysian Electoral Process*, Singapore: Times Books International, 1979.

Jenkins, Peter, *Mrs Thatcher's Revolution: The Ending of the Socialist Era*, London: Jonathan Cape, 1987.

Jesudason, James V., *Ethnicity and the Economy: The State, Chinese Business, and Multinationals in Malaysia*, Singapore: Oxford University Press, 1989.

Jomo, K. S., *A Question of Class: Capital, the State, and Uneven Development in Malaya*, Singapore: Oxford University Press, 1986; 2nd edn., New York: Monthly Review Press and Journal of Contemporary Asia Publishers, 1988.

——, *Beyond 1990: Considerations for a National Development Strategy*, Kuala Lumpur: Institute of Advanced Studies, University of Malaya, 1989.

——, *Growth and Structural Change in the Malaysian Economy*, London: Macmillan, 1990.

——, *The Way Forward?: The Political Economy of Development Policy Reform in Malaysia*, Kuala Lumpur: Institute of Advanced Studies, University of Malaya, 1993.

—— (ed.), *Mahathir's Economic Policies*, 2nd edn., Kuala Lumpur: Institute of Social Analysis, 1989.

—— (ed.), *Undermining Tin: The Decline of Malaysian Pre-eminence*, Sydney: Transnational Corporations Research Project, University of Sydney, 1990.

Jomo, K. S. and Ishak Shari, *Development Policies and Income Inequality in Peninsular Malaysia*, Kuala Lumpur: Institute of Advanced Studies, University of Malaya, 1986.

Kahn, Joel S. and Loh, Francis Kok Wah (eds.), *Fragmented Vision: Culture and Politics in Contemporary Malaysia*, Sydney: Asian Studies Association of Australia in association with Allen and Unwin, 1992.

Kanapathy, V. et al., *The Mahathir Era: Contributions to National Economic Development*, Petaling Jaya: International Investment Consultants, 1989.

Kassim Ahmad, *Universiti Kedua: Kisah Tahanan di bawah ISA*, Petaling Jaya: Media Intelek, 1983.

Kessler, Clive, *Islam in a Malay State: Kelantan, 1838–1969*, Ithaca: Cornell University Press, 1978.

Khong Kim Hoong, *Malaysia's General Election, 1990: Continuity, Change and Ethnic Politics*, Research Notes and Discussion Papers No. 74, Singapore: Institute of Southeast Asian Studies, 1991.

Khoo Kay Kim (ed.), *Beberapa Aspek Sejarah Kedah*, Kuala Lumpur: Persatuan Sejarah Malaysia, 1983.

_____, *Malay Society: Transformation and Democratisation*, Petaling Jaya: Pelanduk Publications, 1991.

Khor Kok Peng, *The Malaysian Economy: Structures and Dependence*, Penang: Institut Masyarakat, 1983.

_____, *Recession and the Malaysian Economy*, Penang: Institut Masyarakat, 1983.

Kua Kia Soong, *The Chinese Schools of Malaysia: A Protean Saga*, Kuala Lumpur: United Chinese School Committees Association of Malaysia, 1985.

_____, *445 Days behind the Wire: An Account of the October 1987 ISA Detentions*, Kuala Lumpur: Resource and Research Centre, Selangor Chinese Assembly Hall, 1989.

Lal, Victor, *Fiji: Coups in Paradise*, London: Zed Books, 1990.

Lasch, Christopher, *The New Radicalism in America, 1889–1963: The Intellectual as a Social Type*, New York: Vintage, 1965.

Lawyers Committee for Human Rights, *Malaysia: Assault on the Judiciary*, New York, 1990.

Leigh, Michael, *The Rising Moon: Political Change in Sarawak*, Kuala Lumpur: Antara, 1988.

Leys, Colin, *Politics in Britain: An Introduction*, London: Heinemann, 1983.

Lim Kit Siang, *Malaysia: Crisis of Identity*, Petaling Jaya: Democratic Action Party, 1986.

_____, *Prelude to Operation Lalang*, Petaling Jaya: Democratic Action Party, 1990.

Lim Lin Lean and Chee Peng Lim (eds.), *The Malaysian Economy at the Crossroads: Policy Adjustment or Structural Transformation*, Kuala Lumpur: Malaysian Economic Association and Organisational Resources, 1984.

Lim Mah Hui, *Ownership and Control of the One Hundred Largest Corporations in Malaysia*, Kuala Lumpur: Oxford University Press, 1980.

Loh, Francis Kok Wah, *Beyond the Tin Mines: Coolies, Squatters and New Villagers in the Kinta Valley, Malaysia, c.1880–1980*, Singapore: Oxford University Press, 1988.

Malaysia, *Dewan Ra'ayat, Parliamentary Debates*, Second Parliament, 1964–9.

Malaysia, *Second Malaysia Plan, 1971–1975*, Kuala Lumpur: Government Printers, 1971.

———, *Mid-Term Review of the Fourth Malaysia Plan, 1981–1985*, Kuala Lumpur: Government Printers, 1984.

———, *Sixth Malaysia Plan, 1991–1995*, Kuala Lumpur: Government Printers, 1991.

Malaysia, Ministry of Information, *Profile of Dato' Seri Dr Mahathir Mohamad*, Kuala Lumpur: Federal Department of Information, 1982.

Marina Yusoff, *Time for Change*, Kuala Lumpur: Champ Press, 1990.

Marquand, David, *The Unprincipled Society: New Demands and Old Politics*, London: Fontana Press, 1988.

Marx, Karl, *Capital*, Vol. 1, New York: International Publishers, 1967.

———, *The Eighteenth Brumaire of Louis Bonaparte*, New York: International Publishers, 1977.

Mauzy, Diane K., *Barisan Nasional: Coalition Government in Malaysia*, Kuala Lumpur: Marican and Sons, 1983.

Mead, Ronald, *Malaysia's National Language Policy and the Legal System*, Yale University Southeast Asia Studies Monograph Series No. 30, New Haven, 1988.

Means, Gordon P., *Malaysian Politics: The Second Generation*, Singapore: Oxford University Press, 1991.

Mehmet, Ozay, *Development in Malaysia: Poverty, Wealth and Trusteeship*, London: Croom Helm, 1986.

———, *Islamic Identity and Development: Studies of the Islamic Periphery*, Kuala Lumpur: Forum, 1990.

Miller, Harry, *Prince and Premier*, London: George G. Harrap in association with Donald Moore, Singapore, 1959.

Minchin, James, *No Man Is an Island: A Study of Singapore's Lee Kuan Yew*, Sydney: Allen and Unwin, 1986.

Mohammed Amin and Caldwell, Malcolm, *Malaya: The Making of a Neocolony*, Nottingham: Spokesman Books, 1977.

Mohammed Ayoob, *The Politics of Islamic Reassertion*, New York: St. Martin's Press, 1981.

Morais, J. Victor, *Hussein Onn: A Tryst with Destiny*, Singapore: Times Books International, 1981.

———, *Mahathir: A Profile in Courage*, Singapore: Eastern Universities Press, 1982.

_____, *Anwar Ibrahim: Resolute in Leadership*, Kuala Lumpur: Arenabuku, 1983.

Muhammad Ikmail Said and Saravanamuttu, Johan (eds.), *Images of Malaysia*, Kuala Lumpur: Persatuan Sains Sosial, 1991.

Muhammad Syukri Salleh, *An Islamic Approach to Rural Development—The Arqam Way*, London: ASOIB International, 1992.

Mustafa bin Ali Mohamed, *Mahathir Mohamad*, Petaling Jaya: Pelanduk Publications, 1986.

Mustafa Johan Abdullah and Shamsulbahriah Ku Ahmad (eds.), *Penswastaan: Tanggungjawab Sosial atau Untung Kapitalis*, Kuala Lumpur: Ikraq, 1988.

Nagata, Judith, *The Reflowering of Malaysian Islam: Modern Religious Radicals and Their Roots*, Vancouver: University of British Columbia Press, 1984.

Parti Gerakan Rakyat Malaysia, *The National Economic Policy—1990 and Beyond*, Kuala Lumpur, 1984.

_____, *Into the Mainstream of Development*, Kuala Lumpur, 1986.

Pathmanathan, Murugesu and Lazarus, David (eds.), *Winds of Change: The Mahathir Impact on Malaysia's Foreign Policy*, Kuala Lumpur: Eastview Productions, 1984.

Perpustakaan Negara Malaysia, *Bibliografi Dr Mahathir*, Siri Bibliografi Rujukan No. 35/1990, Kuala Lumpur: Perpustakaan Negara Malaysia, 1990.

Rahmanmat, *Benarkah Dr Mahathir Pembela Bangsa Melayu?*, Kuala Lumpur: Golden Books, 1982.

Raja Aziz Addruse, *Conduct Unbecoming*, Kuala Lumpur: Walrus, 1990.

Ramanathan, Sankaran and Mohd. Hamdan Adnan, *Malaysia's 1986 General Election: The Urban–Rural Dichotomy*, Occasional Paper No. 83, Singapore: Institute of Southeast Asian Studies, 1988.

Ranjit Gill, *Razaleigh: An Unending Quest*, Petaling Jaya: Pelanduk Publications, 1986.

Ratnam, K. J., *Communalism and the Political Process in Malaya*, Singapore: University of Malaya Press, 1965.

Rodan, Gary, *The Political Economy of Singapore's Industrialisation: National State and International Capital*, Kuala Lumpur: Forum, 1989.

Rodinson, Maxime, *Islam and Capitalism*, translated from the French by Brian Pearce, New York: Pantheon, 1973.

_____, *Marxism and the Muslim World*, London: Zed Press, 1981.

Rodney, Walter, *How Europe Underdeveloped Africa*, London: Bogle-L'Ouverture Publications, 1972.

Roff, W. R., *The Origins of Malay Nationalism*, Kuala Lumpur: University of Malaya Press, 1974; reprinted Kuala Lumpur: Oxford University Press, 1995.

Rosnah Majid, *Koleksi Temuramah Khas Tokoh-tokoh*, Kuala Lumpur: Utusan Publications and Distributors, 1985.

Sahabat Alam Malaysia, *Papan Radioactive Waste Dump Controversy*, Penang, 1984.

Said, Edward, *Orientalism*, Harmondsworth: Peregrine, 1985.

Salleh Abas, *The Role of the Independent Judiciary*, Kuala Lumpur: Promarketing Publications, 1989.

Senu Abdul Rahman (ed.), *Revolusi Mental*, Kuala Lumpur: Utusan Melayu, 1971.

Shafruddin B. H., *The Federal Factor in the Government and Politics of Peninsular Malaysia*, Singapore: Oxford University Press, 1987.

Shaharuddin Maaruf, *Malay Ideas on Development: From Feudal Lord to Capitalist*, Singapore: Times Books International, 1988.

Shamsul A. B., *RMK: Tujuan dan Pelaksanaannya. Satu Tinjauan Teoritis*, Kuala Lumpur: Dewan Bahasa dan Pustaka, 1977.

———, *From British to Bumiputera Rule*, Singapore: Institute of Southeast Asian Studies, 1986.

Shaw, William, *Tun Razak: His Life and Times*, Kuala Lumpur: Longman Malaysia, 1976.

Sopiee, Mohamed Noordin, *From Malayan Union to Singapore Separation: Political Unification in the Malaysian Region, 1945–65*, Kuala Lumpur: University of Malaya Press, 1976.

Sopiee, Mohamed Noordin; Chew Lay See; and Lim Siang Jin (eds.), *ASEAN at the Crossroads: Obstacles, Options and Opportunities in Economic Cooperation*, Kuala Lumpur: Institute of Strategic and International Studies (ISIS), n.d.

Stenson, Michael, *Industrial Conflict in Malaya: Prelude to the Communist Revolt of 1948*, Kuala Lumpur: Oxford University Press, 1970.

———, *Class, Race and Colonialism in West Malaysia: The Indian Case*, St Lucia: University of Queensland Press, 1980.

Steven, Bob, *Japan's New Imperialism*, London: Macmillan, 1990.

Stockwell, Anthony J., *British Policy and Malay Politics during the Malayan Union Experiment, 1942–48*, Malaysian Branch of the Royal Asiatic Society Monograph No. 8, Kuala Lumpur, 1979.

Strauch, Judith, *Chinese Village Politics in the Malaysian State*, Cambridge: Harvard University Press, 1981.

Tan Chee Khoon, *Without Fear or Favour*, Singapore: Eastern Universities Press, 1984.

———, *Sabah: A Triumph for Democracy*, Petaling Jaya: Pelanduk Publications, 1986.

Tengku Razaleigh Hamzah, *Mengapa Saya Tentang Mahathir*, Petaling Jaya: AZ Distributors, 1989.

Tibi, Bassam, *Islam and the Cultural Accommodation of Social Change*, translated from the German by Clare Krojzl, Boulder: Westview Press, 1990.

Tunku Abdul Rahman, *Something to Remember*, Singapore: Eastern Universities Press, 1983.

Turner, Bryan S., *Weber and Islam: A Critical Study*, London: Routledge and Kegan Paul, 1974.

Vasil, R. K., *Politics in a Plural Society: A Study of Non-communal Political Parties in West Malaysia*, Kuala Lumpur: Oxford University Press, 1971.

_____, *Tan Chee Khoon: An Elder Statesman*, Petaling Jaya: Pelanduk Publications, 1987.

Von Vorys, Karl, *Democracy without Consensus: Communalism and Political Stability in Malaysia*, Princeton: Princeton University Press, 1975.

Wang Gungwu, *Community and Nation*, Singapore: Heinemann, 1981.

Williams, Peter Alderidge, *Judicial Misconduct*, Petaling Jaya: Pelanduk Publications, 1990.

Worsley, Peter, *The Third World*, London: Weidenfeld and Nicolson, 1974.

Yoshihara Kunio, *The Rise of Ersatz Capitalism in South-East Asia*, Singapore: Oxford University Press, 1988.

Young, Hugo, *One of Us: A Biography of Margaret Thatcher*, rev. edn., London: Pan Books in association with Macmillan, 1990.

Zainah Anwar, *Islamic Revivalism in Malaysia: Dakwah among the Students*, Petaling Jaya: Pelanduk Publications, 1987.

Zakry Abadi, *Mahathir 'Machiavelli' Malaysia?*, Kuala Lumpur: Sarjana Enterprise, 1990.

Articles

Ahmad Kamar, 'The Formation of Saberkas', in Asmah Haji Omar (ed.), *Darulaman: Essays on Linguistic, Cultural and Socio-economic Aspects of the Malaysian State of Kedah*, Kuala Lumpur: University of Malaya Press, 1979, pp. 179–84.

Amsden, Alice, 'The State and Taiwan's Economic Development', in Peter Evans, Dietrich Rueschemeyer, and Theda Skocpol (eds.), *Bringing the State Back In*, Cambridge: Cambridge University Press, 1985, pp. 78–106.

Anderson, Benedict O'Gorman, 'A Time of Darkness and a Time of Light: Transposition in Early Indonesian Nationalist Thought', in Anthony Reid and David Marr (eds.), *Perceptions of the Past in Southeast Asia*, Singapore: Heinemann Asia for Asian Studies Association of Australia, 1979, pp. 219–48.

Arasaratnam, Sinnapah, 'Indian Society of Malaysia and Its Leaders: Trends in Leadership and Ideology among Malaysian Indians', *Journal of Southeast Asian History*, 13, 2 (1982): 236–51.

Brennan, Martin, 'Class, Politics and Race in Modern Malaysia', in

Richard Higgot and Richard Robison (eds.), *Southeast Asia: Essays in the Political Economy of Structural Change*, London: Routledge and Kegan Paul, 1985, pp. 93–127.

Cham, B. N., 'Class and Communal Conflict in Malaysia', *Journal of Contemporary Asia*, 5, 4 (1975): 446–61.

Cheah Boon Kheng, 'The Erosion of Ideological Hegemony and Royal Power and the Rise of Postwar Malay Nationalism, 1945–46', *Journal of Southeast Asian History*, 19, 1 (March 1988): 1–26.

Colquhon, Keith, 'At Bay: A Survey of Malaysia', *Economist*, 31 January 1987, pp. 3–18.

Craig, James, 'Privatization in Malaysia: Present Trends and Future Prospects', in Paul Cook and Colin Kirkpatrick (eds.), *Privatization in Less Developed Countries*, Brighton: Harvester Press, 1988, pp. 248–58.

Crouch, Harold, 'Authoritarian Trends, the UMNO Split and the Limits to State Power', in Joel S. Kahn and Francis Loh Kok Wah (eds.), *Fragmented Vision: Culture and Politics in Contemporary Malaysia*, Sydney: Asian Studies Association of Australia in association with Allen and Unwin, 1992, pp. 21–43.

Drucker, Peter, 'The Changed World Economy', *Foreign Affairs*, 64, 4 (Spring 1986): 768–91.

Fatimah Halim, 'Capital, Labour and the State: The West Malaysian Case', *Journal of Contemporary Asia*, 12, 3 (1982): 259–80.

——, 'The Transformation of the Malaysian State', *Journal of Contemporary Asia*, 20, 1 (1990): 64–88.

Fitzgerald, F. Scott, 'The Crack-up', in F. Scott Fitzgerald, *The Crack-up with Other Pieces and Stories*, Harmondsworth: Penguin, 1979.

Fromm, Erich, 'Psychoanalytic Characterology and Its Relevance for Social Psychology', in Erich Fromm, *The Crisis of Psychoanalysis*, Greenwich, Conn.: Fawcett, pp. 163–87.

Funston, John, 'Writings on May 13', *Akademika*, 6 (1975): 1–16.

——, 'The Politics of Islamic Reassertion: Malaysia', in Mohammed Ayoob (ed.), *The Politics of Islamic Reassertion*, New York: St. Martin's Press, 1981, pp. 165–89.

——, 'Challenge and Response in Malaysia: The UMNO Crisis and the Mahathir Style', *Pacific Review*, 1, 4 (1988): 363–73.

Hagan, Stephanie, 'Race, Politics and the Coup in Fiji', *Bulletin of Concerned Asian Scholars*, 19, 4 (October–December 1987): 2–18.

Harding, A. J., 'Turbulence in the Land below the Wind: Sabah's Constitutional Crisis of 1985–86', *Journal of Commonwealth and Comparative Politics*, XXIX, 1 (March 1991): 86–101.

Hing Ai Yun, 'The Development and Transformation of Wage Labour in West Malaysia', *Journal of Contemporary Asia*, 15, 2 (1985): 139–71.

Hirschman, Charles, 'Development and Inequality in Malaysia: From Puthucheary to Mehmet', *Pacific Affairs*, 62, 1 (Spring 1989): 72–81.

Ho Khai Leong, 'Aggrandizement of Prime Minister's Power: The Transformation of the Office of the Prime Minister in Malaysia', *Internationales Asienforum*, 23, 1–2 (1992): 227–43.

Hofstadter, Richard, 'North America', in Ghita Ionescu and Ernest Gellner (eds.), *Populism: Its Meanings and National Characteristics*, London: Weidenfeld and Nicolson, 1970, pp. 9–27.

James, Kenneth, 'Malaysia in 1987: Challenges in the System', in Institute of Southeast Asian Studies, *Southeast Asian Affairs, 1988*, Singapore: ISEAS, pp. 153–69.

Jomo, K. S. and Ahmad Shabery Cheek, 'The Politics of Malaysia's Islamic Resurgence', *Third World Quarterly*, 10, 2 (April 1988): 843–68.

Kershaw, Roger, 'Anglo-Malaysian Relations: Old Roles versus New Rules', *International Affairs*, 59, 4 (Autumn 1983): 629–48.

———, 'Malay Monarchy since Yahya Petra: Riding for a Fall?', *Contemporary Review*, 245, 1424 (September 1984): 113–20.

———, 'Within the Family: The Limits of Doctrinal Differentiation in the Malaysian Ruling Party Election of 1987', *Review of Indonesian and Malaysian Affairs*, 23 (1989): 125–93.

Kessler, Clive, 'Archaism and Modernity: Contemporary Malay Political Culture', in Joel S. Kahn and Francis Loh Kok Wah (eds.), *Fragmented Vision: Culture and Politics in Contemporary Malaysia*, Sydney: Asian Studies Association of Australia in association with Allen and Unwin, 1992, pp. 133–55.

Khong Kim Hoong, 'Results of the 1986 Malaysian General Elections', *Review of Malaysian and Indonesian Affairs*, 20, 2 (Summer 1986): 186–215.

Khoo Khay Jin, 'The Grand Vision: Mahathir and Modernization', in Joel S. Kahn and Francis Loh Kok Wah (eds.), *Fragmented Vision: Culture and Politics in Contemporary Malaysia*, Sydney: Asian Studies Association of Australia in association with Allen and Unwin, 1992, pp. 44–76.

Lim Mah Hui, 'Ethnic and Class Relations in Malaysia', *Journal of Contemporary Asia*, 10, 1–2 (1980): 13–54.

Lim Mah Hui and Canak, William, 'The Political Economy of State Policies in Malaysia', *Journal of Contemporary Asia*, 11, 2 (1981): 208–24.

Loh, Francis Kok Wah, 'Modernisation, Cultural Revival and Counter-Hegemony: The Kadazans of Sabah in the 1980s', in Joel S. Kahn and Francis Loh Kok Wah (eds.), *Fragmented Vision: Culture and Politics in Contemporary Malaysia*, Sydney: Asian Studies Association of Australia in association with Allen and Unwin, 1992, pp. 225–53.

Lowe, Vincent, 'Redefining the "Constitutionality" of the Monarchy: The

1983 Constitutional Amendment Crisis in Malaysia', *Kajian Malaysia*, II, 2 (December 1984): 1–15.

Machado, Kit G., 'Malaysian Cultural Relations with Japan and South Korea in the 1980s: Looking East', *Asian Survey*, XXVII, 6 (June 1987): 638–60.

——, 'Japanese Transnational Corporations in Malaysia's State Sponsored Heavy Industrialization Drive: The HICOM Automobile and Steel Projects', *Pacific Affairs*, 62, 4 (Winter 1989–90): 504–31.

Mansur bin Ismail, 'Sejarah Perkembangan Government English School Alur Star, 1908–1935', in Khoo Kay Kim (ed.), *Beberapa Aspek Sejarah Kedah*, Kuala Lumpur: Persatuan Sejarah Malaysia, 1983, pp. 83–93.

Marican, Malek, 'The NEP from a Private Sector Perspective', Paper presented at the Seminar 'Dasar Ekonomi Baru Selepas 1990: Peranan Sektor Korporat Awam', Kuala Lumpur, 24–26 March 1987.

Mauzy, Diane K., 'Malaysia in 1986: The Ups and Downs of Stock Market Politics', *Asian Survey*, XXVII, 2 (February 1987): 231–41.

Mauzy, Diane K. and Milne, R. S., 'The Mahathir Recovery in Malaysia', *Current History*, 89, 545 (March 1990): 113–26.

Milne, R. S., 'Politics, Ethnicity and Class in Guyana and Malaysia', *Social and Economic Studies*, 26, 1 (1977): 18–37.

——, 'Malaysia—Beyond the New Economic Policy', *Asian Survey*, 26, 12 (December 1986): 1364–82.

Milner, A. C., 'Rethinking Islamic Fundamentalism in Malaysia', *Review of Indonesian and Malaysian Affairs*, 20, 2 (Summer 1986): 48–69.

Mohd. Ismail Ahmad, 'The Economic Upturn in Malaysia', in Institute of Southeast Asian Studies, *Southeast Asian Affairs, 1989*, Singapore: ISEAS, 1989, pp. 236–46.

Nairn, Tom, 'The Modern Janus', *New Left Review*, 94 (1975): 3–29.

Nathan, K. S., 'Malaysia in 1988: The Politics of Survival', *Asian Survey*, XXIX, 2 (February 1989): 129–44.

Radin Soernarno, 'Malay Nationalism 1896–1941', *Journal of Southeast Asian History*, 1, 1 (1960): 1–33.

Rasiah, Rajah, 'Reorganisation of Production in the Semi-conductor Industry and Its Impact on Penang', in Muhammad Ikmal Said and Johan Saravanamuttu (eds.), *Images of Malaysia*, Kuala Lumpur: Persatuan Sains Sosial Malaysia, 1991, pp. 201–23.

Ratnam, K. J. and Milne, R. S., 'The 1969 Parliamentary Election in West Malaysia', *Pacific Affairs*, 43, 2 (Summer 1970): 203–27.

Rawlings, H. F., 'The Malaysian Constitutional Crisis of 1983', *International and Comparative Law Quarterly*, 35, 2 (April 1986): 237–54.

Rustam Sani and Mustafa Mohamed Najimuddin, 'Pilihanraya Umum

1990: Mandat Baru, Cabaran Baru', *Dewan Masyarakat*, November 1990, pp. 24–36.

Saravanamuttu, Johan, 'The State, Authoritarianism and Industrialisation: Reflections on the Malaysian Case', *Kajian Malaysia*, V, 2 (December 1987): 43–75.

Shafruddin Hashim, 'Malaysia 1991: Consolidation, Challenges and New Directions', in Institute of Southeast Asian Studies, *Southeast Asian Affairs, 1992*, Singapore: ISEAS, 1992, pp. 183–201.

Shamsul A. B., 'The "Battle Royal": The UMNO Elections of 1987', in Institute of Southeast Asian Studies, *Southeast Asian Affairs, 1988*, Singapore: ISEAS, 1988, pp. 170–88.

Sivanandan, A., 'Sri Lanka: Racism and the Politics of Underdevelopment', *Race and Class*, 26, 1 (1984): 1–37.

Sothi Rachagan, S., 'The Apportionment of Seats in the House of Representatives', in Zakaria Haji Ahmad (ed.), *Government and Politics of Malaysia*, Singapore: Oxford University Press, 1987, pp. 56–70.

_____, 'The 1986 Parliamentary Elections in Peninsular Malaysia', in Institute of Southeast Asian Studies, *Southeast Asian Affairs, 1987*, Singapore: ISEAS, 1987, pp. 217–35.

Tan Liok Ee, 'The Rhetoric of *Bangsa* and *Minzu*: Community and Nation in Tension, the Malay Peninsula, 1900–55', Monash University, Centre for Southeast Asian Studies, Working Paper No. 52, Clayton, 1983.

_____, 'Dongjiaozong and the Challenge to Cultural Hegemony, 1951–1987', in Joel S. Kahn and Francis Loh Kok Wah (eds.), *Fragmented Vision: Culture and Politics in Contemporary Malaysia*, Sydney: Asian Studies Association of Australia in association with Allen and Unwin, 1992, pp. 181–201.

Tan, Simon, 'The Rise of State Authoritarianism in Malaysia', *Bulletin of Concerned Asian Scholars*, 22, 3 (July–September 1990): 32–42.

Thompson, E. P., 'Time, Work-Discipline, and Industrial Capitalism', *Past and Present*, 38 (1967): 56–97.

Van Fossen, Anthony B., 'Two Military Coups in Fiji', *Bulletin of Concerned Asian Scholars*, 19, 4 (October–December 1987): 19–31.

Wan Abdul Manan Wan Muda, 'The Seventy Million Population Policy: Implications for Health, Nutrition and Aging', in Muhammad Ikmail Said and Johan Saravanamuttu (eds.), *Images of Malaysia*, Kuala Lumpur: Persatuan Sains Sosial, 1991, pp. 224–61.

Wiles, Peter, 'A Syndrome, not a Doctrine', in Ghita Ionescu and Ernest Gellner (eds.), *Populism: Its Meanings and National Characteristics*, London: Weidenfeld and Nicolson, 1970, pp. 166–79.

Worsley, Peter, 'The Concept of Populism', in Ghita Ionescu and Ernest Gellner (eds.), *Populism: Its Meanings and National Characteristics*, London: Weidenfeld and Nicolson, 1970, pp. 212–50.

Zawawi Ibrahim, 'Malay Peasants and Proletarian Consciousness', *Bulletin of Concerned Asian Scholars*, 15, 4 (1983): 39–55.

Newspapers and Magazines

Aliran Monthly, Malaysia
Asian Wall Street Journal, Hong Kong
Asiaweek, Hong Kong
Berita Harian, Malaysia
Business Times, Malaysia
Correspondent, Hong Kong
Dewan Masyarakat, Malaysia
The Economist, United Kingdom
Era, Malaysia
Far Eastern Economic Review, Hong Kong
Guardian, United Kingdom
Inquiry, United Kingdom
Malaysian Business, Malaysia
Malaysian Digest, Malaysia
Mastika, Malaysia
Mimbar Sosialis, Malaysia
National Echo, Malaysia
New Straits Times, Malaysia
Singapore Monitor, Singapore
Star, Malaysia
Straits Times, Singapore
Sunday Mail, Malaysia
Time, United States
Utusan Malaysia, Malaysia
Watan, Malaysia

Index

ABDUL AZIZ BIN ISHAK, 18, 298, 320
Abdul Hadi Awang, 224–6, 302
Abdul Kadir Sheikh Fadzir, 270
Abdul Rahman, Tunku, 17, 22–5, 175, 201, 203, 263, 267–9, 272–3, 275, 290, 298, 300, 312, 320, 322–3
Abdul Razak, Tun, 17, 23, 25, 27, 35, 103, 161, 261, 269, 272–3, 298, 300
Abdullah Ahmad, 18, 280, 313
Abdullah Badawi, 263, 265, 270–1, 339
ABIM, *see* Angkatan Belia Islam Malaysia
Abu Hassan, 263
Abu Talib Othman, 257, 291
Adibah Amin, 3
Adshead, Robin, 5, 20, 24, 183
Afghanistan, 78
African countries, 76
Agriculture, 336
Ahmad Boestamam, 17
Ahmad Noordin, 231, 257
Ajib Ahmad, 263, 270
Alatas, Syed Hussein, 11, 112, 273, 309
Aliran Kesedaran Negara, 161, 235, 277–8, 286, 301
Alliance, 18, 22
Angkatan Belia Islam Malaysia (ABIM), 37, 160–1, 187, 225
Angkatan Perpaduan Ummah (APU), 2, 324, 326
Antarctica, 75–6, 97
Anti-Westernism, 42–7, 57–65, 75–81, 199, 332
Anwar Ibrahim, 207, 226, 263, 270–1, 273, 282, 302, 309
APU, *see* Angkatan Perpaduan Ummah
ARE, *see* Asian Rare Earth Sdn. Bhd.
ASEAN, 74
Asia–Pacific Economic Cooperation Summit, 332
Asia–Pacific Economic Council, 332
Asian Rare Earth Sdn. Bhd. (ARE), 223–4, 252, 278
Asian Wall Street Journal, 277, 288, 312
Atomic Energy Licensing Board, 224
Australia, 332
Authoritarianism, 261–303, 325
Azlan Shah, Sultan, 289

BANGSA MALAYSIA, 331, 334, 338
Bank Bumiputra, 209–12, 214–15, 231
Bank Islam Malaysia Berhad, 177–9
Bank Negara, 217–18
Bank Rakyat, 211
Bank Simpanan Nasional, 214
Barisan Nasional, 35, 104–5, 161, 221, 223, 232, 235–7, 274, 281–2, 286, 324–6, 332
Basir Ismail, 214
Berita Harian, 207
Berjaya, 219–23
Berthelsen, John, 277, 288
BMF, *see* Bumiputra Malaysia Finance Limited
Bowring, Philip, 3, 56, 80
British, 33, 43, 47, 90, 92
British–Malaysian Industry and Trade Association, 90
Bumiputera, 104–6, 128, 139, 334–5
Bumiputera economic congresses, 108, 126

Bumiputra Malaysia Finance Limited (BMF), 209–12, 231, 233–4
Burhanuddin al-Helmy, 17
Business: Malay participation, 28–9, 337–8
'Buy British Last' policy, 54–7, 78, 332
By-elections, 323–4

CABINET, 22, 26, 270
Capital flight, 137
Carrian Group, 209–11, 234
Challenge, The, 11, 13, 35–48, 54, 61, 65, 72, 88, 182; alarmist tone, 36; criticisms of Malays, 36, 42, 72; on dangers from a West in decline, 11, 43–7; on East–West relations, 45–7, 65; on Islam, 11, 37–41, 162; on materialism, 38–9; on nationalization, 55; as a transitional point in the evolution of Mahathir's nationalism, 11, 42, 47–8
Chamil Wariya, 21, 75
Chan Chin Cheung, 214
Chandra Muzaffar, 161, 243
C. H. E. Det, 12–13, 81–8, 199–200, 205; categories of writings, 82; chronology of articles in the *Sunday Times*, 81–3; journey from Kedah to Singapore, 87; pseudonym of Mahathir, 12, 81; as a 'sophisticated town Malay', 87–8; 'world of C. H. E. Det', 12, 81–8; writings: on Malay customs and social life, 82–3; on the problems of the Malays, 83–4; on political issues, 84–5
Chen Man Hin, 294, 317
China, 75, 135
Chinese, 18–21, 28, 31–3, 87–8, 109, 137, 205, 226–7; ambivalence towards the New Economic Policy, 105, 142, 216; business–politics mix, 205, 216–17, 218–19; compared to Malays in Singapore, 85, 87–8; criticism of Industrial Co-ordination Act, 137; 142; dilemma, 274, 279, 281–2; 'economic domination', 26, 31–3, 54, 85; in government after 1969 election, 21–2; losses through DTCs, 218; meeting at Thean Hou Temple, 282–3; stereotypes of, 28, 31–4, 109; urban electorate, 235–6, 238–9
Chinese Chamber of Commerce, 142, 282
Chinese schools, 281–2
CHOGM, *see* Commonwealth Heads of Government Meeting
Chooi Mun Sou, 231, 257
Chun Doo Hwan, 68
Chung Chin Man, 209
Civil rights, 275
Civil service, 29–30, 129–30, 180–2, 272–3, 337
Clad, James, 311
Commodities, 57–8, 61, 115–17, 324
Commonwealth, 62, 74–5, 78
Commonwealth Heads of Government Meeting (CHOGM), 4, 75, 78, 99, 332
Confederation of British Industry, 80
Congress of Unions of Employees in Public, Administrative and Civil Services (CUEPACS), 93
Constitution, 289
Constitution (Amendment) Bill 1983, 202–9
Corruption, 37, 272, 333
Court cases, 277–9, 287–9, 323
Crouch, Harold, 271
CUEPACS, *see* Congress of Unions of Employees in Public, Administrative and Civil Services

DAIM ZAINUDDIN, 128, 134, 214–15, 231, 233–4, 248, 263–5, 278, 306, 324–5
DAP, *see* Democratic Action Party
Darul Arqam, 37, 160–1, 186–7
Darwin, Charles, 31, 51, 169
Das, K., 3, 23, 74, 108
Democracy, 46, 261, 275–6
Democratic Action Party (DAP), 2,

232, 235–8, 282–5, 293, 323–4, 326
Deposit taking co-operatives (DTCs), 217–19, 231
Diplomacy, 74–81; Antarctica, 4, 75–6, 97; CHOGM, 4, 75, 78, 99, 332; dilemmas of the Third World, 76, 79, 88, 273; priorities, 74–5; Mahathir's style of, 78–9, 272; maverick stance, 79; Non-Aligned Movement, 74, 76, 80; trade and, 330; *vis-à-vis* superpowers, 75
Diversification, 115–16, 330
Dongjiaozong, 281–2
DTCs, *see* Deposit taking co-operatives
Dunlop, 56
Dutch, 33

EAST ASIAN ECONOMIC CAUCUS, 332
East Timor, 78
Economic growth, 324
Economic restructuring, 103–8
Eda Investments Limited, 210
Education, 39–40, 83–4, 86–7, 167–9
Education Ministry, 281–2
Elections: 1969, 18, 21–2; 1982, 205, 232; 1986, 231–9; 1990, 1–2, 325–7
Employees Provident Fund (EPF), 214–15, 231, 233
Environmental groups, 77, 235
Environmental Protection Society of Malaysia (EPSM), 253, 286
EPF, *see* Employees Provident Fund
EPSM, *see* Environmental Protection Society of Malaysia
Ethnic tension, 104–5, 280–6; Abdullah Ahmad's speech, 280; Bukit China, 279; Christian proselytization, 280–1; conversion of non-Malay minors to Islam, 279; deteriorating situation in 1987, 280; 'disunity' in Barisan Nasional, 274, 281–2; Kelab Sultan Suleiman rally, 283–6; mandarin oranges, 279; May 13 1969, 18, 22, 26, 103; mosque arson, 281; New Economic Policy related, 274, 279; non-Mandarin-educated teachers, 282; Operation Lalang, 284–7; *pendatang* statement, 280; polarization in the 1960s, 19–24; real and imagined slights, 274, 279; Thean Hou Temple meeting, 282–3; UMNO rally, 283–6
European Economic Community, 45

FADZIL NOOR, 224
Federation of Malaysian Manufacturers, 137
Fiji, 78
Finance Ministry, 214
Financial scandals, 209–19
Foreign exchange rates, 60, 325
Foreign investment, 55, 79, 118, 137–8, 140–2, 325
Foreign Investment Committee, 106
Foreign policy, 74–81
Free trade, 57–65, 69, 330, 332
Free Trade Zones, 35, 118–19

G-7, 60, 76
G-77, 76, 78
Gagasan Rakyat Malaysia, 2, 324, 326, 332
Gerakan Rakyat Malaysia, 232, 236–8, 282, 285, 312
Ghafar Baba, 233, 262–3, 269–70, 278, 282, 284, 286
Ghani Ismail, 304
Ghazali Shafie, 74, 223, 339
Government English School, Alor Star, 185, 196
Grand United Holdings, 216–17
Growth Industrial Holdings, 216
Guide for Small Businessmen, 11
Guthrie Corporation, 55–6, 130

HAMID OMAR, JUSTICE, 292–3
Hamzah Abu Samah, 137
Harris Salleh, 219–20
Harrisons and Crossfield, 92
Harun Hashim, Justice, 289–90

Harun Idris, 18, 211, 265, 298, 300, 305, 323, 338
Hasan Hj. Hamzah, 6
Hashim Ghani, 100
Hashim Shamsuddin, 211
Hatibudi, 278
Heavy Industries Corporation of Malaysia (HICOM), 119
HICOM, *see* Heavy Industries Corporation of Malaysia
Highway projects, 155
Ho, Bentley, 211
Home Affairs Ministry, 277
Hong Kong, 66
Hudud laws, 332, 341
Hussein Onn, Tun, 35, 212, 261–3, 266, 267, 272–3, 298, 300, 304

IBRAHIM JAAFAR, 211, 234
Ibrahim Mahmood, 227–8, 232
Ibrahim Yaakob, 17
Idris Shah, Sultan, 204
IIU, *see* International Islamic University
Immigration Department, 277
Industrial Co-ordination Act 1975, 106, 137, 140, 142, 156
Industrialization, 109, 117–24, 130, 328
Information Ministry, 5
INSAN, 286
Intellectuals, 161
Internal Security Act (ISA), 161, 232, 275, 284, 288
International Conference on Drug Abuse and Illicit Trafficking, 78
International Islamic University (IIU), 175–7
International Tin Council (ITC), 212
Investment Coordinating Committee, 214–15
ISA, *see* Internal Security Act
Ishak Shari, 105
Islam, 37–41, 52–3, 74, 159–74, 328
Islamic state, 161–2
Islamic Summit, 67, 77–8
Islamic Youth Force of Malaysia, *see* Angkatan Belia Islam Malaysia
Islamization policy, 174–81, 332–3
Ismail, Tun Dr, 17, 20, 23, 261, 269, 294
ITC, *see* International Tin Council

JALIL IBRAHIM, 210–11
Jamaat Tabligh, 160
Japan, 62, 66, 68–72, 95, 124, 135, 325
Japanese occupation, 86, 101
Jayasankaran, S., 3, 182
Jesudason, James V., 137
Jomo, K. S., 3, 105
Judiciary, 275, 286–94; Aliran case, 277–8, 289; Berthelsen case, 277, 288, assault on, 286–94; deregistration of UMNO, 290–1; independence of, 289; Karpal Singh's case, 289; Lord President's suspension, 292; Mahathir's interview with *Time*, 288, Mahathir's statement in relation to ISA amendment, 288; Papan case, 289; Supreme Court judges' suspension, 292–3; Team A–Team B split, 287; UEM case, 287, 288; UMNO-11 case, 287–8

KALONG NINGKAN, 275
Kampuchea, 78
Karpal Singh, 289
Kassim Ahmad, 161, 273, 309
Kedah Islamic Religious Council, 232
Kee Yong Wee, 219
Kelantan, 161, 224, 237, 326, 332
Kerk Choo Ting, 273, 309
Kershaw, Roger, 3, 265, 272
Kevin Hsu Group of Companies, 209–10
Khir Johari, 298
Khoo Khay Jin, 264
KLSE, *see* Kuala Lumpur Stock Exchange
Koperasi Belia Bersatu (Kosatu), 217–18
Koperasi Serbaguna Malaysia Berhad (KSM), 218

Kosatu, *see* Koperasi Belia Bersatu
KSM, *see* Koperasi Serbaguna Malaysia Berhad
Kuala Lumpur Stock Exchange (KLSE), 214, 216

LABOUR PARTY, 18
Labuan, 221
Lady Templer Hospital, 155
'Lagu Setia', 321
Lazarus, David, 6
Lebanon, 78
Lee Kim Sai, 280, 282, 314–15
Lee Kuan Yew, 18–20
Lim Chong Eu, 19–20, 90–1, 282, 294
Lim Kit Siang, 271, 278, 288
Ling Liong Sik, 282, 315
London Metal Exchange, 56, 63, 212–13
London Stock Exchange, 55, 63
'Look East' policy, 65–74, 182, 328
Lorraine Osman, 211
Luping, Herman, 233

MAHATHIR BIN MOHAMAD, DATUK SERI DR: administration, 78, 275; anti-Westernism, 42–7, 57–65, 75–81; appointment as Prime Minister, 2, 3; character, 3, 10, assault on the judiciary, 286–94; assimilation of Islamic values, 37–41 (*see also* Islam; Islamization policy); austerity drive, 143; authoritarianism, 261–303, 325; *Bangsa Malaysia*, 331, 334, 338; beatification of loyalty, 303, 321; *bersih, cekap dan amanah* campaign, 180; biographies of, 4–6; 'Buy British Last' campaign, 4, 54–7, 75, 78, 332; *The Challenge* (*see Challenge, The*); constitutional crisis, 1983, 202–9; coronary bypass operation, 1; diplomacy, 74–81; as a doctor-politician, 2, 294–301 (*see also* medical background below); expulsion from UMNO, 2; freedom of the press, 275–7 (*see also* Press); foreign policy, 74–81; general elections (*see* Elections); *Guide for Small Businessmen*, 11; Japanese occupation, 86, 101; *kepimpinan melalui teladan* campaign, 180, 200; letter to Tunku Abdul Rahman, 22, 201; liberalism, 275–6; 'Look East' policy, 10, 65–74, 182, 328; loss in 1969 election, 21; MAHA Clinic, 5, 18; *The Malay Dilemma* (*see Malay Dilemma, The*); Malay rulers, attitude towards, 204–9, 331–2 (*see also* Malays); Malaysia Incorporated policy, 132–4, 328; May 13 1969, 18, 26, 103; medical background, 5, 8, 11, 18; *Melayu Baru*, 336–8; as Minister of Education, 275; as Minister of Home Affairs, 285; as Minister of Trade and Industry, 78, 118; National Development Policy, 328–9; nationalism (*see* Nationalism); New Economic Policy (*see* New Economic Policy); political rallies, 207–8, 237, 301–3; populism, 198–202, 231–9, 273, 333; Privatization policy, 129–36; purge of Team B Ministers and Deputy Ministers, 270–1; reputation as a Malay 'ultra', 4, 12, 17–24, 273, 279; religiosity of the self-made man, 181–6; revolt against his party presidency, 2, 262–9; Sabah politics, 219–23, 326, 332; SEMARAK campaign, 303, 321; Social Darwinism, 9, 31–4, 66 (*see also Malay Dilemma, The*); 'South–South cooperation', 76; speeches, 12–13; Third Islamic Summit, Taif, Saudi Arabia, 67, 77–8, 172; as a Third World spokesman, 2, 61, 76–81, 199, 201, 332; as UMNO Deputy President, 35; as UMNO President, 1, 2–3, 232; on value of time, 5, 33, 110, 111–13, 336; on Vietnamese

refugees, 77; on work ethic, 68–71, 172–4, 181–3, 274, 328; *Wawasan 2020*, 2, 327–31; *see also* Capitalism; Chinese; Industrialization; Islam; Islamization policy; Malays; Nationalism; Nationalization
Mahathirism: as a coherent ideology, 2, 7–14, 331; core components of, 7, 329; culmination in *Wawasan 2020*, 327–38; paradoxes of, 9–10
Mahmood Iskandar, Sultan, 204
Mak Foon Than, 211
Makuwasa Securities Sdn. Bhd., 215, 231
Malay Dilemma, The, 10–11, 13, 24–36, 40, 42, 47–8, 54, 72, 85, 108–14, 162, 173, 182, 187, 201, 205, 298–9; association with the New Economic Policy, 25, 27, 108 (*see also* New Economic Policy); ban on, 24–5; criticism of Tunku Abdul Rahman, 26; on Chinese economic domination, 32–3, 54, 88, 205; definition of Malay dilemma, 28; illustrating medical approach to politics, 298–300; lifting of ban, 25; on Malay attitudes towards: land, 110–11; money, 110–13; time, 111–13; on Malay backwardness, 26–8, 63, 72; on Malay character and traits, 30–6, 173–4; on Malays as definitive people, 10, 27; on marriage, 31, 83; no change in Mahathir's views, 25; post-mortem on May 13 1969, 26; rehabilitation of the Malays, 28–30; 201; Social Darwinism, 30–4, 114; stereotypes of Chinese, 28, 31–4, 109; *see also* Chinese; Malays
Malay Land Reserve, 29
Malayan Banking Berhad, 214
Malayan Union, 86–7, 207
Malays: capitalist class, 105, 337–8; character, 30–6, 72–4, 83–4; class division, 159; economic backwardness, 26–8, 63, 72–3, 103; economic decline, 109–10; indigenous people, 27; poverty, 27, 37, 86–7; royalty, 204–9, 331–2; special position, 29; values, 42–4, 53, 110–13; working class, 35, 336–7
Malaysia Airlines System, 155, 275
Malaysia Incorporated, 132–4, 328
Malaysian Business Council (MBC), 327
Malaysian Chinese Association (MCA), 22, 26, 105, 216, 218–19, 232, 236–8, 274, 282–5, 323, 326
Malaysian International Shipping Corporation, 155
Malaysian Muslim Welfare Organization, *see* Pertubuhan Kebajikan Islam Malaysia
Malaysian People's Socialist Party, *see* Partai Sosialis Rakyat Malaysia
Malek Marican, 106, 138–9, 264
Maminco Sdn. Bhd., 212–15, 231, 234
Manan Osman, 305
Manufacturing sector, 117–18, 324–5, 335
Marina Yusoff, 265, 305
Ma'sud Abdul Rahman, 323
May 13 1969 riots, 18, 26, 103
MBC, *see* Malaysian Business Council
MCA, *see* Malaysian Chinese Association
Medicine, 18, 294–303
Megat Junid, 284, 312
Melayu Baru, 336–8
Memali incident, 227–8
Merdeka University, 105
Middle East, 78
Mohamad Iskandar, 183, 185–6
Mohamed Suffian, Tun, 289
Mohammad Asri Muda, 224
Monetary Authority of Singapore, 216
Money politics, 10, 233,
Morais, J. Victor, 4–5
Morgan Guaranty Trust Company, 137
Multinational companies, 64, 118–19, 138, 336
Multi-Purpose Holdings Berhad, 56, 145, 216

Munir Majid, 75, 77
Musa Hitam, 18, 23, 25, 50, 52, 123, 220–1, 224, 226, 228–31, 240, 261–6, 268–70, 275, 298, 302, 304, 325
Muslim Unity Force, *see* Angkatan Perpaduan Ummah
Mustafa bin Ali Mohamed, 5
Mustapha Harun, 220

NADI INSAN, 99
Najib Tun Razak, 314–15
Nakasone, Yasuhiro, 68
Nakhaie Ahmad, 224
National Consciousness Movement, *see* Aliran Kesedaran Negara
National Development Policy, 328–9
National Economic Consultative Council (NECC), 326, 339
National Equity Corporation, *see* Permodalan Nasional Berhad
National Language Act, 18
National Operations Council (NOC), 35, 103
National Union of Journalists, 277
National Unity Department, 104, 107
Nationalism: Malay, 17–48, 72–4, 329–30, 333; Malaysian, 54–88, 273–4, 329–30
Nationalization, 55, 79, 131
NECC, *see* National Economic Consultative Council
Neo Yee Pan, 232
NEP, *see* New Economic Policy
New Economic Policy (NEP), 27, 73, 80, 103–9, 124–9, 136–43, 159, 264, 325; bureaucratic expansion, 129–30; and Chinese businesses, 106, 136–7; criticisms of, 104–6; and economic growth, 106, 130, 136; end of, 141; held 'in abeyance', 141–2; Malay dependence on, 104–6, 138; Malay disagreement over, 139; and multinational corporations, 138; objectives, 103–4; poverty eradication, 103, 104, 105, 107; promulgation, 103; restructuring targets, 103–4, 108; success of, 334–6; state interventionism, 106, 129
New Investment Fund, 140
New Malay, *see Melayu Baru*
New Straits Times, 203, 207
New villages, 145
Newly industrializing countries (NICs), 3, 66, 68, 124, 135
NGOs, *see* Non-government organizations
NICs, *see* Newly industrializing countries
Nik Abdul Aziz, 224
Non-Aligned Movement, 74, 76, 80
Non-government organizations (NGOs), 223, 232, 235, 237, 253, 277–8, 284–6
North America Free Trade Agreement, 332
North–South Highway, 278, 288

OCCIDENTALISM, 47
Official Secrets Act (OSA), 276–7, 306, 311–12
OIC, *see* Organization of the Islamic Conference
Ongkili, Roger, 219
Onn Jaafar, Dato, 17, 85
Operation Lalang, 284–7, 289
Organization of the Islamic Conference (OIC), 176
OSA, *see* Official Secrets Act
Othman Saat, 305

PACIFIC COUNTRIES, 76, 98
Pacific Rim, 68
Pairin Kitingan, Joseph, 219–22, 233
Palestine, 78
Pan-Electric Industries Berhad, 214–17
PAP, *see* People's Action Party
Papan, 223–4
PARC, *see* Perak Anti-Radioactivity Committee

Partai Sosialis Rakyat Malaysia (PRSM), 37, 161, 285, 323
Parti Bersatu Sabah (PBS), 219–23, 233, 312, 326, 332
Parti Islam SeMalaysia (PAS), 2, 37, 160–1, 175, 205, 224–7, 232, 237, 324, 326, 332
PAS, *see* Parti Islam SeMalaysia
PASOK, *see* Pertubuhan Kebangsaan Pasok Ragang Bersatu
Pathmanathan, Murugesu, 6
PBS, *see* Parti Bersatu Sabah
Pemuda UMNO, 105, 207, 263, 274, 281, 283–4, 286, 314
People's Action Party (PAP), 18–20
Perak Anti-Radioactivity Committee (PARC), 223–4, 278, 286
Perkim, *see* Pertubuhan Kebajikan Islam Malaysia
Permodalan Nasional Berhad (PNB), 55, 129, 153
Pertubuhan Angkatan Sabilullah, 187
Pertubuhan Kebajikan Islam Malaysia, 160, 175
Pertubuhan Kebangsaan Pasok Ragang Bersatu (PASOK), 220
Perusahaan Otomobil Nasional (PROTON), 119–20
Perwaja Trengganu Sdn. Bhd., 119
Petroleum Development Act 1974, 137, 156
PNB, *see* Permodalan Nasional Berhad
Population, 122
Populism, 198–202, 231–9, 273, 333
Portuguese, 33
Poverty eradication, 103–6, 145
Press, 46, 78, 203, 206–7, 210, 234, 275–7, 284, 312
Prime Minister's Department, 55, 119, 203
Privatization, 129, 131–6, 328, 333
Promotion of Investments Act, 140
PROTON, *see* Perusahaan Otomobil Nasional
PRSM, *see* Partai Sosialis Rakyat Malaysia
Public enterprises, 130–1, 180
Pura, 277
Puspati, 224

RADZI SHEIKH AHMAD, 270
Rafidah Aziz, 263, 306
Rahim Bakar, 305
Rahmah Othman, 270
Rahmanmat, 6
Rais Saniman, 211
Rais Yatim, 263, 265–6, 270, 302
Rallies, 283–4, 300–2
Ramli Ibrahim, 257
Rampai Muda, 155
Razaleigh Hamzah, Tengku, 1–2, 18, 56, 137, 211, 229–31, 257, 261–70, 293, 300, 302, 304, 322–3, 325
Recession, 128, 138
Religious freedom, 274
Rodinson, Maxime, 123
Rodney, Walter, 109
Rukunegara, 27

SABAH, 219–23, 326, 332; abrogation of Tambunan's district status, 219; anti-Muslim allegations, 220–1; attempted coup, 220, 221; elections in 1985 and 1986, 219–222; Labuan issue, 221; PBS joins Barisan Nasional, 220–1, 223; PBS joins Gagasan Rakyat, 326; 'Sabah formula', 222, 223; Tambunan by-election, 219; violence in, 220
Sabry Sharif, 311
Safar Hashim, 264
Salleh Abas, Tun, 287–8, 291–3
Samy Vellu, 282
Sanusi Junid, 263, 278–9, 283
Saravanamuttu, Johan, 272
Schoolmasters, 183–5
Second Malaysia Plan, 107–8
Sedition Act, 205, 226
Semangat 46, 1–2, 323–6
SEMARAK campaign, 303, 321
Senu Abdul Rahman, 203

Shaharuddin Maaruf, 11
Shahrir Samad, 263, 270–1, 293, 323
Shamsul A. B., 264
Sigma International, 216
Sin Chew Jit Poh, 284
Sistem Televisyen Malaysia Berhad, 155
Slogans, 180, 303, 328
Smith, Patrick, 55
Social Darwinism, 31–4, 66
Socialist Front, 18–19
Societies Act, 160, 300
Socso, 214
South Africa, 78
South Commission, 76
South Korea, 66, 68–72, 120–1
Soviet Union, 75
Spirit of '46, *see* Semangat 46
Star, 203, 284
Stock Exchange of Singapore, 215–16
Suhaimi Kamaruddin, 265, 305–6
Suhaini Aznam, 3, 226
Sulaiman Palestin, 261, 304
Sultan Abdul Hamid College, 185, 196
Sunday Times, 2, 11–12, 81
Supreme Group, 216
Swain, Jon, 3
Syarikat Telekom Malaysia Berhad, 154–5
Syed Ja'afar Albar, 18, 22
Syed Nasir bin Syed Ismail, 17–18, 22

TABLIGH, *see* Jamaat Tabligh
Taiwan, 66, 71–2, 325, 339
Tan, George, 209, 211
Tan, Simon, 272
Tan Chee Khoon, 13, 20, 25, 57, 121, 125, 272, 294, 317
Tan Kok Liang, 217
Tan Koon Swan, 216–19, 232, 280
Television, 207, 228, 321
Tenaga Nasional Berhad, 154–5
Teoh, Bob, 312
Thai Malays, 78, 84
Thong Yaw Hong, 214
Thrift, 169–71
Time, value of, 111–12
Tin market misadventure, 56, 63, 212–14
Trade unions, 46, 64, 69–70, 77, 336
Tunku Abdul Rahman College, 281

UEM, *see* United Engineers (M) Berhad
'Ultras', 18–24, 49, 273
Ummah, 67, 94
UMNO, *see* United Malays National Organization
UMNO Baru, 1, 290, 323–7, 332
UMNO Malaysia, 290, 323
United Engineers (M) Berhad (UEM), 278, 288
United Malayan Banking Corporation, 105, 145, 306
United Malays National Organization (UMNO), 1, 19, 23, 35, 86–7, 160–1, 208, 225–7, 230–1, 237–9, 261–71, 274, 283–91, 322
United Nations, 75–8, 97
United Sabah National Organization (USNO), 220–3
United States of America, 43–4, 47, 75
Universiti Islam Antarabangsa (UIA), *see* International Islamic University
Universiti Teknologi Malaysia, 281
Universities: Malays, 35, 52
Universities and University Colleges Act 1975, 275, 311
University of Malaya, 83, 281, 295
USNO, *see* United Sabah National Organization
Utusan Malaysia, 228

VIETNAMESE REFUGEES, 77
Vision 2020, *see Wawasan 2020*
Von Vorys, Karl, 21

WAN MOKHTAR, 270
Wang Choon Wing, 219
Wanita UMNO, 263
Watan, 284
Wawasan 2020, 2, 327–31
West: decline, 43–7, 66–7
Work ethic, 68–71, 172–4, 181–3, 274, 328

YANG DI PERTUAN AGONG, 202–9, 292
Yong, Amar Stephen, 223
Yoshihara Kunio, 137
Yusof Rawa, 21, 224

ZAIN ASRAAI, 214–15, 231
Zainal Abidin Zin, 270